D0319456

THE LAST DAYS OF
MUSSOLINI

RAY MOSELEY

SUTTON PUBLISHING

First published in the USA by Taylor Trade Publishing, 2004
First published in the UK, 2006 by
Sutton Publishing Limited · Phoenix Mill
Thrupp · Stroud · Gloucestershire · GL5 2BU

British Library Cataloguing in Publication Data
A catalogue record for this book is available from the British Library.

ISBN 0-7509-4449-8

For Jennifer, Ann and John

Typeset in 10.5/15pt Photina.
Typesetting and origination by
Sutton Publishing Limited.
Printed and bound in England by
J.H. Haynes & Co. Ltd, Sparkford.

CONTENTS

Acknowledgements

In first place I wish to thank the superb, highly professional staff of editors at Sutton Publishing with whom I have had the good fortune to be associated in bringing this book to completion: Hilary Walford, Nick Reynolds, Jonathan Falconer and Julia Fenn. Throughout the process, it has been a pleasure to work with people of such dedication and ability. I am also grateful to Elizabeth Stone for her skilful editing and my wife Jennifer, who read the manuscript with a critical eye, saving me from numerous mistakes and some infelicitous phrases.

Special thanks also go to the late Urbano Lazzaro for providing additional details to his previously published accounts of his capture of Mussolini in April 1945. My critical judgement of his published account of how Mussolini was killed by partisans in no way reflects any lack of appreciation for his generous assistance. Licia Cusinati came to my rescue splendidly in resolving some tricky problems of translation from Italian texts. Leonora Dodsworth, with her usual efficiency, ferreted out vital information from archives in Rome, with the kind assistance of Wladimiro Settimelli.

Giorgio Delle Fonte, director of the municipal library in Dongo, Italy, and his wife Edda Cecchini contributed valuable archival material and were very helpful in suggesting other sources of information.

Others I wish to thank for their encouragement and help in various ways are Bill Landrey, Robin Knight, William Tuohy and Marco Donghi. Finally, I would like to mention Alberto Botta, who will disagree with nearly everything about this book but who was kind and helpful when I sought his assistance.

Abbreviations

CLN	Committee of National Liberation, the political group that directed partisan warfare
CLNAI	Committee of National Liberation for Upper (Northern) Italy
CVL	Corps of Volunteers for Freedom, the partisan military command organisation
GAP	Gruppi di Azione Patriottica, partisan death squads operating in the cities
OSS	Office of Strategic Services
RSI	Italian initials for Mussolini's Italian Social Republic
SAP	Squadre di Azione Patriottica, partisan death squads operating in rural areas
SD	Sicherheitsdienst, the internal security service of the SS
SS	Schutzstaffel, the Nazi security service

Chapter 1

THE LAST SPECTATOR

I work and I try, yet know that all is but a farce.

(Benito Mussolini, March 1945)

In early 1945, Benito Mussolini found himself acutely aware that his life had nearly run its course and ahead lay only a few agonizing weeks or months that were sure to bring more disasters, more defeats. His mood was black, and, almost obsessively, he began to speak about his approaching death. He may have clung to a thread of hope that he could survive, but he was in a room without exits. The German armed forces that had sustained his puppet government since its creation in September 1943 were inexorably being driven out of Italy, the frontiers of his Fascist republic were shrinking almost daily and Mussolini was aware that German military leaders were negotiating with the Allies behind his back in neutral Switzerland. With Soviet forces and those of the Western Allies steadily sweeping towards the heart of the Nazi empire, Germany offered no refuge, nor did Mussolini seek one. He was determined to die in his own country. In February, seeing with sudden clarity the inevitable destruction of all he had lived for, Mussolini suffered what his German doctor called a nervous breakdown, and his physical and mental powers deteriorated noticeably. He slept badly, ate little and once again grew thin, as he had earlier when he suffered from an ulcer.[1] By now he probably regarded death as a welcome release. From the moment he had been overthrown in July 1943, arrested, then rescued by the Germans and forced by Hitler to take up the reins of government once again, Mussolini had been a miserable figure in the grip of anger, shame and depression. The Germans had lost faith in him and humiliated him almost daily, denying him any real exercise of power, brutalising and even enslaving his people and stealing his country's assets. He hated some of the Fascists around him, hated where he lived in remote isolation beside Lake Garda, the most melancholy of the Italian lakes and not a place of his choosing. His private life was turbulent as always. Sometimes he and his peasant wife

Rachele would pass each other coldly in the villa they shared without recognising each other's existence.[2] His mistress, Claretta Petacci, lived 6 miles away in another lakeside villa and his moments of comfort with her were few.

'Death has become my friend, it doesn't frighten me any longer. Death is a grace of God for one who has suffered too much. . . . For me the doors will not open except for death. And it is also right. I have made mistakes and I will pay, if this poor life of mine can serve as payment.' Thus did Mussolini unburden himself to Madeleine Mollier, wife of the press attaché at the German Embassy and a Red Cross volunteer in a German military hospital in Italy. She had interviewed him for a German magazine in 1938, when he was at the height of his powers in Rome, and he remembered that well. 'Seven years ago I was an interesting person. Now I am a corpse.' Mollier had won his consent to be interviewed and photographed again, one of the last interviews he would give and an exceptional one in that it contained no hint of dissimulation or self-serving distortion of the facts. He could be more frank than he had ever been before, because in effect he was speaking from the grave; he had asked her not to publish anything until after his death, and it was not until 1948 that Mollier did so. 'Yes, madam, I am finished,' he said. 'My star has fallen. I work and I try, yet know that all is but a farce. . . . I await the end of the tragedy and – strangely detached from everything – I do not feel an actor any more. I feel I am the last of the spectators.' He said he had begun to die in January 1944, when extreme Fascists in his regime had compelled him to acquiesce in the execution of his son-in-law and former foreign minister, Count Galeazzo Ciano, after Ciano had helped vote him out of office. That had brought a rupture with Edda Mussolini Ciano, his favourite child, a painful break for both that would not be repaired in his lifetime. 'The agony is atrociously long. I am the captain of the ship in a storm. My ship is broken. I am in the furious ocean, on a piece of wreckage. This impossibility to act, to put things right! No one hears my voice. . . . Now I am enclosed in silence. But one day the world will listen to me.'[3]

He was now sixty-one, and, in the twenty-third year of his tumultuous leadership, prematurely aged and a shadow of the dynamic figure – shoulders back, jaw thrust forward imperiously – who had once held millions in thrall. He had brought backward Italy into the modern world, his oratory had electrified a nation, he had once been widely admired abroad and his ambitions for conquest had initially won approval among his own people. He was a man of genius, his followers never tired of declaiming in the glory days, but now that description rang hollow. 'The Duce is always right' had been the guiding slogan of Fascist rule, plastered on walls and lampposts around the country. The man who had aspired to be a modern Caesar, to share with Hitler in the domination of Europe, to bite off a part of France and annex it to Italy, to be the iron-fisted overseer of the Mediterranean and to create an empire in Africa, had been reduced to the role of provincial governor in his own diminishing domain. Sometimes he referred to himself bitterly as simply the mayor of the little town of Gargnano, where he was forced to live. Even that could seem an exaggeration of his powers. Germans guarded his villa there, Germans exerted full control on the battlefield, Germans censored his newspapers and monitored his telephone calls, Germans appointed provincial officials without reference to him, Germans ignored his complaints about the state to which he had been reduced. More to the point, Mussolini often described himself as a prisoner in Gargnano. His life was one long, unceasing humiliation and, worst of all, Hitler himself, who once looked to Mussolini with genuine admiration, now ignored him and considered him of little consequence. Mussolini was equally disillusioned with a Nazi dictator who had also failed; but he retained, or pretended to retain, a childlike faith that Nazi secret weapons would be unveiled at the last minute and achieve a miraculous victory.

Through his own folly, Mussolini had lost almost everything he sought to achieve in life, had lost most of his followers and finally had lost the will to live. 'I am the most hated man in Italy,' he told his secretary, Giovanni Dolfin, in late 1943.[4] To a friend he said: 'If I promised every Italian gold coins, no one would believe me. If I had them poured into their hands, they would take them but would be convinced within themselves of their falsity. And when an expert guaranteed that they were of pure precious metal, then they would think gold wasn't worth anything.'[5]

He had once boasted that Italy's frontiers would be protected by 8 million bayonets, but now his pitiful little army – steadily dwindling through desertions – was held in so little regard by the Germans that they had until recently declined even to allow it to engage in the life-or-death struggle for control of Italy.

But Mussolini would not simply wait passively for death. In March, he told Ottavio Dinale, an old trade unionist friend whom he had first met in Switzerland at the beginning of the century, that the Allies would never take him alive.[6] As their offensive pushed northwards towards the total conquest of Italy, he was seized by a romantic image of a last stand in the Valtellina, a valley along the Swiss border, where he would lead 50,000 armed Fascists in a fight to the death. It would be a Fascist Thermopylae, but one without hope of success. The idea had been promoted by Alessandro Pavolini, the fanatic who had been chosen by Mussolini as secretary of the Fascist Party. He convened several meetings of Fascists and Germans to discuss the plan. Each time the Germans were resolutely opposed, his own armed forces minister, Marshal Rodolfo Graziani, no less so. But Mussolini clung to the idea.

On 20 March, he gave another farewell interview, this one to the journalist Ivanoe Fossani. Bizarrely, he asked Fossani to meet him at 9 p.m. on the island of Trimellone in Lake Garda, perhaps the only place he believed he could talk away from German listening devices. The abashed tone of the Mollier interview was replaced by recriminations and self-justification as he ruminated beneath the stars. Mussolini blamed the fall of fascism on selfish Italian industrialists and financiers, complained of the ill will of France and England towards Italy before the war and defended his alliance with Germany. But he blamed Hitler for not having listened to him more. He had reacted to Hitler's invasion of the Soviet Union with enthusiasm, and volunteered to send Italian soldiers to the battlefront, but now he pretended he had opposed it. 'In Germany they all despise me except Hitler, who has respect for me.' He said he had been a prisoner of the Germans throughout the life of his little republic, and, if Hitler and Germany had been able to win the war, 'Mussolini and Italy would have equally lost.' He feared that Russia, once in possession of central Europe, could not be dislodged; could the Americans and British really fail to avert this great danger?

He expressed admiration for ordinary working people and disdain for the middle class, which had contributed to his downfall. 'The stars of the dictators burn a short while among Latin people. In other people, instead, dictatorship is an organic necessity. . . . I believe I ennobled dictatorship.' Yet, he observed bitterly, 'Stalin is on his feet and wins, I fall and I lose.' Then he returned to the subject of his own death. 'Who fears death has never lived, and I have lived too much. . . . I will go where fate takes me. . . . After the defeat I will be covered furiously in spit but then they will come to clean me with veneration. Then I will smile because my people will be at peace with themselves.'[7]

These last, introspective interviews reveal a man who was resigned to death but hardly serene. Another remarkable thing about them is what is absent from Mussolini's thoughts. He dwells at the end on his place in history, his successes and his failures, his approaching death, the betrayal of his cause from many quarters. He expresses no thoughts or concerns for the future of his people in a defeated country, no views on how Italians might extract themselves from their current dilemma and find their way back into a self-regarding role in the new Europe. It is a truly self-obsessed performance. It might be too much to expect that such a man would offer his people an apology for his mistakes, but even any element of compassion is lacking.

In mid-April, Mussolini had finally decided to break out of the isolation of Lake Garda and act. He would go to Milan, then move from there to the Valtellina. But before he left Gargnano, he had another conversation with Dinale. It was a valedictory commentary on his life and his rule.

> Recriminations are useless, there's nothing left but to fall back on oneself, there is nothing to be done. Nothing to be done. The curtain falls. . . . In this moment, for example, I feel an overwhelming desire to return to being a little boy, a little scamp of thirteen years, to still write affectionate letters to my little girl friend, to ask her what she would do in my place. . . . I tested fortune, and it revolted. I evoked violence, and it was thrown back on me a hundredfold. I challenged the world, and it has been the stronger. I despised men, and they are vindicated. . . . I have fought to the extreme. They have defeated me. We are equal. One goes where one must go. And I will go there without recriminations, without hatred, without pride. Farewell.

Dinale replied: 'Goodbye.' And Mussolini responded: 'No, no more illusions. Farewell.'[8]

It was the last time Dinale saw him. On 18 April, the Duce left for Milan. Ten days later, he would be dead.

Chapter 2

AFTER THE FALL

The Germans are difficult friends and dangerous enemies.

(Benito Mussolini, September 1943)

Mussolini had, of course, experienced a political death in 1943. Allied troops had landed in Sicily on the night of 9/10 July, and it was a matter of time before the mainland was invaded. Even for many of the Fascists who had been blind followers of Mussolini for years, it was now imperative to replace the Duce and bring the war to an end. From 1940 onwards Mussolini's star had been in decline. Italy had tried to conquer Greece, a poor country with a fraction of Italy's population, and had been humiliated. It had been shorn of its nascent African empire, driven from Ethiopia and then from Libya. In the Soviet Union its forces, along with those of Hitler, were being relentlessly driven back. By mid-1943, and especially after the Sicily landings, there could no longer be any doubt that defeat was inevitable and Mussolini bore the major responsibility. King Victor Emmanuel III himself was deeply implicated in the regime's flawed policies, but he was determined to get rid of the Duce to save himself.

Dino Grandi, Mussolini's former ambassador to Britain, led a small group that drew up a resolution calling for the Duce to share his wartime powers with the king. In effect, if the resolution were adopted, it would be a vote of no confidence in the regime. Mussolini called a rare meeting of the Fascist Grand Council for 24 July to resolve the issue. Accustomed to dominating his subordinates ('electric light bulbs which I turn on or off as I wish'), he went into the meeting curiously sanguine and emerged a shaken man. The vote had gone against him, nineteen to eight with one abstention. Most wounding of all, Count Galeazzo Ciano had spoken out firmly in favour of the resolution and joined in the vote against him. Ciano, the husband of Mussolini's favourite child Edda, was the young diplomat who had been his foreign minister for six years and his closest adviser. But the rift between them had been growing ever since Germany invaded Poland, and Ciano, disillusioned with the Nazi leadership, had tried vainly to persuade his father-in-law to break with Hitler. Just five months before the Grand Council meeting, Mussolini had removed Ciano as foreign minister and made him ambassador to the Holy See. Ciano had bided his time, and now he had struck out against the man he had once virtually worshipped. With Ciano's vote, Mussolini observed bitterly, treason had entered his own house.

The Grand Council meeting lasted into the early hours of 25 July, and that afternoon, after Mussolini had gone to the Villa Savoia royal residence to discuss the crisis with the king, he was arrested on the king's orders. The Duce was whisked off to a Roman barracks in an ambulance that raced through the streets of Rome at high speed, and was transferred from there to imprisonment on the island of Ponza, near Naples, where he had previously exiled some of his political enemies.[1] Then a nervous government moved him to La Maddalena naval base off the north coast of Sardinia, but, ever fearful the Germans would find him, brought him back to the mainland on 28 August by Red Cross seaplane and planted him on the Gran Sasso, the highest mountain in the remote Abruzzi region south-east of Rome.

There he remained until 12 September, when he was rescued in a daring German raid and flown to Germany to be reunited with Hitler, his family and his Fascist minions. Mussolini held the bizarre conviction that the rescue had saved him from the certainty of a show trial in Madison Square Garden in New York, and commented that a hanging in the Tower of London would have been preferable.[2]

* * *

Mussolini had whiled away his time at Ponza jotting down his thoughts in a notebook, and although not a religious man read one of the few books available to him, Father Giuseppe Ricciotti's *Life of Jesus Christ*. Evidently he compared his travails with those of Christ, for he underlined passages about the betrayal of Jesus, the flight of the Apostles and the solitude of Christ. He passed his sixtieth birthday, on 29 July, at La Maddalena and there received from Hitler as a birthday gift the complete works of the philosopher Friedrich Nietzsche. When he was being transferred there from Ponza, he alluded to the government's fears of a German rescue attempt, telling Admiral Franco Maugeri that he would never have tried to return to power with German support.

The Gran Sasso rises 6,970 feet amid the Abruzzi mountain chain, and on a wide plateau at the top sits the Hotel Campo Imperatore, which became for Mussolini, as he commented to his guards, 'the highest prison in the world'. The only means of access to the mountaintop was a funicular railway. Mussolini was ensconced in a suite on the second storey of the hotel, where he took his meals alone – usually rice, an egg, a cooked onion, a little meat, milk and a lot of fruit. He was guarded by forty-three Carabinieri officers and three other policemen, who protected their fortress with two heavy machine guns and rifles. One guard was always present in the suite to keep an eye on Mussolini. Overseeing the guard force were Giuseppe Gueli, an inspector general of the army, and Lieutenant Alberto Faiola, whom the new Italian leader Marshal Pietro Badoglio had known in Ethiopia in 1935.

Mussolini spent his days in talks with these officers, walking around the hotel grounds and observing the surrounding panorama through a viewfinder, playing an Italian card game, *scopone*, with the officers and listening to the radio – in Italian, German and English – and always remaining impassive when he heard himself being denounced in broadcasts.

The Germans had received a number of early indications about Mussolini's presence on the mountain, and their suspicions were confirmed when they intercepted a coded message that Gueli sent to Italian Police Chief Carmine Senise in Rome about his security measures. On 8 September, Badoglio signed an armistice agreement with the Allies, about which Mussolini was informed as he was reading a book: he hurled the book across the room, accused Badoglio of treason and said of the Germans: 'They will never tolerate this betrayal.' For years he had suffered from an ulcer and his psychological condition had deteriorated markedly during his captivity. After this outburst, he became so ill that a military doctor had to be called in the next day. He diagnosed a worsening of Mussolini's ulcerous condition, aggravated by nervous tension.

On the night of 11/12 September, Mussolini happened to listen to a German radio broadcast, which reported that the Italian armistice agreement called for him to be handed over to the Allies. In despair, he cut both his wrists with a razor blade, but the Carabiniere officer in his suite saw the blood streaming down his hands and rushed to stop the bleeding. He found the cuts were only superficial, and Mussolini expressed regret for his half-hearted attempt at suicide. All metal objects were removed from his suite. At 3 a.m. on 12 September, he sat down and wrote a letter to Lieutenant Faiola: 'You know from hard experience what it means to fall into enemy hands. I beg you to spare me such shame and ruin. Send me your pistol.' Faiola, who had been taken prisoner in North Africa while seriously wounded and felt he had been treated badly by the British, naturally declined Mussolini's request, but told him: 'I would never hand over an Italian to the English.' He promised to give him an hour's warning if the British came for him, presumably to give him time to flee.

In the days that followed the armistice, those on the Gran Sasso observed German planes flying low over the hotel. They also received reports that

German officers had checked into a hotel in nearby Aquila. Gueli spoke to Police Chief Senise, who advised him to use 'prudence' if there were a German rescue attempt. Badoglio had ordered Mussolini shot if there were any attempt at escape, but Gueli and his fellow officers interpreted Senise's advice to mean there should be no bloodshed. The lower-ranking Carabinieri also decided among themselves they would not put up a fight.

Hitler had assigned General Kurt Student, celebrated in Germany for the capture of Crete, to effect Mussolini's rescue. Student had come to Rome immediately after the overthrow of Mussolini with a contingent of troops headed by an Austrian Waffen SS captain, Otto Skorzeny. Their mission then was to capture Badoglio and his ministers, members of the royal family and other prominent personalities. Nothing came of that plan, but they were then detailed to free Mussolini. The operation was planned by Student with the assistance of Major Harald Mors and a Lieutenant von Berlepsch, but German propaganda later gave full credit for the rescue to Skorzeny. Student protested to Luftwaffe commander Hermann Göring over this, but Göring could do nothing because Hitler had accepted the story that Skorzeny was the principal hero. Göring suspected that SS chief Heinrich Himmler had manoeuvred to make Skorzeny the hero to promote the SS over the Luftwaffe.

The rescue, code-named Operation Eiche (Operation Oak), began at 2.20 p.m. on 12 September when fifty German armoured cars, ten tanks and forty trucks full of soldiers arrived at the base funicular station and took it over without resistance. Ten minutes later, a fleet of German transport planes arrived over the Gran Sasso and disgorged nine gliders, which proceeded to land on the mountain in front of the hotel. One crashed into rocks on the plateau. Mussolini and Osvaldo Antichi, a Carabiniere inspector, watched the landings from the little window of the Duce's suite. Antichi said Mussolini looked worried and commented: 'This was not wanted.'

After the gliders landed, parachutists climbed out, dropping to the ground on all fours, then lying flat. Last of all, Italian General Fernando Soleti emerged, walking along a path toward the hotel while the parachutists remained prone. It had been Skorzeny's idea to bring an Italian officer along on the theory that this would confuse the Carabinieri. Behind Soleti walked a giant of a man carrying a machine gun, Skorzeny. About 100 other men got up and walked single file behind Skorzeny, while other troops guarded them from behind rocks. Approaching the hotel, Soleti shouted: 'Don't shoot!' While this was going on, a small, single-engine German plane, a Fieseler Storch, flew in and landed.

Just in front of the main door to the hotel, Soleti shouted again: 'Don't shoot!' and a voice from a window above, that of Mussolini, shouted: 'Don't shed blood, don't shoot.' Skorzeny began shouting in German, then went in the hotel and found a radio operator transmitting a message. He kicked the chair from under him and smashed the radio with his pistol. Then he ran up the stairs, three steps at a time, with a pistol in his hand, and burst into Mussolini's suite. Others crowded in behind him, and Skorzeny made what amounted to a short speech while Mussolini wearily sat down on the edge of his bed and replied to him in German.

'Duce, the Führer sent me to free you,' Skorzeny said.

Mussolini embraced the SS officer and said: 'I knew that my friend Adolf Hitler would not have abandoned me.'

Skorzeny said that at first glance Mussolini seemed to be a seriously ill man, and this image was reinforced by the Duce's three-day-old growth of beard. But then he saw that Mussolini's eyes still shone with the brightness of 'the great dictator'.

Skorzeny asked Mussolini where he wanted to be taken, and, after a moment of uncertainty, Mussolini decided on Rocca delle Caminate, a castle in his home province of Romagna that had been fitted up as a summer retreat for him and his family years earlier. Skorzeny ordered Gueli's driver to take all Mussolini's belongings to Rocca delle Caminate, then invited Mussolini to follow him outside. In front of the hotel, Mussolini turned to Antichi and said: 'I would have preferred to have been freed by Italians.'

The pilot, a Luftwaffe ace named Captain Heinrich Gerlach, got out of his plane and embraced Skorzeny. He tried to persuade Skorzeny that such a small plane could not take off safely with three men aboard, but Skorzeny insisted. He ordered his men to clear the plateau of rocks and invited the Carabinieri to help. He then asked Mussolini who were the members of his immediate guard escort, and Mussolini indicated Gueli, Faiola and Antichi. 'Fine,' said Skorzeny, and moved off. The three men feared they were about to be deported to Germany. Antichi said he approached Mussolini and took him aside.

'My family has always taught me to hate you,' he said. 'If you take me with you, you take an enemy. I beg you to leave me to my fate.'

'Fine, my dear Antichi, fine,' Mussolini responded. 'I will remember you.'

Shortly after, Antichi saw him speak to Skorzeny and heard him mention his name. He was in no doubt that Mussolini had saved him from deportation: 'I confess I felt in those last moments some sympathy and compassion for that man.'

Another Carabiniere who watched Mussolini climb aboard the plane with a half smile said it was 'the smile of a man freed by a foreign hand and aware of having drawn the country into the abyss'. The pilot revved the plane's engines to full throttle while a group of parachutists held it back. Then, at a gesture from the pilot, they let go and the plane jerked forward, bounced along, rolled toward the edge of the plateau, finally rose into the air, then struck a rock and rose again. Immediately after it cleared the mountain, it dropped out of sight, falling into the abyss. But Gerlach gained control of the plane, and once he had gained altitude, he circled the mountain once before flying off as the men below cheered. Mussolini was flown to Pratica di Mare, just outside Rome, and transferred to a larger German plane that took him to Vienna in the evening. The next morning, he was off again to Munich, where he saw his wife Rachele briefly at the airport before continuing to Hitler's hideaway in the East Prussian forests. Rachele said he was pale, wearing ski boots and an old black coat she had sent him. His first words to her were: 'I thought I wouldn't see you again.'[3]

* * *

The Mussolini who met Hitler after his rescue was not the swaggering, confident Duce of old. He was a seriously ill man, so weak that the Germans feared for his survival. During his captivity on La Maddalena, he vomited often and ate only a few spoonfuls of rice each day, the effects of the four years in which he had been suffering from an ulcer, insomnia and loss of appetite. In Germany, everyone who saw him remarked on the fact that he looked ill and had aged in just a short time. Rudolf von Rahn, who was to become ambassador to Italy after Mussolini returned to office, said: 'It was evident he would have preferred to go and bury himself quietly in a library.' SS Colonel Eugen Dollmann, who had often translated at Hitler–Mussolini meetings, said: 'I believe Mussolini would have preferred to remain on the Gran Sasso to admire the flight of eagles.'

While he was in office, his Italian doctors had prescribed a spartan diet of tea, toast, a little butter, occasionally stewed fruit and milk – ever increasing quantities of milk – that only worsened his condition. It is worth dwelling on this fact because it raises the question of whether Mussolini was led into serious errors of decision-making by his physical illness. Could a man fixated on the pain in his stomach and unable to sleep be relied upon to think clearly? A report to Berlin in April 1943 by the German secret services in Rome had referred to the Duce's continuing physical and mental deterioration.[4] Dr Georg Zachariae, a German physician who treated Mussolini in Germany and later in northern Italy, wrote in his memoirs: 'One must suppose he was not always in full possession of his clear physical equilibrium and of his total energies, that therefore he may not have understood sometimes the importance of decisive steps he was called upon to carry out.'[5]

Mussolini's relationship with Hitler had evolved gradually over the years they had known each other. At first Hitler deferred to the Duce, the more senior dictator, and seemed genuinely to admire him. Later, and especially after Mussolini began to play second fiddle to Hitler as war leader, summit meetings between the two men had consisted mainly of long monologues by Hitler, with Mussolini barely able to get in a word now and then. At one memorable meeting in 1942, when Hitler talked uninterruptedly for an hour and forty minutes, General Alfred Jodl, the Führer's chief of defence staff, dozed off while Mussolini kept looking at his wristwatch. Even at this stage, Hitler was professing admiration for Mussolini. But now, owing his life to the Führer, Mussolini was to see Hitler at his most brutal.

At their meeting in East Prussia, Hitler was smartly turned out in military uniform, Mussolini a bedraggled wreck. The Duce arrived by train wearing an old overcoat, a rumpled white shirt, a tie that was badly knotted and a rather dusty black cap. Assorted papers and folded newspapers protruded from the pockets of his overcoat.[6]

Hitler got down to business right away, and his message was a stern one: 'I don't doubt that you will agree with me in believing that one of the first acts of the new government will have to be to sentence to death the traitors of the Grand Council,' he said. 'I judge Count Ciano four times a traitor: traitor to his country, traitor to fascism, traitor to the alliance with Germany, traitor to his family. If I were in your place perhaps nothing would have stopped me from rendering justice with my own hands. But I advise you: it is preferable that the death sentence be carried out in Italy.'

'But you're talking of the husband of the daughter whom I adore, the father of my grandchildren,' Mussolini protested.

'All the more reason Count Ciano merits punishment in that not only has he failed in fidelity towards his country, but in fidelity to his family,' Hitler replied.[7]

Gripped by the conviction he had developed stomach cancer, Mussolini later told Hitler his only desire was to leave public life and rest. But Hitler, stripping away a mask of concern for his fellow dictator, insisted he return to Italy and head a new Fascist government. If Mussolini refused, he said, he would have to carry out a 'punitive plan' to use his secret weapons – 'diabolical arms' – to destroy Milan, Genoa and Turin just as he intended to destroy London. 'Northern Italy will have to envy the fate of Poland if you don't accept,' he said. 'In such a case, Count Ciano will naturally not be handed over; he will be hanged here in Germany.'[8] Logically, Hitler might have seemed to be making a hollow threat. Poland had been a defeated, dismembered country, where the Germans could do as they liked. In Italy, they were fighting a war against Allied invaders, and the last thing the German military needed at that point was to antagonise the Italian population and add a civilian uprising to its problems. But the Germans were perversely immune to logic, and Mussolini could not be sure Hitler was not ruthless enough to carry out his threats.

So incensed were the German military leaders by the Italian betrayal that they treated Italy as an occupied country, took what they wanted, inflicted suffering on the people and thus triggered the hostile reaction they had every reason to try to avoid. Mussolini always contended afterwards that he had returned to Italy because of a duty to his people to try to stay the hand of German repression and to save Italian honour by remaining faithful to the alliance with the Nazi regime. The first argument might have some merit, but the second is entirely spurious. The Nazi treatment of the Italian people represented a gross violation of the terms of alliance and thus removed any obligation on Mussolini's part had he chosen to recognise that. His hesitations about returning to office were so quickly overcome that one must conclude he was either genuinely frightened by the consequences of arousing Hitler's wrath or the Führer's threats served as a convenient rationale for overcoming his own hesitations. Perhaps he went back because he could not easily relinquish the habit of power, and, above all, because he thirsted for revenge against the king and Marshal Pietro Badoglio, the man who had been appointed to replace him. He also wanted revenge against those Italians who had cheered his downfall.

In a conversation in Germany with the extreme Fascist Roberto Farinacci, Mussolini raged against the king and Badoglio. 'Think what I, with my defects as a man, have done for this country. Think with what clemency I have governed. Think of that king I would have been able to pulverise and have elected to the dignity of a Roman emperor. Think of that sinister marshal I could have sent before an execution squad and whom I have enriched, promoted and given a title of nobility. Think also of those three or four hundred thousand sheep who shouted like lunatics and bleated at my every word . . . and who in the hour of defeat cursed me and repudiated me.'[9]

Hitler might be determined that Mussolini should return to office, but many of his Nazi associates were not at all enthusiastic. Even if the Duce could be trusted to remain loyal to Germany, he was fatally flawed, a man whose own weakness in dealing with his subordinates had brought about his downfall. 'Duce, you are too good, you will never be a dictator,' Hitler told him. The Germans smugly told themselves the treachery that resulted in Mussolini's downfall could not have happened in Germany, where the people were solidly behind the Führer. Hitler himself had informed Mussolini: 'Italy will be considered the country of traitors without distinction.'[10] The Duce himself was perhaps excluded from that indictment, but the German General Staff did not want him present in Italy to interfere in its conduct of the war. Foreign Minister Joachim von Ribbentrop shared that sentiment. Propaganda Minister Joseph Goebbels thought the Duce was finished, and favoured Farinacci. Alfred Rosenberg, the so-called philosopher of the Nazi regime, preferred Giovanni Preziosi, a defrocked priest, former journalist and rabid antisemitic pamphleteer who had been flown to Germany to meet Hitler the day after Mussolini's arrest.

Of all this Mussolini quickly became aware, but he told his son Vittorio, who had fled to Germany after his downfall: 'Only my person is beyond any suspicion and can be useful today to the Italians.' He also said Hitler had assured him that the Wehrmacht, the German armed forces, would soon have very modern weapons capable of reversing setbacks on the battlefield. If the Germans won the war without his presence, he said, they would be more inexorable and intransigent with Italy. 'The Germans are difficult friends and dangerous enemies,' he told Vittorio. 'My presence in Italy will be decisive, especially if we can demonstrate with facts that the people did not engage in betrayal, only a clique of politicians and military men, of courtesans and Communist intellectuals.' He assured Vittorio there would be 'no servitude, no phantom government'. Badoglio, he said, was trying to incite Italians to a guerrilla war against the Germans and was evidently unaware he could unleash a civil war. 'He will earn the contempt of the entire world,' he said.

'Hitler gives his support but I don't know how much he will be able to support me considering the mistrust of Goebbels, Ribbentrop and Rosenberg, and the resistance of many members of the Wehrmacht General Staff.'

He said that the king, at their last meeting before his arrest, told him: 'If there remained to you only one friend, I would be that one.' Mussolini said the king had never had a more devoted chief of government than himself but 'a man of small stature also became small in spirit. However things go, his fate and that of his house will certainly not be happier than mine.'[11]

Vittorio showed his father a collection of Italian newspaper articles that followed his overthrow, attacking him, his family and the Fascists in general. After reading the articles, Mussolini said: 'I thought there were plenty of hyenas and jackals in Africa, but not that they disembarked with the Anglo-Americans in Italy. Is it possible that such things are written in Italy? Are there people who believe these lies?'

Speaking to the little group of Fascists clustered around him in Germany, Mussolini said: 'Italy must return to the battle; her honour requires it. Besides there is the need of a lightning rod against German anger and internal chaos. . . . Should we stand at the window and watch as they burn the house? Hitler leaves the decision to me, but he has made me understand clearly that the German people . . . will not tolerate a weak attitude of the German forces toward the Italy of Badoglio.'[12]

Once Mussolini had accepted the decision to return to a semblance of power, Hitler called in his personal physician, the quack Dr Theodor Morell who was treating his own physical ailments with a cocktail of possibly dangerous drugs, and ordered him to restore Mussolini to health. Fortunately for Mussolini, Morell enlisted the services of Zachariae, an internal medicine specialist who had been in the army since 1939 and shared none of Morell's crackpot ideas. Zachariae diagnosed a large duodenal ulcer, and determined that Mussolini suffered from enlargement of the liver, a relatively high sugar content in his blood and a deformed colon. There had long been rumours that Mussolini suffered from syphilis as well. Zachariae established that he had no active syphilis, and the Duce assured him he never had been so afflicted; these rumours had simply been spread by his opponents.

Morell read Zachariae's reports and wrote out a number of prescriptions that appalled and frightened Zachariae on his patient's behalf. Among other things, Morell wanted to give Mussolini intravenous iodide to protect his heart and veins against syphilis infection. Zachariae knew this would not only be superfluous but actually harmful. 'I absolutely did not intend to make of the Duce a walking pharmacy,' he wrote afterwards. He decided secretly to defy Morell and follow his own course of treatment.[13]

Mussolini spent two weeks in Germany, undergoing medical exams, being reunited with his family and meeting Fascist Party and government officials who had fled to the safety of the Reich after his overthrow. Others had gone to safe havens such as Spain, taken refuge in extraterritorial religious institutions around Rome or been imprisoned by the Badoglio government before its ignominious flight from the capital. Those who gathered in Germany were naturally the most extreme Fascists, among them Alessandro Pavolini, a former minister of popular culture who had been dismissed by Mussolini in February 1943; Farinacci, the fervently anti-Jewish former secretary of the Fascist Party; Renato Ricci, a longtime Fascist and former minister of communications; and Preziosi. While Mussolini was still in captivity, German authorities provided the Fascists with a radio station, Radio Munich, to beam broadcasts to Italy. The Germans insisted they should set up a provisional Fascist government, but Vittorio later wrote that the Italians resisted taking such a step in the absence of Mussolini. Instead, they began in their broadcasts to advise Italians to remain united and calm and not to exacerbate the Germans by resort to armed resistance.[14]

Mussolini told his associates at one of their first meetings in Germany that enemy invasion of Italy was intolerable and a German occupation would be insupportable. For that reason, he said, Italy must take up again its position in the front line of battle alongside Germany. As to the shape of his new government, he recognised that the authoritarian style he had followed for more than twenty years – 'the system from on high' – had failed. 'Because men failed,' he argued. 'Not fascism, men.' The new order, he said, would be a 'system from the bottom up'. But then he asked what would happen if the masses were to fail. 'The same need they had of a Duce, doesn't that tell you anything? I myself will ask the nation to confirm its confidence in me.'[15] In short, the 'system from the bottom up' had its limitations; there would always be a Duce to guard against the failings of others.

Mussolini, his wife Rachele and their two youngest children, Romano and Anna Maria, were ensconced during their stay in Germany in the Hirschberg Castle, 50 miles south of Munich, and remained there about a week. From their residence, near the winter resort of Garmisch-Partenkirchen, they could see on the horizon the gleam of fires caused by the Allied bombing of Munich.[16]

Ciano and his wife Edda had been in Germany nearly three weeks before Mussolini arrived. After Mussolini's downfall, those who had drawn Ciano into the plot to overthrow Mussolini wanted nothing to do with him. The Badoglio government placed him under house arrest in Rome and drew up plans to imprison him on charges of financial corruption. His strong-willed wife Edda, who had always been sympathetic to the Germans, finally arranged with SS Colonel Eugen Dollmann to have the couple and their three children spirited out of the country on 27 August. They were under the impression the Germans would fly them to safety in Spain, but instead they were taken to Munich, where Ciano was placed under house arrest. Edda later flew to Hitler's secret headquarters in the forests of East Prussia to try to negotiate her husband's release but succeeded only in offending the Führer, telling him among other things that the war was lost and his only alternative was to make a separate peace with the Russians. Hitler leapt to his feet. '*Nein*! *Nein*!' he cried. 'Anything but that! I shall never negotiate with the Russians, madam. You cannot marry water with fire. Peace with them is impossible.'[17]

Edda, who met her father on 13 September, beseeched him to receive Ciano: the Duce agreed, and a meeting took place several days later. 'The greeting was warm and they embraced with emotion,' Edda noted. 'Then they were closeted together for some time. Upon leaving my father's office Galeazzo seemed quite serene. He told me that he had explained his role to my father, who had seemed to believe him, and that he had asked to be permitted to return to Italy and work in no-matter-what capacity, including going into the Air Force. According to my husband, Papa had agreed to this.'

Rachele Mussolini shared the German dislike of Ciano, whom she could not forgive for his vote in the Grand Council. 'I will spit in his face if he comes near me,' she said. But she was present at the first meeting between the two men and said that, for love of Edda, she suppressed her resentment. A few days later, however, she scolded Ciano severely: 'If you didn't like the post the Duce had assigned you, you could have resigned.' Ciano tried to say he had always acted in good faith, but she cut him off. 'The Duce is not a piece of furniture that you can put in the sunroom when someone is tired of it,' she said. 'You have erred and it may be that one day you will have to pay for this.'[18]

* * *

On 18 September in Munich, Mussolini made his first radio address to the Italian people since his rescue. He harked back to his arrest and said he was convinced the Badoglio government had intended to hand him over to the enemy. 'I had, however, the clear impression, even though I was completely isolated from the world, that the Führer would not have abandoned me,' he said. He went on to describe how Hitler, during his imprisonment, had sent him a 'truly monumental edition' of the works of Nietzsche. 'The word loyalty has a profound, clear-cut, I would say eternal significance in the German soul,' he enthused.

He contrasted Hitler's steadfastness with the perfidy of the king: 'It is not the regime that has betrayed the monarchy, it is the monarchy that has betrayed the regime . . . When a monarchy fails in its duties, it loses every reason for being. . . . The state we want to establish will be national and social in the highest sense of the word; that is, it will be Fascist, thus returning to our origins.'

He outlined the four principal points of his new government's programme:

1. Take up arms again alongside Germany and Japan.
2. Prepare the reorganisation of armed forces around militia units without delay.
3. Eliminate traitors, particularly those who voted against him in the Grand Council on 25 July and 'passed into the ranks of the enemy'.
4. Annihilate the 'parasitical plutocracies'.

'I call you again to work and to arms,' Mussolini exhorted. 'Our will, our courage, our faith will give back to Italy its face, its future, its possibility of life and its place in the world.'[19]

These words were those of the Duce of old, an attempt to rally his people behind him once again. But the voice was another thing, the voice of a man so ill and tired that it was unrecognisable to many Italians. Word spread quickly inside the country that Mussolini was dead and the man who gave the speech was an impostor trying to preserve the fiction that he was alive. Claretta Petacci, Mussolini's mistress, heard the speech at an airfield near Bergamo in northern Italy where she and her family had stopped en route to Merano. She was so overcome with emotion that she fainted.[20]

After finishing his speech, Mussolini told Rachele: 'I am convinced that Italy can still be saved. My appeal will be heard by all those who have faith, by all who have fought.'[21]

Ciano had another two meetings with Mussolini, offering once again to enter the armed forces if he were allowed to return to Italy. 'My husband naturally let himself be affected,' Rachele said. On 19 September, the Cianos dined with the Mussolinis. Romano, the sixteen-year-old son of the Mussolinis, went into another room during dinner and began playing American jazz on the piano. He was made to understand that American music was not much appreciated, so he switched to Viennese waltzes. Vittorio Mussolini later described the family gathering:

> My father sat at the head of the table, in an old wooden chair. He was in a dark civilian suit, with a tie that had been hurriedly and carelessly knotted. . . . He was thinner and obviously suffering, and only his eyes, deep and commanding, had conserved something of their force. After some minutes the orderlies served the soup: a rather watery vegetable broth. Papa took only a few spoonfuls, with no relish. I saw him lost in thought far from us, and perhaps from himself. On his right sat my brother-in-law Galeazzo in his usual aloof manner, which so angered my mother.
>
> He was wearing a light grey suit, perfectly cut, and out of his breast pocket a crisp white handkerchief protruded with casual elegance. His hair was carefully combed, his nails immaculately cut. From time to time he even managed to make us smile, commenting to me on the modest lunch, which after the soup consisted only of a duck, a few boiled potatoes and a piece of horrible synthetic yellow butter. . . .
>
> Next to me Edda, silently trying to swallow a few mouthfuls, was oblivious of everything other than how to save her husband. It was her instinct, rather than specific German opposition to plans for the whole Ciano family to escape to Spain, that told her Germany was the really mortal danger for her family. Galeazzo, immediately after the talk with my father, had tried to give him courage, showing he felt sure of his innocence and therefore of the understanding and protection of the Duce. But in that moment Edda, the Duce, the Führer, the war, the alliance, were words devoid of meaning. To flee, this was the only thing that needed to be done and therefore whoever might have a different opinion became for her, automatically, an enemy: even my father. . . .
>
> The meager meal of roast duck and boiled potato was over, and my father was picking up the crumbs around his plate – a habit of his.

> Next to him Galeazzo lightly wiped his lips with a corner of his napkin and slowly drank a glass of Mosel wine. Edda and my mother watched them both silently. . . .
>
> My father left us with a tired wave. When he had gone out of the room, Edda and Galeazzo got up to go back to the villa at Allmanshausen. . . . Only my mother and I had remained in the big dining room. I shall always remember the look she had in her eyes. She was staring into space, but she wasn't crying.[22]

The apparent reconciliation of Mussolini with Ciano did not go unnoticed by the Germans, and Goebbels commented in his diary on 23 September: 'Edda Mussolini has succeeded in completely reversing the Duce's opinion of Ciano. . . . That means this poisonous mushroom is again planted in the midst of the new Fascist Republican Party. It is obvious that the Duce cannot start criminal proceedings against the traitors of fascism if he is not willing to call his own son-in-law to account. . . . If after all his bad experiences the Duce again puts himself in the hands of his daughter Edda, who is really a vulgar and mean wench, he can't be helped politically.'[23]

Mussolini's first official act on resuming the reins of power was to send Alessandro Pavolini, who was to become the new Fascist Party secretary, and Renato Ricci, who would head the militia units, to Rome to begin the work of forming a new government and armed forces. Vittorio also went to Rome to collect his father's archives and to arrange for the transfer of his office staff to a new location, yet to be decided. On 23 September, Goebbels wrote in his diary that Pavolini was having little luck building up the Fascist Party and Fascist militia in Rome. 'In response to his first appeal for recreating the Fascist militia, exactly fifteen men in the Italian capital reported! . . . One can see from it to what depths fascism has already sunk in public esteem.'[24]

The writer Felice Bellotti said Pavolini's humiliation was worse than that. He went to Rome with a list of forty people he hoped to recruit for high posts in the new government, and promised Mussolini that all would accept. Only three did so.[25]

Before Mussolini's radio speech, Hitler had spoken to Mussolini of re-establishing an Italian Fascist state, and Mussolini told him the state must be a republic. There was no dispute on that point; both men believed the Italian monarchy was finished. Hitler suggested the new state be called the Italian Fascist Republic, but Mussolini objected, saying fascism belonged to the past and the name would be a subject of discord. He must appeal to all Italians outside and above fascism, he argued. Hitler continued to insist on 'Fascist Republic', and Mussolini continued to resist. He did refer in his speech to a return to fascism, but his Cabinet decided on 25 November that the new regime would be known as the Italian Social Republic, or by its Italian initials, RSI. The name harked back to Mussolini's Socialist past, before he invented fascism in the 1920s.[26]

* * *

On the day after Mussolini's arrest, British Prime Minister Winston Churchill had sent a telegram to President Franklin D. Roosevelt, forecasting that the new Badoglio government would seek an early armistice with the Allies and suggesting they should now agree among themselves on what they wanted from Italy. 'The fury of the Italian population will now be turned against the German intruders who have, as they will feel, brought all these miseries upon Italy and then come so scantily and grudgingly to her aid,' he wrote. 'We should stimulate this process in order that the new liberated anti-Fascist Italy shall afford us at the earliest moment a safe and friendly area on which we can base the whole forward Air attack upon South and Central Germany.'

Churchill went on to discuss what treatment should be meted out to Mussolini and his retinue, or what Roosevelt had described as 'the head devil together with his partners in crime'. 'Some may prefer prompt execution without trial except for identification purposes,' Churchill wrote. 'Others may prefer that they be kept in confinement till the end of the war in Europe and their fate decided together with that of other war criminals. Personally, I am fairly indifferent on this matter, provided always that no solid military advantages are sacrificed for the sake of immediate vengeance.'[27]

Unfortunately, Churchill's hopes for establishing an early platform in Italy for air attacks on Germany were misplaced. The choice of Badoglio to head the government was a disastrous one, made by a king who had himself played a compromising role throughout the Fascist era. Badoglio was a vacillating 72-year-old who had been dismissed by Mussolini after the disaster of the Italian campaign in Greece in 1940 and should have been left to enjoy retirement. Marquis Blasco D'Aieta, the newly arrived Italian counsellor in Lisbon, gave the British ambassador there an alarming account of conditions in Rome, which Churchill passed on to Roosevelt in a telegram on 5 August. 'Fascism in Italy is extinct. . . . Italy turned red overnight' was D'Aieta's estimation. As he saw it, only the king and those who had rallied around him remained as a bulwark against a Communist takeover. D'Aieta said the king and Badoglio wanted to make peace but had no alternative to putting up a show of going on with the fight. He reported that a communiqué would be issued in Rome the following day affirming that Italy would continue the war at Germany's side, but this would be only a pretence. The Italians wanted to be rid of the Germans and were anxiously awaiting liberation by the Allies. When the Allies landed in Italy, they would find little opposition and perhaps even active cooperation on the part of the Italians.

In Berlin, Hitler foresaw that Badoglio would proclaim loyalty to the Axis but would then betray the Germans. He threatened to send in a tank division to arrest the king, crown prince and the Badoglio government, then march into the Vatican and clean out 'that bunch of swine' represented by the diplomatic corps. Hitler also ordered eight German divisions from France and southern Germany to secure the Alpine passes, vital for the supply of German troops already in Italy.[28]

Fearing an overthrow and possible execution by the Germans, Badoglio did proclaim that Italy's war alongside its Axis ally would continue. There were German troops stationed not far from Rome, and their presence evidently preyed on his mind. The king was impatient for negotiations with the Allies in order to arrange a quick exit from the war, but Badoglio dithered. Raffaele Guariglia, the new Italian foreign minister and one of the few competent people in government, shared the king's impatience with Badoglio. He sent envoys to Tangiers on 3 August to sound out the Allies and inform them that Italy was ready to change sides. The Italians were told there could be no negotiation; only unconditional surrender would be accepted.

General Dwight D. Eisenhower, the Allied commander in Europe, was anxious to obtain an early Italian surrender because he had fixed 9 September as the date for invading the Italian mainland at Salerno in the south and he did not want to face opposition from Italian forces. Badoglio continued to equivocate, but Guariglia took charge of events and on 3 September dispatched General Giuseppe Castellano to Sicily to sign a short surrender document. The Allies agreed with Castellano that airborne landings on Rome would follow within hours of the announcement of the armistice, with seaborne landings at the mouth of the Tiber near Rome twenty-four hours later. The Allies planned to announce the armistice on 8 September.

General Maxwell Taylor, second-in-command of the 82nd Airborne Division, arrived in Rome on 7 September to coordinate plans for the air landings, only to discover the Italians had made no preparations. Badoglio evidently still feared the Germans would march in and execute him, and he argued for a postponement of the air landings. Eisenhower was furious and called them off. On the morning of 8 September, Badoglio sent him a radio message to the effect that it was no longer possible to accept an immediate armistice as this could provoke German occupation of Rome. But Eisenhower was determined to go ahead, and the king overruled Badoglio. On the evening of 8 September, the marshal went on the radio to announce the armistice – but failed to exhort his troops to fight the Germans. On the following day, a frightened Badoglio and the king fled to Brindisi in south-east Italy, gaining protection behind the advancing British Eighth Army, which had landed unopposed in the deep south. In his flight, Badoglio could easily have gone to the Gran Sasso and taken Mussolini to southern Italy with him as a prisoner, but he chose to ignore the clause in the Italian surrender agreement that called for Mussolini to be handed over to the Allies. In his haste to leave Rome and save his own skin, Badoglio even failed to alert his ministers he was going, and gave no instructions to his generals concerning the defence of Rome. After the ignominious flight of Badoglio and the king, an Italian diplomat based in Rome, Luigi Bolla, recorded in his diary: 'I feel a shame, a bitterness, a humiliation, an indescribable pain. For the first time I regret having been born Italian.'

At the time of Mussolini's overthrow, the Germans had seven divisions in Italy; by 8 September, they had twenty-four or twenty-five, poured in over Alpine passes that Badoglio had neglected to defend. Churchill later told the House of Commons there had been no negligence or lack of faith on the part of the Badoglio government in failing to hand over Mussolini, but that clearly was not true. Churchill blamed the Carabinieri who were guarding Mussolini, saying they had orders to shoot him if he were in danger of getting away, but they had failed in their duty. In fact, as noted above, Police Chief Carmine Senise had countermanded the order to shoot the Duce and had told the Carabinieri to act with 'prudence' if there were any attempt at rescue.

Badoglio's abandonment of his troops, and his failure to order them immediately to fight the Germans, resulted in the German capture of 600,000 soldiers, including 22,000 officers, and a huge amount of war material, stretching from the Italian mainland to southern France, Yugoslavia and the Greek islands. The soldiers were loaded into cattle trucks, taken by rail to Germany and interned in concentration camps in miserable conditions, most for the duration of the war. The Allies also had missed, thanks to Badoglio, a golden opportunity to capture Rome; it would take another nine months of hard fighting before they could achieve that goal.[29]

* * *

On the Greek island of Cephalonia, 200 miles across the Ionian Sea from Italy's south-eastern coast, Italian soldiers of the Acqui Division who shared control of the island with a smaller German force learned that their fellow troops were being sent to Germany for internment, and decided to resist. Fighting broke out between the Italians and Germans on 15 September and raged until 22 September when the Italians, nearly out of ammunition and under attack from Stuka dive-bombers, capitulated.

The Germans received an order from the Führer to massacre all the Italians who had fought. As the Germans moved into the positions of the surrendering Italians, they cut them down with machine-gun fire. Those who escaped this first attack were marched off to the town hall and executed by detachments of eight German soldiers. The Germans then forced twenty Italian sailors to load the bodies on rafts and sink them in the sea. Once this was accomplished, the sailors were shot too.

Of 12,000 Italian troops on Cephalonia, 1,250 fell in combat and 4,750 were put to death after their surrender. Another 4,000 who had surrendered without fighting were put on three ships to be taken to the Greek mainland, but all the ships hit mines and sank. A few Italians who managed to jump into the sea were machine-gunned. The remaining Italians on the island escaped after the surrender, joined Greek guerrillas and later fought under the Italian royal banner.

Italians on the Greek island of Corfu also decided to fight, and on 13 September they overran a German post, later sending 400 German prisoners back to Italy. The Italians evacuated 1,760 of their own troops before the Germans put down the resistance. On 25 September, a number of Italian officers were captured and shot, and forty-one more were shot on the field of battle. Four days later, more officers were shot or put in sacks that were thrown into the sea. The remaining Italian troops were put aboard ships to be transferred to the mainland for later internment in Germany. One ship was attacked by Allied planes on 10 October and was sunk. Once again the Germans machine-gunned Italians trying to swim ashore.

The Cephalonia massacre in particular was one of the worst German atrocities of the war, but the German commander on the island, General Hubert Lanz, received only a twelve-year sentence when he went before the Nuremberg war crimes tribunal in 1948, and was released after serving five years. He claimed that fewer than a dozen Italian staff officers had been shot, and his testimony apparently was believed. Curiously enough, the Italian government produced no evidence at the trial.[30]

* * *

In Rome, the Germans had wasted little time after the flight of the king and Badoglio in taking over the capital and plundering Italy's wealth. There had been relatively few Germans in the capital at the time of the 8 September armistice, but two days later they began shelling the city. Many Italian soldiers hastily put on civilian clothes. They said their officers had told them they were out of ammunition, had told them to 'do what you can for yourselves, boys', and had fled. During the evening of 10 September, the

Germans occupied Rome.[31] That same day Goebbels recorded in his diary that the only certainty about the war was that Italy would lose it. 'Its pusillanimous treachery to its own leader was the prelude to cowardly treachery toward its ally. The Duce will enter history as the last Roman, but behind his massive figure a gypsy people has gone to rot.'[32]

Almost immediately the German troops in Rome began looting houses on a wide scale and robbing Italians. 'They stop people in the street and take their jewels, rings, chains, watches and money from them at the muzzle of a revolver,' reported Mother Mary St Luke,* an American nun who lived in Rome throughout the occupation. 'They are also stealing bicycles and motor cars.' She said German troops had even forced Monsignor Rosignani, who had been secretary to Pope Pius XII when the pope was still a cardinal, from his car and had driven it away.[33] Other Germans broke into the apartment of the pope's sister, killed her lodger who opened the door, then ate and drank their fill before looting and going away. M. de Wyss, a Swiss journalist based in Rome, said the Germans also violated many girls, including one who was seven years old.

On 21 September, she said, Germans passing along Via Nomentana in a truck suddenly opened fire at a group of civilians, killing four and wounding five others. 'Why?' de Wyss wrote. 'Nobody knows. It was apparently just a German whim.'[34]

Germans were also reported to be going into restaurants in Rome and, at the end of a meal, tearing up the bill saying: 'Badoglio pays for this.'[35]

Luigi Bolla, the diplomat who was in Rome at the time, wrote in his diary on 10 September: 'Our units have received no orders and don't know what to do. Some let themselves be captured by the Germans, who have disarmed them, removed their badges of rank, beaten them and sent them away. I have seen soldiers tear off stars and tabs on uniforms. I have seen Carabinieri run without purpose, saying that their officers fled, advising them to steal away and get civilian clothes. I have seen military men strip off in the street and put on old trousers.' One report noted about 60,000 disbanded Italian soldiers were wandering through the city, begging for food and civilian clothes.

Nine days later, Bolla observed: 'That Mussolini today is the only possibility of safeguarding us before the Germans is without doubt. That Mussolini can still be the Duce is impossible.'[36]

On 20 September, Major Herbert Kappler, the head of the Gestapo in Rome, met Vincenzo Azzolini, the governor of the Bank of Italy, and ordered him to hand over the Italian gold reserves. Subsequently, 120 tons of gold were sent

*Mother Mary St Luke, who worked at the Vatican, described her wartime experiences in a book written under the pseudonym Jane Scrivener. Her real name was Jessica Lynch.

to Milan under German control and later transferred to Fortezza, a small town near the Austrian border. Sixteen thousand sections of rail track and a large quantity of mercury and precious metals were also seized and sent to Germany. The Germans transferred the Military Geographic Institute of Florence to Merano in northern Italy and to Innsbruck, Austria, obliging the 230 people employed there to move to those cities.[37]

Not content with having disarmed and interned most of the Italian armed forces, Field Marshal Albert Kesselring, the German military commander, gave orders on 28 September that the army's horses and mules be handed over. With typical German meticulousness, he specified that each animal must have a good halter and reins six feet long, and each must come with ten pounds of hay. Any attempt to thwart this order, he said, would be punished according to the German law of war.[38]

On 9 October, Bolla wrote: 'Today all the people hate the Germans profoundly, inextinguishably. . . . It is superfluous to add that the new Fascist Republican Party has no following.'[39]

The German repression would soon become more intense, in ways even Kesselring had not anticipated.

Chapter 3

BIRTH OF THE SALÒ REPUBLIC

This republic begins to lose ground every day.

(Benito Mussolini, 1 October 1943)

In late September, Mussolini decided to return to Italy. Rachele asked him why he was in such a rush, and he replied: 'Badoglio's declaration of war has thrown Italy into an absurd situation. I have to go to see what is happening there and place relations between Italians and Germans on the right footing.'[1] By now the Germans, at least according to Goebbels, had all but given up on Mussolini. In his diary on 23 September, Goebbels wrote that Hitler believed the Duce had no great political future. 'His whole political conception is without real clarity because he is too much bound to his family. He is undoubtedly an exceptionally inspired thinker and a high-grade political strategist, but in the last analysis he is nothing but an Italian and can't get away from that heritage. . . . We must begin slowly to write off the Duce politically. However much we may like him personally . . . there must be a limit somewhere, especially when the interests of the Reich are involved.'[2]

Mussolini, wearing a militia uniform and a borrowed black shirt, piloted a German warplane which brought him back to Italy on 25 September. This was, in effect, the birth date of his new republic. He landed at Forlì and was driven to Rocca delle Caminate, his summer residence near his birthplace at Predappio.

He had insisted that his new regime should not be a phantom government, but he was to be quickly disabused of that notion. His return to power was not a true political rebirth; the new government was an infant who, because of a brutal parentage, never really grew or learned to walk unaided. Hitler despised what he had created and dealt Mussolini a severe blow even before he returned, annexing eight provinces of Italy near the Austrian border. Bolzano, Trento and Belluno were united in what was called the Austrian Voralpenland. Udine, Gorizia, Trieste, Pola and Fiume – the latter two in what is now Croatia – were incorporated in the Adriatisches Kustenland and united to the Austrian province of Styria. The first six of these provinces covered 1,500 square miles and had a population of 3 million. Nazi gauleiters were appointed by Hitler to head each of the two new political units.[3] As a result of the Versailles Treaty that followed the First World War, Austria had lost the South Tyrol to Italy, and at the time of this transfer, the region was renamed the Alto Adige. Now Austria regained the South Tyrol, and more. In November, the Croatian Fascist regime, whose leader Ante Pavelic had enjoyed Mussolini's support before he came to power, took advantage of the Italian surrender by annexing, with German consent, part of Venezia Giulia, Istria and Dalmatia.[4]

Naturally, Mussolini was extremely upset. 'I am not here to renounce even a square metre of state territory,' he told his associates. 'We will go back to war for this. And we will rebel against anyone for this. Where the Italian flag flew, the Italian flag will return. And where it has not been lowered, now that I am here, no one will have it lowered. I've said these things to the Führer.'[5] The Germans assured him the annexation was not permanent, merely a security measure for the duration of the war. Mussolini was not placated, and with good reason. Goebbels wrote in his diary that Hitler wanted to extend the German border as far as the Veneto, and include that region in the Reich 'in a sort of loose federation'. Goebbels imagined the Veneto would accept this 'since only the Reich could supply it with tourist trade, to which Venice attaches the greatest importance'.[6]

At his overthrow in July, Mussolini had controlled all Italy and Albania, a sliver of southern France, part of Croatia and several Greek islands. Just two months later, the territory that was left to his new republic was but a fraction of that. The French, Croatian and Greek territory was gone and, apart from the German-annexed provinces, he had lost most of the land south of Rome. Four provinces in the far south were under the control of the Badoglio government, and the rest of southern Italy was a battleground between the Germans and the Allies. Even in the area Mussolini nominally controlled, the German military exercised effective power in many instances. Still, Mussolini could claim that he governed the richest part of Italy – the industries of the north, especially in Milan and Turin; the ports of Genoa, Livorno and Venice; and the fertile Po valley, the country's breadbasket.

Just eight countries gave diplomatic recognition to the republic – Germany, Japan and their satellites, including Manchukuo, the Japanese puppet regime in Manchuria. It was undoubtedly a bitter blow to Mussolini that his troops had helped bring his fellow Fascist dictator Francisco Franco to power in Spain during that country's civil war, yet Franco withheld recognition and the Italian embassy in Madrid passed to the Badoglio government. This was a disappointment to the Germans as well, as they had hoped to gain control of Italian ships blocked in Spanish ports at the time of the armistice.[7] The Vatican also refused recognition, but high-ranking clerics sometimes came to the republic to bless its people, not its government.

Gina Ruberti, the widow of Mussolini's son Bruno, who had been killed in an air accident, joined the Duce at Rocca delle Caminate and was fully aware of the problems he faced in trying to win back public approval. It would be difficult, she told him, to get Italians to respond to the old Fascist slogan 'Believe, Obey, Fight'. Mussolini responded: 'It will be necessary to replace it with the three theological virtues: Faith, Hope, Charity. Faith in Divine Providence, hope in victory, charity of the country.'[8]

Mussolini held his first Cabinet meeting at Rocca delle Caminate two days after his return, with ministers escorted from Rome by SS Colonel Eugen Dollmann, the suave, sophisticated German who had arranged the departure of the Cianos from Rome. A long-time resident of Italy with good contacts in Italian high society, Dollmann had been recruited into the SS after Hitler came to power and had often functioned as interpreter at meetings of Hitler and Mussolini. When the party of ministers stopped at Spoleto for lunch en route to Rocca delle Caminate, the new armed forces minister, Marshal Rodolfo Graziani, told Dollmann: 'It's best that you know this immediately: I have never been a Fascist, but always a soldier who obeyed orders.'[9]

The appointment of Graziani had been imposed on a reluctant Mussolini by Hitler, whose opinion perhaps had been influenced by the antisemite Giovanni Preziosi. Preziosi saw in Graziani a fellow Jew-hater and opponent of Freemasons. The Masonic Order, with its secret rituals, was regarded by the Nazis and extreme Fascists such as Preziosi as a subversive society, and was banned in Germany in 1935. The Duce had never forgiven Graziani for his humiliating defeat at the hands of the British in North Africa in 1940 and the subsequent loss of the Italian foothold there. At the time he had considered having Graziani arrested and tried, and confided to his police chief, Carmine Senise, that he thought an exemplary shooting might be in order. 'Here is another man', he said, 'with whom I cannot get angry because I despise him.'[10] In disgrace, Graziani had retired to his farm in southern Italy. Hitler said Graziani did not enjoy his confidence but was the only Italian general with the prestige and popularity to do the job. Mussolini's acceptance of Graziani, he said, was an 'indispensable condition' for his renouncing a plan of reprisal against Italy. A tall, barrel-chested man with a thin moustache, Graziani was one of the few Italian military leaders who looked the part. Before the débâcle in North Africa, he had been viceroy of Ethiopia (1936–7) and honorary governor of Italian East Africa (1938). He was reluctant to leave the farm, but he finally bowed to pressure from Rudolf von

Rahn, Hitler's plenipotentiary in Italy who would become the German ambassador to the republic. Although he later denied it, Graziani was undoubtedly swayed by a desire to bring down his old foe Badoglio, who had condescendingly referred to him as 'a good battalion commander'. Mussolini commented: 'Of the two military evils I have had to suffer in my life, Badoglio and Graziani, the least has remained to me.'

Mother Mary St Luke, an American nun living in Rome, said people there were 'horrified' by Graziani's appointment. 'Graziani is a great soldier, though a butcher by reputation; it seems impossible that such a man should have put himself at the service of such a gang,' she wrote.[11]

Graziani was at least a well-known figure in a Cabinet of largely mediocre and, in some cases, suspect figures. Some of Mussolini's former ministers had deserted him, while some men he had wanted to appoint were reluctant to serve in what clearly would be a puppet government. Several of his ambassadors also gave their allegiance to the Badoglio government. In the new government, Fascist extremists – men most disliked by a majority of Italians – were in the ascendancy.

A principal figure was Alessandro Pavolini, who as secretary of the Fascist Party was in many respects the No. 2 to Mussolini. The small, thin, cultivated Pavolini was one of the genuine intellectuals of the regime, but a flawed one. The son of a professor of linguistics, he had been a journalist and a talented poet. At twenty-six he had been the Fascist Party leader in Florence, and the historian Marco Innocenti described him as one of the best journalists of his generation, with a dry, modern, incisive style.[12] He had been raised to prominence in the Fascist movement by Galeazzo Ciano when Ciano served as foreign minister. But after Ciano helped to vote Mussolini out of office, Pavolini became Ciano's most ardent opponent and demanded his execution. This was perhaps typical of a man who always proved difficult in his relations with other people. One of the first acts of the new Cabinet was to approve the establishment of extraordinary tribunals intended to punish traitors, Ciano first among them. The writer Felice Bellotti described Pavolini as 'the most unbalanced man who ever climbed to a post of responsibility', and the diplomat Luigi Bolla said Pavolini was 'an old maid of notable intellect and bad character'. Giovanni Preziosi, who remained behind in Germany, was furious at Pavolini's appointment because Pavolini's brother had a Jewish wife.[13]

The most controversial member of the new Cabinet, intensely disliked by many Fascists as well as anti-Fascists, was the principal political survivor from an earlier Mussolini government. Guido Buffarini-Guidi, appointed interior minister, had held the post of undersecretary for the interior in Rome until Mussolini dismissed him in February 1943, partly because of his involvement in illicit gold and currency dealings in league with Marcello Petacci, the brother of Mussolini's mistress Claretta Petacci. Buffarini was jailed by the Badoglio government but freed on 12 September by the Germans, who insisted on his appointment as interior minister. Filippo Anfuso, Mussolini's last ambassador to Germany, aptly described both Buffarini and Pavolini in terms that would have made them recognisable to a fellow Tuscan of an earlier age, Niccolò Machiavelli: Pavolini was a fourteenth-century Tuscan with an intolerance inspired by medieval conformism, Buffarini a Renaissance Tuscan in his 'diabolical shrewdness'. Luigi Bolla was more cutting: Buffarini was 'an astute and greasy grocer, inside and out'.[14] Goebbels commented on the new government in his diary: 'Apart from Graziani, there is no personality of importance in the lot.'[15]

Dino Campini, secretary to Education Minister Carlo Alberto Biggini, later wrote of Mussolini: 'The man did not know how to avail himself of capable men and surrounded himself indifferently with nobodies, insensible often to the protests that these nobodies provoked.' In an earlier time Elisabetta Cerruti, wife of Italian ambassador Vittorio Cerruti, expressed a thought that was still relevant: 'The members of Mussolini's immediate circle were no better than he. They were glad he authorized them to be rude, and they hid their ignorance of manners and foreign languages behind insolence, which they called patriotism.'[16]

If some members of the new government were mediocre, Buffarini thought the same of the 250,000 Italians then enrolled as Fascist Party members. 'Very many members, above all those most in the public eye, represent the refuse of what was the Fascist Party in the past and are regarded by the population with disgust, disdain and sometimes even real terror,' he wrote. In truth, the support for Mussolini that had extended through several strata of Italian society had begun to dissolve after the Allied military victories in the winter of 1943 and would never be recaptured. One Allied report estimated that diehard Fascists now represented less than one-fifth of the population. Max Salvadori, a British Special Forces officer who spent most of his early life in Italy, said the principal groups flanking the Fascists had been the three C's, crown, capital, clergy, and all three had now deserted to other camps.[17]

Mussolini received his new Cabinet in his office while his son Vittorio, 'as always unshaven, ill-mannered and discourteous, made it clear that the hospitality was offered with ill-will', according to Colonel Dollmann, who said Vittorio later made insistent requests to General Karl Wolff, the SS commander in Italy, for millions of lire as compensation for losses suffered by the family when it was forced to flee from its Rome residence.[18]

Mussolini told the Cabinet that Italy was 'in a state of chaos like a drunk who has become disoriented'. He acknowledged the difficult position in which the country had been placed in regard to relations with Germany. 'It is a tragedy for the Italian people that Germany has remained alone to fight,' he said. 'But given things as they are, Germany alone must have the complete direction for everything that refers to the conduct of the war in Italy.'[19] One of his first acts was to free Italian military officers from their oath of loyalty to the king.

After the Cabinet meeting, Mussolini met alone with Dollmann and complained that the Romans had not lifted a hand to free him after he had been taken prisoner in July. 'When one thinks of what this city owes me, the most ungrateful of them all!' he exclaimed. 'From the time of the Caesars there has not been a government that, like fascism, made its supreme aspiration the greatness and magnificence of Rome. . . . I will not re-enter Palazzo Venezia except as a winner, and it will be another Mussolini who returns. Until that day, however, I will make that ungrateful city feel my disdain.'[20]

The ingrates in Rome were probably too concerned with survival to give much thought to Mussolini at that time. With the beginning of German occupation, food shortages had set in almost immediately, and only a thriving black market kept many residents from starvation. Mother Mary St Luke described the situation in meticulous detail in her diary:

> Many shops are boarding windows to save glass or discourage looting. Even when the shop windows are not boarded up there is next to nothing in them. . . . The lira is worth next to nothing. . . . There is no salt and there are no matches. Gas goes on only for a brief period three times a day. Smokers are to be allowed three cigarettes a day. Salt is to be had at 150 lire a kilo on the black market, its original price being one lira. . . .
>
> Little sugar is allowed, a tenth of a liter of [olive] oil. Green vegetables are difficult, if not impossible. No fruit, fresh or canned. Flour and rice in the black market at terrific prices. Potatoes the same, but rare. Milk is next to unobtainable. No meat or fish, no eggs except on the black market. Tea, coffee and cocoa, no.

Mother Mary said there had been 'an avalanche' of requests from Romans for English lessons, with some saying: 'We want to know how to welcome the Allies when they come.'[21]

Thousands of Roman men had gone into hiding to escape German attempts to call them up for labour service in either Italy or Germany. A few hundred escaped Allied prisoners were also hiding in the city. Some of the men, Romans as well as Allied soldiers, took refuge in private homes, some in convents, seminaries and other church institutions that enjoyed extraterritorial sanctuary. 'Another famous [refuge] is the Lunatic Asylum,' wrote the journalist M. de Wyss. 'Scores of people have entered it and have filled it to bursting point: Rome never had so many madmen.'[22]

Many who were not fortunate enough to escape were tortured at Herbert Kappler's notorious Gestapo headquarters in a modern building at 155 Via Tasso, or in Fascist Party torture chambers. Even the Germans were disturbed by reports of some of the excesses carried out by the Fascists, and they organised a raid on the headquarters in late November, finding men in a pitiable state from starvation and torture. 'Some details of the torture are too revolting for description,' Mother Mary wrote in her diary. The raiding party also found the Fascists had concealed large stocks of foodstuffs, a live cow and gold, silver and jewellery stolen from houses. Forty of the Fascists were sent to northern Italy for trial.[23]

The Germans were no less eager than Mussolini himself to have the Duce back in Rome. He suggested putting his capital in Merano or Bolzano, both in provinces that had been annexed by Germany, but of course the Germans would not entertain such an idea. Field Marshal Erwin Rommel, the military commander in Italy before Kesselring replaced him, had his command on Lake Garda, and the Germans decided Mussolini should be near him. So, reluctantly, Mussolini accepted that the little town of Gargnano, about 20 miles up the west side of the lake, should be his capital.

He arrived there on 8 October and ensconced himself in the nineteenth-century Villa Feltrinelli, owned by the Lombard industrialist Antonio Feltrinelli, on the shores of the lake. Mussolini's immediate impression was that his new home, a gloomy villa of thirty-seven rooms furnished with fake antiques but surrounded by well-tended gardens and olive trees, was 'lugubrious and hostile', and he never learned to like it. The diplomat Luigi Bolla shared that assessment, saying the villa was almost vulgar in its furnishings and had 'the air of a waiting room in a provincial doctor's office'. At first the Villa Feltrinelli – today transformed into a luxury hotel heavily patronised by wealthy German tourists – functioned as Mussolini's home and office, but in November the office was transferred to Villa delle Orsoline in the centre of Gargnano, also owned by Feltrinelli. The doorways to his home and office were each guarded by one SS man and one Fascist Blackshirt. SS men swarmed all over the grounds of Villa Feltrinelli.

Other government ministries were widely scattered across northern Italy, which became a major obstacle to their effective operation and coordination, especially with the communication systems in chaos. The Germans controlled the only functioning telephone lines, and until December 1943 they forbade government officials from using them. Telegrams often took two or three days to reach their destination. When the Germans finally relented and opened the phone system, they monitored all conversations by government officials, and it still sometimes took hours to get a call through from one town to another. The government had no communication with provinces in the south, and only sporadic links with Rome and central Italy.[24]

The reborn Mussolini regime has gone down in history as the Republic of Salò, but only the Foreign Ministry and the Ministry of Popular Culture were located at Salò, a town of 7,000 people near the southern end of Lake Garda. The Ministry of Popular Culture (a euphemism for a ministry of propaganda) was responsible for issuing government communiqués, all reported by the Fascist news agency Stefani with a Salò dateline. Journalists became accustomed to writing such phrases as 'Salò has announced' or 'Salò says'. But some Italians insisted on calling the new government 'Pinocchio's Republic'. The Interior Ministry was at Maderno, Defence at Cremona and Desenzano, Economy at Verona. Other ministries were at Bogliaco, Asolo, Monza, Vicenza, Montecchio, Iseo, Milan, Bergamo, Treviso, Padua and Brescia. One was at Venice, nearly 100 miles away. The general direction of the police was at Valdagno and the Fascist Party headquarters at Maderno, a few miles south of Gargnano. The dispersion of the government ministries in widely scattered localities was a deliberate move by the Germans to cripple any effective functioning of the regime. Compounding the new government's problems, most civil servants in Rome gave up their jobs rather than move north. Others simply found excuses not to move. 'In Rome 90 per cent of the civil servants are at present seriously ill,' Mussolini commented sarcastically on 7 November. 'And there is no shortage of doctors who issue their declarations for a price.'[25]

Milan would have been the natural capital of a government in the north. But Mussolini complained to his secretary, Giovanni Dolfin, that the Germans had not wanted to establish the government in any city on the pretext that it was necessary to save him and urban populations from Allied bombing. 'The cities become "ploughed" without us,' he said. 'Distances divide us and this is the real reason they have put us in this hole.'[26] A few weeks later he told Dolfin: 'Here we are at the extreme terminus of that Italy we want to govern and that the Germans, in perfect accord with the Anglo-Americans, are reducing ever more.' He had learned that, in the Alto Adige, Italian street signs and other writings were disappearing and at Limone, near the north end of Lake Garda, the Germans had established a frontier barrier. Mussolini described Gargnano as an oppressive, dark alley (*budello*).[27] He gave an accurate description of the mood of the Italian people at that time. He said there were three Italies – that of the king, his own and that 'of the multitude, which believes neither in us nor in them, which aspires only to peace'.[28]

With good reason. Allied air raids on Italy had contributed to war-weariness, but not all Italians blamed the United States or Britain; many held the Fascist government responsible for these attacks. In Milan alone, 200,000 people lost their housing because of Allied bombing, 300,000 were evacuated from the city and 80,000 lived in damaged houses. A large part of the city's population left the city each night aboard special trains, slept in the open in the countryside, then returned in the mornings. Turin and Genoa also were hard hit. Many houses that had not been damaged lacked light, water and heating.[29] Mussolini's dilemma was that the last of the Italies he enumerated overlapped the other two: war-weary Italians were an overwhelming majority in his republic and in the south. The Duce had never achieved quite the godlike status Hitler had acquired in Germany, or Stalin had in Russia, but he had come close. After 1940, the leader who was 'always right' was very often wrong, and by 1943 Italians only wanted to be rid of the war at almost any price. If he had any hope of regaining his popularity, Mussolini needed to get out of his hated cul-de-sac at Gargnano and travel about his republic, using his oratorical skills to rally people behind him. But, strangely, he did not take this course; it was as though he were resigned to failure, or content to remain a ghostly presence in the republic he headed. The Germans might argue it was unsafe for him to travel with Allied warplanes constantly overhead and sometimes strafing cars, and with opponents of his regime ready to shoot him in one city or another. But, had Mussolini insisted on breaking out of his isolation, the Germans undoubtedly would have had to cut him some slack. Over the succeeding months, he became extremely passive, taking little interest in the day-to-day affairs of government and fobbing off German officials when they brought problems to him by telling them to deal with his ministers instead. The reason undoubtedly was shame at the role he had taken on as a puppet ruler. He told Dolfin that he preferred to remain out of sight 'even on the action of the government'. He added: 'At least some people will continue to believe I am dead.'[30]

The diplomat Luigi Bolla said that while some described Mussolini at Gargnano as a prisoner of the Germans, he was even more a prisoner of himself,

> a prisoner of the myths created by him to his design, a prisoner of his past . . . of having destroyed and not created, of not having formulated any message that could survive him. He knew the game was up. . . . In the squalid corner of the Villa Feltrinelli, almost hallucinatory in the days without sun like a Kafka scenario, he followed in slow motion the false routine of the old times, the routine of a functionary awaiting tasks to be got rid of, and of long, dead hours, almost the parody of himself.[31]

One early question that had to be settled was Mussolini's salary as head of state. Whatever else Mussolini may be criticised for, he was never found to be personally involved in robbing the public purse, although he tolerated corrupt officials around him throughout his years in power. He claimed never to have taken a salary when he headed the government in Rome, living from his earnings as an author and as owner of the newspaper *Popolo d'Italia*. Now he needed money; he had left Munich with only 15,000 lire given to him by Rachele, and that was soon exhausted. His daughter-in-law Gina Ruberti arrived at Rocca delle Caminate with 80,000 lire from the sale of some furniture in his former home in Rome, but even that would not last long. The Finance Ministry proposed setting his salary at 150,000 lire a month, but he considered that excessive and also rejected a suggestion from Buffarini that he take 100,000 a month. He finally had to accept 12,500 lire, the same as his ministers and undersecretaries. With a family to support and relatives crowding into Gargnano, the amount was entirely insufficient. But he later received some additional royalties from his books.[32]

The Germans continued to behave in many respects as though the new republic did not exist. German authorities appointed officials in various prefectures in north and central Italy. In Turin, they objected to Mussolini's appointment of a prefect for Piedmont and insisted on another man. 'No people', Mussolini wrote, 'likes the presence in their own territory of foreign armed forces giving out decrees and orders and exercising acts of imperium.'[33] Effectively, the new government held sway in little territory south of the Po valley. A secret circular from Führer headquarters to German military commands described the territory of the new Fascist government as comprising the lowlands of northern Italy, excluding the coastal zones, the Alps and the Apennines. That meant the government controlled the six richest and most populated regions of Italy: Piedmont, Liguria, Lombardy, Veneto, Emilia and part of Venezia Giulia. The total population of those regions was 17.2 million, in a country of 44 million.

* * *

Within days of Mussolini's return to Italy, the boundaries of his little republic shrank with the liberation of Naples – a liberation achieved not by the Allies but by the Neapolitans themselves against a greatly reduced German garrison. This represented the first successful uprising in occupied Europe against the Germans and the first serious instance of what would become a widespread Italian resistance. Naples was already a beleaguered city, subjected to 120 Allied air raids between July and 8 September that caused heavy damage and left 22,000 people dead. So many people left the city that its population was reduced by about half. The daily bread ration had been lowered to 3½ ounces per person, and still bread was hard to find. The Germans had pillaged the city and Colonel Scholl, the German commander, was fond of saying that for him one German soldier was worth the whole of Naples.

By mid-September the Germans had only a few hundred men left in the city. They began a systematic destruction of the port and the few remaining industrial plants. People living near the port were ordered to evacuate a strip 300 yards wide. Field Marshal Kesselring had wanted to evacuate an area three miles deep – practically the entire city – but the Fascist Prefect Soprano persuaded him to drop that idea. The Germans did set fire to the 300-year-old University of Naples, and students watched as archives, collections and libraries went up in flames. Some of them tried to intervene, but fifty students were surrounded in front of the building and shot while their relatives looked on helplessly.

On 22 September, Colonel Scholl issued orders for all men between the ages of eighteen and thirty-three to present themselves within three days to be sent to Germany for forced labour, and threatened punishment for those who failed to obey. Some 30,000 men fell within the stated age-bracket but, three days later, only 157 of them had shown up. These few were registered and sent home. Scholl began an attempted roundup of the missing men and ordered that those who resisted be shot.

At noon on 27 September, rumours spread that Allied troops had penetrated the city or were about to make a landing from the sea. This rumour apparently triggered the four-day Naples uprising, which started when a group of young men came out of a large farm, saw a German on a motorcycle and killed him. Then other Neapolitans hurled bombs at a motorcycle carrying two Germans, killing one and wounding the other. In reprisal, the Germans killed five young men and took another fifty into their barracks as hostages.

On the morning of 28 September, Allied ships were spotted off Capri and the Neapolitans believed a landing was imminent. Attacks on the Germans resumed, particularly in the Vomero district on the west side of the city. Spontaneous uprisings began all over Naples. People seized weapons from the arsenals of the disbanded Italian armed forces, which had been left unguarded by the Germans, and by the afternoon of the next day the Germans were under attack. Bands of gunmen darted out of hiding places to strike at the Germans, then disappeared into the maze of alleys and side streets that honeycomb Naples. The first impulse of Colonel Scholl was to leave the city, but Hitler ordered that Naples be reduced to 'mud and ashes'. Scholl threatened to kill 100 civilians for every German soldier wounded or killed. The Germans destroyed scores of houses and businesses, cut off water supplies and left port facilities in ruins. They planned to blow up aqueducts and power plants before they departed.

On 29 September, the Germans sent a long line of tanks towards the city centre, but partisan units destroyed several with cannon fire, immobilised the rest and blew them up with mines. The Germans had now lost control and in the evening began moving out of Naples. They placed cannon on Capodimonte, a hill rising above the city centre, and fired into it that day and the next, killing many people. The Neapolitan insurrectionists issued a manifesto on the morning of 30 September, declaring that they were taking power. As the Germans moved out, they stopped in San Paolo Belsito, near the suburb of Nola, and set fire to the irreplaceable historical archives of Naples. Lost were more than 50,000 parchments, 30,000 volumes of documents and precious accounts of the early history of the city, Italy and Europe.

Allied forces entered Naples on 1 October and received a jubilant greeting from its liberators. Estimates of the number of Neapolitans killed in the fighting varied widely. Major Max Salvadori of the British Special Forces, who fought with the partisans elsewhere, put the figure at around 300.[34]

* * *

'This republic begins to lose ground every day,' Mussolini commented when he learned that Naples had fallen.[35] The philosopher Benedetto Croce, observing all this from Naples, exulted that Mussolini was 'a patched puppet that has lost his sawdust and fallen down limp'. Croce, who had once recognised the extraordinary force of Mussolini's personality, now saw him as lacking in intelligence, conscience and moral sensitivity. He described him as ignorant, incapable of self-criticism, extremely vain, devoid of taste, vulgar and arrogant.[36]

Mussolini wrote to Hitler on 4 October, emphasising that his government must have autonomy within the shrunken borders in which it operated or it would fail. The German military, he said, must cease its interference in Italian civil life, and its various commands must stop issuing contradictory orders. Hitler did not respond. Ambassador Anfuso noted that Mussolini's exalted view of Germans had evaporated and he now saw them as 'a crowd of small, sinister, disquieting and at times monstrous people. . . . The Germans mutated, from historical lithographs . . . into hysterical, complicated and tendentiously hostile creatures.'[37]

The effective political rulers of occupied Italy were two men: Rudolf von Rahn, as ambassador to the republic, and General Karl Wolff, the SS commander for Italy. Rahn, a tall, intelligent man in his forties, was close to Foreign Minister Joachim von Ribbentrop. He had previously served in Syria and had been Nazi gauleiter in Bohemia where, according to Badoglio's memoirs, he had become famous for his ruthless oppression. Mussolini's secretary Dolfin wrote of Rahn: 'He knows . . . how to mask with well-studied courtesy the obvious hardness of his character.' According to Dolfin, Mussolini was always agitated and nervous in Rahn's presence, and after meeting him remained tired and in a bad humour. As an Italian diplomat, Luigi Bolla came to know Rahn well and described him as cultivated, intelligent and versatile. 'He didn't correspond at all to the stereotype of the German and even less to that of the Gauleiter, even though he was capable of ruthlessness,' he wrote. The SS Colonel Eugen Dollmann, who took a dislike to Rahn, described him as a man of 'threatening eyebrows and manners that betrayed a bad upbringing. Rahn was a strange mixture of goodness and wickedness, culture and natural instincts, snobbism and simplicity.'

A letter from Rahn to Field Marshal Kesselring somehow fell into Allied hands and caused the Germans embarrassment when it was published. 'I consider my task', he wrote, 'to squeeze the neo-Fascist and therefore Italian lemon beyond the possible, and what matters is only the means of succeeding in that.'[38]

Mussolini called Rahn 'the viceroy of Italy' and Wolff 'the interior minister of Italy'. Initially he considered Wolff a personal friend and a friend of Italy, a judgement that would later change drastically. Dolfin described Wolff as cunning, pliant and intelligent. A sophisticated, handsome and athletic man, Wolff had been No. 2 in Berlin to Heinrich Himmler, the head of the SS, but had fallen out of favour when he divorced and remarried; in the SS, all marriages and divorces required the personal approval of Himmler, but Wolff secured Hitler's approval of his divorce after Himmler had refused him. Wolff liked to boast that Mussolini could do nothing without his approval. 'I don't give him orders,' he said. 'In practice, however, he cannot decide on anything against my will and my advice. I had to prevent him from carrying out acts harmful to the re-established alliance. . . . I controlled all his acts.'[39]

Even Rahn thought the German military was too heavy-handed and was undermining the authority of the new government. In a letter to Hitler he wrote: 'It is senseless to create a government that then must not govern . . . and reorganise an administration to which nothing is left to administer.' The Italian poet Salvatore Quasimodo observed that Italy lived 'with a foreign foot on its heart'.[40]

Still, the few able Italian ministers had some successes. Finance Minister Gaetano Pellegrini-Giampietro succeeded in persuading the Germans to dispense with the German occupation mark from 25 October and revert to using Italian lire. He also prevented the Germans from transferring the Italian Mint to Vienna, where they could have printed as many lire as they wished. And he persuaded them to return some of the gold they had taken from the

Bank of Italy. Rahn, who endured long and difficult negotiations with Pellegrini-Giampietro, once referred to him as 'the Napolitaner ball-breaker'.[41]

Communications Minister Augusto Liverani, according to Anfuso, ambassador to Germany, spent his time in office hiding railway carriages from the Germans, changed the names of railway stations to confuse them, suppressed production figures, invented accounts and statistics and established a system of control to block the removal of rail carriages.[42]

But the Germans prevailed more often than not. Pellegrini-Giampietro was forced to sign an agreement under which the republic would reimburse German occupation costs to the tune of 7 billion lire a month. That would rise to 12 billion in 1945. Mussolini observed dryly that the Salò Republic was 'a cow that must guarantee its daily milk'.[43]

Economics Minister Angelo Tarchi tried to exercise control over Italian industry but General Hans Leyers, responsible for recruiting Italian labour for German factories, hampered his work. In March 1944, Leyers denied Italians any use of cement, reserving it all for the Todt organisation that was building fortifications in Italy. He left Italian industry 15,000 tons of steel per month instead of the 70,000 it had used in 1943.[44]

Mussolini's relations with Field Marshal Rommel were as fraught as those with Rahn and Wolff. The two men did not like each other, and Mussolini was not pleased when Rommel told him he favoured withdrawing to a defensive line along the Po valley and conceding all Italian territory south of there to the Allies. Rommel was replaced in November by Kesselring, which relieved Mussolini. But Anfuso said that despite the personal differences between Mussolini and Rommel, the Duce later learned that 'all the gestures of Rommel were favourable, if not to the newly born Republic, at least to the Italians'. If the SS Colonel Dollmann is to be believed, Anfuso was wildly mistaken. Dollmann said Rommel thoroughly disliked the Italians. Dollmann admired Kesselring and said: 'Among the German generals he was, perhaps, the best, even if he modestly defined himself in these terms: "I as a commander am not worth much but I have the advantage that the others are worse than me."' Dollmann noted that Kesselring was later to spare Rome and Florence from destruction and said that, without him, 'Italy would have become a desert.'[45]

* * *

While Mussolini grappled with a malignant German administration eating away at his authority, his own state of health remained perilous. Dr Zachariae, the specialist who had treated him in Germany, arrived at Gargnano on 5 October together with a physiotherapist named Horn who worked for the Gestapo and gave Mussolini a daily massage. Zachariae was shocked on seeing his patient again. 'I found myself before a ruin of a man who evidently was on the brink of the tomb,' he said. Mussolini was lying on a sofa in the Villa Feltrinelli wearing a nightshirt, his face pale, yellowish and very thin. His cheekbones stood out and made his cheeks seem emaciated. Mussolini told the doctor that, since 1940, the pain from his ulcer had been severe, especially for two or three hours after meals, and at night he suffered cramps. He could not sleep and dreaded the coming of night. He also suffered from acute constipation. He ate very little, was anaemic and suffered from low blood pressure (100 over 70) for a man his age. His skin was dry and had little elasticity, and the upper part of his abdomen over the liver was very enlarged and hard.

Zachariae learned of the poor diet Italian doctors had prescribed for Mussolini, which was worsened by his daily consumption of about two quarts of boiled milk. Mussolini's cook told the doctor it was impossible to convince the Duce to eat mashed potatoes or vegetables, as he complained these caused pains in his head. Zachariae told Mussolini he must change his diet, and said his milk consumption was causing great knots in his intestine that were responsible for his constipation. The milk intake was initially reduced to half a pint per day, then cut off after a week.

Zachariae decided to initiate treatment with hormones and vitamins he had brought with him, beginning with relatively small doses to avoid a counter-reaction. Within a week he found his patient improved, and fifteen days after that Mussolini commented: 'I must tell you I feel liberated. I no longer feel pains in my stomach and I don't fear the night.' His liver returned to normal size after four weeks. It took another two months before the sensitivity in the Duce's stomach had disappeared. In place of his spartan diet of tea, toast and stewed fruit, he was given light vegetables such as carrots and potatoes. He drank tea with a little sugar but no milk. Zachariae said it helped that Mussolini did not smoke and his only alcohol consumption was an occasional glass of wine at parties or official dinners. Like Hitler, Mussolini preferred a vegetarian diet, and Zachariae had trouble persuading him to eat boiled chicken or fish from Lake Garda to restore his protein levels. Mussolini finally agreed to eat meat, but only so long as his weakness made it essential. This was accompanied by injections of vitamins B and C, and after four weeks his red blood cell count rose.

'He walked erect again, his skin returned to normal and there was more colour in his face,' Zachariae wrote. 'He became more energetic and showed a new interest in political affairs, work and affairs of state.' But within a few months, the doctor was puzzled to find his patient's weight was slowly going down. He finally learned from the cook the reason: the Italian people had been forced to adopt meagre wartime food rations, and the Duce refused to eat better than they. Once a prefect sent him a package of food. Furious, he immediately sent it to a hospital in nearby Gardone and wrote a scolding letter to the prefect. But his health continued to improve, and Zachariae boasted that he had restored Mussolini to the physical condition of a man of forty.[46]

* * *

While his illness persisted, Mussolini habitually arose at 10 a.m. and met Zachariae half an hour later. But once he had recovered his health, Zachariae's appointment was pushed back to 9, then 8. Mussolini settled into a routine of working until 2 p.m., stopping for lunch, then resuming work at 3 p.m. He scheduled a second meeting with the doctor at 8 p.m. but these sessions were often cancelled because of urgent affairs of state. After dinner, he returned immediately to work. Each day before he began work, Zachariae reported, Mussolini sat at a desk at home reading Italian history or the poetry of Goethe. He always kept at his hand a copy of Plato's *Republic*, which he consulted from time to time. His only 'luxury' was a manicure every fifteen days.[47]

At Gargnano, Mussolini talked to Zachariae at considerable length, not just about his health but also about his interests in literature, philosophy, history, art, music and current affairs. These daily talks reflected the fact that he was no longer the busy government leader of old, but a figure who had been sidelined. Zachariae wrote admiringly of the fact that Mussolini spoke English, French, Spanish and German, and commented that Hitler was inferior to Mussolini in culture, acuity, intelligence and memory.

Mussolini told the doctor he had had influence on Hitler at an early stage, but not in the latter years of the war because Hitler wanted to be the only one who commanded. 'Today I feel tied to the Führer and Germany in an eternal friendship, even if sometimes I am forced to criticise German policy,' he said. But he had only hatred for Foreign Minister Ribbentrop, whom he denounced as a clown and incompetent. He expressed concern that an Allied victory over Germany would destroy the only people capable of stopping a Soviet takeover of Europe.

Mussolini also expressed great admiration for Churchill, but never in his life appeared to have a kind word for Roosevelt. In the early years of fascism, when he was bringing Italy into the modern world, Mussolini was widely admired abroad, and Churchill once called him 'the greatest living legislator' and said he would have donned the Fascist black shirt if he had been Italian. Roosevelt and members of his Cabinet joined in the praise, but Mussolini's scorn for the American president appeared to arise mostly from Roosevelt's physical infirmity caused by infantile paralysis. Speaking to his son-in-law

Galeazzo Ciano, Mussolini once said: 'Never in history has one seen a nation led by a paralytic. There have been bald kings, fat kings, handsome and even stupid kings, but never a king who, in order to go to the toilet, the bath or the table, had to be held up by other men.'

He told Zachariae that America would have remained out of the war except for Jewish influence on Roosevelt and on the media. 'America is a country without ideals, a country in which money, the power of money, the greed for money, take the place of all that for us still has a cultural and moral power,' he said. Americans, he added, did not understand that material comforts 'cannot compensate for the spiritual void of a people whose only god is the dollar'. Mussolini's only god, it might be noted, appeared to be military power; he had long ago abandoned his religious beliefs.[48]

In a meeting with his old friend Nino D'Aroma, Mussolini expressed his bitterness towards those who had participated in his overthrow in July. 'They are starved and goitrous gravediggers,' he said. 'They are like some families of insects that want to live in the carcass, in the inanimate remains of me, now and forever.'[49]

* * *

As his health recovered, Mussolini became more active physically. Almost every day he went bicycling around the extensive grounds of the Villa Feltrinelli, and when it was not raining he played tennis. Rachele said it surprised her to learn that he won almost all his matches, but then she discovered that his opponents were letting him win. 'He was very embarrassed,' she said.[50]

Mussolini's office routine also changed. In Rome, he had kept his ministers standing at meetings in his grandiose office. In his much smaller office in Gargnano, he adopted a more informal pose and allowed his visitors to sit. And in deference to those Fascists who wanted a more democratic regime, he abolished the salute to the Duce and barred the display of his photograph in public offices.

As he settled into his new routine, Mussolini was unaware of what the German masters of Italy were preparing to try to carry out in Rome: the deportation of the entire Jewish population of the city to the death camps in Poland. The decision by the Germans neither to advise nor consult him in this matter was the most visible sign yet that his voice counted for nothing.

Chapter 4

THE FATE OF THE ROMAN JEWS

These things can't happen in Italy.

(Ugo Foà, leader of the Jewish community in Rome, speaking of German atrocities against Jews elsewhere, September 1943)

The Roman Jewish community is the oldest in Europe, having been established in the second century when the Jews were first brought from Palestine as slaves of the Roman Empire. For centuries afterwards, Jews and Christians lived peacefully side by side in the capital, and Jews came under a certain amount of papal protection. Gregory the Great rejected attempts to ban the Jewish liturgy, and in the twelfth century Innocent III put a stop to enforced conversions and violation of Jewish burial grounds. But in 1555 the newly elected Pope Paul IV decided to restrict the Jews to a ghetto of just 7½ acres, a section of narrow medieval streets bordering the Tiber and extending almost to the base of the Capitoline Hill, the seat of power in ancient Rome. Just over 3,000 Jews then living in the city were shut off from the rest of Rome by high walls and were allowed to leave the ghetto only during certain hours of the day. Outside the ghetto, Jewish men had to wear a piece of yellow cloth on their caps and women were required to wear a yellow shawl or veil. Their property was assigned to non-Jews to whom the ghetto residents had to pay rent. On the Jewish Sabbath, Jews were required to attend church services at which priests tried to persuade them to convert to Christianity.

These restrictive measures remained in effect until 1870, when the Jews were allowed to leave the ghetto and their civil rights were restored. Many of the more prosperous Jews gravitated to other parts of the city, but the ghetto, an atmospheric district of old buildings set amid Roman ruins, of small shops and restaurants, remained the centre of the Jewish community and the home of most of the poorer Jews, many of them itinerant pedlars. Charles Dickens described the nineteenth-century ghetto as 'a miserable place, densely populated and reeking with bad odours'.[1]

Until Mussolini attempted to foster a degree of antisemitism in 1938, a subject that will be discussed in Chapter 10, Jews and Christians lived amicably together in Rome and elsewhere in twentieth-century Italy. The painter Amedeo Modigliani was one widely admired product of the Roman Jewish community. Luigi Luzzati, the thirteenth prime minister of modern Italy, was another. Such antisemitism as existed was largely confined to an extremist fringe, but when Jewish refugees from other parts of Europe began arriving in Rome and reports of the Nazi extermination programme filtered through, some Jews became alarmed.

Rabbi Israel Zolli warned Jews to 'disperse and go as far away as you can'. He urged Ugo Foà to close the temple and offices, but Foà rebuked him: 'You should be giving courage instead of spreading discouragement. I have received assurances.'

Zolli's concerns were shared, however, by Ernst von Weizsäcker, the German Ambassador to the Holy See, and Embassy Secretary Albrecht von Kessel. They were worried about possible papal reaction if the Nazis undertook a pogrom in Rome, and Kessel asked a Swiss friend to warn the Jews they must leave the city and seek shelter elsewhere. Renzo Levi, president of a Jewish relief organisation known as Delasem (Delegazione di assistenza agli emigranti ebrei, or Commission of Assistance to Jewish Emigrants), and Settimio Sorani, secretary of the organisation, knew of the Nazi extermination programme from Vatican diplomats and the International Red Cross, and they told Foà the time had come for all Roman Jews to go into hiding. 'These things can't happen in Italy,' Foà replied. He believed the Germans would respect Rome because of the city's special character as an 'open city'.[2]

Some Jews, expecting a German takeover, did flee after Mussolini's downfall in July, and some took refuge in summer resorts around Lake Maggiore, just below the Swiss border. Between 15 and 24 September, the SS's Leibstandarte Adolf Hitler unit butchered forty-nine of them, with some tied hand and foot and drowned in the lake. Mussolini was then still in Munich and may not have known of this atrocity; if he did, he made no protest.[3]

After Mussolini's rescue from the Gran Sasso on 12 September, Giovanni Preziosi broadcast to the Italian nation from Germany calling for the 'total elimination' of Italian Jews. Rabbi Zolli then went to see Dante Almansi, President of the Union of Italian Jewish Communities, but Almansi refused to take the threat seriously. He said he and Foà had had 'categorical assurances from high personages in whom we have unshakeable confidence'. Zolli then urged Foà to destroy the community's list of Roman Jews, but Foà did nothing.[4]

Once the Germans had taken control of Rome on 10 September, SS chief Heinrich Himmler wasted no time in tackling the Jewish issue. Just two days later, the city's Gestapo chief, Major Herbert Kappler, received a phone call from Berlin advising him that Himmler wanted him to round up and deport all Jews still in Rome. Although himself an antisemite, Kappler opposed such a step, which he regarded as a 'gross political stupidity'. As far as he was concerned, there was no Jewish problem in Italy; the Jews had not grown rich, as they had in Germany, and they were orderly and passive. But Himmler sent a top-secret dispatch to Kappler on 24 September, demanding the Jews be sent to the Reich for 'liquidation'.[5]

General Rainer Stahel, the German military commander in Rome, read Himmler's secret message to Kappler and went to Eithel Moellhausen, the German consul in Rome, to say he would have nothing to do with this kind of *Schweinerei* (mess). Moellhausen himself was also opposed. He had a woman friend who he knew was hiding a family of Jews in her home. Moellhausen took up the Himmler order with Kappler, who said he would have to consult Field Marshal Kesselring. The marshal objected to the deportation of Jews; he said this would require the use of troops who were needed for the defence of Rome in case of an Allied landing at nearby Ostia, and he favoured using Jewish labour to build defensive fortifications around the city.

Kappler came up with a strategem that he may have thought would satisfy Himmler and forestall the roundup. He called in Almansi and Foà on 26 September, and told them they had thirty-six hours in which to deliver to him 110 pounds and 3.68 ounces of gold, worth $56,000 on the international market at that time. If they failed to produce the gold, Kappler said, 200 Jews would be deported to the Russian frontier or would be 'otherwise rendered innocuous'. When questioned, he agreed he would accept dollars or sterling in lieu of gold, but not lire. He ended the meeting with a lie: 'Mind you, I have already carried out several operations of this type and it has always ended well. Only once did I fail, but that time a few hundred of your brothers paid with their lives.'

The Jewish leaders feared they would not be able to find enough gold in such a short time and they decided to buy as much as they needed. The acquisition of gold was forbidden, but Italian authorities still serving in Rome decided to turn a blind eye. The Jews appealed to the Holy See, which agreed to lend gold, but in the end this was not needed. Through their own community, and with contributions from other Italians including many priests, the Jewish leaders amassed 170 pounds of gold, much of it in the form of wedding rings and personal jewellery. The excess amount was hidden in filing cabinets and the amount that was demanded was turned in. The Germans weighed it and tried to pretend it amounted only to ninety-five pounds, but the Jewish leaders protested and the Germans gave in. They refused, however, to give a receipt for the gold.

Kappler sent the gold to the Berlin office of Ernst Kaltenbrunner, Himmler's No. 2 as head of the Reich High Security Office, along with a letter expressing reservations about the consequences of Jewish deportation. The case of gold, never opened, was found in a corner of Kaltenbrunner's office after the war.[6]

On the morning of 29 September, the day after the gold was handed over, the Germans blocked off Jewish community institutions and sent in experts in Hebrew to make a minute examination of documents. The Germans took away 2,021,540 lire and all the documents, including a list of all the Jews living in Rome. Several times they returned, seeking information on the richest Jews and examining the Jewish Library.

Himmler contacted Adolf Eichmann, the Austrian SS officer in charge of Jewish affairs, and Eichmann sent to Rome a special team of forty-four SS men under the command of Captain Theodor Dannecker, a thirty-year-old zealot who had previously headed teams responsible for deporting Jews from Paris and Sofia. Dannecker arrived on 6 October and showed Kappler an order he had received to arrest the 8,000 Jews in Rome. Eithel Moellhausen contacted Ribbentrop and urged him to have the order rescinded. But Ribbentrop told Moellhausen the SS had exclusive jurisdiction in such matters and ordered him not to interfere. Von Weizsäcker informed the pope of what was about to happen, and the pope secretly ordered the heads of all extraterritorial religious institutions in Rome to open their doors to those in need of refuge. In all, 477 Jews took shelter in the Vatican and 4,238 in more than 150 monasteries and convents. All these institutions enjoyed extraterritorial protection under Italian law.[7]

Two Germans showed up in the ghetto and told Foà they were Orientalists, one of them a professor of Hebrew language studies from Berlin. They requested permission to examine books in the two community libraries, the Biblioteca Comunale and the Rabbinical College Library. The Biblioteca had one of Europe's richest collections on Judaica and early Christianity, including the only copies of books and manuscripts dating from before the time of Christ and the era of the first popes. Foà acceded to their request, and a few days later they returned to say the contents of the two libraries were being seized. On the morning of 13 October, two German railway freight wagons rolled up on trolley line tracks to the front door of the Jewish temple and the next day took away the entire contents of the Biblioteca Comunale and most of the books from the Rabbinical College Library.[8]

Soon thereafter, all prominent Jews in Rome, led by Almansi, disappeared from their homes and took refuge elsewhere. Rabbi Zolli had left his home with his family much earlier and had found shelter with a Catholic family living not far from the Vatican.[9]

Dannecker did not have enough men to round up all the Jews in the ghetto and those hiding elsewhere, so he went to Kappler and General Stahel and eventually put together a force of 365 SS police and Waffen SS troops. He scheduled his raid for the early hours of 16 October, the Jewish Sabbath. Shortly before midnight, residents of the ghetto heard shooting in the streets, then the sound of exploding hand grenades. The firing broke off, but resumed periodically through the night. At about 4 a.m. the soldiers who were responsible drifted away.

'It was cold, and the dampness of the rainy night penetrated the walls,' said a Jewish writer named Giacomo Debenedetti. 'Everyone stood about in their nightshirts and slippers, a few with shawls or overcoats draped around their shoulders. Perhaps the abandoned beds still held a little warmth.' After the soldiers left, people went back to bed.

At 5.30 a.m., amid a pouring rain, Dannecker and his men struck. A non-Jew arriving at his shop from outside the ghetto heard the drumming beat of boots on the pavement and saw two rows of German troops marching by. They took up positions at street corners and set up roadblocks at entrances to the ghetto. Then the roundup began. Jews were told they were being transferred to a camp and were given twenty minutes to pack and leave. They were advised to bring money and anything else of value because it would be needed to buy things at the camp store.

Many young men fled across rooftops or hid in cellars. One old woman, paralysed by a stroke, was carried on a kitchen chair by two Jewish men to a waiting truck. A number of non-Jews gathered behind roadblocks to watch what was happening. One of them, Francesco Odoardi, described the scene: 'The men, some in jackets, some in overcoats, were sitting on the ancient stones, or on suitcases, boxes or sacks. . . . The women . . . were tidying the little clothes and coats of their children. . . . One of the women, with a baby at her breast, covered the child with a shawl. Another put a kerchief on the head of her daughter, who was crying. She wiped the girl's tears and the drops of rain on her face, but always in silence. She had no words to comfort her.' Another Roman described what he saw as 'like a scene out of hell'.[10]

Arminio Wachsberger and his family were arrested at their home in Trastevere, across the Tiber. His brother-in-law and sister-in-law had left their two-year-old son Vittorio with them for the weekend, and a Catholic woman, Assunta Fratini, saw them aboard a parked truck. When the German guard turned his head, Wachsberger threw his nephew, who landed in Fratini's arms. She disappeared into the hallway of her building.

Among those arrested was the retired Admiral Augusto Capon, father-in-law of the Nobel Prize-winning physicist Enrico Fermi who would help develop the atomic bomb. Capon was seventy-two and paralysed from the waist down, and he left his home on crutches, taking with him a personal letter from Mussolini that he was sure would prove helpful.[11]

When the roundup started, one Austrian SS trooper pushed an old man forward with the butt of his rifle, shouting incomprehensible words. They reached a half-open door and the soldier gave the old man a last kick, whispering in Italian: 'Quickly, get inside. I am a Catholic, I'm not like these others.'

Sarina Vivanti, aged sixty, who owned an electrical shop in the ghetto, had left home early and escaped. But the soldiers took her mother, her three sisters, the three children of one of the sisters and a sister-in-law with her three children. All died in the camps. The Germans returned on 24 February and took her husband, her brother and her brother-in-law. Then on 16 April they grabbed her only son and her last brother.[12]

The Marchioness Fulvia Ripa di Meana, walking through a rain-swept Rome that morning, saw trucks full of Jewish children. 'I read in their eyes dilated by terror, in their little faces pallid with pain, in their little hands that gripped spasmodically the sides of the trucks, the maddening fear that invaded them, the terror of what they had seen and heard. . . . They didn't even cry, those little children; fear had rendered them mute and had burned the infantile tears in their eyes. Only in the bottom of the trucks, thrown on wooden planks, some new-born babies, hungry and frozen, wailed piteously.'

One working man, who had been a fervent Fascist, watched a truck full of children driven away and started cursing Mussolini for his cowardice in having 'teamed up' with Hitler in the persecution of 'people who had done nothing wrong'. Other Romans shook their fists with rage as the trucks passed.[13]

Mother Mary St Luke did not witness the pogrom but wrote in her diary: 'It is a nameless horror. They came for the father of a family we know. He was out. The Germans said in that case they would take his wife. Whereupon the daughter said: "Where my mother goes, I go too."'[14]

Rosetta Loy, a Catholic schoolgirl who lived with her family in the Prati district not far from the Vatican, returned from school to find that two Jewish families in their apartment building had been taken away. They were never seen again. Loy later collected the stories of a number of Jews, such as that of the Calò family. The family had been warned on 15 October that the Germans were planning a roundup, and the head of the family took his wife and four children to a nearby bordello where the madam was disposed to hide them in her cellar. Then he fled to the countryside. The mother and three little girls remained in the cellar for eight months, living in an enforced silence so as not to alert clients of the bordello, including German soldiers, to their presence. Sometimes 'Signor Adolfo', an employee of the bordello, would come down to the cellar to play cards with the girls to keep them quiet.

Hundreds of other Romans, at risk to their own lives, sheltered Jewish families throughout the German occupation. Some Jews escaped the roundup by killing themselves, and others died of fear. Loy recorded that in the following eight months of occupation another 723 Jews were arrested in Rome. Of these, 644 were deported to Auschwitz, 4 died at an Italian concentration camp and 75 were executed in reprisal for a partisan attack on German troops in Rome.

Alberta Levi, twenty-four, and her family had been persuaded by Roman relatives to leave their home in Ferrara and come live with them because Rome was safer. At 6 a.m. on 16 October, when the SS rang the bell of the apartment, Alberta went out onto the balcony in her nightgown. She heard a hard voice say: '*Kommt! Kommt!*' Then the door to the balcony closed behind her; her mother was determined to save her. After the Germans left with the members of the two families, Alberta went back inside through a door to the kitchen that had been left open, got dressed and made her way across town to join her father, who had been sleeping elsewhere. Later her mother and sister convinced the Germans they were Catholics from Bologna who had come to Rome after that city was bombarded, and they were set free. But three other Levis, members of the family that hosted them, remained prisoners and later died in the concentration camps.[15]

Iris Origo, an Anglo-American woman married to an Italian marquis and living in Tuscany, received a letter after the roundup of the Jews from a friend in Rome working with the Red Cross. The friend told her that in one house a woman and a child of eight had hidden in the attic when the Germans came, leaving a one-month-old baby in the room below for fear that its cries would give them away. When they returned, the baby was gone. 'In short, all that we had heard about the treatment of the Jews in Poland we have now seen here,' the Red Cross worker commented.[16]

Settimio Calò, aged forty-four, a Jew who had left home early that fateful morning to join a queue at a tobacconist's shop for scarce cigarettes, returned to find his wife and nine children gone. A married daughter living around the corner had also disappeared. He ran down the street in a mad panic and eventually made his way to the Collegio Militare, a building along the Tiber not far from the Vatican, where the Jews had been taken. Calò threw himself against the doors but an Italian guard took him by the arm and said: 'Are you crazy? Get out of here. Don't you know they'll grab you too if they see you?' Calò kept pushing but the guard threw him out. 'I walked a little, sat on the ground and began to cry,' he said.

The Jews taken to the Collegio Militare passed St Peter's Square, shouting to Pope Pius XII to save them. Albrecht von Kessel, the German secretary in the embassy to the Holy See, spoke to Father Pankratius Pfeiffer, the pope's personal liaison with the Germans in Rome, to try to find a way to stop the arrests. Pfeiffer in turn went to Bishop Alois Hudal, rector of the German Catholic Church in Rome, and persuaded him to sign a letter requesting General Stahel, the German commander in Rome, to order an immediate suspension of the arrests. The letter expressed fear that unless this happened the pope would take a public position that would be used by anti-German propagandists as a weapon against the Germans. The letter was sent on to the Foreign Ministry in Berlin without comment. Ambassador von Weizsäcker followed this up with a report of his own: 'The Curia is especially upset considering that the action took place, in a manner of speaking, under the Pope's own windows.' He suggested Jews should be used in labour service in Italy instead of being deported.[17]

Cardinal Luigi Maglione, the papal secretary of state, met Weizsäcker on the day of the arrests and asked him to intervene with his fellow Germans for the sake of 'humanity and Christian charity'. Weizsäcker apparently tried to persuade Maglione to ask Pius XII to protest over the arrests, but stressed that their conversation was confidential. 'What will the Holy See do if these things continue?' the ambassador asked. Maglione said he replied: 'The Holy See would not wish to be put in a situation where it was necessary to utter a word of disapproval.' Weizsäcker then suggested the Holy See should consider whether it was worth 'putting everything in danger just as the ship is reaching port'.[18]

While the Jews were going into the Collegio Militare, one woman ran up, grabbed a baby from an old woman and said: 'This is my baby, this is my son, this one is not Jewish.' She pushed the Germans away and went off with the baby; she was a Catholic woman who risked her life to save a child she didn't know.[19]

The last German trucks drew up to the Collegio Militare just after 2 p.m. The men were separated from women and children and the Germans counted 1,259 captives, of whom 363 were men. Almost all the Jews were convinced they were going to be sent to a labour camp. Dannecker sought to confirm that impression, and also announced that non-Jews who had been caught in the roundup would be freed. But he warned that any Jews who tried to pretend they were not Jewish would be shot on the spot. Despite that, several Jews, including the Levi women, accepted his challenge and succeeded in passing themselves off as Christians. A total of 252 people were eventually released, including some Jews who had converted to Catholicism and some non-Jewish household employees. But one Catholic woman remained inside; she was the nurse of a Jewish orphan boy who suffered from epilepsy, and she did not want to desert him.

That night, some SS men took house keys from their prisoners, returned to the ghetto and plundered the apartments. Many people arrived at the Collegio Militare in the evening with food and clothing for the prisoners but were driven away. Inside, there were only meagre food rations, not enough to go around, nothing to drink and no proper sanitary arrangements. A pregnant woman, Marcella Di Tivoli Perugia, was dragged into a courtyard to give birth during the night after having been refused the services of a doctor. Lazzaro Anticoli, a Jew chosen for the distribution of available food, made his rounds, turned a door handle and found himself standing on the street. Instead of making good his escape, he went to a nearby tobacco shop, bought ten packages of cigarettes and returned to the Collegio Militare; he could not abandon his wife and three children, one of them ill with diphtheria and apparently on the point of death. Alone among his family members, he would subsequently survive the death camps.[20]

Before dawn on 18 October, the Jews were driven across Rome to the Tiburtina railway station on the eastern side of the city, and loaded into twenty freight wagons. It took until early afternoon to complete the loading, and those who had first gone into the wagons had to wait up to eight hours in almost total darkness before the train moved out. Word of what was happening spread across the city. Costanza Calò Sermoneta, who had been in the countryside when the arrests were made two days earlier, arrived at the rail station and began shouting: 'Fascists! Fascists! Open up! I want to go too. I want to go with my husband.' Her husband and other Jews shouted to her from the wagons to run away, but she kept shouting and finally the Germans unlocked a freight wagon and put her with her husband and five children. All of them died in the concentration camps.

At 2.05 p.m. the train departed. A short distance outside Rome, Allied fighter aircraft strafed it and the SS returned fire. One German was wounded slightly in his hand before the planes departed. Inside the wagons, temperatures were rising and the prisoners were in the grip of extreme thirst. Some were already dying. At Orte, 49 miles north of Rome, prisoners called out that they needed to relieve themselves. The Germans opened a few wagons and about fifty people got out. Suddenly two or three youths made a dash across an open field, but they surrendered when the Germans opened fire.

Three or four people died during the night. When the train reached Padua, a Red Cross representative at the station offered food and medicine, which the Germans refused. Fascist militiamen who were at the station threatened to open fire unless the Germans relented. Finally, the Germans allowed a few Jews to come out to take water for the others. The Red Cross distributed bread, fruit, jam, powdered milk and medicine. The dead bodies were removed from the cars, and the train went on its way. Leone Sabatello, urinating beside the track on the far side of the train, ran after it, calling for it to stop so he could remain with his family. A German heard his cry and obliged.[21]

Before the train left Padua, Lazzaro Sonnino had tampered with the lock on his wagon. Now he pushed the door open and jumped. No one else in the wagon attempted to do so. They closed the door behind him. At 11 p.m. on Friday 22 October, the train finally arrived at the Birkenau death camp in Poland. But other trains were being unloaded and this one had to wait until the following morning to enter the camp. The camp commandant, Rudolf Höss, and Dr Joseph Mengele, the Nazi doctor notorious for his cruel medical experiments on prisoners, were on hand to see the Jews off the train. The prisoners were quickly divided into two groups: those who would be assigned to work, which included 154 males and 47 females, and the remainder who were sent immediately to the gas chamber. They had been told that, after taking showers, they would go to a nearby camp to rest and do very light work.

Of seventy-five men put to work in coal mines at Jawiszowice, all but eleven soon died. Another forty-two were shipped to Warsaw to recover bricks from the ghetto, and only three survived. Settimia Spizzichino, a young woman who had been spared the gas chamber, was transferred to Block 10 where she became a guinea pig for Mengele's experiments. Later she was transferred to Bergen–Belsen, and at the war's end British troops found her among a pile of corpses, where she had slept for the previous two days. In the summer of 1945, the fifteen survivors came home.[22]

Luciano Camerino, aged sixteen at the time of the arrests, was among them. He saw his mother sent off to the gas chamber, while he, his father and brother were assigned to work in the mines and on the roads. He said they worked in light cotton clothes in severe winter weather, and their only food consisted of a thin, watery soup distributed once a day with pieces of black bread. 'My father died in my arms the evening of 5 January, and so escaped the gas chamber,' he said. He and his brother, having passed through six camps, escaped at the end of April 1945 and hid in a forest until the Russians arrived and saved them. At the time he weighed just over 6 stone.[23]

Rabbi Zolli gave an interview to the *New York Times* after the liberation of Rome in 1944 in which he bitterly attacked Ugo Foà, and accused him of letting the lists of Roman Jews fall into German hands. Zolli resigned his posts and in February 1945 converted to Catholicism, taking a job in the Vatican Library. He was denounced as a traitor by the Jewish leadership. Foà and Almansi, the head of the Union of Italian Jewish Communities, were slowly rehabilitated by new Jewish leaders and given honorary positions. Ambassador Weizsäcker, then aged fifty-five, was put on trial for war crimes in 1947 and sentenced to seven years in prison, but the sentence was reduced after a number of people protested on his behalf. Then the sentence was cancelled and he was released in 1950. There is no doubt he was unjustly tried but Eithel Moellhausen, the German consul who was opposed to Hitler, thought Weizsäcker could have done more for the Jews. 'Baron Weizsäcker was an aesthetic man, a gentleman, honest but rather cold and not particularly intelligent,' he wrote. 'In tendency he was nearer the planet of the Pope than the meridian of Hitler, but he would never have had the strength to rebel openly, nor to compromise himself seriously with the adversaries of the regime, his "career" being for him his raison d'être.' Theodor Dannecker, the SS killer who organised the Nazi pogrom, disappeared after the war.[24]

There is no record of Mussolini ever having protested to the Germans over the pogrom. Neither, of course, did the pope, and that has remained a matter of intense controversy. Whether his silence was justified morally or not, the pope had a reasonable concern that the Germans would take over the Vatican and seize him. On several occasions, Hitler threatened to do just that, and had to be dissuaded by his aides. General Wolff said after the war that Hitler had told him on 13 September 1943 that he wanted the pope to be deported, and Wolff only managed to dissuade the Führer in a meeting three months later. Pius was aware that after Dutch bishops had protested over the persecution of the Jews the Gestapo arrested 40,000 people and put them in concentration camps. The pope wrote a protest over the treatment of the Poles that was intended for publication in the Vatican newspaper, *L'Osservatore Romano*, but then he burned it, fearing his protest would cause as many as 200,000 Poles to be incarcerated.[25]

In a book published in 2003, the American author Robert Katz contended that the Vatican had received one unsubstantiated report of German intentions to round up the Jews before the pogrom took place, but the pope did nothing to warn the Jews or to intervene with the Germans to try to block their plans. Likewise, he said recently released archive material demonstrated that British intelligence learned of the German plan in advance, but the British did not warn the Jews.[26]

Eighty survivors of the death camps met the pope on 29 November 1945 and thanked him 'for his generosity towards those persecuted during the Nazi-Fascist period', a reference to the sanctuary he provided in ecclesiastical institutions.

But in 1995, Settimia Spizzichino, the lone woman survivor, gave an interview to the BBC in London in which she said: 'I came back from Auschwitz on my own. I lost my mother, two sisters, a niece and one brother. Pius XII could have warned us about what was going to happen. We might have escaped from Rome and joined the partisans. He played right into the Germans' hands. It all happened right under his nose. But he was an anti-Semitic Pope, a pro-German Pope. He didn't take a single risk. And when they say the Pope is like Jesus Christ, it is not true. He did not save a single child. Nothing.'[27] That, of course, was untrue.

Chapter 5

MUSSOLINI AND CLARETTA

You are the most beautiful part of my life.

(Benito Mussolini to his lover Claretta Petacci, summer 1939)

On 28 October, after an absence of three months, Mussolini was reunited with Claretta Petacci, his lover and the woman fated to die alongside him just six months later. As Claretta's sister Myriam related, Mussolini sent a car driven by a German officer to collect Claretta from a villa where she and her family were staying at Merano in northern Italy and take her to Gargnano, where he was then living alone. She returned the following evening and told Myriam: 'I have seen him again. He was marvellous. We remained embraced for hours, looking into each other's eyes without saying a word. Then he began to speak and it went on all night, his telling me what happened after 25 July. He's a little thin, and tired, but he is well. Between us it is all as before. . . . His wife is in Germany and he hopes she will remain there. Any moment now, we will also move to Gargnano.'[1]

During Mussolini's captivity, the Badoglio press had given wide coverage to his affair with Claretta, never previously mentioned in the newspapers, and to her brother Marcello's illegal dealings. Upon his return to Italy, Mussolini read a collection of these articles and was mortified and resentful. 'I believed every man had the minimum right to a private life,' he told Goffredo Coppola, rector of the University of Bologna. 'For me they have wanted to tear everything apart, try to besmirch me and present me to the Italian people as a childish Don Giovanni.'[2]

Claretta was then thirty-one years old, Mussolini's junior by twenty-nine years. She was just the latest, and the last, of a long string of lovers he had had and eventually discarded. Some of these love affairs, such as those with the Russian Jewish emigré Angelica Balabanoff and two Italian women, Fernanda Facchinelli and Ida Dalser, occurred before he began living in 1910 with Rachele Guidi, the peasant woman from his birthplace of Predappio whom he would marry five years later. Facchinelli was a married woman when Mussolini met her in 1909, and he had a son by her, but the child lived only a few months. He also had a son by Dalser, Benito Albino, who disappeared mysteriously in the 1940s when he was in his mid-twenties; one version is that he served in the Navy and was killed on active duty. Later mistresses were Margherita Sarfatti, a Jewish novelist and wife of a wealthy Milanese lawyer, and Angela Curti Cucciati, also a Milanese. It was widely assumed that Mussolini was the father of Curti Cucciati's daughter Elena, who took up residence in Gargnano after he had moved there.[3]

To what extent he may have loved any of his mistresses is unclear. To his secretary Giovanni Dolfin, Mussolini once remarked: 'Women have always provoked in me a sense of indifference and boredom because of their tendency to make a drama of an instant that could also be pleasurable.' On another occasion, when the German artist Paul-Mathias Padua was painting his portrait, Mussolini remarked on the 'solitude' of his life and so the artist's wife asked him if he did not have a close friend, or a woman to whom he was close. 'I have never had a close friend,' he replied. 'As for women, they never get into the heart of a man.'[4] Mussolini's friend Nino D'Aroma, who saw a great deal of him, wrote after the war: 'The women he preferred – before arriving in Rome – had to be not too intelligent if they wanted to last with the future Duce. Anyone who was cultivated and perhaps even clever ended by making herself hated. He never wanted to give excessive importance to women.' The first part of that statement is a questionable judgement; Balabanoff and Sarfatti were both highly intelligent, and both those affairs lasted a long time. D'Aroma also quoted Mussolini as telling him: 'A man must be observed and judged only down to his belt. The rest must not concern anyone.'[5]

Mussolini and Claretta first met on Sunday, 24 April 1932, at the seaside town of Ostia, near Rome. He was then fifty and she was twenty-one, the daughter of a Vatican physician, Francesco Saverio Petacci. Her name was Clara, but she was usually known by the diminutive Claretta. Mussolini had stopped his car near the waterfront and Claretta, on a Sunday outing with her family and her fiancé, Air Force Lieutenant Riccardo Federici, spotted him and went over to talk to him. From her teenage years, she had been fascinated with Mussolini, and had written him letters and poems. As one of her biographers, Roberto Gervaso, observed: 'Claretta did not love the Duce; she venerated him to the point of idolatry. . . . He felt for her a physical attraction, mixed, at least at the beginning, with paternal or infantile tenderness.' The conversation between the two went on for a half hour, and when Claretta gave her name and told him of the letters and poems, he remembered them and said he had kept them, tied with a tricolour ribbon.

Two days later he rang her home and asked to speak to her. 'I have phoned to tell you I have found your poems,' he said. 'I am here at my desk. Ask the permission of your mother and your fiancé and, if you like, come to me at 7 o'clock. I am waiting for you.' Claretta hurried to change her clothes, and accompanied by her mother, went to Palazzo Venezia. Claretta went in alone, and she and the Duce had only a brief conversation. He spoke to her of her poems and asked her about her interests in books, music and sport. Then he remarked: 'Do you know you have given me a strange sensation? I haven't slept, thinking of you.' Immediately, he observed that the hour was late, but invited her to come to him again.[6]

Twenty days later, he phoned again, telling Claretta he had had more sleepless nights because of her. In a book about her sister, Myriam quoted this exchange between them:

Mussolini: 'With you a breath of spring enters my heart. . . . I have no friend, I have no one. I am alone. My family doesn't get along with me. But why do I tell you these things? What can it matter to you?'

Claretta: 'No, Duce, don't say this. Every word of yours is a gift for me.'[7]

Over the next twenty months, they met about a dozen times, never for longer than about fifteen minutes. Federici naturally grew jealous over Mussolini's attentions to his fiancée and her obsession with the Duce, and Myriam said Federici renewed a relationship with an old flame, a girl named Fernanda. Despite all, however, Federici and Claretta were married on 27 June 1934. It was a big society wedding, attended among others by the Vatican secretary of state, Cardinal Eugenio Pacelli, later to become Pope Pius XII.

Myriam said the marriage started to go sour on the first night of the honeymoon, and a few days after they returned Federici told Claretta he wanted a separation. They soon patched up their differences, but within a short time he started beating her. Things steadily worsened. Claretta once surprised him with another woman in a hotel in Naples. At the Trastevere train station in Rome, he pushed her off a stationary train. And once when they had a dispute in a coffee bar, he slapped her and she fell down. Finally, in the autumn of 1935, Federici obtained a legal separation from her and he was later posted to Tokyo as a military attaché, remaining there throughout the war.[8]

For a long time afterwards, Mussolini continued to meet Claretta but made no advances towards her. But on the evening of 16 October, 1936, he invited her mother Giuseppina to accompany her to the Palazzo Venezia. When they met, he brusquely asked: 'Signora, will you permit me to love Clara?'[9] Giuseppina did not hesitate long before giving her assent. The Petaccis were a scheming, opportunistic family who would take advantage of Claretta's relationship with the Duce and eventually create a national scandal. The family included Claretta's younger sister Maria, who became a film actress and adopted the stage name of Myriam di San Servolo; and her older brother Marcello, in the 1930s a medical student who figured at the centre of the Petacci scandals.

Nino D'Aroma, who had little regard for Claretta, described her as being of medium height, a typical Latin brunette with a languorous step and soft features. 'But she was very common and equal to so many beautiful women of our country,' he said. 'One thing about her I will never forget: a sad and timid smile in which one felt, more than one saw, something that anticipated the victim and resignation. . . . For years she counted for nothing or less than nothing. Only in 1941 did she take a certain upper hand.' He said she often recommended for appointments men whom she regarded as very faithful, and believed she rendered a service to Mussolini by doing so.

Marcello, he said, was 'a sort of eternal madman, full of a hundred thousand projects'. At one time D'Aroma was a newspaper editor, and a friend brought Marcello to his office to meet him. 'He showed he was a neurotic . . . capable of spicing all his conversation with huge lies. . . . He seemed more a clinical subject than a man with whom one could have a common and civil conversation.'

Myriam, he said, was a mediocre actress and in other respects 'gave a painful impression. She was the subject of widespread gossip.' He was more kind to Claretta. 'She was a simple woman who had just one unpardonable defect, that of being absurdly and madly enamoured of a man named Mussolini.' But one of Claretta's biographers said she complained about her body, her teeth, her health and the size of her breasts, and if given the chance would stay in bed all day eating chocolate.[10]

Elisabetta Cerruti, the wife of an Italian ambassador, encountered Mussolini's new lover in the 1930s and afterwards offered this description: 'Miss Petacci, his last lady love, although she had beautiful legs and unbelievably small feet like her predecessors, was hardly a fitting companion for a chief of state [*sic*]. I saw her once at the opera and found her very attractive in a certain way. She had too many curls and her makeup was unnaturally heavy. Her mink coat was too big; her jewels too showy; but it could not be denied that she attracted attention.'[11]

Mussolini came to devote an inordinate amount of time to Claretta. One Italian writer said that, during Italy's war with Greece in 1940 and its involvement in the war against the Soviet Union the following year, the Duce spent 'every afternoon' with her, frequently making it impossible for his generals to contact him at crucial moments.

One Italian writer quoted Mussolini as saying to her: 'I love you so much, so much. I don't know why I love you like this. I only love you! The perfume of your kisses stuns me, kills me. When I look into your eyes I read to the bottom of your soul. The world vanishes and I forget everybody and everything.' During the summer of 1938 and 1939, the Mussolinis took a holiday by the sea at Rimini while the Petaccis were just up the Adriatic coast at Riccione. Claretta later recalled that she and Mussolini met on a deserted beach, he called her 'baby' and said he adored her. 'You are the most beautiful part of my life. You are my youth,' she quoted him as saying.[12] In the summer of 1940, Mussolini arranged for a Carabiniere guard to be placed at the door of her house.[13]

Like some of Mussolini's previous lovers, Claretta longed to have a child by the Duce. In 1940 she had an extrauterine pregnancy, and when peritonitis set in doctors performed an abortion. Claretta's recovery took four months, and during that time Mussolini phoned her several times a day and visited her in the evenings when he could. In the winter of 1941 she phoned him one day to say she thought she was pregnant again, and the call was recorded by the Italian secret services.

'The important thing is that you are not displeased,' she said at one point.

'Why should it displease me?' he said. But at no point in the conversation did he say he was pleased. In any case, Claretta was mistaken; she was not pregnant, and doctors had told her she could never have children after her abortion.[14]

As divorce in Italy was unlawful, Claretta travelled to Budapest and obtained a divorce from Federici on 29 December 1941. Galeazzo Ciano noted with amusement in his diary that after she came back someone asked her about her trip and she replied: 'I have had neither receptions nor parties. I went strictly incognito.' Gino Sotis, the lawyer who handled her divorce, was shortly afterwards appointed by Mussolini as a national councillor.[15] It was one of the first instances that proved to many that she was not merely the Duce's lover, but a woman who mixed in politics and especially political appointments.

Some Italians began to speak of her as a 'little Pompadour' and of her brother Marcello as a sort of Lorenzino de' Medici,* who did 'more harm to the Duce than fifteen lost battles'. Education Minister Giuseppe Bottai wrote in his diary in November 1942: 'The regime is Pompadourising, with what a low species of Pompadour!'[16]

Some of Mussolini's collaborators who did not approve of Claretta tried to interest him in a young film star, Alida Valli. For a time they succeeded but, as a journalist in Rome wrote: 'Unfortunately, however, after a short time Mussolini returned to Claretta. He could not live without her.'[17]

Renzo De Felice, Mussolini's principal Italian biographer, judged that she was not an intriguer nor did she have ambitions to play a political role. He quoted one writer as saying she 'didn't have nerves strong enough to use her sceptre. She cried easily and had the heart of a little sentimental bourgeois

*Lorenzino de' Medici was banned from the papal court for misbehaviour and in 1537 murdered the tyrant Alessandro de' Medici, his cousin.

woman.' Despite that, De Felice concluded she did have a certain influence over some appointments, but not the most important ones. She was certainly not involved in a major Cabinet shakeup in February 1943, which Mussolini told her about casually in a phone call after the fact, De Felice said.

'That the relationship contributed to discrediting Mussolini and the regime is without doubt,' he said. British radio broadcasts to Italy made much of the relationship during the war.

In 1939 the Petacci family built a gaudily luxurious house in the upmarket Camilluccia district of Rome, and De Felice said it was only then that people began to whisper about her.[18]

Adelchi Serena, secretary of the Fascist Party in 1941, showed Bottai a letter that Marcello Petacci had written to Interior Under-secretary Luigi Gatti, 'threatening and blackmailing for certain affairs'. Serena said he could not rule out the possibility Mussolini had fired Gatti to rid himself of a witness to Marcello's 'excesses'.[19]

Galeazzo Ciano and his wife Edda were among those most strongly opposed to Mussolini's relationship with Claretta, and Edda claimed Claretta took her revenge by engineering Ciano's removal as foreign minister in February 1943. That seems unlikely; Mussolini already had been aware for some time that Ciano opposed his wartime policies and had denigrated him in private.

Ciano noted in his diary on 12 November 1941 that everyone in the Navy was whispering that a certain Admiral Riccardi owed his post to Claretta, 'and this is certainly not a rumour destined to increase his prestige'. The following month Ciano observed that Guido Buffarini-Guidi, then under-secretary of the interior, was making a monthly payment of 100,000 lire to Claretta. Later he quoted an Italian minister as saying Buffarini was paying her 200,000 lire monthly 'and from that he draws the security of his impunity'. He also reported, without elaboration, that Myriam had 'caused a great scandal in Venice'.

In March 1942, Ciano wrote that the Petacci family 'intervenes on the right, protects on the left, threatens above, intrigues below. . . . It is without doubt that the scandal is spreading and by now invests the person of the Duce.'

Mussolini's sister Edvige came to Ciano a month later and said she had proof of 'the profiteering of the Petacci couple and the scandal that arises from it'. She said she had decided to speak to the Duce about it.

Raffaele Riccardi, minister of exchange and currency, discovered that summer that Marcello Petacci, along with Buffarini, was involved in illegal currency dealings and the smuggling of gold from Spain. He went to Mussolini to report his findings, and Ciano said the Duce became very indignant and gave orders 'to proceed against the guilty according to the law'. But no action was taken against Marcello, and it was not just Petacci family members but also those associated with them who seemed exempt from punishment. Riccardi showed Ciano a confidential report by a Carabiniere officer, who wrote that he had evidence against a certain 'rogue' but he was the lover of Myriam Petacci, 'hence he cannot touch him'.[20]

Edda Ciano claimed in her memoirs that one high official owed his appointment to the fact that he was a friend of Claretta's, and another lost his job because he had helped expose Marcello's illegal dealings. Edda said she had known of the existence of Claretta for some years but had not thought until then that the affair was anything serious. But she said there was now a great discussion everywhere of 'the most important minister', Claretta, and careers were created and destroyed at the Camilluccia residence of the Petaccis.[21]

In July 1942, Galeazzo Ciano said Osvaldo Sebastiani, who had lost his post as secretary to Mussolini, attributed his fall 'to the sinister influences of the Petacci house'.

'The girl isn't bad but the rest of the family are a band of exploiters,' Ciano commented. He said Mussolini had once told Sebastiani that 'this affair also will end soon'. But at the same time, Alessandro Pavolini, then minister of popular culture, told Ciano that Mussolini had taken an extraordinary interest in Myriam's wedding to an Italian marquis, a greater interest than he would have shown for any of his own children, even going so far as to telephone at midnight to learn how the Roman newspaper *Il Messaggero* had worded the wedding announcement.

In August 1942 Ciano noted that Claretta, enjoying a seaside break at Rimini, 'judges and intrigues', and that her factotum was 'a certain Spisani, dance master in a third-rate dance hall'.[22] In that same month, the public scandal was such that Edda decided to raise the matter at a private lunch with her father. 'I recognise that I don't have great diplomatic ability and I don't know how to present things with delicacy,' she wrote. 'Therefore I entered brutally into the argument. I told him, without minding my words, all that I knew' about Marcello. She also observed tartly that Marcello had never 'spent a single day at the [war] front' and benefited from promotions 'as unusual as they were promising'.

Mussolini later told Edda he had called in Marcello, who resigned from a Milanese firm in which he was involved and had promised to embark on a naval ship. The Duce also said he intended to put an end to his affair with Claretta because the only woman who really counted for him was Rachele. Edda was sceptical; he had kept his distance from Rachele in recent years, and when they did meet they always ended by arguing.

Edda went to Umberto Albini, the new under-secretary of the interior, and asked him to furnish her with proof of Marcello's crooked dealings. With Albini's file under her arm, she went to see her father and showed him contracts Marcello had made in Spain, which included kickbacks to him and which provided for the supply of materials that proved unusable. She also showed him a contract under which Marcello had bought a villa in Merano in northern Italy, paying more than a million pengö, the Hungarian currency. She told Mussolini that Marcello, instead of embarking on a ship, had become director of a Venetian hospital and was the subject of much gossip there.

This time, she said, Mussolini was indignant and thanked her for what she had shown him. 'The woman will be liquidated, and all these affairs will come to an end,' he said. 'What an imbecile to sign with his own name a contract of purchase in pengö.' Edda commented that Mussolini seemed more scandalised by Marcello's naïveté than by 'the serious dishonesty of his conduct'. She was still sceptical, and rightly so. She went to Sicily as a war nurse, and when she returned Ciano told her that Mussolini had severed his relationship with Claretta but in less than a week had allowed her to return.[23]

A few months later Albini whispered to Education Minister Bottai: 'I will be capable of taking her out, if it becomes necessary.' Bottai said it was clear Albini meant killing her.[24]

The Petacci affair became the subject of discussion at a meeting of top Fascist officials at Lucca in October 1942. Mussolini got wind of it and told Pavolini that 'no one has the right to investigate and judge on the sentimental life of others'.

A Sicilian princess, whom Ciano discreetly avoided naming but described as having 'a cordial friendship' with Mussolini, came to Ciano in December 1942 and told him: 'Mussolini would have the head of Claretta, her brother, her sister, all of them, but he would not succeed in getting them off his feet because they are riffraff, ready for blackmail and scandal.' Ciano said he didn't know whether this was true or due to jealousy on the part of the princess. 'The princess attributes to the Petaccis all that goes badly in Italy, including the illness of the Duce,' he wrote. 'Which, honestly, seems to me a little exaggerated.'[25]

The Mussolini–Petacci relationship had not been without its ups and downs earlier. Once, according to Myriam, Claretta followed his car and saw that he stopped at the house of a former lover. She refused to take his next phone call. When Mussolini learned why, he told Myriam: 'I do not permit myself to be followed. I have already told her that I do not tolerate being shadowed.'[26]

Marcello's illegal operations did provoke Mussolini to bar Claretta from Palazzo Venezia for a time. On 23 April 1943, she wrote to him to protest, saying: 'When I think that a little while ago I was the dear, delicious little girl worthy of being adored, and a little later everything becomes a piece of buffoonery . . . I wonder if I am crazy or about to become so. . . . I would want to fall dead instantly rather than hear that you can betray me, that you can no longer love me.' She kept writing in that vein almost daily, without response.[27]

While Claretta was *persona non grata*, General Giacomo Carboni, the chief of military intelligence, arranged a meeting with her at her house. In a report he wrote after the war for the US Office of Strategic Services, Carboni described the house as looking like 'a large can on a bar of ice'. He described walls covered with mirrors, pink furniture, a bathroom all in black marble.

'A setting for an American film, but of evident bad taste,' he wrote. Claretta, wearing a dressing gown, received him in her bedroom. She complained that Mussolini was always lacking in attention to her, always rude. Carboni brought up the name of Enzo Galbiati, a member of the Grand Council, and Claretta claimed that Mussolini had appointed him as chief of the militia forces at her insistence. She also described Buffarini, the ousted interior under-secretary, as her most devoted friend, and said she was working to help him get back into power. Had she known in advance of Mussolini's decision to dismiss him, she said she 'would have impeded it'. She went on to claim she was responsible for the appointment of other men as prefects in Aquila and Varese. As they chatted, the phone rang and Mussolini was on the line. Carboni claimed to have overheard both ends of the conversation, with Mussolini saying: 'I beg you to leave me alone. I cannot interest myself now in your personal case. I need to remain alone.'

Claretta protested that she was not a drawer that could be closed at any moment. 'I am not a whore. I hope that you will remember that I am not only your lover. Basically I don't ask anything extraordinary of you except to see you again.'

Carboni said Mussolini repeated that he wanted to be left alone, and not forced to adopt unpleasant measures.

'Then tell me frankly that you don't want to know of me any more and I will go away,' Claretta said.

'It would be more opportune,' he replied.

She put down the phone, dissolved in tears, cursed Edda and said: 'He has treated me like a loose woman, like all his other loose women. He has never understood me. He has always kept me in the same consideration as the others, while I have sacrificed twelve years of my youth for him. . . . He shows me the door without giving me the means of escaping the ire of his enemies and mine.'[28]

But shortly afterwards Mussolini agreed to meet her.

'I had decided not to see you again,' he said.

'But why? What have I done to you?'

'I had serious reasons.'

'Why haven't you wanted to tell me? What have I done?'

'You, nothing. But there are serious accusations against someone in your family.'

'Accusations? What accusations?'

'Trafficking in foreign currency and contraband of gold. . . . I will show you the report.'

She read the report and asked why he believed such lies from people who wanted to destroy them. Myriam, who described this conversation, claimed Mussolini apologised to her in the end, and told her Marcello had fallen into a political trap. They resumed their relationship.[29]

One evening he told the Palazzo Venezia doorkeeper: 'I didn't want to see her again, but now she's back here. She is silly like an honest woman. Because of this she doesn't understand that it is necessary to end it.'[30]

On 24 July, the day of the Grand Council meeting that set the stage for his overthrow, she sent him a note: 'Only three or four [Council members] are with you. All the others are against you. If you get to a vote, they will overthrow you. If you let them leave Palazzo Venezia it is finished. . . . Order them arrested and you are safe.'[31]

Rachele later claimed that she had known nothing of Claretta until someone mentioned her name after Mussolini's overthrow, but Myriam and Edda both believed Rachele had known of her much earlier. After his rescue, when Rachele and Mussolini were reunited in Munich, she said they made a pact to consider 'the Clara incident' past and as something that never happened.[32]

On 28 July, three days after Mussolini's overthrow, the Petacci family left Rome for northern Italy. Claretta wrote him a note, which he never received, expressing worry over his fate and telling him: 'I love you, and more than before.'

On the night of 12 August, the Petaccis were arrested on orders of the Badoglio government and imprisoned at Novara, a city west of Milan.[33] From jail, Claretta wrote thirty-seven extravagantly sentimental letters to Mussolini – one for each day she was behind bars – even though she had no address to which to send them. Published later as her 'diary', they appear to have been written by someone who spent too much time reading cheap romances. She referred to herself often as 'your little girl' and 'your little dear one in jail'.

> *19 August*: Yesterday evening you thought of me, I felt it and I know also of what you thought; I also thought the same thing of you: Love. You were with me and everything seemed sweet, everything was bearable, even the laceration of the flesh. Your caress, your love, your voice were my medicine. . . . Oh! my Ben, I will not see you again. . . !
>
> *23 August*: Ben, tonight I dreamed of you, such sweetness, your voice, your caress! Oh! No one can take away from me this joy of flying to you

> in dreams. . . . Neither distances, walls, bars, jails and jailers exist. You are with me and I with you. . . . You have said with your inimitable voice: 'I love you, I love you, I think of you night and day, not a minute passes that I don't think of you, that I don't remember you. I didn't believe I could love you so deeply, I didn't believe I loved you still so much. . . .' My adored one, is it true, is it true?

On 18 September, the day after the Petaccis were freed and were at a military base, she wrote:

> Suddenly they tell us you will speak on the radio at 9.30 from Germany. I have a shock to the heart, I begin to tremble. . . . And there in the little nearby room where the bunks are, in the profound silence, the radio sends me your voice, your voice, your voice, my Ben, Ben! A convulsion, a shudder, a burst of unstoppable crying, sudden, violent sobs that I try to suffocate in the arms of Mimi [Myriam], who trembles but keeps control of herself. I cannot, I cannot stop myself, it is all my soul that overflows, that weeps. I hear you, I hear you, you speak, you are love, it is your voice, alive, I still live and I listen to you and cry with joy, with tenderness, with passion, I live still to hear you, it's you! . . . Your soul passed into mine by drops and I felt you inside me, as before, transfused as always. The officers were moved and wept, amazed and surprised. I fell ill and I fainted.[34]

The Petaccis made their way north to Merano, where Marcello had his villa. SS Commander General Karl Wolff arrived soon afterward and told Claretta he needed her help. He said the fact that the regime had not asked for the extradition of Ciano from Germany was worrying the German government. 'Now, given the consideration which you enjoy with the Duce,' he began, but she raised a hand to stop him.

'My relations with the Duce are of a personal and private nature. If the government of the Reich wishes to make him know something it may follow the normal procedures.'

Wolff told her that her influence could be precious. Ciano must return to Italy. She turned to the interpreter and said: 'Tell the general that, first of all, he is speaking with an Italian and that, in second place, the Duce doesn't need someone to make suggestions. Tell him also that I am not in the service of the Reich. And, finally, let him note that, even if I had the influence he attributes to me, I would not use it ever to turn the Duce against one of his family.'

She gave Wolff a letter for Mussolini, which was handed to him when he returned to Italy. He replied on 10 October, and their first meeting occurred on 28 October.

When she returned to Merano, her mother pleaded with her to end her relationship with Mussolini and get on with a new life. 'Now you must also think of your parents, your sister, your brother,' she admonished. 'We have been close to you, beyond every human limit. Our name has been compromised.'

'You are right,' Claretta replied. 'Leave me alone.'

Myriam, who quoted that conversation, said: 'At times I wanted to hit her for her hard-headedness, for her selfishness.' She said Wolff and Buffarini subsequently tried to relocate the family to Malcesine, on the eastern shore of Lake Garda, 'in a sort of cold and squalid hovel'. To reach there, Mussolini would have had to drive about 100 miles round-trip, or go by motorboat across the lake from Gargnano on the west side. Myriam herself went to the lake and found a more comfortable residence for them at Gardone Riviera, just 6 miles from Gargnano, in the Villa Fiordaliso (Italian for lily), which Wolff agreed to put at their disposal. German and Japanese diplomats occupied the third and fourth floors of the villa, which today is a luxury hotel, and the Petaccis were ensconced on the first and second floors. Vittorio Mussolini and his family lived nearby.

The Petaccis moved in in mid-November, but they returned to Merano to celebrate Christmas and see in the New Year. When they returned to Gardone, they received threats from extreme Fascists, who accused Claretta of weakening the Duce and provoking the ruin of Italy.

The SS Colonel Eugen Dollmann said Wolff wanted to get rid of Claretta, but Mussolini told him: 'I will never separate myself from her and I would prefer to sacrifice my life rather than consent to such a separation.'

Myriam said Mussolini arranged trysts with Claretta in the tower of a building across the road that had belonged to his friend, the late poet Gabriele D'Annunzio. Rumours circulated that Claretta was an agent of foreign secret services, either German or American, depending on who was doing the talking. Claretta spent nearly all her time at the Villa Fiordaliso, swimming and sunbathing in the daytime or taking motorboat rides with Franz Spoegler, an SS lieutenant who had been assigned to look after her and who hailed from the German-speaking Alto Adige region of northern Italy. In the evenings, she stayed in, awaiting Mussolini's phone calls.[35]

Vittorio Mussolini said his father never allowed his love affairs, even the one with Claretta, to detract from his relations with Rachele or the rest of the family, 'and they never lessened the respect and affection that we all felt for him'.

Vittorio had the impression the Germans encouraged Claretta's presence near the Duce, as did Interior Minister Buffarini. 'They obviously thought that Clara Petacci could have an influence over my father which in fact she didn't seek to have and indeed didn't have,' he said. 'But the really fanatical Fascist Republicans were convinced she wielded this influence . . . and to them Clara

Petacci was a disgrace and a source of danger.' In light of this, Vittorio went to his father, told him what was being said about him and his lover, and begged him to send her away.

From Mussolini's replies, Vittorio realised his father had a deep affection for Claretta but did not appear to attach overriding importance to the affair. Mussolini said he had nothing against sending her away. But afterwards he clearly told her of his conversation with Vittorio, because two days later a militia officer handed Vittorio a seven-page letter in Claretta's tiny handwriting. She rebuked him for being small-minded in judging the situation and said: 'I ask nothing from your father and I would have you know that I would give him anything, including my life.' She said Mussolini lived in an atmosphere of disloyalty and treachery, and she spent her few precious hours with him consoling him for the difficulties he faced. 'If I went he would be even more alone, with not a single friend – nobody,' she wrote.

Rachele later said she learned of Claretta's presence from anonymous or signed letters sent to her. She went to Mussolini, who confirmed Claretta was nearby and said he had made only one visit to Gardone with General Wolff to resolve the question. Rachele then went to Buffarini, who promised he would send Claretta away. Rachele soon learned that Claretta was still in Gardone, but she bided her time.[36] A spectacular showdown between the two women would come later.

Chapter 6

A Most Unhappy Family

The Italians are Fascists out of cowardice.

(Vittorio Mussolini, 1929)

Rachele Mussolini rejoined the Duce on 3 November, and their two youngest children, Romano, sixteen, and Anna Maria, fourteen, returned from Germany a few weeks later. Other Mussolinis crowded into Gargnano and the Duce appointed Vittorio, now aged twenty-seven, to head a political secretariat that was often in conflict with the official secretariat run by Giovanni Dolfin. The police estimated that about 200 Mussolinis were living around Gargnano. Many of them were dependent on the Duce for their livelihood, and Mussolini was not above resorting to nepotism. Not only did he appoint Vittorio to a job for which he was not suited; he named Vanni Teodorani, the husband of his late brother Arnaldo's daughter, as an envoy extraordinary. 'This . . . has upset my stomach. . . . It is something that surpasses the limits of the tolerable,' the diplomat Luigi Bolla wrote. Serafino Mazzolini, the under-secretary for foreign affairs, protested over the appointment. Mussolini agreed he was right and cancelled it.

The return of Rachele and their children was not a happy family reunion. As Dr Zachariae noted in his diary, Mussolini and Rachele often passed each other in their residence without speaking. Rachele sought always to convey the impression that she had a devoted husband and claimed they laughed together about his affairs. 'Benito was always not only the best of fathers but also an attentive and affectionate spouse who, until the last, surrounded me with every kindness,' Rachele wrote in her memoirs. 'Never, I can swear it, did he pass a night outside the house, never did he allow himself to introduce Claretta to someone of our family. (In Italy there are few men who pass all their evenings with their families.)'[1]

In fact, Rachele was deeply wounded by his straying from the marital nest and they quarrelled frequently. Edda later told a Swiss psychiatrist that she had asked as a child to be sent to a school in Florence to get away from the tempestuous family atmosphere. She said her mother reviled Mussolini constantly in front of the children and the servants, and both parents tried to make her the witness and arbiter of their marital disputes.[2]

There was nothing close-knit about the Mussolinis as a family. 'At home the Mussolinis were not communicative,' said Nino D'Aroma, who knew them well. 'Each lived his own life, had his own friends. And they spoke little.'[3] Rarely did they have friends or even close relatives to dine with them. But Filippo Anfuso, Mussolini's ambassador to Germany, was once privileged to get a dinner invitation in Gargnano, and he described a curious scene.

> He [Mussolini] ignored his guests at meals. He ate quickly and badly, in a sort of irritable race towards the food. . . . He rose when he finished, and left the others to remain with their forks in the air! But that day he remained at the table, to describe the beauty of the edition of Nietzsche that Hitler sent him in prison. He mentioned it contained some passages in Greek by Nietzsche and praised . . . the doctrine of the philosopher.
>
> During a pause, the very young son Romano, who was seated in front of him and seemed to be absent from the conversation, addressed himself to his father: 'But papa, you do not know Greek.'
>
> Mussolini ignored the interruption and continued his praise of his Greek Nietzsche. But Romano persisted: 'But you don't know Greek, papa! Why do you say you know Greek if you don't know it?'

Mussolini got up from the table and went away.[4]

Rachele took pride in her peasant background and her practical management of household affairs. Edda once spoke to D'Aroma of her mother's 'peasant fanaticism'. Zachariae, who observed the family closely in their months at Gargnano, said he often saw Rachele ironing clothes even though the family had five servants. Elisabetta Cerruti, wife of an Italian ambassador before the war, said: 'Rachele was an extraordinarily simple woman, not especially attractive except for her legs, which seem to have been Mussolini's first criterion in women. She had good common sense and never wished to appear on public occasions. . . . What was important, she knew how to handle her man.'[5]

Romano irritated his father by going about the Villa Feltrinelli playing jazz on a saxophone; he would become a jazz pianist after the war, and would grow up to have perhaps the most pleasant temperament of any of the Mussolinis. While at Gargnano, he attended secondary school in a nearby town and did not do well at his studies. He had previously been found by teachers in Rome to have a short attention span. Anna Maria was mentally slow and had suffered an attack of polio in early childhood. In the spring of

1944, Mussolini sent her for treatment to an orthopaedic hospital in Mecklenburg, Germany. But she showed little improvement and the Duce quarrelled with the director, saying he had promised a complete cure.[6]

Rachele said Mussolini would sometimes take walks with Romano, and the Duce was no doubt indulgent toward Anna Maria because of her handicaps, allowing her to burst in on him frequently at his office in the Villa delle Orsoline. D'Aroma said Anna Maria was 'a serious, courageous girl, full of spirit'. Despite undergoing a number of operations and being often in pain, he said, 'she knows how to smile and give a hand to her mother'.[7]

Mussolini and his wife suffered a nasty shock at Christmas, a few weeks after the family's return from Germany, when they feared Romano had drowned in Lake Garda. He and Anna Maria had gone to visit their cousin Vito on an island in the lake. They left in a car driven by Vittorio and went to San Felice, then crossed from there to the island by motorboat. At dinner time on Christmas Day, Vittorio, his wife and Anna Maria returned, but Vittorio informed his parents that Romano was returning directly from the island to Gargnano by motorboat with three other people, including Second Lieutenant Hans Heinrich Dyckerhoff, an SS officer who lived in Villa Feltrinelli to keep an eye on the family.

The Mussolinis waited until late evening, growing increasingly worried, and Rachele phoned Vito, who confirmed the motorboat carrying Romano had left the island at 7 p.m. Through the night, Mussolini paced back and forth in the villa, reproaching Vittorio for having allowed Romano to take such a long motorboat ride at night in winter, when the lake was often choppy. Neither Mussolini nor Rachele slept that night, but around 5 a.m. the door opened and Romano and his three companions appeared, tired and frozen. Mussolini, who until then had threatened Romano with severe punishment, took him in his arms without speaking. The four explained that, because of darkness and fog, they hadn't managed to find Gargnano and finally had run out of fuel. The motorboat drifted along the rocks until a fortunate change in the wind pushed them toward the shore and they made land a long way from Gargnano. They had walked all the way back from there.[8]

The incident could not have endeared Vittorio to his father. They had never been close, at least not until after the death of Vittorio's brother Bruno in 1941, and Vittorio gave a bad impression to many outside the family, both on account of his character and his manners. He had no talent for politics but was pushed into attempting to play a political role by Alessandro Pavolini, the fanatical Fascist who was the party secretary. The diplomat Luigi Bolla described Vittorio as 'one of the greatest boors who exists on the face of the Earth'. Lieutenant-Colonel Johann Jandl, the German armed forces liaison officer with Mussolini, once spoke about Vittorio to Bolla after a dinner attended by Mussolini and Hitler and asked: 'Is it possible they haven't even taught him to eat soup?' Bolla commented: 'In fact Vittorio eats in a disgusting way.' He said Dr Zachariae had asked: 'Why is the son of the Duce so ill-bred?' Bolla said Zachariae added that Vittorio was 'anti-German, of an invincible ignorance, surrounded by hair-raising boors and that – incredible to say so – the Duce listens to him.' But, at Gargnano, Mussolini developed a closer relationship with Vittorio than before, and used him as a courier to take letters to Hitler when he began to suspect his letters were not reaching their destination. 'I noted with pleasure that his esteem for me grew with the passage of time,' Vittorio wrote.[9]

But not the esteem of those around Mussolini. Bolla said that as Mussolini often allowed himself to be influenced by Vittorio this difficult son was the cause 'of very serious damage and of many sorrows to the country'. Vittorio, he said, was given to extremism based on presumption, ignorance, boorishness and a total misunderstanding of present reality.[10]

Ruggero Zangrandi was a friend of Vittorio's for ten years starting in 1929 when they attended school together. He described him as 'good, loyal, simple, a little indolent' and as having little contact at that time with his father. He also said Vittorio was gifted with an acute intelligence and a critical spirit but ended by conceiving a disdain for other people.

Once when Zangrandi was waxing enthusiastic about fascism, Vittorio said: 'It's useless. Fascism is entirely a bluff. Papa has not succeeded in doing anything he wanted. The Italians are Fascists out of cowardice and they don't give a damn about the revolution.' Together Zangrandi and Vittorio put out a student newspaper in which they boldly criticised 'Fascist art' and denounced profiteering by those who benefited from the regime.

The young Zangrandi often visited the Mussolini family home in Rome, Villa Torlonia, and said Mussolini gradually revealed himself as an odd individual. 'When Mussolini played ball with us, he always wanted to win, although he was a very poor player,' he said. 'His comments and advice . . . were pronounced in a sententious oratorical form as if, instead of finding himself before three or four boys, he spoke to an audience of exalted Fascists.'

Zangrandi later broke with Vittorio. He became an opponent of the regime and served time in prison for his dissent.[11]

In his memoirs, Vittorio wrote:

> I believe no one ever enjoyed the full confidence of my father. It is known that he was 'a solitary man'. In his youth he had male friends and girl friends, but such friendships did not last. Intimacy with men and the exterior forms of friendship, with embraces and slaps on the shoulder,

> with spontaneity and the happy, noisy company of friends, were very foreign to him.
>
> He never invited friends to Villa Torlonia, nor collaborators. Even his brother Arnaldo and his sister Edvige seldom frequented our house. Having known men and their misery close-up, he had not only a psychic but a physical intolerance for them, this being not the least among his reasons for insisting on the abolition of handshakes in favour of the more hygienic Roman salute.[12]

After leaving school, Vittorio and his brother, Bruno, then just seventeen, served in the Air Force during the Ethiopian war. In January 1936, Bruno's plane was repeatedly hit by anti-aircraft fire but he returned safely, and two months later Marshal Badoglio, then the Italian commander in Ethiopia, awarded Bruno and Vittorio the silver medal for valour after they had flown 110 hours in combat. Afterwards, Vittorio wrote a book about his experiences and said it was 'very amusing' to see bombs falling on Ethiopians.[13]

Police reports suggested that as young men Vittorio and Bruno spent a lot of time in high-class brothels. Both loved fast cars, and Bruno killed Teresa Velluti, an elderly Roman woman, when she was crossing a street, but an official report blamed her and he was not prosecuted. Bruno also had to contend at one point with a claim by a poor Roman girl whom he seduced and abandoned.[14]

D'Aroma described Bruno and Vittorio as having 'a closed and fundamentally sad temperament' and said both were indifferent to being sons of the Duce. He said Bruno was by nature quiet, shy and timid, was usually bad tempered and reserved, wore a sad face and had a serious and taciturn character. He wanted nothing to do with politics and his only ambition was to be a pilot. In the summer of 1937 he transferred to Spain and fought in the Spanish Civil War from a base in Palma de Majorca. But Generalissimo Francisco Franco, the Spanish Fascist leader, told Mussolini he could not risk having Bruno captured, so he returned home at Christmas that year. 'It wasn't worth the trouble of going to Palma to stay there such a short while,' he commented.

Bruno had a passion for music, especially opera. In 1938, he married Gina Ruberti, the drama critic of a Roman newspaper and the daughter of a minor official in the Education Ministry. Their only child, a daughter named Marina, was born in 1940. Long air flights were still a novelty at that time, so Bruno reaped widespread publicity when, in 1938, he flew to Rio de Janeiro with a stop en route in Dakar, Senegal. He ducked out of interviews after his return from the 6,000-mile round trip.[15]

After his return from Ethiopia, Vittorio went into the film business, producing several Italian films. At the Cinecittà studios outside Rome, he met the American producer Hal Roach, who in 1937 invited him to the United States. Vittorio made the rounds of Hollywood, met Shirley Temple and other stars, then went on to Washington where he was invited to meet President Roosevelt. The president expressed interest in meeting Mussolini and asked Vittorio to try to arrange it, but nothing came of this.

Vittorio also became co-editor of a new theoretical journal called *Cinema*, but he left most of the work to his fellow editor Luciano De Feo. Vittorio married a Milanese woman, Orsola Bufali.

When Italy entered the war against France in 1940, Vittorio was called up as an air force lieutenant and took part in bombing raids on Malta and Greece. Bruno had remained in the Air Force, and the brothers were together in the great Italian naval port of Taranto when it was subjected to a heavy British bombing raid.[16]

On 7 August 1941, Bruno was killed when a plane he was piloting developed engine trouble and crashed near the Pisa airport. Vittorio was present and rushed to the scene of the crash, just in time to hear his dying brother murmur: 'Papa . . . the field . . .'. Two other fliers died with him and five men aboard the plane survived. Mussolini rushed to Pisa and sat by Bruno's body all night. He was pitched into such grief that he contemplated suicide at one point. 'From that sad day,' Vittorio wrote, 'my father always wanted me nearer to him, and even if I couldn't fill the void left by the exuberant youth of Bruno, our relations became more steady and affectionate.'[17]

Vittorio returned to war service on the North African front in 1942.

In late 1941, Mussolini published a 166-page book, *Parlo con Bruno* ('I Speak with Bruno'), cast as a fatherly conversation with his departed son and recounting his exploits and his interests, ranging from opera to boxing.

'A Fascist born and bred, you were intransigent in your faith,' he wrote. 'All that I have done or will do is nothing by comparison with what you have done. Just one drop of the blood that will arise from your lacerated temples and runs down your pale face is worth more than all my works, present, past and future.' He concluded with these words: 'I take leave of you, Bruno. How much time will have to pass before I descend into the crypt of San Cassiano (the family cemetery) to sleep beside you the sleep without end?'[18]

Throughout his captivity on Ponza, La Maddalena and the Gran Sasso, Mussolini kept a photograph of Bruno on his bedside table.[19]

At Gargnano, it was not only Bruno who was missing from the family circle. There was Edda, the favourite of his children, now estranged from him and on the point of a nervous breakdown as he prepared to give passive approval to the trial and execution of her husband, Count Ciano. It was to be one of the most painful episodes of Mussolini's life, and one of the most shameful.

Chapter 7

GALEAZZO CIANO AND EDDA

From that morning I began to die.

(Benito Mussolini on hearing of the execution of his son-in-law, January 1944)

Mussolini once wrote to Edda to say: 'As in your adolescence, when times were tough, today you were and are the special favourite of my soul.'[1] Edda was the first of the Mussolini children, born in 1910 when her unmarried parents were living in dire poverty. She had her father's intelligence, his headstrong temperament and even his looks. She and Galeazzo Ciano had met in 1930 when he was a young diplomat, just returned to Rome from a tour of duty in China. He was the son of Costanzo Ciano, Mussolini's minister of communications and a man he once designated as his successor. After a courtship of just seventeen days, Galeazzo proposed to Edda, and she accepted with a nonchalant air. With Mussolini's blessing, they were married on 24 April 1930, and shortly afterwards went to China together where the first of their three children was born. In 1935, back in Rome, Ciano was made minister for press and propaganda, and a year later, at the age of thirty-three, he was elevated to become Europe's youngest foreign minister. He was evidently too young for the job, and, although highly intelligent, had a frivolous nature and was devoted to the *beau monde* of film stars and Italian and foreign nobility; his little circle of friends and admirers fluttered about him at the Acquasanta Golf Club outside Rome, where Ciano held court in the afternoons. Despite these shortcomings, he became Mussolini's closest confidant and was widely regarded as the dauphin of the regime. Ciano worshipped the Duce to the point of imitating his gestures and his style of speaking, making himself look ridiculous in the eyes of others.[2]

His marriage to Edda had been happy at first, but he soon began a series of affairs, causing her to contemplate leaving him at one point. She eventually found lovers of her own, or male companions who satisfied her need for attention. The lover to whom she appeared to be closest was a young air force captain, Emilio Pucci, who would become a world-famous dress designer after the war.[3]

Ciano was initially a strong supporter of the Axis partnership with Germany, and together with Foreign Minister von Ribbentrop signed the Pact of Steel that established a military alliance between Italy and Germany. His disillusionment with the Germans, and Mussolini, began after he went to Salzburg in August 1939 to learn of German intentions, and was bluntly told that Germany was preparing – without consultation with Italy – to go to war with Poland. 'We want war,' Ribbentrop told him. Ciano did not believe Hitler's bland assurances that Britain and France would sit on their hands in such a war, and on his return to Rome, he tried in vain to persuade Mussolini to break with the Germans. Mussolini declared a state of nonbelligerence and waited until June 1940 to join Germany, belatedly, in an attack on an already prostrate France. Ciano did egg on Mussolini to attack Greece in the autumn of 1940, and Italy found itself bogged down in a disastrous war from which it had to be rescued by Germany.[4]

Edda, resolutely pro-German until the tide of battle turned against Hitler in the Soviet Union, did her part in the war as a Red Cross nurse. She was aboard a hospital ship that was sunk by British bombers off the Albanian coast, but was rescued. She went on to serve on the Russian front, then later in Sicily after the Allied invasion there.[5]

Ciano's friends who sponsored the resolution against Mussolini in the Fascist Grand Council in July 1943 tried to dissuade him from speaking in support of it because they did not want to compromise him with his father-in-law. But by now openly contemptuous of Mussolini, Ciano was determined to play his part. He embarrassed Mussolini by revealing that Germany had violated terms of the Pact of Steel by attacking Poland without prior consultation.

'The Germans lighted the fuse ahead of time, against every pact and understanding with us,' he said. 'And they did not abandon this method during the entire course of the war. All the attacks that followed the one on Poland were equally communicated to us at the last hour: from that on Belgium and Holland to the last one, against Russia. . . . In short, our loyalty was never returned. Every accusation of betrayal made by the Germans to us could be incontrovertibly turned back on them. We were not, in any case, traitors, but the betrayed.'

Rachele had tried to persuade Mussolini before the meeting to arrest Ciano and the other plotters, but he had remained confident he could corral members of the council who were 'modest, very modest, in intelligence, vacillating in belief, hardly gifted with courage'. Now he was aware he had underestimated his opponents, and in the early hours of 25 July the vote went decisively against him. Rachele met him at the door of Villa Torlonia when he returned after 3 a.m., and urged him to arrest those who had voted against him.

'No, I'll do it tomorrow,' he answered dully.

'Tomorrow will be too late,' she said.

By the afternoon of 25 July, Mussolini was inside an ambulance, speeding through the streets of Rome, being carried into captivity on the orders of the king. The Cianos took refuge in their apartment in the prestigious Parioli district of Rome, but Badoglio and those around him did not want Ciano's support. He resigned as ambassador to the Holy See on 31 July and was placed under house arrest. Edda made an appeal to the Vatican for refuge that was rejected. Friends urged Ciano to leave Italy, but he refused to go without his family. Adversity had drawn him and Edda together as never before.

Rumours were circulating in Italy that Ciano had enriched himself in office, and on 4 August the Badoglio government announced it was setting up a commission to look into the illicit wealth of high Fascist officials. It was now a matter of time until Ciano was arrested, and the couple grew desperate. Edda persuaded Ciano that they must appeal to the Germans to help them fly to exile in Spain. A friend arranged a meeting between Edda and SS Colonel Dollmann at which the two discussed an escape plan. On 22 August the Milanese newspaper *Corriere della Sera* carried an article on the riches of Ciano's father and on those allegedly amassed by his son. Ciano sent a letter of protest to Badoglio, saying his father's 'billions' actually amounted to 800 million lire, apart from the value of a family-owned newspaper. Badoglio did not reply.

On the night of 23/4 August, the prominent Fascist Ettore Muti was killed at his house in Fregene outside Rome. The official version was that Carabinieri shot him as he tried to escape arrest. Badoglio ordered his police chief to arrest Ciano and other high-ranking Fascists, but Ciano learned of the order and the police chief, who was sympathetic to him, delayed acting.

The Cianos made their escape on 27 August in accordance with the plan Dollmann had outlined to Edda. Edda went out with their three children, as though going for a walk, and when they were well away from the apartment building an American car carrying two Germans pulled up and they were whisked away. Moments after they left home, Ciano stepped out of the front door of the building and, before Carabinieri guards had time to react, climbed into a slowly moving car that had its door open. The Cianos were then taken to an airport south of Rome. Edda later insisted that the Germans had told them they would be flown to Spain, but instead their plane landed at Munich where it was met by SS General Karl Wolff. They were driven to Oberallmannshausen, on the lake of Starnberg in Bavaria, and put up in a magnificent villa; once again, they were under house arrest.

Edda demanded to see Hitler, who until then had admired her, and she was flown to his headquarters in the East Prussian forest. She not only infuriated him by suggesting he had lost the war and should make peace with the Russians; Goebbels said she asked permission to exchange 6 million lire the Cianos had brought with them for Spanish pesetas, and offered Hitler the difference in the exchange rate, 'a tactlessness that nauseated the Führer'. Hitler declined her request that they be flown to Spain, and the Cianos fell into despair, even beginning to contemplate suicide.

After Mussolini's rescue and flight to Germany, the reconciliation between him and Ciano was of little solace to Ciano, who evidently did not fully believe Mussolini's assurances that he would be allowed to return to Italy and serve the regime: his nerves began to crack and he considered how he might save himself. He thought he had one card to play that might prove decisive: throughout his term as foreign minister, he had kept a diary that was a politically explosive document. If it were ever published, it would lay bare before the world the duplicity of Germany toward its Italian ally, Mussolini's private outbursts against the Germans, his frequently expressed disdain for the qualities of his own people, Ciano's own disenchantment with the Germans and with Mussolini and the personal and political foibles of the leaders in both Axis powers. The Germans and Mussolini were well aware of the general tenor of the diary, and Ciano had good reason to suppose they might be willing to spare his life in exchange for his handing it over. Towards the end of September, Ciano sent Edda back to Italy to try to retrieve the diary from its hiding place, but she suffered a nervous collapse and went into a clinic at Ramiola, near Parma.

Ciano remained under house arrest in Germany until 19 October, when he was flown to Verona on a German military plane and incarcerated in the Scalzi prison, a former sixteenth-century Carmelite monastery, to await trial for treason. Two days later, Edda rushed to see her father at Gargnano to deliver a furious protest and to demand to see her husband. 'There undoubtedly will be a trial,' Mussolini assured her, 'but don't worry. I shall make the necessary provisions for the outcome.' This was a lie, but it bought Mussolini a brief moment of peace with his daughter.

Edda managed to see her husband just twice, on 22 October and 27 November, and in the first meeting she managed to whisper to him that she had retrieved some of his documents. But the prison authorities were determined to block most of her requests for visits, and Mussolini acquiesced. While many members of the Grand Council who had voted against Mussolini had fled the country, four who remained in Italy were arrested and were transferred to the Scalzi prison on 4 November to go on trial with Ciano. They were Giovanni Marinelli, former administrative secretary of the Fascist Party; Tullio Cianetti, former minister of corporations; Luciano Gottardi, president of the Confederation of Industrial Workers; and Carlo Pareschi, former minister of agriculture and forests. Later, on the eve of the trial, one more defendant arrived at the prison. He was Marshal Emilio De Bono, one of the founders of fascism in 1922 and the leader of the military forces that invaded Ethiopia in 1935.

Ciano, of course, was the real target of the judicial proceedings. The others had been arrested to give consistency to the idea that anyone who voted for the Grandi resolution was guilty of treason. Goebbels wrote in his diary on 9 November: 'It's true that Mussolini had his son-in-law, Ciano, arrested, but those in the know are certain he will not let him be condemned to death.' Mussolini told his secretary Dolfin: 'You are my witness that I am the least convinced of all of the usefulness of this trial, which will not resolve anything. But there will be no shortage of those who will say we have carried out a crime.' In short, Mussolini was resigned to Ciano's death. The Duce's friend Nino D'Aroma urged him to avoid death sentences, but Mussolini said that was not possible. In Germany after his rescue, he said, he had almost convinced Hitler to postpone proceedings until after the war, but Göring, Ribbentrop, Goebbels and Himmler all persuaded Hitler that Ciano should be condemned without delay.[6]

Members of the Fascist Party opened a party congress in Verona on 14 November to draw up an eighteen-point political programme for the new republic, and delegates were in an angry mood. Whipped up by Alessandro Pavolini, the party secretary, they demanded death for members of the Grand Council who had voted against Mussolini, and in particular for Ciano. 'Death to Ciano!' cries rang out on the floor.[7]

While Ciano was considering how to exploit his diary to save himself, an avenue of assistance opened up to him. The SS had assigned an attractive young woman agent, Hildegard Burkhardt Beetz, to visit Ciano in prison, win his confidence and get him to reveal where he had hidden the diary. But the SS had not counted on the ability of Ciano, a notorious womaniser, to win her sympathy. Beetz, married to a Luftwaffe officer fighting in Russia, had acted as an interpreter for Ciano during his discussions with German officials in Bavaria and already had developed a soft spot for him. In Verona she became determined to help him and Edda, who was still in the Ramiola clinic.

Edda also had enlisted the aid of her former lover, Emilio Pucci, and he helped to smuggle the three Ciano children – Fabrizio, twelve, Raimonda, nine, and Marzio, six – across the border into Switzerland on the night of 12 December, with their mother planning to follow. From prison, Ciano wrote letters to the king and to Winston Churchill, and an introduction to his diary that placed all responsibility for the war on Mussolini. Beetz smuggled these documents out of prison and turned them over to Edda. The letter to the king assured him of Ciano's loyalty, while that to Churchill denied that he had been Mussolini's accomplice in siding with the Germans.

'The crime which I am now about to expiate is that of having witnessed and been disgusted by the cold, cruel and cynical preparation for this war by Hitler and the Germans,' Ciano wrote to Churchill. 'I was the only foreigner to see at close quarters this loathsome clique of bandits preparing to plunge the world into a bloody war. Now, in accordance with gangster rule, they are planning to suppress a dangerous witness.' But he said they had miscalculated, because his diary would prove the crimes committed by people 'with whom later that tragic and vile puppet Mussolini associated himself through his vanity and disregard of moral values'.

By now Mussolini left no one in doubt he had washed his hands of Ciano. 'For me, Ciano is already dead,' he told his secretary Dolfin. 'He could not now go about in Italy, be seen, have a name. . . . Whoever voted for the Grandi resolution will be condemned.'

Edda saw her father again on 18 December, and he told her there was nothing he could do to save her husband. 'You are all mad, you are all mad!' she stormed at him. 'Between us it is finished, finished forever, and if you knelt before me dying of thirst, and asked me for a glass of water, I would throw it on the ground before your eyes.' She was still boiling with rage two days later when she met Filippo Anfuso, the Italian ambassador to Germany, and told him: 'If my husband had to vote again in the Grand Council, I would press him again to vote against the Duce.'[8]

Rachele said Mussolini had been given a document drawn up by Ciano before 25 July 1943 that demonstrated his participation in the plot against him. He commented: 'One day it will serve to demonstrate the facts and justify my position in Edda's eyes.'[9]

Despite the bad blood that existed between the Cianos and Claretta Petacci, Claretta was moved by Ciano's plight and wrote to Mussolini to save him. 'My Ben, I have had a long, terrible night,' she wrote. 'Nightmares, anxieties, blood and ruins. Among the figures, known and unknown, appearing in a red cloud, was that of Ciano. Ben, save that man! Show the Italians you still control your own will. Fate, perhaps, will be kinder to us.' Beetz told Ciano of Claretta's intervention, and he gave Beetz a note for Claretta expressing his gratitude.

Edda had planned to escape to Switzerland on 27 December, but Beetz urged her to delay her departure because she had a plan to save Ciano's life. She urged her superiors to barter Ciano's diary for his life, and she found that Heinrich Himmler, the head of the SS, and Ernst Kaltenbrunner, head of the SS security service, the SD, were interested. They hated Foreign Minister Ribbentrop and hoped to find material in the diary that would drive him from office. Himmler concocted a plan under which two SS men, disguised as Italian Fascists, would pretend to overpower Ciano's guards and kidnap their prisoner. Ciano would be taken by plane to Hungary and from there smuggled into Turkey. He would then phone Edda and she would hand over the diary and other documents to the Germans.

Through Beetz, Ciano smuggled out a letter to Edda instructing her to get some of his documents from their hiding place in Rome and turn them over to the Gestapo as a proof of his good intentions. The diary itself was hidden near Milan. Pucci collected the documents after an arduous journey over snow-covered roads, then he and Edda set off for a rendezvous point on the Verona–Brescia road at which they were supposed to meet the freed Ciano. But Pucci's car developed two flat tyres, so Edda continued alone, partly on foot, partly by hitching lifts. She arrived late at the rendezvous point in the early hours of 7 January, only to find her husband was not there, and she curled up by the roadside on a night of bitter cold. That morning, after finally hitching a lift and reaching Verona, she discovered that Hitler had learned of the plan to free Ciano and had cancelled it. The plan had fallen apart on 6 January, two days before Ciano and his fellow Fascists were scheduled to stand trial. Through Beetz, Ciano sent a farewell message to Edda, telling her all hope was gone and urging her to send threatening letters to Mussolini and Hitler and to flee to Switzerland with his diary.

Edda and Pucci then put into operation the plan for her escape. She would go to Switzerland with the Ciano diary and turn it over to the Allies unless her husband were freed. On 8 January, Edda slipped out of the Ramiola clinic through a cellar door, and walked across fields to join Pucci, who was waiting in his car. An SS unit arrived at the clinic the next day to try to retrieve the diary and discovered she had fled. SS and Gestapo units immediately fanned out across northern Italy in a desperate search for her, under orders to prevent her crossing into Switzerland at all costs. But Edda and Pucci, with the advantage of a day's head start, drove to the frontier town of Viggiù and spent the night at a small hotel there. Edda wrote letters to the Gestapo chief Wilhelm Harster, to her father and to Hitler, threatening to disclose to the Allies all the information she possessed unless her husband were freed within three days.

In the early evening of 9 January, Edda crossed into Switzerland with Pucci's help. A guide he had hired spotted a German patrol passing when they were still a few hundred yards from the border, and he pushed Edda to the ground. Then he said: 'Go now!'

'Instead of running, I crossed the moonlit field with tranquil steps, standing quite erect,' Edda wrote later. 'I don't know why, but at that point I didn't care what might happen to me.' She carried the Ciano diary in a pyjama shirt under her dress, fashioned by Pucci so the bulge would make her look pregnant. The Swiss had been told to expect the Princess d'Aosta and were astonished to hear her identify herself as Edda Ciano. She went the next day to join her children. When Mussolini learned of her flight, he commented: 'The tragedy of the son-in-law has finished and the comedy of the daughter begins.'[10] But he was deeply hurt by Edda's estrangement, and he would later send an emissary to Switzerland, a priest who had known Edda for many years, to try to persuade her to return.

After leaving Edda at the border, Pucci headed for Sondrio, but he was ill and had hardly slept in eight days so he pulled over to the side of the road and fell asleep. Shortly before 4 a.m. on the morning of 10 January, finding his car wouldn't start, he flagged down a passing car. Unfortunately, four German soldiers were in the car and they got out and demanded his papers. When they discovered his identity, they thrust machine guns against his throat, demanded he tell them where Edda was and shoved him against a wall. Then they beat him and drove him to Gestapo headquarters in Verona. From there he was transferred to the Hotel Regina in Milan, the SS headquarters, and was subjected to two days of relentless torture. He became blood-soaked and fainted from pain every few minutes, but he refused to talk.

At the end of the second day, Pucci decided to kill himself with a razor blade he had hidden in his underpants. With his hands tied, he had to reach the blade with his mouth and managed to open a vein in his wrist but he could not make a cut deep enough to produce the desired result and only succeeded in cutting his lips and tongue. The torture resumed the next morning but suddenly stopped when Beetz arrived. She had persuaded the authorities to release Pucci on the grounds he might dissuade Edda from doing anything against Germany. Pucci was smuggled into Switzerland by boat during the night and, three days later, he collapsed and went to a hospital. Doctors found his skull was fractured in several places. He managed to join Edda only in late 1944.

The trial of Ciano and his co-defendants began on schedule on 8 January in the Castelvecchio, a fortress on the banks of the Adige river in Verona that dates from 1354. The courtroom was crowded with local Fascists and Germans, most of them in black shirts. Ciano indignantly rejected the charges against him, amid cries from spectators: 'To death!', 'Traitor!', 'It's not true.' He knew his fate already had been decided. The trial testimony lasted two days and on the morning of the third day the nine judges condemned four of the defendants to death by a five-to-four margin. The vote to condemn Ciano was unanimous. Only Tullio Cianetti was spared a death sentence; he was given thirty years. The trial, Rachele said afterward, was 'a continual torment for all of us, a real nightmare'.

That evening the condemned men signed a petition to Mussolini for pardon, with Ciano initially reluctant to do so but finally yielding to the argument that his obstinacy imperilled the others. Mussolini learned of the verdicts that afternoon and spent a sleepless night worrying about his son-in-law. He only received Edda's bitter letter that evening and, in a disturbed state, he phoned General Wolff to ask what he should do. Wolff advised allowing the execution of Ciano to proceed. Mussolini never telephoned the prison to find out if pardon requests were en route to him, an omission that was no doubt deliberate. In fact, Fascist Party Secretary Alessandro Pavolini and other extreme Fascists were determined not to refer the requests to Mussolini, and they tried all through the night to find a competent official willing to reject the requests. Finally an obscure officer of the Republican National Guard in Verona was persuaded to turn down the requests at 8 a.m. on 11 January.

Ciano spent his last night in conversation with Beetz and Zenone Benini, an old friend and former public works minister who had been imprisoned on lesser charges for having asked Cianetti, at Ciano's behest, to vote for the Grandi resolution in the Grand Council. Once during the evening Ciano revealed to Benini that he planned to cheat his executioners by swallowing a phial of potassium cyanide that Beetz had given him. He retired to his cell to take the poison, but returned half an hour later. 'It was a false poison. Thus I must die two times,' he said. Beetz claimed later she had asked a doctor for potassium cyanide but he had given her a harmless solution of chlorate of potassium. During the evening the prison director informed Benini that Edda had succeeded in reaching Switzerland, and Ciano was overjoyed when Benini relayed the news.

Just after 9 a.m., prison authorities arrived to inform each of the condemned men individually that their requests for pardon had been turned down. The five men were then put in a police van and driven across the city to a firing range at Fort Procolo outside the ancient city gates. On a cold, overcast morning, they were ordered to sit on rickety wooden folding chairs lined up near a wall. Ciano and Marshal De Bono asked to face the rifles, but they were refused. Thirty federal policemen – six for each prisoner – formed the execution squad. As their commander, Nicola Furlotti, prepared to give the order to fire, several prisoners shouted: 'Long live Italy!' Ciano remained silent but, at the command 'Fire!' he turned to face the firing squad. The fire was so inaccurate that four of the men lay on the ground writhing and screaming while the fifth, Carlo Pareschi, remained seated, apparently untouched by the bullets. Furlotti and other militiamen finished off their victims with pistol shots.[11]

At 10 a.m. Mussolini learned of the executions from his secretary, Giovanni Dolfin. 'He cried in desperation. We all cried,' Rachele said later. The Duce asked how Ciano had comported himself and Dolfin replied: 'He died like a man, like the others, with a courage that commands respect. He tried, turning at the last instant, to look death in the face.' Mussolini, pale and tense, drummed his fingers on his desk, then exclaimed: 'Justice was required; and we, we will carry it out in depth so that it is equal for all.' General Renzo Montagna, one of the judges at the trial who had voted against execution, later met Mussolini, who reeled off names of members of the Grand Council he said should have been condemned to death. 'The men shot at Verona were all excluded, including Ciano,' Montagna wrote in his diary. The prison chaplain, Don Giuseppe Chiot, also called on Mussolini, who told him that in the 'horrible night' preceding the executions he turned on the light in his room and 'discovered the irresistible attraction of the revolver on my night table'. Several days later Mussolini discussed the executions with his wife, who had long been opposed to Ciano, and he commented: 'From that morning I began to die.' Shortly afterwards, Rachele recorded: 'He no longer wished to live. He was like a sick man who still has the possibility of saving himself but refuses and abandons himself to the current of his destiny.'[12]

In her memoirs Rachele wrote: 'Only after the death of Bruno have I and my children seen him so upset and crushed, indifferent to everything. Afterwards, if anyone in his presence referred unintentionally to what happened at Verona, he made them get quiet, fixing his eyes on them with a burst of rebellion.'[13]

There is no reason to doubt the sincerity of Mussolini's reaction. He genuinely wanted to spare Ciano, if only for the sake of Edda and her children, but he knew he risked the implacable wrath of Hitler and the dangerous opposition of the extreme Fascists in his regime if he intervened to save his son-in-law. His actions were nonetheless cowardly, by contrast with the courage Ciano showed in facing death. In the fifteen months that remained to him, Mussolini tried repeatedly but never succeeded in achieving a reconciliation with Edda. Don Giusto Pancino, a childhood friend of Edda's who had been a military chaplain in Albania and later in Russia when Edda served there as a nurse, went to Switzerland repeatedly at Mussolini's request to try to end the estrangement between father and daughter. At Pancino's first meeting with Edda on 23 March 1944, she said of Mussolini: 'Tell him that his situation causes me pain; tell him that only two solutions could rehabilitate him in my eyes: to flee or kill himself.' When Pancino returned to Italy and repeated those words, Mussolini showed no emotion.

Four months later, after suffering another nervous collapse, Edda sent a similar message: 'All is so black, but everyone must pay. For my part, the injustice and cowardice of men and of you have made me suffer so much that by now I cannot suffer more. I pray only that everything finishes soon.'

Allen W. Dulles, the head of American espionage operations in Switzerland, learned soon after Edda's arrival in Switzerland that she was in possession of the Ciano diary and began a search for her. But it was not until December that he made contact with Pucci and began negotiating through Pucci to obtain the diary for the US government. The negotiations, eventually held face to face with Edda, proved long and difficult, but she finally handed over the diary in January 1945 and sold it in April to the *Chicago Daily News*. She had waited too long to use the diary as a weapon against her father and the Germans; it had to be translated into English, and was only published by the newspaper a month after the war in Europe had ended.[14]

In his war memoirs, Winston Churchill taunted Mussolini over having allowed the execution of his son-in-law. 'The end of Ciano was in keeping with all the elements of Renaissance tragedy,' he wrote. 'Mussolini's submission to Hitler's vengeful demands brought him only shame, and the miserable neo-Fascist republic dragged on by Lake Garda – a relic of the Broken Axis.'[15]

This story is probably apocryphal, but worth repeating: Churchill was said to have been approached once by a son-in-law he disliked, Vic Oliver, and asked what historical figure he most admired. 'Mussolini,' Churchill responded. The astonished Vic Oliver asked why, and Churchill explained: 'Because he had the courage to have his son-in-law shot.'

Chapter 8

TROUBLES ON ALL FRONTS

We call each other allies and know we lie.

(Benito Mussolini on his relations with the Germans, 11 December 1943)

The fate of Ciano wasn't the only problem weighing on Mussolini's mind in the closing months of 1943. He would have to contend with the first industrial strikes against his regime, and with acts of violence by Fascists and their opponents that would soon lead to all-out civil war. In Germany, Goebbels continued to fulminate in his diary against Mussolini, whom he had once admired. 'Nothing is to be expected either of fascism or the Duce,' he wrote on 9 November. 'The Duce hasn't the faintest idea of his real position. . . . He is living a life of make-believe and struts around in a heroic pose that has no place in a world of realities.' Goebbels said it was 'out of the question' that the Italian nation should re-enter the war at the side of the Germans, and he went on to deplore the Duce's conduct with his mistress, 'a cause for much misgiving. One can see from it that he has no clear understanding of the seriousness of his situation.'[1]

On 20 November Goebbels wrote: 'The English and the Americans are in for a lot of joy with the Italians. That serves them right. The Italians gave us so much trouble in the earlier years of war that it is only fair that our enemies should also get their share.' Ten days later, goaded by a report he had received from the antisemitic extremist Giovanni Preziosi, Goebbels wrote that Mussolini was 'still surrounded by traitors, former Freemasons and Jew-lovers who give him consistently wrong advice.' He said Vittorio Mussolini was playing a loathsome role, not so much because of his lack of character as because of his stupidity. 'The Duce has learned nothing and forgotten nothing.'*[2]

The Germans had learned nothing either about how to treat the Italians under their thumb. The diplomat Luigi Bolla, making his way to Lake Garda

*Goebbels was quoting French statesman Charles-Maurice Talleyrand's taunt about the Bourbon monarchs in France.

from Rome, observed that in every village along the way the population hated and feared the Germans, whom they regarded as being 'like dangerous beasts'. Some Italians already had begun to carry out sabotage against the Germans in reprisal for their heavy-handed behaviour, and the north Italian towns of Bardolino and Peschiera were fined 250,000 lire each after German military phone lines had been repeatedly cut. The Germans ordered Italian guards placed at each 100 yards of phone line, and warned that if any section were cut the guard would be shot.[3]

The Duce did not attend the Fascist Party congress in Verona in November, an indication of the passivity that now characterised his behaviour, but he did prepare a brief opening speech that Party Secretary Alessandro Pavolini read on his behalf. It was an unruly meeting, with many members demanding new policies and others clinging to their old Fascist ideals. But delegates appeared united in expressing their discontent over Mussolini's choice of ministers, particularly Buffarini, and there was widespread condemnation of Claretta Petacci. In the end, the party congress adopted an eighteen-point programme, which Mussolini had drawn up in consultation with Pavolini. It affirmed the republican character of the state and its determination to maintain independence and territorial unity. The programme also called for nationalisation of private firms and worker participation in management.

While the congress was under way, news arrived from Ferrara that the Fascist Party leader there, Igino Ghisellini, had been assassinated by anti-Fascist elements as he was leaving for Verona. 'He will be immediately avenged!' Pavolini cried out as he announced the news. The Ferrara delegates to the congress and a squad of federal police left the congress hall immediately to wreak vengeance. That night, seventy-four Ferrarese citizens were arrested, and at dawn eleven bloody bodies lay on the ground in front of Ferrara Castle. Some young students brought flowers to the feet of the victims, while Fascist militants sang a party hymn. It later turned out that Ghisellini had not been killed by anti-Fascists, as Pavolini reported, but by one of his 'comrades' who had quarrelled with him.[4]

Mussolini privately called the Ferrara massacre 'a stupid and bestial act', and had a heated argument with Pavolini about it. Pavolini gave him a list of sixty-three Fascists who had been killed in recent months, sometimes in front of their wives and children. Mussolini remained angry. 'Today in Italy the law of the forest prevails, that is, the law of the beasts,' he told Dolfin. 'This law responds basically to the nature of the Italians, accustomed for centuries to factional vendettas. At present a real national feud is under way.'[5] It would soon get much worse.

An Italian woman in Florence wrote to the world-renowned art expert Bernard Berenson, hiding in the hills above the city, about the arrogance of the Fascist militias. 'One sees Blackshirts strutting about with the faces of convicts, but behind their arrogant mien lurks a good deal of wholesome fear. . . . They seem to be quite oldish men with grey hair, or young *beceroni* [riffraff] under twenty. . . . The Germans have handed over the guarding of the Ponte Vecchio to the Blackshirts. The first night I was startled out of my sleep by wild shooting, which was kept up half the night; and this morning the house shook from hand grenades being hurled into the Arno. These people are so terrified of being pounced upon in the dark that they bolster up their courage by warlike display.'[6]

As if in defiance of the Verona congress, workers at the Fiat–Mirafiori plant near Turin went on strike on 18 November, four days after the congress had concluded. It was the first strike to occur in any German-occupied land, and it not only caught the regime by surprise but also Communist leaders who had counted on a longer period to organise the working class. The Fiat workers walked out because of poor economic conditions and to protest over the deaths of workers killed because the authorities had refused to allow them to leave the plant during bombing raids. The Germans promised to increase food rations but threatened severe sanctions if the strike continued. Other Turin factories joined in and continued the strike for forty-eight hours, and the Germans were forced to make concessions to them too. On 25 November, Genoese tram workers struck to protest the arrest of three of their members by the Gestapo. Strikes also occurred in several other towns.[7]

Serafino Mazzolini, the under-secretary for foreign affairs, met the Duce on 26 November and found him very depressed. Mussolini was upset over German high-handedness in the Italian frontier provinces. He also had read Italian press reports that had appeared during his captivity about his affair with Claretta, which had soured his mood. These reports, he grumbled, were all lies intended to make him look ridiculous. The news reports had referred both to Claretta and her sister Myriam. Luigi Bolla commented in his diary: 'It is very possible that these two people are profiting from his name to draw big profits, but it is undeniable that both have taken up their posts again, along with innumerable delinquents.'[8]

Talking two days later to his secretary Giovanni Dolfin, Mussolini was preoccupied with Hitler's mistakes. He complained that the Führer 'hasn't known how to manoeuvre politically to avoid Germany finding itself, as in 1918, isolated and against the whole world'. He said if the supreme political command of the war had been in his hands, and the military command entrusted to Hitler, the war would already have been won. Hitler's 'fatal errors', he claimed, included the attack on the Soviet Union, the failure to set up an independent Polish state and the treatment of people in occupied lands.[9]

Mussolini was disgruntled not merely with Hitler but with those Italians who refused to adhere to his republican government. He told Mazzolini on 3 December that he would like to send them all to concentration camps, together with the Jews. Luigi Bolla took an indulgent view of the Duce's low spirits. 'I couldn't look at him without feeling inside myself something worrying, a combination of affection and pity. . . . He has a sense of impotence, a paralysing lack of confidence in himself.' A month later Bolla recorded in his diary: 'Mussolini is always very down, lacking will power and not at all in good health.'[10]

The Communist Party organised a strike in Milan factories on 13 December. Municipal police or Carabinieri were sent to the factories to break up the strikes but were hesitant to attack the workers and warned them the Germans were coming. On the third day of the strike, General Otto Zimmermann, an SS brigade leader who had been sent to Italy by Hitler to deal with the situation, sent in armoured cars to intimidate the strikers and ordered workers in every factory seized as hostages. But when the workers remained defiant, he said their demands would be met if they agreed to resume work on a Saturday to make up for lost time. On Saturday, most of the workers remained on strike. Zimmermann went to one factory and announced: 'Anyone who doesn't resume work, get out of the building. Those who leave are declared enemies of Germany.' All the workers left, and returned to work only on Monday. Zimmermann arrested some activists to be sent to Germany for forced labour, but at the same time raised salaries and distributed food to workers. The strike spread to Genoa's shipyards, where three workers were killed in clashes, and to other towns. In Genoa, the strikers retaliated by setting off a bomb at a dinner of Fascists and Germans, killing seven and wounding fifteen. A month later the Fascists killed seven hostages in reprisal.[11]

Mussolini might fear the consequences of strife among Italians, but he had lost none of his authoritarian instincts. In December, he thought the Fascist press was engaging in dangerous polemics in a time of war and called their editors on the carpet. 'For twenty-three years the 190 million Russians have read only one newspaper and listened to only one radio,' he told them. 'It seems this severe radio-newspaper diet hasn't harmed the public and moral health of the Muscovite people.'[12] Buffarini had announced on 9 October the death penalty or life in prison for anyone publishing news that could damage the Axis. He also decreed life sentences for holding non-authorised meetings and ten years in prison for those who abandoned their jobs without permission. The regime arrested some aristocrats and industrialists, and Pavolini recommended that 'plutocrats' and people who had grown rich be excluded from party membership.[13]

Towards the end of the year, violence was increasing across the country. The Germans had ordered the evacuation of the village of Pietransieri, in the Abruzzi mountain region, on 21 November, and when some people were slow to carry out the order, the Germans slaughtered 130 civilians, many of them women and children. On 9 December, the Germans captured seventeen partisans and an escaped prisoner of war, Private David Russell of New Zealand, after they had attacked a German headquarters at Porto Canavese. All eighteen men were shot dead on the spot. In Praticello, a village near Reggio Emilia, a Fascist patrol in November surrounded a farm owned by a family named Cervi after being tipped that the Cervis were hiding six escaped prisoners of war and one Italian anti-Fascist in their barn. After an exchange of gunfire, the Fascists set fire to the barn and captured the escaped POWs. They took nine members of the Cervi family to prison to await trial, but when partisans assassinated a Fascist Party official at Bagnolo-in-Piano on 27 December eight of the men were condemned to death and shot. Aldice Cervi, the head of the family, remained behind bars but escaped when an Allied air raid destroyed the prison.

On 18 December, partisans assassinated Aldo Resega, the Fascist Party leader in Milan, their most important victim to date. The Fascist Muti squad went into poor, anti-Fascist districts of Milan and retaliated with widespread vandalism. Then the squad attacked police headquarters and Francesco Colombo, the thuggish leader of the squad, slapped the police chief in the face, later demanding that Interior Minister Buffarini remove him. An extraordinary military tribunal was convoked and condemned to death eight political detainees, who were immediately shot. Fascists from all over northern Italy came to Resega's funeral on 20 December, and when the cortege reached the Piazza del Duomo, the large square in front of the cathedral, Fascists began shooting into the air and pandemonium ensued. Anti-Fascists fired at the funeral procession from nearby windows, and people in the crowd fled in panic. The Fascists fired back and thousands of shots were exchanged, but, miraculously, no one was killed.[14] The country was now on the road to civil war.

Mussolini complained to his officials about arbitrary arrests being carried out in many areas. 'All this is not republican or Fascist but confusion, arbitrariness and anarchy . . .', he said. 'Such episodes must absolutely stop.'[15]

In southern Italy, the quick advance that Allied forces had hoped to make towards Rome had eluded them. They were bogged down around Monte Cassino, where the Germans were heavily dug in around the ancient monastery of St Benedict, one of the most important historical sites in Italy.

In October, Churchill had been so confident of the fall of Rome that he had wanted to withdraw several divisions from Italy to fight the Germans in

Rhodes, but Roosevelt had vetoed that idea. Now Churchill had realised its impracticality, and in November he and Roosevelt turned to discussion of the new political situation in Italy, finding themselves once again in disagreement. Churchill wanted to keep King Victor Emmanuel on the throne and Marshal Badoglio at the head of government at least until Rome was captured, but Roosevelt thought the king should abdicate in favour of his grandson Victor Emmanuel, the Prince of Naples, and he was not wedded to the idea of keeping Badoglio in office. The debate continued for several months, and behind it lay an unspoken contest for influence in postwar Italy. Churchill thought Britain would be better placed to play a dominant role by maintaining the status quo, but the Americans believed a new political order would be less inclined to accept British guidance and would look to Washington for leadership. Roosevelt ultimately would prevail, and the United States exercised predominant influence in Italy after the war.[16]

* * *

At the beginning of 1944, Mussolini was barely treading water above a floodtide of political and personal problems, and he was more deeply depressed than before. German atrocities against Italians intensified, as did German rapine and German interference in civil life. The Allied offensive in the south gathered momentum. Fascist murder squads were alienating the population, and the anti-Fascist partisan movement was slowly gathering adherents, making it a real threat for the first time. The unpopularity of the regime grew, and soon industrial strikes began to spread. Most vexing and humiliating of all was the problem of the Italian military, facing continual obstruction by Hitler and the German High Command. Would the Salò Republic be allowed to have an army at all? Not least, Mussolini also faced frequent quarrels with his wife, who was jealous over the presence of Claretta Petacci nearby.

'I cannot live here any more,' Mussolini exploded to Dolfin on 5 January. 'The domestic area has become suffocating. Every day troubles, anger, scenes. My human ability to support this has touched the extreme limit. . . . My wife, who doesn't give me peace for the usual story, is now carrying out real investigations, interrogating even the household staff. All that cannot but complicate . . . my life. She tries to make me ridiculous.' After a pause he added: 'We must move elsewhere as soon as possible.'[17]

On 13 January, two days after Ciano's execution, a new problem assailed Mussolini. Workers in Genoa went on strike, and the strikes spread across northern and central Italy. Then, on 22 January, the Allies staged a landing at Anzio, south of Rome, in an attempt to break out of their stalemate further south, and sent radio calls to Italian partisans to sabotage enemy communication lines and 'to strike against him everywhere'. Right-wing members of the Badoglio government did not approve of partisan activity, believing it was wiser to 'express one's anti-fascism by carrying out intelligence for the Allies and fighting the Nazis with a clandestine press'. But around Rome, anti-Fascists attacked petrol and ammunition dumps and shot isolated groups of German soldiers. The Anzio operation, however, did not go as planned. An overly cautious US General John Lucas failed to move his men off their beachhead in time to make a quick strike for Rome, and the Germans brought in reinforcements who pinned down the Allied troops.[18] General Mark W. Clark, the principal American commander under General Harold Alexander, hesitated for an entire month to relieve Lucas of his command, and only did so when Alexander pointed out that the Allies still could be pushed back into the sea and Clark would certainly be relieved of his command if that happened.[19] The Anzio débâcle was a setback, and an impatient Churchill cabled Alexander: 'I expected to see a wildcat roaring into the mountains – and what do I find? A whale wallowing on the beaches.' On another occasion he grumbled: 'What are you doing, sitting down doing nothing? Why don't you use your armour in a great scythe-like movement through the mountains?'[20] But Mussolini could take little heart from the Allied mistake at Anzio. It was a matter of time until the Germans were worn down and Rome fell. Monte Cassino was finally destroyed by Allied bombing on 15 February.

A debate over the wisdom of this act went on for years after the war. Clark maintained the bombing of the abbey that dominated the plain below was a mistake. Ernst von Weizsäcker, the German ambassador to the Holy See, had notified the Allies through the Vatican that the abbey was not occupied by German troops, and General Clark had taken him at his word, but others had not. In the event, Weizsäcker and Clark were proved to be correct. 'Not only was the bombing of the Abbey an unnecessary psychological mistake in the propaganda field, but it was a tactical military mistake of the first magnitude,' Clark wrote in his memoirs. 'It only made our job more difficult, more costly in terms of men, machines and time.' Clark's point was that the destruction of the abbey left the Germans free to use the ruins of the buildings as defensive positions, which for them was more effective than if the buildings had still stood.[21]

Alexander admitted that destroyed buildings can be more valuable to defenders than intact buildings; nonetheless, he authorised the bombing at the insistence of a New Zealand general, Bernard Freyberg, whose troops were involved in the fighting. Alexander quoted US Air Force General John Cannon as telling him: 'If you let me use the whole of our bomber force against Cassino, we will whip it out like a dead tooth.' In just one day, 255 Allied bombers wiped the abbey off the face of the Earth, dropping 576 tons of explosives. 'Was the destruction of the monastery a military necessity?' Alexander wrote in his own memoirs. 'The answer . . . is "yes".' It was necessary more for the effect it would have on the morale of the attackers than for purely material reasons. How could a structure which dominated the fighting field be allowed to stand? The monastery had to be destroyed.' He said Pope Pius later told him he understood the military necessity for the bombing. But on 18 February, three days after the monastery had been destroyed, the Vatican newspaper *L'Osservatore Romano* said the Holy See had shown a 'timely and insistent solicitude . . . that this wonderful monastery be spared every damage'. The patrician Harold Rupert Leofric George Alexander, elevated to field marshal rank after the Cassino battle and later made Earl Alexander of Tunis, was one of Churchill's favourite commanders, but the British historian Max Hastings said Alexander had 'the brains of an ox'.[22]

Alexander's argument was a weak one, for it did not take into account the effect of the bombing on the Italian population's view of the Allies. The abbey of Monte Cassino had been founded by St Benedict in about AD 529 and, although it was destroyed and rebuilt several times in later centuries, it was a centre of learning through the dark years of the Middle Ages and renowned throughout Europe. Its final rebuilding took place in the seventeenth century.

The art treasures of the National Museum at Naples had been hidden at Monte Cassino well before the bombing. But two officers of the Hermann Göring Division, Colonel Schlegel and Captain Becker, arrived in October 1943 and persuaded the abbot that all the art works gathered there should be moved to Rome for safekeeping. Over a period of nearly three weeks, German trucks took away the art treasures. Some were delivered to the Vatican in December 1943, and the Germans made a public display of handing others over to the Fascist government in Rome the following month. In fact, long before that, some of the art works had been shipped to Germany. A Titian and a Claude Lorrain from the Naples collection were presented to Göring as birthday presents, and he also acquired works by Raphael, Brueghel, Lippi and Palma Vecchio as well as a folio of drawings from the Naples museum and various sculptures and bronzes. These were returned to Italy after the war.

Bernard Berenson dismissed the destruction of the abbey with the insensitive insouciance of an aesthete lacking any sense of history. 'The buildings and decorations were no earlier than of the seventeenth century and in no way remarkable for that period,' he wrote in his diary. 'There are in Catholic countries hundreds of structures far more valuable.' He was sure the abbey would be rebuilt and said: 'Instead of erecting an exact copy of the mediocre edifices that we have known, why not do something more interesting?' In fact, the abbey was rebuilt after the war as an exact copy of the one that was destroyed. Likewise, Berenson took a loftily dismissive view of the bombing of the Mantegna chapel in the Eremitani Church at Padua by American bombers a month later. 'I would not weep my eyes out,' he wrote. 'They [the frescoes] were not over-suitable for the space they covered and their colouring was not harmonious.'[23] Berenson was then seventy-eight, and, while he gave no other signs of mental decline, his remarks were difficult to understand. One can only be thankful that he was not responsible for safeguarding other works of art that failed to meet his approval.

The Germans had suggested on 29 January that Mussolini go to Rome to boost morale, but he refused. 'I don't want to come to Rome until Italians are on the Italian front alongside the Germans,' he said. 'I will come to Rome when the city will be defended by my people.'[24] He had another reason not to go to Rome: he had never forgiven the Romans for cheering his overthrow the previous July. Mussolini, incidentally, was clearly aware at this time of rumours about his failing mental powers. After he had addressed some Fascist generals with a promise to restore Italian honour and saw that they were deeply moved, he told Dolfin: 'They will have understood, I hope, that I am not in fact impoverished cerebrally, as some dare to say here and abroad. My brain functions in a perfect way and I see things, as always, with absolute clarity.'[25]

In northern Italy, the Germans continued to act as they pleased, with little or no regard for Fascist sensitivities. General Wolff ordered twenty-one Foreign Ministry employees and twenty members of their families to clear out of a Gardone hotel within forty-eight hours because it was needed by the SS. The commissioner of prices returned from Milan to find his office at Montichiari occupied by Germans, and he had to find new quarters. Buffarini was called in by SS Captain Eugen Wenner and ordered to declare how many gold ingots he possessed. The accusation did not stand up, but there were no apologies afterwards. Radio Munich, the station beamed at Italy and controlled by Goebbels, delivered broadsides against various Fascist ministers. Rahn demanded that the Interior Ministry inform him beforehand of the appointment of prefects and other officials, and made clear he intended to control municipal budgets. Mussolini wrote to Goebbels, noting that Germany needed more soldiers, and said there were 'hundreds and thousands' of Germans in Italian offices who could be better used on the front lines. Germans, he said, had created 'a series of little states within the state', undermining the authority of the republic.[26]

'I am only the first actor in a vast comedy that we all recite together,' he told Dolfin. 'The Germans do likewise, reciting also. We don't love each other and we say we love each other. We call each other allies and know we lie. I have no effective power. We are a group of freed slaves commanded to govern a people of slaves.'[27]

The 'slaves' were having a hard time of it. Allied bombing left more than 60,000 homeless in Milan in one month alone. Not only were they being bombed, but Italians living in the north found it increasingly difficult to make ends meet. Factory workers received starvation wages of about 1,100 lire per month, while prices shot up. Ration books allowed people just over two pounds of potatoes per month, the same amount of rice and pasta, 3½ ounces of beans, seven ounces of butter, 10½ ounces of salt and about one-sixth of a pint of cooking oil. They could buy 5¼ ounces of bread per day and 3½ ounces of meat. Rationing gave to each Italian less than 1,000 calories daily; without the black market, many would have starved. About 3½ ounces of soap had to last two months. Men eighteen and older – no women – were allotted forty cigarettes a week. With the republic required to subsidise German forces in Italy, the state budget went into deficit and the government resorted to printing money. Inflation skyrocketed.[28]

Mussolini, in another talk with Dolfin, said he would prefer to live under Soviet rather than German domination in a future Europe. 'In the struggle that is under way among the great colossi, Germany, Russia and America, we are destined after our voluntary exile from the war to be crushed like nuts whatever may be the course of events to come. In this eventuality, which by now seems certain, I as an Italian citizen would not hesitate a moment in choosing Stalin. . . . Between becoming an English dominion, or a German province or a Soviet federal republic in the tragic game of events that is being determined, the choice leaves no doubts.'[29]

German Ambassador Rahn complained on 2 February to Serafino Mazzolini, the Foreign Ministry under-secretary, that 3,000 Fascist recruits had deserted and the authorities were taking no action to arrest them. Mussolini told Mazzolini the desertions had occurred because the Germans had not seen fit to give the recruits proper uniforms or arms. A soldier who is not dressed, or is badly dressed, has the right to return home, he said.[30]

The sixth meeting of Mussolini's Cabinet on 12 February approved a legislative decree on nationalisation of industry, carrying out one of the eighteen points of the Verona declaration. The decree did not provide for nationalisation of capital, but of management, and unions were brought into company management. There were at least three reasons for this decree: it responded to the basic instincts of a man who had begun his political life as a Socialist. Secondly, he may have hoped it would shore up his government's sagging popularity. Thirdly, he knew it would upset the Germans, who tended to equate anything of a Socialist nature with communism. 'I entered political life as a Socialist, and as such I will leave it,' Mussolini told Dr Zachariae at one of their daily meetings.[31]

The Germans reacted swiftly, expelling the commissioner of prices, Carlo Fabrizi, from his office and blocking nationalisation of war industries. Mussolini went to Rahn to warn that the workers would act to defend nationalisation. But the Germans were not alone in their hostility to nationalisation; the Swiss accounted for one-quarter of investments in northern Italy and demanded that their firms be exempted.[32]

On 16 February, Dolfin wrote in his diary: 'I often have the impression that the Duce is more tired than all of us and that in himself he feels an immense irritation for at least 90 per cent of what he must say and do.' Later he quoted Mussolini as saying: 'I prefer . . . a concentration camp to the ridiculous fact of passing into history as a puppet.'[33]

Adding to his woes, corruption and 'brutal overbearing' on the part of leading Fascists and government officials were spreading, and Luigi Bolla said the Italian people therefore hated the Fascist Party and above all the militia. Dolfin told Bolla that he had advised Mussolini repeatedly that the dishonesty of his officials was alienating the people, and the Duce seemed convinced. But then Party Secretary Pavolini and Republican National Guard Commander Ricci would persuade him otherwise.

Armed Forces Minister Marshal Graziani learned from his generals interned in Germany and Poland that they were being treated brutally. They had been transported to internment camps in cattle trucks, then housed eight to one small room, subjected to roll calls three times a day and given little food: bread and soup daily with less than one ounce of meat and bone in the soup. In one camp three out of twenty had died and their bodies had been transported for burial on wagons used for coal and rubbish.[34]

Mussolini remained dissatisfied with Gargnano and thought of transferring to Valeggio or Mantua, but was advised that no buildings there could provide a defence against bombardment. At Gargnano, Allied planes passed over frequently, but never bombed the town. It is one of the mysteries of the Second World War that they never attempted to kill Mussolini or his ministers, as they might easily have done. The Germans surmised, probably correctly, that the Allies wanted to keep a Fascist government in power for the time being because it generated opposition among many Italians and thus had advantages for them. Mussolini always refused to join his family and officials in air-raid shelters when planes were overhead. But even he was surprised that Villa Feltrinelli was never bombed. 'They could cut me in half very easily,' he told his wife. Once when she knocked on his door, begging him to join her in the shelter, he said: 'Not all the Italian people can have access to a shelter.'[35]

Italian workers responded to the nationalisation decree not with the support Mussolini expected but with a general political strike initiated by the Communist Party, the first and only general strike to occur in occupied Europe under the Nazis. The resistance movement claimed 1 million workers took part in the 1 March walkout, while the Fascists estimated 207,000. Claims about the length of the strike also varied, from fifteen minutes to four days. Buffarini favoured a violent repression of the strikes, but Mussolini ruled that out.[36]

Hitler, enraged by the strikes, demanded the forced transfer of 70,000 workers to Germany in reprisal. Rahn objected that the Germans lacked the means of transport to take them there, and said any such order would only force most of the workers to take to the mountains and join the partisans. 'The order of Hitler is simply crazy,' Mussolini commented. He said fewer than 300,000 workers had taken part in the strikes, out of a workforce of 5 million, so even the organisers considered them a failure.[37]

Italian industrialists were not particularly bothered by the nationalisation decree because, with the exception of a few pro-Fascists, they thought it would be a dead letter when the Nazis and Fascists were defeated. In early 1943, they had tried to convince Mussolini that the country must make peace because of its desperate economic condition, and when he refused they gave up on him. Some industrialists offered financial help to the resistance, but others, such as executives at the Fiat automobile works, also tried to remain on good terms with the Germans.[38]

* * *

Roosevelt and Churchill continued to disagree about the future of the king and Badoglio. Adlai Stevenson, after a fact-finding mission to Italy in January, had reinforced the president's lack of enthusiasm for the two men, saying their government 'receives scant respect or support from the people'. But in deference to his British partner, Roosevelt wrote to Churchill on 11 February to say he had instructed the State Department to take no action about changing the Italian government until the military situation improved sufficiently to warrant disaffection in Italian ranks. This, he remarked, was only 'a temporary reprieve for the two old gentlemen'. Churchill came back with a plea for keeping the present government 'tame and completely in our hands' and more likely to obey Allied directions than any other that might take its place. A new government, he said, would have to make its reputation with the Italian people by standing up to the Allies, and might try to wriggle out of the armistice terms.[39]

But Churchill was swimming against the tide of Italian public opinion, as well as that of resistance political leaders and his own advisers. British General

Sir Maitland Wilson, the Allied commander for the Mediterranean zone, concluded that only the king's abdication and replacement of the Badoglio government could prevent a serious civil disturbance. Opposition political parties had circulated an appeal asking the Italian people to treat the king and the government as rebels, and on 20 February they forced the king to agree to invest Crown Prince Umberto as Lieutenant of the Realm on the day the Allies entered Rome. On 22 February, the State Department drafted a cable approving the abdication of the king and the resignation of the government, and Roosevelt dispatched this to Wilson. Churchill, speaking to the House of Commons that same day, reiterated British support for the king and government until Rome was occupied. Three days later, he cabled Roosevelt saying he was surprised by Wilson's attitude, and he urged the president to reconsider his stand if the fall of Rome were unduly protracted. 'If the Italian political parties think they can play one of us off against the other, we shall have the worst of both worlds,' he wrote. The next day Roosevelt tried to mollify Churchill, saying he had not intended to give approval to action against the king and government without Churchill's concurrence.

But, to Churchill's intense annoyance, the United States continued to hold out for abdication of the king and replacement of the Badoglio government. On 13 March, Roosevelt said in a telegram to him that American public opinion would never understand continued tolerance and apparent support for Victor Emmanuel. Churchill replied the same day: 'I fear that if we drive out the King and Badoglio at this stage we shall only have complicated the task of the armies.' The dispute dragged on for another four months.[40]

In March, the Badoglio government dropped a bombshell on the two Allied capitals. Without bothering to inform the Allies or even the Italian Communist Party, it agreed to establish diplomatic relations with the Soviet Union. The Americans and British, anxious to avoid any Soviet involvement in Italian affairs, were furious. But when they expressed their displeasure, Badoglio complained about interference in every aspect of the political life of the country. Like Mussolini, he had become dissatisfied with foreign tutelage, but he had undercut Churchill's arguments for keeping him in power.[41]

Badoglio's dealings with Moscow coincided with the return to Italy of Palmiro Togliatti, the Communist leader who had been living in the Soviet capital for years. Formerly the Italian Communist Party had refused to cooperate with the government, but Togliatti, carrying out instructions from Stalin, began manoeuvring immediately to get his party into the government and to persuade other parties of the Left to join in a united front to defeat the Nazis and Fascists.[42]

* * *

The Germans carried out one of their many atrocities in late March. The US Army's 2677th Special Reconnaissance Battalion landed fifteen men along the Ligurian coast in northern Italy with a mission to demolish a rail tunnel between La Spezia and Genoa. But the men were captured on 24 March, and two days later all of them were shot on the orders of General Anton Dostler, commander of the 75th Infantry Corps.[43]

Churchill attacked Mussolini in a radio speech on 26 March. 'Mussolini indeed escaped to eat the bread of affliction at Hitler's table, to shoot his son-in-law and to help the Germans wreak vengeance upon the Italian masses whom he had professed to love,' he said. 'This fate and judgement more terrible than death has overtaken the vainglorious dictator who stabbed France in the back and thought that his crime had gained him the empire of the Mediterranean.' Churchill went on to proclaim that the Allies then held one-third of the Italian mainland, had swept sixty-six Italian divisions out of the struggle and were holding down in Italy nearly twenty-five German divisions and a part of the German air force, 'all of whom can burn and bleed the land of their former ally while other even more important events which might require their presence are impending elsewhere'.[44]

Mussolini replied three days later in an unsigned article in his occasional publication called *Corrispondenza repubblicana*: 'It would be said that Mr Churchill has a strictly personal quarrel with Mussolini. It is necessary to explain this singular phenomenon by referring to the criminal tendencies of Mr Churchill, tendencies that Churchill himself revealed and confessed in his memoirs at the time of the war against the Boers.'[45] Later Mussolini told his friend Ottavio Dinale that the enemy who would never forgive him was England. 'It is the Italy of Mussolini that has begun the liquidation of the very powerful English empire,' he said. 'This is my most legitimate pride, even if it signifies more certainly my condemnation. England is the only enemy of Italy, therefore of Mussolini.'[46]

In March, Police Chief Tullio Tamburini, sensing that fascism was on its last legs, presented Mussolini with a plan to enable him to escape when the regime fell. It involved building a giant submarine in which he and other Fascist leaders could remain at sea for a long period, then find refuge in some distant port in the Far East or South America. Mussolini rejected the idea out of hand.[47]

Mussolini's tendency to revert to a hierarchical and authoritarian system within the Fascist Party met at this time with growing disquiet that was expressed in the Fascist newspapers. Even the American poet Ezra Pound, a Fascist sympathiser living in Italy, joined in the dissent with a letter to the newspapers. In February, the Venetian periodical *Fronte Unico* had been closed because it had attacked Pavolini as 'the most unpopular man in the government'. The editor of the Florentine newspaper *La Nazione* had also been forced out of his job, and eighty of his journalists transferred, because of criticisms of regime policies. In March, Fernando Mezzasoma, Mussolini's youthful minister of popular culture, sent the newspapers a warning – probably written by Mussolini – that was intended to shut off all debate and any public meetings that could be dangerous to public order. But the dissent continued, backed by at least two Cabinet ministers and some of the Duce's closest associates.[48]

Towards the end of March, Mussolini again sought escape from Gargnano. He sent Dolfin to a place near Verona to see if a certain villa could be used as his office. But Dolfin conferred with various authorities and reported the villa was too exposed to possible enemy air attack.[49] So Mussolini remained at Gargnano, and on 29 March he sacked Dolfin because of his inability to get along with Vittorio and other members of the Mussolini family. Luigi Bolla noted in his diary: 'Vittorio, however, continues to play the fool in Germany and draw to himself the antipathy of all the German authorities.'[50]

Mussolini was fretting most of all at this time about the state of his army, and on 22 April, armed with a report prepared by Graziani, he went to Austria for a showdown meeting with Hitler on the subject. Graziani said the troops he had available for antipartisan warfare were mostly without arms. This was a longstanding Italian complaint against the Germans, who had seized tons of Italian weapons at the time of the surrender. In many cases troops were also lacking proper food and clothes. 'Since 8 September, the Germans have made an enormous booty of our things,' Mussolini said. 'I prefer to keep quiet so as not to have to confess to the Italians and the world our present miserable state.' But on 24 February, he had complained to Rahn, who was blunt in his response. 'The English have many weapons, we Germans, no,' he said. 'And we must therefore give them only to those we trust.'[51]

* * *

In attempting to put together a proper fighting force after his appointment as armed forces minister in 1943, Graziani had been thwarted by a combination of factors: German obstruction and mistrust, competition from Fascist militias and German labour recruiters for the limited pool of manpower that was available and a lack of competent officer material. When the republic was formed, 300 generals pledged their loyalty to Mussolini, 63 in Rome alone, but the quality of many republican officers was questionable. Some were too young, some too old and some insisted on wearing civilian attire for fear of being assassinated. The retired Marshal Enrico Caviglia, then in his eighties, watched a film on officers being sworn in and wrote: 'I have never seen such generals. . . . Where have they gone to dig them up? I would not have trusted them to command even a kitchen corporal. . . . You don't make war with stuff like this.'[52]

The German High Command was resolutely opposed to an independent Italian army it feared could never be trusted and would interfere in its conduct of the war. Field Marshal Wilhelm Keitel, the chief of staff, commented: 'The only Italian army that will not betray us is an army that doesn't exist.'[53] He had grudgingly allowed three Italian divisions that remained loyal at the time of the surrender to fight alongside German forces, and in early 1944 they were acquitting themselves well at Anzio. The only other Italian troops the High Command was willing to accept were a few 'auxiliaries' recruited to man anti-aircraft defences and the like.[54]

On 13 October 1943, Graziani met Hitler, who was still fuming over the Italian 'betrayal'. He told Graziani that if Badoglio and the king had gone to him directly and explained why Italy couldn't continue to fight, he would have understood – provided Italy did not then join any other belligerent and guaranteed its neutrality and defence of its territory. Graziani, of course, could hardly be expected to believe that kind of reasonableness from Hitler.

Graziani requested that twelve divisions be formed out of the 600,000 Italian troops interned in Germany since the Italian surrender a month earlier. Hitler refused and barred Graziani from visiting the internment camps to raise volunteers for his army. As far as Hitler and the German High Command were concerned, the internees were *Badogliotruppen*, disloyal and still wedded to a treasonable monarchy, or else Communists. Hitler told Graziani he would consider finding equipment for four Italian divisions to be given six months of training in Germany, and their armament would be equal to that of the German infantry. Later, perhaps, there would be eight and finally twelve divisions. A certain number of Italian officers and NCOs would be drawn from the camps and would lead soldiers recruited or drafted in Italy.

Meanwhile, the SS enrolled 13,000 volunteers among the internees for an Italian SS, but 10,000 of them disappeared when they returned to Italy. Hitler insisted the Fascist government should call up fresh recruits in Italy to provide soldiers for the four divisions. Mussolini agreed and the call-up began on 16 October. Many of the draftees refused to answer the call and either went into hiding or joined the partisans. Among those who did turn up, desertions soon started, which Graziani blamed on lack of supplies, lack of proper barracks and 'stupid German interference'. The regime had to use Fascist militias, local police and Carabinieri to hunt down the deserters, and it threatened heads of families if sons failed to report.[55]

A grocer at Sondrio lost his licence to do business because his three sons deserted to Switzerland. At Vercelli, seven shops were closed, with signs displayed on their doors: 'Closed because father of a deserter.' Authorities in Milan threatened to remove driver's licences from all relatives of deserters, suspend payments of pensions and dismiss state employees whose sons were involved. Graziani said a very high percentage of draftees showed up in some areas – 98 per cent in Emilia, 'much above what we wanted'. But many who reported for duty deserted soon afterwards. Others went off to training camps singing 'Bandiera Rossa' (Red Flag), the Communist hymn. One government report said recruits travelling to Cremona by train sang subversive songs, and Carabinieri escorting them allowed this to go on for two hours without intervening. About 100 recruits fled their barracks at Sassuolo near Reggio Emilia because of bad treatment, nondistribution of food rations, dirty mess tins, lack of blankets and other conditions.

In a letter to Graziani of 12 February, 1944, Field Marshal Kesselring stated that 3,500 draftees had fled in the previous five weeks: 'In recent times the cases of desertion . . . have reached unsupportable proportions.' But Kesselring had been so impressed by the fighting qualities of the three Italian divisions engaged at Anzio that he withdrew his reservations about equipping the four divisions being formed in Germany, and Hitler ordered this to go ahead. In his reply, Graziani said the desertions were the result of German delay in furnishing clothing and decent barracks. 'One cannot wonder if, in full winter, men badly dressed and badly housed in barracks lacking almost any comfort have not known how to resist the temptation to go away,' he wrote.[56]

The Mussolini regime issued a decree on 18 February providing the death penalty for refusal to serve and desertion, but said there would be no punishment for those reporting after the 8 March deadline if they asked to be sent to the front. At his trial after the war, Graziani denied he was the author of the decree, claimed he had opposed it to the last and blamed Mussolini and the Germans. But it was signed by Mussolini, Graziani and Piero Pisenti, the minister of justice. Graziani's reply to Kesselring's letter also was found. In his letter, Graziani said he hoped the decree would help to reduce, if not halt, 'this sad phenomenon' of draft evasion. Despite the decree, Mussolini himself could be lenient with draft evaders. When a Parma war tribunal condemned to death thirty-five such men who were arrested carrying arms, he ordered the sentences to be suspended. The Fascist historian Attilio Tamaro said that while the Duce was inexorable with his Communist opponents, considering them true enemies of civilisation, he was sometimes truly liberal toward other anti-Fascists.[57]

Some Fascist officials went beyond the 18 February decree. Giovanni Alessandri, Prefect of Alessandria, ruled that anyone helping partisans, deserters or escaped prisoners of war would have their livestock confiscated and their ration cards suspended, except those who were sick and children under twelve, who would be allowed meat and sugar. Fines would also be imposed, and shop licences suspended for an indefinite time. Such actions, of course, only increased the unpopularity of the regime. 'The majority of the population . . . holds little sympathy for fascism or the action of the republican government,' Mussolini's police chief told him on 29 April.[58]

From the moment Graziani assumed command in the autumn of 1943, his attempts to recruit soldiers had met competition from two other organisations, the Fascist militias known as the Republican National Guard and the Todt organisation, the German unit responsible for recruiting Italian civilian labour for German factories.

One of Mussolini's first acts when he was restored to power was to appoint Lieutenant-General Renato Ricci, aged forty-seven, as commander of the militias. Ricci was a former minister of corporations and former head of the Fascist youth organisation who had close ties with Himmler. He had dreamed of becoming head of a new republican national army and instead found himself as chief of the Fascist Party's principal police force. The writer Felice Bellotti said Ricci was disliked even by his fellow Fascists. 'All were agreed that Renato Ricci was an imbecile and they said it openly to discredit him in the eyes of the Germans.'[59]

In his first speech, Mussolini had said only an army of the party could defend Fascists from a repeat of his overthrow on 25 July. But when Graziani was then named armed forces minister, he submitted a memorandum to Mussolini objecting to the appointment of Ricci and the establishment of a party army. 'The militia is hated and must be dissolved immediately,' he wrote. 'The army must be national and apolitical, also absolutely unitary. . . . The police forces of every type must depend on the Minister of the Armed Forces.' At a Cabinet meeting on 28 October 1943, Mussolini announced the militias would be an integral part of the army and would form the Corps of Black Shirts. The fundamental law of the armed forces approved that day referred to the army, navy and air force and made no mention of the militias.[60]

Ricci told Mussolini he would not take orders from Graziani and continued to press for an autonomous militia. Mussolini accused him of personal ambition and assured Graziani on 17 November that he would stand by his decision. But on 19 November, after another talk with Ricci, he told Graziani that the militia would be autonomous and would be called the Republican National Guard. In a letter to Buffarini, Ricci said all police operations against anti-Fascist partisans would be carried out by the Guard at the express request of the German Command. The Guard initially had 30,000 men, most of them former Carabinieri, but Graziani said the marriage between the

Carabinieri and the militias was a 'hybrid and unsuccessful union'. A Guard report accused many Carabinieri of sabotaging the work of the Fascists, refusing to arrest wanted people and inviting peasants to hide when the Germans were passing so as to avoid being called up. Some Carabinieri fled from northern Italy with their families and their weapons.[61]

Many new Guard members recruited by Ricci were boys between the ages of fifteen and seventeen, undisciplined and lacking training. Mussolini was dismayed. 'We can only count on the very young and on old men, on those who are under twenty and over forty; we can't count on men in between,' he told his journalist friend Ermanno Amicucci. Most Italian men between twenty and forty, Amicucci noted, were in Allied and Russian prison camps or in concentration camps in Germany. At the end of January 1944 Ricci wrote to Graziani that he had no more than 3,000 men available to fight the partisans. He complained that because the Germans had failed to equip his forces properly there was one machine gun for every twenty Guard members, one pair of shoes for every three, one armoured car for every five hundred. Desertions soon began.[62]

* * *

All these problems were on Mussolini's mind when he met Hitler at Klessheim castle, near Salzburg, on 22 April. None troubled him more than the fate of the 600,000 Italian soldiers interned in Germany for the past seven months in wretched conditions. Hitler reiterated his distrust of these troops and told the Duce about sedition among internees at Linz, in Austria. 'These Italian Communists of Linz put themselves under the protection of the Italian embassy in Berlin,' he said. 'They do not deserve anything and, believe me, Duce, anything you do for them will only bring you disappointment.' But Hitler, who wolfed down multicoloured pills throughout the meeting, promised to sort out the younger and more reliable men among those infected with treason.[63]

In a telegram to Field Marshal Keitel shortly before the conference, Graziani complained that while the German was asking him for more troops to help the war effort, German authorities in Italy were demanding not less than 1 million men for labour service in Germany. Now he laid out his problems in greater detail. He told the conference that 60,000 to 70,000 young men had reported for duty, many as a consequence of the threats against their families, but many others had remained defiant. 'There are not enough police available to oblige the draftees to show up,' he said. Hitler asked the reason for the resistance, and Graziani replied: 'In Italy the population is now convinced that for Germany the war is already lost.' Hitler responded that Germany would soon win the war, thanks to secret arms, a renewal of submarine warfare and air superiority to be achieved by new fighter planes.

He said the German people had been taken to the extreme limit of effort and sacrifice. In the past year, he had drawn 136 new divisions from the people, but now there were no more people to be mobilised. The Germans had suffered colossal losses in Russia and 64,000 had been killed in one raid on Hamburg, 'and yet despite that, production has not in fact diminished. I must say we have achieved a miracle.' He commented that Churchill would have to attack within six to eight weeks because he could not indefinitely keep his people in the present state of tension. If Churchill did not attack, Hitler promised he would take the initiative and destroy London.

Hitler assured Mussolini that his secret weapons would have a range of 150 to 180 miles, would 'transform London into a heap of ruins' and would change the course of the war. 'We will never capitulate, never, never, never,' he declared.[64]

'From the exposition of the Führer,' Luigi Bolla wrote, 'those present drew a strange rather than profound impression, the impression of finding themselves before an altar without any ornament on which a madman, horribly wounded, sacrifices with crazy firmness the last fibres of his life to redeem his destiny in eternity.'

Mussolini's ambassador, Filippo Anfuso, urged the Duce to press for the release of Italian internees in Germany, even with the proviso that they could remain in Germany as workers, but under Italian authority. To Anfuso's annoyance, Vittorio Mussolini opposed this, saying: 'Let's forget about these lame sheep.'[65]

Mussolini not only got little satisfaction from Hitler; he got a humiliating lecture about the performance of Italian troops in Russia, especially the Alpine units ('our worst enemies'); about Italian workers in Germany; and about the breakup of Italian fascism. Hitler said most internees were Communists and could not be allowed freedom in any form. 'I had never known a Hitler so brutal and so similar to his legend,' Mussolini remarked afterwards. He tried in vain to persuade Hitler to open peace negotiations with the Soviet Union. He also urged a German declaration of solidarity with the Fascist Party and said the Italian people must be given the impression their government was independent and exercised complete control in certain areas. At the moment, he said, only a minority of the population favoured the republican regime, and the clergy had adopted a reserved or even hostile attitude. He described himself as the most hated man in Italy, and Hitler replied that both of them were the most hated men in the world. One of the few things Mussolini got out of Hitler was the gift of a magnificent new armored car.[66]

Despite Hitler's harsh treatment, Mussolini phoned Rachele to tell her the talks had been 'very cordial'. On his return, he said he had succeeded in persuading Hitler that German plans for a wholesale transfer of Italian industries from the Po valley would be unwise, as it was 'in Germany's own interest to have a zone of production decentralised in northern Italy'.[67]

From Klessheim, Mussolini went on to Grafenwöhr, near Nuremberg, where the San Marco Division was training, and received a rapturous welcome from his troops. In a speech he told them that on their return to Italy, they would be fighting Allied troops from many nations, including 'Negroes and Communists. . . . You will therefore have the joy of opening fire on this mixture of bastard races and mercenaries who respect nothing and no one in an invaded Italy.' His warm reception proved that some of the old Mussolini magic remained, but that was hardly surprising; his presence offered the troops, isolated and treated with contempt by the Germans, some hope of regaining the self-respect of which they had been robbed.[68]

Upon his return to Italy, Mussolini ignored strong objections from Graziani and acceded to a German demand that he call up men for labour service in Germany. The result, Graziani said, was 'more or less nothing', and the Germans gave up this attempt.[69]

In late May, the Allies staged a breakthrough in the south and began their advance on Rome. In a speech to army commanders four months earlier, Mussolini had said: 'Now it is for us, for you, a humiliation that burns the flesh, I would say almost physically, to have to witness as spectators the defence of Rome, entrusted for now only to the indisputable valour of soldiers of the Reich.'[70] Kesselring decided on a strategic withdrawal, and, as his forces pulled back, bringing the front line closer to the north, German authorities began to transfer Italian industries to Germany and to destroy some of those they could not move.

Economy Minister Tarchi signed an agreement with the Germans in which it was suggested that plants taken away would be returned after the war. But the people more directly involved were not so complaisant; Italian obstruction was immediate. Industries began hiding their equipment in tunnels and in the countryside. The Germans also stepped up the transfer of workers to the Reich, and helped themselves to livestock on Italian farms. In Genoa, the SS divided workers into three categories: the very young to be sent to Germany, more mature workers to be transferred to other north Italian provinces to help the German war effort and older workers to be kept in the city. Shortages of milk and cheese occurred because of the steady German slaughter of milk cows. Peasants became increasingly reluctant to hand over products to the Germans, hiding them and selling them on the black market or turning them over to the partisans.[71] The resistance had assumed more than a military character. German mistrust, brutality and short-sightedness were just beginning to produce a reaction among Italians that the Nazi forces would come to regret.

Chapter 9

THE PARTISAN WAR DEVELOPS

They think they can treat Italians like Poles.

(Benito Mussolini on German cruelty, 29 March 1944)

In August 1943, the Badoglio government proclaimed Rome an 'open city', a declaration to which Pope Pius XII lent his ecclesiastical weight. The Germans naturally enough supported the idea; it was clearly to their advantage that no Allied bombs should fall on a city they had occupied. The Allies refused to recognise a special status for Rome, however, because German military supplies to Cassino and then to the Anzio front continued to pass through Rome by rail and road. In further violation of the concept, the Eleventh Company of the German Third Battalion SS Police Regiment marched through the centre of Rome each day, a reminder to the populace of its power to carry out repressive police measures and to round up young men for labour service in Germany. These were not fighting troops; most of the men in the regiment were beyond the age of forty-five and most came from the German-speaking Alto Adige region of Italy. They were used primarily to safeguard government ministries and some military objectives.[1]

For some time, Italian partisans living in Rome had watched the police unit's movements, planning how to launch an attack, and on 23 March 1944, they put their plan into operation. The spot chosen was along the Via Rasella, a street in central Rome not far from the Trevi Fountain. The partisans placed an explosive charge, forty pounds of TNT, in a rubbish bin on the street. Rosario Bentivegna, a medical student, and Carla Capponi, who had worked in a chemical laboratory, were the principal partisan agents designated to carry out the attack. They were lovers and hoped to marry soon.

Bentivegna, dressed in a street cleaner's attire, waited by the bin. He would light the fuse when the Germans approached, while Capponi, a raincoat over her arm, waited at the top of the street where it joins the Via delle Quattro

Fontane. The plan was for Bentivegna to walk up the street towards her after he had lit the fuse; she would cover him with the raincoat and they would make their escape.

Three times Bentivegna lit his pipe, intending to use it to light the fuse, but the police unit was late in arriving and when it finally did so, at 3.45 p.m., he was out of tobacco. So, when he finally saw the 156 men of the unit marching up Via Rasella with an escort of armoured vehicles, he used pieces of paper in his pocket and matches to light the fuse. Bentivegna made his way up the street to Capponi, and they ran to her mother's house several streets away in Piazza Foro Traiano, near the Roman Forum.[2]

After the bomb went off, thirty-two Germans lay dead in the street and many more were wounded. Hand grenades worn on the belts of some of the Germans exploded, either because they were hit by shrapnel or were set off by the heat from the resulting fire, and they added to the carnage. Three partisans waiting in a side street stepped into Via Rasella and hurled grenades, but one failed to detonate. Partisans also engaged the surviving Germans in an exchange of pistol fire, and were joined by some civilians.[3]

Luftwaffe Lieutenant-General Kurt Mälzer, the German commandant in Rome, rushed to the scene when he got word of the explosion. Mälzer, who lived in the Excelsior Hotel on the Via Veneto, was called by Romans the 'king of Rome' or 'Tiberius' because of his penchant for the *dolce vita*, and he was often drunk. In fact, he had been drinking heavily just before he arrived, and when he saw the scene of carnage in Via Rasella he burst into tears and, gesticulating wildly, shouted: 'Revenge, revenge for my poor comrades!' He threatened to blow up houses along the street with dynamite but Eithel Moellhausen, the German consul in Rome, and SS Colonel Eugen Dollmann told him he could not do that, touching off a heated argument. Mälzer turned on Dollmann and shouted: 'Perhaps you want to help the killers?' Moellhausen contacted General Siegfried Westphal, chief of staff to Field Marshal Kesselring, and urged him to restrain Mälzer. Herbert Kappler, the Gestapo chief in Rome and now a lieutenant-colonel, also arrived at the scene and proceeded to arrest about 200 men living in the neighborhood. This was the same Herbert Kappler, of course, who had extracted gold from the Roman Jews before they were arrested. He had come to Rome in 1939 at the age of thirty-two as a police attaché at the German Embassy, and he spoke Italian perfectly. Ambassador Rahn once called him 'a cruel policeman', and Albrecht von Kessel, the anti-Nazi counsellor at the German embassy to the Holy See, said he was 'a ferocious beast'. General Westphal said: 'I never wanted to have anything to do with him.' Earlier Kappler had arrested Princess Mafalda, the daughter of King Victor Emmanuel who was still living in Rome. He had called her to Gestapo headquarters on the pretext that her

German husband, Prince Philipp of Hesse, was on the phone from Germany waiting to speak to her. She later died in the concentration camp at Buchenwald. Among those Kappler arrested in Via Rasella was a nephew of Marshal Graziani, the Italian armed forces minister, but when his identity became known he was released. Mälzer wanted all the arrested men shot on the spot.[4]

Hitler was enraged when he received word of the massacre and ordered a savage reprisal: he wanted to blow up an entire quarter of houses around Via Rasella, with their occupants inside, and thirty to fifty Italians were to be shot for every German killed. But he was later persuaded to forgo blowing up the houses and to accept a figure of ten Italians for each dead German. Kesselring issued this order to the commander of the Fourteenth Army, General Eberhard von Mackensen: 'Kill ten Italians for every German. Carry out immediately.'[5]

Kappler assured his superiors he could find 320 hostages who had already been condemned to death, but he searched his records and found there were only 3. He then came up with 270 names of Italians under German arrest, and asked the Italian Fascist police chief, Pietro Caruso, to produce another 50. Caruso consulted Interior Minister Buffarini-Guidi, who was in Rome at the time, and Buffarini said: 'Give them to him, give them to him. . . . If not, who knows what those people will do?' By midday on 24 March, the list of 320 prisoners was complete. Another German soldier died of his wounds that day, so Kappler added 10 innocent Jews to the list without consulting Kesselring. Altogether the list included 75 Jews. Now the list numbered 330, or so the Germans thought; in some confusion, they had failed to count properly and 335 men were marked for death.[6]

Dollmann later said he had tried to forestall the reprisals by suggesting an elaborate ceremony for the dead Germans. Their bodies would be taken in a cortège through the streets of the city, the bells of all the Roman churches would sound together and special editions of newspapers would carry photographs of all the bomb victims. Kesselring would make a speech in which he would announce that the city of Rome must make financial compensation to the families of the men killed and this would be 'the last act' of German clemency. If there were further incidents of this nature, the entire responsibility would fall on Rome and its people; the fate of the city was in their hands. This suggestion went nowhere.[7]

Weizsäcker telephoned Kesselring repeatedly to try to stop the reprisals. Moellhausen said he entered Kappler's office that evening and saw him drawing up a list of names of men to be shot.

'Listen, Kappler, if I were in your place my conscience would tremble in doing what you are doing,' he said. 'I don't know how I would act, but certainly I would feel I was at a turning point in my life. Think that one day you also will be called to render accounts at the tribunal of God.'

Kappler looked up and said: 'I promise you what I can, and it is this: for every one of the names that I am writing, I will think three times.'[8]

Pope Pius XII, apparently more concerned about armed Communists in Rome than about German reprisals, did not intervene in the matter. The Vatican newspaper *L'Osservatore Romano* cautioned against 'ill-judged violence' because those who had to maintain public order would react 'with a series of painful reprisals which cannot be estimated'.

On 24 March, the same day that article appeared, Kappler arranged for the execution of his hostages to take place in the Ardeatine caves south of Rome. Wehrmacht officers had refused to become involved, but Kappler had twelve Gestapo officers and sixty-nine men available to carry out the order. He threatened that if any man refused to take part in the shooting, he would be sent before an SS tribunal and his family would be dispatched to a concentration camp. Truckloads of prisoners, many under the impression they were being taken for forced labour, were transported to the site from Rome's Regina Coeli jail and, with hands tied behind their backs, the victims were ordered to walk inside the caves and kneel. Kappler later said he did not allow a priest to comfort the victims beforehand because he could not spare the time. They were killed, five at a time, by revolver shots in the back of the head. The killings began at 2 p.m. and were completed at 8.30. Kappler spent much of that time chatting with those waiting to be killed.

According to one account, a German soldier identified only as Wotjan shouted that Kappler could kill him but he would not fire on anyone. He became ill and vomited. But Kappler, in testimony at his postwar trial, said he found Wotjan reluctant to shoot, spoke to him 'in a comradely manner' and went into the cave with him and fired a shot at his side as Wotjan also opened fire. Another soldier, Gunther Ammon, failed to shoot because when he entered the cave and saw a mound of bodies before him, he fainted and had to be carried out. Kappler did not punish him.[9]

At a trial after the war, Kappler testified that he told his men to get drunk on brandy after the massacre because they were so upset by what they had done. He also said he had shot many victims himself to encourage the others. Then German engineers sealed the caves. 'I must recognise that I did not order the exclusion of minors,' Kappler testified. One of the victims was fourteen years old, one was fifteen and two were seventeen. The oldest was a Jew, Mosè Di Consiglio, seventy-four, who was killed along with his two sons and three nephews. One victim was a priest, Don Pappagallo. Besides Italians, the victims included three Germans and three Russians and one man each from Belgium, France, Hungary, Turkey and Libya. Bruno Spampanato, editor of the Roman newspaper *Il Messaggero*, described the killings in his newspaper the next day as an exemplary act of justice.[10]

Testifying before the International War Crimes Tribunal in Nuremberg after the war, Kesselring said he told Kappler he was 'to a certain extent grateful to him that this very distasteful matter had been settled in a way which was legally and morally above reproach'. He said he did so in the belief that all those executed in the Ardeatine caves had already been sentenced to death.

Several hours in advance of the massacre, the Vatican learned of German intentions to execute ten Italians for every dead German, but the pope did not intervene. When news of the executions became known later, the pope maintained his silence, unwilling to speak out after the unjustified slaughter of many of his flock as bishop of Rome. On 26 March, *L'Osservatore Romano* commented: 'Thirty-two victims on the one hand, and on the other three hundred and twenty persons sacrificed for the guilty parties who escaped arrest. . . . We call upon the irresponsible elements to respect human life, which they have no right whatsoever to sacrifice.' The comment seemed to equate the guilt of partisans and Nazis.[11]

Kappler testified at his trial that General Karl Wolff, the SS commander in Italy, arrived in Rome on the evening of 24 March and declared the killings were not a sufficient measure. Kappler said he lost his temper and shouted in Wolff's face: 'It's enough for me, general!' Wolff told Kesselring that SS chief Heinrich Himmler was inflexible, insisting that all Communists or suspected Communists had to be eliminated from Rome through 'a forced exodus from the capital'. Dollmann, who met Wolff on his arrival, agreed with this account. He quoted Wolff as saying: 'Himmler is right. We need to give an example here.' The entire male population between the ages of eighteen and forty-five in the most dangerous neighbourhoods – San Lorenzo, Trastevere and Testaccio – was to be rounded up and shipped north. Kesselring said it would require two or three divisions of soldiers to carry out such an operation and he could not spare the men. Wolff was reported to have agreed to a temporary delay, but the matter eventually was forgotten. Wolff's own version of the facts was that he had gone to Rome to try to stop the reprisals.[12]

The partisans issued a communiqué on 26 March warning that revenge for the Ardeatine caves massacre would be 'pitiless and terrible. . . . Patriotic and partisan guerrilla actions in Rome will not cease until the city is totally evacuated by the Germans.'[13]

Mussolini was horrified by the massacre and ordered the release of all political prisoners not accused of murder to prevent their being seized by the Germans for future reprisals. Rachele said he sat silently through dinner that evening until her questioning finally provoked him to speak.

'What happened is terrible,' he said. 'They think they can treat Italians like Poles, without understanding that in this way they only create new enemies. . . . I didn't act in time to stop it, only to protest.' He said those who carried out the bombing on Via Rasella had not altered the outcome of the war 'by one inch'. He added: 'With their cruel reprisal, the Germans certainly cannot avoid the repetition of similar acts.'[14]

After the war, Mackensen and Mälzer were tried before a British military court martial, found guilty and sentenced to be shot. But the sentences were commuted to life imprisonment. Mälzer died in prison and Mackensen was released in 1952. Kappler and five of his staff were tried by an Italian military tribunal in 1948; he was sentenced to life, plus fifteen years for the theft of Jewish gold, and his co-defendants were acquitted. While in prison, Kappler married a German masseuse who had begun visiting him regularly. He became very religious in prison, and attended mass regularly. Then he developed cancer and was transferred to a military hospital, but escaped and was smuggled out of Italy by his wife on 15 August 1977. He died on 9 February 1978, in Germany.[15]

Pietro Caruso, the Fascist police chief who assisted in finding victims for the Ardeatine massacre, fled from Rome on the morning of 4 June 1944, the day on which the city fell to the Allies, but he crashed his car into a tree near Lake Bracciano north of Rome and was taken to a hospital in Viterbo with a broken leg and other injuries. When the Allies captured Viterbo, he was arrested and found to have a lot of jewellery and money on him. Scheduled to go on trial in Rome on 18 September 1944, he had to wait because a mob stormed the courtroom and seized Donato Carretta, the former director of the Regina Coeli jail who had opposed the German use of his prisoners in the Ardeatine caves massacre and who was to have been a prosecution witness. Carretta, hated for his own crimes, was pinned to tram tracks but the driver of a tram refused to run over him. He was then thrown into the Tiber and drowned. His body, fished from the river, was taken by the mob to his house and presented to his wife. Caruso was sentenced to death after a one-day trial on 20 September and was executed by a twenty-man Carabiniere firing squad.[16]

In 1949, Carla Capponi, the partisan involved in the Via Rasella massacre, was given the Gold Medal, Italy's highest military honour, and was later elected to Parliament. Her husband, Dr Rosario Bentivegna, who had ignited the bomb, was given the Silver Medal.[17]

The Via Rasella attack on the German military was one of the first significant acts of a partisan war that took shape slowly after the overthrow of Mussolini and that waxed and waned at different times over the next thirteen months. The Italian resistance campaign, which led to a bloody civil war, has never received the attention in books and films that has been accorded the French resistance. But it played a significant role in reducing German and Fascist military strength and in helping escaped Allied prisoners of war and airmen who were shot down over Italy to reach safety. There were more than 60,000 escaped prisoners of war in Italy immediately after the 8 September surrender. Many of these fought with the partisans and others were sheltered by Italian families at great risk to their own lives. In his memoirs, written after his own trial as a war criminal, Marshal Kesselring had the effrontery to denounce the partisan war as contrary to international law. But he admitted that from mid-1944 onwards, 'the Partisan war was an actual menace to our military operations'. Max Salvadori, a British Special Forces officer who fought with the partisans, wrote after the war: 'Of all the European resistance movements, the Italian was the one that had the best organisation. . . . More than elsewhere, the Italian resistance succeeded in presenting a single, united front.'[18]

Leaders of the main Italian political parties met in Rome in the autumn of 1943 and organised the resistance under the name of the Committee of National Liberation (CLN). In a resolution adopted on 12 September, just four days after the Italian armistice, the CLN openly declared war. 'The Committee of National Liberation notes with pain that the abandonment of their posts on the part of the sovereign and head of government have impaired and destroyed the possibility of resistance and struggle on the part of the army and people, and decides on insurrection for [the restoration of] Italian honour.' It called on Italians 'to reconquer for Italy the place that belongs to it in the assembly of free nations'. At that point the committee's influence did not extend much beyond Rome, and the leftist parties represented on it took the military initiatives into their own hands.[19] In January 1944, the party representatives in northern Italy formed the CLNAI (Committee of National Liberation in Upper Italy), and the focal point of the struggle was from that point in the north, especially the Piedmont region around Turin.

The Allies viewed the partisan movement with mixed feelings. They wanted the partisans to confine themselves to harassing the enemy, providing intelligence and helping Allied troops to escape. The political parties behind the movement had a broader aim: they wanted to conquer and hold territory as the basis for an independent Italian government to challenge the Badoglio regime in the south, and they naturally vied with one another for pre-eminence. The fact that the Communists played a dominant role in the resistance, particularly in the north, aroused more concern among the British than it did among the Americans, who were happy to accept help from any party willing to fight the Germans and Fascists. But the Allies were slow to provide significant military help. Initially, the Yugoslav and French partisans got priority. But by the end of the war the Allies had dropped more than

6,490 tons of supplies in Italy, 68 per cent of it coming from the US Air Force. More material came by sea or overland. Financial help to the movement was provided by many Italian bankers, financiers and industrialists, who also transferred Allied funds to the partisans. Three major banks supplied a total of 35 million lire, which went on their books as fictitious loans to the Edison, Falck and Pirelli companies, with directors of those firms signing the receipts.

Some of the first partisans were anti-Fascist Italian soldiers who had escaped the German roundup and deportation immediately after the armistice. In the Boves region west of Turin, about 1,000 troops and officers from the disbanded IV Armoured Brigade gathered in the mountains with arms and material, expecting an imminent Allied landing on the Ligurian coast and hoping to assist in the ensuing battle. But the Germans attacked on the afternoon of 19 September 1943, and the resistance crumbled in the unequal battle. The Germans burned the entire village of Boves and killed twenty-four people, including a parish priest and an industrialist who were burned alive. This was the first reprisal action by the Germans after the armistice; there would be many more.

Near Teramo, in the remote Abruzzi mountain region north-east of Rome, 320 disbanded soldiers joined 100 escaped war prisoners and 1,200 young men from Teramo holding out in a wooded area called Bosco Martese. Hoping to survive there until the Allies arrived, they came under German attack on 25 September and the Germans were surprised by the strength of the resistance. The partisans captured a German major and shot him on the spot. In a battle that lasted three days, fifty-seven Germans were killed or wounded and the partisans lost just six men. The Germans brought up heavy reinforcements and the partisan forces melted away.[20]

Some former soldiers who fled to the mountains had no intention of fighting but merely wanted to hide out until the war ended, and some stole food and money to survive. One partisan commander said 200 men might turn up if there was a hot meal available, but when it came to fighting the number could be reduced to 50. The northern Communist leader and Spanish Civil War veteran Luigi Longo said these men 'were of the opinion they had to do nothing other than await the day of liberation'. Salvadori once asked a partisan commander in Milan how many men he could count on. 'On 600 in any event, 6,000 if there is any hope of success, 60,000 if the Germans refuse to defend themselves,' the commander replied. Partisan units sent away many 'useless mouths' who had to be fed but showed little propensity to fight. But not all the partisans were men; an estimated 35,000 women took part, either as fighters or as messengers. Many were young girls barely out of school.[21] Some partisan units were poorly armed, and Mussolini dismissed the importance of the movement in a letter to Hitler on 1 November 1943. 'It's a matter in great part of disbanded soldiers . . . and they do not represent a danger,' he said.[22] He would change his mind later.

Ferruccio Parri, leader of the left-wing Action Party, took the initiative in making contact with the Allied Secret Services in Switzerland in November 1943 and requesting their help. The Secret Services were surprised by his idea of forming a large partisan army, not at all to their liking, and the meeting, although described as 'very cordial', ended inconclusively.[23] The Communists in Milan decided to ignore the Allied reservations and push ahead with what became known as the Garibaldi Brigades in northern Italy. Longo became commander of the Garibaldi Brigades and Pietro Secchia, another Communist, was named commissar. The Brigades were organised in units of just five or six men, usually with two units forming a joint squadron. Few of the early recruits had any idea what communism was. Most had joined because they were fleeing the Fascist draft or compulsory labour service in Germany, or because the Germans had burned their houses and in some cases killed their families in reprisal actions. The first Allied air drop of war material for the partisans occurred on 23 December 1943, but it consisted of equipment for only thirty men. Later, Communist partisans sometimes seized arms and money dropped to other units. At the time the Communist Party was purely Stalinist in outlook, not the moderate party that evolved later and pioneered so-called Eurocommunism as an alternative to the Moscow variety.[24]

The Italian Supreme Command in the south, under Badoglio, gave a half-hearted endorsement to the resistance movement on 10 December. It said the Italian land and people lent themselves poorly to guerrilla warfare, but concluded that a war of liberation must be carried out.[25] With the beginning of winter, the partisans stepped up their attacks. A great railway viaduct at Vernante, in Piedmont, was blown up on 24 December, interrupting rail traffic along that route for more than a year. The partisans also occupied the village of Vinadio in the Val di Stura, the first inhabited centre in which they raised the tricolour flag. Further south, partisans mined the Sette Luci bridge near Rome on the night of 20 December and a stretch of the Rome–Cassino rail line. About 500 Germans were killed when the partisans blew up a train carrying troops, munitions and fuel to Cassino. The Germans attributed the attacks to British paratroops 'because they were carried out with too much precision to be the work of partisans'. In the Castelli Romani, the Alban Hill towns south-east of Rome, partisans established their first radio links with the Allies. In a coordinated action, they put nails on the roads and the Royal Air Force bombed German vehicles immobilised with flat tyres.[26]

At the beginning of 1944, the Germans carried out a wave of arrests of partisan suspects in the cities and began large-scale search operations in the

Piedmont valleys. They burned villages that supported the partisans and massacred the civilian residents. The partisans also suffered heavy losses. The CLN leadership responded with the strikes in northern Italy that were intended to deepen the struggle, stop the deportation of workers to Germany, reduce the production of war material and impede the dismantling of machinery in factories.

In a speech on 22 February 1944, Churchill belittled the CLN and praised the Badoglio government. For its part, the CLN was bitterly upset over Allied bombing, which had caused heavy civilian casualties in Italy and provided useful propaganda to the Mussolini government and the Germans. When Palmiro Togliatti, the Communist leader, returned from Moscow to southern Italy in March and decided to join the Badoglio government, the CLN agreed to accept the authority of the government. That improved the climate of CLN relations with the Allies.[27]

The leftist parties in the CLN took the initiative in organising assassination squads called Gruppi di Azione Patriottica (GAP), in the big cities. The Communists in particular believed a terror campaign was necessary, an act of 'revolutionary morality', even at the risk of alienating people. Partisan terror would provoke a reaction of the Fascists and Germans, and thus, in the Communist view, popular indignation towards them would grow. That many innocent Italians would die as a result of reprisals did not trouble the Communists; that was the whole point of the GAP actions. Not only would the population as a whole turn against the Fascists and Germans, but many of them would be moved to take up arms on the partisan side. The campaign was also intended to demonstrate to the people the activism and efficiency of the Communists by comparison with the passivity of other parties. Some women took part in GAP squads. Longo told of a young woman of nineteen in Rome who was stopped by German soldiers as she pedalled across town with a load of bombs in her bicycle basket. They asked her what she was carrying, and with a smile she replied: 'Bombs'. The soldiers laughed and waved her on.[28]

Ather Capelli, publisher of the Fascist newspaper *Gazzetta del Popolo* and one of the exponents of a Fascist faction that wanted peace, was shot dead in Turin on 31 March by a GAP operative. On 15 April, the most notorious of the GAP actions took place when several young men on motorcycles assassinated the philosopher Giovanni Gentile as he was getting into his car outside his home in Florence. Gentile had been Mussolini's first minister of education in the 1920s, was editor of the *Enciclopedia Italiana* and was president of the Academy of Italy. He enjoyed a worldwide reputation and was perhaps the most illustrious living Italian. Furthermore, he was an advocate of peace and of an end to the fratricidal struggle among Italians.

His secretary had been killed earlier by the Germans, and he had threatened to complain to Mussolini about this. Renzo De Felice, Mussolini's chief biographer, wrote: 'Gentile could have become the most authoritative supporter of the party of conciliation; for this he was killed.' Even anti-Fascist parties repudiated the murder, but Radio Bari, the mouthpiece of the Badoglio government, applauded it. Longo likewise endorsed the killing, calling Gentile a traitor who had 'prostituted science to fascism'. Mussolini ordered his Fascist squads to refrain from reprisal but in a note titled 'Basta!' (Enough!) he wrote: 'This shedding of blood must absolutely stop, this anarchy must end, it must be fought and snuffed out.' At a meeting of his Cabinet called to commemorate Gentile, it was announced that 1,023 Fascist Party members plus 535 officers and members of the Republican National Guard had been assassinated.[29]

The most famous of the GAP operatives was Giovanni Pesce, who headed the organisation first in Turin and then Milan. He had fought aged seventeen in Spain with the International Brigades against Franco, and he was twenty-five when he launched his GAP career in Piedmont, carrying out bloody reprisals for arrests, hangings and shootings by Fascist militias. On 1 January 1944, Pesce waited near the entrance of a Turin café frequented by German officers, and shot down the first two who came out. Two other officers rushed out with machine guns. Pesce threw himself to the ground and opened fire, killing both before making his escape. He was later held responsible for the murder of Capelli, and he joined two other men in blowing up the antenna of a Fascist radio station on the outskirts of Turin.

He used the name Ivaldi in Turin, and in June when he moved to Milan he became Visone. He also carried an ID card in the name of Antonio Chilotti, born in Cagliari, Sardinia. He blew up five locomotives and two other railway carriages before carrying out his most notorious attack, which will be discussed in Chapter 12. In early 1945, Pesce blew up a bar in Milan frequented by Fascist militiamen, and thirteen days later a liquor store. After the war the Italian government gave him the Gold Medal.[30]

Iris Origo, an Anglo-American woman married to an Italian marquis and living in central Italy, noted in her diary that partisan bands operating in the area were resorting more and more to looting. She said that on 4 April they had broken into a large farm nearby and stolen 150,000 lire, twelve pairs of sheets and some food. Partisan assassination squads in the countryside were known as Squadre di Azione Patriottica (SAP). One partisan writer said that although people in the countryside hated the Fascists, they often did not hesitate to denounce partisans because they wanted to keep away from both sides. Partisan actions had led the Germans to kill many peasants or burn their houses in reprisal.[31]

The Germans launched a big search-and-destroy operation on 6 April, using 20,000 men to try to ferret out partisans on the high ground of Tobbio near Alessandria, and 800 rebels were disarmed. The next day the Germans and Fascists surrounded the old semi-destroyed monastery of Benedicta there and captured seventy-five young men who had escaped the Fascist draft. They were shot in groups of five and their bodies dumped into a large open grave. The Fascists refused to allow relatives to take the bodies, and the prefect of Alessandria said they were 'unworthy of burial'.

In the Tuscan village of Stia, east of Florence, German troops who had been fired upon from the window of a house killed 137 civilians between 13 and 18 April, including every male resident and 45 women and children. Thirteen partisans were shot dead at Villa Bagnara, sixteen at Voltaggio. In Genoa, seventeen were shot on 19 May along with forty-two political detainees.[32]

The Germans calculated that in the nine months between September 1943 and the following May, they had killed, wounded or captured more than 16,000 partisans. Field Marshal Kesselring stated that an intelligence officer reported to him that in the period June–August 1944, the partisans killed 5,000 German soldiers and wounded or kidnapped between 25,000 and 30,000. 'Casualties on the German side greatly exceeded in proportion the total partisan losses,' he said, and attributed this to the fact that the Germans had no training in guerrilla warfare. Kesselring accused the partisans of a 'whole calendar' of crimes, and he divided the partisans into two main categories: professionally trained, gallant men, and criminals and riffraff who robbed, murdered and pillaged wherever and whatever they could. There were, in fact, criminal elements in the partisan movement who joined principally to steal, but Kesselring undoubtedly exaggerated their importance. He said there were partisan-occupied villages and zones in which every man, woman and child was in some way connected with them, but also whole zones that were free of partisans.[33]

Mussolini offered an amnesty to those partisans who would turn themselves in by 25 May, and promised severe military action to wipe out those who failed to comply. The Fascist government claimed 44,000 young men availed themselves of the amnesty. But partisan numbers kept going up, reaching 70,000 to 80,000 in northern Italy and registering big increases in Tuscany and elsewhere in central Italy.[34]

Iris Origo, whose diary gives much of the flavour of life in Italy at the time, wrote on 3 May that punitive expeditions of the SS, especially those of the Hermann Göring Division, had been 'indescribably brutal'. The village of San Pancrazio was burned to the ground, and at San Godenzo women were raped and a child killed. 'Everywhere farms have been plundered and burned,' Origo noted.[35]

Initially, Allied air drops to the partisans were limited, partly by a refusal to believe the partisans could achieve much and partly because the Allies had only 134 planes in the Mediterranean and had to use some of them to supply the Balkans, Eastern Europe and southern France. The Italian partisans were resentful and felt they were being short-changed. In early May 1944, the Eighth Garibaldi Brigade in Romagna theoretically had 8,050 men, but 450 of them were without arms. Five months later, two of every three men in three brigades had no weapons. But Allied respect for the partisans grew as their successes became apparent, and supplies were increased.

Field Marshal Harold Alexander's Allied headquarters at Caserta, near Naples, reported to the Allied governments in May that assistance to the partisans had produced good dividends in terms of bridges blown up, locomotives derailed and Germans killed. The report said large bodies of German and Fascist troops were constantly tied down in trying to curtail partisan activity, and sometimes the enemy forces suffered losses in pitched battles comparable to those they might have sustained in a full-scale Allied attack. The report said the partisan force, which originally had numbered a few thousand, had grown to about 100,000 and the partisans controlled mountain areas while the Germans only held the main roads and railways. Alexander told *The Times* of London that the partisan movement was holding down up to six of the twenty-five German divisions.[36]

Graziani likewise estimated in this period that partisan strength had grown to 82,000, just below that of the Republican National Guard, which had 93,000 men including 48,000 controlled by the Germans. His report said the partisans had begun operating within sight of the big cities and controlled the Alpine and Apennine mountains.[37]

The partisan war, and reprisals by Germans and Fascists, were steadily intensifying. In the second half of 1944, the war reached levels of savagery that had become commonplace among German forces throughout Europe, and partisan units were sometimes guilty of excesses as well. Mussolini's Fascists, often operating beyond his control, also waged war with atavistic brutality. The primary blame for this undoubtedly rested with the Germans and Fascists, whose atrocities beginning after the 1943 armistice spurred the development of the resistance movement.

While the battles raged in the countryside and city streets, Mussolini further stained his record with a policy of partly cooperating in German persecution of the Jews while seeking on occasion to modify the harshness of this policy.

Chapter 10

IL DUCE AND THE JEWS

For Italy a Jewish problem does not exist.

(Benito Mussolini, January 1945)

Benito Mussolini was a racist, but by the standards of his time a mild one. For most of his time in office, he was akin to that familiar bumpkin who stands around the pool hall or village café, making crude antisemitic remarks, but not the oaf who goes out and burns synagogues or desecrates graves. Then you find that despite the bluster he had a couple of Jewish mistresses and he actually protected some Jews, and you wonder just what sort of man this was. As for blacks, he was much harsher in both his views and actions, a virulent racist who didn't mind using poison gas to kill them in Ethiopia, something he never contemplated against white enemies. But hostility toward blacks was fairly commonplace in Italy at the time, as elsewhere, and there was no great outcry in the country over the poison gas attacks.

His most notorious act of antisemitism in the prewar period occurred in 1938 when he announced his Charter of Race. This was harsh by any democratic standard but relatively mild compared to what had happened in Nazi Germany. Jewish children could no longer go to state schools, and Jews were barred from jobs in public administration, schools and universities and were expelled from the armed forces, various professions, banks and state-owned enterprises. Marriage between Catholics and Jews was prohibited. This was accompanied by a number of humiliating decrees that, among other things, prohibited the publication of Jewish funeral announcements in newspapers, barred Jews from listings in telephone directories and prohibited them from working in the entertainment field or from holding jobs as obstetricians or nurses. Texts written by Jews were eliminated from schoolbooks, and Jewish names were removed from streets. Plaques honouring Jewish benefactors were removed from hospitals and asylums. Mussolini also ordered Count Galeazzo Ciano, then his foreign minister, to recall Jewish diplomats stationed abroad to Rome. Ciano did so, and ordered that Jews employed locally by diplomatic missions be dismissed.[1]

The Duce appeared to have decided on these measures less out of conviction than from a desire to ingratiate himself with Hitler. The regime declared Italians were Aryans and 'Jews do not belong to the Italian race'. But, as has been noted previously, Mussolini at an earlier stage had two Jewish mistresses, Angelica Balabanoff and Margherita Sarfatti, and he helped Sarfatti to emigrate to the United States when she found his legislation too onerous. A few months before his laws were enacted, he had had a sudden outburst of racial consciousness, declaring the Mussolinis were 'Nordics', sharing racial characteristics with the English and Germans. He said Edda Mussolini's marriage to the Tuscan Ciano and Vittorio's marriage to a Lombard demonstrated the instinct of his family to ally with people 'who were purer from a racial point of view'.[2]

In the view of the British Special Forces officer Max Salvadori, who had spent much of his life in Italy, among Italians who had lived through the First World War and thus resented the Germans, Mussolini's racial laws were proof that Italy was becoming a province of the German empire.[3] It was a point Mussolini failed to comprehend. His policy towards the Jews may have been erratic in some respects, but it was consistently and slavishly opportunistic.

Before 1938, he had occasionally fulminated against Jews but had denied there was a Jewish problem in Italy and had taken no action against them. A number of prominent Jews were among the early supporters of fascism and helped finance the movement.

In the 1930s, Mussolini told Vittorio: 'We have not invented the Jewish problem and as regards racism the Jews can give us some credit.' He said he had received Chaim Weizmann, the head of the Zionist movement, three times and told him he was not opposed to a Jewish state in Palestine. On another occasion, he agreed to give refuge to Jews fleeing Germany. 'But I don't hide from you,' he said, 'that the collusion of the Jewish world with the plutocracy and international left is ever more evident, and our politico-military situation doesn't permit us to keep in our bosom eventual saboteurs of the effort that the Italian people are making.' Then he appeared to contradict himself: 'For another thing it is not a serious problem: the Jews in Italy are not more than 50,000 [out of a population of forty-four million], and not a hair of any of them will be harmed.'[4]

After his 1935–6 Ethiopian war, he had noticed that large numbers of Jews were among those who were critical of the war. 'World Jewry is doing a bad business in aligning itself with the anti-Fascist sanctions campaign against the one European country which, at least until now, has neither practised nor preached antisemitism,' he said.[5] At about the same time, speaking to

Elisabetta Cerruti, wife of one of his ambassadors, he was contemptuous of the Nazi attitude towards Jews, saying it was a serious historical mistake and would have grievous consequences. 'Fancy, they went so far with their persecutions that the bishop of Nice felt called upon to pray for the Jews in his church,' he said.[6]

* * *

After Italy had entered the war at Germany's side in 1940, Mussolini resisted pressures to further emulate Nazi racial laws. In the Italian zone of occupation in southern France, Italian officials cancelled an order by the French Vichy regime set up with Hitler's blessing that required Jews to wear the Star of David emblem. Likewise, Italians in Dalmatia gave protection to Jews who had fled to their zone to escape persecution by the Croatian Nazi regime of Ante Pavelic.[7]

After Mussolini's overthrow in July 1943, Badoglio allowed his racial laws to remain on the books. Badoglio said he could not abrogate them without a violent clash with the Germans, but he told Jewish leaders the laws would remain a dead letter. Some minor modifications were made, and Jewish community leaders expressed hope the government would abrogate the laws. But that was before the government fled south. There were 14,000 Jewish refugees in Italy at the time, many coming from Germany, and plans were afoot to arrange the entry of 15,000 others from the Italian zone of France so they could be evacuated to Algeria, Tunisia and Morocco. The announcement of the Italian surrender on 8 September, followed by Germany's decision to make the whole of Italy an occupied territory, scuttled those plans. Several hundred Jews in France did cross the Alps to take refuge in Italy, but some were later captured by the Germans.[8]

In his new republic, humiliated by the Germans and thoroughly disillusioned with them, would Mussolini reverse his anti-Jewish measures as a way of thumbing his nose at the Nazis? He would not. Throughout his remaining months in power, he remained as equivocal as he had been in the past, denying he was antisemitic but acquiescing in or promoting antisemitic measures. His silence was his greatest crime. Never did he protest to Hitler over the Nazi pogrom in Rome, the subsequent German deportation of other Italian Jews or Germany's treatment of Jews elsewhere. Standing up to Hitler on this question would have been a bold stroke of independence, but Mussolini lacked the moral courage to do so. This was one of the most severe blots on the record of a man who claimed to have returned to power to save his people from German excesses. His people did not include Jews.

Yet many Jews convinced themselves the new government would not take harsh measures against them. At Ferrara, Jews were concentrated in one wing of the city jail, and when the building was damaged in an Allied bombardment, the Jews escaped. After the bombardment, they returned and handed themselves over to Fascist authorities. A *modus vivendi* was then established: whenever there was bombing, the Jews could take refuge elsewhere, but afterwards they came back to the jail. A handful fled, but the rest eventually ended up in a concentration camp.[9]

In a speech at Gargnano on 14 October 1943, Mussolini denounced 'the voracity of Jewish capitalism, which is aiming at . . . the scientific exploitation of the world'. In his new republic, this was his only publicly spoken reference to the 'Jewish peril'. In thirty-nine articles he wrote for his occasional publication, *Corrispondenza repubblicana*, he mentioned Jews only seven times.[10]

In November 1943, the Fascist Party Congress in Verona adopted its eighteen-point manifesto whose seventh point stated: 'Those belonging to the Jewish race are foreigners. During this war they belong to an enemy nationality.' This was drafted by Mussolini with the help of Pavolini and Nicola Bombacci, a former Communist and friend of Lenin's who had gravitated to fascism and become one of the Duce's closest associates. Buffarini followed this up on 30 November by decreeing that all Jews resident on the national territory must be arrested, with their property seized and handed over to people made indigent by Allied air raids. Those citizens born of mixed marriages between Jews and Christians were to be subject to special vigilance but not jailed. Buffarini's son Glauco later claimed his father timed the publication of this decree to give Jews twenty-four hours in which to flee the country or hide, and thousands did so. Buffarini was apparently willing to leave the Jews enough money to live on, especially those who were old and sick, but Finance Minister Pellegrini-Giampietro was implacable, pointing out that the regime needed money and the Jews had money.

The final part of Buffarini's communiqué was omitted in Fascist radio and newspaper reports; it said Jews were to be put in provincial concentration camps. Some Fascists said later the purpose of concentrating Jews in camps was to save them from deportation by the Germans, a foolish intention if true because the gathering of Jews in camps merely facilitated eventual deportations. On 10 December, Police Chief Tullio Tamburini instructed province chiefs to exempt from internment certain Jews, including the aged, the sick, those who had been 'Aryanised' and those with Aryan spouses.[11]

In December, Mussolini, while ignoring the republic's anti-Jewish measures, repented of his earlier policy in a conversation with his journalist friend Bruno Spampanato, saying his 1938 Charter of Race could have been avoided. It was, he said, 'a scrupulous German essay translated into bad

Italian. . . . I have always considered the Italian people an admirable product of diverse ethnic fusions on the basis of a geographic, economic and especially spiritual oneness. . . . Men who had different blood were the carriers of a unique, splendid civilisation. This is why I am far from the Rosenberg myth. This is also a position to be corrected.'[12] Little that followed bore out these noble intentions.

Mussolini's most expansive comments on Jews were made to his German doctor Zachariae, and were quoted in the doctor's memoirs. Typically, they included expressions of respect for Jews coupled with blatantly antisemite remarks. He declared:

> The Jew succeeds very well in camouflaging himself and no one perceives the noose that he puts on the neck of his victim. For Italy a Jewish problem doesn't exist, since in Italy there are very few Jews and they in general have not succeeded in occupying the key posts of the economy that instead they possess in America and in other European countries, and possessed especially in Germany before Hitler came to power. Since they have succeeded in concentrating in their hands, beyond the money market, also the newspapers, the radio and the great networks of trade, they possess still today a force very superior to their importance and numerical efficiency. I am not antisemitic and recognise that Jewish scientists and technicians have given to the world exceptional individuality. However, I judge it necessary to try to limit the decisive Jewish influence and the domination of the Jews in every field of production and capital. . . . I cannot approve the manner with which the Jewish problem has been resolved in Germany, since the methods adopted are not reconcilable with the free life of the civil world and redound to the damage of German honour. But still I must recognise that some incidents have been provoked by Jews, although certainly not in a way such as to justify the Nazi violence.

He went on to say that Jews 'with their typical lack of scruples' had unleashed bloody wars so as to acquire the riches of other countries.[13]

* * *

In Germany, the renegade priest Giovanni Preziosi had received a sympathetic hearing from Hitler and Goebbels, and he remained behind to spout a continuous flow of venom against Jews and Masons over Radio Munich, the station that broadcast to Italian listeners. On 30 October 1943, he lashed out at 'Jew-lovers' of the Salò Republic, naming among them Fascist Party

Secretary Pavolini and Interior Minister Guido Buffarini-Guidi. Just seven days earlier, Mussolini had told Rudolf von Rahn, the German ambassador, that Preziosi was a 'loyal' friend and 'an expert on the Masonic-Jewish question'. The German consul Moellhausen said many Italians believed Preziosi had the evil eye, and Moellhausen described him as 'mean, vindictive, wretched . . . incapable of speaking well of other people. . . . Preziosi was the true incarnation of hate.' Moellhausen said Rahn would willingly have interned in an insane asylum 'that authentic psychopath and excommunicated priest, whose ill-omened influence was evident in all fields'.[14]

Preziosi had been anti-German as a young man, and wrote a book attacking the Germans. In 1920, when he was thirty-nine, he started to give his first signs of antisemitism, describing all Jews as enemies of Italy and naming among them three men who were not Jewish – Woodrow Wilson, David Lloyd George and Georges Clemenceau. Later he translated from German the infamous and bogus antisemitic tract, *Protocols of the Elders of Zion*. Before coming to power, Hitler wrote an article for Preziosi's publication, *Vita Italiana*, signing it 'a Bavarian'. On the day Mussolini was overthrown in 1943, Preziosi flew to Germany and met with Hitler, accusing Mussolini of being weak, faulty in his judgement of people and surrounded by Freemasons.[15] Leading personalities with Jewish sympathies, he told Hitler, included Mussolini himself, his daughter Edda, his son-in-law Count Ciano, Buffarini, Pavolini and Giovanni Marinelli, former administrative secretary of the Fascist Party.

Preziosi sent Mussolini a twelve-page memorandum on 31 January 1944, calling for the 'total elimination' of Jews, half-breeds and Jew-tainted Gentiles from Italian life. Mussolini was furious when he received the memorandum and described Preziosi as 'a repulsive creature, a real figure of an unfrocked priest'.[16] Eventually he adopted toward Preziosi what could now be described as the Lyndon Johnson solution. That is, as the American president said of one of his opponents, he decided it would be better to have Preziosi inside the tent pissing out rather than outside the tent pissing in. On 15 March the Duce appointed Preziosi as inspector-general of race, but limited him to an office staff of four and very modest funds.

Preziosi devised a new racial code modelled on the Nazi Nuremberg laws, but according to Meir Michaelis, a leading authority on the Italian Jews, he never advocated the extermination of the Jews. He proposed barring marriage or procreation between those of Italian blood and those of foreign or mixed blood, excluding Jews from every public, professional and artistic activity and confiscating what remained of their property. His draft legislation, never adopted, defined Italian citizens as those whose antecedents, going back to 1800, 'are of the white Caucasian race and immune from cross-breeding with Jews'. Buffarini wrote to Mussolini protesting that if the legislation were adopted all Italians born in provinces occupied by the Allies and therefore unable to furnish documentation of their racial purity would be automatically suspected of being Jewish. Almost all government ministers and under-secretaries would have to be dismissed and imprisoned, he said, because they were related to Jews and Masons. 'This law is an aberration,' he told the Duce, and Mussolini agreed. He told Eithel Moellhausen 'that Preziosi wants to create Jews for the pleasure of persecuting them'.

On 5 June Preziosi persuaded the SS to confiscate from the Ministry of the Interior the archives that had been taken from Jewish communities and synagogues, and a census of Jews that had been carried out in 1938. Four months later, he insisted on having in his possession the archives of all Italian synagogues.[17]

* * *

The Germans had made clear, with the Rome pogrom of September 1943, that they were determined to encompass Italian Jews in the roundups and deportations that were occurring elsewhere in conquered Europe. Eichmann sent two extermination experts, Theodor Dannecker and Friedrich Bosshammer, to carry out this grim task. When Dannecker had completed the Rome operation, they extended their activities to central and northern Italy. Mussolini and Buffarini argued that Italian law exempted all Jewish members of mixed families and those over seventy years of age. Bosshammer disputed this, complained that the Salò laws were not rigid enough and demanded that even Jews who had converted to Christianity be included in the roundups.

Iris Origo, the Anglo-American woman living in Tuscany at the time, wrote in her diary about German roundups of Jews in Florence. 'Many are hiding in friends' houses,' she said. 'Even those who were lying in bed in hospital, and some old men and women of over seventy, were hunted down, while the houses of those who had previously been left alone have been burned or looted.' This sort of persecution went on elsewhere within the domain of the Salò Republic.

An emissary of Bosshammer's visited Giuseppe Jona, president of the Jewish community in Venice, and demanded a list of all the 2,000 Jews living there. Jona promised to comply and asked him to come back the next day. During the night, Jona warned all Venetian Jews to go into hiding. Then he destroyed the list and committed suicide.[18]

Tried after the war, Bosshammer said he was opposed to mass murder but favoured the evacuation of Jews to the East for 'security reasons'. He had deported inmates of Italian mental hospitals and homes for the aged, and he sent Jews with Aryan spouses to their death in violation of Fascist laws.[19]

Some Fascist officials cooperated zealously with the Germans in hunting down Jews; Renzo De Felice, Mussolini's chief Italian biographer, wrote that hundreds of documents examined after the war demonstrated that military and government officials of the republic collaborated with the Germans on a vast scale and were responsible for the extermination of thousands of Jews. At the trial of Adolf Eichmann in Israel after the war, Herbert Kappler, the former Gestapo chief in Rome, testified that after October 1943 all arrests of Jews in Italy were made not by Germans but by Italians.[20]

The notorious Celeste di Porto, a Roman Jewish woman known as the Black Panther, betrayed to the Nazis for 5,000 lire each the whereabouts of fifty Jews, including twenty-six who were killed in the Ardeatine caves massacre. After the war she was sentenced to twelve years in prison, but was then given a pardon covering five of those years. She later married, became a Catholic and appeared to have repented of her crimes.[21] On 3 February Rome Police Chief Pietro Caruso permitted his men to raid the Roman basilica of St Paul's Outside the Walls, which enjoyed extraterritorial immunity under the Lateran Pacts, and seize six Jews who had taken refuge there, including two who were Swiss. Mussolini rebuked Caruso after Pope Pius had protested over this violation.[22]

But there were Fascists who were sympathetic to the plight of the Jews. The famed Jewish art expert Bernard Berenson, hiding out in the hills above Florence during the Nazi occupation of the city, recorded in his diary that the Fascist prefect of Florence privately warned Jews when he took up his post to leave their homes and go into hiding. Some German officials joined with Italians in undermining the anti-Jewish policy. The German consul in Florence, Gerhard Wolf, and Fascist Police Chief Virgilio Soldani Benzi knew that Berenson was in hiding at the home of the Marquis Filippo Serlupi Crescenzi, the ambassador to the Vatican of the tiny state of San Marino. But Wolf and Soldani spread the word that Berenson had fled to Portugal. Wolf, a career diplomat, a Catholic and a secret anti-Nazi from Munich, was given honorary citizenship by the city of Florence in 1946.[23]

Many Italians – at the risk of their own lives – did all they could to help the Jews, providing them with hiding places and false documents, and some of these benefactors were jailed and shot as a result.[24] In Florence, a parish priest was arrested for harbouring a Jew, but was released when Cardinal Elia Dalla Costa went to the authorities, declaring he was the real culprit and requesting to be jailed in place of the priest. Of course, no Fascist official was about to arrest a prince of the church, as Dalla Costa well knew. A Florentine Jewish woman who testified at Eichmann's trial in Jerusalem said: 'Every Italian Jew who survived owed his life to the Italians.'[25]

The main Fascist concentration camp set up under Buffarini's decree was at Fossoli, near Modena in northern Italy, on land that was lacking in vegetation. Life for the Jews interned there was not pleasant but far from the harsh conditions that prevailed in German camps. Almost all those interned received food parcels from friends and relatives to supplement the meagre camp rations. Among the prisoners were a ninety-year-old woman, Elena Servi, sent there by Bosshammer, and Primo Levi, who was later transferred to Auschwitz and after the war wrote a classic of Holocaust literature, *If This Is a Man*. Levi had left his home in Turin and tried to set up a group of partisans in the mountains but was captured in December 1943 by a Fascist militia group.[26]

Buffarini instructed his officials to impress on the Germans the need for Jews held in Italian camps to remain there. But in January 1944 the Germans took over the camps and SS units arrived on 20 February, ordering all the Jews in Fossoli to be ready for departure the following day. Their destination was Auschwitz.[27] Dannecker's operations throughout northern Italy resulted in the deportation of about 2,000 Jews. Contrary to Fascist laws, the deportees included Jews married to non-Jews, sick people, the aged and the insane.

At the end of July 1944, with the Allies advancing in central Italy, the Gestapo decided to evacuate the camp at Fossoli and opened a new one near Bolzano, close to the Austrian border. The last of the Jews in the Fossoli camp were hurriedly deported. With bridges across the Po river knocked out by Allied bombing, they were taken across in boats and from Verona were sent to concentration camps in Germany and Poland. Jews continued to be sent to Auschwitz from the Bolzano camp until 24 October 1944. But other Jews were sent to camps in Germany as late as February 1945.[28]

Meir Michaelis reported that there were 44,500 Jews in Italy and Italian-occupied Rhodes at the time of the 8 September 1943 armistice, and about 12,500 of them were foreigners. By the end of the war, he said, at least 7,683 had perished, including the 173 murdered on Italian soil. But more than four-fifths of Italian Jews survived the war.[29] Between 2,000 and 3,000 Jews fought in the resistance, and the postwar government posthumously awarded seven of them the Gold Medal. More than 5,000 Jews escaped to Switzerland during the last period of Mussolini's rule. Another 4,000 had fled there earlier or had escaped to liberated areas in the south.

Mussolini's Socialist friend Carlo Silvestri said the Duce was aware that the prefect of Milan, Piero Parini, had saved the Jewish lawyer Leone Del Vecchio, his family and other Jews. 'In effect, they lived in Milan under the protection of Mussolini,' Silvestri said. He claimed Mussolini and Graziani also kept safe numerous Jews who had not wanted to leave Italy.[30]

The Germans had their own concentration camps in Italy. In the one at Bolzano, prisoners were divided into four categories: dangerous political, nondangerous political, hostages and Jews.[31] Another camp was established in a rice factory at San Sabba, near Trieste, and was a staging post for Jews in transit to Dachau, principally from Dalmatia. Some Italian historians have claimed that San Sabba contained the only gas chamber on Italian territory, but Richard Lamb, a British military historian who investigated the claim, said it was not true. He said the camp had a large furnace for drying rice and that was used not to incinerate Jews but to burn the bodies of some partisans killed in fighting and brought there by truck.[32]

By January 1944, when the Nazi holocaust machine was moving into top gear, Mussolini was claiming to see a worldwide Jewish conspiracy against Italy and Germany. 'Now these Jews of the entire world have surrounded our nations with an insidious and very tenacious ditch and in the calculus of the struggle it is necessary to recognise that they are valid and feared enemies,' he told his friend Nino D'Aroma. But he said that, 'as a Christian', he considered unduly harsh legislation against Jews to have been 'a formidable stupidity. Stupidities in politics are paid in small change, that is, dearly and for a long time.'[33]

That last remark was puzzling, for in the same month a Fascist decree prohibited Jews from owning shares or land and ordered their property to be sequestrated. A partisan report in April said province chiefs in Piedmont and Liguria had issued 45,850 orders to seize the property of Jews. In June, Finance Minister Pellegrini-Giampietro told the Duce that seizures by then had included 75,089,047.90 lire in bank deposits, 36,396,831 lire in stock in state-owned companies, 731,442,219 lire in private industrial shares, 855,348,608 lire in furnishings and 198,300,003 lire in factory holdings. The seizures were partly determined by the precarious economic condition of the government.[34]

On 2 March, a further decree ordered the sequestration of works of art held by Jews, including Jewish organisations. By the end of 1944, the Fascists had seized about 1.9 billion lire worth of Jewish property, and by the time the regime collapsed about 8,000 confiscation orders had been issued. Pietro Koch, a particularly notorious Fascist militia leader, sacked the Milan synagogue. The whole treasure of Florence's synagogue was found by Fascist Republican National Guard members in farmhouses near Fiesole and Prato and was confiscated.[35]

Mussolini's Cabinet, at its last meeting on 16 April 1945, adopted legislation to dissolve the Union of Jewish Communities and to suppress all Jewish welfare organisations.[36] So much for a man who thought that 'for Italy, a Jewish problem does not exist'.

Chapter 11

THE LIBERATION OF ROME

Rome is Italy, Italy is Rome.

(Benito Mussolini, June 1944)

The Swiss journalist M. de Wyss went out onto the streets of Rome on the afternoon of 4 June 1944 and witnessed a scene she had almost despaired of ever seeing. 'The Huns are retreating!' she wrote excitedly in her diary when she rushed back home. 'The Huns are leaving the city!' After 268 days of a harsh German occupation, Field Marshal Kesselring had decided, against the orders of Hitler and against the will of his own army and Mussolini, to abandon the Eternal City and establish a new battle line to the north, sparing Rome the destruction that would have resulted from street-to-street fighting. He had communicated his intentions to Pope Pius XII before he also abandoned his own headquarters at Frascati, in the Alban Hills south east of Rome.[1]

It was a bedraggled, chaotic German fighting force that made its way lumberingly out of Rome over the ancient roads leading north. The evacuation had actually begun on the night of 2 June when thousands of cows and oxen were driven through the city en route to the north, accompanied by a large number of trucks. Now more trucks and wagons, carts and peasant vehicles crammed with dead-tired German soldiers were streaming along the same route. One soldier rode an ox. Then came endless rows of those on foot. 'Their faces gray with fatigue, eyes popping out, mouths wide open, they limped, barefoot, dragging their rifles after them,' de Wyss observed.

The Marchioness Fulvia Ripa di Meana watched the same dispirited procession. 'In rags, dirty, dispersed, often wounded, the Nazis cross Rome on foot, while the citizens watch the sad spectacle, amazed and impassable,' she wrote.

Peter Tompkins, a bilingual American spy who had been in Rome since the time of the Anzio invasion, noted: 'The Germans . . . are leaving in a pathetic state. Some are trying to get away with cars that no longer have tires, driving on the rims. One motorcyclist had a flat tire but went right on. Some were on bicycles, but the most pathetic were the ones on foot who had been walking so long they could hardly stand.' A few hours earlier, as the Germans were abandoning their headquarters in the city, an informant told Tompkins that General Mälzer, the German commander of Rome, was 'stinking drunk, speaking in lamentable French, the place in complete confusion'.[2]

Allied planes showered leaflets on Rome during the day, urging people to do all they could to prevent destruction of the city. The leaflets said they should protect power stations and railways and remove street barriers so Allied troops could pursue the retreating Germans. Crowds of Romans gathered on the steps of churches or sat at the tables of the few cafés still open, awaiting their deliverers. The last of the Germans tried to make a little money before the exodus, selling typewriters on the Via Veneto for 1,000 lire apiece and cars at bargain prices ranging from 25,000 to 40,000 lire. These Germans, Tompkins said, wanted to collect enough money to buy civilian clothes with which to hide out or desert.[3]

That morning, when the German retreat began and the guards had disappeared, thousands of political prisoners, Jews and ordinary criminals were freed from Rome's Regina Coeli jail by their determined friends and relatives. Some of the freed prisoners wandered the city in rags, starry-eyed, hardly able to believe what had happened. The Mussolini Barracks in Prati, near the Vatican, was evacuated by its Fascist battalion, going out with the Germans, and was sacked by women and children. On Via Flaminia, departing Germans had been distributing food shortly before Fascists, following them in trucks, shot into a crowd on the same street and killed three women.

Before they departed, the Germans carried out the last of their own atrocities. At 4 p.m. a man, stripped naked, was shot publicly in front of the Quirinale Palace, and Tompkins learned that four others had been summarily executed. A Gestapo truck carried fourteen prisoners out of Rome on the ancient Via Cassia and, at the kilometre 10 (six mile) marker, the truck stopped, and the men were marched off to the side of the road and shot. They included one English prisoner and Bruno Buozzi, the secretary of one of Italy's leading trade unions.

As the last of the Germans disappeared from the city, partisans moved in to take over ministries, barracks, bridges and the radio station without a struggle.[4] Then, as the dying rays of the sun touched Rome, a young girl raced across a piazza and told Tompkins that the Americans were at St Paul's Outside the Walls, the great church on the southern outskirts of the city.

'How do you know?' he asked.

'Because one of them gave a man a can of meat and beans,' she replied.

Tompkins commented: 'Some thought this was a rumour, but I knew damned well it was the truth. . . . Only a GI could be dishing out those goddamn "C" rations to the populace!'

In the faint light of early evening, he made his way to the Piazza Venezia, the great square in which thousands had once gathered to cheer the speeches of Mussolini, and saw a wide semicircle of GI halftracks and Jeeps beneath the balcony from which the Duce harangued his followers. 'The Fifth Army had entered Rome,' he said.[5]

Mother Mary St Luke, who had stayed in Rome through the occupation, looked out of a window from the residence she shared with other nuns near the Via Veneto:

> The electric light which had been cut off was turned on abruptly, and uncurtained windows flashed out brightly like a signal of liberation to come. . . . Suddenly, from the direction of Porta Pia, came a burst of wild cheering. The Allies had entered Rome. . . . There was talk and laughter in all the streets, even in the narrowest ones; there was cheering and the sound of clapping everywhere.
>
> The column that came through Porta Pia, and whose welcome we heard, went straight on through the city in pursuit of the enemy, and did not even stop for food or rest. There was fighting on some of the bridges. At about 11 p.m. some Americans fell at Ponte Sublicio, and on Ponte Margherita German dead lay all night. . . . An exuberant Italian rushed forward, took an embarrassed American infantryman in his arms, kissed him on both cheeks and returned home with the bridge of his nose severely cut by the rim of his hero's helmet.[6]

Rome had become the first European capital liberated by the Allies, just two days before the historic Allied landings on the beaches of Normandy, and its loss was a huge psychological trauma for Mussolini, 'one of the most severe blows he suffered in his life', according to Rachele. 'Much of his confidence which had been regained dissolved in a flash and the phenomenon of the partisans appeared more serious. Mussolini's soul was wounded by the tragic spectacle of Italians fighting other Italians.' He told Rachele: 'Rome is Italy, Italy is Rome. I tried to ensure the food provisions until the last. It was all I could do for the beloved Roman people.' These were, of course, the same people he had denounced as ungrateful some months earlier. Mussolini ordered three days of national mourning, exhorted his people to stand firm and, in this moment of supreme defeat for his own cause, he gave vent to a crude racial comment more worthy of the racist extremist Giovanni Preziosi than of a national leader. In an article for his

Corrispondenza repubblicana, he wrote: 'The thought that coloured troops are bivouacked between the Colosseum and Piazza del Popolo assails our spirit and gives us a suffering that from hour to hour is made more acute. The Negroes have passed under the arches and on the streets that were built to exalt the old and new glories of Rome.' Fascist newspapers in the north began publishing cartoons showing black soldiers stealing from the altars of churches and raping women.[7]

Mussolini had got wind of Kesselring's plans to abandon Rome several days before it happened, and he sent an emissary to ask him to make an all-out defence of the capital. Kesselring replied in tones of irony: 'I thank Mussolini for the invitation. I am, however, sorry not to be able to accept because of the small number of divisions at my disposal.' The Germans pointed out that evacuation would preserve the historic and artistic value of the city, but Mussolini replied that in war those who want to win 'do not act as though they are visiting a museum'. According to the SS Colonel Eugen Dollmann, he grudgingly agreed that any last-minute fighting should be limited to the zone along the Tiber bridges, as he considered the historic and artistic value of those quarters of little importance.

Hitler had sent orders to Kesselring at midnight on 3 June, ordering him to defend the city until the last German soldier had left and to blow up the Tiber bridges to facilitate his retreat. But Kesselring refused to destroy the bridges.

After Kesselring had decided to abandon Rome without a fight, the Germans, acting on orders from Hitler, asked Mussolini if their communiqué should say this decision was taken at his request. He replied with an indignant 'no'.[8]

President Roosevelt announced the fall of Rome in one of his famous fireside radio broadcasts to the American people on 5 June. 'Yesterday, on June fourth, 1944, Rome fell to American and Allied troops,' he said. 'The first of the Axis capitals is now in our hands. One up and two to go!'

He gave no thanks to the Germans for sparing Rome the devastation that had been wreaked on Naples and other Italian cities. 'The Allied generals maneuvered so skillfully that the Nazis could only have stayed long enough to damage Rome at the risk of losing their armies,' he said. Then he described the miserable condition in which the liberating troops found the people of Rome.

'In Italy the people had lived so long under the corrupt rule of Mussolini that, in spite of the tinsel at the top . . . their economic condition had grown steadily worse. Our troops have found starvation, malnutrition, disease, a deteriorating education and lowered public health – all by-products of the Fascist misrule. . . . We have already begun to save the lives of the men, women and children of Rome.'[9]

The following day, Prime Minister Winston Churchill addressed the House of Commons: 'This is a memorable and glorious event.' Like Roosevelt, he said the liberation had saved Rome from famine.

But Field Marshal Alexander, the Allied commander based at Caserta, was less than jubilant. He wrote in his memoirs that he had instructed General Mark W. Clark, the commander of the American Fifth Army, to attack the German main supply line to troops still holding out at Cassino, but instead Clark switched his point of attack north to the Alban Hills, then marched on to Rome. Alexander contended that his own plan would have resulted in the destruction of most of the German forces south of Rome. 'I can only assume that the immediate lure of Rome for its publicity value persuaded him to switch the direction of his advance,' he said.[10]

When the German occupation of Rome began in September 1943, many residents thought it would last only a few days, or weeks at the most, before the Allies came to their rescue. The following nine months, as has been noted previously, tested their resilience to the limits. A city of 1.5 million had taken on an extra 1 million people, refugees from the countryside and surrounding towns being bombed by the Allies, which had put a further strain on food stocks. Most refugees had no food ration cards and depended on a Vatican relief effort that was never able fully to meet the needs of all. In addition to near-starvation, the Romans had had to put up with German theft of property, German attempts to impress them into labour service, German and Fascist arrests and torture and, of course, the terrible pogrom against the Jewish community.

De Wyss noted in her diary on 30 January: 'People look hungry and frozen. Many young boys go barefoot. . . . Everybody cares only for food.' Later she wrote: 'There is starvation in the city. Dog meat costs 40 lire a kilo. . . . People are selling all they possess to get food.' Mother Mary wrote on 31 May: 'The lack of food has had an alarmingly slimming effect on everyone in Rome, not only on the poor. . . . It gives one a heartache to see it.'[11]

The Romans had not accepted all this passively. Just days after the occupation began, Mother Mary reported that on the night of 18 September twenty-three Germans had been killed on Monte Mario, a hill overlooking Rome. Later she said that people in one of the slum suburbs had thrown spikes onto roads, flattening German tyres; phone wires in the city had been cut; and hundreds of inscriptions had appeared on walls of buildings: 'Long live Russia', 'Stalin and communism', 'Down with the Germans', 'Mussolini and fascism'. On 18 December, she reported that some Germans having dinner in a café were killed by a partisan bomb, and another bomb went off in a lift shaft of the German-occupied Hotel Flora on the Via Veneto, killing a soldier and one woman. Another bomb in a cinema killed one civilian, and hand grenades were thrown into a German barracks. A detachment of former Carabinieri, dressed in Fascist police uniforms, entered the San Gregorio prison on the Caelian hill and presented false orders for the handover of prisoners. They escaped with six prisoners.[12]

The Germans and the Fascists reacted to the resistance by raids on ecclesiastical institutions harbouring people who had sought protection there. Under the Lateran Accords Mussolini had signed with the Vatican before the war, these institutions were supposed to enjoy extraterritorial immunity from such acts. But on 23 December, Fascist police and the Gestapo raided the Lombard Seminary and the Pontifical Russian College, capturing some partisans and Jews and stealing watches, cameras and money. After the pope had protested to the German ambassador to the Holy See, they released nine of the twelve men they had captured at the Lombard Seminary, but kept the well-known Communist trade union leader Giovanni Roveda and two other men. Then, on 4 February 1944, as noted in the previous chapter, Fascist Police Chief Pietro Caruso led his men in a raid on the abbey of St Paul's Outside the Walls. They ransacked the building, smashed furniture, slashed pictures with knives and arrested sixty-two men who had taken refuge there. Six were Jews, including two who were Swiss.[13]

In March, a pregnant woman went to a Fascist barracks and begged permission to see her husband, who had been arrested so he could be used for forced labour. A Fascist guard shot and killed her. Roman men who witnessed the killing shouted 'murderer' at the guard, and Fascist police attacked them. The men brought out arms and killed five of the Fascists.

A few days later, a partisan bomb destroyed a truck loaded with petrol not far from the Palatine Hill that overlooks the Roman Forum. Ten prisoners were taken from the Regina Coeli jail and shot in reprisal.

In May, the Germans, who had been torturing prisoners at the Gestapo headquarters in Via Tasso, opened another torture house in the Pensione Jaccarino. 'People living nearby hear screams and groans and say it is diabolical,' wrote Mother Mary.

On 3 February and again on 16 February, General Mälzer marched long columns of Allied prisoners through the most crowded parts of Rome, up the Corso and from there to the Colosseum, where the men were put in trucks. The parading of prisoners was a violation of the Geneva Conventions, and one of the crimes for which Mälzer was tried after the war. Many prisoners gave a 'V' sign to onlookers, and one Italian man was arrested for giving a prisoner a cigarette.

Not only was food in short supply in the city; coal for heating had become virtually non-existent. Many Romans cut down trees for fuel, or carried away park benches at night.

All the while, the Allies kept up bombing and machine-gun attacks on the city and many civilians were killed. In one raid on 18 March, sixty people aboard a tram were killed in Piazza Bologna. The notorious Fascist propagandist Virginio Gayda, who edited the newspaper *Giornale d'Italia*, was killed when a bomb hit his house.[14]

When the Allies entered Rome, they found water supplies had long been cut off from private houses, and people spent much of their day lined up to collect water from public fountains. A friend in Rome told Iris Origo that handcarts went from house to house in the city, selling flasks of water at prices that once would have seemed expensive for wine. Part of Rome was without electric lights. Some trams still ran but there were no buses. Pharmacies had almost completely run out of medicines. The economy had returned to a barter system, with shopkeepers selling some items only in exchange for food.[15]

On 5 June, the day after the liberation, crowds of Romans flooded into St Peter's Square at dawn and again later in the morning, calling for the pope. On both occasions he appeared at his study window and gave them his blessing. Authorities advertised that the pope would speak to the people of Rome in the evening, and they streamed into the square from all over the city. The bells in Rome's 400 churches pealed, and more than 100,000 people had gathered by nightfall. In his speech, the pope asked the people to put aside feelings of anger and revenge, and he thanked the 'mutual collaboration' of Germans and Allies for having spared Rome physical damage.

'For many it was a matter of five or six miles there and back, not to mention standing in the piazza,' Mother Mary wrote. 'But apparently no one minded. Quite the contrary. They didn't mind anything. Fascism was gone; Nazism was gone; and the horror of war had passed from Rome.'[16]

With the fall of Rome, King Victor Emmanuel stepped aside in favour of Crown Prince Umberto, who was named Lieutenant of the Realm. Umberto asked Badoglio to form a new government, but Italian opposition parties – with tacit American approval – demanded Badoglio's resignation. He yielded at a Cabinet meeting in Rome on 4 June and Ivanoe Bonomi, aged seventy, a conservative Socialist, was appointed as his successor.

In a telegram to Roosevelt on 10 June, Churchill grumbled: 'I think it is a great disaster that Badoglio should be replaced by this group of aged and hungry politicians. I thought it was understood he would go on until we could bring the north in. Instead we are confronted with this absolutely unrepresentative collection . . . without the slightest pretence of a popular mandate.'

The irony of these remarks evidently escaped Churchill. At the age of seventy, he denigrated other 'aged politicians'. He spoke of their lack of a popular mandate, as though Badoglio enjoyed one. Two days later Stalin told Churchill he also had been opposed to replacing Badoglio. But Roosevelt, in a telegram to Churchill on 15 June, said it would have been 'a grave mistake' not to permit the Bonomi Cabinet to be promptly installed. 'The Rome CLN seems to be the best available channel existing in Italy today for the expression of the popular will.' Churchill gave in. The Allies transferred the new government to Salerno, but it was allowed to return to Rome on 15 July.[17]

Chapter 12

A Terrible Summer

We will pay very dearly for the blood of Piazzale Loreto.

(Benito Mussolini referring to a Fascist atrocity in Milan, August 1944)

By the summer of 1944, Italy was in the grip of two wars that were only partially distinct in territorial terms: Allies versus Germans and Fascists, mainly in the south but now moving rapidly into central Italy, and partisans versus Germans and Fascists, from just north of Rome to the Alps. Much of the country was being hammered by Allied bombing, and the clash between partisans and Fascists had developed into an increasingly ferocious civil war, as partisan numbers rose steadily and their armament and equipment improved. Innocent Italian civilians were increasingly the victims of savage atrocities carried out by combatants on both sides of the conflict, and the Salò Republic was in a state of gradual disintegration with little popular support remaining. This ancient land, stained with blood repeatedly through the centuries, was undergoing the most severe trial in its history.

'After the fall of Rome [the partisans] became more aggressive, far more in fact than I had reckoned with, and this date may be called the birthday of the all-out guerrilla war,' Kesselring wrote in his memoirs.[1] On 17 June, he issued the following order to his troops: 'The fight against the partisans must be carried on with all means at our disposal and with the utmost severity. I will protect any commander who exceeds our usual restraint in the choice and severity of the methods he adopts against partisans. . . . A mistake in the choice of methods in executing one's orders is better than failure or neglect to act.' Three days later he issued another top-secret order: 'It is the duty of all troops and police in my command to adopt the severest measures. Every act of violence committed by partisans must be punished immediately. . . . Wherever there is evidence of considerable numbers of partisan groups, a proportion of the male population of the area will be arrested; and in the event of an act of violence being committed, these men will be shot.' He said if German troops were fired upon from any village, it should be burned down. 'Perpetrators or the ringleaders will be hanged in public.'[2]

As for the Salò Republic, it could not count on the loyalty of its forces or of the population. Ten Italian torpedo planes attacked Gibraltar on 5 June and claimed to have sunk four ships. But three of the crews preferred to land in Spain rather than return to Italy – just one of a wave of defections from Fascist ranks that summer.[3] The Fascist press announced on 21 June that 110 draft dodgers and deserters had been shot in Novara province west of Milan. About seventy prisoners were massacred at Fossoli the next day.

In BBC broadcasts to Italy on 19, 20 and 27 June, Field Marshal Alexander exhorted the partisans to shoot German soldiers wherever they found them. 'Kill all German soldiers who are left in the rear. Act in the same way as the patriots of Teramo,' he instructed. (At Teramo, in south-east Italy, partisans killed German soldiers cut off from the main body of troops just after the Italian surrender in September 1943.) On 27 June, Alexander ordered partisans in Siena to attack the enemy from the rear while the Allies attacked from the front and from the air. In a broadcast from Bari, Marshal Badoglio ordered the partisans to attack the German Command Headquarters and other operational centres. 'Kill the Germans from behind in order to prevent their retaliation, and thus kill even more,' he said.[4]

On 29 June, Germans carried out a reprisal in Civitella in Val di Chiana after two German soldiers were killed and a third wounded in a clash in the Tuscan village. They killed 212 men, women and children, and some of the dead women were found completely naked. The ages of the dead ranged from one year to eighty-four years. About 100 houses in the village were destroyed by fire, and some victims were burned alive in their homes.[5]

By the end of July, Kesselring had broadened his orders. Captured partisans were to be shot on sight, and troops were to kill civilians who supplied the partisans with any kind of help, who carried arms or failed to report concealed weapons and who committed any hostile act against German armed forces. In the case of brutal attacks on German forces by partisans, civilian hostages were to be taken from districts in which partisan bands operated and shot. If German soldiers were killed by civilians, up to ten able-bodied Italians would be shot for each German who lost his life. All civilians captured in battles with partisans and in reprisal actions would be sent to Germany for forced labour.[6]

Kesselring's orders gave carte blanche to his troops to carry out the most brutal atrocities, acts that soon would lead even Mussolini to protest. In seeking to justify himself, Kesselring harked back to Alexander's incitement to the partisans to kill Germans wherever they found them. 'As a man I condemn . . . the invitation to kill people behind their backs,' he said. 'The sorrow brought to Italian families who have no guilt, following our reprisals, will be immense. Until now I have demonstrated with facts that respect for human principles is for me something of normal logic. As a responsible leader, however, I cannot hesitate to prevent with the most repressive means this extremely despicable and medieval system of combat.'[7]

Fulminating against the partisans in his memoirs, Kesselring wrote: 'Patriotism was often merely a cloak for the release of baser instincts. The partisan war was a complete violation of international law and contradicted every principle of clean, soldierly fighting. In the whole calendar of crimes – from ambushing, hanging, drowning, burning, freezing, crucifying and every kind of torture, not forgetting the poisoning of wells and the repeated abuse of the Red Cross – there is not one which was not an everyday occurrence.' He said partisans went about dressed as Germans or Fascists, rarely accepted a fair fight and when they did 'forgot all human decency'.

He admitted that 'abominable things' also were done on the German side, but said there were only three or five exceptional instances of this. 'The excesses or acts of barbarity that occurred in Italy must be equally shared among Partisan bands, neo-Fascist organisations and German deserter groups,' he wrote. 'The stories of crimes against civilians reported to me by Mussolini turned out when investigated at my insistence by Germans to be lies or exaggerations.'[8] This was a blatant falsehood. After the retreat from Rome, the Germans rested for a time on a line around Lake Trasimeno in central Italy, and atrocities became more frequent. Thirty-eight hostages were shut inside a chestnut-drying shed, which was mined and blown up. Seventy-seven miners were killed at Val Cecina for trying to prevent Nazi destruction of their mines.[9]

The fall of Rome unleashed panic among Fascists in much of central Italy. Fascist provincial chiefs and other officials and party members began defecting to the Allies. In Lucca, the police chief fled and Fascists there had to disarm 400 police officers who were threatening to defect. Jail guards in Pistoia freed all political prisoners. Everywhere Carabinieri officers began fleeing. An Italian Fascist battalion stationed on the island of Elba went over to the Allies. Fascist officials in Pisa took to their heels. Renato Ricci, commander of the Republican National Guard, informed Kesselring and General Wolff on 12 June that some of his units had had to give way to the partisans because they lacked arms, equipment, uniforms and shoes. He said there was a continual defection of Republican National Guard units that had been recruited from the Carabinieri.[10]

At one point Mussolini, holding a radio intercept in his hand, remarked to Foreign Under-secretary Mazzolini: 'See how well my Bersaglieri strike? There are still those who know how to die for Italy.' He was not referring, as one might expect, to Fascist troops fighting with the Germans; the intercept was an Allied broadcast praising the valorous behaviour of the Bersaglieri – an elite unit of Italian troops – fighting alongside the Allies in the Apennines. Likewise, he was later to say that Communist leader Palmiro Togliatti was one of the few personalities in the Italian regime in the south capable of leading a government. It seemed he admired Italians of ability, no matter which side they represented.

But his praise of the Bersaglieri perhaps betrayed the weakness of his own leadership. 'He has lacked coherence, the capacity to carry out his plans, understanding of men and above all a sense of history,' Luigi Bolla remarked at this time. 'He is a demiurge, not a statesman.'[11]

The partisans went on the offensive that summer, liberating valleys and setting up mini-republics in some places. At one time or another, fifteen 'partisan republics' were established. When the Allies reached Assisi on 17 June, they found it was already in the hands of the partisans. Mussolini learned that the army, the police and the Republican National Guard were not fighting, and he charged Graziani with mounting a counter-offensive. Graziani told him that, in recent months, the party had offered 50,000 men to the army, but gradually reduced the number to 3,000 and in the end supplied barely 1,000. He was able to send to the front only four battalions of volunteers, armed just with rifles and a few machine guns. In a report to Mussolini on 28 June, he wrote: 'In practice the government of the Italian Social Republic controls, and that only up to a point, the stretch of plain astride both banks of the Po. All the rest is virtually in the hands of the so-called rebels who are supported by large sections of the population. . . . All our "peripheral" organisations have been destroyed.' He said the situation had been aggravated by a plan to send 10,000 Carabinieri to Germany and force them to wear the Fascist black shirt. Graziani said the Republican National Guard was on the point of collapse, with units throwing down their arms at the first sight of partisans. He demanded that Ricci be dismissed, saying the Guard commander, along with Party Secretary Pavolini and Interior Minister Buffarini, had 'alienated the sympathies of the great majority of Italians to Republican neo-fascism'. Partisan numbers were shooting up, to which each Fascist draft call-up contributed. In Novara, the partisan commander Cino Moscatelli made a joke of this. He put up posters addressed to the Fascists saying: 'Please don't make any more call-ups because our ranks are full.'[12]

Allied air drops to the partisans increased dramatically in the summer, and more officers from the US Office of Strategic Services (OSS) and the British Special Operations Executive, the two Allied intelligence agencies, joined them. They sent back reports that some Communist units not only were fighting the enemy but were murdering political opponents. The OSS itself had been too lax in recruiting Italian speakers from the US Mafia. When OSS Major William V. Holohan parachuted down near Lake Orta in northern Italy, carrying a large sum of money, he was poisoned by fellow Americans and his body dropped in the lake.[13]

In July, Mussolini telephoned a Fascist official in Piedmont and asked him to send fifteen trucks to transport police needed in Forlì, which was surrounded by partisans. The trucks were sent to Lake Garda and parked in the open during the night. The next morning, they were gone – seized by the Germans. Likewise, the same Piedmont official sent 5,000 pairs of shoes for militia forces, and these were taken by the Germans.

With conditions in the Salò Republic rapidly deteriorating, the editor of *La Stampa*, a Turin newspaper owned by Fiat, published an article on 21 June likening the government to a spectre that shows itself during a spiritual gathering around a table. The editor, Concetto Pettinato, said partisan units were robbing, sacking and killing as if government authority did not exist, and he demanded that some government organs be transferred to Turin, the former Italian capital, or people in Piedmont would take matters into their own hands. Mussolini's minister of popular culture, Mezzasoma, described the article as 'the worst blow inflicted on the prestige of the RSI'.[14]

In Piedmont, the partisans carried out a daring theft of a German train loaded with ten cannon at the village of San Francesco al Campo, near Ciriè. After the cannon had been put aboard the train, partisans went into the railway station at night, disarmed troops who were on guard there and convinced the railway staff to help them. They drove off in a train consisting of six carriages and two locomotives, giving a prolonged blast of the train whistle to SS troops as they passed through Ciriè and continued to a nearby valley, where they destroyed two carriages, damaged the other four carriages and the locomotives, and made off with the cannon. A German armoured column went into the valley to retrieve the wrecked train, and partisan artillery seriously damaged one tank.

In the Fonteno pass in Piedmont, partisans threatened with encirclement attacked German troops, forcing them to surrender and release 100 civilian hostages. The German commander Fritz Langer commented: 'If the Fascists were like the partisans, the war would have ended two years ago.'[15]

On 15 June, eleven partisans staged a daring rescue of seventy-three political detainees, some of whom were awaiting execution, from the Belluno jail. Seven partisans dressed in German uniforms escorted four comrades handcuffed as prisoners to the jail, and Carabinieri guards opened the iron gates. The partisans then disarmed the Carabinieri, freed the detainees and locked the Carabinieri in cells. Another rescue effort a month later in Verona did not go so well. Partisans entered the Scalzi prison and rescued Giovanni

Roveda, the trade union figure who had been captured in Rome, while he was enjoying a visit from his wife. But most of the partisans were killed while trying to get away.[16]

In June, a Fascist government report said the partisans enjoyed the sympathy of the mass of the Italian population. The report attributed this to an aversion towards fascism, antipathy towards the Germans, a desire for the war to end quickly, opposition to the drafting of young men, abuses by Fascists during mopping-up operations, lack of protection of the population (especially in the valleys), German transfer of industrial machinery to Germany and fear of being taken to Germany for forced labour.[17]

The big partisan successes during the summer, particularly in Piedmont, led to large-scale German search operations and reprisals. The Germans began shooting civilians suspected of helping the partisans, and they also burned their houses. The population had a growing hatred of the Germans and Fascists, but many also accused the partisans of abandoning them to fierce reprisal. To escape from the Germans, some partisans in the Cuneo valley crossed into France, where they were disarmed and put into prison camps. Later, through American and British intervention, some were re-equipped and sent back to Italy.[18]

On 21 June, Mussolini decided to militarise the Fascist Party and set up new militia units known as Black Brigades, an idea that had long been pushed by Pavolini. But Mussolini feared a further division of the republic's scant military forces and knew Graziani would not take well to the idea. The Duce did not allow Pavolini to announce the birth of the Black Brigades until 25 July. All party members between the ages of eighteen and sixty-one who were not part of the armed forces were ordered to form Blackshirt action squads. The first Black Brigade units began operating in Piedmont in August under the direct command of Pavolini, who promoted himself to general and was lightly wounded in a skirmish with partisans. Some of the worst elements of the Fascist Party went into the Black Brigades, and they became notorious for thefts and unbridled violence. Ultimately even the Germans would complain of their excesses.[19]

Their crimes were sometimes more than matched by those of Fascist militia squads that had operated since Mussolini's return to power. One of the worst of these was headed in Milan by Pietro Koch, an Italian with a German father, who became immensely rich from dealing in hard drugs and running protection rackets. Koch himself was a cocaine addict, and so were some of his men. Tall, elegant and well-groomed, Koch was a former second lieutenant of grenadiers, and sold cars between the two world wars. He married a woman ten years older than himself, whom one writer described as little more than a prostitute. But he abandoned her almost immediately and persuaded a sixteen-year-old girl in Florence, named Tamara, to run away with him to Rome. She organised parties and orgies for him there.

The Koch squad was set up with Mussolini's permission and paid and armed by the Interior Ministry. After Rome fell, it shifted its operations to Florence, then to Milan. The Koch headquarters in Milan ran its own private prison and torture chamber. The methods included the use of electric current, keeping prisoners in cells no higher than 3½ feet, whipping, putting matches in toenails and setting them alight, crushing genitals, hitting people in the kidneys with sacks of sand to provoke internal lesions, making prisoners drink glasses of motor oil, forcing them to swallow salt and putting them in cellars with no light, water or sanitary facilities. Piero Pisenti, Mussolini's decent justice minister, persuaded the Duce to put a stop to the Koch operation. The squad was dissolved when it was found to be working for the Germans and disobeying government orders. Buffarini had to bring in the rival Muti Legion to assist the police in suppressing it. The Muti Legion freed forty-three prisoners, including some who couldn't walk and five who had to be hospitalised. The police arrested fifty-three members of the gang and found a considerable quantity of morphine and cocaine on the premises. The gang members were released by the Germans after a few hours and later assigned to police duties. Some of the prisoners the gang had held were deported to Germany. Koch was arrested again in December 1944 and held until 25 April, 1945. After the liberation of Italy, his mother and girlfriend were arrested in Florence and he went to the police to inquire about them, confessing his identity. He was arrested, tried in Rome and shot on 5 June 1945. He was then thirty-seven. Before his execution, the pope sent him a pardon, a blessing and a rosary.[20]

The Muti Legion, named after the prominent Fascist Ettore Muti who was assassinated by Badoglio's Carabinieri after the fall of Mussolini in 1943, was also known for its sadistic tortures. The Cardinal of Milan, Ildefonso Schuster, in a letter of September 1944 to a priest who was close to the Salò officials, protested against the tortures. He said some priests had been arrested without sufficient cause, tied to trees for hours, whipped with lashes and had their teeth broken. Some curates were in prison or under house arrest. The Muti Legion was headed by a foulmouthed former army sergeant and self-promoted colonel, Francesco Colombo. His first recruits were young men who had escaped from a reformatory. His men beat prisoners with rifle stocks and other implements, hit them with their fists, whipped them, kicked them with their boots, removed fingernails and injected prisoners with chemicals. Colombo was captured by partisans and executed in the closing days of the war.[21]

In Florence the ill-named Fascist secret police chief Mario Carità (*carità* means charity) conducted a reign of terror as head of a gang of torturers.

'I suffer in seeing you suffer,' Carità would say to prisoners. Typically, he would pretend to reproach one of his men for hitting a man in the nose, then punch the prisoner in the stomach. He delighted in putting out cigarettes on the stomachs of women, giving electric shocks to the genitals of men and pulling out nails with pliers. Carità was described as the headmaster of torturers, and his two daughters participated in beating prisoners while sleeping with their father's torturers. Finally, a GAP unit decided to assassinate him. Tosca Buccarelli, aged eighteen, the daughter of a long-time anti-Fascist, and Antonio Ignesti, aged twenty-five, were chosen to kill him at a café in the centre of Florence that Carità frequented. Their plan was to plant a bomb under a table near the one at which he always sat. After reconnoitring the cafe for several weeks, pretending to be sweethearts, Buccarelli and Ignesti made their attempt on 8 July. But the bomb missed a hook that had been screwed under the table and fell to the floor. In the ensuing confusion, Buccarelli escaped but looked back and saw several men were holding Ignesti. She went back, and as Fascists moved in to seize her, Ignesti escaped.

Buccarelli was questioned at Fascist police headquarters by Carità, then by the Germans. She was tortured, with Carità and his mistress watching, then transferred to a women's prison. At dawn on 9 July, several men in Nazi uniform arrived at the prison and showed guards a document ordering her release. A guard went to the phone to confirm the order with the SS, but one of the uniformed men drew a pistol and forced him to drop the phone. The partisans in Nazi uniform proceeded to free Buccarelli and all other political prisoners.

Cardinal Elio Dalla Costa suggested to SS Colonel Eugen Dollmann that Carità should be removed from Florence. Dollmann went to Carità's office to investigate, and as he approached he heard a 'frightening shout', then a window above him was shattered and a bloody body fell to the street. Soldiers accompanying Dollmann kicked open a door inside the building, and found themselves in a torture chamber, with Carità and his half-naked mistress on one side of the room. From the walls hung bloody spikes, and blood stained the floor and the walls. In the centre of the room was a table with leather straps. Dollmann and his men trained their guns on Carità and his lover and told them to explain what had happened. 'In Florence, I am in command,' Carità said. Referring to the man who had jumped from the window and died, he said: 'This cowardly pig escaped too soon from the treatment he deserved. . . . Can I offer you something to drink?'

Dollmann said he went to Pavolini, who was then in Florence, and told him Carità and his lover must leave Florence within an hour. Pavolini reluctantly obeyed and Carità moved to Padua, where he resumed his work as a torturer and killer under the protection of Lieutenant-Colonel Herbert Kappler, the man responsible for the Ardeatine caves massacre in Rome. Education Minister Carlo Alberto Biggini denounced Carità's crimes to Kappler, after which the Germans compiled a dossier on Biggini and sent men to watch his house. Biggini was an upright man who only reluctantly agreed to become education minister, played a significant role in hiding Italian art treasures from the Germans, resisted pressures from Mussolini and the Germans to dismiss anti-Fascist professors and refused to allow troops on to university campuses to search for draft dodgers. He survived the war but died of pancreatic cancer in November 1945.

One writer has described the exchange that took place between Kappler and Biggini when the minister made his complaint about torture:

KAPPLER. If we don't use certain systems, we achieve nothing.
BIGGINI. These systems have turned the world against you and, consequently, against us. The Italian people cannot bear it. You are mistaken, for in this way no war has ever been won and is lost even if won on the field of battle.
KAPPLER. Are these your sentiments?
BIGGINI. Certainly, my sentiments of yesterday, today and always.
KAPPLER. May I refer them to higher authority?
BIGGINI. You may refer them to whomever you want.

After the war, American soldiers tracked down Carità in an Alpine *pension* in northern Italy, and found him in bed with his lover. When they burst in, he grabbed a pistol and shot the woman, then killed an American soldier. He was cut down in a burst of machine-gun fire.[22]

* * *

During the summer of 1944, the level of violence on both sides in northern Italy mounted steadily. In Venice, a GAP unit blew up the office of the Fascist federation on 26 July, killing a number of people. Twelve anti-Fascists were shot in reprisal.[23]

Like the Fascists, some partisan units tortured their prisoners. Members of the Garibaldi Legion in the town of Varaita systematically resorted to simulated shootings to try to get people to talk, and one of their commanders forced a prisoner to sit on a red-hot stove. Those suspected of spying were sometimes tortured to force them to reveal the names of other spies.[24]

Dollmann wrote after the war: 'The appalling methods of torture employed in the prisons of the Salò Republic were rivalled only by the painful inquisitorial techniques of partisan interrogators. Sensitive parts of the body were singed with red-hot irons and soles branded with horseshoes, orgies of beatings were a regular part of interrogation and shootings had become so commonplace that they no longer caused a stir.' He spoke of rotting bodies of partisan victims piled by roadsides, stinking in the summer heat. 'In many cases,' he said, 'bands of Communist guerrillas had shot their fathers and mothers, carried their sisters or fiancées off to the mountains as spoils of war, taken the last cow from their stables.'

Dollmann told also of helping save two girls from Fascist Black Brigades members when he stopped at a farmhouse that was a Brigades outpost. The girls had been stripped naked, lashed face upwards to a bench in the barn and smeared with butter and salt. A young Fascist claimed his family had been killed by partisans after the girls fingered them as Fascists. He led into the barn a billy goat and huge white sheep dog, both of which pounced on the girls. A German soldier with Dollmann shot the frantic animals and untied the girls. The Fascists gave them back their clothes and the Germans drove them to the nearest German military post.

In December 1944, the bishop of Reggio Emilia came to Dollmann and asked him to accompany him to what proved to be Fascist torture cellars in the town. The smell of burning flesh greeted him when he entered, and he saw a number of naked men strapped to tables, their torturers brandishing hot irons they were about to apply to their victims. Two German soldiers with Dollmann pushed the torturers aside and the captured partisans were taken by ambulance to a German military hospital.

On another occasion Dollmann drove into the mountains to exchange a couple of hundred partisans in German hands for an equal number of captured German soldiers. He claimed the partisans told him they would rather be fighting alongside the Germans against the Allies if only the Germans had not allied themselves with the *cadavere vivente* (the living cadaver, i.e., Mussolini): Dollmann was not always completely reliable.[25]

Dollmann told of another occasion, on which he was invited to visit a German hospital in Emilia, where he lived. The doctors showed him a young man on the operating table, whose feet were tied together. Horseshoes had been nailed to his heels, and pus was oozing from the wounds. The German doctor said the young man had fallen into the hands of Communists in the mountains, who took him for a spy, and he had been left before the hospital door that morning by peasants who had come upon him as he was near death.[26]

In July, the German Command began hanging captured partisans in the streets of Turin. The Germans also took prisoners out of Fascist jails in Bologna and shot them. Seven bodies were found with placards declaring they were 'killers and saboteurs'.

Some peasants turned against the partisans because partisan actions had caused the Germans to burn their houses and kill civilians. Partisans also antagonised peasants in the countryside by requisitioning their cows or part of their harvest, seizing food, forcing them to pay 'taxes' and robbing banks. Sometimes villagers went without meat because small partisan units had killed all their livestock, and peasants often saw partisans who were drunk.[27]

Alexander and General Sir Maitland Wilson, the Allied commander for the Mediterranean, were anxious that summer to push on to the Po valley, and they were supported by Churchill. On 6 June, Alexander had even issued a proclamation inviting the partisans to be ready for an insurrection that summer, a decidedly premature action. The Americans overruled the British on 14 June, insisting on diverting seven divisions to an invasion of southern France by mid-August so as to support Allied troops on the Normandy beachheads. Churchill was so angry that on 30 June he drafted a telegram to Roosevelt – which was never sent – stating: 'The whole campaign in Italy is being ruined.' On 1 July, after moderating his language, he sent a message in which he described the diversion of troops from Italy as 'the first major strategic and political error for which we two have to be responsible'. If Roosevelt insisted on Operation Anvil, the landing in southern France, His Majesty's Government would have to enter a solemn protest, he said.

Churchill and the British military leaders had wanted to push up the Italian peninsula and into Vienna, Budapest and Prague before the Russians got there, and they were undoubtedly right. As Warren F. Kimball, the editor of the Churchill–Roosevelt correspondence, noted: 'The drain of troops caused the Italian front to become a backwater, merely tying down German forces.' The Allies settled for pushing forward to the Gothic line, the line of German defence in central Italy, but it took them three months to reach even that. Alexander was left with 153,000 men, and began integrating into the British Eighth Army 45,000 Italian combat troops who had remained loyal to the Badoglio government after the surrender.[28]

On 25 June, the Allies designated General Raffaele Cadorna to command the partisan war. Cadorna, a career cavalry officer, was the son of General Luigi Cadorna, the ruthless Italian commander who had led his forces to disaster in the battle of Caporetto against the Austrians in the First World War. The son, living in Rome at the time of the Italian surrender, had become disillusioned with the Mussolini regime because of the lack of adequate material for the army and the losses suffered in North Africa and Greece. His sympathies were resolutely monarchist. After the surrender he made contact with the Rome CLN, but learned later that the republican government there was preparing to arrest him so he went to northern Italy to hide out for a time. When he later returned to Rome, he took refuge in the Vatican Palace of the Congregations. After Rome was liberated, the CLNAI asked that he be sent to the north as its military adviser. The British parachuted him into Piedmont on the night of 11 August, and fifteen days later he had his first meeting with CLNAI leaders in Milan.

Cadorna quickly saw that the partisan movement was dominated by the Communist Party and the left-wing Action Party. In September, these two parties and the Socialists expressed opposition to his appointment as commander of the partisan military units, which were now called Corps of Volunteers for Freedom (CVL). British Captain Oliver Churchill (no relation to the prime minister), who had parachuted into northern Italy with him, told the CLNAI that the Allied Command wished to see Cadorna as commander, but Luigi Longo for the Communists and Ferruccio Parri for the Action Party refused to budge. Cadorna stayed on as military adviser rather than commander. But in November he was named supreme commander of the CVL, with Longo and Parri as deputy commanders, an arrangement that suited all sides.[29]

* * *

In July, Mussolini went to Germany to visit the four Italian divisions training there, and, as happened during his visit in April, he was received amid scenes of exultation. Speaking to men of the San Marco division at Grafenwöhr on 18 July, he said: 'Rome, which during thirty centuries of its history never saw Africans if not chained behind the chariot of the winning consuls, today has its walls profaned by these uncivilised and bastard races. If on the one hand all that saddens us, on the other it serves us as a spur for the necessary recovery.'

That same day he addressed officers of the Littorio Division at Heidelberg and gave vent to one of his antisemitic outbursts. He said the 'supreme shame' of the Italian Navy, led by a half Jew such as Admiral Da Zara, was to have handed over its ships to the enemy fleet at Malta following the surrender in September 1943. He also told the officers: 'I hope none of you wants to establish in Italy a Roosevelt-type plutocratic republic, or realise a Stalin-type Communist one. I think that even less you want an arch-parliamentary republic, drenched in Judaism and Masonry, like that of the French.'[30]

There were 57,000 Italian soldiers in the German camps. Some were volunteers, but most had been captured and sent to Germany by rail in freight wagons. The German training regime was harsh and the men were not given enough to eat; thirteen in the Littorio died from fatigue.[31]

Mussolini went on to Rastenburg on 20 July for his final meeting with Hitler. 'These trips to Germany were not very pleasant for Benito,' said Rachele, as he constantly had to appeal for arms, fuel and other supplies, and provisions for the interned soldiers. But he told her: 'There is too much defeatism about; I want to satisfy myself with my own eyes about many things I have learned only from diplomatic reports.' As Mussolini's train approached the Wolf's Lair, Hitler's headquarters in the forest near Rastenburg, the train was stopped and the blinds of his carriaged lowered without explanation. Several hours later the train resumed its journey and the blinds were raised only when it reached its destination. As Mussolini stepped from his train, Hitler greeted him and exclaimed: 'Duce, they have thrown at me a real infernal machine.' Mussolini, puzzled, thought at first Hitler was referring to a political machine. Then Hitler showed him his burned hair and explained what had happened: a disloyal officer, Claus von Stauffenberg, had attempted to assassinate the Führer by setting off a bomb hidden in a briefcase during a staff meeting. Hitler had been saved by the heavy oak table in front of him, which had taken the full force of the explosion, but eleven men were seriously injured and four died of their wounds. Stauffenberg got away, but was captured in Berlin and shot, along with a number of co-conspirators. Vittorio Mussolini said Hitler told the Duce: 'The explosion ripped my clothes and I came out semi-naked. Luckily, there were no ladies present.'

Hitler was eager to show Mussolini the wooden barracks where the bomb went off. There was a wide crater in the centre of the barracks, and windows and furniture lay scattered on the grass outside. Hitler noted that if the explosion had happened in the much more solid shelter where he normally held his conferences, the blast would have been contained and no one would have come out alive. This shelter was not used because it was under repair.

As the Hitler–Mussolini meeting got under way, Hermann Göring, Admiral Doenitz and Martin Bormann assured Hitler the German people were behind him and the attempt on his life had only drawn them closer. Göring said Stauffenberg's treachery explained why German troops were being defeated in the East; their generals had betrayed them. 'We noted a growing reciprocal animosity, as if each of them intended to accuse the other of having protected or allowed a handful of plotters to act,' wrote Filippo Anfuso, Mussolini's ambassador to Germany. 'For us Italians it was all frankly unpleasant and disturbing, also because it prejudiced the outcome of the conversations we had planned to conduct. . . . At a certain point Mussolini looked at me as if to ask me what we should do.'

Throughout the talks, Hitler had a distracted air, obviously thinking more about wreaking revenge on those involved in the plot against him than on what Mussolini was saying. He got up from time to time to take phone calls from Goebbels in Berlin, or broke off to read messages. Anfuso said the Italians noticed their presence was an irritation. The Duce gave Hitler a rundown on the deteriorating situation in the Salò Republic and commented: 'Now we can count only on the Republican Fascist Party and its organisations.' He added that enemy propaganda had hindered the enrolment of military recruits. He also insisted that if the Germans yielded on the Gothic line, this would prevent any possibility of recovery by the republican government.[32]

It was a strange meeting, Hitler sitting on an overturned box and Mussolini on a stool, the Duce uncharacteristically drinking brandy and nervously tearing apart but not eating the tea snacks offered to him, Hitler fiddling with the green, blue and yellow tablets provided by his quack doctor Morell and Vittorio Mussolini sitting nearby, wolfing down one slice of German cake after another. Hitler remained silent for a long time, his silence disturbed only by rain beating on the windows. Finally he said: 'Never had I felt with such force that Providence is with me. The miracle achieved in the last hours has reinforced in me the conviction that bigger tasks await me and that I will lead the German people toward the greatest victory in their history. I want, however, to destroy and crush the criminals who today have tried to oppose Providence and me. Betrayers of their own people, they deserve a shameful death and they will have it. This hour will be a punishment for whoever has taken part and for the families if they help them. The nest of vipers that seeks to impede the ascent of my Germany will be wiped out once and for all.' Hitler began speaking in a low tone, but by the end he was shouting. 'When I go through it all again . . . I conclude from my wondrous salvation . . . that nothing is going to happen to me.'

Mussolini seemed to be under the same spell, reading much into Hitler's escape. 'Our position is bad, one might almost say desperate, but what has happened here today gives me new courage,' he said. 'After the miracle that has occurred here in this room today it is inconceivable that our cause should meet with misfortune.' When he returned to Italy, he told Rachele that, if he had not been delayed at the Brenner Pass by an air-raid alarm, he would have been in the room with Hitler when the bomb went off.[33]

The German chief of staff, Field Marshal Keitel, met in another barracks with Graziani and said he wanted to keep the Italian divisions in Germany and use them for anti-aircraft defence on the Eastern Front. Graziani threatened to resign and the matter was dropped. Mussolini won from Hitler an agreement to return the divisions to Italy, and also obtained an important concession concerning the 600,000 Italian troops who had been interned in Germany after the Italian surrender. With the backing of Wolff and Rahn, he proposed they be allowed to join the labour force in Germany. Hitler, apparently ready to agree to anything to get rid of his visitor, said: 'I believe that from today we can begin to transform the military internees into free workers, also because this can have a favourable impression in Italy.' Having won that point, Mussolini then requested a pardon for four Italian Navy officers under sentence of death in occupied France, and Hitler promised it would be granted.[34]

At the end of the meeting, Hitler said to Mussolini: 'Please believe me if I tell you that I consider you my best and perhaps the only friend that I have in the world.' Rahn said later that the Führer looked at the Duce like a woman in love, forcing those around to lower their eyes in embarrassment. Then, as Rahn was leaving, Hitler assumed a different aspect and whispered to his ambassador: 'Rahn, keep an eye out.'[35]

Some of the Italian soldiers who figured in the discussion between the dictators had already been put to work and their treatment, along with that of Italian civilians, was horrendous. Anfuso, the Italian ambassador in Berlin, had drafted a report on 1 June that described the treatment as 'contemptible and inhuman'. Attached to the report was a rundown on conditions in various camps visited by Italian authorities. At Saarbrücken, the percentage of deaths in all camps was very high, some because of hunger and illness, some because of beatings. At Stammlager VII in Goerlitz, 'The moral and material conditions of these internees are worse than it is possible to imagine.' Workers were subjected to heavy labour and given meagre food rations. The Germans opened packets of food sent from Italy and broke up chocolates, salami and other food into little pieces. Canned meat, milk and sardines were opened before being given to prisoners, so some of the food went bad before it could be consumed. Many men were forced to work even though they were clearly sick, and were beaten. One man who was ill was forced to work until 6 p.m. on 15 March, and died three days later of exhaustion. His body was buried without military honours in a nearby wood. 'It has become a habit to beat internees for ridiculous and even non-existent reasons,' and some were hospitalised as a result. 'Treatment in this camp is worse than that inflicted on French prisoners of war and even Russians.'

At a camp in Breslau, workers were underfed and weak, subjected to various humiliations and dying in greater numbers than were those in other camps. At Petersdorf, the 250 Italians were beaten, called traitors and required to work seventy-two hours a week on short rations. 'The treatment is so bad one cannot imagine.' At Luckenwalde, Italians were beaten and sometimes stabbed. Italian doctors certified some as ill but the camp commander refused to recognise that and made these men go around the camp ten times with a sack on their shoulders until they collapsed. They also had to crawl on their hands and knees along half a mile of road. The workday was twelve hours, plus two hours of shovelling. An interpreter who surprised one soldier searching in a rubbish bin for turnip peelings stabbed him in his left shoulder with a bayonet. An Italian doctor ordered rest for the injured man, but the camp commander beat him for not working. A German major told the Italian authorities than any prisoner who refused to work could be beaten with a rifle butt, bayoneted or shot. In another Luckenwalde camp, Italians worked twelve hours a day and spent one to two hours walking to work, and many had swollen stomachs caused by hunger or had died of starvation. Some men still wore the only set of underwear they had when they were captured, and their clothes were in rags. They were given wooden clogs or wore sandals they made themselves from wood. Every fifteen days they were allowed a bath. Of 1,370 men in the camp, 367 were in hospital, many with tuberculosis, and 232 in the camp infirmary. Between October 1943 and April 1944, seventy-three of them had died. At Hennerstein, many Italian officers had contracted TB because their quarters were close to Russian quarters that were infected with TB and typhus. In his report, Anfuso noted: 'Men who are good Italians and good Fascists slide ever more towards communism. In the Europe of tomorrow, thousands and thousands of internees, after their return from internment camps, will see in Germans only the tyrants of yesterday.'[36]

Luigi Bolla had the responsibility in the Italian Foreign Ministry of trying to improve conditions for the Italians in Germany, and a report sent to him by an army officer was equally gloomy. At Stammlager XIII D in Nuremberg, the report said, the Italians had developed a shameful loss of hope and dignity. 'In a corner of frightening filth, there is a full flowering of thefts, spying, shamming and robberies that disgusts the German military guards of the camp . . . and creates prejudices against the Italians, considered the worst elements among all the races in Germany. And yet since last November, slowly but continuously, the situation has improved.'

But the report said the Italian internees had developed a 'ferocious hatred' of the Germans and of Italy, which they felt had betrayed and abandoned them. At Stalag 367 in Poland, it said, police lined up prisoners in a courtyard for a body search that lasted five and a half hours, and many of the Italians fainted. The police removed trousers from two officers because they did not seem proper military attire, and the men were left in their underwear. The camp director intervened to restore the officers' trousers. In other camps, there were men who had been reduced to walking skeletons from hunger. TB and other diseases were rife, and beatings were common.

To make matters worse, Vittorio Mussolini was appointed secretary of the Fascist organisation in Germany with responsibility for the internees, and he surrounded himself with profiteers and spies. Red Cross packages sent from Italy for the internees were regularly tampered with, and medicines were sometimes removed from the packages.

It was at that point that Bolla wrote in his diary:

> Vittorio Mussolini, 'the commander', secretary general of the Fascist Republican Party in Germany, is one of the greatest boors that exists on the face of the Earth. He shows it in every way, partly by his own behaviour, partly by pushing his following of athletes and boxers and ex-companions of sport. He argues with everybody, including Anfuso, and also the Foreign Office, which refuses to see either him or his secretary. The Duce proclaims him an idiot and promises to recall him every two days. . . . Perhaps the Duce already has too many troubles that embitter his life, also in the family, and he doesn't want to add another. Mussolini shows his lack of will power also in private life, which he conducts in a static way . . . refusing even a boat trip to get out of this depressing and slovenly environment. . . .
>
> He repeats often that he knows he is the most hated man in Italy and asserts that he attributes no weight to that fact. Instead he resents it with profound bitterness, and that is why he repeats it often. He . . . lacks or has lost his sense of history and reality, the capacity to know people and not fear them, a man who suffers from an incredible weakness in facing the pressures of people near him.[37]

Forty thousand of the former soldiers refused to work for the Reich and remained in concentration camps in miserable conditions. The Germans had even put Italians in one camp considered too bad to house Russian prisoners of war. It was not until March 1945 that the Germans agreed to repatriate 7,000 men who were seriously ill.[38]

The San Marco Division returned to Italy at the end of July, the Monterosa in August, the Littorio in November and the Italia in December. Some of the soldiers were sent across the Brenner Pass on foot. Getting the soldiers back was Mussolini's one significant success in his dealings with Hitler. A functioning army participating in the defence of the country was essential to the credibility of his government. But the success was dissipated soon after the troops came home. The first three divisions were immediately incorporated into an Italo-German armoured unit on the Ligurian coast and in the Piedmont Alps under the nominal command of Graziani. But Kesselring, of course, was the real boss. Some of the troops were without arms and lacked proper clothing and equipment. The partisans blew up one train loaded with Alpine troops from the Monterosa, killing many of them. Soon desertions began – 1,015 from Monterosa, 1,400 from San Marco, according to a German general. Anfuso complained in his memoirs that Wehrmacht propaganda made the desertions seem bigger than they were.

By September, one-third of the returnees had deserted, many joining the partisans, and a partisan report said morale was low among 50 per cent of those remaining. Some of the deserters were captured and shot, or sent to prison. Graziani admitted to Rahn there were 5,000 deserters from the first two divisions that returned to Italy. Rahn corrected him: there were 10,000. Relatively few of the Italian troops were allowed by the Germans to serve in frontline posts; most were used in fighting against the partisans rather than the Allies. The Germans were hard pressed and in need of help, but they still stubbornly refused to trust the Italians to fight against the Allies. On 3 July, Siena was occupied by French troops. Arezzo fell on 26 July, and Ancona and Livorno on 19 July. 'Why does every one of our battalions, brought to the firing line, desert?' Bolla wrote in his diary. 'Not for love of the English nor hatred of the Germans, but for aversion to the Fascists and a desire to hasten the end.'[39]

As they advanced, the Allies continued to view the partisans with some mistrust, and the US Fifth Army greeted many partisan bands in the Apennines by putting them in internment camps. Partisans in red shirts, flaunting revolutionary banners, had not endeared themselves to American officers. On 12 July, the Communist Party delegation in Piedmont instructed the Garibaldi Brigades to avoid using red shirts, displaying the hammer and sickle and singing 'Bandiera Rossa', the party hymn, but to continue 'carrying out with intelligence all the political work of the party that we must never neglect'.[40]

On 29 July, after his return to Italy, Mussolini observed his sixty-first and last birthday. There is no record of how he marked the occasion. Five days later, he left for Rocca delle Caminate, then went on to visit German and Italian frontline units along the Metauro river. In places where his car could not proceed, Mussolini got out and walked on the battlefield, 'often amid a real tempest of fire', Rachele recounted. He told her: 'I seemed really to have returned to the trench life of the other war.' Men of one frontline Italian unit left their trenches to acclaim the Duce when he showed up; the Allies spotted them and turned their fire on them.[41]

One of the largest pitched battles of the war between partisans and Germans was fought 28 July–3 August around Montefiorino, south-west of Modena. The Allies dropped a battalion of Italian parachutists behind the Gothic Line at Piandelagotti to help the partisans, and the Germans employed three divisions in attacking the Italian forces with artillery, mortars, armoured units and flamethrowers. Some partisan units withdrew, but others resisted. The resulting losses were 250 partisan dead and 70 wounded, and 2,080 German dead. The Germans succeeded in relieving a threat to the Gothic Line, but at a high price.[42]

In early August, partisan units began the liberation of Florence without waiting for the Allies to arrive. Kesselring had proclaimed Florence an open city in February, but there would be hard fighting in its streets before it was free. Even from late June, the Germans had begun abandoning the city. The art expert Bernard Berenson, calmly reading Schiller and Goethe while admiring Turner sunsets from his hideout in the hills above Florence, recorded in his diary on 20 June: 'For miles together the highway to Bologna is crowded with German soldiery tramping, motoring, employing carts, any and every obtainable vehicle, in their trek northwards. They take along all they could lay hands on. . . . Not inanimate things alone, but cows and calves, oxen and horses, mules and asses, rabbits, geese, chickens, anything alive and edible.'

He also said the Germans were taking 'all the valuable and admired masterpieces of art to be found in Florence', on the pretext of saving them from 'Judeo-American predatoriness'. Retreating German troops also stole the car of Fascist Party Secretary Alessandro Pavolini, and were selling stolen goods in Florence at a tenth of their value, rushing to the shops 'to buy underwear and other dire necessities' with the proceeds, Berenson said.[43]

The Fascists opened negotiations with the CLN, promising to free political prisoners in exchange for immunity and a pledge of non-interference with the German withdrawal. But the talks eventually broke down and the Fascists, led by Pavolini, hastened to abandon Florence. The Germans also held talks with CLN representatives. They ordered people living on the left bank of the Arno to leave their homes, and threatened terrible reprisals if their retreat were opposed. The CLN decided the only way to save the city was to drive out the Germans. A state of emergency was declared on 3 August; lights went out, water supplies were cut off, bread supplies disappeared and no one was allowed to leave home. That same day, Berenson recorded that Germans had taken refuge in a villa that housed many people, including five Jews, and a German soldier, dandling a Jewish baby, 'never guessed that he was caressing an offspring of the calamitous, infectious, subhuman, verminous Jewish race'.[44]

The Germans planned to blow up the Arno bridges, but Colonel Dollmann, the artistically minded SS officer, said he went to Kesselring and urged him to spare them. Kesselring told him he had lost a lot of soldiers by not blowing up the Tiber bridges in Rome, in defiance of Hitler, and he could not do the same again. He said he could save either the Ponte Vecchio or the Trinità bridge if Cardinal Dalla Costa could obtain the agreement of the Allies not to fight in Florence. Dollmann said he and General Wolff argued in favour of saving the Trinità bridge, superior to the Ponte Vecchio from an artistic standpoint. But on the night of 4 August, the Germans spared the Ponte Vecchio and blew up all the other Arno bridges.[45] The Trinità bridge was restored to its original appearance after the war, with many materials retrieved from the river.

The Germans abandoned the centre of the city on the night of 11 August, and the Allies began arriving on 13 August. By 31 August the battle for Florence was over. Two hundred and five partisans died in the battle and 400 were wounded. Most of the city's invaluable art treasures were hidden in Tuscan villas or in northern Italy at an early stage. The Germans discovered many of them and sent truckloads of paintings to Germany, including Titian's *Danae*, which wound up on the bedroom wall of Hermann Göring, but most of the loot was returned after the war.[46]

* * *

As the Germans were being pushed back throughout central Italy, General Wolff sent a circular to SS forces on 4 August: 'Every act of violence must immediately have adequate countermeasures. If in a district there are (partisan) bands in large number, then in every single case a certain percentage of the male population of the place is to be arrested and, in cases of violence, shot. If someone fires on German soldiers etc. from villages, then the village is to be burned. Those guilty, or the heads of the bands, are to be hanged publicly. . . . The honour of the German soldier requires that every measure of repression be hard, but fair.'[47]

At this point, Major Walter Reder enters the story. In the long and tragic list of atrocities carried out on the German side, no one matched his record of cruelty and barbarism. Like many of the more fanatical Nazis, Reder was an Austrian. At the age of eighteen, he had been suspected of murdering the Austrian Chancellor Engelbert Dollfuss. Early in the war, he commanded troops in Poland and Russia, and lost a hand in battle. He wore an artificial hand covered with a black glove. He drank heavily every night, tried to rape a woman in one village and violated a nun in another. Reder was twenty-nine years old when he began a rampage of murder and destruction across central Italy, no doubt encouraged by Wolff's circular. In less than a month, between 8 September and 5 October, he and his men killed 1,830 civilians, including five priests, in the town of Marzabotto and surrounding villages south of Bologna, the worst single atrocity of the war in Italy. But his depredations began earlier and in all led to about 3,000 deaths.

On 12 August at Sant' Anna di Stazzema, his SS troops made 150 people come out of their houses and gather on the village piazza. All were cut down by machine-gun fire. The SS rushed into other houses, drove the people out and shot them down as they ran. Straw and faggots were spread over the bodies, petrol poured on them and the bodies set on fire. When the work was nearly finished, SS patrols arrived with more people. They took them to the edge of the fire, shot them in the back and pushed them in. Eleven members of one family, the Tuccis, were among the victims. Altogether 560 people were killed there, and another 107 at Valla.

Fifty-three young men rounded up at Lucca and Pisa were brought on 18 August to Bardine San Terenzo, where Reder had a command post. He had them strangled with barbed wire tied around their necks, then left their bodies hanging. On 24 August, assisted by the Black Brigades, the SS burned Vinca to the ground and killed 174 people.

At Caprara, fifty-five people were herded together in a single room, then killed when the building was burned down. Three girls were tied to separate chestnut trees. Their skirts were raised above the waist, and each had a long stick inserted by force into the vagina. Altogether, 107 people including 24 children died in Caprara. Between Caprara and Villa Ignano, two pregnant women were disemboweled, and beside the cheek of one of them her killers placed the head of her foetus. Giorgio Laffi, nine months old, was the only survivor of a family of nine. He crawled in the rain among the bodies of those who had been shot, and was found dead from cold the next day.

At Casaglia, a crowd took refuge in a church to pray for safety. Germans burst in and killed the officiating priest and three old people who could not obey an order to get out quickly. The remaining 147 villagers were gathered together in a cemetery. A survivor described what happened: 'They crowded us together against a chapel, between the gravestones and wooden crosses. They went into the corners and kneeled down to take aim. They had machine guns and rifles and continued shooting.' Twenty-eight families were wiped out, and the Pirini family lost seven children. 'A Nazi with a big pistol killed them one by one,' a surviving family member said. 'A crying little boy grabbed the leg of the executioner. He gave him a kick and finished him off with a blow to the head.' A boy of six, crying that he wanted to die with his mother, was killed by a grenade. A boy about three or four years old had a stake driven into his anus. The other end of the stake was planted in the ground, leaving him swaying on the end of the stick like a mini-scarecrow. At Casolari, 282 people were killed, including 38 children and 2 nuns.

Fifty-five people were locked inside a chapel at Cerpiano and machine-gunned. Then the SS smashed bronze statuettes and painted vases in the chapel. Some of those who were shot were extracted from the heap of bodies and found to be still alive. The Germans decided to let them live for another two hours, then finished them off with revolver shots to the neck. A woman teacher named Rossi, among the wounded, begged them to stop. They laughed at her and killed her with a burst of machine-gun fire.

At Colalla, an old woman was burned in her bed because she could not get up. Her pregnant daughter of sixteen was cut in two. One young woman who had just given birth tried to flee with her baby. The Germans reached her in a vineyard, killed her, threw the baby in the air and shot it. In Creva, eighty-one died.

One thing that survivors of some of these massacres remembered was the music. 'They had a record player in the priest's house, and they didn't stop playing it during the slaughter,' said one. A woman recalled: 'They had a little organ and they played it while they passed from one house to the other.' Reder's troops ate all the food they found in the houses, and destroyed everything else.[48]

While Reder carried out his reign of terror, German and Fascist forces elsewhere were also committing atrocities. In Milan on 8 August, Giovanni Pesce, the bold GAP leader who had earlier carried out a wave of terror in Turin, led an attack on a German truck carrying food; nine people were killed and fifteen were seriously wounded. Gestapo posters later spoke of six innocent children, women and men among the victims, but Vincenzo Costa, the Fascist inspector in Milan, claimed the dead included five German soldiers. At German instigation, Fascist authorities took fifteen 'Communists and terrorists' from the San Vittore jail at 6 a.m. on 10 August and killed them in reprisal. A squad of the Muti Legion commanded by Captain Pasquale Cardella lined them up in the vast Piazzale Loreto and shot them dead while two companies of Black Brigades men surrounded the square. On German orders, the bodies were left where they fell until 6 p.m., and relatives were forbidden to approach them. Militiamen standing guard in the square ate slices of watermelon, and every now and then sang war songs.

Piero Parini, the Fascist provincial chief, resigned in protest over the killings, but Mussolini told him: 'Marshal Kesselring has his valid reasons. Every day in the north, German soldiers and officers are treacherously killed. He has decided to carry out a reprisal.' But to Eugenio Apollonio, the head of the Fascist secret police, Mussolini said: 'We will pay very dearly for the blood of Piazzale Loreto.' Mussolini's wife Rachele also claimed in her memoirs that Mussolini was indignant over the killings. 'The Germans lack any sense of justice,' she quoted him as saying. 'It is not possible to humiliate a city like Milan, inflicting on it such an exhibition of summary justice.' She said he sent a violent protest to Rahn the next day, asking him to tell Hitler no one could carry out reprisals against Italians in Italy without his consent. On 9 June 1999, a military tribunal in Turin condemned to life imprisonment, in his absence, the former SS officer Theodor Emil Sävecke for having instigated and organised the execution of the partisans shot in Piazzale Loreto. The court said Fascist and German documents proved indisputably that all the victims of the GAP attack on the truck were Italian civilians and did not include German soldiers as Costa had claimed. Sävecke died in December 2000 while German proceedings against him were under way. After the war, he had served in the German police and had risen to become deputy director of West German security services before retiring in 1971.

GAP carried out a reprisal for the Piazzale Loreto killings on 28 August, setting off a bomb in a rest area for German troops at Milan Central Station. A German nurse was killed and many others were wounded.[49]

Atrocities by German forces everywhere were now so frequent and well known that Mussolini wrote to Rahn on 17 August to protest. He included details of atrocities at Borgo Ticino, near Novara, where thirteen civilians were shot and fifty houses burned after four German soldiers had been wounded. He gave eleven examples of similar atrocities. At Torelino, near Udine, for example, thirty-two civilians were machine-gunned to death after a firefight between Germans and partisans. After partisans sniped at German soldiers in the Fucchio Marshes on the River Arno near Florence, Germans blew up houses and killed 100 civilians 'to frighten the partisans'. They left dead and wounded lying in the road.

Rahn later showed Mussolini a circular Kesselring had sent to his commanders on 22 August, deploring the killing of innocent civilians. The letter said these acts had undermined confidence in German forces, gained the Germans new enemies and aided enemy propaganda. All measures must be taken against actual partisans, he said, and not innocent civilians. Kesselring threatened to bring to justice anyone acting against such civilians.[50]

By mid-August, Mussolini was not only concerned over German atrocities but over the ineffectiveness of his Republican National Guard under Ricci. Graziani had wanted Ricci to be dismissed, and on 14 August Mussolini began the process by issuing a decree ending the autonomy of the Guard and providing for its integration into the army. Four days later, Graziani asked that 7,000 members of the Guard be made available for anti-aircraft defence, but Ricci refused. Graziani renewed the request, Ricci again refused and the two men had a bitter quarrel. On the evening of 18 August, Mussolini called in Ricci, who refused for a third time and denounced Graziani in strong terms. Mussolini dismissed him in a letter of the morning of 19 August, saying he could no longer tolerate Ricci's treatment of Graziani and had decided to assume personal command of the Guard. Ricci remained head of the Opera Nazionale Balilla, a Fascist youth organisation.[51]

On 16 August, Mussolini ordered partisans captured in fighting shot and those captured without arms to be sent to Germany.[52]

Acting on orders from Hermann Göring, Colonel General Wolfram Freiherr von Richthofen sent a German colonel to see Manlio Molfese, Mussolini's under-secretary of the air force, in Bellaggio on 24 August and inform him that the Germans had occupied all Italian airfields. He said the Italian aviators had a choice either of joining a flying legion under German orders or anti-aircraft units of the Luftwaffe. Mussolini protested to Hitler, and dismissed four air force officers who supported the German manoeuvre. Richthofen was also in conflict with Kesselring and was recalled to Germany. On 6 September, Mussolini was dismayed to learn that 450 officers, NCOs and airmen at Vicenza had agreed to join the German forces and were being sent to Germany. Some pilots were trained in Germany to fly Messerschmitts and returned to Italy to take part in combat missions. Most other Italian Air Force personnel ran away.[53]

Chapter 13

MORE ATROCITIES, GREATER DESPAIR

German lack of understanding is digging ever deeper furrows.

(Benito Mussolini, 8 October 1944)

On 25 August, the British Eighth Army attacked along the Adriatic littoral and on 1 September it broke through the Gothic Line towards Rimini. General Mark Clark's US Fifth Army launched a parallel offensive in the Apennines on 10 September, and after a week of hard fighting drove the Germans from a key position of the Gothic Line, the Giogo Pass. Pisa was occupied in early September, followed by Lucca and Pistoia, and Rimini fell to the Allies toward the end of the month. But the diversion of seven divisions to France earlier in the summer had weakened the Allied ability to sustain an offensive. It soon ran out of steam, and the Allies would be stalled for months. Field Marshal Kesselring had only half the forces of the Allies, and his divisions included conscripts from prison camps of dubious fighting ability. He was also at a clear disadvantage in artillery, tanks and planes. Twice he asked Hitler – in vain – to be allowed to retire behind the Po and concentrate on defence of the Alpine valleys that would provide an escape route to Germany. But when that was refused, his highly motivated forces held back the Allied offensive.[1]

Mussolini's concerns now were threefold. He was frustrated and angry over the German refusal to make full use of his small army. Divisions within his government had come into the open, with some moderate Fascists agitating for the removal of hardliners such as Interior Minister Buffarini. And, finally, the Duce faced the prospect that a renewal of the Allied offensive could see all that remained of the Salò Republic overrun. He would need to find a safe refuge, if not for himself, at least for Fascist families, and he would have to plan where to make his last stand. At a Cabinet meeting on 31 August, he outlined with 'profound bitterness' his complaints about German high-handedness and decided to have a talk with

Ambassador Rahn. Either the Germans would allow the Fascist government to operate normally or he would resign. But Rahn cared little for Fascist complaints, and Kesselring, while attacking partisan strongholds, was preoccupied with negotiating truces with partisans in some areas along the eventual German line of retreat. 'The German lack of understanding is digging ever deeper furrows,' Mussolini commented. Rumours spread that he was contemplating suicide; they gained currency when he asked Goffredo Coppola, editor of *Civiltà fascista*, to publish an essay on suicide he had written in his youth.[2]

The Fascist prefect of Bologna, Dino Fantozzi, reported to Mussolini that in his area the Germans were taking away everything 'from sewing machines to calves, from artistic vases to pieces of fabric, from match boxes to bottles of liquor'. German atrocities were continuing as well, as Mussolini noted in a letter to Rahn on 15 September. 'I draw your attention above all to the fact that many women and many children have been killed and entire villages have been burned, putting hundreds of families in the blackest desperation.' The consequences of that, he said, would be to increase the number of partisans and feed enemy propaganda. Six days later he wrote again: 'As a man and as a Fascist I cannot much longer bear even the indirect responsibility of this shedding of innocent blood that is added to the indiscriminate bombardments of enemy aviation.'[3] His relations with Rahn had just about touched bottom. Later that year, when Allied bombings and low-level strafing attacks around Lake Garda had become almost a daily occurrence, three bombs fell on the villa where Rahn lived and hit his office, killing a guard and a cook. When Mussolini learned that Rahn had been unhurt, he exclaimed: 'What a shame!'[4]

Mussolini expressed his concern about 'stupid reprisals' by the German military at a Cabinet meeting on 18 September. He also set up an interministerial commission under Party Secretary Pavolini to arrange the exodus of the government in case the Po valley were invaded. At the end of the meeting, however, he reaffirmed his faith in victory. A few days later, a report from Ambassador Filippo Anfuso in Berlin may have bolstered Mussolini's expectations of victory. Anfuso said the Germans were preparing to use three devastating new weapons: the V2 rockets, that were soon to rain on Britain; the V3, an anti-aircraft missile capable of destroying every plane within a range of half a mile, and the V4, a rocket that would suck all the oxygen from its point of impact to a zone of up to several miles. These last two weapons, of course, never came into existence.[5]

The Germans were not acting alone in the brutalities of which Mussolini complained; Fascist forces also were continuing to resort to terror. The Fascist prefect of Novara, Enrico Vezzalini, ordered all male relatives of known partisans between the ages of fifteen and sixty-five to be arrested and sent to an Italian concentration camp. In Turin and elsewhere, the partisan command was decimated by arrests, tortures and shootings.

One immediate consequence of the deteriorating situation was a new strike in Milan on 21 September, followed by demonstrations and brief work stoppages in Turin and elsewhere that the Fascists tried in vain to halt by conceding salary rises and sending in officials to discuss working conditions. The workers concentrated on sabotaging arms production. Tank production came to a halt, and the output of armoured cars slowed to a trickle.[6]

Rahn referred Mussolini's complaints about atrocities to Kesselring, who replied in a letter to the ambassador on 23 September. Kesselring said he would repeat an order to his troops that all reprisals be directed only at the partisans. The following day, he issued a new order in which he said German atrocities were 'revolting' and were 'driving even the best elements of the population and those willing to fight on our side into the enemy camp or that of the partisans. I am no longer ready to stand by and see such things take place. . . . I further order that in future courts martial are to be immediately set up on the spot.' But this was intended as a sop to Mussolini and was not taken seriously by Kesselring's officers. Soon after he issued the order, a poster went up in Milan bearing his name: 'For each German shot, ten Italians will be shot.'[7]

Major Reder, the Austrian SS officer responsible for the worst atrocities of that summer, would, as previously noted, soon be responsible for carrying out the biggest massacre in Italy of the war, centred on the village of Marzabotto south-east of Bologna. The partisan Stella Rossa (Red Star) band, one of the most renowned units of the resistance, had gathered on Monte Sole, near Marzabotto. Allied forces were fighting nearby and had urged the band, composed mostly of local people and escaped prisoners of war, to stay on the mountain until they arrived. But one man in the unit turned informer, going off to tell the Germans where they were located. SS troops under Reder encircled Monte Sole on 28 September, and launched an attack. The partisans soon ran out of ammunition and were liquidated. Then the SS began a three-day rampage in which all houses in Marzabotto were surrounded and set on fire. People running out to escape the flames were shot dead. The final death toll was 1,830, including 5 priests. News of the massacre eventually reached Mussolini, who questioned Dino Fantozzi, the prefect of Bologna. Fantozzi assured him the attack against the partisans had involved no reprisal against the civilian population. But the Bologna police chief went to Marzabotto and came back to confirm the slaughter. Mussolini telephoned Hitler: 'You cannot protest about the Katyn forest massacre* when in Italy Marzabotto has happened.' Hitler ignored the protest.

SS General Max Simon, Reder's commanding officer, was held responsible for his crimes and tried in August 1947 by a British court martial. He was sentenced to death on six war crimes charges, but the sentence was later commuted to life imprisonment. Reder, denying he ordered the killing of civilians, was tried by a Bologna military court in 1951 and sentenced to life imprisonment. In 1980, the sentence was commuted to thirty-four years, and in 1985 he was allowed, over the protests of most Italians, to return to Austria. Back home, he sent a long plea of forgiveness to the people of Marzabotto.[8]

On 1 October at Bressanone, near Bolzano, three escaped British prisoners of war were butchered in a barn by German soldiers. Two months later two British soldiers were murdered by the SS at Borgo, near Tranto in Val Sugano. The Germans ordered a gravedigger to dig two graves and an undertaker to prepare two coffins. The captives were taken to a cemetery with their hands tied and shot from behind. The bodies were left for the Italians to bury.

Mussolini wrote to Kesselring on 4 October, demanding that Italian troops be used against the Allies. 'What are they doing? Why are they not used?' he asked. 'Why are the enemy armies using the people of five continents to attack Italy, while the Italians, the best Italians, are not allowed to contribute to her defence?' Four days later, Mussolini seemed very depressed over the issue when Foreign Under-secretary Mazzolini met him. Not only was Kesselring not using his troops, but the Germans were threatening to break up the two divisions still in training in Germany and use them for anti-aircraft defence on the Russian front. 'The tragedy of the country consumes this man, who had dedicated himself entirely to making Italy great,' Mazzolini wrote in his diary. Mazzolini himself fretted that the Germans were unwilling to use Italian forces while 'on the Adriatic riviera soldiers of all colours and all races advance!' Kesselring yielded to the extent of using the Monterosa Division on a quiet part of the western end of the Gothic Line near Lucca in mid-October. The division assisted the Germans in capturing Barga from the Americans on Christmas night, but British-led Gurkhas later recaptured the town.[9]

The Allied offensive in August–September had raised hopes of an early victory, spurring the partisans to go on the offensive as their numbers

*In April 1943, the Germans uncovered the bodies of thousands of Polish officers in the Katyn Forest, near Smolensk. The Nazis and Russians blamed each other, and only in 1989 did Soviet authorities admit that Russians had been responsible for executing 15,000 Polish officers.

multiplied rapidly. But Kesselring began a counter-offensive, involving five or six German divisions and all the Salò Republic forces, which culminated in the second week of October. Kesselring urged his forces to use 'maximum harshness' in an attempt to reoccupy all key points that had been lost to the partisans.

The fighting was particularly ferocious in the Veneto region, and most of the partisans there were wiped out. Clorinda Menguzzato, aged thirty, a woman known as 'the lioness of the partisans', was captured and raped by German soldiers, then bitten by vicious dogs unleashed on her. She died under torture without betraying the whereabouts of her comrades. At Domodossola, near the border with Switzerland in north-west Italy, the partisans had driven out German and Fascist forces and established one of their mini-republics in September. Under the new German assault, the republic fell and many partisans fled to Switzerland while others regrouped around Omegna on Lake Orta, where the partisans had set up an independent entity in August. The Domodossola republic, encompassing more than 650 square miles and a population of 82,000, had lasted thirty-four days. Another short-lived free republic was established in September in the Friuli area of north-east Italy, covering just over 1,000 square miles and with a population of 90,000. But German and Russian Cossack forces attacked on 3 October, and the partisan forces had scattered in disarray by the end of the month.[10]

Mussolini told Mazzolini on 27 October that he was worried over German intentions to transfer his government to Klagenfurt, in Austria. He said he intended to remain in Italy as long as possible and found the idea of a 'phantom government' distasteful. Pavolini's interministerial commission recommended the government transfer to Trevigiano as an intermediate measure.[11]

On 31 October, Mussolini approved a government protest over German high-handedness in Emilia, involving violence against civilians and the theft of livestock and other property.[12]

The north Italian Communist leader Luigi Longo described other German and Fascist depredations in the countryside: thousands of cows drowned in the Po, pigs killed and their meat sent to Germany, grain that couldn't be transported over bad roads destroyed. 'Even the equipment of the hospitals, clinics and insane asylums of Bologna, Imola and Castel San Pietro, etc. have been emptied of everything they contained, and patients, those with tuberculosis and people sick in their minds, have been strewn along the road,' he wrote. 'Tunnels, overpasses, bridges, electric plants, railway tracks, railings, telephone and telegraph poles . . . have been destroyed with German meticulousness. . . . At Casalecchio di Reno twenty-four young men have been hung on butchers' hooks and steel wires from trees along the road and their remains exposed for several days.'[13]

* * *

Rachele Mussolini and the Duce's mistress provided a touch of *opéra bouffe* amid all these crises. Dowdy Rachele, fifty at the time and a peasant woman without any refinement, had been fuming for months over the presence of her more glamorous rival a few miles away, and she determined upon a showdown. She telephoned Mussolini on 24 October and told him she was going to the Villa Fiordaliso to confront Claretta. 'Do as you wish,' he replied wearily.[14]

Many Fascists saw Claretta as a malign influence upon the Duce and resented her presence at Gardone. When she went to Merano for Christmas in 1943, Mussolini asked her not to return and to await better times; but she refused.[15] He defended her to his secretary, Dolfin, and said she had stood by him while many Fascist supporters had melted away. Badoglio, he said, had put her in prison like a common delinquent and she had wasted away to just six stone. 'I need to be left a little in peace, at least for my intimate affairs,' he said.[16]

He was fascinated by her and evidently unaware of the degree to which she was disliked even in Fascist circles. But he was not alone in succumbing to her charms; other men found her captivating as well, including the Duce's German doctor Zachariae, who wrote:

> She was an intelligent woman, simple and transparent. She played no political role of influence on the Duce. She loved to dress well and had many jewels given her by the Duce. She confided to me one day she had sold part of her jewels abroad to be able to lighten the expenses of the Duce and finance herself independently. She possessed charm in exceptional measure. It happened not only to me but many others to be completely conquered by the fascination she emanated. She was for the Duce the only suitable woman. She could give him courage and reanimate him. When he was with her his humour was always excellent and his mind serene.

Rahn described Claretta as 'a beautiful woman, vaporous, a little oriental, with deep eyes, intelligent, sensitive'. But General Giacomo Carboni, a former chief of military intelligence who met her in 1943, described her then as 'an insignificant little being with an upturned nose and two lively little black eyes'.[17]

In October 1944, Mussolini was informed that Claretta was making copies of his letters to her and giving them to the Germans, and he sent Police Chief Emilio Bigazzi Capanni to investigate. Claretta was still in a dressing gown, her head wrapped in a pink turban and wearing men's slippers, when he arrived. She asked him the reason for his visit, and he said he had been sent by the Duce 'to sequester your correspondence with the head of government, as well as papers, books and photographs that you have received from him'.

'This is gross. I cannot imagine such a thing,' she said. 'Of what photographs are you speaking? Photographs of his letters do not exist. . . . Word of honour, I have never thought to have the letters of Mussolini photographed.' Bigazzi insisted on having the letters, and she tried to telephone Mussolini but the switchboard operator at his office said he was very busy and did not want to be disturbed. Claretta burst into tears, ran upstairs and locked herself in her bedroom. The police chief, followed by three of his men, forced the lock and found her standing before a mirror holding a Beretta 7.65mm pistol. As Bigazzi rushed over to disarm her, she pulled the trigger but she had forgotten to release the safety catch. The police chief found five of Mussolini's letters lying on a table and photocopies of eight others in a leather case. He put them into his briefcase, together with the pistol.

Claretta fell on the bed and drank a small glass of cognac. Then she handed over two photographs of Mussolini with a dedication to her, a few books, another pistol and a machine gun. She asked Bigazzi if she could send a letter to the Duce, and he agreed. She sat down and wrote a four-page letter that began: 'Something irreparable has truly happened between us, and it has been the revelation that your love is finished. . . . I can no longer remain beside you. Now it is really finished, now truly there is nothing more to be done.' But Mussolini pardoned her and she remained at the Villa Fiordaliso. Unknown to Mussolini, Buffarini recorded telephone calls between the Duce and his lover. And once, during her absence, the Fascist secret police chief, Eugenio Apollonio, went into her bedroom and stole her diary.[18]

Rachele, after phoning her husband to tell him she was going to the Villa Fiordaliso, went first to the office of Buffarini. She demanded that he, as 'the accomplice of that woman', accompany her. 'This time I will kill everyone, even you, and thus your double game will end,' she raged. Mussolini phoned Claretta to warn her of the storm that was about to break: 'She is coming to you. I tried to dissuade her, but it was not possible. Don't let her in. She's out of control and I fear she may be armed.' Claretta summoned Spoegler, her SS minder, and he had the gate closed.

Rachele arrived with Buffarini and several others, pressed the bell a couple of times and, getting no answer, held her finger there. Spoegler came out through a steady rain and told her she could not be received and should go away. Rachele began shouting, grabbed the bars of the gate and tried to climb over, Buffarini tugging at her skirt to hold her back. Spoegler asked her if she was armed, and when she said no, he let her enter with Buffarini. She met Claretta on the ground floor.

'What are you, signora or signorina?' Rachele asked. Claretta told her she was married although, of course, she had obtained a Hungarian divorce not recognised in Italy. 'Then, good evening, signora,' Rachele replied. There are four accounts of what followed – from Myriam Petacci, Rachele, Spoegler and Rachele's biographer, Anita Pensotti. First, Myriam's account, which she said she learned from Claretta:

'You wanted to see me?'

'Yes, I wanted to. I wanted to see you, to tell you something: that you must go away, that here there is no need of you. No one wants you. Go away and leave my husband in peace.'

'I beg you to believe me that, if you try to give me orders, you commit an error.'

Rachele got angry. 'He doesn't love you at all,' she taunted her rival. 'He told me even yesterday that he doesn't love you and that if you get off his feet it would give him pleasure. Not only him, but everyone. He loves only me, understand?' Claretta left the room and returned with thirty-two letters from Mussolini that she said were proof of his feelings for her. She said she knew she was in the wrong, but she loved him and was prepared to go away if necessary, provided that he asked it of her.

Rachele said she didn't want to see the letters. 'They don't interest me.'

'I must tell you that the Duce has always shown the greatest respect for you, as the mother of his children,' Claretta said.

'How do the children come into this? When people marry, they have children, no?' Rachele told Claretta that, with her figure, she was probably not capable of having children. Myriam thought it likely that Rachele knew Claretta had had an abortion in 1940 and after that was told she could never have children.

Rachele stepped forward, grabbed Claretta by the arms and began insulting her. Claretta shouted: 'Signora, moderate your language. Remember that you are in my house.' Buffarini and Spoegler intervened and Rachele said: 'If you love him truly you must sacrifice yourself. All the worse for you if you don't go away. You will end badly.'

At that point the phone rang. Mussolini was on the line, and he spoke first with Claretta, then told Rachele to calm herself and return home. Rachele lost control and Myriam found her words unrepeatable. The meeting lasted more than three hours.[19]

In her own version of events, Rachele said that when Spoegler asked her if she were armed, she replied: 'I don't make visits carrying weapons.' She added that when Claretta finally appeared, she held between her fingers 'a handkerchief of crepe, like a French woman, and seemed to me defenceless, like a fragile plant of our countryside'.

Rachele said she told Claretta she had not come to threaten her and had not acted out of jealousy; her husband needed peace and it was necessary 'to put an end to the scandal created by your presence here. . . . If you truly love him, you must give up seeing him'. Claretta burst into tears. Exasperated, Rachele told her she could not suffer women who resolved every problem with tears and fainting. She accused Claretta of photographing and sending to Switzerland and Germany some very delicate letters the Duce wrote, and of having permitted a direct phone line to be installed between their houses. Claretta fainted from time to time, with Buffarini rushing up with a bottle of cognac to revive her. Between faints, she insisted Mussolini could not live without her.

'It isn't true,' Rachele replied. 'My husband knows I am here, you can ask him if you don't believe me.' She said she pushed Claretta towards the telephone and Mussolini confirmed what she had said: 'Yes, I know my wife is there, but she is right. It's time to end it.' Rachele told Claretta she was hated by all, Fascists and partisans, and her life was in danger.

Rachele said in her memoirs she had received an anonymous letter with a poem that repeated the line: 'We will take you all to Piazzale Loreto.' That was the square in Milan where fifteen partisans had been murdered by Fascists in August 1944 in reprisal for a partisan attack on a German truck. Rachele looked at Claretta and said: 'They will take you to Piazzale Loreto.'[20]

Spoegler's version contained many of the above details but he added that Rachele said to Claretta: 'What elegance! You dress just like a kept woman. Look at how the kept woman of a head of state dresses! And look at me who is married to him.' When Claretta showed Rachele her husband's letters, Spoegler said Rachele tried to seize them but was held back by a German official.[21]

SS Colonel Eugen Dollmann, who was not present but may have learned this from Germans who were, said Rachele launched this 'fatal arrow' at her rival: 'Signora, I am no longer young, and I know it. But do you believe that the Duce, if he saw you as you are now, without makeup and without face powder, would continue to consider you his idol?'[22]

Anita Pensotti added one more detail. After this stormy meeting, Rachele told Pensotti she returned to Villa Feltrinelli, cried and swallowed bleach. She became very sick and was confined to her bed for three days. Towards the evening of the first day, according to Vittorio Mussolini, the Duce sent her a note asking if he could come to her. Vittorio said she brightened up, got out of bed to improve her appearance, then received her husband and they stayed together the whole evening, patching up their differences.[23]

In her memoirs, Rachele was rather indulgent in her judgement on Claretta. 'She was more an instrument of others than personally guilty. Around her developed a web of shady political interests and financial speculation, above all involving Marcello.'

Rachele said she learned from an informant one day that Marcello Petacci, whom she had never met, had acquired on the opposite bank of Lake Garda a large motorboat that he planned to use to kidnap Mussolini. It was at that point, she said, that she decided to go to Buffarini and confront Claretta.[24] Strangely, Rachele did not elaborate on Marcello's alleged plot or what followed from her hearing about it.

* * *

As the Allies advanced, Mussolini sent out feelers to the apostolic nuncio in Bern, the pope's representative to the Swiss government, asking him to intercede to obtain asylum for his family. The nuncio informed Cardinal Schuster in Milan, who suggested he could help in return for the liberation of some priests and a promise to end cruel police measures against the population.[25] Later, Mussolini's Cabinet met, in his absence, to discuss a proposal to send families of government ministers to Switzerland. Some were opposed, but a majority approved the proposal. When Mussolini was informed, he agreed to an approach to the Swiss commercial representative in Milan, Max Troendle, to sound out Swiss views. Troendle consulted his government and replied that the Swiss wanted assurances that the families would have enough money to support themselves for two years, and wanted an exchange of Italian sugar for Swiss watches as part of the deal.

The Italians informed Rahn and found him opposed. Wolff also rejected the plan and suggested they must find another solution, for example some place in Austria near the Swiss border, so the families could flee to Switzerland if the Axis were defeated. Finally, the Germans suggested Zurs, a famous winter sports venue approximately 8,000 feet up in a remote corner of the Austrian mountains near Lake Constance. Rahn said he could offer a refuge to 20,000 Fascists. The Fascist families – Mussolini's excepted – went there on 10 December and found that because of deep snow they had to travel the last six miles on sleighs driven by Russian and Yugoslav war prisoners. An Italian diplomat, Capasso-Torre, remarked jokingly: 'It seems to me an elegant concentration camp for highly regarded people.' The Germans learned of his remark and threatened to put him on trial for treason but were finally dissuaded. The heads of families joined their relatives for Christmas, but by early January most of the families had tired of their isolation and elected to return to Italy.[26]

Mussolini meanwhile was making his own preparations in anticipation of the collapse of the Salò Republic. He stunned and outraged many of his followers when, on 7 November, he sold his newspaper *Il Popolo d'Italia* to the Milanese industrialist Gian Riccardo Cella for a reported 75 million lire to be paid in Swiss francs. He had founded the newspaper in 1914, and it had been the principal mouthpiece of his regime and a major source of his income. Nothing could have given a clearer indication that he believed the game was up and he was out to save his personal wealth for his family. His daughter Edda, then in exile in Switzerland, later said she received from a Mussolini emissary 5 million lire, her share from the sale of the newspaper. It closed on 25 July 1945, and never appeared again.[27]

On 13 November, Field Marshal Alexander broadcast a proclamation to the 'patriots beyond the Po'. He said the summer campaign had ended and the winter campaign was about to begin. He asked the partisans to put an end to their activities, prepare for a new phase of struggle by conserving their munitions and await new orders. The Allied commander had failed to understand that the partisans could not simply hide their arms and go back to the towns and villages from which they came; they would be recognised and rounded up by the Fascists. 'With the Germans in Upper Italy there was no way [for the partisans] to retreat to solid "winter quarters",' wrote Leo Valiani, one of the political leaders of the resistance. 'Either we continued to resist . . . or the anti-Fascist army would break up and the liberation movement would be buried under the snow.' Communist leader Luigi Longo said the partisans could not afford 'the luxury of a "vacation"'. Basil Davidson, a British Special Forces liaison officer with the partisans, said Alexander had 'as well as told the partisans to disband and the enemy to come up and finish them off while they were doing it'. An American officer liaising with the partisans, Max Corvo, was equally appalled. He said the partisans concluded they had been abandoned by the Allies. Shortly afterward, US Treasury Secretary Henry Morgenthau and other American officials complained the Allied Command was following a British line and the British were interested in maintaining the Fascists in power, a wildly mistaken accusation. The British provided the bulk of the troops fighting against the Fascists and Germans in Italy, and a principal reason for Alexander's order was that at American insistence his forces had become bogged down and weakened by the diversion of troops to the invasion of southern France. He could not continue his offensive in winter with reduced forces.[28]

The Corps of Volunteers for Freedom (CVL), the body directly in charge of the partisan military struggle, sent a message to Alexander on 2 December protesting that his order for a winter stand-down was 'absolutely unjustifiable'. Longo drafted the message, which went on to say the partisan struggle had not been 'a caprice or a luxury which one can renounce when one wants' but was necessary to defend the material, political and moral patrimony of the Italian people day by day. Far from scaling back their struggle, the partisans would intensify it. The Allies partly made up for the damage they had done to the partisan cause by increasing air drops of supplies during the winter.[29]

Mussolini wrote to Hitler on 14 November, urging a resumption of the military initiative on the Italian front. He said 'the partisan phenomenon is dying out' and a recent amnesty had brought several thousand young men back to Fascist barracks and factories. Hitler did not reply, but Kesselring had already made his plans. Within a week of the Alexander stand-down order, the partisan movement was under heavy fire and roundups everywhere. The entire Garibaldi Brigades command in Piedmont was captured and one member killed. Similar arrests took place in the Veneto, Liguria and Lombardy. The entire Committee of National Liberation in Ferrara was arrested by Fascists and handed over to the SS; their seven bodies were found in a common ditch only in 1946. It was the beginning of a hard winter, of constant rain and snow, and many partisans were without winter clothing. They lost much of the territory they had controlled, and a great deal of their equipment, arms and food. They were forced to extort food from civilians or pay high prices. Rampant inflation had set in throughout northern Italy because of scarcities.[30]

Ferruccio Parri, the Action Party leader who represented his party on the CLNAI, returned to Milan after a long trip to the south, and was arrested by chance but not recognised immediately. A search of his quarters turned up a suitcase full of compromising documents that identified him, and he was taken to the SS headquarters in the Hotel Regina. Edgardo Sogno, one of the outstanding figures of the resistance movement, developed a bold plan to rescue Parri. He and several other men would go into the hotel from the roof and snatch Parri away under the eyes of the SS. But before Sogno could fully develop his plan, he learned Parri was about to be transferred to Verona. He had to act quickly. He and several companions, dressed as German soldiers, were spotted in an adjoining building before they could reach the roof and, after a brief fight, he was captured. One of his men managed to escape.[31]

On 23 November, workers in more than seventy factories in Milan went on strike. The walkout spread to Turin, Genoa, Bergamo and other cities.[32]

In Rome on 26 November, Bonomi resigned as prime minister and proposed Count Carlo Sforza, who had returned to Italy from exile in the United States, as his successor. But Churchill disliked Sforza and the British vetoed this choice. Crown Prince Umberto asked Bonomi to form a new government and he put out feelers to the leftist parties in the CLN, only to find some of them hostile. But Communist leader Palmiro Togliatti eventually accepted Bonomi's proposal to become deputy premier and a new government was formed, with the Socialists and the Action Party in opposition. The unity of the CLN had been broken.[33]

Ravenna fell to the Allies on 6 December and Foreign Under-secretary Mazzolini found the Duce 'very nervous'. He complained about systematic pillage by German forces everywhere.[34]

On 9 December Mussolini informed his Cabinet that he intended to transfer his government to Milan. Alberto Mellini Ponce de Leon, now his principal Foreign Ministry contact with Rahn and Wolff, said the Duce would have preferred to establish a redoubt at Trieste for its symbolic value, but the Germans opposed the plan because of 'technical and military difficulties'.[35] Several Fascist officials had earlier suggested the government should make its last military stand in Milan, but Mussolini had rejected that. 'Samson could tie the Philistines to his fate, I cannot,' he said. 'Milan is not the temple of Baal, nor are the Milanese Philistines.' But he promised to share the fate of his men. 'Life does not interest me, nor will I move a single finger to save myself,' he said.[36]

In mid-December, the Germans launched a counter-offensive in the Belgian Ardennes against Allied forces and were reported to be advancing in the north of Belgium. The news gave a moment of hope and relief to the Fascists, which Mussolini sought to exploit in a speech to his followers in Milan on 16 December. It was his first visit there since his return to power. Rahn had suggested he go to Milan to show his people they had not been abandoned, but Mussolini had initially been reluctant, saying he didn't feel he had anything to say. Rachele also had opposed his going to Milan, where he could be exposed to danger from anti-Fascists, but when he decided to go he told her: 'For too long I have been closed up here. I want to renew contact with the people.'

He arrived secretly on 15 December and sent word to Fascist officials he would speak the next day at the Lyric Theatre. The officials began telephoning around the city and the next morning a crowd of 20,000 marched toward the Lyric, most in Fascist uniform.

The speech was his greatest public triumph since his return to office. He extolled the Italian contribution to the war – 786,000 men, plus former internees and tens of thousands of Italian workers in the Reich – and asserted that this gave Italians the right to demand that their effort was 'equally and comradely valued' by the Germans and Japanese.

He spoke of the fall of Rome as a 'culminating date' in the history of the war, followed by the hard fighting in Normandy, and said the Allies expected to make a triumphal entry into Berlin by Christmas but would be foiled. He said:

> In the period of such euphoria the new German arms, improperly called 'secret', are undervalued and scoffed at. It is not a matter of secret arms, but of 'new arms', that obviously are secret until they are used in combat. That such arms exist, the English know from bitter experience. That the first will be followed by others I can, with knowledge of the matter, affirm. That they are such as to re-establish the balance, and then to return the initiative to German hands, is, within the limits of human forecasts, almost sure and also not far away. . . .
>
> Germany is in a position to resist and to determine the failure of enemy plans. . . . Now the German armed forces are not only not destroyed but are in a phase of growing development and power. While not exaggerating, one can observe that the political situation is today not favourable to the Allies. . . . Politically, Albion [England] is already defeated. . . . The Communist parties, that is the parties that act in the pay of and according to the orders of Marshal Stalin, are partially in power in countries of the West.

He went on to taunt President Roosevelt for having promised American mothers that their sons would not have had to fight and die overseas. 'He lied, as is the custom in all the democracies.'

He was nearing his peroration, and soon the crowd was on its feet, shouting: 'Duce, Duce, Duce!'

'We want to defend, with our nails and our teeth, the valley of the Po.' (*Shouts of 'Yes!'*) 'We want the valley of the Po to remain republican while waiting for all of Italy to be republican.' (*'Yes! All!'*) 'The day in which all the valley of the Po might be contaminated by the enemy, the destiny of the entire nation would be compromised. But I feel, I see, that tomorrow an irresistible and armed type of organisation will arise that will render life practically impossible to the invaders. We will make just one Athens of all the valley of the Po.'

Six times Mussolini was called back to the podium by the applause of the crowd, and he basked in a reception such as he had not experienced since the glory days of his rule in Rome. Then he rode across Milan in an open car to Piazza San Sepolcro, where fascism had been born in 1919, for another speech and another enthusiastic reception. 'Now everyone knows of what pasta these "liberators" are made,' he said. 'They bring us only political slavery, economic servitude, moral degradation. A people worthy of the name is never defeated unless it puts down its arms. And we will not put them down until the day of victory.'

On 17 December, a large contingent of Fascists marched through Via Dante to the headquarters of the Fascist Ettore Muti Legion, and Mussolini addressed them from the balcony.

'If some among our multicoloured enemies, and I say multicoloured because alongside a few white bastards are people of all races, had witnessed the march today in Via Dante, they would be convinced that, despite the greyness of this autumn, the grand spring of the nation is imminent,' he proclaimed.[37]

On his return to Gargnano, Fascist officials congratulated him on his triumph and he replied with a sad smile: 'What is life? Dust and altars, altars and dust.'* In his speech at the Lyric Theatre, he had sought, by stressing the Italian contribution to the war, to absolve his people of the charge of betrayal of the Germans, and he reacted bitterly when he saw that German press accounts omitted those passages.[38]

But in conversation with Rachele, he seemed clearly buoyed up by his reception in Milan. 'In twenty years of fascism I never had a reception like this,' he said. 'The Lyric was linked with the radio and so all of Italy suddenly knew of my presence. After my speech there was a triumph, a real triumph. . . . A sea of people, so enormous that it had no end. I was pleased to pass among the people, standing in the car, while they shouted their faith in me.'[39]

*A quotation from Alessandro Manzoni's poem about Napoleon, 'Cinque Maggio', signifying that someone who has risen to great heights can be trampled in the dust.

Chapter 14

'I HAVE RUINED ITALY'

We have been snatched away by a hurricane of frenzy.

(Benito Mussolini, January 1945)

In 1945 Benito Mussolini concluded a half century of political life. Whatever he may have achieved in his first four decades had been more than cancelled out by the unbroken series of disasters of the last ten years. Long past the age of empire-building and colonialism, he had set out to achieve an empire at the expense of hapless Africans whom he despised on purely racist grounds and against whom he did not hesitate to use poison gas. He had helped to bring to power a Fascist dictatorship in Spain, and attacked Albania and Greece with catastrophic results. He had tied his country to one of the most evil regimes in human history, and, like a jackal, had run after Hitler in his every act of aggression, even attacking the underbelly of France so he could have his share of the spoils after the Führer had brought that democracy to its knees. He had caused his country to be overrun, occupied by Germans, bombed by Americans and British, reduced to grinding poverty and subjected to appalling atrocities. He bore partial responsibility for German action against the Jews in Italy, and had himself stained his name with an opportunistic antisemitism. He might deservedly have faced a firing squad for all these acts; instead he put his son-in-law before one. In all the long, turbulent history of the Italian people, he represented an unparalleled disaster. None of the tyrants of the past had inflicted so much suffering on so many people, nor created so little that was enduring and ennobling. He was a Faustian figure who had gambled on a compact with the devil and lost. His besetting sin was greed, a greed for personal and national glory that blinded him to Italy's true national interests. Finally, mercifully, it was about to end. But first there was some unfinished business.

He began in January to try, over German opposition, to implement on a larger scale the nationalisation measures he had decreed earlier. 'My German allies are hostile from the depth of their souls,' he told his sister Edvige.

'In fact, their generals insist on declaring as many industries as they can protected from this nationalisation for reasons of war. Hitler, he is a Ghibelline: the political asset he would give to Europe corresponds to a new Holy Roman German Empire. As to my Guelph nationalisation, I will be able to live on as an inheritance to a Catholic–Socialist combination that perhaps will govern Italy when this pandemonium has passed.'*

Never far from his mind, amid a winter military stalemate that was sure to be broken as spring approached, was the matter of finding the appropriate place to make his last, heroic stand. Fascist Party Secretary Pavolini had been pushing the idea of an Alpine redoubt in the Valtellina since September, describing it as 'the most logical and worthwhile solution'. The 44-mile-long valley, 85 miles north of Milan between the Swiss border and the Adige river, was still ringed with First World War fortifications. It was sparsely inhabited but had electricity generating stations and a hospital for tuberculosis patients. Mussolini, who had never been there, approached Rahn, who advised against the Valtellina. 'Men are men and after a little while the solution of a Swiss internment would entice the less convinced and you would remain alone with a handful of men,' he said. But Mussolini was not dissuaded, and in November and December the Milan Fascist leader Vincenzo Costa carried out some preparatory work in the Valtellina, erecting barriers at the entrance, digging an anti-tank ditch and beginning construction of houses. He sent four cannon, ten machine guns, other munitions and food stocks. Another Fascist official, Paolo Zerbino, warned that the zone was controlled by partisans. Giorgio Pini, the under-secretary of the interior, went to the valley for an inspection and said there were 3,000 Fascists in the valley and 3,000 partisans on the mountains behind it. If the Valtellina were to be the last Fascist redoubt, intensive work should have been under way by January. But the matter was allowed to drift, with no final decision taken.[2]

Rachele said Vittorio Mussolini had kept in contact with an agent of the American secret services and hoped to persuade his father not to refuse a chance to save himself. 'You cannot tie your fate to that of the Germans. You must think also of yourself,' Vittorio told him. Mussolini replied that it was useless to insist, as he had already decided to resist in the Valtellina. 'It is a crazy undertaking and they will always say you just tried to save yourself,' Vittorio responded.[3]

The month of January mostly passed in drift and resignation. Mussolini told his close confidante Nicola Bombacci: 'We've lost completely, without possibility of appeal. One day history will cast up the balance and will declare

*In medieval Italy, the Ghibellines were the party of the German Holy Roman Emperors, and the Guelphs were the party of the pope.[1]

that I built many buildings, many streets, that I threw many bridges across rivers; but it will have to admit that so far as the spirit is concerned we were only common pawns in the present crisis of human conscience and that we remained pawns to the end. . . . We have been snatched away by a hurricane of frenzy, we are all going mad.'[4]

Towards the end of January, Mussolini made one of his infrequent trips outside Gargnano to visit troops of the Italia Division in the snow-covered Apennines of central Italy. He slept on a wooden camp bed in a mountain hut, covered with two horse blankets, then went on the next day to inspect his troops. Some were in good shape, while others appeared depressed and had few arms. Some, he found, had deserted to join the Todt organisation, which at least offered them work in more comfortable conditions in Germany. Mussolini returned from the trip with renewed energy but was bitter toward the Germans over their neglect of his troops.[5]

Some of the mountain villages he passed through had been heavily damaged by bombing, but Mussolini told Rachele he found people who still believed in him and even kissed his hands. One woman said her son had been with the partisans, but she wanted to enrol him in the republican army, and Mussolini naturally agreed.[6]

By the end of January, the Russians were on the German border and the Allies were fighting within Germany. In one of his notes for the *Corrispondenza repubblicana*, Mussolini said every country that was prey to the winners in the war could not but be alarmed. 'As to Germany, it is today historically and morally justified if it will put aside every scruple and, threatened with catastrophe, will provoke damage to its enemies, beginning with Great Britain, the nation responsible in its immeasurable and cynical egoism for the blood pouring across Europe for six years.'[7]

At a meeting of German and Italian military leaders on 31 January, Graziani said the military situation was unsustainable. Kesselring thought the Germans and Italians could still put up a resistance, but he admitted he lacked the means to undertake an offensive proposed earlier by Graziani. In the following month, Kesselring gave orders for the arrest of relatives of partisans, the execution of partisans and those who gave them assistance and the destruction of houses or portions of towns in which the inhabitants supported the partisans.[8]

Cardinal Schuster of Milan, who would play an increasingly active role in efforts to end the war in the coming months, was deeply worried at the prospect of Milanese and other north Italian industrial plants being destroyed by the Germans when they began their retreat. He wrote to Mussolini on 13 February, urging the Duce to exclude the city from future war operations and warning that 'the destruction of Milan would constitute such a historical crime that all the centuries would condemn it'. Mussolini already had decided against a last stand in Milan, but at the same time was determined to transfer his government there in its dying days. The hopes of some Fascists of transforming Milan into the Stalingrad of fascism had vanished after General Filippo Diamanti, the city's military commander, had called in forty-eight construction firms to bid on building fortifications around the city. Forty-four failed to attend the meeting, two managed to show they were not equipped to do the work and two accepted. But after threats from the CLNAI, the directors of those two firms fled the city. It was a hard winter in Milan, Genoa, Turin and other cities. People were forced to denude parks and avenues of trees to get wood for heating and cooking, and food supplies were increasingly scarce.[9]

On 14 February, Mussolini angered the Germans, perhaps deliberately so, by authorising Professor Edmondo Cione, a little-known philosophy professor, to establish what amounted to an opposition political movement, the National Republican Socialist Grouping. Cione had first approached Mussolini with the idea in August 1944. He said he wanted to set up a group of non-Fascist intellectuals who would accept a critical function within the Salò Republic. Mussolini was interested and gave Cione permission to publish a newspaper for his party. But he soon had to close it because of a violent reaction by hardline Fascists. Cione again met Mussolini in December and told him he did not want a rebirth of the parties but was seeking a forum in which critical voices could be heard. He asked Mussolini to secure the release of some Christian Democratic politicians who had been arrested in Como. Mussolini agreed in principle to Cione's ideas but waited until February to give formal approval. In Berlin, Ribbentrop, who believed Cione was in contact with the British Labour Party, was furious. He called in Italian Ambassador Anfuso and asked if Mussolini were moving away from fascism.[10] In his diary, Goebbels wrote: 'What a piteous spectacle the Duce is. . . . He now lets it be known through his newspapers that fascism intends to revert to a two-party system. This is again some new quirk of Fascist intellectualism, which is totally off the rails and now, to cap it all at this stage of the war, is saying farewell to its own principles.'[11]

But the rumpus over Cione was but the prelude to another Mussolini bombshell that upset the Germans even more. He dismissed Buffarini, the corrupt and conniving interior minister whose presence in the government had become unsupportable to moderate Fascists. Buffarini was seen as a divisive force, heavily involved with some of the more disreputable militia groups and an intriguer suspected of corruption. Mussolini had sounded out the Germans in late 1944 and found they were opposed to a change. They considered Buffarini a trusted and loyal figure. Carlo Silvestri, Mussolini's Socialist friend, said Buffarini had been kept at Mussolini's side as the direct representative of Himmler and the SS. 'Intelligent and sly, he was the personification of the worst fascism; he was the worst enemy of the policy of national conciliation of Mussolini and Graziani.'[12]

When Buffarini got wind of Mussolini's plans to dismiss him, he went to see Rachele. She said he placed before her his revolver and 'insisted I kill him, protesting that everybody was hostile to him, including his wife. I sent him away.' She said she had earlier had to restrain some people who wanted to kidnap Claretta or kill Buffarini.

Spurned by Rachele, Buffarini appealed to Mussolini, claiming that his merits as a Fascist were clearly demonstrated by the fact he had been condemned to death by the partisans as a war criminal on several occasions. He said he had been profoundly wounded by accusations of betrayal and corruption coming from 'a very high person'. He apparently alluded to Claretta Petacci, who had become hostile to him. Mussolini passed on to Buffarini anonymous letters accusing the minister of having trafficked in foreign currency and stolen the property of a prominent Jewish family named Morpurgo.[13]

On 16 February, Mussolini called in Alberto Mellini Ponce de Leon of the Foreign Ministry and told him: 'There is a very important question and one that requires an energetic intervention: the situation with the Germans isn't going well. Some time ago I decided to send away Buffarini-Guidi and they know why very well: he is a man who has many merits but is hated by all, anti-Fascists and Fascists. He is hated even more than I. I am not discussing his technical capabilities, but the Fascists can no longer see them and for some time have been asking me for his head. For the rest, the Germans themselves, who have such good organs of information in all the Italian cities . . . know by now that the firing of Buffarini will provoke everywhere manifestations of joy. I say manifestations of joy, and it is painful to say it, as if it were a matter of a military victory.'[14]

Rahn had asked Mussolini to postpone the announcement of Buffarini's dismissal until he could let Berlin know, but Mussolini refused. He informed Buffarini in a letter of 21 February of his removal, and closed with this pointed command: 'Hand over to the bearer of this letter the secret funds in your possession.' He later shifted Paolo Zerbino from Piedmont to be Buffarini's successor. When German censors threatened to prevent the news of Buffarini's dismissal being broadcast, Mussolini ordered Mellini to go to Rahn with a protest, and said he would go on the air personally to announce his decision. Wolff was indignant at not having been informed of the removal, especially as he had oversight of Italian police who operated under Buffarini's ministry. 'From that moment my good relations with Mussolini ceased,' he said. In retaliation he ordered the immediate arrest of former Police Chief Tullio Tamburini and Eugenio Apollonio, head of the secret police. Mussolini instructed Mellini to demand their release, and in a note to Wolff said the arrests 'could lead to very serious political consequences'.[15]

'This is the drop that makes the vase overflow,' he told Mellini. 'I intend to have satisfaction and as soon as possible. Otherwise it is better that the Germans arrest me, dissolve the republican government and transform this disguised and humiliating occupation into a real and true occupation.' He instructed Mellini also to deliver a protest over acts of violence by German troops, especially in Emilia. He said he had learned of unjustified executions carried out with no semblance of legality and with the condemned people not allowed to see a priest before they died. The Germans, he said, also were guilty of spoiling crops and livestock and making minute preparations to destroy industrial plants and public works, especially port facilities in Genoa and hydroelectric plants.[16]

His emissaries were unable to meet Wolff or Rahn immediately. Wolff pretended to be in bed with an injured foot and Rahn was tied up in a long talk with Buffarini. Mussolini told Mellini to try again: 'Either the Germans have confidence in me and my government, and therefore concern themselves with making war and let me govern . . . or it is useless that I continue to stay in this post and that a republican government exists.'[17]

Rahn eventually saw Mellini and told him the atmosphere around the Duce was very anti-German and was made worse by Mussolini's lack of confidence in him and Wolff. But he said the German censors had been overly zealous, and he ordered the broadcast about Buffarini to go ahead. He complained that his position as ambassador was becoming untenable, and suggested that Mussolini have him removed. As to the arrest of the two officials, he said that was outside his competence. But he said Apollonio was of Jewish descent and had conspired against the Duce and the Germans, while Tamburini had had secret contacts with the Allies in Switzerland and had been involved with them in contraband currency dealings. Mellini observed that Rahn appeared very nervous during their meeting. When Mellini reported back, Mussolini exploded. 'I've swallowed so many toads, but now enough,' he said. He was not looking for Rahn's resignation, he said, but he wanted the Germans to let him govern and let his troops fight. The Germans ignored his demands, eventually deporting Apollonio and Tamburini to the Dachau concentration camp. Buffarini remained in close contact with Rahn and some SS commands.

In a talk later that month with Mellini, Mussolini said he wanted to leave 'this cul-de-sac' of Gargnano for Milan, and it had been an error on his part not to base his government there: 'Rome having been lost, the capital of Republican Italy is Milan. . . . From this lost and faraway corner one cannot govern. Besides I have never liked lakes. The lake is a compromise between the sea and the river: because of this, like all compromises, I don't like it.

For that matter the Social Republic is a compromise.' He said some people had told him Britain could use him, at the right moment, as a moderating and anti-Bolshevik influence, but he did not believe it. 'England doesn't want to treat with and serve itself of anyone,' he stated. 'It wants to win and put aside Germany and Italy for a long time.'[18]

In a separate meeting with his friend Nino D'Aroma, Mussolini railed against Churchill as 'a very genial ham actor who has ruined, by his mania of reciting his part too much, his island and our continent together'. He said Churchill's 'very theatricality will end by condemning him among his people'.

He also sounded off against Generalissimo Franco, the Spanish dictator. 'This Franco with his neutrality cost us and costs us still more than a bitter battle in open field on Spanish territory,' he said. 'He is just an able, cold and calculating Galician who, from a bloody and passionate revolution, has made a wretched dictatorship.'[19]

Preziosi, the antisemitic extremist and excommunicated priest, came to Mussolini to push another of his obsessions to the last. All Masons or former Masons must be removed from republican posts, he demanded. Mussolini let him know he had more important matters to consider. 'The question today is this: if the game were lost, do you believe it is better for the Axis in general and Italy in particular to surrender to the Anglo-Saxons or the Soviet Union?' Preziosi ignored the question and returned to the issue of Masons and Jews. As though he hadn't spoken, Mussolini resumed his own train of thought: 'If it were only a matter of the United States, I could be undecided. But there is England in the middle and because of this I do not deny my sympathies for Russia. . . . I am an old Socialist.' He went on to attack the bourgeoisie, with its 'materialistic mentality and greed for riches', as the ruin of Italy. 'If I must disappear, the inheritance of power in Italy must be by the Socialists . . . the true Socialists. In Italy there are very many of them, even if many believe themselves to be Communists.'[20]

Count Serafino Mazzolini, the under-secretary for foreign affairs, died of septicaemia on 23 February. Mussolini told his sister: 'Poor Mazzolini. I appreciated him and his death saddens me. But he died in his bed, as used to happen, and has had a solemn funeral. Who knows how we will die and where they will throw our bones.' Earlier that month, he had admitted to Mazzolini that Germany had lost the war, and Hitler's secret weapons were probably an illusion. But in December he had assured Rachele and Vittorio that the arms did exist.[21]

Mussolini's physical and mental state began to deteriorate again at the beginning of February, and no doubt the strains of the Buffarini episode contributed to his decline. His German doctor Zachariae said there was no sign of a return of his ulcer, but the Duce slept badly, grew thin and no longer gave an impression of freshness and vitality. 'In the days preceding the collapse, where there was no longer any doubt that the war was lost, he, who was gifted with a physical and spiritual capacity much superior to that which is normal for his age, had a serious nervous attack, a true breakdown,' Zachariae said. 'He became apathetic and showed an absolute lack of energy and intelligence. . . . He did not sleep and ate almost nothing. In these circumstances even the medical art could do nothing for him.' Around this time, Mussolini was overheard exclaiming to himself, as he walked in the garden of Villa Feltrinelli: 'I have ruined Italy! I have ruined Italy!'[22]

Chapter 15

THE SECRET NEGOTIATIONS

There is no possibility of understanding and honest collaboration with the Germans.

(Benito Mussolini after suspecting the Germans were acting behind his back, 5 March 1945)

Few Italians today would recognise the name of Baron Luigi Parrilli, and outside Italy his obscurity is almost total. But he deserves to be remembered, because he played a role of no little importance in ending the war in Italy. Short, slightly built and bald, Parrilli was in 1945 a businessman in northern Italy. SS Colonel Eugen Dollmann described him as 'a great bon viveur and woman chaser' who smoked a hundred cigarettes a day and 'looked like a character in a late nineteenth-century French novel'. He said Parrilli had wasted a family fortune on the gaming tables at Monte Carlo, then had recouped his fortunes by marrying the daughter of a rich industrialist. For fifteen years before the war he represented the US appliance firm Nash Kelvinator in Italy and he had business interests in various parts of Europe. A member of a noble Neapolitan family, he was also a Knight of Malta and a Papal Chamberlain of Cape and Sword. He had no prior experience of politics or diplomacy. Yet this improbable figure, at considerable risk to his life, was the catalyst who brought together American secret agents and German SS officers, behind the backs of Hitler and Mussolini, to forge a surrender on the Italian front and to save northern Italy's industrial and public infrastructure from wanton destruction.

Parrilli seems to have stepped on to the world diplomatic stage purely as a result of a chance meeting with SS Lieutenant Guido Zimmer, chief of counter-espionage in Genoa, in a hotel breakfast room towards the end of 1943. Over the succeeding months, they became friends. Zimmer was a practising Catholic who had joined the SS only at the urging of his fanatical father. Zimmer's wife had refused baptism to their two children, and he had been discovered trying secretly to have them baptised. This went into his military file, blocking his promotion. Parrilli used his friendship with Zimmer to get one of his household servants exonerated from military service. It was then that Zimmer began to confide in Parrilli his worries about the war. He revealed that the Germans had prepared a plan of vast destruction to be carried out before their departure from Italy, and he was deeply troubled, concerned above all to save the country's art and religious treasures. At Parrilli's urging, Zimmer confided his concerns to Dollmann, who was General Wolff's emissary in dealing with Catholic Church leaders in Italy, and Dollmann agreed to pass on Zimmer's views to Wolff. Zimmer told Parrilli about several previous failed attempts at negotiations between Germans who wanted to end the war in Italy and Allied officials who were sceptical of their intentions and unwilling to accept their terms. For reasons known only to himself, Parrilli then decided he could succeed where others had failed; he would be the angel of deliverance. He consulted his friend Marshal Enrico Caviglia, now in his eighties and living in retirement, and Caviglia encouraged him to act. In February 1945, Parrilli wrote to a friend, Professor Max Husmann, who was the director of two youth institutes in Switzerland, asking for his help in getting him into Switzerland. Husmann eventually advised him he had cleared the way, so Parrilli applied for an exit permit from Italy for 'economic reasons', and the Germans approved. He crossed into Switzerland at Chiasso on 21 February, met Husmann in Zurich and told him of his mission.[1]

Fortunately, Husmann had some important connections. He was in touch with Major Max Waibel of the Swiss Military Intelligence, who was in St Moritz. Husmann phoned him and said it was urgent that they meet but gave no details. Waibel took the first available train to Zurich and, after talking to the two men, he sent an urgent message to Allen W. Dulles, head of the US Office of Strategic Services in Switzerland. Dulles happened to be in Hegenheim, in Alsace, for a meeting with an American army intelligence officer. Dulles and his principal aide, Gero von Schulze-Gaevernitz, a tall, elegant, naturalised American of German origin, took a train to Lucerne at Waibel's suggestion and had dinner with him that Sunday evening, 25 February, at a quiet restaurant near Lake Lucerne. Waibel filled them in on his talk with Parrilli and Husmann. Dulles was not impressed; this latest peace feeler had the earmarks of earlier soundings from Italian industrialists that had come to naught.[2]

Dulles left it to Gaevernitz to meet these two dubious characters at the Hotel Schweizerhof in Lucerne on 26 February. Gaevernitz was not immediately impressed. Parrilli had an ingratiating manner and struck him as 'a bit like the keeper of a small Italian hotel who is trying to persuade you to take your dinner there'. Husmann was talkative, given to sweeping generalities and prone to lecture in a slightly pompous manner about peace and international understanding. Parrilli was evasive when asked whom he represented. He told Gaevernitz the SS, not the German army, was capable of independent action and did not favour a scorched-earth policy as the Germans fought their way out of Italy. He was confident certain SS people could be used to sabotage such a policy. Gaevernitz pressed for names, and Parrilli mentioned two relatively minor German figures in Italy. Gaevernitz was dismissive; these were small fry, men without influence. Parrilli, sweating by now as he saw 'the ground collapsing under my feet', came up with the name of Zimmer. He noticed that Gaevernitz became more attentive. Then he added the name of Dollmann, and Gaevernitz displayed even more interest, according to Parrilli. In fact, Gaevernitz was not as impressed as Parrilli believed. Gaevernitz thought Zimmer was a misfit in the SS and doubted Zimmer and Parrilli could influence Wolff and Dollmann. He asked Parrilli if he could get Dollmann and Wolff into Switzerland, adding that a meeting with Field Marshal Kesselring would be even more worthwhile. 'I had the impression Gaevernitz thought nothing more would happen,' Parrilli wrote. He was correct. Gaevernitz thought he had seen the last of Parrilli. But Waibel, more optimistic, gave Parrilli a password to be used with Swiss border guards if he should return. He also gave him a code name: Pietroluigi.[3]

* * *

Certain German officials had been interested in a peaceful departure from Italy for months, and had tried to make contact with the Allies, but the failure of these attempts gave Gaevernitz ample reason for scepticism. The first approach was inspired by Heinrich Himmler, who had come to fear a Communist takeover of Germany and was determined to act even behind Hitler's back. Through Wilhelm Harster, head of the Gestapo in Italy, he sought to find an Italian not compromised with fascism who might enjoy the confidence of the Allies and be willing to act as an intermediary. Harster lighted upon Franco Marinotti, the president of the giant textile company Snia Viscosa, who had been jailed for opposing Mussolini's attempts to nationalise industry. The Germans secured his release, and Harster met him at the SS-controlled Villa Locatelli at Cernobbio on the banks of Lake Como. Harster told him the Germans wanted to explore the possibility that the Allies would join them in a common front against the Soviets. He pointed out the advantage to the Allies of the deal the Germans had in mind: they could shift twenty-five divisions from Italy to Central Europe and thereby prevent the Russians from overrunning Europe. The Germans, he said, would only ask that German territorial integrity be respected at the end of the war. Marinotti was more than willing to act as an intermediary with the Allies; he feared the Germans would carry out a scorched-earth policy in northern Italy if there were no accord. He approached the British consul in Zurich, a man named Cable, who reported the conversation to the Intelligence Service in London. The British rejected the German conditions out of hand and reprimanded Cable for acting on his own initiative in encouraging Marinotti to continue meeting with Harster. Monsignor Filippo Bernardini, the papal nuncio in Bern, learned of this in November 1944 and hoped the Americans would be more accommodating than the British. He showed Dulles a document signed by Harster that guaranteed Marinotti safe passage in and out of Italy, and suggested the Americans make contact with him. Dulles was not convinced of German good faith, and when he sounded out Washington he was instructed to let the matter drop.

Later that November, the Reverend Giuseppe Bicchierai, secretary to Cardinal Schuster, made a secret visit to Switzerland to contact Dulles. Schuster wanted to act as mediator between the Germans and partisans to avoid further bloodshed and the destruction of the Italian economic infrastructure, and he had had discussions with Wolff and Rahn. In a message to them on 14 October, he said German destruction of industrial and public utility installations would only facilitate 'Bolshevik infiltration in Italy' by creating disorder and unemployment. Through Bicchierai, Schuster passed along a proposal from the Germans that their forces would refrain from destroying Italian industry, public services and power installations if the partisans would agree not to obstruct German withdrawal from Italy. Schuster was confident Wolff and Kesselring would be prepared to sign an accord to that effect. Contacted by Dulles, the Allied command in Caserta advised that partisan leaders were working for a general uprising against the Germans and would not entertain the German proposal. The Allies clearly were not inclined to try to persuade the partisans to change their minds.[4]

In late December, Gaevernitz learned that the German consul in Lugano, Alexander Konstantin von Neurath, was also discreetly taking soundings about a peace agreement. He was the son of Konstantin von Neurath, the former German foreign minister, and Dulles suspected he was working for German Intelligence. Gaevernitz met Neurath, who told him he was in direct touch with Kesselring, Wolff and Harster. He was convinced the war was lost and he was prepared to take any personal risk to bring it to an early end. He went to Italy in January 1945 and met Kesselring, who said he was not prepared to come to terms with the Allies just yet but would be willing for Neurath to explore peace possibilities through other Germans. In February, Kesselring visited his father's estate near Stuttgart and arranged for Neurath to secretly meet him and two German generals at a small village inn nearby.

The generals told Neurath they considered it futile to continue the war, and they would be willing to allow German divisions in the West to be overrun so the Allies could capture Germany ahead of the Soviets. But they were nonetheless worried they might be tried as war criminals. Gaevernitz hoped one of the generals, Siegfried Westphal, might be smuggled into Switzerland with Neurath's help for talks. Westphal was chief of staff to General Alfred Jodl, chief of operations of the Armed Forces High Command.

While this was afoot, Walter Schellenberg, a top aide to Himmler, had established contact with a British official in Zurich, who said he had obtained Churchill's authorisation for unofficial exploratory conversations. Schellenberg discussed the matter with Himmler, who got cold feet and suggested putting the matter to Ribbentrop first of all. Ribbentrop was unwilling to take responsibility, so the matter went to Hitler. Ribbentrop then sent a note to Schellenberg, forbidding any contact with enemy nationals and threatening dire punishment if talks went ahead. Despite this, Schellenberg decided to avail himself of longstanding, secret connections in Switzerland to try to bring peace closer. He held talks with Brigadier Masson, chief of the Swiss Secret Service. In early February, Dulles was informed that Schellenberg had arrived in Switzerland and wanted to see him. Schellenberg had passed word to Masson that if the Allies were prepared to drop their demand for unconditional surrender, the Germans would be interested in talks. Dulles declined to see him. A German Embassy official in northern Italy also arrived in mid-February and relayed word that Kesselring was ready to abandon the war if the Allies offered acceptable terms. Then, in late February, an Austrian agent arrived from Vienna. He had been sent by Ernst Kaltenbrunner, No. 2 to Himmler in the security apparatus as chief of the Reich High Security Office. Kaltenbrunner wanted him to tell Dulles that he and Himmler were anxious to end the war and were contemplating liquidating Nazi warmongers, especially Hitler's aide Martin Bormann. Dulles viewed all this with complete scepticism. 'As we saw it, the SS appeared to be chiefly trying to get some good marks with the Allies to offset what was otherwise an unmitigated record of black criminality,' he wrote.[5]

* * *

On 27 February, the same day Parrilli returned to Italy from Switzerland, Wolff met Mellini of the Italian Foreign Ministry to reply to Mussolini's recent complaints about German military actions in Emilia and Tuscany. Wolff said these actions were justified by the necessity of war and the hostile attitude of the population. Then he alluded indirectly to his discussions with Schuster about ending the war in Italy, telling Mellini he had recently taken initiatives that were 'very delicate' concerning his personal position and would like to talk to the Duce about it were it not for Mussolini's 'coldness and mistrust'. He went on to say he would be happy to meet the Duce and show him proofs of the guilt of Tamburini and Apollonio, the two police chiefs he had arrested after Mussolini's firing of Buffarini as interior minister. Mellini reported to Mussolini, who replied: 'I will submit myself also to this conversation.' But he said it would serve no purpose, and the Germans should have listened to him before carrying out 'useless cruelty and unjustified violence and rapine'. He complained that Hitler had gone to war with Russia against his advice, and still declined to listen to him. 'There was still time to make a satisfactory peace with Russia when he was at the gates of Stalingrad. In vain I implored him to do it. One sees today the consequences of his not having listened to me.' His remarks suggested that Wolff's mysterious initiatives had failed to pique his curiosity, but he subsequently had several meetings with Wolff and Rahn. To what extent they briefed him on their peace initiatives has never been satisfactorily explained.[6] On 2 March, Mussolini received a report from Ambassador Anfuso in Berlin that the Germans were still confident of being able to use secret weapons, which at least would improve the military situation and make possible negotiations with the Americans and British. Anfuso said Ribbentrop wanted to sound out the possibility of separating the Allies from Russia. Mussolini scoffed that Ribbentrop's face concealed only 'a pneumatic vacuum. Pneumatic vacuum and the most boundless and ridiculous presumption.'[7] He had so little regard for Ribbentrop's intelligence that he did not take the report seriously.

* * *

Parrilli may have been rash in his meeting with Gaevernitz in presuming to know the intentions of SS leaders. But he was now about to find out how far they were prepared to go. Zimmer, who had transferred from Genoa to Milan, arranged for Parrilli to meet Dollmann on 1 March. Parrilli said Dollmann was persuaded that 'I was a sort of emissary of the Allies', and Dollmann had convinced himself the Allies would break with Russia and make a separate peace with Germany. Dollmann tried to phone Wolff on the spot but found he was at Kesselring's headquarters in Recoaro, a small town east of Lake Garda, discussing how to end the war in Italy. Dollmann phoned Harster in Verona, told him of Parrilli's contacts with the Americans and said this must be reported to Wolff at once. Harster learned that Wolff was on his way back to Fasano, so he drove out to meet him and flagged down his car outside Verona. The report struck Wolff as so promising that he and his aides decided Dollmann and Zimmer should go to Switzerland with Parrilli to pursue the contact. Dollmann meantime had gone to Fasano and reported to Rahn, who also approved his meeting with the Americans. In his memoirs, Rahn said he advised Dollmann that it would be hopeless to try to drive a wedge between the Allies and the Soviets.

A few days later, Kesselring called on Rahn, who was sick in bed, and Rahn told him the moment had come to save what was left of Germany from destruction. Kesselring referred to his oath as a soldier and said he thought the Führer would be able to turn the fortunes of war in their favour. Rahn replied: 'Field Marshal, this is no time for either of us to resort to propaganda slogans for each other's benefit. If you cannot make a decisive move now, I hope you will be ready the moment we hear the Führer is dead.' Kesselring did not reply but, as he was going out, he turned and said: 'I hope your political plans succeed.'[8]

Dollmann had lived in Italy since 1927. A member of a Munich family that had served the royal courts of Bavaria and Austria, he had gone to Italy to research Renaissance history, and earned his living initially as a translator and writer. He moved in both Roman and German aristocratic and clerical circles and hardly seemed the type likely to become an SS officer. But Dollmann went to Germany in 1937 as interpreter for a group of touring Italian Fascist youths, and when Hitler's interpreter fell ill he was asked to step into the breach. Hitler was impressed, and Himmler asked Dollmann to serve as his interpreter when he went to Italy that autumn. From then on he frequently served as an aide and interpreter to important Nazi visitors to Italy, including Hitler, and Himmler enrolled him in the SS. By 1944 he had become a colonel and was Wolff's liaison officer with Italian Church officials. He seldom wore the SS uniform so as not to give the wrong impression to his Italian artistic friends. Dulles later described him as 'an intellectual, highly sophisticated, somewhat snobbish and cynical', and a man of almost effeminate gestures. Dollmann offered his own more highly coloured assessment of Dulles: 'He always struck me as a leather-faced Puritan archangel who had fled from the European sink of iniquity on the *Mayflower* and now returned to scourge the sinners of the old world. He was incorruptible and totally humourless.'[9]

Parrilli crossed into Switzerland on 3 March and Dollmann and Zimmer, dressed in civilian clothes and travelling under false names, joined him in Chiasso early the next morning. The Swiss Major Waibel had meanwhile informed Parrilli that he had been unable to locate Dulles, and Gaevernitz was in Davos watching some German spies and could not leave. (Dulles's version was that Gaevernitz was on a skiing holiday.) Parrilli, the two Germans and Husmann left by car for Lugano while Waibel set off for Zurich to try to find Dulles. When he finally located him, Dulles decided to send another of his operatives, Paul Blum, to Lugano.

Parrilli, Husmann, Dollmann and Zimmer gathered in the Ristorante Biaggi in Lugano to await Blum. They had lunch in an upstairs private dining room normally used for meetings of the local Rotary Club, and Parrilli introduced Husmann to the Germans as Dulles's envoy. Over cold cuts and wine, Husmann made an impassioned speech in which he said an unconditional German surrender was the only way out. Dollmann was taken aback. As Parrilli described the scene, 'the veins in his neck were ready to explode, he got up, furious, with a violent movement of his chair'. Dollmann shouted at Husmann: 'But in short, what are you asking of us? Treason?' Husmann replied he was not asking anything of anyone. He asked Dollmann exactly what he meant by the word treason; were the German officers who tried to assassinate Hitler on 20 July traitors or patriots? Husmann said he was aware that Germans who contributed to ending the war were all afraid of being put on trial as war criminals, and he offered assurances that the Allies would view them more leniently than that. Writing about this later, Dollmann made no mention of his outburst but said Husmann's speech could easily have been published verbatim as a lost oration of Cicero. Dollmann asked permission to withdraw from the room and reflect. When he and Zimmer returned, Parrilli said, 'we perceived that the battle was won'. Dollmann was a different man, commenting gaily on the food and wines. He drank copiously and told his audience anecdotes about Rachele Mussolini's jealousy of Claretta Petacci. He also revealed unpublished details of how Mussolini had been rescued from the Gran Sasso in 1943.

Blum still had not arrived, but after 3 p.m. he sent word he was waiting at the Hotel Walter, a small hotel facing Lake Lugano. Swiss Lieutenant Fred Rothpletz, who had escorted the party to Lugano, went off with Husmann to fetch him while Parrilli remained with the Germans, who were 'drowning in liquor'. When Blum arrived at the restaurant, Parrilli went out to meet him and asked if he were willing to shake hands with the Germans. 'To whomever I speak, I cannot refuse my hand,' Blum replied. He did shake hands, and sounded out the Germans on the terms they were willing to concede and on their ability to carry out their promises. Are you convinced, he asked, that it would be impossible to separate the Allies from the Russians? Are you persuaded that the war is lost for Germany? Do you understand that Americans in Switzerland can deal only with Italian, and not German, territory? That the Americans will not speak with representatives of Hitler or Himmler? That the only basis of discussion is the unconditional surrender of the German army in Italy? To each question, Dollmann answered 'yes'.

Parrilli intervened to ask if the Allies would accept Himmler as their partner if he led a separatist movement in northern Italy. Until then the discussion had been conducted in French, but Blum blurted out in English:

'Not a Chinaman's chance.' Parrilli asked Blum how Germans who contributed to shortening the war would be treated. Blum replied in French: 'Because of this war, the material and moral destruction in Europe is so colossal that the Allies need every man of goodwill for reconstruction. All people who help to shorten the war give proof of their goodwill.' Dollmann struck Blum as a slippery customer who no doubt knew more than he was telling, while Zimmer hardly opened his mouth. Dulles had given Blum a slip of paper on which two names were written, and instructed him to hand it to Dollmann. The names were Ferruccio Parri, the Action Party leader who had been arrested in Milan, and Major Antònio Usmiani, an Italian who had been doing military intelligence work for Dulles before his arrest. Dulles wanted to test Wolff's seriousness by asking him to release the two men. Parri was held in Verona and Dulles believed Usmiani was in Turin; if Wolff could obtain the release of men in two widely separated locations, it would demonstrate how far his authority extended. Dollmann agreed to try to meet the American demands, but Dulles and Gaevernitz thought it was unlikely they would see him again. Blum was less sure.[10]

Parrilli accompanied the two Germans back to Italy that evening. He said Dollmann was dark and sullen, looking worried and fearful of the consequences of the position he had taken. He complained that the Allies 'have the effrontery to ask us for favours. Why should we free Parri and Usmiani?' Dollmann continued to Fasano and met Rahn on 4 March. He said Rahn told him: 'The best thing is that I go immediately by plane to the Führer and have him put me in charge of the conduct of the negotiations.' Dollmann was taken aback; he told Rahn he would do better to obtain three one-way tickets for Dachau for himself, Wolff and Dollmann.

Parrilli, upon his return from Switzerland, spent the night at Zimmer's house in Milan. Around midnight, Zimmer received a phone call ordering him to leave immediately for Fasano. When he arrived, he was asked to make a written report on the Lugano meeting, then met briefly Wolff, Dollmann, Rahn and Wolff's adjutant, Major Eugen Wenner. Then Wolff sent a car for Parrilli, and they met late that afternoon, 4 March.

'Recently the Führer assured us that soon he would experiment with a new, very powerful weapon, such as to decide the outcome of the war,' Wolff said. 'Kesselring is persuaded the weapon exists and told me that if it were too cruel he would refuse to use it.' Parrilli said he gathered from Wolff's tone that Wolff did not believe in the weapon. Wolff went on to say the Allies could not possibly want the Bolshevisation of Germany and should be willing to use the German army to maintain order in Central Europe; he clung to the illusion the Americans and British could be separated from the Soviet Union. Parrilli said he assured Wolff this was impossible but, if he approached the

Allies, 'many prejudices would fall on both sides and certain problems would assume an entirely new aspect'. Wolff got up, paced the floor and finally said: 'Fine, propose to Dulles to send me his emissary. My word of honour that he will be treated with all respect.' Parrilli suggested it would be better if Wolff came with him to Switzerland to speak to Dulles. Wolff continued pacing, then agreed. He had now crossed his personal Rubicon, and was aware that he would be putting his life on the line. He told Parrilli he would be prepared to travel on 8 March. Parrilli told him Dulles would not be willing to talk unless Wolff showed goodwill by releasing Parri and Usmiani. Wolff was hesitant; Parri was under surveillance by Harster, who worked for Kaltenbrunner, and he did not want to involve him. What explanation could he give Harster for freeing Parri? Parrilli suggested Wolff try to work out an exchange of prisoners. Wolff agreed, saying he would ask the Allies to hand over a Colonel Max Wuensche, a former adjutant to Hitler who had been captured in Brittany after the Allied invasion of France; the Führer was particularly fond of him. But there was one problem: Wolff had never heard of Usmiani and had no idea where he was being held.[11]

At this time Mussolini was still unaware of the talks between the Germans and the Allies, but he knew something was up. On 5 March, the day after the Wolff–Parrilli meeting, he told Mellini of the Foreign Ministry that he was aware that Wolff and Rahn were negotiating with the Committee of National Liberation. 'It may be opportune to do it,' he said. 'But I believe I have at least the right to be informed of what is happening. I can say the same about the relations they have with Cardinal Schuster. I convince myself ever more that there is no possibility of understanding and honest collaboration with the Germans. Apart from the fact they understand absolutely nothing of politics.' Mellini went to Rahn the following day and reported what Mussolini had said. Rahn confirmed the Germans were negotiating with the CLN but said the talks were of a local character, dealing more with military than political questions, and were out of his hands. He said the talks with Schuster were concerned only with limiting the damages of war. He wanted to assure the Duce that nothing concrete was happening and all initiatives by himself and Wolff, often taken without Berlin being informed, were aimed at doing everything possible to protect the interests of Italy, the Duce and fascism. Mellini reported back to Mussolini and wrote in his diary: 'The reply of Rahn has interested and reassured the Duce very little.' Mussolini instructed Mellini to tell Rahn that some of his ministers would soon transfer their offices to Milan and he would go there also, returning to Gargnano from time to time.[12]

Parrilli crossed into Switzerland on the morning of 5 March, after some difficulty with a German SS guard at the border, to inform Husmann of his meeting with Wolff and reveal the SS general's willingness to come to

Switzerland. Then he returned to Italy. Meanwhile, Zimmer found Usmiani in the San Vittore jail in Milan. The SS had had difficulty locating him because he was a prisoner of the Wehrmacht, not of the SS. A bewildered Parri was brought from Verona to SS headquarters at the Hotel Regina in Milan on 7 March. Parrilli and Zimmer were waiting for him, told him he was a free man and would be taken to Switzerland the next morning. Parri collapsed in a chair and had to be revived with a martini cocktail. The three men dined together that evening at the hotel, with Parri's wife present, and Zimmer opened a bottle of champagne. They all joined in a toast to peace.

At 5 a.m. the next day, they left for Switzerland, stopping at San Vittore to collect Usmiani. Then they proceeded to the Villa Locatelli at Cernobbio to join Wolff, Dollmann and Major Wenner before going on to Switzerland. The German officers, who had left Fasano in uniform, changed into civilian clothes at the villa. Wolff regretted not having a hat to his liking, and they lost time trying to find him one. At 7.30 a.m. the entire party headed for the frontier post at Chiasso in two cars, with Parrilli, Zimmer and the two freed Italians in the lead and Wolff and his party following. Parri and Usmiani had no documents but SS Captain Josef Voetterl had advised Parrilli to show any paper and the soldier at the frontier would pretend to examine it and make notes. Parrilli pulled out the first document he found in his wallet, an old Michigan driver's license that had expired. The ruse worked. Parri and Usmiani were driven to Zurich by Zimmer, and the rest of the party went by train.[13]

In Zurich, Major Waibel phoned Gaevernitz, who was in Davos, and said: 'Gero, are you standing or sitting? Because if you're standing, you might fall over when you hear the news. Parri and Usmiani are here. They were delivered safe and sound a few hours ago to my man at the Swiss–Italian frontier at Chiasso. SS Captain Zimmer has driven them up from Milan.' Gaevernitz quickly caught a train to Zurich, and arranged to join Dulles at an apartment they used only for sensitive meetings. Waibel had concocted a cover story for the party travelling by train: they were members of a German–Italian commission that had come to discuss the use of port facilities at Genoa. They travelled in two compartments reserved for them, with the doors closed and curtains drawn. En route, their train was blocked by an avalanche near the Gotthard Pass and they had to walk up the tracks with other passengers to get another train. Some Italians who knew Wolff were in the crowd, so Wolff stalled and ducked until they had passed him.[14]

After the five-hour train journey, the party was taken to Husmann's apartment at 80 Sonneggstrasse, where they had lunch, followed by coffee and liqueurs. Approaching 4 p.m., there was still no word of the Americans and the Germans were getting nervous. Husmann turned on the lights because it was a grey day. Dollmann, angry at being kept waiting, took

Parrilli aside and said: 'If it were not out of respect for the house that hosts us, I would propose to the commander to leave immediately. There are protocol forms that must be respected. It is unheard of that a mission led by a general is kept waiting for an entire afternoon without even being offered a justification.'

Meanwhile, Dulles had learned that Kaltenbrunner had flown to Constanz, just over the border from Switzerland, and held a meeting with a Professor Burckhardt, president of the Geneva-based International Red Cross. Kaltenbrunner had sent word through Burckhardt that he wanted to enter the country to speak with Dulles. Dulles had no wish to see him, and he was not allowed into Switzerland.[15]

Husmann came to meet Dulles for the first time, and suggested for security reasons Dulles call on Wolff at Husmann's apartment. But Gaevernitz thought it appropriate that Wolff should come to Dulles, not vice versa. Dulles wondered if Wolff wanted to trap him. 'I could see the headlines: "Envoy of President Roosevelt Receives High SS Officer".' He told Husmann that Wolff would have to wait because he wanted first to see Parri and Usmiani, who had been admitted as patients to an expensive clinic in an elegant section of Zurich. Dulles told Husmann he only wanted to hear one thing from Wolff: how he planned to carry out an unconditional surrender. Husmann handed over papers that Wolff had given him, and they proved to be letters of recommendation for Wolff from Rudolf Hess, the pope and other churchmen and aristocrats. 'They were somewhat like the material that a man applying for a job prepares for the company he hopes to serve,' Dulles observed. There were also notes attesting that, on Wolff's orders, several hundred paintings in the Uffizi Gallery had been removed to safety when Florence was bombarded, along with sculptures and the king's famous coin collection. Wolff claimed that, together with Kesselring, he had saved Rome from German bombardment, settled without bloodshed the strikes in Turin, Milan and Genoa in 1944 and negotiated an agreement with the partisans in November 1944 so north Italians no longer needed fear being drafted into the Italian Army or sent to Germany as labourers.

At the clinic, Parri burst into tears when Dulles arrived, and threw his arms around him. He had no idea why and how he had been rescued, and had assumed until that moment that he was to be shot or deported to Germany. 'What sort of deal have you made with the Germans to get me out?' he asked Dulles. Parri said he would accept no restrictions on his freedom of action and wanted to return to Italy immediately to continue the fight. Dulles assured him he had made no deals, and Parri was free to return at any time but it would be inadvisable to go immediately. Dulles was aware that it would be difficult to explain his escape if he returned and was recaptured. Parri agreed to his suggestion that he wait at least a week or two. Parri told him how Edgardo Sogno had tried to rescue him from the Hotel Regina, and urged Dulles to get Sogno released too. Dulles promised to do what he could.

Dulles returned to the secret American apartment that was on the ground floor of a bleak building at the end of Genferstrasse, facing Lake Zurich. He laid a fire in the fireplace and, just before 10 p.m., Husmann arrived with Wolff. On the way to the apartment, Husmann asked Wolff: 'Did Himmler send you here or did you come of your own initiative?' Wolff replied: 'Himmler knows nothing about my trip.'

Gaevernitz met first with Wolff while Dulles waited in the library. Gaevernitz offered Scotch, and the two men spoke in German, with Wolff stiff at first and saying little. Husmann summarised the talks he had had with Wolff on the train journey, emphasising that Wolff considered the war lost, was aware the Allies and Soviets could not be divided and affirmed that Hitler and Himmler knew nothing of his trip. Wolff nodded his agreement, and Husmann left the apartment. Dulles then entered the room, and the American spy and the SS general came face to face. They talked for an hour. Wolff admitted that from the early days of Nazism until the previous year he had had complete faith in Hitler but now realised the war was lost and to continue it would be a crime against the German people. 'I control the SS forces in Italy and I am willing to place myself and my entire organisation at the disposal of the Allies to terminate hostilities,' he said. But he stressed the necessity to win over Kesselring and other military commanders, and said he would try to arrange for Kesselring or his deputy to come to Switzerland to discuss surrender.[16]

Dulles later described Wolff as 'neither a troop commander nor police official but a kind of diplomatic or political adviser to the SS leaders' who had slipped into very high places because of his ability to manage other people through the force of his personality. He had become chief liaison officer between Hitler's command posts, the Foreign Ministry and SS headquarters at the start of the war. Later he was chief of Himmler's personal staff and his liaison officer with Hitler. He also acted as liaison between Himmler and Ribbentrop. But when he went over Himmler's head and won Hitler's approval for his divorce, Himmler banished him to Italy, where he commanded more than a million men. He held the title of plenipotentiary general of the armed forces for the rear combat areas of Italy, a title that meant he adjudicated in disputes of authority between the SS and the military.[17]

When Wolff returned that night to Husmann's house, he said to Parrilli: 'You were right, Parrilli. How different these Americans are from the descriptions that are made of them.' He went to a window and looked out on the lights of Zurich. 'For five years I haven't seen a city illuminated,' he said. 'But this visit has given me also an interior light: I know what I must do now.' To Dollmann he remarked how much finer it would have been if the lights of Europe had not been extinguished in August 1939. Over dinner, he said he had agreed to several demands by Dulles: renounce destruction in northern Italy, save the lives of all hostages in German hands, halt attacks on the partisans, suspend offensive action, order German troops to limit themselves to self-defence and prepare to surrender independently of Berlin.[18]

Dulles returned that night to Bern to notify Washington and the Allied command at Caserta of what had been discussed. Gaevernitz stayed in Zurich and had a long talk the next morning with Wolff and Dollmann. Wolff proposed to see Kesselring over the weekend to get his commitment, then draft together with Kesselring a declaration to be signed by them, Rahn and others on the uselessness of the struggle. It would call on German military commanders to dissociate themselves from Hitler and Himmler and announce the Germans were terminating hostilities in northern Italy. Wolff also said he was prepared to take several steps immediately: stop the war against the partisans, while keeping up a pretence of continuing; release several hundred Jews interned at Bolzano; and take full responsibility for the safety and treatment of 350 American and British prisoners held at Mantua, of whom 150 were in hospital. He also promised to release Edgardo Sogno if he could find him, and to facilitate the return to northern Italy of Italian officers held in Germany.[19]

In fact, he never found Sogno, who had been held for a long time in Milan, then transferred to Verona and finally moved on to the German concentration camp in Bolzano in mid-April 1945. In the closing days of the war, he escaped, made his way to Switzerland and returned to Italy on 9 May.[20]

After Wolff's departure from Zurich, Dulles's mistress, Mary Bancroft, told him she had been strolling past a suburban Zurich train station on 8 March and had seen Wolff getting off a train. 'You must be crazy,' Dulles said, laughing. 'What would an SS general be doing in Zurich? And why were you hanging around the Bahnhof Enge instead of doing something useful?'[21]

On 9 March, a Friday, the Allies made their breakthrough into Germany, crossing the Remagen bridge. That afternoon Wolff and his party returned to Italy, so euphoric that they indulged during the journey in a game of deciding on posts in the first post-Hitler government in Germany. They 'appointed' Wolff as interior minister, Hjalmar Schacht as finance minister, Hans Georg von Mackensen to his old post as ambassador to Rome and Rahn as chief of propaganda. They couldn't decide if the new foreign minister should be Konstantin von Neurath, who held the post when Hitler came to power, or Ernst von Weizsäcker, the German ambassador to the Holy See.[22]

En route back to Italy, Wolff's aide Major Wenner told Parrilli that the Germans had 2 billion lire worth of cash and state bonds at Bologna that must be transferred urgently to northern Italy. He also said many of the Uffizi Gallery paintings from Florence and the king's stamp collection were near Bolzano. He made a list that he asked Parrilli to hand over to the Allies, to ensure Allied planes would not attack buildings where these treasures were held. At the Chiasso border post, they were met by Colonel Walter Rauff, SS inspector for Lombardy, Piedmont and Liguria. He handed a telegram to Wolff, who read it and said to Parrilli: 'You, Baron Parrilli, get in the car with me.' The telegram was from Kaltenbrunner. It prohibited any further contacts with American representatives in Switzerland and ordered the arrest of the 'very dangerous' Baron Parrilli. Kaltenbrunner also pressed Wolff to meet him in Innsbruck. Wolff remained silent as they drove to Cernobbio, then got out of his car, smiled and told Parrilli: 'Don't be afraid, everything will go well.' He locked Parrilli in a room of the Villa Locatelli without further explanation. When Wolff returned an hour later, he immediately challenged Parrilli to say if he thought Colonel Wuensche would be handed over to him in exchange for Parri and Usmiani. 'Baron Parrilli, you will answer with your head for the handover of Colonel Wuensche,' he said. He insisted that the next time Parrilli went to Switzerland he must return with Wuensche. He advised Parrilli not to sleep at his home in Milan, or at the house of Zimmer, but to keep in touch and stay away from Rauff. Wolff returned that night to his headquarters at Fasano and sent Kaltenbrunner a teletype message begging to be excused from a trip to Innsbruck because of the pressure of work. He was aware Kaltenbrunner might try to arrest him. He was also dismayed, when he phoned Kesselring's headquarters at Recoaro, to learn he would not be able to meet the field marshal as he had hoped. Kesselring had been summoned on 8 March to the Führer's headquarters in Berlin, and the likely explanation was that he would be transferred from Italy to the defence of Germany.

At German behest, Parrilli returned to Switzerland to explain to Dulles what was happening and ask instructions. On 11 March, a Sunday, Parrilli met Dulles for the first time at the Hotel Schweizerhof in Lucerne, with Gaevernitz present. After Parrilli had explained the situation, Dulles told him to go to Fasano and put these questions to Wolff: was he in a position to act alone? If so, what help would he need from the Allies? If Kesselring were replaced, would Wolff be able to involve his successor in his plans, or could he act without him if he refused? Parrilli gave Dulles the list of treasures to be safeguarded in the palace of the Duke of Pistoia in Bolzano. Dulles dismissed this issue as trifling. Parrilli then raised the question of Wuensche, but saw that Dulles was not pleased. Dulles had learned from London that Wuensche was in a prisoner-of-war camp in Canada and not available for handover.[23]

That same day, Field Marshal Alexander, in a telegram to the US and British governments, had expressed strong scepticism about the approaches from the Germans. 'Please note that two of the leading figures are SS and Himmler men, which makes me very suspicious,' he said. The US and British governments informed the Soviet government during the day about the contacts with the Germans. Soviet Foreign Minister Vyacheslav Molotov told US Ambassador Averell Harriman on 12 March that his government did not object to the talks but wanted to send three Soviet officers to Switzerland to take part. He did not explain how that might be possible, since the Soviet Union had no diplomatic relations with Switzerland. The State Department cabled Harriman on 15 March that the Soviet representatives would be welcome at Caserta when the surrender became an actuality. Molotov reacted aggressively, saying the refusal to accept Soviet officers in Switzerland was 'unexpected and incomprehensible', and he demanded that negotiations with the Germans be terminated. The dispute would become increasingly heated in coming weeks.[24]

Dulles learned from Caserta on 11 March that two envoys of Field Marshal Alexander would be arriving in Switzerland via France to pursue the talks with Wolff. They were US Major-General Lyman L. Lemnitzer, then deputy chief of staff to Alexander, and British Major-General Terence S. Airey, chief intelligence officer to Alexander. Lemnitzer, who would become one of the first NATO commanders after the war, had been involved in the surrender negotiations with the Badoglio government in 1943. Caserta decided upon the code name Sunrise for the secret negotiations. Churchill later baptised the operation 'Crossword'. Dulles sent a message to Lyons, where the two generals already had arrived, and asked them to come alone to the Swiss border at Annemasse.[25]

Parrilli returned to Italy and met Wolff at Fasano at 6 a.m. on 13 March. Wolff told him: 'Put to Dulles . . . the premise that I am firmly decided to carry out the pledges agreed with him in the talk of 8 March in Zurich. He will soon have proof of that.' He said he was ready to act alone, but the results would not be as complete as he would wish. Kesselring had been appointed to command on the Rhine front, and no successor had been named for Italy. Wolff hoped to be able to persuade the new commander to join in his plot. 'I have several effective arguments, not least that of force,' he told Parrilli. 'I have sufficient means to impose myself at the right moment on Kesselring's successor if necessary.' He also suggested he could arrange for an Allied parachute drop to clear airfields and coastal areas in Italy and for coordinated seaborne landings.

Wolff convened a meeting of German command officers that morning and told them: 'From today, pending new instructions, violence against persons and property in all Italian territory controlled by the SS is prohibited. Nothing must be destroyed, nothing taken away. In the zone under occupation by the Wehrmacht or the Navy, SS and SD commanders must carry out moderating work and seek to impede every act of injustice.' He gave Parrilli lunch and sent him back to Switzerland. Dulles waited at his apartment in Bern, and Parrilli arrived there at 8 a.m. on 14 March, not having slept for forty-eight hours. Husmann sent him to the Bernerhof Hotel to sleep while Dulles went to France to receive the Allied generals. He was back that night and Parrilli saw him at 11 p.m., giving him a full report on his talk with Wolff. He also relayed a report from Wolff that Mussolini was considering fleeing to Spain, and gave Dulles a burned piece of cloth from Wolff's overcoat; while Wolff was on the road on 12 March, an American fighter-bomber had shot up his car. What Parrilli did not say, and probably did not know at the time, was that Wolff had been travelling with Mussolini, who was going to Mantua to attend an exercise of a Black Brigades unit. Just beyond Desenzano, at the south-western tip of Lake Garda, their column of cars came under air attack. Mussolini's driver, Giuseppe Cesarotti, swung the car off the road into a farm, with the other cars following. One SS officer was killed and two men wounded, but Mussolini emerged unscathed. Dulles told Parrilli he wanted to see Wolff a few days hence. Parrilli returned to Italy and continued to Fasano that night to report to Wolff.[26]

Five days later Wolff was back in Switzerland to discuss terms of surrender with Lemnitzer and Airey.

Chapter 16

IN SEARCH OF A WAY OUT

Fascism cannot be cancelled from the history of Italy.

(Benito Mussolini, March 1945)

While these secret negotiations were under way, Mussolini launched a peace initiative of his own. Don Giusto Pancino, a childhood friend of Edda's, had been entrusted by the Duce to go to Switzerland and try to win back her favour, and on 9 March Pancino met, at Mussolini's bidding, Monsignor Filippo Bernardini, the papal nuncio in Bern. Pancino told the prelate that Mussolini wanted to propose an alliance of Germany, the Salò Republic and the Americans and British as a bulwark against communism in Germany and Italy. He coupled this with an offer to dissolve the Republican Fascist Party. Pancino observed that Mussolini was now subject to sudden mood swings, having told him in December it was 'urgent' to talk to the Allies and a month later telling him such discussions were 'three months too late'. Bernardini wrote to the Vatican that there was no possibility the Allies would entertain the absurd Mussolini proposal.[1]

But the Duce, without waiting for a reply, decided to try another tack. On 13 March, he sent his son Vittorio to Milan to meet with Cardinal Schuster and put forward a proposal that was equally far-fetched but more elaborate. It was a stark demonstration of the fact that Mussolini, like Himmler and Ribbentrop, was at the extreme limits of desperation and detached from reality. If the Germans were forced to withdraw from Italy, he said, the Salò Republic army might have no alternative but to gather in a preselected locality and fight 'to the last man and the last cartridge'. But to save the country further damage and the people more suffering, he was prepared to sign a preliminary accord with the Allied command on these terms: Graziani's troops would maintain order in cities and towns until a final accord could be reached with the Allied Command. Every uncontrolled and extremist movement of irregulars or of street gangs would be fought by republican forces and the Allies. The Allied Command would block indiscriminate actions by partisans and make sure they were disarmed before Salò Republic troops were disarmed (thus weakening the Communist element among the partisans, in Mussolini's view). No Fascists or soldiers would be subject to arrests, trials, dismissal or other persecutions.

Vittorio told Schuster his father envisaged both Germany and the Salò Republic moving into the Anglo-American camp to block the spread of communism. Schuster asked Mussolini to put the proposal in writing, and he then passed it to Bernardini for relay to the Vatican. In an accompanying note, Schuster dismissed the proposal and said he believed there was no alternative to unconditional surrender. The Holy See eventually responded: 'Allies do not intend to enter into negotiations and demand unconditional surrender.' That reply was not communicated to Mussolini.[2]

Shortly before taking these initiatives, the Duce had spoken to officers of the Republican National Guard at Brescia and exhorted them to make not merely a last-ditch defence of his tottering republic but a victorious drive back into the lands that had been lost. 'We have promised . . . we will defend the Po valley, city for city, house for house,' he said. 'This is a sacred promise we must carry out. If then events permit us to break out beyond the Apennines – no one can exclude it – I believe we will find a wave of enthusiasm as perhaps not even we supposed. . . . Fix it in your minds that Germany cannot be beaten. It cannot be beaten for a very simple reason; for it, and for us as well, it is a matter of life or death. . . . Today the German General Staff and the German people are historically justified, before God and men, if they have recourse to all weapons so as not to succumb.' This remark was greeted with prolonged applause.

'Fascism cannot be cancelled from the history of Italy . . . ,' he went on. 'We have left traces in things and in the spirit of the Italians that are too profound to allow anyone to think that these people . . . can combat and defeat our generations and our ideas, that represent and will represent the life and future of the country.'[3]

Goebbels had disparaged Mussolini for months, but he noted this speech with approval. However, he commented in his diary: 'The Italian people are not worthy of the Duce; they are not worth a row of beans.' Six days later, however, he found fault with the Duce: 'Opinion in Northern Italy has turned against us, the Italians are flirting with the French. Even some of the Fascists are making this about-turn. Mussolini has not yet succeeded in finding a common denominator in Fascist policy.'[4]

True enough; he hadn't even been able to stop the excesses of Fascist militias, and in a meeting with Mellini on 9 March he railed against these groups. He said he had received a report that in the Vicenza area some Fascists 'have thought it well to have recourse to electric shocks on the soles of the feet to make suspects talk'. In another village, he said, Fascists had shot a man, then hanged him and left his body suspended in the village square. Someone took pity and buried the body, but the Fascists dug it up and hanged the man a second time. In yet another village, Fascists had captured and killed a partisan who was guilty of several homicides and robbery, then decapitated him and left his head in a shop window for many hours. 'Macabre, inhuman and cretinous more than anything,' Mussolini commented. He said Italians, when they abandoned their natural gentleness of character, could become 'one of the cruellest and most inhumane people in the world'.[5]

He retained a naive faith in Hitler's promises of secret weapons that would change the course of the war. In a conversation with Bruno Spampanato, his journalist friend, he said of the Germans: 'At a certain moment they will be able to use weapons such as to bring enormous damage to the enemy, but above all to annihilate him morally. It is never too late for a political solution. Today it is not foreseeable which it will be. But a solution there can always be, and it can come about only after a breakdown of the military situation.' Spampanato asked him if he would leave Gargnano. 'In this gloomy alley I will not let myself go down,' he said. Would he go to the Valtellina? 'First, leave the lake. Second, take the government to Milan. . . . If one must think of the Valtellina, that will be the last Italian front.'[6]

* * *

The Germans put out feelers to the partisans about a peace agreement in early March, around the time Wolff was preparing to go to Switzerland to see Dulles. Cardinal Maurilio Fossati, archbishop of Turin, and Baron Schmidt, one of the directors of Fiat, contacted General Cadorna, the partisan military commander, and said Wolff was prepared to meet him to discuss an agreement under which the Germans would respect Italian industrial plants if the partisans would refrain from attacking them during the German withdrawal. Wolff also would give the partisans a free hand to continue fighting Fascist units. As a proof of his intentions, Wolff was prepared to release two important prisoners, for example, Parri and Sogno. Cadorna replied that this was a matter that concerned the CLN and not the military command. He considered it unlikely the CLN would agree.

Cadorna and Leo Valiani of the CLN were in Bern in March, and they reported on this conversation to British secret agent John McCaffrey and to Dulles. They went on to Lyons to meet with a Colonel Vincent, an officer of the British Special Forces. Vincent told them the British were opposed to any contacts with the Germans. Cadorna replied that if the Germans were intent on the destruction of Italian plants, the partisans could not stop them. Vincent urged the two men to return to Switzerland and remain there because they were too much at risk in Milan. When they returned to Bern, they found that McCaffrey and Dulles were also strongly opposed to their leaving Switzerland. The Allied agents had information that Cadorna and Valiani had been identified by the Fascists and could be captured at any moment. The two men protested that their place was in Italy, and Valiani, ignoring the warning, returned to Milan to prepare the way for Cadorna.

Cadorna lunched with Dulles on 23 March and was surprised to find the American was accompanied by Parri. He and Parri later went to McCaffrey to insist on returning to Italy. McCaffrey seemed disposed to let Cadorna go, but not Parri. Cadorna finally returned to Italy on 18 April.[7]

* * *

Mussolini convened his Cabinet on 15 March for a further discussion about the proposed Alpine redoubt in the Valtellina. When some ministers expressed reservations, he told them: 'The retreat in the Valtellina is not obligatory for anyone. . . . Everyone will decide spontaneously.' Graziani came out against the idea, and those who favoured the redoubt criticised Pavolini for having failed to make any serious preparations until now. The matter was put off for further discussion, ensuring that the redoubt would never be prepared in time.[8]

Father Pancino returned from Switzerland on 17 March and had a last meeting with Mussolini. He reported that Edda was still bitter towards her father because of the execution of her husband, but when she learned of his attempts to reach an agreement with the Allies she said: 'What hope is there then? Will he be able to save himself?' As he bade farewell to Pancino, Mussolini asked him to pray for him. 'Father, let's say goodbye here, because I know I will be killed,' he said. Pancino urged him to think of his soul. Mussolini smiled but did not reply.[9]

On March 19 Anfuso sent him a report suggesting Germany was on the brink of an inevitable defeat. 'Fate marches inexorably, nor is there any way of escaping it and by now only a miracle can modify its line,' Mussolini observed. Anfuso said some Germans hoped the British and Americans could be separated from the Russians, but Mussolini commented: 'A compromise between the Anglo-Americans and the Nazis will never happen if the new inventions [weapons] don't come out finally, with indisputable and lightning success.' He arranged for Anfuso, while remaining as ambassador to Germany, to return to Italy to fill the vacancy left by the death of Mazzolini as effective head of the Foreign Ministry. Goebbels was characteristically caustic about the appointment: 'Fascism and the social–Fascist republic are so impotent that it is fairly immaterial who occupies the various ministerial posts in Mussolini's Cabinet.'[10]

The Cabinet decided on 22 March, at Mussolini's suggestion, to proceed by 21 April to the nationalisation of enterprises with at least 100 workers and 1 million lire in capital. Until then nationalisation had been a half-hearted affair; only about seventy firms, all of them media organisations, had been affected. Now Mussolini was determined to proceed, if only to unsettle the Germans. Shortly afterwards, most government ministers began transferring their offices to Milan. Wolff, back in Italy, asked the Duce if he proposed to apply the nationalisation law, and Mussolini said it must be applied without delay. Goebbels observed that Mussolini's earlier nationalisation had produced 'a certain favourable reaction among the Italian working class. Its psychological effect has been considerable'. Rahn took up the theme with Mellini on 23 March, saying some of Mussolini's positions were worrying the Führer and in particular the Duce's nationalisation had aroused suspicion in Germany. When Ribbentrop took leave of Anfuso, he repeated these same complaints. Mellini reported on his conversation with Rahn, and the Duce exploded: 'Look at how the German gentlemen in this moment lose themselves. They occupy themselves with Italian internal politics, and even the little kitchen. It would be better if they thought about their houses. The enemy razes to the ground their most beautiful cities. . . . Let them make war and leave me to govern Italy.'[11]

On 23 March Mussolini went to Bogliaco for a ceremony celebrating the twenty-sixth anniversary of fascism. He noted that the Italian flag had once flown over Ethiopia, but now 'the traitors have brought the Negroes into the land of Tuscany, of that Tuscany which has given the world a flowering of geniuses such as no other people on earth ever gave'. In such a situation, he added, it was a thousand times better to die than to continue to live.

Diplomats from Spain and several South American countries at this time offered planes so that Mussolini could take refuge in their countries. Francesca Lavagnini, a woman with whom he had had an affair in 1938, also wrote from Argentina urging him to save himself. He refused all offers and entreaties.[12]

With the military situation worsening, Mussolini told Rachele he needed to move to Milan, where communications were better. On 24 March, a German officer came to see Mussolini and then talked to Rachele, saying the German Command was opposed to the transfer. In broken Italian, the officer said: 'Duce niente lasciare Gargnano' (literally, '*Duce nothing to leave Gargnano*'). Rachele observed: 'I am also of this opinion. I don't know why. I feel calmer here.'[13]

Anfuso arrived from Berlin on 26 March and told Mussolini that Ribbentrop had sought contacts with the Americans and British. He also reported that Göring was in disgrace because of the failures of the Luftwaffe. Mussolini told Anfuso he knew of 'certain acts' of Wolff in Switzerland, but he had no precise details. He also affirmed that he favoured a retreat to the Valtellina.[14]

In his memoirs, Anfuso said the Duce talked to him of possible peace initiatives. 'Until some time ago I thought my mediation through Churchill would be possible,' he said. 'Now when one speaks to Hitler of England it seems he is bitten by the asp. He wasted two years in Africa and in the end we left there. Our greatest possibility of winning the war remained buried in Libya. . . . One-quarter of the forces employed in Russia would easily have held North Africa, the real vital space of the Axis. If we had remained in Africa, today I could still address myself to Churchill, even without the consent of Hitler, but now in England it is easy to answer no, even if he is convinced that communism prepares difficult days for him.'

Anfuso said Mussolini did not then imagine that Wolff's intrigues in Switzerland foreshadowed the total surrender of the Germans in Italy and abandonment of the Salò Republic. 'He believed they were limited to regional accords circumscribing German military actions against the partisans and exchanges of hostages. Did he hope to serve as intermediary between the Europe that was falling and the winners? Yes; perhaps because he didn't understand the depth of the hatred that had accumulated.'[15]

Goebbels wrote in his diary on 28 March that the Germans had received an interesting report from the Duce's headquarters that the pope was keen to know German peace conditions for possible negotiations with the Western Allies. 'The Führer says there can be no question of peace negotiations,' he added.[16]

Angelo Tarchi, the economy minister, came to Mussolini on 29 March and suggested making approaches to the Western Allies to spare Italy the further ravages of warfare. The Duce told Tarchi to go ahead. The minister was confident an agreement with the West could leave room for a future role for Mussolini. The Duce replied: 'You know that my initiatives, supported by Hitler, to overturn the front met with silence on the part of Churchill. In my proposal I put no conditions either for my person or the party. The aim was still only that of saving Europe from a Russian invasion, of concluding a war without the immediate necessity of having to fight another.' Afterwards, Tarchi began soundings through the Italian Red Cross commissioner with a lawyer representing the CLN.[17]

Mussolini met Rahn on 31 March and the ambassador repeated criticisms he had voiced earlier to Mellini, including suspicions that Mussolini was turning away from fascism. The Duce told Rahn this was injurious and senseless. Rahn said the Germans feared a new Italian betrayal, and he lamented that ministers had transferred to Milan while his embassy remained on Lake Garda. Mussolini told him he also planned to go to Milan soon as he had no real contact with the country in Gargnano. He said Ribbentrop lacked perspicacity and that the 'real betrayal' was being carried out by Wolff, as Rahn well knew.[18]

Chapter 17

PEACE HOPES IN THE BALANCE

The important thing is not to lose our heads. Not only metaphorically.

(General Karl Wolff, 31 March 1945)

In mid-March, Parrilli discovered that he had attracted the suspicions of the partisans. One of his trusted employees told him the CLN thought his trips to Switzerland and his dealings with the Germans meant he was involved in illegal currency dealings, with German connivance. Such suspicions, of course, could result in a bullet in the head, but that was a chance Parrilli knew he would have to take. He could not afford to let the CLN know the nature of his mission. On 17 March, he returned to Switzerland to inform Dulles that General Wolff would arrive two days later for talks with Lemnitzer and Airey, the Allied generals who had come from Caserta. Dulles cabled Washington that an agreement with Wolff 'may present a unique opportunity to shorten the war, permit occupation of northern Italy, possibly penetrate Austria under most favorable conditions and possibly wreck German plans for establishment of a *maquis*'.[1]

He arranged for the meeting to take place at the Swiss resort of Ascona, beside Lake Maggiore. Gaevernitz had the use of two houses there belonging to his brother-in-law Edmund H. Stinnes, who had emigrated to the United States. One was a villa directly on the lakeside and the second was a smaller house some distance above it on a hillside. As a security precaution, Lemnitzer and Airey were given the dog tags of two senior sergeants in the OSS. Lemnitzer became Nicholson, a resident of Long Island City, New York, and Airey was transformed from a Briton to a New Yorker named McNeely.

Dulles needed to concoct some explanation for the presence of the two men in Switzerland. He discovered that Airey was a dog lover, and Switzerland was home to a breed of dachshund he had long wanted to acquire. So Airey whiled away the hours of waiting in Switzerland by visiting kennels, and he bought a dog whom he christened Fritzel. It accompanied him everywhere he went. Dulles's mistress Mary Bancroft warned him that 'something had to be done about the small dog' that the Swiss police had spotted waiting forlornly outside some unlikely places.

On 15 March Lemnitzer received a message from Alexander saying the Soviets were claiming the right to send a representative to any talks in Switzerland. Lemnitzer saw no objection to one Russian joining the talks if he could speak English. But, as the Soviet Union had no diplomatic relations with Switzerland, a Russian would have to be brought in under false pretences and Dulles wondered how he could be passed off as American or English.

Dulles took his wife Clover with him to Ascona to provide cover for the meeting. Lemnitzer, Airey and Fritzel went by separate train with a crew of OSS radio technicians, who managed to plunge the lakeside villa into darkness when they plugged in their electrical gear. Once that was repaired, they taped black paper over the windows and the two generals withdrew to the hillside villa so Dulles could start the discussions with Wolff on his own. Clover was sent off to take a rowing boat on the lake.[2]

Wolff arrived promptly on 19 March, a clear, sunny day, accompanied by his adjutant, Major Wenner, and Zimmer. Dulles and Gaevernitz met Wolff alone, spending an hour and a half in the living room of the villa, with Allied agents in machine-gun nests keeping watch around the house and other armed agents in boats on the lake – a bold undertaking in neutral Switzerland. General Heinrich von Vietinghoff had been named as Kesselring's successor in Italy, and the talks initially focused on the issue of getting him on board in the negotiations. He had been commander in chief of the German Tenth Army defending Monte Cassino, then had been transferred to Latvia. Wolff described him as a rather stiff and proper aristocrat of Baltic origin, and – contrary to what Wolff had told Parrilli – said it would not be easy to win his backing unless he had the support of other senior army officers. Dulles later wrote that Vietinghoff was 'a stiff, broad-shouldered man with a long, straight nose, hair parted in the middle, clipped mustache, polished riding boots, unexcitable, a man of few words'. Wolff suggested three possible courses of action: he could act with the men under his command, ignoring Vietinghoff; he could try to persuade Vietinghoff to accept surrender; or he could go to Kesselring and try to get him to persuade Vietinghoff. Wolff said his own preference was to go to Kesselring. Dulles commented: 'It is easy to start a war, but difficult to stop one.'* Wolff reiterated his determination to prevent wholesale destruction in northern

*Adlai Stevenson paraphrased that remark in 1956: 'Making peace is harder than making war.'

Italy, including its art treasures and industry, and he asked for five to seven days to come up with an answer.

The talk then turned to the question of Wolff surrendering on his own. He said his men were armed only with light weapons and a few old tanks, and were widely scattered. His SS forces included three German divisions numbering about 30,000 men, and a few battalions of anti-Soviet Russian and Ukrainian troops. In his dual capacity as a Wehrmacht general, he also controlled more than 50,000 troops, but only 10,000 were in tactical units and the rest were in supply and transport. Thus it was apparent that most German forces were not under Wolff's control, and to achieve their surrender, he would have to win over the Wehrmacht leaders. Dulles inquired about Mussolini's position. Wolff replied that the Duce was largely under the influence of Rachele, Claretta and Claretta's relatives. In any event, he was of no consequence concerning a surrender. Dulles asked about reports that the Nazis would establish a final Alpine redoubt in southern Germany, and Wolff simply replied: 'Madness'.

Dulles told Wolff that Caserta would be the best place to hold technical military discussions about surrender, and Wolff agreed. Dulles also suggested the OSS should send a wireless operator who spoke German like a native to Wolff's headquarters to ensure speedy communications as negotiations reached a critical stage. Wolff agreed this could be done after he had seen Kesselring. Dulles chose for the task a Czech citizen, Vaclav Hradecky, who was about twenty-six and was known to all as Little Wally. He had been forced into the German army, had deserted, been caught and imprisoned at Dachau. But he had escaped and lived three years underground in Germany. He was finally caught again but convinced the Germans he was an escaped military prisoner, not a former concentration camp inmate. He was put in a prisoner-of-war camp, escaped a second time and made his way to Switzerland, where he went to work for the OSS.

Dulles's talks with Wolff broke for lunch, with Dulles summoning Clover from the lake to prepare a picnic for Wolff and his aides. Dulles and Gaevernitz went up to the smaller house to join the two generals. After they had been briefed, Lemnitzer and Airey agreed Wolff should proceed immediately to meet Kesselring.

The Allied generals agreed to meet Wolff at 3 p.m., and Dulles proposed introducing Lemnitzer and Airey as unnamed military advisers. Airey insisted he would not shake hands with an SS general. Gaevernitz suggested the Allied generals enter the small room where the meeting was to take place through the kitchen door, while Dulles and Wolff would enter from the terrace. That way they would be at opposite sides of an antique octagonal table taking up most of the room, too far apart to shake hands. But when Wolff entered he squeezed his way around the table, shook Airey's hand and then Lemnitzer's. With Gaevernitz interpreting, Lemnitzer said the only topic for discussion was the unconditional surrender of all German forces in Italy. He suggested the Germans should send two officers to Switzerland and they would be flown to Alexander's headquarters to sign the surrender document. Wolff nodded and promised to comply. He raised the issue of freeing Wuensche, but Dulles explained this was impossible. Wolff then suggested the Allies find someone else; he needed a freed German prisoner to justify to his superiors his release of Parri and Usmiani. Questioned by Gaevernitz, Wolff promised he would refuse to carry out any order to kill political prisoners held in Italian concentration camps. He said there were several thousand, of many nationalities. He also promised to suspend all actions against partisans, and asked if this needed to extend to Communists. To his surprise, he was assured the Allies made no distinction among partisans.

Wolff reluctantly handed over to the Allies a suitcase full of maps and military documents on the disposition of German forces in Italy. He promised to return by 27 March, eight days hence, and the two generals agreed to wait for him. The meeting ended at 5 p.m. and as the men came out of the villa, Dulles remarked to Parrilli: 'We've done some good work.' But two days later Washington informed the Soviets that the talks with Wolff had been inconclusive. On 13 March, Molotov accused the Western Allies of negotiating with the Germans behind the back of the Soviet government. President Roosevelt cabled Stalin on 24 March rejecting a Soviet demand to break off the talks and assuring him the Allied initiative carried no political implications.[3]

Wolff returned to Milan on the evening of 19 March after agreeing on what now seems a rather amateurish code for communicating with his officers while he was in Germany seeing Kesselring. He would frame his conversations in terms of a commercial transaction concerning two patents: the first was surrender on the Italian front, the second surrender on the Rhine front in Germany. The president of the firm was Dulles, the technical director Kesselring, the sales manager Wolff. Parrilli was a lawyer who dealt with the shareholders, Waibel and Husmann. The two Allied generals were general directors.[4]

Dollmann saw Rahn on 20 March, and the ambassador showed him a note he had prepared for Wolff to take to Hitler. The note advised Hitler he should choose between two things: go at the head of a Waffen SS unit and find heroic death in battle, or go to Stalin. Stalin would either have him shot, in which case Hitler would make the supreme sacrifice for Germany, or the Soviet leader would reach a peace agreement with him. Rahn asked Dollmann to take this bizarre note with him to Emilia, where it would be safer than in Fasano. Dollmann, thinking of his own safety, declined. 'I preferred to fix the date of my suicide myself,' he remarked caustically in a later book.[5] (I have cited this reference, but have doubts about its authenticity. Dollmann intensely disliked Rahn, and it is not inconceivable he made this up. It is difficult to imagine a diplomat stupid enough to put his head in a noose with such a memo.)

Because of Allied control of the air Wolff could not risk flying to Germany, so he travelled by car and took longer than he had expected to get back. At one point he phoned Zimmer in Milan and said: 'Tell the lawyer to alert the president that I have informed the technical director. Because of events, he is very busy and it is extremely difficult to speak to him at length and with a certain calm. Assure the stockholders that, of the two patents, we will certainly have the first.' He added that he wanted to remain as long as necessary to complete the business and he still had hope of obtaining both patents. Zimmer relayed this information to Parrilli.

Rauff called in Zimmer, said he had received information that Parrilli was up to something suspicious and he had decided to arrest him. So now Parrilli was in danger both from the CLN and the Germans. Zimmer promised to track down Parrilli. When he told Parrilli of his conversation with Rauff, Parrilli concluded that Rauff was probably offended at having been left out of the action; the best course would be to take him to Switzerland and let him meet the Allied representatives. So Parrilli went to see him at the Hotel Regina, told him the Allies had become suspicious over delays in hearing from Wolff and it was vital that Rauff go and talk to them. Rauff replied that he had learned Wolff would be back at his Fasano headquarters on 29 March. Then you must go to Switzerland and tell the Allies, Parrilli insisted. After some hesitation, Rauff agreed.

He went to Lugano and was introduced to Allied representatives in the meeting room of the Rotary Club at the Ristorante Biaggi. They played to his sense of self-importance and told him they wanted to proceed to an exchange of prisoners, handing him a list of twelve partisans held by the Nazis. First on the list was Edgardo Sogno, the man who had tried to rescue Parri from the Hotel Regina. Over a lunch at which the wine flowed freely, Rauff agreed to facilitate the prisoner exchange. On 26 March, several partisans were freed in exchange for a German non-commissioned officer held by the partisans.

While Rauff was in Switzerland, Parrilli set off from Milan to Fasano in his car but was stopped at a Black Brigades roadblock and ordered out of the car by armed men. He feared he would be shot summarily, but as the Fascists questioned him, Zimmer and two German soldiers arrived, burst in with machine guns and angrily ordered the Fascists to release him. When Parrilli arrived in Fasano, Wolff was back and told him Kesselring was favourable to negotiations for surrender on the Italian front but could not bring the Rhine front into the discussions. Kesselring said he could resist the American forces of General Patton only another three or four weeks, and after that there was nothing he could do but die fighting. At the Führer's headquarters, he said, there was still talk of secret weapons being employed at the last minute but Kesselring didn't believe they existed. He authorised Wolff to relay to Vietinghoff his consent and encouragement. Wolff had not been able to see Vietinghoff straight away because the general was on a frontline inspection tour and would not return to his headquarters until two days later, on 31 March.

Wolff told Parrilli that while he was in Germany Himmler called him in at Kaltenbrunner's insistence. He discovered that Himmler and Kaltenbrunner knew of his contacts with the Americans, but clearly were not aware of the Ascona meeting. Wolff acknowledged the contacts and assured them he had simply been following earlier instructions from Himmler and Hitler to test the ground for a separate peace with the Western Allies. Himmler allowed himself to be persuaded but forbade him to return to Switzerland. Himmler asked about the release of Parri, and Wolff said Wuensche was to be freed in exchange as a birthday present for Hitler. The Führer's birthday was 20 April. At Himmler's insistence, Wolff and Kaltenbrunner went on to Bavaria to discuss the matter with intelligence specialists there. Wolff had suggested they all go instead to Hitler and try to convince him of the need for German surrender in Italy at the earliest possible date. But Himmler and Kaltenbrunner feared this would put Hitler in a rage, with unforeseeable consequences for all of them. After Wolff had met intelligence officers in Bavaria, he was given a mild admonition to keep away from Americans and was sent on his way.[6]

Himmler informed Ribbentrop of the surrender negotiations, who fearing that Rahn's part in it would bring down Hitler's wrath upon his head, decided to recall the ambassador. But Rahn, warned in time, sent a long and sensational report about Mussolini and his entourage that convinced Ribbentrop he was indispensable. Some of his report was true, and some was fictitious.[7]

Parrilli stressed to Wolff the importance of an early return to Switzerland, where the Allied generals were becoming increasingly impatient, and said he must go with some concrete development, at least the agreement of Vietinghoff. 'I know what I must do,' Wolff replied. 'Provided Dulles doesn't lose patience, I will hand Italy to him on a silver platter.' He decided to send Zimmer to Switzerland to let the Allies know where matters stood, and Zimmer left at dawn on 30 March. Wolff went off to see Vietinghoff and returned, satisfied, to Fasano at 2 a.m. on 30 March; it had not been difficult to convince Vietinghoff. General Hans Roettiger, chief of staff of the Wehrmacht in Italy and commander of the Panzer divisions, also had agreed to surrender.

But Wolff's good humour was short-lived. Himmler telephoned from Germany, saying he had learned that Wolff had transferred his family to a place in Austria near the Brenner Pass crossing into Italy. 'It was an imprudent act, which I have allowed myself to remedy, taking your wife and children directly under my protection,' Himmler said. He promised to call often to give Wolff news of his family and hoped to find him in Fasano. Wolff was staggered. 'Perhaps, while we are here engaging in trifles, an executioner is on his way to assassinate me,' he told Parrilli. 'Perhaps he is already hidden within these walls. Evidently, someone has betrayed us.' He suspected Harster, and possibly Rahn and Rauff as well. 'If it were indispensable for the cause, I would not hesitate to sacrifice what I hold most dear, my wife and my children,' he said. 'But in these conditions I wonder: is it useful to take the risk? The conclusion would be very certain: my funeral at state expense. And national mourning, as in the case of Rommel.* But the Allies would not know what to do with my cadaver, nor as a dead man could I be useful to the German people.' Therefore he would remain in Fasano and try to determine what to do next. 'The important thing is not to lose our heads. Not only metaphorically,' he told Parrilli.

Zimmer rang from Switzerland on 1 April, Easter Sunday, and spoke to Parrilli. He asked to know the date and modalities of a new meeting of the sales manager with the general directors, who were prepared to wait until 8 p.m. on Tuesday 3 April. 'The affair doesn't interest us any more,' Parrilli told him abruptly. 'Neither Tuesday nor Wednesday nor ever.' A stunned Zimmer handed the phone to Husmann, but Parrilli told him: 'Don't insist. However, tomorrow morning at 7 o'clock I will be with you. Goodbye.' He left that night, wearing a military overcoat and helmet so as not to arouse the suspicion of German guards around Fasano. For added safety, Wolff sent a motorcyclist ahead of his car and put two armed men in the car with him. At 7 a.m. on 2 April, having shed his overcoat and helmet, Parrilli crossed the frontier and met Waibel and Husmann at Chiasso. They went on to Ascona, and Parrilli, unshaven and 'looking like an escapee from a concentration camp' in his own words, met Dulles and the Allied generals. They gave him a glass of cognac to revive him, and he told them of Himmler's phone call to Wolff. For a moment there was silence, then Lemnitzer spoke: 'It is not half as bad as it looks.' Airey chipped in: 'We all know Himmler and we know what he is capable of. It is best that Wolff does not move from Fasano. It's a matter now of working out a satisfactory solution for both sides.'

*Rommel was forced by Hitler to commit suicide on 14 October 1944, after the Führer learned of his involvement in the July plot against his life. He was given a state funeral with full honours.

The Allies drafted a message for Parrilli to take to Wolff. The Germans who would sign the surrender document could come to Switzerland and be taken to Caserta, or they could show up at an agreed point on the Gothic Line, carrying a white flag, and give the code word Nuremberg. Then they would be taken overland to Caserta. Parrilli spent the night at a Lugano hotel, memorising two typed pages of instructions that he could not risk taking across the frontier, and returned to Italy the next morning.[8]

* * *

On 3 April Roosevelt received an insulting message from Stalin. In response to Roosevelt's message of 24 March, assuring him there had been discussions but no negotiations, Stalin in effect called him a liar. 'It may be assumed that you have not been fully informed,' he wrote. He said he knew negotiations had taken place and had ended in an agreement with the Germans under which Kesselring would allow the Allied armies to advance through Germany in return for Allied agreement to ease the peace terms for Germany. Stalin said German troops had ceased to make war against Britain and the United States but were continuing to fight the Russians. Roosevelt replied to Stalin on 5 April, again saying there had been no negotiations in Bern. He said the only purpose of the Bern meeting was to test the credentials of the German emissary and to try to arrange a meeting between Alexander and a nominee of Kesselring. Alexander, he affirmed, had the full right to accept the surrender of a German army of twenty-five divisions on his front, and Soviet representatives would be welcome to attend the surrender ceremony in Italy. Roosevelt said the United States and Britain would continue to demand unconditional surrender, and so far nothing had resulted from the Swiss contacts. Stalin's information, the president suggested, must have come from German sources, and he speculated that Wolff's aim in initiating the discussions may have been to sow mistrust among the Allies. He said he was astonished by Stalin's allegations and felt 'bitter resentment toward your informers concerning the vile misrepresentations of my actions or those of my trusted subordinates'. Dulles was informed of this exchange and discerned what was troubling the Soviets: if the Western Allies obtained a quick German surrender, they would have occupied Trieste. If they failed, either Soviet forces or the Communist troops of Marshal Tito would reach Trieste first and gain a toehold on the Adriatic. The westernmost tip of the Iron Curtain would have come down there.

Stalin replied to Roosevelt on 7 April, in somewhat more moderate terms than he had used previously, but still insisting the Soviets should have been invited to take part in the discussions. Churchill, in a cable to Roosevelt, said that if the Russians 'are ever convinced that we are afraid of them and can be bullied into submission, then indeed I should despair of our future relations with them and much else'. On 12 April, Roosevelt, resting in Warm Springs, Georgia, approved a conciliatory response to Stalin. A few hours later he suffered a stroke and died.[9]

* * *

When Parrilli reported to Wolff on 6 April, he was told that Mussolini had learned from a Swiss radio broadcast of the release of Parri and Usmiani and had demanded an explanation from Rahn. The ambassador told him Wolff hoped to get Wuensche released in exchange, and this seemed to pacify Mussolini. Wolff invited Parrilli to tea with Vietinghoff and Roettiger, who had just come in full dress uniform from a meeting with the Duce. They had assured Mussolini the Germans would fight on to victory. But at Wolff's tea party, Vietinghoff spoke of damage in Milan and Genoa and told Parrilli: 'Enough of this destruction. Too many sorrows, too much pain, already have been sown. Any further destruction to the civilian population can and must be avoided.' After he had left the room, Wolff explained that Vietinghoff was ready to surrender provided it was done in a way that would salvage military honour. He was prepared to accept prisoner-of-war status for his men, but only if they were allowed to do some useful work of reconstruction on roads and railways and return to Germany after a short interval with sword belt and bayonet, showing they had not been disarmed but yielded only to overwhelming force. Vietinghoff also wanted a copy of the act of surrender so he could examine it before sending officers to sign it.[10]

Parrilli was irritated, fearing the OSS would never accept such terms, and he asked that Vietinghoff's demands be put in writing for him to take to Switzerland. Wolff agreed and called Dollmann to come to Fasano from his residence at Reggio Emilia to help draft the document. It included a sentence written by Vietinghoff, who asked for 'the maintenance of a modest contingent of Army Group C as a future instrument of order inside Germany'. Wolff also included a phrase to the effect that he could not guarantee what would happen in port areas such as Genoa because neither he nor Vietinghoff controlled German naval units. Parrilli crossed into Switzerland on 8 April and presented the document to Dulles, who realised the terms were unacceptable. But he had the document translated into English and sent on to Caserta, Washington and London. Parrilli also told Dulles that Wolff was pleading for the release of a high-level prisoner. On 10 April, Alexander replied to the Vietinghoff terms: 'Impossible to send draft of capitulation document as this could only be handed to parlamentaires on arrival at an appropriate Allied headquarters in accordance with the usages of war.' He added that the Germans sent to sign the document must have 'absolute authority' to act in the name of the German commander. Gaevernitz offered to go to Vietinghoff's headquarters to try to talk sense to him, but Caserta considered this too risky.[11]

Parrilli got a cold reception when he returned to Italy and informed Wolff of Alexander's response to Vietinghoff's terms. Wolff told him the Germans were prepared for a 'strategic retreat' on all fronts, averaging six miles a day, and would refrain from destruction, respect hostages and neutralise the opposition of Fascist militias. If the Allies agreed, this could begin immediately. Parrilli told him the proposal was absurd, and Wolff agreed; he said it had come from Vietinghoff. He also said he had obtained the collaboration of General Maximilian Ritter von Pohl, the Luftwaffe commander in Italy. Pohl had discussed the need for a peace settlement with Dollmann as far back as early 1944. He told him then he had never been a Nazi, and Dollmann hinted that Wolff might also be inclined to take initiatives for a settlement.

Parrilli learned that Himmler had phoned Wolff again, insisting he come to Berlin. Wolff replied that his absence from Italy could have unpleasant consequences; Mussolini was disturbed and given to a thousand fantasies, and it would be dangerous to leave him uncontrolled. Since Himmler knew of Wolff's initiative with Dulles, he felt that returning to Berlin would amount to suicide. He wrote to Himmler saying he was pursuing talks with the Western Allies with a view to separating them from the Soviets, and further fighting in Italy would only kill more Germans to no advantage. He invited Himmler to come to Italy to join him in an attempt at peace. If Himmler had accepted, Wolff later told Dulles, he planned to arrest him upon arrival. Wolff sent his letter by SS courier on 14 April. Himmler tried twice that day to phone him, but Wolff absented himself from his headquarters until his letter arrived.[12]

Parrilli, not knowing of Wolff's hopes of arresting Himmler, later wrote that Wolff had become fearful and indecisive. 'He half believed in secret weapons that would give Germany victory,' he said. Parrilli asked him how he thought the Allies would regard a man who proved himself a modest pawn whom Berlin could move at its pleasure. 'Wolff recognized the justice of the criticism,' he wrote. Himmler, he said, had allowed Wolff's family to return to the Brenner area, but they were closely watched.[13]

Dulles was called to Paris to meet his boss, OSS Chief William Donovan, while Lemnitzer and Airey returned to Alexander's headquarters at Caserta. While Dulles was in Paris, he heard the announcement of Roosevelt's death. During his absence Wilhelm Höttl, the SS intelligence chief in Austria, arrived in Switzerland and asked to see him, as Dulles learned upon his return.

An aide to Dulles went to Zurich to meet Höttl, who claimed he wanted to help the Allies prevent the establishment of an Alpine redoubt by the Fascists under Mussolini. He hinted that the Austrian Nazis wanted to make some kind of separate settlement. Höttl was undoubtedly acting for Kaltenbrunner, trying to learn more details of what was happening in Switzerland.[14]

Wolff went to Gargnano on 14 April to meet Mussolini. In an account of the meeting that Wolff wrote for an Italian magazine in 1950, he said he told Mussolini he was aware of feelers the Duce had put out to the Allies through the Italian clergy, and asked him to suspend those talks and await with confidence the outcome of negotiations Wolff was conducting in person. Wolff said he guaranteed Fascist forces would receive the same treatment as German troops. He claimed he also told Mussolini there was no longer any hope of military success, and the only possible salvation could come from a political compromise that involved dissolving the Salò Republic and halting the nationalisation programme Mussolini had undertaken. He promised to report on further contacts with the Allies and urged that meanwhile Mussolini should not turn against the Germans as Badoglio had done. Wolff claimed Mussolini agreed to suspend his own peace feelers, but in fact he began negotiations with the CLN a few days later after he went to Milan. Some Fascist historians have contended that Wolff's account of this meeting was a lie and ridiculous.

Anfuso was present but his brief account of the meeting did not mention Wolff's references to negotiations. He said Wolff told Mussolini that if northern Italy could not be held a line of alpine defences would allow the Germans and Fascists to arrive at a *heroischer Untergang* (heroic sunset). When Wolff left, Mussolini asked Anfuso: 'What is this story of the *heroischer Untergang*? And why speak of *Untergang*?' Anfuso suggested Wolff was the type who would arrange sunsets for others, but not for himself.[15]

* * *

Unknown to Dulles and Wolff, on 14 April, Vietinghoff sent an urgent message to Führer headquarters, saying he could no longer maintain his position on the Po and asking permission to withdraw. Jodl answered three days later, rejecting the appeal and accusing Vietinghoff of defeatism. 'The Führer expects . . . the utmost steadfastness in fulfilment of your present mission, to defend every inch of the north Italian area entrusted to your command.' He warned there would be 'serious consequences' if Vietinghoff failed to carry out orders.

Zimmer arrived in Lugano on 15 April. He said he and Wolff had met Vietinghoff three days earlier and had been given a very cold reception.

According to Zimmer, a British major had turned up in civilian clothes in Genoa, claiming he had been sent by Alexander with a message for Vietinghoff: he was on the wrong track in negotiating with the Americans in Switzerland, and should talk directly with the British. The major said he would return soon to get Vietinghoff's reply, but he was never seen again. Vietinghoff was now very upset that his contacts were no longer secret, and he feared for his life. He threatened to write to Jodl about his contacts with the Americans and to ask his advice. It took the combined efforts of Wolff, Roettiger and Rahn to dissuade him, and he had become even more difficult as a result, Zimmer said. Dulles cabled Caserta and was told the British had never sent anyone to Genoa. He suspected the 'British major' may have been a Soviet intelligence operative.

Zimmer brought Dulles a letter of condolence from Wolff on the death of Roosevelt. It was written on his official stationery, but at the top he had deleted three lines spelling out his titles and had penned 'Personal'. Zimmer said Roettiger and von Pohl were now fully behind Wolff, who had talked to army commanders under Vietinghoff and was confident they would back him regardless of what Vietinghoff might do. Zimmer brought this verbal message from Wolff: 'I beg you to do everything possible that the Allies do not make useless sacrifices in an intensified offensive. I take full responsibility and guarantee that during the coming week all will be surrendered.' But Zimmer then told of how Himmler had phoned from Berlin ordering Wolff to report to him at once.

Himmler phoned three times to say he wanted to discuss the 'interesting' reasons Wolff gave in his letter for negotiating with the Americans. Wolff continued to argue for staying in Italy, but Himmler sent his personal plane to take him to Berlin. Wolff left on 16 April, but before going he gave Parrilli a document to present to Dulles; in effect, it was his will. If Wolff were put to death in Berlin, he wanted Dulles to 'rehabilitate my name, publicising my true, humane intentions; to make known that I acted not out of egotism or betrayal but solely out of the conviction and hope of saving, as far as possible, the German people'. He also asked Dulles to obtain terms of an honourable surrender for German and Italian troops, and to protect his two families 'in order that they not be destroyed'.[16]

Parrilli returned to Switzerland on 17 April, disguised as a priest. He wrote later that Dulles now seemed tired and aged. Parrilli told him that Wolff had arranged for Rauff in Milan to remain in close touch with Cardinal Schuster to avoid clashes between retreating German troops and the Italian population and partisans. Wolff also passed word that he believed he had won over Franz Hofer, the gauleiter of the Tyrol, for surrender. Wolff arranged to have any messages he sent from Berlin relayed to Milan, and Zimmer would carry them

Mussolini visits Cardinal Ildefonso Schuster, Milan, 1 November 1936. *(Farabola Photos)*

Opposite, top: Mussolini, saluted by a German officer, visits a training camp for Italian soldiers, Monza, 2 August 1944. Soldiers are to be transferred to Germany to form the Monterosa Division. With Mussolini is Francesco Maria Barracu, who will be among the Fascists shot at Dongo in April 1945. *(Farabola Photos)*

Opposite, bottom: German Ambassador Rudolf von Rahn, waving, attends a celebration in the Milan Public Gardens of the Balilla, a Fascist youth organisation. Fascist Party Secretary Alessandro Pavolini is on his left. *(Farabola Photos)*

Above: Mussolini giving his last official speech at the Lyric Theatre, Milan, 16 December 1944. Pavolini is on the left. *(Farabola Photos)*

Partisan leader Pier Luigi Bellini delle Stelle with Lia De Maria in the bedroom of her farmhouse where Mussolini and his lover Claretta Petacci spent their last night. Bellini visited there after the war. *(Farabola Photos)*

Opposite: Crowd in Milan's Piazzale Loreto, gathered around bodies of Mussolini, Claretta Petacci, and several Fascists, 29 April 1945. *(Farabola Photos)*

Walter Audisio, the presumed killer of Mussolini, speaking 9 July 1950, at a Communist Party rally celebrating the wartime Resistance. *(Farabola Photos)*

Opposite: The bodies of Mussolini and Claretta Petacci, hanged in Milan's Piazzale Loreto on 29 April 1945, the day after their execution. *(Farabola Photos)*

Site of the execution of Mussolini and Petacci. *(Jennifer Moseley)*

to Switzerland for delivery to Dulles. If not, Little Wally, who had been ensconced in Zimmer's SS attic in Milan since 13 April, could radio the messages to Switzerland.

Shortly afterwards, Wolff sent a message saying he had met Himmler and had an appointment to see Hitler at 5 p.m. on 18 April. He planned to fly back to Italy immediately afterwards.[17] Wolff had reached his point of maximum danger. How could he hope to escape the lethal wrath of the Führer now that his actions were exposed? The little group of people awaiting him in Switzerland knew there was every possibility they would never see him again, but, to their great relief, Wolff returned safely to Italy on 19 April. There was no immediate word from him about the state of negotiations, and Parrilli, instead of being thankful that the man who was key to these negotiations was still alive, was angry at being kept waiting to see him, and distrustful. Parrilli told Dollmann: 'If the general doesn't receive me, and immediately, to give me formal assurances that he intends to remain faithful to what he freely agreed, the radio operator Wally will know what to do. Wolff will be officially proclaimed a war criminal and squadrons of bombers will attack the headquarters, destroying this den of incompetents.' Of course, Parrilli had no authority to make such threats, as the Germans well knew.

Wolff finally called in Parrilli at 11 a.m. on 20 April at Fasano, opened a bottle of champagne to celebrate his safe return and recounted the full details of his remarkable trip. After crossing into Germany, he was flown from Munich to Prague at treetop level to avoid Allied planes. From Prague he was flown to an airfield near Berlin and met by a Professor Gebhardt, one of Hitler's doctors and Himmler's close associate. Gebhardt drove him into Berlin, and Wolff was so exhausted that he slept through air raids in his fourth-floor room at the Adlon Hotel instead of going to a shelter.

The next day, 17 April, Gebhardt drove Wolff to his clinic 60 miles north of Berlin, where Himmler was waiting. Wolff found Himmler physically and morally depressed. Himmler had destroyed Wolff's letter outlining his hopes of separating the Western Allies from the Soviets because he thought it was too compromising. He accused Wolff of ingratitude and of having overreached himself by taking an initiative without consulting him. Wolff showed him a letter Rahn had written to Hitler, which indicated that contacts with the Allies had been useful in achieving Hitler's objective of holding up the Allied offensive in Italy. Himmler seemed pacified, and returned the letter to Wolff without comment. Himmler called in Kaltenbrunner, who brought a voluminous dossier 'proving' the betrayal of Wolff. The two men argued heatedly in front of Himmler, with Kaltenbrunner accusing Wolff of having met with Schuster to reach a surrender agreement with the CNLAI. He also claimed Wolff had told the Allies by radio that he would be ready to conclude an armistice within five days. Wolff swore he had not met Schuster. He showed Kaltenbrunner the Rahn letter, but that did not pacify him. The argument went on until midnight, and finally Himmler proposed letting Hitler be the judge. Wolff accepted enthusiastically and suggested the three of them go to see Hitler, but Himmler declined.

Wolff and Kaltenbrunner went to the Führer's bunker below the Chancellery at 3 a.m., each eager to make his case. Before they entered, Wolff warned Kaltenbrunner that if he started accusing him of secret negotiations or showed Hitler the reports of his agents, Wolff would tell Hitler he had already informed Himmler and Kaltenbrunner on 24 March about his contacts with the Americans and they both asked him not to bring Hitler into the picture at that time. Kaltenbrunner turned pale. The meeting did not proceed as either had expected. 'I found myself in the presence not of a man but of a spectre,' Wolff told Parrilli. Hitler greeted Wolff cordially but called his approach to the Allies 'a colossal disregard of authority'. Wolff reminded Hitler of a meeting they had on 6 February at which Hitler had not opposed exploratory contacts with the Allies. Wolff said he met Dulles on 8 March without informing Berlin so that Hitler could disown him if things went wrong. Hitler expressed understanding, and asked Wolff what the terms of surrender would be. Wolff said unconditional surrender could not be avoided. Hitler then broke off the talks, saying he had to get some sleep, and he asked the men to return at 5 p.m. Wolff went back to the Adlon Hotel to sleep.

In the afternoon, Wolff found a desperate and frightened atmosphere in the bunker, everyone there aware the Russians would seal off Berlin within days. The city was subjected to another air raid while Wolff was below ground, and when it was over Hitler invited Wolff, Kaltenbrunner and Hitler's SS aide General Hermann Fegelein to join him for a walk along the terrace in front of his office. Wolff regarded the Führer as 'on the edge of madness'. Hitler told them he could hold out at least six weeks, possibly eight, and Wolff must maintain the Italian front that long. Meanwhile, the new German weapons would be ready and the outcome of the war changed. 'We must only concern ourselves with gaining time,' Hitler said. 'As soon as we make use of new arms, the fracture between the Anglo-Americans and the Russians will be inevitable. And then I will accept the better proposals, from whichever side they will come.' Wolff referred to the overwhelming Allied strength and German losses, but Hitler said: 'Go back to Italy, maintain your contacts with the Americans but see that you get better terms.' He went on to say that when the war was over he would realise an old dream of retiring to private life to influence from a certain distance the destiny of the German people. Wolff had the impression the Führer was in a trance, with no grasp of the real situation. The talk ended at 5.55 p.m. Kaltenbrunner told Wolff afterwards to eliminate all important civilian prisoners in Italy before they could fall into Allied hands. Wolff flew from Tempelhof Airport in Berlin to Munich at dusk, and at dawn on 19 April he flew to Bergamo, then continued by car to Fasano.

But he was not in a mood to continue negotiations; he had lost his nerve after his narrow escape in Berlin. Parrilli told him the confidence of the OSS and the Swiss in him was shaken and he must hurry to conclude the negotiations. Wolff replied: 'It is a real miracle if I have my head still on my shoulders. I have re-entered legality and I cannot go out of it again twenty-four hours later. I cannot come to Switzerland and I must forbid Zimmer also to go there, at least until we have succeeded in unmasking the spies who denounce our movements to Berlin. It is not a lack of goodwill; it's a matter of looking at the situation in a realistic way. I have remained alone still. Vietinghoff, to whom I have had to transmit the opinion and directives of the Führer, lives under the nightmare of being replaced from one minute to the next and no longer wants to hear about surrender.' He said he would be free to act only when Berlin fell and Hitler was dead.

Zimmer, who was present, suggested eliminating Vietinghoff if there was any likelihood he would betray those involved in the negotiations. 'And who would dare do it?' Wolff asked. 'I would, general,' Zimmer replied. Wolff returned to his old idea of allowing Allied troops to advance six miles a day, then launched into a defence of his latest stand. While the meeting was under way, Roettiger phoned to say Vietinghoff's headquarters at Recoara had been subjected to a massive Allied bombardment. Damage was extensive, but there were only three dead and fifteen wounded. Parrilli left, wondering if Wolff was now betraying the Allies.[18]

Chapter 18

LOOMING DEFEAT AND PARALYSIS

The game is up for me. It's finished.

(Benito Mussolini, 18 April 1945)

At the beginning of April, Mussolini was drawing near the end of his confinement at Gargnano and the Allies were preparing to launch their long-awaited spring offensive. In a sign of desperation, the national directorate of the Republican Fascist Party met on 4 April and ordered the mobilisation of all available Italian men, without limit as to age, into the Black Brigades. Graziani told the Fascist Party leadership that if the Po front fell, any further resistance would be impossible. On the same day, the Milan Catholic Curia again asked the German Command for an agreement to safeguard the city as German forces withdrew. The Fascist Prefect of Trieste, Bruno Coceani, telegraphed an urgent appeal for forces to fight off Slav partisan bands closing in there.[1]

The Allied offensive began on 5 April with a diversionary attack by the US Fifth Army along the Ligurian coast. Massa-Carrara was captured that day. On 9 April, the main thrust was delivered by the British Eighth Army in the flooded Lake Comacchio region, on the opposite coast of Italy north of Ravenna, with the British then advancing toward Argenta and Ferrara. General Mark W. Clark, the American commander, feared the offensive would trigger partisan insurrections that could be premature, and urged the partisans to be patient. They ignored him. Communist Party headquarters in Milan issued Directive No. 16 on 10 April, laying the basis for an insurrection there.[2]

On 9 April, the SS Command drew up a report on the forces available to do battle with the partisans. The Fascists had 102,514 men in the Republican National Guard and militia units, and another 30,000–35,000 men in their four divisions. There were nine German reserve divisions in the Po valley, numbering 90,000 men, that were designated to fight the partisans. This represented a total of more than 220,000 troops opposing a partisan force of about 100,000 frontline fighters. Vietinghoff issued a circular on 14 April stating that captured partisans must be treated as prisoners of war and sent to German concentration camps. But partisans wearing German or Fascist uniforms were to be shot after questioning.[3]

What was Mussolini doing during these crucial days? Holding urgent talks with the Germans to ensure they would spare the infrastructure of northern Italy as they retreated? Trying to get to the bottom of what Wolff was up to in Switzerland? Following up the success of his December speech in Milan by rallying his followers? Visiting the front lines to encourage the troops? None of the above. He did send an emissary to Rome, but too late, to ask the Bonomi government to recognise the military character of troops the Salò Republic had sent to defend Trieste. He also hoped to arrange a peaceful handover of power, if that were possible, but seemed in no rush to do it. Otherwise, he was preoccupied with three matters: moving his government to Milan, dreaming of a heroic last stand in the Valtellina and indulging in rambling musings about various subjects with friends and journalists as he awaited the end. As Zachariae had noted, he suffered a nervous collapse in February, and now he had mostly sunk into apathy.

On Easter Sunday, 1 April, Mussolini had a talk about Hitler with his old friend of forty years, Ottavio Dinale. He recalled a meeting in the library of Hitler's Alpine retreat at Berchtesgaden at which Hitler showed him a row of volumes in red morocco leather by philosophers and German occultists. Of the many philosophers, Hitler admitted he had read fully only Schopenhauer and Nietzsche but had delved deeply into the works of the occult writers of the sixteenth and seventeenth centuries. 'He tried to make me believe he was mystically and scientifically convinced of being possessed not by a demon but by a spirit of prehistoric Aryan mythology,' Mussolini said. 'At that moment I understood the strange, inexplicable sensation always produced in me by his speeches, which were characterised by a prophetic tone that could not but surprise his listeners.' Hitler, he said, had learned from the occult sciences how to deceive his people and the entire world with the cunning of a swindler. In a later meeting with Dinale, Mussolini explained why for a long time he had not believed the United States would intervene in the war. He had given too much weight to Roosevelt's promises to American mothers that their sons would not be sacrificed in battle.[4]

Soon after the Allied offensive began, many Fascists saw the writing on the wall, and the CLNAI in Milan was bombarded with offers of surrender, according to Leo Valiani, its Action Party representative. 'The big rats and the little rats are equally anxious to save themselves from the boat that is taking on water,' he wrote in his diary. 'Montagna, Zerbino, Buffarini and Tarchi are among the tens of Fascist *gerarchi** who let us know, by the most tortuous means, they would be disposed to negotiate their surrender. But we require immediate total surrender and reject every individual negotiation.' He said hundreds of lesser Fascists also wanted to switch sides at the last moment.

Mussolini threatened a seventy-two-hour curfew during which he claimed Fascist forces would drive all the rebels from the cities. The CLNAI's insurrectional committee passed the word that it would violate the curfew and its armed squads would circulate in the streets when and where they wanted. Unwilling to face an open battle, Mussolini dropped the threat.[5]

At Pavolini's suggestion, Mussolini also considered making a last stand of Fascist forces in Milan, and the two men spoke of turning Milan into 'the Italian Stalingrad', an idea the Duce had previously rejected. Graziani said Mussolini abandoned the idea, and reverted to the project of a redoubt in the Valtellina, after Graziani refused to allow his forces to become involved against Milan. Mussolini attended a German–Italian military conference on the morning of 6 April to discuss the Valtellina question. Pavolini, still the main promoter of the scheme, had christened it 'the Epic of the Fifty Thousand', referring to the number of Fascist troops he imagined would gather in the mountain valley.

Dollmann, who attended the talks, said most of the Germans were 'outraged by the idea and the lack of organisation behind it'. The primary aim of Wolff's negotiations with the Americans, he said, not quite truthfully, was 'to avert any such lunatic last-minute massacre'. He claimed later Rahn was the only German to approve Pavolini's 'macabre fantasies'. Vietinghoff insisted the Fascists should only go into the Valtellina with food supplies for three months, which had not been arranged. Filippo Anfuso, now the Italian under-secretary for foreign affairs, told Mussolini: 'Imagine a little the hunger your men will experience after a march into the high mountains.' Four days later, the partisans compiled a secret report that estimated the number of Fascists in the Valtellina at 8,000 and suggested the number could rise to 40,000. Both figures were wildly excessive. The Fascists had only a handful of troops in the Valtellina, and most were under partisan siege in their village garrisons. Despite the opposition to his plan, Pavolini sent reinforcements numbering just 750 men.

After the meeting, Mussolini called Dollmann aside and said he wanted to see him alone that afternoon. Dollmann was apprehensive; he feared the Duce had discovered the German surrender plan and wanted to confront him. The Germans, he later claimed, had not informed Mussolini of the contents of the

**Gerarchi*, literally hierarchs, was the Fascist name for high-ranking government and party officials.

talks with the Americans because of the machinations of the Petacci clan. Dollmann was relieved to find Mussolini just wanted a chat. The Duce reminisced about trips they had taken together, talks with Hitler at which Dollmann interpreted and the 1938 Munich conference at which Britain and France sold out Czechoslovakia. 'That was my great day,' Mussolini mused. 'I was the only one who spoke and understood all the languages. All eyes were on me, not on Mr Chamberlain or Monsieur Daladier. It was an occasion worthy of the Caesars – do you remember?' Then, standing and gesticulating like an actor, he recited lines from Shakespeare's *Julius Caesar*. Mussolini went on to other topics. He justified his dismissal of Buffarini, which he said Fascists – without exception – had wanted. Then he turned to religion, asking what was the precise Nazi conception of divinity. From Dollmann's explanation, he concluded the concept was rather confused.

Mussolini pulled from a drawer the draft of a letter he had written to Hitler after he had returned from his July 1944 meeting with the Führer at Rastenburg. The letter asked Hitler to leave troops in Italy for a year or two after the end of the war so that the Fascist government could secure a firm hold on the country from the Brenner Pass to Sicily. As Dollmann took his leave, never to see the Duce again, he urged him not to leave Lake Garda. 'We still believed that our negotiations in Switzerland might save his life provided he remained close at hand,' he wrote afterwards. That, of course, was untrue; there is no evidence the Germans negotiated with the Americans for Mussolini's safety. They were interested in saving themselves.

Dollmann asked Mussolini what fate he foresaw for Claretta, and the Duce replied: 'Signorina Petacci has been beside me in good times and will be with me in extreme misfortune.' Before leaving Lake Garda, Dollmann also saw Claretta and urged her to take one of the last flights to Spain. But she replied: 'Never. I loved Benito when times were good. I shall love him even more now that they are bad.'[6]

Mussolini learned from Spampanato that day that German radio technicians in Milan had received an order to pack for immediate departure. But the Duce was blind to facts; he expressed the hope there would be a sudden stiffening of German resistance that would push back the enemy. He also lamented, once again, German refusal to make full use of the four Italian divisions, and confirmed his intention to go to the Valtellina after moving first to Milan. He thought a final battle in the Valtellina would save republican troops from fratricidal slaughter at the end of the war because they would be recognised as regular soldiers.[7]

The Germans were then attempting through their contacts to persuade the partisans not to interfere with their withdrawal from Italy, with a promise that they would leave the electric power plants in Piedmont and the Valtellina intact and would free partisan prisoners. Partisans asked for instructions from their superiors and were told, according to Valiani, 'Fight, don't negotiate'. The CLNAI now figured Mussolini could count on 20,000–30,000 Blackshirts who would be ready to die for fascism in a showdown. They also calculated that once Allied troops arrived on the lower Po, the Germans would have to concentrate all their efforts on opening a passage toward Germany and would not have time to think about laying waste to the Po valley. They estimated the partisans could count on 83,000 to 156,000 men plus fifty-two autonomous mountain brigades and an undetermined number working clandestinely in the cities.[8]

Mussolini received the writer Pia Reggidori Corti on 7 April, and after a philosophical discussion on the meaning of love he admitted: 'By now everything is finished. I remain here beyond good and evil and I continue only for Italy. . . . Yes, the Italian people hate me, I know. But I, I have loved them so much.' He spoke longingly of Rome, a city he would never see again. 'I am alone, alone and, faced with danger and difficulties, man is cowardly, recoils, denies, betrays. . . . Not everyone, however.'[9]

To Carlo Silvestri, his old Socialist adversary who had become his friend, Mussolini spoke of handing over power to workers and Socialist organisations before the government in the south took control. Silvestri had another matter on his mind. Pavolini was threatening to order a general roundup of anti-Fascists to be used as hostages in case the partisans intended to execute Fascist militiamen. Silvestri urged Mussolini to put a stop to this, and the Duce gave Pavolini a written order to drop his plan. 'Let's entrust ourselves to the judgement of God and history,' he said. 'I want it known that, until the last instant, I did what I could to reduce the fatal consequences of the situation and humanise them against uncontrolled passions.'[10]

When Roosevelt's death was announced in mid-April, Mussolini exulted. A few days later he wrote in one of his notes for the *Corrispondenza repubblicana* that the president had been 'struck down by the justice of God and the curses of millions of mothers in all the world, including the United States'.

Rahn went to see Anfuso at the Foreign Ministry around mid-April to suggest that Mussolini attempt to persuade Hitler to seek a separate peace settlement with the Soviet Union. Anfuso said such a proposal would get nowhere and would only arouse the ire of Ribbentrop. But Rahn took the proposal to Mussolini, who agreed to make the attempt. He told Rahn the death of Roosevelt had opened the possibility of a separate peace. Anfuso drafted a note on the subject and Rahn telephoned it to Hitler's headquarters. 'I don't know if it was ever answered,' Anfuso wrote later, 'because Rahn let me know it was absolutely necessary for me to return to Berlin, where the absence of an Italian ambassador could be commented upon unfavourably, and said that's what Ribbentrop wanted.'

The entire diplomatic corps in Berlin had, in fact, moved to Bad Gastein in Austria, near the border with Bavaria, and Rahn insisted Anfuso at least go there. He suggested they could fly together to Berlin to support the request for a separate peace with the Russians, then changed his mind. Mussolini told Anfuso it was perfectly superfluous to make the proposal to Hitler, who was hoping one of the two parts of the Allied coalition would offer him better terms than the other. From Bad Gastein, Anfuso contacted Mussolini to suggest he could arrange for a plane to take him to Spain, or he could go to Switzerland. The Duce replied he would go to the Valtellina. 'I cannot leave my country,' he said. Anfuso said Mussolini was convinced that if he went to Switzerland he would be handed over to the Allies.[11]

Tarchi, the economy minister, told Mussolini on 13 April that he had reached a preliminary accord with the CLN, aimed at guaranteeing public order and safety for Fascists in case the Germans withdrew. Interior Minister Paolo Zerbino, who was present, said he was favourable to such an agreement but insisted he should be in charge of further negotiations. Tarchi said that would be unwise because the CLN would not like it. That same day, Mussolini received Giorgio Pini, the under-secretary of the interior, and asked him for his views on the war. 'By now there is no doubt that it is lost,' Pini replied. Mussolini objected that the Germans were still resisting, but Pini said the situation was hopeless. Mussolini was silent, then said: 'Yes, you are right. It is like that. There's nothing more to be done.'[12]

The final Italian–German meeting to discuss the Valtellina project took place on 14 April with Wolff, Vietinghoff and Rahn present. This followed the Mussolini–Wolff private meeting that day at which, Wolff claimed later, he had urged the Duce to suspend his peace feelers and rely on him instead. At the Valtellina meeting, Pavolini continued to wax enthusiastic and was supported by Francesco Maria Barracu, the Cabinet Office minister. Pavolini talked of setting up a printing press, newspaper, radio station and hospital in the valley. Vietinghoff interrupted: 'How many arms do you have? How much food?' Pavolini admitted this was still to come, but he had sent 400 soldiers and 350 members of the Black Brigades to the Valtellina. Vietinghoff suggested it would be better to transfer the Salò Republic and its forces to Klagenfurt, in Austria, to an enclave that could be protected by the Wehrmacht.

Graziani objected to the Valtellina plan on the grounds that his troops could not act except in agreement with the German High Command. In any case, he said his experts had made a preliminary study and found the plan impractical. Buildings in the valley lacked central heating and the area was thick with Communists, who threatened to blow up generating stations if the Fascists moved in. The Todt organisation had promised to provide 200 labourers to build defences but they had never shown up. General Filippo

Diamanti, the Fascist military commander in Milan, said the plan was unworkable and Allied aviation would have destroyed the entire valley in a day. He proposed that Fascists gather in the Castello Sforzesco in Milan and await the arrival of the Allies, but Mussolini said: 'No, we must die fighting.' Vietinghoff concluded the plan had not been studied sufficiently from a military point of view, and now it was too late to do so. Wolff agreed but showed little interest; no doubt his mind was more on his negotiations with Dulles. The meeting broke up without agreement after two hours.[13]

Claretta had earlier suggested to Mussolini a plan of escape. She told him that Franz Spoegler, her SS escort, owned a hut 9,000 feet up in the Dolomite mountains where she and the Duce could hide. The hut, kept by an old couple in a pine forest on the Joecherhof peak, was a two-hour trek above the remote village of Lengmoos. Spoegler showed a photograph to Mussolini and said: 'Duce, it's the ass-end of the world.' Mussolini expressed some interest, but never came to a decision.[14]

Pavolini, who had left his wife and children for the film actress Doris Duranti, had her smuggled into Switzerland on 15 April. The next day, the Mussolini Cabinet met for the last time and discussed sending to Switzerland the families of ministers and leading party officials. Mussolini announced that he was preparing to transfer to Milan, and the next Cabinet meeting would be held there. Some Cabinet ministers suggested he go instead to the royal villa at Monza but Mussolini remembered that King Umberto I had been assassinated there, and, always superstitious, he rejected the idea.[15]

Graziani clashed with Rahn at a meeting about this time, telling the ambassador that the Germans should stop accusing Italians of being traitors. He said Italians were paying for their loyalty to Germany – 25,000 deaths each month. Rahn replied that the Germans were losing 25,000 people every day.[16]

The Mussolinis had begun to pack their bags, and the Duce told Rachele on 15 April: 'You must believe, there is something in the Italian people that cannot perish and will never perish. Not even Italians, as much as they try, can destroy it because it is linked to our entire past.' He told her he would leave for Milan first and she and the children would follow later. He also reaffirmed his intention to make a last stand in the Valtellina.[17]

On 17 April, Mussolini called in his sister Edvige, who had been living on Lake Garda with her family for some months. He urged her to go to Milan, and said he was going there to meet Cardinal Schuster. 'If there exists even a minimum possibility to carry out the transfer of powers without blood and shame, it is necessary to look for it,' he said. 'The war is about to end everywhere. Germany is at the extreme limits and Japan will not be able to continue fighting for long. I think I am sufficiently serene in this hour to understand how men and ideas of which I have been the adversary have won.' He predicted that Germany would remain for a long time divided between the West and the Soviet Union. He told her Churchill and Stalin were the principal winners of the war, by contrast with Roosevelt whose vision had been distorted by 'a sort of rough amateurism'. He said he and Churchill had had an exchange of ideas before Italy entered the war, and he had been struck by the British leader's open-mindedness. In case of extreme need, he advised, she should turn to Churchill. He pronounced a benediction on his Salò Republic, saying it would appear to some future historian 'as the only means by which the prostrate Italy existed among the huge armed forces at the end of the Second World War'. As for himself, he said: 'I really don't feel the need of being vindicated or rehabilitated. I have run my course.' He recalled a line from Hamlet: 'The rest is silence.' 'I have been ready for some time to enter into a grand silence.'[18]

That night Silvestri phoned and awakened him, saying that Fascists at Mantua were preparing to carry out a death sentence against Tomaso Solci, the local president of the CLN. At Silvestri's request, Mussolini ordered the sentence to be suspended. He had earlier saved Solci's son from a death sentence.[19]

Mellini went to see Rahn on 18 April and found him in an optimistic mood, speaking of underground factories in Germany and the development of jet fighter planes. Wolff joined the meeting and was equally optimistic. He had earlier told Mellini he was confident the Italian front would hold, and asked him to reassure the Duce. When Mellini reported the conversation, Mussolini erupted angrily: 'Recklessness or bad faith. Or perhaps both. I don't know what to make of the generic reassurances. I would only like to know what plans they have and if and what measures they intend . . . to prevent the entire Po front from falling like a ripe pear. But they are too presumptuous to keep me up to date on what they have in their conceited heads. And I have swallowed one humiliation after another to avoid the worst.' He said Hitler had never understood the importance of the Mediterranean and of keeping Italy at all costs. A collapse of the Po front, he said, would unleash a bloodbath against Fascists by the partisans and have perhaps fatal repercussions on the Italian and German war fronts. 'And to think they haven't permitted the magnificent Italian divisions trained in Germany to defend the Apennines. . . . Italy could save its honour only if foreigners in the north and in the south had let the Italians fight to defend their country. In the north, against the Anglo-Americans, in the south against the Germans. The dead would not have died in vain.'[20]

The Fascist Prefect Gioacchino Nicoletti came to see Mussolini that day to ask him to stop proceedings against a woman arrested at Mantua, and the Duce did so. He had a long talk with Nicoletti, bemoaning German failure to create a free Poland and an independent Ukraine, thus ensuring that these lands remained hostile to Germany, and he blamed Ribbentrop. 'Inside that cranium there is absolutely nothing.' He spoke of Goebbels and said: 'Not even an idiot baby believes the stupidities this false werewolf keeps repeating.' Göring, he recalled, once said that 'you can call me Mr Smith' if British planes ever flew over Berlin. As for Kesselring, he said the field marshal had had only one plan since he had been in Italy: 'to retreat, retreat systematically, always retreat, it doesn't matter if it is a hundred yards, a mile or ten miles. . . . Has he ever tried an encirclement, a surprise attack, a simple manoeuvre based on the most elementary tactical schemes?' The outcome of the battle, he said, certainly would not improve with Kesselring's successor.

'The Germans always lose an hour, a battle, an idea. . . . The game is up for me. It's finished.' After the war, he said, Italy would rise again but Germany would be 'cruelly dismembered'. All this would signify the end of Europe and the Bolshevisation of the West.

Nicoletti asked him what he would do. 'I don't know yet exactly. . . . But if necessary, for the honour of the flag, we will make an extreme resistance in the Valtellina, where everything has been predisposed to create a defensive valley.' Contradicting what he had told Edvige just a day earlier, he said Churchill knew perfectly well that Britain would be the major loser from the war. 'The heavy chain of war debts will tie England forever to the will of America, which will be the true arbiter, with Russia, of the new situation. A mortal duel between the two antagonistic giants already is delineated. England, in the new conflict, will be nothing more than a pawn and shield of the United States of America. All that is tremendous and will signify . . . the end of civilisation, at least in the terms in which that is understood by us.'

He said he would never have taken the helm of 'this broken-down [*fatiscente*] republic' if Hitler had not forced him to. He would have wanted to go to Florence, Bologna or Milan, to be in contact with the people, but instead the Germans had relegated him to 'this cul-de-sac of Gargnano. . . . Here I see practically no one any more, and here my very breathing is controlled. . . . The Germans are responsible for everything. They torpedoed my army, police, nationalisation, the very acts of my civil administration. It is because of this that the Germans always lose an hour, a battle, an idea.'[21]

In a conversation with Police Chief Renzo Montagna, Mussolini said: 'Hitler will die in Berlin and nobody will find his body. Within ten or maybe a hundred years the Germans, who love creating myths, will say the Führer went to heaven in the heart of the flames and they'll make him a national hero. If something similar happened to me . . .'.[22]

Late in the afternoon of 18 April, he left for Milan in a convoy of five cars and a truck loaded with baggage, escorted by SS troops commanded by

Lieutenant Fritz Birzer and Lieutenant Otto Kisnatt of the SD. He was accompanied by Interior Minister Zerbino, his secretary Luigi Gatti, Dr Zachariae and other officials. He stopped at the Villa Feltrinelli to say goodbye to Rachele and his children, Romano, eighteen, and Anna Maria, sixteen. Romano was playing the 'Blue Danube' waltz on the piano as Mussolini approached. He slapped his son on the shoulder and said: 'Since when have you liked waltzes?' Romano started to get up to accompany him to the car, but his father said: 'No, no, continue playing.' He added that he would return in two or three days.

He told Rachele, alarmed by his departure, that he would soon return, but that was not to be; it was the last time he saw her. In her diary she wrote: 'He referred vaguely to agreements of a certain gravity he will have to make in Milan, mentioning the name of Cardinal Schuster. But I fear that today more than ever he is too loyal in a moment in which snares are hidden everywhere.' As he was getting into his car, he turned back for a last look at the garden and the villa, then at his wife. 'There were no other words between us. In my desperation I understood his soul,' she said.[23]

Mussolini arrived in Milan at 7 p.m. and told the Fascist Prefect Mario Bassi: 'This is not an official visit. I will receive only those I wish to see. I must work.' On the same day, the Allies launched another big offensive east of Bologna and the Germans suffered heavy losses.

Graziani dined that night with Rahn, who presented him with a new Beretta pistol. Graziani was so depressed that he wondered whether this was an invitation to commit suicide. He left for Milan that evening.[24]

As soon as Mussolini left Gargnano, Claretta ran to Spoegler and asked him to take her to Milan. She left that night.[25]

Dulles's radio operator, Little Wally, learned during the afternoon that Mussolini was on his way to Milan. He radioed the news to Caserta and said Mussolini would stay at the Palazzo Governo for three or four days. He described the building and suggested the Allies dive-bomb it, while taking care to avoid his own quarters 300 yards to the south-east. But, as Dulles said later, the Air Force had other priorities.[26]

Chapter 19

A Temporary Loss of Nerve

Probably never in history had plenipotentiaries desiring to surrender a great army received such a strange reception.

(Allen W. Dulles, 23 April 1945)

At dawn on 21 April, Allied troops entered Bologna. The race to the Po had begun. Dulles went to his office that morning, a Saturday, and received a severe jolt when he found an urgent top-secret message had come in overnight from the joint Chiefs of Staff in Washington: the OSS was ordered to break off all contact with German emissaries at once. The combined Chiefs in Washington had concluded that Vietinghoff did not intend to surrender on acceptable terms, and because of the complications with the Soviets the US and British governments thought it best to end the talks. The Allied representatives in Moscow would inform the Russians.

Stopping everything in its tracks was not a simple matter. Dulles needed to get Wally out of Italy, where he could be prey to the SS. There was also the problem of how to handle Parrilli and what to tell Major Max Waibel, the Swiss military intelligence officer who had been involved in the negotiations from the start. Dulles outlined his dilemma to Washington, and officials there replied that they appreciated his problems but he would have to solve them in a way that would comply with their instructions. Dulles sent a radio message to Milan, claiming that Bern was not picking up Wally's signals satisfactorily and asking him to come to the frontier for consultations.[1]

On 22 April, Parrilli met Wolff's adjutant, Wenner, in Fasano and launched into a furious complaint against Wolff, again referring to him as a war criminal. Wolff was not there because he had gone to see Vietinghoff at Recoaro to insist he draw up a written authorisation for surrender and name someone to represent him. The trip had been suggested by Rahn, who together with Roettiger had succeeded in stiffening Vietinghoff's resolve. Vietinghoff designated Colonel Victor von Schweinitz to go to Caserta to sign for him. Schweinitz was chosen because he spoke English fluently, having been an exchange officer in Britain before the war. He was descended on his mother's side from John Jay, America's first Supreme Court chief justice and one of the signatories of the Declaration of Independence. But Vietinghoff still conditioned his acceptance of surrender on the right of his soldiers to return to Germany with sword belt and bayonet, and complained he had received no guarantees on this point. Wolff argued that Caserta had not refused, and he was sure a convenient formula could be found at the moment of signing. Vietinghoff yielded, but in the document he gave to Schweinitz he inserted this phrase: 'in the limits fixed by me'. Wolff designated Wenner to sign in his name, and announced he would go to Bern to explain the delay to Dulles.[2]

Vietinghoff insisted that an emissary be sent to Kesselring to get his final consent to surrender. Dollmann was chosen for this mission, and he had a preliminary meeting with Franz Hofer, the Austrian gauleiter for the Tyrol. Hofer argued the Germans should hold out for measures that would guarantee political autonomy for the Tyrol and leave him in charge. Before continuing his mission, Dollmann thought he had persuaded Hofer to abandon the idea. This and subsequent developments involving Kesselring were not known to the Allies until after the war.[3]

On the night of April 22/3, Wolff left Fasano, ordered his headquarters to be moved to Bolzano and set off for Switzerland. He and his party stopped at Cernobbio to exchange their uniforms for civilian suits. They could not find civilian shoes for Schweinitz, who was mortified to have to settle for a pair of white tennis shoes. On the morning of 23 April, Waibel phoned Dulles with the 'astounding news' that Wolff and his party were on their way to Switzerland to surrender and had proposed an immediate meeting with Dulles in Lucerne. Dulles, of course, was in a bind; he was under strict military orders to have no dealings with them. He radioed Caserta and Washington, asking for new instructions. Waibel offered to stall the Germans until he received an answer. Alexander informed Dulles that he had asked the Combined Chiefs in Washington to reconsider. The response that eventually came from Washington was equivocal: avoid any action that could be construed as a continuation of Operation Sunrise. But if the Swiss were acting on their own in talking to the Germans, any information they passed on could be transmitted to Allied headquarters.

Waibel and Husmann went to the frontier to escort the Germans to Lucerne. When Waibel met Wolff, he said the general's delays and his meeting with Hitler had made Washington and London sceptical of his intentions, but he should come to Lucerne to see what could be done. The party arrived that evening at Waibel's house overlooking Lake Lucerne. Meanwhile, Himmler had sent a telegram to Fasano that read: 'It is indispensable that the Italian front is maintained unaltered. I forbid any negotiation, even of a local character.' The telegram was relayed to Zimmer in Milan, and he went to the border to read it over the phone to Wolff. Zimmer also advised that Mussolini was planning to go to the Valtellina. When Wolff was off the phone, he remarked: 'Himmler doesn't frighten me any more.' He said before leaving Fasano he had agreed with Vietinghoff, Pohl, Roettiger and Hofer that they would not accept any more orders from Himmler regarding the Italian zone.[4]

Dulles and Gaevernitz reached Lucerne shortly after the Germans arrived there, and went to the Hotel Schweizerhof, with Dulles suffering from an acute attack of gout. Dulles learned that Wally was now safely back in Switzerland. Dulles informed the Germans through Waibel that he was under orders not to see them, but he urged patience. He wanted to know the text of Vietinghoff's authorisation to Schweinitz before taking any initiative. So Waibel awoke Schweinitz after midnight and asked him for the document. He handed it over, but then, fearing a trap, grew alarmed and protested loudly. He did not calm down again until the document was returned to him. The Germans agreed to stay in Lucerne for a day or two, and meanwhile Dulles relayed the Vietinghoff document to Caserta and Washington. On 24 April, the Germans went to a shop in Lucerne to buy a pair of shoes for Schweinitz. That evening Wolff, no longer fearing Kaltenbrunner's spies, took his party to a popular restaurant in Lucerne for dinner.[5]

By 25 April, having waited two days with no word on what would happen next, the Germans were getting impatient. 'Probably never in all history', Dulles wrote later, 'had plenipotentiaries desiring to surrender a great army received so strange a reception.' He feared that with the Allies now pushing north, Berlin would order the destruction of industrial and power plants in northern Italy and the port facilities in Genoa. Dulles had another problem: he was in such pain from his gout that Gaevernitz had to call in a doctor, who gave him morphine, enabling him to continue working.

Wolff sent word to Dulles on the afternoon of 25 April that he had to return to Italy immediately. He feared Himmler might come and try to take control of his forces, and Vietinghoff might change his mind. The Duce was also unpredictable and might try to prevent an orderly surrender. Another consideration was the possibility that partisans would cut off the road to Wolff's headquarters. He gave Wenner full written powers to represent him, and left Dulles a longhand memorandum listing Tyrolean castles and other hideouts where he had stored priceless Italian art objects to save them before the battle for Florence. He suggested the Allies should send army detachments to these areas to rescue the treasures. Then Wolff took an evening train to the frontier, while Dulles and Gaevernitz returned to Bern.[6]

The partisans launched their uprising in Milan that same evening. Wolff had ordered his troops not to move from their barracks and not to attack for any reason but only to defend themselves if attacked. He ordered Rauff, who was in command of SS forces in Milan, to put himself at Cardinal Schuster's disposition to prevent any bloodshed, and said in extreme cases the Germans should surrender to partisans rather than use their arms. A young Italian priest, Giovanni Barbareschi, carried Wolff's order to Rauff. Wolff telephoned Zimmer in Milan and instructed him to facilitate Wally's transfer to Bolzano, as Wally had to establish a radio link between the German commands and Caserta to make sure the surrender proceedings went smoothly.[7]

From Cernobbio, Wolff dispatched a courier-delivered report to Husmann, expressing concern that he might not be able to leave there because partisans were moving up to seal the border area. He also disclosed that Mussolini had held a three-hour conference with Schuster on the evening of 25 April to discuss an armistice between partisans and Fascists. Dulles was at a low point, fearing that all his efforts were about to end in confusion. To make matters worse, Schweinitz was threatening to show his surrender authorisation to the press if something didn't happen soon. The world would learn who had led the Germans down the garden path and who was responsible for a needless slaughter. Waibel succeeded in calming him.

In the early hours of 26 April, Waibel learned that partisans had surrounded Wolff's villa in Cernobbio and might storm it and kill him. Waibel and Gaevernitz headed for the border to see what they could do. They spoke by phone with Wolff, who proposed going to Milan and issuing a surrender proclamation over German-controlled radio. He had spoken to Colonel Rauff in Milan about this, who relayed his intentions to Cardinal Schuster. But Gaevernitz and Waibel opposed any attempt by Wolff to go to Milan because they feared partisan attacks on him. Gaevernitz also thought Allied troops would not know what to make of Wolff's broadcast and would go on fighting. He proposed that Wolff return to Switzerland and cross the Austrian frontier, going from there to Bolzano. But he would need help to do that. Fortunately, Waibel and Gaevernitz had been met at Chiasso by OSS agent Don Jones, a former journalist whose code name was Scotti, and OSS Captain Emilio Q. Daddario, who had learned from a Swiss intelligence officer that Wolff was in a serious predicament.

Jones organised a convoy of three cars and brought along three Swiss, two SS officials from the dissolved German border post and several partisans. The first car displayed white flags, but the convoy was fired on as it left Chiasso. At Como, the men got papers authorising them to pass through partisan lines. En route to Wolff's villa, they encountered more rifle fire and the occasional grenade was thrown at them, but they arrived safely. While they were on their way, Rauff informed CLNAI and church officials in Milan that he was prepared to ask Wolff for powers to sign a surrender in his name and those of Vietinghoff and Rahn. The men who reached Wolff's villa in Cernobbio found the general in full SS uniform. Jones told him to put on civilian clothes and hurry. Wolff, in continuous phone contact with Rauff in Milan, learned that the centre of the city was held by the SS and the suburbs by partisans, but no shots had been fired. Wolff ordered Rauff to release all political prisoners at once. Rauff had tried to send an armoured car to Cernobbio to collect Wolff, but it could not get past partisan lines. Schuster had sent a car with a priest and an SS officer, but this attempt also failed. Rauff had presented to Wolff his idea of signing the surrender in Wolff's name but was told the general felt 'bound by his word to the Allies' to complete the surrender negotiations in Switzerland. Wolff and the Allied representatives returned to the Swiss frontier at 2.30 a.m. on 27 April.[8]

Later that morning, Dulles received three messages marked 'TRIPLE AUTHORITY'. The combined chiefs had accepted the Vietinghoff document and instructed Alexander to arrange for German envoys to come immediately to Caserta for the surrender. There were to be no conferences or discussions in Switzerland. The Russians had been invited to send a representative to Caserta. A plane was coming that day to Annecy, in France, to collect the surrender team. The messages suggested that Gaevernitz and Waibel should accompany the German emissaries if possible.[9] Finally, two months and seven days after Parrilli had launched his improbable peace mission, success was at hand.

Chapter 20

The Fall of Fascism

At this point of my existence death becomes a rest.
(Benito Mussolini, speaking three days before his death, 25 April 1945)

In Milan, Mussolini had many of his ministers with him in the same city for the first time since he had returned to power. He was finally freed from the oppressive atmosphere of Lake Garda, and was in the thick of things just as the Allied offensive was gaining momentum. All of this should have galvanised him to begin acting in a decisive manner, but in the week he would remain in the Lombard capital he was for the most part a pathetic, indecisive leader whose grip on reality was sometimes questionable. He had come to Milan expecting his government could continue to function rather longer than proved to be the case. The Po river runs west to east across Italy just 25 miles south of Milan at its closest point, and although the Allied offensive was concentrated further east, any crossing of the river put the city in imminent peril. As German defences along the Po began to crumble with alarming rapidity, Mussolini discovered he had little time left.

On 19 April, residents of Bologna began an insurrection against Fascist and German forces even as Mussolini was meeting with officials in Milan for yet another fruitless discussion about the retreat to the Valtellina. Pavolini now spoke in terms of 100,000 men converging there, but Vincenzo Costa, the Fascist Party leader in Milan, said they could count on 16,000 at most. Mussolini told his officials he wanted to speak to the Milanese on 21 April after a ceremony in the cathedral dedicated to all the Fascists who had fallen in the war. In liberated Siena, Captain Max Corvo, an American OSS officer, drew up a bold plan to capture Mussolini and his *gerarchi* now that they were in Milan. He and thirty OSS agents would parachute onto the San Siro racetrack, 3 miles north-west of the city, and sneak into Milan to seize the Fascist leaders after a partisan insurrection had begun. Allied headquarters in Caserta vetoed the plan.[1]

Soon after his arrival, Mussolini absolved the military from its oath to the republic, contradicting his promise in December to go down fighting.

He ordered salaries for the coming six months to be distributed to ministerial employees, including a hypothetical last month of service. In other respects, he carried on the ordinary business of government as though nothing had changed. He appointed a new prefect for Varese, promoted the Fascist Party leader in Turin to become party chief for the Piedmont region, ordered elections for town hall officials and discussed the republic's finances with Finance Minister Pellegrini-Giampietro. He also called in Education Minister Carlo Alberto Biggini and gave him 'very important personal documents' to save in case the government collapsed. The documents may have included his diary, which was never found after his death. He also received Japanese Ambassador Shinrokuro Hidaka and there were reports he gave him some documents for safekeeping, but Hidaka denied that after the war.[2]

Zachariae witnessed a continuing decline in his patient. 'His physical state worsened day by day, and he almost didn't eat or sleep any more,' he said. 'Also he became very reserved with me.' Others who saw the Duce at that time shared Zachariae's view. The Italian diplomat Bolla spoke of 'a sense of impotence . . . a paralysing lack of confidence in himself. . . . He is without doubt a man . . . who has lost the sense of history and reality . . . a man who suffers from an incredible weakness before the pressures of people near him.' Zachariae saw Mussolini on the morning of 20 April, told him the war was lost and said he must avoid becoming a prisoner of the British or the partisans. He suggested Mussolini allow him to go to the Swiss frontier and plead for asylum for a seriously ill patient. Otherwise, he thought Mussolini should try to reach Spain by air and continue to a neutral country. 'He was visibly moved and shook my hand without responding,' Zachariae said. After a pause, the Duce promised to think over his proposals and asked Zachariae to return at 5 p.m. When he did so, Mussolini said he could not follow his advice because abandoning his friends in that extreme hour would be a betrayal. Zachariae tried in vain to dissuade him.[3]

A few scattered strikes occurred in Milanese industrial plants on 20 April, the first signs of an impending insurrection. Throughout the day, Milan and routes leading to it from Lake Garda and Lake Como were machine-gunned at low altitude by Allied planes. Even a Swiss doctor, travelling with a big Swiss flag on his car, was killed. Mussolini ordered the closure of provincial offices of government ministries so all their employees could concentrate in Milan and follow the government to its Alpine redoubt. Because of the deteriorating military situation, he also decided to forgo the 21 April ceremony for the fallen, and he ordered that munitions be sent to the Valtellina. Just two truckloads of arms subsequently departed for Rogolo in the valley.[4]

Giorgio Pisanò, a young officer of the Republican Guard, was sent to the Valtellina to survey the situation and was shocked by what he found.

'Where is the Alpine redoubt?' he asked. 'What does it consist of? Along the 24 miles from the roadblock at Sondrio I saw only blocked-up houses, deserted lands, no concentration of troops, no fortifications. I knew also that all our garrisons formerly existing along the route . . . had been withdrawn to Sondrio.'[5]

Rahn arrived in Milan on 20 April to try to persuade Mussolini to return to Gargnano and found him 'apparently calm, and even imperturbable and serene'. Mussolini refused to leave Milan. 'Here I feel myself at home and here I must remain,' he said. 'It is from here that I must govern.' Leaving the meeting, Rahn murmured: 'The rupture on the Po front will unleash a slaughter of the Fascists by the partisans.' Mussolini told members of his Cabinet later that he did not believe the end of the war was near. 'It is a great drama that has not five acts but may have six, seven or eight,' he said.[6]

Mellini, acting on Mussolini's instructions, met the Swiss representative in Milan, Max Troendle, to renew their discussions on a Swiss refuge for families of Fascist officials. Troendle told him it was neither possible nor advisable to try to obtain visas for the families, but he felt confident that women and children who appeared at the Swiss frontier under serious and immediate threat would be allowed to enter. Political personalities under threat also might be allowed in, he said, provided they were not wanted for crimes and had not in the past carried out acts of hostility against Switzerland. But he said they would be interned, and he asked for a list of those who would want to enter the country. Troendle offered his advice unofficially; he had not consulted his government.[7]

Economy Minister Tarchi met Mussolini in the afternoon of 20 April and told him that Giuseppe Brusasca, a lawyer representing the Christian Democrats on the CLN, had agreed to sign an accord regulating the passage of powers to the CLN at the moment of German withdrawal. Under the agreement, Graziani would surrender together with the Germans, and the Black Brigades would be dissolved and integrated into the armed forces. But Interior Minister Zerbino, still trying to muscle in on the act, insisted it was up to him to sign the agreement. The signing was fixed for 22 April, with the question of who would sign left in the air.[8]

Mussolini found time in the afternoon of 21 April for a long interview with Gian Gaetano Cabella, editor of the newspaper *Il Popolo di Alessandria*. Cabella said that, contrary to rumours, he found Mussolini in very sound health, with a good complexion, vivacious eyes and quick movements. Mussolini said that if he were killed in coming days, Cabella should withhold publication for three years. The interview was published in book form in 1948 as Mussolini's political testament. He reaffirmed his plan to go to the Valtellina, then said: 'For me it is finished. I haven't the right to demand sacrifices from the

Italians. The life of Italy will not end this week or this month. Italy will rise again . . . and will be great again, as I wanted.'

He sought to defend his decision to go to war alongside Germany in 1940, asserting that he had been heavily criticised earlier for remaining neutral. 'Germany had won. . . . And what did Mussolini do? He went soft. A golden occasion would never again have presented itself. So everyone said, and especially those who now shout that we should have remained neutral and that only my megalomania and my love of power and my weakness before Hitler had carried us to war. . . . The truth is this: I had no pressure from Hitler. Hitler had already won the continental game. He didn't need us. But we could not remain neutral if we wanted to maintain that position of parity with Germany that we had had until then.' He said the coming victory of the Allies would give the world only an ephemeral and illusory peace.

He was usually fond of expressing his admiration for the Italian masses, as opposed to the middle and upper classes. But now he said:

> I overvalued the intelligence of the masses. In the dialogues I had with the multitude so many times, I was convinced the cry that followed my questions was a sign of consciousness, understanding and evolution. Instead, it was collective hysterics. The extremity that our enemies have obtained is that the proletarians, the poor, the needy, lined up body and soul on the side of the plutocrats and the profiteers of big capitalism. . . . This crisis, which began in 1939, has not been overcome in the Italian people. They will rise again, but their convalescence will be long and sad. . . . I am like the great clinic that hasn't known how to find a cure and no longer has the confidence of the families of the important patient.

He defended his decision to return to power at German behest in 1943. If he had not, he said, the Germans would have named a military government that would then have burned the land, brought hunger, deported masses of people, sequestrated property, introduced forced labour and taken Italian industry and art treasures as war booty. Mussolini evidently said all this without irony, ignoring the fact that the Germans did precisely all these things. 'I reflected a long time. . . . I had the very precise conviction I was signing my death sentence,' he said. 'I had no more importance. I had to save as much life and property as possible. I had to try yet again to do good to the Italian people. . . . I prevented many shootings, even when they were just. I tried, with three amnesty decrees, to pardon and put off as long as possible the repressive actions the German Commands demanded. . . . I distributed to poor people . . . many millions. I tried to save the saveable.' He insisted Germany did have secret weapons, and suggested nonsensically there would have been time to use them had there not been the July 1944 attempt to assassinate Hitler. 'Betrayal also in Germany provoked ruin, not of a party, but of the country.'

Mussolini pointed to a leather briefcase and said it contained proofs of his efforts to prevent war, enabling him to be tranquil and serene about the judgement of posterity. 'I do not know if Churchill is, like me, tranquil and serene. Remember well: we have frightened the world of the great profiteers and speculators. They did not want to give us the possibility to live. If the outcome of this war had been favourable to the Axis, I would have proposed to the Führer, victory achieved, world nationalisation.' He predicted the partisans would soon regret having helped the Allied invaders, and he foresaw a new conflict of 'capitalist democracies against capitalist Bolshevism. Only our victory would have given the world peace with justice.'[9]

Mussolini went to see Claretta and vainly urged her to follow her parents and her sister Myriam, who had decided to flee to Spain. She told him she would not leave him. She had written to a friend at Gardone, asking her to send some personal objects and clothes to her, and had said: 'What will become of me? I don't know. I don't interrogate fate, since I have chosen this fate. . . . Now I am alone, alone with myself and this ideal that burns and consumes me.'[10]

In the Hotel Regina, SS officers and troops celebrated Hitler's birthday with a reception. Mussolini ordered Prefect Mario Bassi to attend, hoping he would be able to glean some information on what the Germans might be planning. But Bassi was unable to learn anything.[11]

On 21 April, the Allies entered Bologna and partisans there began to kill Fascists and even non-Fascists they considered their political adversaries. Partisans also liberated Modena on 21–2 April, just before the arrival of the US Fifth Army, and Reggio Emilia was freed. The Allies were pushing on toward Verona, their offensive now unstoppable. Although the fighting was concentrated far to the east of Milan, Graziani told Mussolini: 'If they are bold enough, they could be in Milan even tomorrow. What have you decided to do?' Mussolini replied that events would decide, and Graziani objected that such passivity was not appropriate. In his memoirs, Graziani said of Mussolini at this point: 'He showed he was dominated by a fatalist waiting into which he had fallen some time back.' He recalled that Mussolini had once told him: 'My cycle closed on 25 July 1943. This is only an appendix.'

Mussolini's friend Nino D'Aroma, meeting him for the last time, told him the Germans were retreating. 'This strange Rahn has plotted something,' Mussolini replied. 'He is unctuous and slimy with those eyebrows of a rug merchant. Why must they burden us?' He asked D'Aroma what the people were saying, and D'Aroma replied: 'They hope in you still. Many still believe in secret weapons. Others are convinced you have a card up your sleeve.' Mussolini asked D'Aroma what he thought, and was told: 'I think it is truly finished for you and for us. . . . Now it is time to take our leave.' Mussolini said he was determined to see that Milan was not destroyed, but blood would flow all the same. D'Aroma pleaded with him to save himself and Mussolini said: 'My sacrifice is necessary. My salvation serves nothing. . . . Mussolini must die. I will be born again much sooner than our enemies believe, in the hearts of all Italians. . . . I have committed some errors. I see it, I understand them now, but in time they will be pardoned even by my most obstinate detractors.'

Railway workers throughout Lombardy began an unlimited strike. The CLN issued a proclamation calling on Fascists and Germans to 'surrender or die', and during the night copies of it were affixed to walls near enemy barracks in Milan.[12] In Germany, Russian forces had reached the outskirts of Berlin. Mussolini convened a military meeting in the Milan Prefecture, where he had his office, to discuss the Valtellina project. Pavolini spoke of 25,000–50,000 men he planned to concentrate around Como before proceeding to the valley. Graziani blew up. 'You know very well it is absurd to think of a resistance in the Valtellina. Even so, you go on betraying the Duce,' he shouted at Pavolini. He told him it was 'puerile and silly' to continue trying to delude Mussolini. Pavolini reacted bitterly and Graziani replied that after the fall of Bologna the situation was hopeless and the only reasonable option was surrender. Pavolini stormed from the room and went off to Como to make preparations. That evening, Graziani dined with Rahn, who said nothing about the secret peace negotiations in which Wolff was involved.[13]

Later that day Mussolini saw the editors of the Milan newspapers. Drawing some papers from his jacket pocket, he told them: 'It's necessary to resist for one month. I have in hand so much for winning the peace.' He asked their opinion of the Valtellina project, and their embarrassed silence told him all he needed to know. To his friend Ermanno Amicucci, he said: 'This war will never finish. Before we see peace, we will all have long white beards.' He added that he would go to the Valtellina and 'linked with the German redoubt in Bavaria, we will resist there'.[14]

That evening, Mussolini wanted to see again a film of his December triumph in Milan, the speech at the Lyric Theatre, then a film of the Allied bombardment of Gorla, in which several hundred children were found buried under the ruins of a bombed school. Allied planes flew over Milan all that night, carrying help to the partisans.[15] Zerbino informed Red Cross Commissioner Coriolano Pagnozzi, who had taken over Tarchi's negotiations with Brusasca, that Mussolini had rejected the proposed agreement with the CLN because he regarded it as an act of surrender. Mussolini confirmed this to Tarchi the next morning, but offered a different justification. He said the negotiations had been conducted by the conservative wing of the CLN and there was no guarantee the Communists and Socialists would respect the agreement. He repeated this to members of his Cabinet, adding that other negotiations were under way, but he gave no specifics. Brusasca said later that, if the agreement had been signed Mussolini would not have been shot because he would have become a prisoner of war.[16]

At 8 a.m. on Sunday, 22 April, Mussolini received reports on the military situation and concluded that the end of the war in Italy was imminent. Preparations for a withdrawal to the Valtellina, he said, must begin. Pavolini came to him to advise that the partisans were preparing an insurrection in Milan for the night of 25/6 April. Mussolini issued that day the ninety-ninth *Corrispondenza repubblicana*, entitled 'Anticipated Chronicle of an Unexpected Speech'. More than anything, it revealed his detachment from reality. With his regime on the point of collapse, he devoted precious time to a document dwelling on the fact that defeated small countries such as the Baltic States would be excluded from the forthcoming San Francisco conference to organise the United Nations: 'Was it right to consent to their disappearance? Wasn't this the old story of the wolf and the lamb. . . ?'[17] Bruno Spampanato called on Mussolini, and later claimed he found him in better physical condition than some people said at the time. 'The physical condition of Mussolini was normal. If anything, he showed a greater calm,' he wrote. Mussolini told him: 'It is impossible to avoid that which rains upon us now. But it is still possible to lighten the consequences. I speak of the political consequences. But we must know first what Berlin decides. From Vietinghoff I know nothing. Basically, the situation indicates only a worsening, not a collapse. . . . We can still face the enemy and negotiate.' Spampanato told him German offices were being moved to the Alto Adige as a measure of security.[18]

Biggini, the education minister, went to see Mussolini on 22 April to discuss what Biggini considered the 'most urgent' matters: not matters pertaining to the war but to his Ministry, as though the end were not near. He proposed a new law regarding teachers, and discussed a news release he planned to give to the radio on his work in the past year concerning the University of Trieste. He also produced a list of teachers who had been killed in the war.[19]

That afternoon Mussolini saw Silvestri. They agreed he should not negotiate with conservative forces in the CLN or with the Allies but should arrange a transfer of powers to republican and Socialist forces among the partisans. Silvestri wrote a letter to the Italian Socialist Party of Proletarian Unity to this effect, and asked that the exodus of Fascists be allowed to take place unopposed. He also planned to make the same offer to the Action Party, which had a Socialist element, but not to the Communists. Silvestri added that Mussolini asked a guarantee for the safety of Fascist families and isolated Fascists who remained in their homes, with the understanding they would hand over their arms. Fascist militias, he said, would promise not to take initiatives against partisans or troops of the government in Rome, but would continue the struggle in Italy or elsewhere against the Allies. Mussolini had no illusions that the Socialists would accept the proposal, and he was correct. Silvestri later met Riccardo Lombardi, a Socialist leader, who gave him a flat rejection.[20]

Graziani went to the nearby residence of Cardinal Schuster at 7 p.m. on 22 April and had a talk that lasted seventy-five minutes. Vietinghoff had asked him to inform Schuster that the Germans would save the industrial plants, art works and infrastructure of northern Italy if the clergy could help persuade the partisans not to interfere with a German withdrawal. He showed Schuster a letter written by Vietinghoff, and the cardinal promised to do all he could to achieve such an outcome. Graziani also said he was ready to make contact with General Cadorna, the partisan commander, but Schuster told him that was not possible; Cadorna was being watched and couldn't risk such a meeting.

Graziani asked the cardinal's opinion of his old plan to withdraw his troops toward the Brenner Pass and save them from destruction. Schuster replied that events had bypassed that plan, and asked if the Church could intervene to save Italy from further war. He said Mussolini had spoken of fighting in Milan to the last man and the last bullet, and this represented a programme of desperation. Graziani responded that it was his duty to resist an invader, and he could count on 1.5 million men. 'I remained silent and listened,' Schuster wrote afterwards. Graziani later observed that he found Schuster cold and uncaring.[21]

Gerhard Wolf, the former German consul in Florence who was now performing the same role in Milan, called on Schuster later that evening. He regretted that German negotiations with the Church for saving industries had leaked to the Swiss press, and he expressed concern that this could compromise the outcome. Schuster urged him to save Germans and Italians from a useless slaughter and seek an honourable surrender. Wolf assured him the Germans were prepared to negotiate.[22]

By the morning of 23 April, the Fascists around Mussolini were beginning to panic. Parma had fallen to the partisans, and Cremona and Mantua were isolated. The Japanese–American 442nd Battalion from Hawaii captured the La Spezia naval base. Yugoslav forces under Tito had occupied Fiume (now known as Rijeka, and part of Croatia) and French units had crossed into Italy. A report had come in that the SS Command in the Hotel Regina was burning its papers. A systematic killing of isolated Fascists across northern Italy was under way, and German defences had disintegrated. At Fornovo, 6,000 men of the 148th German Infantry Division were captured. The 75th Infantry Corps surrendered in Liguria and 40,000 men were taken prisoner. The 1st Parachute Division at Bologna had been pulverised and ceased to exist.[23] But Mussolini gave his last, brief public remarks that day to the Republican National Guard and urged them to fight on. 'This adorable country of ours must not perish,' he said. 'If Italy were to die, life for us wouldn't be worth living. We will reach the Valtellina to prepare the last, desperate defence: to die with the sun in our face and our gaze directed at the tops of the mountains, the last smile of the country. The hour is grave but, whatever is our destiny, my veterans of the militia, I launch the ancient and new cry to you: one for all, all for one.'[24]

The rapid military collapse threatened to cause panic in Milan, and Graziani wanted to go on the radio to appeal to the Milanese to remain calm and avoid fratricidal fighting. He put the proposal to Mussolini and also suggested he could meet members of the CLNAI, but the Duce refused to give his approval. 'It's necessary to do something,' Graziani grumbled.[25]

Party Vice-Secretary Pino Romualdi returned from a tour of the front and told Mussolini: 'It's disastrous. There's nothing left.' Mussolini responded that the Germans were defending the Po. Romualdi told him they were defending nothing. 'The Germans think only of retreating and returning home. They have finished fighting.' He urged an immediate retreat to the Valtellina.[26]

Mussolini phoned Rachele in Gargnano, sounding tired, and told her he would be back in Gargnano by 7 p.m. She asked if she and the children should leave Gargnano immediately with him. 'I don't know,' he said. 'I will explain everything to you later.' Mussolini's secretary Luigi Gatti arrived at the Villa Feltrinelli and made a selection of the Duce's documents, some to take away with him, some Mussolini wanted destroyed. An hour after Mussolini first called, he rang again to tell Rachele that Mantua had fallen and the road to Brescia was blocked, so he was unable to come to her.

'It isn't true,' she said. 'They are deceiving you. A militia truck arrived a short time ago from Milan. I myself spoke with them, and they ran into no difficulty.'

But Mussolini insisted she and the children should head for the old royal residence at Monza, and he had arranged for a Fascist official to accompany them. With Allied planes passing overhead, they set out in a car with its headlights turned off and eventually switched to back roads because the main national road was crowded with German trucks. They reached Monza at dawn on 24 April, and twice during the morning Mussolini phoned to say he could not come and would send Gatti to take them on to Como. When Gatti arrived, he told Rachele he hoped to persuade the Duce to go to Spain and take refuge with the family of Gatti's Spanish wife. Gatti escorted Rachele and the children to Como in the afternoon and, as he was leaving, Rachele told him: 'I expect some news soon. Don't ever abandon the Duce.'

'If necessary, I will die with him,' Gatti replied.[27]

Claretta went out to Linate Airport in Milan on 23 April to see off her parents and sister as they left for Spain. Her brother Marcello, with his wife and children, were also in Milan, having returned from a trip to Switzerland. Claretta imagined she could save Mussolini by faking his death in a car accident. She gave Myriam a letter that she opened only when she reached Spain, entrusting her with the custody of her papers including her correspondence with Mussolini. 'I follow my destiny which is his,' she wrote. 'I will not abandon him ever, no matter what happens. I will never destroy with a cowardly gesture the supreme beauty of my offer. I will not fail to help him.'[28]

Wilhelm Höttl, the German SD commander for Italy and southern Europe, said former Interior Minister Buffarini approached German security police that day to propose a scheme for getting rid of Mussolini. Buffarini suggested the security police could issue false passports to Mussolini and his party, and he himself would then persuade the Duce to flee to Switzerland, taking a route via Como and Menaggio to the frontier. But there partisans would be lying in wait for him. Höttl said Marcello Petacci approached a German police official in Merano with an almost identical proposal at almost the same moment. Marcello promised to ensure that Mussolini took all the funds of the Salò government with him, and he would claim 'only a modest fraction of the loot for his pains'. A senior German Secret Service officer in Merano, Höttl claimed, rejected these proposals out of hand and forbade further communication with the two men.[29] Although Buffarini and Marcello were both capable of such actions, this account does not ring entirely true. At the time Höttl claimed Marcello was in Merano, he was in Milan. Even if it were just a matter of getting the date wrong in his case, it seems unlikely a German officer in Merano would know about the approach on the same day by Buffarini, who was 125 miles away in Milan.

General von Meinhold, in charge of German troops in Genoa, made known to a partisan doctor that afternoon that the German commands had received an order to evacuate the city. He wanted the archbishop of Genoa to be informed, and hoped for negotiations with the CLN that would guarantee that retreating German troops would not be attacked. He did not ask for any safeguards for Fascist forces. The doctor, before going to the archbishop, informed the partisan commander in Genoa of his talk with Meinhold. A few hours later, partisan squads began attacking Fascist barracks in an attempt to capture arms. The Fascists were caught by surprise and were roundly defeated. At dawn the next day, the partisans launched an attack on German forces in the port, where 6,000 were concentrated. The Germans surrendered four days later.[30]

In Gargnano, Mellini had a last meeting with Rahn, who said he had put off a planned trip to Milan because he was waiting from one moment to the next for the conclusion of secret negotiations with Alexander. He said he hoped for a solution that would avoid a massacre and save Mussolini, who would be useful in future for the struggle against Bolshevism. Rahn said he expected an emissary to arrive on 24 April with information that would allow him to present to the Duce concrete and satisfying proposals that already had been agreed. Rahn said he wanted to keep this secret because everything could be wrecked if Berlin learned about it, and he told Mellini to say nothing to Mussolini because he wanted to inform him personally. Afterwards Mussolini rang Mellini, who told him Rahn would soon come to him with an interesting communication. 'The news didn't seem to interest him,' Mellini wrote. Thus Mussolini missed his only opportunity to learn firsthand about the German negotiations in Switzerland.[31]

That evening the Fascist leader in Milan, Vincenzo Costa, told a group of Fascists: 'Let's go to the Duce. He must tell us what death we have to die.' Mussolini later joined them in the courtyard of the Prefecture and said: 'Dear Milanese comrades, the hour is grave. I can pass on, but you must hold the ties of comradeship.' He told Costa to come to him the next morning, and bring maps of the Valtellina.[32]

On the morning of 24 April, the Prefect of Piacenza phoned to say German troops had thrown down their arms, asked for civilian clothes and abandoned the city. The US Tenth Mountain Division became the first Allied unit to cross the Po at San Benedetto Po, a small town just south of Mantua. Partisan forces helped to safeguard the Po bridges from German destruction so that the Allies could cross. Fresh strikes broke out in Milan, and Black Brigades members began deserting. At 7 a.m. a few bombs fell on the centre of the city, followed by low-level machine-gunning, and there was no reaction from German or Italian forces. A partisan brigade attacked Fascist barracks on the outskirts and captured a large supply of weapons.[33]

At his office, Pavolini received a Catholic journalist, Giuseppe Gorgerino, and two partisans to see if he could persuade them to agree on a united force of Fascists and partisans to maintain public order after the Germans withdrew and before the Allies arrived. Pavolini also offered to surrender, asking only some guarantees for his personal safety and immunity. No agreement was reached, but the two men decided to meet again the following day. Later, Gorgerino contacted Leo Valiani of the CLNAI, who regarded Pavolini's offer as hardly worthy of a response. He said Mussolini must surrender in person, without conditions, and hand over his Blackshirts with their arms.[34]

In a meeting with Mussolini and Graziani, Pavolini said: 'Duce, I have ordered all the Black Brigades of Liguria and Piedmont to fall back on Lombardy. The movement is under way.' Graziani, knowing the Black Brigade units were deserting, erupted: 'It is an ignoble thing to lie like this at the last moment.'

Pavolini replied: 'Marshal, respect for your person and your age is one thing. To suffer an insult is another.'

At that, Graziani said: 'But if everything is in ruins, if by now we are at the every-man-for-himself stage, why go on deceiving?' Mussolini intervened to ask if the regime were facing a second 8 September, meaning a surrender to the Allies. 'Much worse,' Graziani replied. Pavolini remained silent.[35]

Mussolini, in a meeting with Spampanato, said: 'No one knows what will happen tonight or tomorrow or the day after. But . . . in some way, it will be necessary to remake a powerful Italy. Power equals space, influence, wealth. The social revolution is not an affair for sedentary people or miserable nations. Any social revolution needs these terms; this is the correction fascism has brought to socialism, otherwise reduced to a paper revolution. No one will be permitted to ignore it.' As for himself, he said: 'Nations have a longer life than their leaders. Italy is reduced to Milan. But this is only a year, 1945. The life of nations does not stop with one year.'[36]

SS Kriminalinspektor Otto Kisnatt, who had escorted Mussolini to Milan from Gargnano, barged into his office to find out his plans. He said cars packed with Fascist families were pouring into Milan, and Fascist troops were disappearing. He urged the Duce to move to Merano near the Austrian border. Mussolini produced a map on which he outlined a route via Como and Menaggio to Sondrio, on the edge of the Valtellina. The more direct route to Sondrio was via Lecco on the east side of Lake Como, not Menaggio on the west side, and Kisnatt argued that Mussolini had chosen a dangerous route controlled by partisans. But Mussolini observed that it was close to the Swiss border, and if need be he could take refuge there. Kisnatt said the Germans insisted that he should not try to enter Switzerland, and he would not be given asylum there anyway.[37]

The last message from Hitler to the Duce arrived that day. 'The struggle for being and not being has reached its culminating point,' the Führer wrote. 'Employing great masses of men and material, Bolshevism and Judaism are engaged in depth to reunite their destructive forces on German territory with the aim of precipitating our continent into chaos. Yet, in its spirit of tenacious disregard for death, the German people and many others are animated by the same sentiments. They rush to the rescue, for as long as the battle lasts, and with their unmatchable heroism will change the course of the war in this historic moment in which the fate of Europe is decided for centuries to come.'[38]

Lieutenant Krause of the German Command held a news conference at the Ministry of Popular Culture. He confirmed Bologna had fallen but claimed the population of Ferrara had risen against the partisans. By afternoon, shops in Milan were shuttered, cinemas almost deserted. But in some places a kind of surreal atmosphere prevailed. At 4 p.m. the La Scala opera company, bombed out of its own theatre, went ahead with a performance of *Don Giovanni* at the Lyric Theatre before a relative handful of spectators, with Gino Marinuzzi conducting. Fascist General Filippo Diamanti brought his young son to see Mussolini because the boy wanted a signed photograph of the Duce. Directors of RAI, the state broadcasting company, called on Mussolini to outline their work programme for the months ahead. An executive of the publishing firm Mondadori presented to Mussolini a copy of a new book by Emilio Settimelli, *Thirty Years of Comments*. Settimelli had once been editor of the Fascist newspaper *L'Impero*, but, having fallen out with Mussolini, had been sent into internal exile then expelled to France. Paul Gentizon, a Swiss writer, attempted to enter Italy with the first copies of Mussolini's last book, *Storia di un anno*, but a German lieutenant at the border turned him back with these words: 'When it rains stones it is better to stay at home.' Retreating German troops passed through Milan, their clothes muddy after three days of rain on the Po plain. SS Commander Rauff called in Deputy Mayor Elio Bracco and told him he was needed for negotiations with the CLN. 'Within twenty-four hours, I will say with extreme frankness before you and a CLN representative whether Milan will be destroyed or not,' he said. Finance Minister Pellegrini-Giampietro told Mussolini that Gerhard Wolf, the German consul, had demanded that the Salò Republic hand over its monthly cheque of 10 billion lire for support of German troops, and warned that if it was not forthcoming the Germans would seize the money from banks. 'If they try, open fire,' Mussolini replied.[39]

That evening, Police Chief Renzo Montagna completed a surrender agreement with Renzo Garbagni, a Milanese lawyer who represented the Bonomi government. They had begun their discussions in December and met three or four times since. The agreement proposed to guarantee prisoner-of-war status to republican armed forces, ruled out the establishment of people's tribunals, included safeguards for Fascists and provided that republic police could help keep public order until the Allies arrived. It would allow Fascist armed units to concentrate in a zone formed by the Milan–Lecco–Como triangle to await undisturbed the arrival of Allied troops, to whom they would surrender. At the last minute, a clause was inserted providing safeguards for Mussolini. Zerbino typed up the agreement and the three men took it to the Duce, who approved it and established that Graziani would sign it the next day.[40]

Young Socialists attacked German tanks on the Milan fairgrounds that night and disabled a number of them. Also that night, Rahn tried to telephone Mellini, who had been bombed out of his house and was staying with a friend some distance from Salò in an apartment that had no telephone. Rahn called the Foreign Ministry and asked how long it would take him to reach Mellini, and was told it would take an hour and a half. Rahn said he could not wait and had to leave urgently. The next day, Mellini learned that the ambassador and all his staff had left Lake Garda, with Rahn and some others going to Bolzano, the rest to Sondrio.[41]

By dawn on 25 April, it was clear that Mussolini could not remain in Milan much longer. Varese, on the Swiss border 25 miles north-west of Milan, had been occupied by partisans, and they had appeared just 15 or so miles away at Busto Arsizio and Gallarate. Allied troops would soon enter Padua, only to find the partisans already had locked up 5,000 German soldiers. Public offices in Milan were mostly empty, with employees melting away and taking with them typewriters, radios and even telephones. The Fascist radio gave orders for all military units converging on Milan to go to Como instead. Bassi, the prefect of Milan, had to intervene that morning to stop Germans mining the city's four electric power stations and the telephone network. Political detainees at Milan's San Vittore jail started to break out and Italian guards made no move to stop them. But German guards opened fire, killing nine prisoners.[42]

Yet, in a week of dithering in Milan, Mussolini had made no firm plans for his escape, had authorised a patently unrealistic attempt to hand over power to a party of his choice and had made only half-hearted efforts through his aides to reach an accommodation with the CLN that would spare Milan a senseless, last-ditch battle between Fascists and partisans. He had done nothing at all about negotiating with the Germans on the terms of their withdrawal. As the end beckoned, the Duce was in a state of near paralysis, walking trance-like toward disaster.

The CLNAI issued what was in effect Mussolini's death sentence. Article 5 of a decree establishing popular courts stated: 'Members of the Fascist government and the *gerarchi* of fascism who are guilty of suppressing the constitutional guarantees, destroying popular liberties, creating the Fascist regime, compromising and betraying the fate of the country and leading it to the present catastrophe are to be punished with the penalty of death, and in less serious instances life imprisonment.'[43]

Graziani stopped at the Prefecture and learned from Montagna about the agreement he had reached with Garbagni. It only awaited Graziani's signature, and Mussolini had planned to announce it over the radio that evening. Graziani and Montagna went to see Mussolini, but he seemed to have lost interest in the agreement, saying he planned to go personally that afternoon to Cardinal Schuster to negotiate in the presence of General Cadorna, the partisan commander, the fate of republican forces. A Milanese industrialist, Gian-Riccardo Cella, the same man who had bought Mussolini's newspaper *Il Popolo d'Italia* several months earlier, had arranged the meeting in talks the previous day with Cadorna and Achille Marazza, a Christian Democrat member of the CLNAI.

According to Leo Valiani of the CLNAI, Cella told them Mussolini wanted guarantees for himself, his *gerarchi* and their families, and asked that Fascist militias be allowed to concentrate undisturbed in the Valtellina to surrender to the Allies. Valiani said that Cadorna and Marazza had responded that Mussolini should surrender by handing himself over to the CLNAI at Schuster's residence, with no conditions attached; only in this way would he be assured a trial by a regular tribunal in due course. Whether Cella passed on that message is not known. It seems probable he did not because it might have dissuaded Mussolini from going ahead with the meeting. At 2 p.m. factory sirens around Milan sounded, announcing a general strike, and the city's trams stopped running.[44]

Vittorio Mussolini, who had been living in Milan with friends, saw his father that morning in his office. 'It seemed to me that he did not discount the eventuality that Milan was the last stop of his peregrination,' Vittorio wrote later. 'Milan had been the birthplace of fascism, it could also in dignity be its tomb.' Vittorio exchanged a few words with his father, mostly regarding family questions the Duce asked him to resolve. After lunch, Vittorio returned. Mussolini was calm but told him factories had been occupied at Sesto San Giovanni, on the outskirts of Milan, and partisans were flooding into the city. Vittorio urged him to take a plane to Germany or Spain. He stressed there was not much time, because the Allies would be in Brescia, 40 miles north-east of Milan, within a few hours.

Mussolini rose suddenly from his chair and told him rudely: 'No one asked you to interest yourself in my person. I will follow my destiny here in Italy.' Vittorio said he expected that answer but 'his words froze my blood'. He then proposed another solution: a friend had left him the keys to his apartment, and he would hide his father there. Mussolini looked at him affectionately. 'I thank you, Vittorio, but can you believe I would, like that, leave the others to the mercy of partisan reprisals and the moral and physical offences of a triumphant enemy?' Vittorio argued that Mussolini's closest friends wanted his salvation above everything. The Duce insisted he would go to the Valtellina for the last resistance, and from there he and his followers could reach Germany. 'For another thing there are negotiations under way to prevent further disasters,' he said. Vittorio told him the war in Italy was finished, and Germany could last but a short time. He asked what had become of Rahn and Wolff. 'Probably they have abandoned us to our fate,' Mussolini replied. Vittorio suggested they remain in the Prefecture, fight off partisan attacks and surrender to the Allies.

'It's possible, but it could be that my presence and that of the government of the RSI will cause aerial bombardments, street fighting, fires and massacres of defenceless people,' Mussolini said. 'Milan has already suffered too much from this war. And you know very well I will never give myself alive to the Anglo-Americans.' He said he hoped the handover of powers to a new Italian government would be carried out without further useless shedding of fraternal blood.

Mussolini asked for news of various family members and was told they had reached Como. The Duce said he was sure Switzerland would give them asylum. He asked about his diaries and Vittorio replied: 'They are safe where you know them to be, and I don't think they run risks.' At that moment Cella arrived to inform Mussolini that Schuster had agreed to meet him at 5 p.m., and Vittorio departed.[45]

Meanwhile Silvestri helped Mussolini fill two cases with the most important papers of his secret archive, which he was determined to take with him when he left Milan. Silvestri later said these papers included documents proving the republican government had done all it could to avoid civil war and total German control over Italy. Also among them, he said, were proofs of British ill-will that had led to war, and secret information on massacres carried out by Communists. Other documents, he said, concerned Crown Prince Umberto, Mussolini's exchanges with Hitler and the record of the Verona trial of Ciano and the others who had voted against Mussolini in the Grand Council.[46]

There is a general assumption among Italian historians that Mussolini assembled these documents, and took them with him, to be used as evidence in his defence at an eventual trial. If so, this indicates he had no intention of achieving a heroic death in the Valtellina but of holding out there for a time and surrendering. But to whom? He repeatedly said he would never allow himself to be taken prisoner by the Americans or the British, yet if he went to the Valtellina those were the forces he would be fighting. He could hardly imagine that the Allies would hand him over to a new Italian government for trial. Secondly, if the documents were intended for his legal defence they represented a curious selection in at least one respect. Those concerning the Verona trial could only have been damaging to Mussolini's defence unless they contained evidence that he had tried to save Ciano, which was unlikely. So why did he take them? There is no available answer.

While Silvestri was with Mussolini, the Duce phoned Colonel Rauff to ask about rumours of a possible surrender of German troops. Mussolini added that personally he didn't believe them. Rauff, although fully aware of Wolff's negotiations, replied: 'It is not at all true. It's a matter of *bobards* [lies] of Allied propaganda to sow dissension between Germans and Italians. It is outrageous that there are among your collaborators those who doubt German loyalty.' Silvestri said Mussolini had first received reports in February of negotiations for the surrender of the German army in Italy but had not then known Wolff was involved. 'He did not trust the information,' Silvestri said. 'His dogmatic conviction about German loyalty was still intact on 25 April.'[47]

Although Schuster's residence was only a few hundred yards from the Prefecture, Mussolini went to his meeting with the cardinal on the afternoon of 25 April by car, accompanied by the industrialist Cella, the Prefect Bassi, Interior Minister Zerbino and Cabinet Secretary Barracu. Marshal Graziani joined them later. In Switzerland at that moment, General Wolff was preparing to return to Italy, his attempts at surrender up in the air because of the lack of instructions to Dulles from Washington. Schuster, who had once admired Mussolini unreservedly, met him alone while they awaited the arrival of Cadorna and the CLN representatives.

'He entered the audience room with his face so worn he gave me the impression of a man almost stupefied by his tremendous misfortune,' Schuster recounted later. The cardinal evidently went into the meeting expecting that Mussolini had come to offer his surrender; he had prepared a room in his palace in which the Duce could be held temporarily as a prisoner of war. Schuster began by saying how he appreciated Mussolini's personal sacrifice in initiating, with his surrender, a life of expiation in prison or exile to save the rest of Italy from ruin. Honest people, he assured the Duce, would recognise the value of his gesture posthumously. Schuster recalled the fall of Napoleon, and Mussolini observed that also his empire was about to end. There was nothing left for him but to face his destiny with resignation, like Bonaparte. Schuster told him he had been served badly by many of his officials.

'Unfortunately, men know these things always too late,' Mussolini replied.

'On the contrary,' the cardinal objected, 'the most difficult art is knowing men. One never knows them well.'

It was a difficult and awkward conversation, which went on for an hour of impatient waiting on both sides. Mussolini let Schuster know he had been opposed to an anticlerical movement led by the Crociata Italica, an extreme Fascist organisation. Schuster saw he was very depressed and gave him a glass of rosolio, a sweet cordial, with a biscuit. Mussolini told him that during his captivity in 1943 he had meditated very much on Father Ricciotti's *Life of Jesus Christ*. He seemed extremely tired. Again the cardinal urged him to accept surrender and spare Italy a useless slaughter. Mussolini replied that he would dissolve the Italian army and Fascist militia the following day and would retire to the Valtellina with 3,000 Blackshirts.

'And so you intend to continue the war in the mountains?' Schuster asked.

Mussolini replied: 'Yet for a little while, but then I will surrender.'

Schuster shot back: 'Don't deceive yourself, Duce, I know the Blackshirts who will follow you will be only three hundred, not three thousand as you believe.'

Mussolini smiled. 'Perhaps there will be a few more, but not many. I don't delude myself.'

Still the waiting continued. Schuster turned the conversation to the Milanese clergy, then to the Russian Orthodox Church, finally to Britain. Mussolini noted that the British had lost only 260,000 civilians and 300,000 soldiers in the war. 'England knows well the secrets of trade: it has saved its men. . . . England is like a ship anchored in Great Britain, but always ready to set sail toward the immense ocean,' he said. But he lamented the fact that Britain had allowed Russia 'to have dominance also in the West. This is the new, real and great danger.'

They were finally notified that Cadorna and Marazza had arrived. Before they entered, Schuster told Mussolini that one day history would say he, to save northern Italy, had put himself on the road to St Helena. 'History?' Mussolini replied. 'You speak to me of history. I only believe in ancient history, that is history that is written without passion and after a long time. I do not believe instead in books and the daily press.' Schuster started to leave the room, feeling it was not proper for him to participate in political talks, but Mussolini begged him to preside over the meeting.[48]

When they arrived, Cadorna and Marazza had found the courtyard of the archbishop's palace full of armoured cars and armed Fascist militia. They were joined by Riccardo Lombardi, who was to be the future prefect of Milan, and Giustino Arpesani, a Liberal Party CLN member. Cella met them and stressed they should not leave the palace without an agreement. When they entered the audience room along with Mussolini's aides, the Duce looked up and walked toward Cadorna with hand extended. Marazza thought Mussolini looked as though he did not sleep at night and suffered from some illness. The Duce wore a wrinkled jacket and a faded and worn shirt.

All took their seats, with Schuster on a sofa to the right of Mussolini. Schuster said afterwards that he limited himself to listening, determined to stay out of political altercations. He said Mussolini opened by asking Cadorna what he wanted, but the general turned back the question, observing that he was the one who had been summoned. Cadorna's version is that he told Mussolini he left negotiations to Marazza. The lawyer then told Mussolini the CLNAI could only offer unconditional surrender and an urgent decision was required because the partisan insurrection would begin that evening. Mussolini, according to Marazza, protested that he had been led to expect something else: an agreement under which his officials would be allowed to gather at Varese with their families while Fascist troops and militias would assemble in the Valtellina, where they could surrender to the Allies. Marazza said these details could be studied later; the important thing now was surrender. He said Mussolini replied: 'If that is so, we can negotiate.'[49]

Cadorna offered a different account of the conversation. After Marazza insisted on unconditional surrender, he said, Mussolini stiffened and said he had accepted the meeting because guarantees had been offered for him, his family and Fascists. Cadorna said he told Mussolini the Allies had decided all republican militias would be guaranteed treatment as prisoners of war, but this did not apply to individual war criminals.

Graziani then intervened to say the Fascists could not sign an agreement without the knowledge of the Germans because 'loyalty to an ally is a title of honour and justifies our past attitude'. Marazza responded that in matters of honour the CLN did not have to take lessons from anyone. At that point Mussolini suddenly learned that the Germans were negotiating a surrender behind the backs of their Fascist allies.

Accounts vary as to how this was revealed. Schuster said Don Bicchierai, his secretary, had disclosed the secret to Fascist officials in the ante-chamber earlier, and Graziani corroborated it, adding that he felt compelled to tell Mussolini what he had learned from Bicchierai. But Cadorna said he was the first to observe that concern for the Germans was entirely out of place because they had been negotiating with the CLN for some time. Marazza, on the other hand, said he took the initiative. Schuster said he was embarrassed and deplored the indiscretion, but he confirmed he had had negotiations with Wolff. Bicchierai entered the room and said, 'Yes, the Germans have confirmed acceptance of the surrender, but they have not yet signed, promising to do so within twenty-four hours.' At midday, German troops in Milan had closed their barracks and handed over their arms to the archbishop. 'Mussolini jumped to his feet, beside himself with rage and indignation,' Marazza said.[50]

Several Italian historians have suggested that Mussolini's rage was faked because he already knew the extent of Wolff's negotiations in Switzerland. But that begs the question of why he went to the meeting to try to arrange surrender terms of his own. As the foregoing record indicates, he never sought to get to the bottom of what Wolff was up to. In his confused state of mind, he had scuppered the attempts of his subordinates to arrange an orderly exit for his regime and had waited until the last minute to undertake an initiative that should have been his first priority upon reaching Milan.

Schuster went out of the room and came back with a packet of papers that documented his negotiations with the Germans. He read various clauses, including a German offer to disarm the Black Brigades. Mussolini exploded:

'Once more we will be able to say that Germany has knifed Italy in the back. The Germans have always treated us as servants and in the end they have betrayed me.' He said he would telephone the German consul Wolf and tell him 'the Germans have betrayed us and we take back our liberty of action'. He also threatened to go on radio to reveal the German treachery. Schuster tried to dissuade him and pointed out the Germans had not yet signed the surrender. 'It doesn't matter,' Mussolini said. 'Having initiated negotiations without my knowing already constitutes a betrayal.'[51]

In the discussion that followed, the CLN representatives stressed the importance of reaching agreement because the masses were restive and the situation could degenerate suddenly into acts of violence. Monza had been liberated, and unless Mussolini decided soon there would be clashes with his men, Marazza observed. In a melancholy tone, Mussolini replied: 'Have no fear, lawyer, mine will do nothing.' Cadorna, watching Mussolini, saw menace in his eyes, then observed that his facial expression and voice became extraordinarily soft. 'Instinctively, I felt a sense of pity, the pity that a generous soul feels for one who has fallen from a pedestal,' he recounted. Lombardi, beside him, murmured: 'Basically, I feel a great compassion.' Then Cadorna remembered Mussolini's past crimes and his feeling of sympathy vanished. The CLN representatives continued pressing for a decision, but Mussolini said he would speak to the German consul and would return with his answer at 8 p.m.[52]

Mussolini went out carrying a *History of St Benedict*, which the cardinal had given to him, saying it would 'bring you comfort in the sad days that are now on the horizon'. Schuster accompanied Mussolini and his party to the antechamber, and as the Duce went down the stairs the cardinal took Graziani aside and urged him not to let Mussolini go on radio as this would lead to 'immense ruin'. Graziani promised to try. While Mussolini was leaving, the Socialist leader Sandro Pertini – later to be president of Italy – was coming up the stairs to join the meeting. Pertini said later he had not noticed Mussolini but, if he had, he would have killed him on the spot with his revolver.

Mussolini, still fuming about the Germans, told Graziani as they were leaving: 'I would have them all shot.' Schuster returned to the room and urged the others to stay. They agreed reluctantly. While they waited, they learned of a proclamation from Vietinghoff to his troops that day, which the general had issued in agreement with Wolff. Vietinghoff admitted the gravity of the military situation and instructed his soldiers to suspend offensive operations, avoid destruction, remain in their barracks, respect the lives of hostages and obey their officers. The proclamation ended with 'Long live the Führer!' It stopped short of an act of surrender, but it was an important first step. At 9 p.m. the patience of those waiting for Mussolini was at an end and they decided to send him an ultimatum. They telephoned the Prefecture and were surprised to be told that Mussolini had left Milan, having decided to break off the negotiation.[53]

On the drive back to the Prefecture, Mussolini had told his aides the meeting had been a conspiratorial pretext to keep him and his government in Milan that night. He was ready for any solution except a new imprisonment. All the ministers who were in Milan were gathered nervously in the Prefecture, along with military chiefs, party officials and Fascist journalists, awaiting the outcome of the talks. Mussolini leaped from his car and bounded up the stairs two at a time. Zachariae, who was present, said: 'His face was extremely tight and pale, like that of a dead man.' To Asvero Gravelli, last chief of staff of the Republican National Guard, Mussolini said: 'You know what the cardinal said to me? Repent of your sins!'

Carlo Borsani, a decorated war veteran who had been blinded in combat in the Albanian mountains, said: 'Duce, they've told me you want to go away, that you want to leave us. But tell us the truth, don't leave us, we want to stay close to you to the end. There are still some men who are faithful to you.' Mussolini thanked him and turned to Justice Minister Pisenti: 'We have been betrayed by the Germans and the Italians.'[54]

He went into his office, very agitated, and told his ministers that the CLN had wanted to arrest him again, to stage a second 25 July, and he must leave Milan. He ordered General Diamanti to free all political prisoners from the San Vittore jail. 'To me he seemed resigned to his fate,' Diamanti said later. 'At a certain point he opened a box, showed a revolver and said: "I will look after myself."'

Mussolini turned on Cella and blamed him for what had happened. 'You have deceived me,' he shouted. 'You led me where nothing less than unconditional surrender has been asked of me. Now, Cella, you will answer to me for it with your life.' Cella protested that the meeting wasn't supposed to have gone as it did; General Wolff should have arrived. 'But he will arrive this evening certainly, and you will see, everything will be agreed,' he said.

Pisenti opened the door, saw Silvestri outside and urged him to try to dissuade Mussolini from leaving rather than staying and surrendering to the Allies. Silvestri pleaded with the Duce in vain to stay. Mussolini turned to Graziani and asked what he planned to do.

'I'm going to join my command between Como and Lecco,' Graziani replied.

'Then let's go to Como,' the Duce said. He turned to Montagna, who had been waiting nervously for someone to sign the pact he had agreed with Garbagni. Mussolini shouted angrily: 'Suspend everything, suspend your negotiations.' Montagna said the negotiations were complete; it was only a matter of signing what had been agreed. Mussolini calmed down and said:

'We will sign then. This evening or tomorrow morning. You keep up the contacts.' Montagna hastened from the room to find Garbagni.

General Wening, the German army commander in Milan, entered the room and confirmed that Mussolini's German escort was ready to leave. The Duce turned to Pisenti and said: 'Perhaps there can still be something to do here. You stay.'[55]

Vittorio returned to the Prefecture in the evening for a final meeting with his father, passing through a nearly deserted and expectant city. 'The trams no longer circulated, the shops were closed, there were few people on the streets, a mantle of lead seemed to weigh on the city,' he wrote. He found Mussolini in a foul humour and his anger was directed at the Germans and the CLN. Vittorio recalled his father having told him earlier the one thing he wanted to avoid was capture by the Allies and a trial by judges whose authority he would not recognise. The man who had authorised poison gas attacks on Ethiopians went on to say: 'We Italians . . . have fought without cruelty. . . . [T]he populations of the occupied countries have been helped, fed and protected. Never inwardly have I held sentiments of hatred or desire for vengeance. In Italy there is no war criminal. As for my twenty years of government, only the Italian people have the right to judge them. . . . If they think they can put me in pillory like a ferocious beast in the Tower of London, or in a cage in Madison Square Garden, they deceive themselves. I have never feared death and at this point of my existence death becomes a rest.' Mussolini told Vittorio to remain in Milan with Pisenti and Bassi, and embraced him.[56]

Mussolini's escort consisted of two armoured cars in a German unit commanded by Lieutenant Fritz Birzer, and a convoy of Fascists in their cars followed. Nicola Bombacci, the old Communist turned Fascist, said: 'Where he goes, I go.' Mussolini came down to the courtyard with a machine gun on a strap around his neck. He had given a police official two cloth bags containing secret documents and 5 million lire he had received from his royalties as an author. All those in the courtyard crowded around him, some in tears.

'Duce, don't leave!' pleaded Borsani, the blind veteran. 'Go to Cardinal Schuster. Don't shed any more blood.'

'Fine, Borsani, you come with me also,' Mussolini replied. 'We will discuss this evening what to do.'

'Duce, don't leave,' Borsani repeated. 'If you don't want to give yourself up to the cardinal, remain with us. Here we are, we will die alongside you, we will die together. But don't flee, Duce. It's useless to flee and . . .'.

Pavolini pushed him back and said: 'Duce, everything is ready.'

Mussolini turned to Borsani. 'Come with us also, Borsani. It's not all over yet.'

'Yes, Duce,' Borsani said. 'It's not all over yet. We still have to die.'

He would be killed a few days later in Milan.

Silvestri also urged Mussolini, once again, to stay. Mussolini embraced both men without saying a word, then got in his car with Bombacci at his side. The convoy left at around 8 p.m. for the 25-mile drive to Como. Montagna returned with Garbagni, hoping to sign the accord they had negotiated, but found he was too late.

Mussolini did not know it then, but Claretta, together with her brother Marcello and his wife and children, would also leave Milan that evening in pursuit of him. Claretta had met Asvero Gravelli, the Republican National Guard chief of staff, earlier that day and asked him to get her the uniform of a Guard auxiliary. 'Asvero, I want it, I am going to die with him,' she said.[57]

With Mussolini's departure on the evening of 25 April, the Fascist era that had lasted for twenty-three long years was at an end, and the Salò Republic had survived for just 582 days. 25 April is celebrated as a national holiday in Italy.

Partisans occupied the offices of Milan's newspapers an hour before Mussolini left, and clashes had begun on the city's outskirts. Shortly afterwards, the German Command telephoned Bassi in the Prefecture to say General Wening had assumed all military and civilian powers in Milan, evidently in order to hand them over to the CLNAI. Bassi remained alone in the Prefecture with three drivers throughout the evening.[58] At 10 p.m., 4,000 Fascists who were gathered in Piazza San Sepolcro exterminated a partisan squad that had arrived by car from Pavia and wandered into the wrong part of the city. Pavolini phoned from Como and spoke with General Diamanti, who told him he had agreed to surrender to the CLN. If Pavolini wanted to save the Black Brigades, he said, he should advise them to take off their black shirts, wear military grey-green shirts and accept his orders. Pavolini shouted: 'Only the Duce must give them orders, have you forgotten that? You have forgotten finally too much. How disgusting.'[59]

Preziosi had come to Milan that evening and had taken refuge in the apartment of friends. At dinner he murmured: 'I cannot bear defeat.' During the night the old antisemitic agitator and his wife threw themselves to their deaths from an upper-storey window. Another extreme Fascist, Roberto Farinacci, fled from Cremona that evening by car with his aristocratic lover, Carla Medici del Vascello. Partisans stopped them at Beverate and she tried to flee but was killed. Later the partisans shot Farinacci.[60]

The Allies were concerned that an insurrection would leave the Communists in control. Back in December General Sir Maitland Wilson, the Allied commander for the Mediterranean, had called a meeting of resistance leaders in Rome and persuaded them to sign a memorandum in which they agreed no insurrection would take place without the authorisation of General Clark. But Togliatti, the Communist leader, cabled Luigi Longo, his commander in northern Italy: 'Don't obey General Mark Clark. It is in our vital interests that . . . the population . . . should destroy the Nazi-Fascists before the Allies arrive. . . . Choose your own moment for insurrection.' Longo issued orders that there could be no mercy shown to those retreating, 'only a war of extermination'. Pertini argued that killing Mussolini 'would be to assert our independence'. The leftist parties were determined to prevent the Allies from installing their own administration as had happened in the south.[61]

Cadorna was anxious to see that the accords with the Allies were respected. Longo tried to persuade him to order an insurrection on the evening of 25 April, but Cadorna argued only the CLNAI could make that decision; he was worried that Milan might face the fate of Warsaw as the Germans pulled out. At dawn on 26 April, the CLNAI issued a proclamation saying it was assuming all powers of administration and government. At 7 a.m., just after the Fascist radio had transmitted its morning news programme, partisans took over the station. Broadcasting was interrupted, but at 8 a.m. the radio announced the CLN had taken power: 'Long live the Socialist republic of Milan.' Partisans occupied the offices of the police and the Finance Guards, a police unit dealing with financial crime, especially smuggling of contraband across Italian frontiers. There was some firing in the air by partisans, but Cadorna told them to save their ammunition.[62]

A Christian Democrat bulletin distributed on the streets of Milan that morning announced that the Germans had agreed to surrender and this had been 'made known only now for military reasons'. It said the partisan command would take control of public order and all police forces from 8 p.m., after which German soldiers in Milan would be disarmed and considered prisoners of war. The bulletin also said German authorities had promised to leave intact public services, electrical installations and industries. The position of Fascists, it said, was to be regulated through separate negotiations.[63]

Partisan groups in the mountains north of Milan began streaming into the city and taking over everywhere. German diplomats enjoying breakfast in the Hotel Principe e Savoia were taken prisoner. There was some localised German and Fascist resistance in the city, and some German columns that were withdrawing were attacked by partisans. But the insurrection did not produce the pitched battle many had expected. Pietro Secchia, the Communist who was assigned to organise it, said just twenty-six people were killed, almost all by accidents and shootings by last-minute partisan recruits. Count Federico Barbiano and five fellow partisans, driving across the city in a car bearing partisan flags, were mistaken for Fascists and were killed. Longo later claimed that 250,000 people in Milan participated in the insurrection and filled the city's piazzas. In fact a large crowd filled Piazza del Duomo, but only on the morning of 27 April after the Allies had arrived.[64]

Cadorna, after riding across the city on a bicycle, was escorted on the evening of 26 April to an elegant bedroom in the Prefecture where Mussolini had slept. He found on the table a sheet of paper headed 'Evidence file' with several sheets attached, and a copy of Mussolini's book *Storia di un anno*. Also in the file was a copy of a song popular among German troops:

Where the Duce governs without a country and without power
Where the partisans give no peace
Where at night in every corner there is shooting and tumult
Where every night the rails are blown up
Where the train flies through the air
Where letters reach us after many weeks
This is not our country; and yet we persevere
From the mouth of the Tiber to the Alps
To hell with this damned country
All Germans cry in chorus:
Don't leave us here, Führer, bring us to the country of the Reich.[65]

Chapter 21

FLIGHT AND CAPTURE

I'm afraid we've been betrayed.

(Benito Mussolini, 27 April 1945)

Mussolini's hasty, ill-organised departure from Milan marked the beginning of a confused, puzzling and, in the end, aimless peregrination along the western banks of Lake Como. This is the most beautiful of the Italian lakes, nestling between Alpine peaks and lined with magnificent villas and floral gardens. By late April it is usually a lovely place, just awakening from the chilly Alpine winter. But in April 1945 the weather was unseasonably cold and wet, which could only have added to the Duce's misery. Mussolini and his party reached the town of Como, at the southern tip of the lake, at 8.40 p.m. They went to the Prefecture, where the Duce was received by Prefect Renato Celio, a man close to Buffarini. Celio already was in contact with the local partisan leadership to discuss surrender.

With hands clasped, Buffarini pleaded with Mussolini to go to Switzerland via Chiasso, a few miles to the west. Graziani slapped Buffarini, accusing him of cowardice. Graziani said the proposal seemed incredible (*rombalesco*), and Mussolini commented that it was hardly serious. He said he had decided to await in Como the column of thousands of armed men that Pavolini would bring from Milan at dawn. Paolo Porta, the Fascist Party inspector for Como, suggested an alternative plan. At Cadenabbia, halfway up the western side of the lake, Mussolini could withdraw to a villa where he would be defended by 900 members of the Black Brigades. Highway tunnels through the mountains north and south of Cadenabbia, which had already been mined, would be blown up, making the area more defensible. Mussolini and his party could wait there for the German surrender, and fight off any partisan attack. Mussolini did not immediately commit himself to this plan, but while he waited the Como police chief arrived and told him the present situation was not tenable; partisans were even then moving towards Como. Mussolini replied that he would go to the mountains with Porta. 'Is it really possible that five hundred men cannot be found who are ready to follow me?' he asked.[1]

Celio's wife prepared dinner for the party, but the meal was interrupted by the coming and going of visitors and phone calls. General Archimede Mischi, Army chief of staff, phoned from Sondrio to say he was awaiting the Duce, but Graziani ordered him to come to Como. Fernando Mezzasoma, the minister of popular culture, telephoned the Milan offices of *Corriere della Sera*, seeking news of what was happening in the city, and found partisans had taken over the newspaper. Mussolini was worried by the fact that a small truck, carrying a large sum of money and his important archive documents, had apparently broken down along the way from Milan. He ordered his secretary, Luigi Gatti, and Vito Casalinuovo, an aide to the Duce, to go in search of it. Vittorio Mussolini, who ignored his father's instructions to stay in Milan, had come across the missing truck a few miles north of Milan as he headed for Como. It was stopped under a bridge, with the bonnet raised. Vittorio nodded to the driver, who had a woman at his side, and asked if he needed help, but the driver waved him on. The truck was never seen again.[2]

As the evening wore on, Celio suggested that Mussolini seek asylum in Switzerland. The Duce replied that he had already been informed Switzerland would not accept him. Celio urged him to try again through the American consulate in Lugano, but Mussolini grew angry and said he wanted nothing to do with Switzerland. In fact, he could not have got into Switzerland if he had tried. US Secretary of State Cordell Hull had sent telegrams to several governments on 23 August, 1944, asking them not to give asylum to Nazi and Fascist war criminals. Switzerland gave definite assurances on 14 November that it would not do so.[3]

Rachele and her children remained at the Villa Mantero in Como, and during the night Mussolini sent twenty militiamen to her to act as an escort. Rachele later claimed that at about 2 a.m. on 26 April, a Blackshirt tiptoed in with a letter the Duce had written in Como. She said she woke the children to read the letter to them. According to her account, the letter read as follows:

> Dear Rachele,
> Here I am arrived at the last phase of my life, at the last page of my book. Perhaps we two will not see each other again. Therefore I write to you and send you this letter. I ask you to pardon all the harm I caused you involuntarily. But you know that you are for me the only woman I have truly loved. I swear it to you before God and our Bruno in this supreme moment. You know that we must go to the Valtellina. You, with the children, try to reach the Swiss frontier. Over there you will make a new life. I believe they will not refuse to let you in because I have helped

> them in all circumstances and because you are outside politics. If this doesn't happen you must present yourselves to the Allies, who perhaps will be more generous than the Italians.

Rachele said the letter was written in blue pencil and signed with a red pencil. She later said she had memorised the contents but burned the letter when she was about to be arrested, a hardly credible statement. Most historians and Rachele's Italian biographer are convinced the letter never existed, that she concocted it after the war to try to salve her injured pride. It was apparently more than she could bear that her husband's mistress had followed him to the end, died with him and trumped her in the accompanying publicity.

Rachele said she tried several times during the night to phone Mussolini, and finally got through to him. He told her he felt alone; even his driver Cesarotti had fled. She told him many people were still ready to fight for him, but he replied: 'But there is no longer anyone. I'm alone, Rachele, and I see that everything is finished.' Then he asked to speak to his children. Romano was desperate and urged his father not to leave them in danger. Mussolini replied that he should not be afraid because the family had not been harmed even after 25 July. 'Benito said goodbye affectionately to Romano and Anna Maria with loving advice,' Rachele recounted. Then he spoke to her for the last time: 'You will make a new life. Hurry. Farewell, Rachele, farewell.'

The militiamen around them, she said, were all crying.

Rachele and her children left the villa at 3 a.m. with her Blackshirt escort to try to reach Switzerland, some 20 miles away. Near the frontier she saw Buffarini in another car, and he suggested they join him. Her Blackshirts threatened to kill him and she had to intervene to save him. When she produced her documents at the frontier, a Swiss police officer handed them back and said: 'Absolutely impossible.' Buffarini was also turned away. Rachele headed back toward Como, along a road now filled with fleeing Germans and Italians, and heard shooting on the outskirts of Como. After going to the Fascist Federation headquarters and learning her husband had left Como, she was persuaded by one of the Blackshirts to take refuge in his house some distance away. They arrived at a small cottage, where Rachele made breakfast for all of them with her remaining provisions. While they were inside, her car was stolen. Shooting broke out nearby, and she looked out of the window at scenes of panic. 'A young man is killed in front of our house because he is recognised as a Fascist,' she wrote later. 'From time to time we listen to the radio that carries orders to hunt down Fascists without mercy. The war wounded flee from a nearby hospital. We no longer seem to be living on the earth, but in hell. The children are alarmed, terrorised.'[4]

Mussolini had left Como at 4.30 a.m. Nervous local officials had insinuated that if he remained there, Como might come under Allied aerial bombardment. Sondrio, the gateway to the Valtellina, was just 60 miles away, beyond the eastern side of the lake. If he wanted to reach the Valtellina, he could have been there within two hours. But Mussolini decided, inexplicably, to follow the western shore of the lake, a somewhat longer route, and wait for Pavolini and his thousands at Menaggio, about 18 miles north of Como. He came out of the Prefecture and leaped into his car, along with Bombacci and Porta. Graziani stopped Buffarini and asked him what Mussolini had decided. Buffarini said he had suggested a second escape plan, and the Duce had accepted it; they would go to Porlezza, a small town west of Lake Como, and try to enter Switzerland from the border crossing near there, which leads to Lugano. Buffarini and Mezzasoma tried to persuade Graziani to follow this plan as well, but he refused. Graziani went over to Mussolini and asked him what he had decided. 'For now we go to Menaggio,' he said. Later, when the party stopped at Menaggio, Graziani questioned Porta, who said the Duce had rejected Buffarini's latest suggestion about trying to enter Switzerland.[5]

Mussolini's sudden move to leave Como alarmed Lieutenant Birzer, his German escort. One of his men ran up and said: 'Karl Heinz is escaping.' Karl Heinz was the German military code name for Mussolini. Birzer ran to his own car and drove it across the road, blocking the way. 'Duce, you must not depart without an escort,' he said. Mussolini replied: 'Get off my feet. I can do what I want and go where I like.' Birzer said later he ordered his twenty men to get ready to fire. Then he and a group of soldiers went with fingers on the triggers of their machine guns to Mussolini's car and he said: 'Duce, now we can leave.' Mussolini gave a gesture of resigned acceptance. Graziani had decided not to follow the Duce but there had been no time to tell him so. Now he felt he had to go at least as far as Menaggio to take his leave of Mussolini. With two generals, he set out for Menaggio, planning to return to Como. Mussolini's convoy proceeded cautiously along the narrow lake road and reached Menaggio in the rain after 5.30 a.m. His machine gun slung across his shoulders, Mussolini went to the home of Emilio Castelli, the local Fascist Party secretary, to try to sleep. Castelli claimed that Mussolini, although looking tired, was 'still full of vitality, ready for battle and discussion'. Castelli assured him there were few partisans in the area. In the previous two days the Black Brigades had killed four partisans on nearby mountains.[6]

The rest of Mussolini's party drove into Menaggio escorted by several companies of republican soldiers in two armoured cars equipped with 20mm machine guns. Gatti ordered them to go back to Cadenabbia, a couple of miles below Menaggio, because the presence of so many people risked attracting attention. They left, but reluctantly. 'We have come to die with

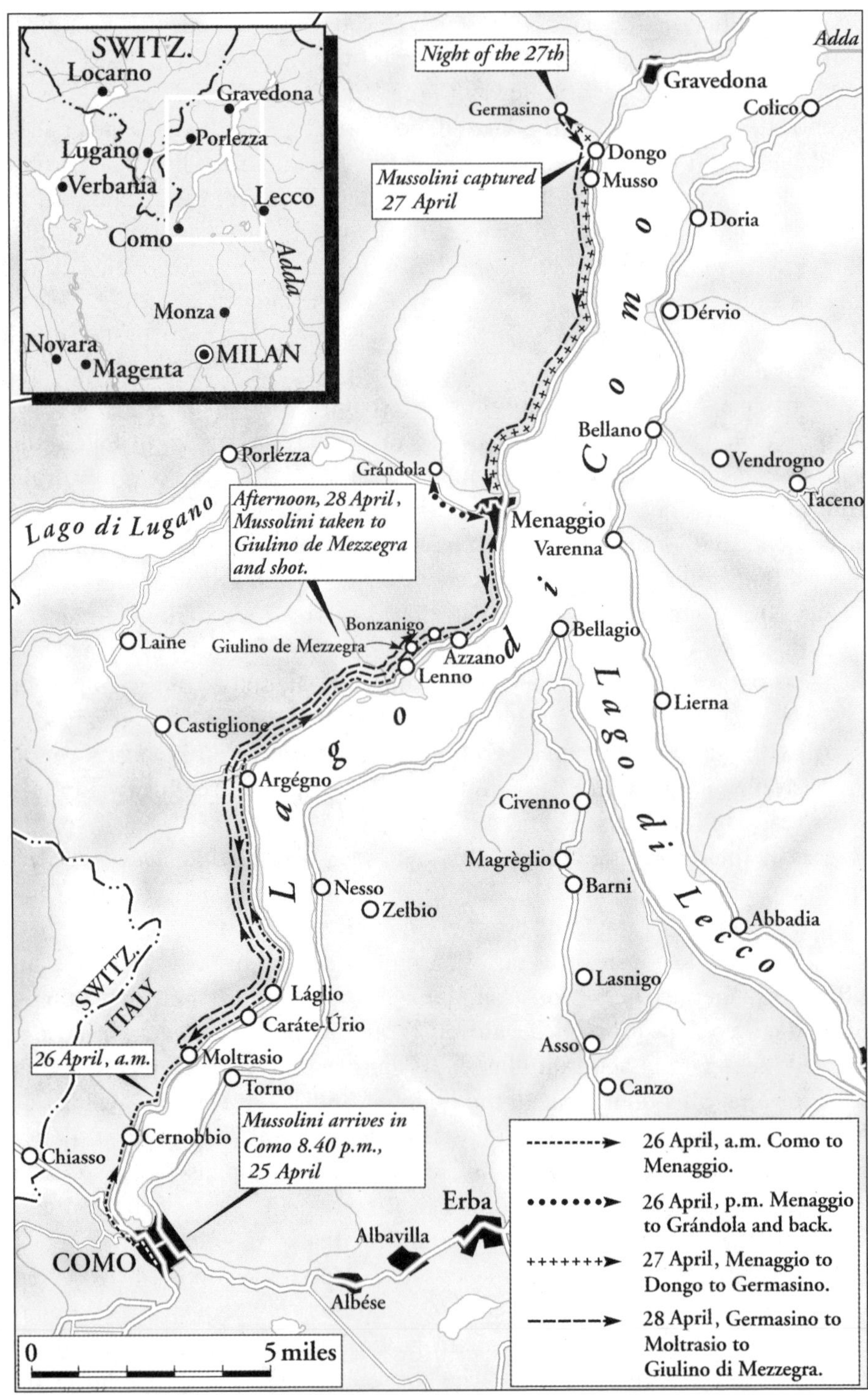

Mussolini's travels in the Lake Como area during the last three days of his life.

the Duce,' one shouted. Another grumbled that Mussolini had abandoned them and wanted to escape alone to Switzerland.[7]

Barracu told Vincenzo Costa, the Fascist leader of Milan, to return to Como and discourage Fascists there from coming to Menaggio. 'We await here an important communication on which will depend what we do in the next few hours. I can't say more,' he told him. Graziani declared that as armed forces minister he had to go to his own command at Mandello, between Como and Lecco, to share the fate of his troops. He left without seeing Mussolini and was followed by General Sorrentino, the under-secretary of aviation, and General Bonomi.

Just one party of late arrivals remained in Menaggio: Claretta Petacci, her brother Marcello, his wife Zita and their two children. Claretta had learned of Mussolini's departure from Milan and set off with her relations to join him. 'Where the owner goes, the dog goes,' she had told a friend. Marcello had befriended the Spanish consul in Milan, Don Ferdinando Canthal, and he was intent on passing himself off as a Spanish diplomat, with the Spanish flag flying from the hood of his car and diplomatic badges on the licence plates.

After the war, Canthal told an Italian reporter that he had met Mussolini and Marcello on the evening of 25 April after the Duce had left Cardinal Schuster's residence, and that Mussolini had asked him to go to Switzerland to meet Sir Clifford Norton, the British ambassador, to present a surrender proposal that would allow fascism to remain as a useful force for the future struggle against communism. Canthal said he agreed, even though the Mussolini proposal seemed 'a chimera', but he found the Swiss frontier closed that evening and returned to Milan. This account is evidently an invention; no one else who saw Mussolini after he left Schuster's residence mentions Marcello and Canthal being present, and there was nothing to indicate that Mussolini was considering surrender to the Allies at that point.[8]

Casalinuovo took Claretta to the villa where Mussolini was resting. After three hours of sleep, the Duce came out and ordered the remaining vehicles to move off the lakeside road and go inland to Grandola, where they would be less conspicuous. Grandola is 5 miles from the Swiss frontier and on the road to Porlezza. Was Mussolini really intent just on becoming less conspicuous, or was he now thinking of going on to the border and trying his luck? Some Italian historians have speculated that he stopped at Grandola to await a message advising him whether he could enter Switzerland. One writer has speculated at length that he was waiting instead for an emissary sent by Churchill to help him get into Switzerland. The first theory is unlikely and the second absurd. Mussolini had frequently expressed a determination never to fall into the hands of the Americans or British, but if he had managed to get into Switzerland he would have been interned there and then, at the end of the war, undoubtedly handed over to the Allies. Carlo Silvestri later said

Mussolini had never intended to go to Switzerland. He said 'a renowned religious figure' offered him that possibility but Mussolini turned it down and his only interest in Switzerland was in sparing the lives of his supporters and their families.[9]

In Milan, Pavolini had assembled by dawn on 26 April several thousand Blackshirts (estimates of numbers vary from 2,000 to 4,600), together with their wives and children. They had armoured cars and a large supply of weapons including artillery. In one of the cars was Elena Curti Cucciati, the 22-year-old daughter of Mussolini's former mistress Angela Curti Cucciati and a student of political science at Milan University. Elena had lived at Gargnano for a time, and it was widely believed that Mussolini was her father. The column of 200 vehicles arrived at Como at 8 a.m. and waited at a railway station while Pavolini tried to find Mussolini. Learning that the Duce was in Menaggio, Pavolini went there to try to persuade him to return to Como so he could take the direct route to the Valtellina via Lecco on the eastern side of the lake. He met Mussolini for a few minutes and returned to Como after evidently failing to persuade the Duce to follow his plan. He would discover on his return that the party he had brought with him was in danger of dissolving.[10]

When Mussolini indicated he was leaving for Grandola, Birzer suspected his intentions and asked where they were now going. 'Follow me, and you'll find out,' Mussolini replied. The Italian cars travelled at high speed up the winding road into the mountains, and Birzer, in his armoured car, had difficulty keeping up. But when he arrived on the outskirts of Grandola, a small, medieval village of houses closely packed along narrow alleys, he found Mussolini in the lobby of the Miravalle Hotel, which was used as a barracks by the Fascist militia. The Duce had gone for a walk in the garden with Claretta and three of his ministers under a dark, rainy sky, but a German sentry who arrived before Birzer insisted they return indoors. Claretta, who evidently did not believe the stories that Mussolini was the father of Elena Curti Cucciati, noticed his pleasure in seeing the young woman and screamed at him when they were alone in the dining room: 'What is that woman doing here? You must get rid of her at once. You must! You must!' Several people walking in the garden were drawn to the dining room window by her shouts and stood there gaping. Mussolini slammed the window shut and shouted: 'Stop!' Claretta turned, slipped on a carpet and fell, bruising her knee. He left her sobbing and returned to the garden.[11]

While other members of his party had lunch, Mussolini began sorting documents he had brought with him, picking out those concerning Mellini's negotiations with Troendle on the question of allowing Fascist families to enter Switzerland. Radio broadcasts from Milan gave the first news of orders issued by the CLN, told of Allied advances and announced the abrogation of the Salò Republic's social legislation. Elena offered to go by bicycle to Como to find out what had happened to Pavolini and his men. Mussolini told her if Pavolini did not come soon, everyone would desert him; enthusiasm for a Fascist last stand was evaporating. One of the Blackshirts in the dining room talked of an eventual surrender to the Allies. The wife of the Black Brigades commander at Grandola said she overheard a woman insisting to Mussolini that he take refuge in Switzerland, and he replied: 'I don't want to become the laughing stock of the world.' He launched into an attack on the British and said they only wanted to make of him a circus-tent curiosity.[12]

Buffarini decided he would try to cross the Swiss frontier at Porlezza. Economy Minister Angelo Tarchi and the former police chief of Bologna, Fabiani, decided to go with him as they did not want to risk falling into partisan hands. Carrying false passports, they left the hotel at 2 p.m. without saying goodbye to Mussolini. Sometime later, Fabiani ran back in, saying their car had been stopped at Porlezza by Finance Guards who had joined the partisans. Buffarini and Tarchi were arrested, but Fabiani managed to escape and ran all the way to Grandola. Mussolini asked Birzer to send SS troops to help the captured men, but Birzer said he did not have enough men to detach for such duty. Alarm mounted among those in the hotel when the prefect Enrico Vezzalini arrived with a bandage on his face. He had been wounded and two militiamen killed when partisans attacked three armoured cars in which a party of Fascists was travelling from Como to Menaggio.[13]

Mussolini told Birzer he had decided to wait no longer. He would go back to Menaggio, then continue north, leaving a message for Pavolini to join them in Merano. Merano is in the Alto Adige just below the Brenner Pass into Austria, suggesting that Mussolini had now abandoned thoughts of stopping in the Valtellina and, contrary to everything he had said before, was ready to abandon his own country and seek refuge abroad.

After the war, Carlo Silvestri wrote a book in which he contended that the Duce never intended to go to the Valtellina. His real intention, he said, was to bypass the Valtellina and continue east from Sondrio where he expected to meet up with a column of well-armed, elite troops coming from Bolzano. Silvestri said Mussolini had learned that the Austrian gauleiter Franz Hofer was planning to annex the Alto Adige to Austria, and the Duce hoped his presence would prevent Hofer from carrying out his plan. There is no evidence to support this supposition, and it is hardly credible that Mussolini, despite having repeatedly expressed in his last months an intention to go to the Valtellina, in fact had another plan that was known only to Silvestri. Birzer objected that his men were worn out and should not be expected, without having had any sleep, to break through partisan roadblocks they were sure to encounter. Mussolini yielded but decided they would move out of

Menaggio at 5 a.m. after they had slept. He was confident Pavolini would have reached him by then.[14]

Arriving in Menaggio in the rain, they went into the semi-deserted Black Brigades barracks where the bodies of the militiamen killed with Vezzalini were laid out. They ate a modest meal while some members of the party silently peeled away to save themselves. Over breakfast, Fabiani said Mussolini poured out his feelings of anger and frustration with the accusatory manner of a prosecutor. The Duce said bitterly that others would take up his 'interrupted march' toward national greatness. He recalled a speech he once made in Forlì in which he promised the people he would have 'stopped throwing the bridle around their necks to make them the masters of their own destiny, to achieve one of the most beautiful horseback rides in history'. But the people had now ceased to understand him. 'If the fault is mine I do hard penance for it.' Before lying down on a camp bed, he appealed to Claretta to save herself and cease to follow him. She refused to listen.[15]

Mussolini did not know it then, but during the night the Fascists in Como had surrendered. The prefect, Celio, favoured an agreement with the CLN and Prefecture employees openly declared themselves partisans. Partisan units moved into the building and removed photographs of Mussolini from the walls. Around 3 a.m., Fascist leaders were invited into the Prefecture to sign an agreement providing for Fascist troops in the city to march unmolested to Val d'Intelvi, west of the lake, to await the Allies and surrender to them. The agreement also specified that Mussolini could join his men there. Graziani and the two generals accompanying him were in an upstairs room of the Prefecture when they got word that Celio was down below signing the agreement. Costa, the Fascist leader of Milan, refused to sign without Mussolini's approval, but at dawn the Fascist column set out for Val d'Intelvi. By early afternoon, its numbers reduced by defections, the column began to dissolve near Cernobbio and some of the men returned to Como. Pavolini's fighting force was no more.[16]

Elena Curti Cucciati arrived in Como in the late afternoon after a three-hour bicycle ride in the rain. She found partisans swarming over the city and Black Brigades members with red bandannas around their necks to show they had gone over to the partisans. She eventually found Pavolini and returned with him, a few soldiers and three armoured cars to Menaggio at 4 a.m. on April 27. The force of 50,000 Pavolini had promised had shrunk to no more than 4,000 and was now down to just twelve men. Mussolini's last great illusion was shattered. The bold leader who was going to make a heroic stand to the death was now simply a man on the run with no place to hide and no real idea of what to do next except to keep running. Worse yet, he had wasted a day and a half; he could have been in the Valtellina on the night of 25 April if he had gone directly there from Milan.

But at least his convoy to nowhere was now greatly enlarged, not by Fascist forces but by Germans. A German anti-aircraft unit, commanded by Lieutenant Hans Fallmeyer and consisting of forty vehicles loaded with troops, had come up to Menaggio from Como en route to Merano. Mussolini distributed money to Black Brigades members in Menaggio and the convoy set out at 5.30 a.m. The Valtellina was 35 miles away. Pavolini put his armoured car at the head of the column, threatening to shoot his way through any roadblocks. Mussolini, driving his armoured Alfa-Romeo, followed Birzer. Claretta was farther behind in Marcello's car.[17]

For a time, the trip proceeded smoothly and Mussolini regained confidence. 'With 200 Germans we can go to the top of the world,' he commented. He saw a man walking beside the road and leaned out of the window. 'Are there any partisans around here?' he asked. The man said they were everywhere. Mussolini signalled for the convoy to stop, then got out and walked up to talk to Pavolini, who suggested he would be safer in the closed military armoured car. Mussolini consulted Birzer, then climbed in and the convoy moved on. At 7 a.m., just after the convoy had passed through the village of Musso and reached its northern outskirts, the right rear tyre of the armoured car was punctured by a three-pointed nail left on the road by partisans. The car kept going but was then forced to stop just short of a bend in the road. (At that time the road wound eastwards along the shore of the lake around the flanks of a mountain. That route no longer exists; the road now continues straight ahead, through a tunnel in the mountain, and emerges on the edge of the next town, Dongo.)

The road was blocked by a large tree trunk and stones that partisans had dragged there. Several shots rang out from the mountain, where the partisans had two 12mm machine guns, and from the bend in the road. The armoured car returned fire, killing an old man who was going to work at a marble quarry on the mountain. Then three men, waving a white flag, appeared.[18]

They were three partisan officers: Count Pier Luigi Bellini delle Stelle, a member of a noble Florentine family who commanded the 52nd Garibaldi Brigade and used the partisan name 'Pedro'; Michele Moretti, the Communist political commissar of the brigade, known as 'Pietro'; and Alois Hoffmann, a Swiss citizen who lived with his Italian wife in a lakeside villa at Domaso, further north. Bellini delle Stelle had joined the partisans after he had seen several women killed or wounded by machine gun fire when they tried to give bread and water to Italian military prisoners on trains from the south passing through Florence in 1943.

Fallmeyer, who spoke Italian fluently, told the three men he had orders to take his troops to Merano and from there into Germany to continue the fight against the Allies. 'We have no intention of fighting the Italians,' he said. Bellini delle Stelle demanded the Germans' surrender. Fallmeyer replied that there was an agreement between the German High Command and the partisans under which the Germans were to be allowed to withdraw unhindered. Bellini delle Stelle said he had no such orders, and warned that the Germans were covered by mortars and machine guns. 'I am in a position to exterminate you in a quarter of an hour,' he said. It was a bluff; there was only a handful of partisans in the area, mostly armed with shotguns, and the Germans could easily have wiped them out. Fallmeyer insisted he would not surrender.

Urbano Lazzaro, a partisan known as Bill, arrived and made a rapid check of the German convoy. Lazzaro, the deputy political commissar of the brigade, told Bellini delle Stelle the Germans had twenty-eight trucks, each carrying a heavy machine gun, several mortars and sub-machine guns and many anti-aircraft weapons. 'There was no doubt that if it came to a fight they could have destroyed us and the entire area we had occupied in next to no time,' Bellini delle Stelle wrote later.[19]

The partisans moved off to confer among themselves as the parish priest of Musso, Don Enea Mainetti, joined the discussion. Mainetti had been celebrating mass when he heard the rumble of the convoy passing through Musso, and he had just gone into the sacristy to remove his vestments when the sacristan rushed in and said: 'The Germans are escaping.' Mainetti ran to the front door of the church and saw a long convoy of trucks, cars and motorcycles. He and a German Protestant pastor travelling with the troops entered into the discussion in their only common language, Latin, with the German asking him to try to arrange safe transit 'in the name of Christian charity'. Fallmeyer asked Mainetti how many partisans were in the area, but Mainetti thought he had asked how many people lived in the area. 'Circiter tri milia', he replied. About 3,000. Fallmeyer was led to believe he confronted a large force. Mainetti asked if there were any Italians in the convoy, and Fallmeyer assured him there were not.[20]

The partisans meanwhile decided their only hope of stopping the Germans was to mine a bridge between Musso and Dongo, but they needed time to find explosives. Lazzaro was sent off to deal with the problem. Bellini delle Stelle asked Fallmeyer if there were Italians among the Germans. Fallmeyer now admitted there were Italians in the armoured car at the head of the convoy, and a few Italian civilians in private cars, but he had no responsibility for them. Bellini delle Stelle said he needed to consult a higher partisan command about letting them through. After further discussion, Fallmeyer agreed to go with him and they set out in a German car with a German driver.[21] When they had left, an Austrian soldier who had been educated in Padua and spoke Italian came up to Mainetti and, contradicting Fallmeyer's assurances to the priest, whispered: 'There are Italians. Don't believe the officer. Have the trucks searched.'[22]

At 8 a.m., just as Fallmeyer was leaving, two Italian radio stations – Radio Monteceneri and Radio Milano – announced that Mussolini had been captured in another locality. The Duce, listening in the armoured car, was understandably surprised to hear the news. As the morning wore on, the waiting Italians became more and more nervous and Pavolini suggested they shoot their way through. Someone else thought they should turn back and look for another route. But most concluded it was best to wait for Fallmeyer's return.[23]

Mainetti was back in his house, preparing to have lunch, when a bearded Italian knocked on his door and identified himself as Nicola Bombacci, the old former Communist who had become Mussolini's friend. He said he wanted to give himself up to the partisans and asked Mainetti's help. 'I am the victim of my stupidity and I see now that I will pay with my life. Until 8 September I was against Mussolini,' he said. 'I am in a trap like a rat. And to think that I have two sons among the partisans, and that I was against fascism for twenty-five years. The Fascists always sang songs against me.' He said he had never been a Fascist, but the Fascists had deluded him with their nationalisation programme, which had been the main aim of his life. 'I made a mistake. I will die. But I don't want a capture with a lot of fanfare,' he said. Later Bombacci told his captors he had become disillusioned with Mussolini at Menaggio because he and Birzer believed the Duce planned to escape to Switzerland with Claretta and leave the rest of his party in the lurch. It was only when Buffarini failed to get into Switzerland, he said, that Mussolini decided to head for the Valtellina.

Bombacci was followed into Mainetti's house by more Fascists. 'In my dining room were gathered the Ministers Zerbino, Augusto Liverani, Fernando Mezzasoma nervously wiping his spectacles and Ruggero Romano with his fifteen-year-old son Costantino. . . . It was now past one o'clock. I managed to get some soup for the fugitives.' The Fascists, whose cars were at the end of the convoy, began discussing Mussolini's whereabouts, and at one point Mainetti heard Mezzasoma say that the Duce was with the Germans. Mainetti said Bombacci also approached his sister and told her: 'He is with us. It is not fair that he should get away.'[24] Outside, a small figure in blue overalls and an aviator's cap appeared at the window of the armoured car in which Mussolini was hiding. Claretta Petacci removed the cap, her hair tumbled down and Elena Curti Cucciati recognised her 'beautiful luminous eyes'. She said Mussolini spoke to Claretta tenderly.[25]

Meanwhile, Fallmeyer, who was away for six hours and returned to Musso only at 2 p.m., had been informed by Bellini delle Stelle that the Germans could proceed, but all the Italians were to be handed over to the partisans. The German vehicles would have to stop in Dongo to be searched and all German personnel would have to produce identification. Fallmeyer was silent for a moment, then asked for half an hour to consult with his officers. He returned to Musso, leaving Bellini delle Stelle and the other partisans sitting on a lakeside parapet in Dongo smoking cigarettes.

When Fallmeyer returned to Musso and informed his officers of the partisan terms, Lieutenant Birzer suggested that Mussolini could still get away with the Germans if he put on a German army overcoat and got into the back of a truck. 'Duce, this is the last chance to save yourself,' he said. 'The partisans will check the convoy and will only let us Germans pass. There is no other way out. I have not found a boat to allow you to cross the lake. The bridges behind us have been blown up and those ahead are mined.'

Mussolini feared Fallmeyer had made a deal to hand him over, and he said: 'I'm afraid we've been betrayed, lieutenant.' But Birzer protested this was not so and told Mussolini his 'only hope' lay in doing as he had suggested. 'The Duce was unshaven, his face waxy yellow and he asked continuously the opinions of others, brokenly, like a man disheartened,' he said. 'He was also afraid, but that seems natural to me.' Birzer went away to separate the Italians from the Germans, and when he returned Mussolini had changed his mind; he would refuse to move if his ministers could not have the same protection.

Birzer told him that this was impossible and Mussolini, glancing at Claretta, said: 'But at least my friend can come with me.'

Birzer replied: 'That is impossible as well.'

Claretta shouted: 'Duce, go, go, you must save yourself.'

Domenico Laghetto, the driver of the armoured car, later said that when Mussolini eventually decided to get on the truck, he commented: 'I am going with the German comrades because I don't trust the Italian comrades any more.' According to Laghetto, it was Pavolini's failure to bring the promised thousands of troops to fight in the Valtellina that had inspired this comment.[26] This was a telling moment. The man who had earlier refused to seek sanctuary abroad on the ground that he could not desert his followers was now abandoning them to their fate while he sought to save his own skin. For what purpose? To die in Germany instead of Italy? He had ignored their entreaties to go abroad in the past. A charitable view would be that Mussolini, sleepless and his nerves shattered, simply was not thinking clearly. A more critical view would be that his courage had deserted him in the face of real danger.

Birzer said some of the Fascist ministers 'exploded angrily' when they saw Mussolini getting on the truck and abandoning them. 'I saw their closed fists, heard their shouts and their curses,' he said. 'The only courageous person, the only one loyal to Mussolini, seemed to me Petacci. The ministers cursed, she cried in leaving him.'

But others insisted that some of those in the armoured car encouraged Mussolini to save himself. A Blackshirt, Pietro Carradori, helped Mussolini into a German coat that was too long for him, and the Duce put on a German helmet back to front by mistake. Carradori carried two cases of documents that Mussolini had entrusted to him. Then some suitcases containing state funds, which Mussolini's secretary Gatti had brought from Gargnano, were loaded on the truck, the fourth from the front of the convoy. Birzer adjusted Mussolini's helmet and gave him a pair of sunglasses and a pistol. Claretta, in tears, tried to get on the truck but was held back and had to return to her brother's car.[27]

Mainetti claimed that a young Italian, Fiorenzo Rampoldi, led him to the German truck and he saw the Duce wearing an overcoat and German helmet. Back in Dongo, Bellini delle Stelle and the other partisans who were waiting for Fallmeyer were approached by a man who came down the road from Musso. He said the convoy contained a number of Fascist VIPs and apparently some Salò government ministers. He said one already had handed himself over and others apparently were trying to get back to Como. Bellini delle Stelle sent ten armed men to Musso with orders to stop anyone trying to get away. Mainetti claimed he had set out on foot for Dongo and along the way he ran into Bellini delle Stelle and Captain Davide Barbiere, another partisan leader, who were returning to Musso. He said he told them: 'Look, Mussolini is here. . . . Don't let him escape, because we are sure he's here.' Bellini delle Stelle said Mainetti was mistaken; he had not set out for Musso and had remained in Dongo. He could not remember who told him Mussolini was in the convoy, but he attached little weight to the report, thinking it was just one of many rumours circulating that day.[28]

When Bellini delle Stelle reached Musso, Fallmeyer told him he accepted his conditions. But Fallmeyer said Bellini delle Stelle would have to inform the occupants of the armoured car of this. Bellini delle Stelle went up to three Fascists sitting on a low wall: Barracu, the minister for Cabinet affairs; Vito Casalinuovo; and a man named Idreno Utimpergher. He told them they could not follow the Germans but would have to surrender. Barracu protested that he had sworn he would go to Trieste to help defend the city against the advancing Slavs of Marshal Tito. Bellini delle Stelle told him that was out of the question. Utimpergher then shouted at Bellini delle Stelle: 'But in short, what kind of Italian are you? Don't you remember that our fathers died to free Trieste?' Barracu finally agreed to continue the discussion on the spot after the Germans had moved on to Dongo. Casalinuovo shouted: 'I warn you we're ready for anything and we will never surrender. Let us leave or it will be the worse for you.' Barracu tried to calm him, but a moment later Casalinuovo erupted again: 'Have you decided, Barracu? Have you decided, yes or no? I warn you we are fed up. . . . We are going. You won't stop us.'

Bellini delle Stelle said: 'Get quiet, for God's sake. Let us talk. Go, if you want, but don't interrupt.' Bellini delle Stelle, assuming Mussolini was in the armoured car, asked to inspect it and Barracu agreed. The partisan leader looked in the car and recognised no one.[29]

At about 3 p.m., the German convoy set off, followed by Marcello's car, which was allowed to continue because of the presumption he was a Spanish diplomat. Most of the Italians who remained behind surrendered, but Pavolini and the other occupants of the armoured car were determined to return to Como. Barracu stood in the driver's seat as the Germans passed, shouting: 'Cowards! Traitors!' When they were gone, he tried to moved forward a short distance so he could turn the car around to head back toward Como. But the partisans thought he was trying to get to Dongo. They opened fire and threw a hand grenade beneath the wheels, killing two men. The armoured car returned fire, and two partisans were wounded. Then a white rag was pushed through the turret.

Pavolini leaped out, shouting to everyone to run to the lake, and was followed by six men. The lake was several hundred yards down a precipice from the road, but Pavolini and Pietro Carradori succeeded in reaching it while the others were captured and Barracu was wounded. The two men jumped in and swam about 100 yards toward Dongo, then, with rain coming down, hid under some projecting rocks. An hour later, they were surprised by partisans in a boat who ordered them to surrender. But Pavolini, cradling a machine gun as he stood waist-deep in water, remained defiant, so one of the partisans fired a shotgun at him. The blast wounded him slightly in the chest and his right eyelid was grazed. Pavolini was then dragged into the boat and Carradori was captured after a struggle in which some of his teeth were broken.[30]

Bellini delle Stelle went with Barbiere to Barbiere's nearby house in Musso, and was drinking a glass of milk when he heard the gunfire. He left a group of partisans to guard the captured Fascists and set out for Dongo again. Along the way, he encountered Lazzaro coming toward him, that afternoon of 27 April, to deliver a historic piece of information. As calmly as though he were speaking of some matter of ordinary administration, Lazzaro said: 'I have captured Mussolini in Dongo. I arrested him myself. Now he is under strict guard in the town hall.'[31]

Chapter 22

MUSSOLINI TAMED: THE POLITE PRISONER

I want to speak to the world one last time before dying.

(Benito Mussolini, 27 April 1945)

After leaving Musso, the German trucks stopped along the lakefront opposite the town hall of Dongo, a little municipality whose German garrison had surrendered to partisans the previous day. The partisans began their inspection of the trucks but did not succeed immediately in finding Mussolini, who was seated in the left rear corner of the fourth truck, just behind the driver's cabin. About ten people subsequently claimed credit for having found him. But two principal witnesses, Lazzaro and Mayor Giuseppe Rubini, agreed that it was Giuseppe Negri, a clog-maker from Dongo who had spent three months in jail for supporting the partisans.

'The ex-sailor Giuseppe Negri arrived at the righthand side of the truck at a certain moment of the long, vain stop,' Rubini recounted. 'Positioning himself to observe it, he ended by perceiving a man . . . apparently sleeping. . . . With amazement and anxiety, he did not doubt he had recognised in the unknown man none other than Mussolini. . . . He remained quiet and limited himself to signalling with his eyes to the waiting marshal of finance Francesco Di Paola, who had told him to climb onto the back of the truck. He had walked away fifty steps into the crowd, seeking help, when he ran into "Bill" [Lazzaro].'[1]

Lazzaro, a young man of just twenty, had been busy checking the documents of German soldiers in the second truck, giving no thought to Bellini delle Stelle's warning that Mussolini might be in the convoy. He heard someone shouting excitedly, 'Bill! Bill!' and saw that it was Giuseppe Negri. 'Oh Bill, we've got the Big Bastard!' Negri whispered in his ear in a Lombard dialect.

'Come on, you're dreaming,' Lazzaro responded.

'No, Bill, it's really Mussolini. I've seen him with my own eyes.'

'You've not. You are certainly mistaken.'

'But Bill, I swear to you I have seen him. It is he.'

'And where have you seen him?'

'He is on a truck near here, dressed as a German.'

Lazzaro still insisted Negri must have made a mistake, but Negri explained further:

> I examined all the documents one by one. There was still one to come from a guy huddled up by the driver's cab with his back against the left side of the truck. I couldn't see his face because he had raised the collar of his greatcoat and pulled his German helmet down over his face. I went to him to ask for his documents but the Germans in the truck stopped me and said: 'Kamerad drunk, Kamerad drunk.' I took no notice and went up to him. Near him there was a pile of blankets and he had one of them over his shoulders. I sat down beside him and pulled his coat collar down. He never moved. I only saw him in profile but I recognised him at once. Bill, it is Mussolini, I swear it. I recognised him. I didn't let on I knew, and got down to come and tell you.

By now convinced, Lazzaro told him to say nothing to anyone. He feared that if the Germans realised they had found Mussolini, there might be trouble. Negri led him to the truck and Lazzaro climbed up to have a look. He tapped Mussolini on the shoulder and said, 'Comrade!' There was no movement, no reply. In a harsh, ironic tone Lazzaro called him again, still tapping him on the shoulder: 'Your Excellency!' Still there was no word and Lazzaro, irritated, shouted: 'Cavalier Benito Mussolini!' Lazzaro continued: 'The form gives a start. I look at the Germans who are watching in silence. Some of them turn pale. Now I am sure of the identity of the individual.'[2] Recalling that moment fifty-seven years later, Lazzaro said: 'I didn't believe at first it was he. I had an impression of Mussolini that was different from the man who was with the Germans. For me, he was the man of Fascist propaganda, a man with a firm jaw. Before me was a man who almost trembled. He was obliging. Later, when he saw I would not kill him like a dog, he recovered his confidence.'[3]

Several partisans and a crowd of local people gathered around the truck. 'I take off his helmet and see his bald pate and the characteristic shape of his head,' Lazzaro's written account continued:

> I take off his sunglasses and lower the collar of his coat. It is he, Mussolini. The man who made the world tremble, who excited me in my younger years, whom I cursed when I was older, is there, squatting at my feet, pale, almost lifeless. Between his knees he holds a machine gun,

> the barrel pointed under his chin. I take the weapon from him. . . . I help Mussolini to get up. 'Do you have other weapons?' I ask. He does not open his mouth, but unbuttons his overcoat. He puts his hand between his belt and trousers and draws a pistol, a 9mm-long-barrelled Glisenti automatic with one butt-face missing, and hands it to me. I put it into my pocket. Now we are on our feet, facing each other. I feel I ought to say something, something which he is expecting now with his head high, with an empty gaze, outside time. His face is waxy, and in that fixed but absent gaze I read extreme fatigue, not fear. Mussolini seems to have no will, spiritually dead. . . . This is the thing that strikes me.

Mussolini tells the German soldiers not to defend him. The crowd is now shouting, and the Germans hand over their weapons, apparently fearing reprisals.

'In the name of the Italian people, I arrest you,' Lazzaro said. Mussolini replied: 'I shall not do anything.' To which Lazzaro said: 'I guarantee you, while you remain in my personal charge, not a hair of your head will be touched.' Mussolini murmured a polite 'thanks'. Only then did Lazzaro realise he had unconsciously made a funny remark; he was talking to a man without hair. Lazzaro and Battista Pirali, another partisan, held Mussolini under the armpits, helped him down from the truck and took him to the town hall, sixty yards away. Shouts erupted from the crowd: 'They've got Mussolini!' and as the shouting grew in volume Mussolini looked apprehensive.

Mayor Rubini came up and introduced himself to the Duce. 'Be calm,' he said. 'No harm will come to you here.'

Mussolini replied: 'I am certain of it. The population of Dongo is generous.'

The Mussolini of old had ceased to exist. From that moment on, the bombast and overweening self-confidence that he had displayed throughout his life were like a fire that had burned itself out. He appeared to some of his captors initially to be frightened, and he was meekly polite. He made no protests about his treatment, and remained courteous even when partisans upbraided him for his past conduct. He never asked what would happen to him, whether he would be handed over to the Allies, put on trial by the Italians or shot summarily. Gradually, over the next twenty-four hours, he became increasingly subdued and sank into a kind of dazed lethargy. Had his German doctor been present, he undoubtedly would have diagnosed a return of the clinical depression that had afflicted Mussolini in the past.

While the German convoy was allowed to proceed beyond Dongo, Mussolini was taken into a long, simply furnished room of the town hall, which had two windows overlooking the square. He took off his coat, which was too long for him, and was found to be wearing a black shirt and a pair of militia trousers. He wore boots but had no jacket. He was made to sit on a bench against a wall. He carried a leather case, which he placed on a wooden chest on his right. Asked if he wanted anything, he requested only a glass of water. Lazzaro asked why he was in the truck while his ministers were in the armoured car. 'I don't know,' he said. 'They put me there. Perhaps they betrayed me at the last minute.'[4]

Mussolini was bombarded with questions from those around him. One man said: 'You are here, finally. I saw you the first time in Albania, years ago, and you disgusted me. You had cigarettes and money distributed to us soldiers, to gain popularity, but we all despised you.' He paused, then said: 'Why did you betray socialism?' Mussolini did not answer.

A former Carabiniere officer, Carlo Ortelli, asked: 'Why did you want the war, why did you stab France in the back in the moment in which France was in agony?'

Mussolini replied: 'The speech I should make to answer you would be too long. I will limit myself to telling you that if we had not entered the war, Germany would have attacked us, not only with arms, but with gas. I will document it in time, to the Italian people.' Rubini, who had been appointed mayor the previous day, also challenged him on why he went to war and Mussolini said: 'I didn't want the war. The representatives of the people wanted it.' When Rubini questioned that, Mussolini said he had always governed with the consent of the people. Rubini retorted that his elections were a farce, without freedom of the press, freedom of assembly and a choice of opposing candidates. Rubini said that by going to war against the Anglo-Saxon powers Mussolini had 'betrayed also our emigrants, most of whom live in America and have learned to love North America as a second fatherland'. Mussolini stammered and replied somewhat incoherently. Ortelli asked about the speech Mussolini made in Germany following his rescue from the Gran Sasso by Skorzeny.

'It was imposed on me,' Mussolini said. 'While I spoke I had around me 150 policemen.' Rubini asked why he had allowed prisoners to be tortured and beaten by Fascists. 'I did not authorise such methods,' Mussolini said. 'I assure you I knew nothing of it.'

Rubini replied: 'Your guilt in all things was exactly that you ignored what a government instead has an obligation to know.'

One man accused Mussolini of having murdered Giacomo Matteotti, the Socialist leader gunned down by Fascist *squadristi* in 1924. 'It wasn't I who killed him,' Mussolini said.

His accuser shot back: 'But it was you who had him killed.'[5]

While this conversation was going on, the door opened and partisans escorted four of the men captured at Musso into the room. They were

Barracu, who had been wounded in one arm; Casalinuovo; Utimpergher; and Porta. Standing at attention, they gave a formal greeting to Mussolini, who responded with an indolent nod. Lazzaro returned to the German trucks to continue his inspection, and a partisan told him there was a Spanish consul in the convoy who wanted to leave at once. The partisan escorted Lazzaro to a yellow Alfa-Romeo that had driven to the head of the column. Lazzaro saw a fair-haired, well-built man with a small birthmark on his fat chin. At his side was a beautiful young woman and in the back seat was another woman with her face half hidden in the collar of a fur coat, wearing a dark brown turban-shaped hat. Two children were beside her, and the car was loaded with suitcases.

'You are the Spanish consul?' Lazzaro asked.

Marcello Petacci turned to him, looking annoyed. 'Yes, and I am in a hurry,' he replied in flawless Italian. Lazzaro asked to see their documents and Marcello said: 'I have already shown them to a hundred persons.' Lazzaro insisted and was handed three passports. One was in the name Don Juan Muñez y Castillo, the second in his wife's name and the third a joint one for man and wife. Lazzaro spotted an error: on the single passports, both were listed as having been born in 1914; on the joint passport, her birth date was 1912. He also thought the stamp on the photos was not embossed properly.

'These passports are false and you are under arrest,' he said. Marcello grew indignant and his wife turned pale.

'But what's this all about?' Marcello said. 'You will pay dearly. I have an appointment in Switzerland at seven o'clock this evening with Sir Norton [the British ambassador in Bern, Sir Clifford Norton]. I am expected. Can you believe such stupidity? . . . When Sir Norton knows . . .'.

Lazzaro replied sharply: 'Be silent. I command here, not Sir Norton.' He took them to the town hall and left other partisans in charge as he went along the road to Musso to find Bellini delle Stelle. Together they went to the Fascist armoured car and found partisans around it. A Fascist riddled with bullets lay dying in the middle of the road. Bellini delle Stelle went with Lazzaro to the Dongo town hall and hardly recognised Mussolini. He looked old, emaciated, frightened. His eyes were staring but seemed unfocused. 'He is a man who is finished,' was Bellini delle Stelle's first thought.

Bellini delle Stelle went into an adjoining room and spoke to Marcello, who insisted on going to Switzerland. He denied knowing Claretta, saying she was merely someone who had asked for a lift along the road. Bellini delle Stelle turned to her and asked who she was.

'Oh, I am nobody in particular,' she replied. 'I was in Como by chance during these disturbances, and to avoid the danger of finding myself in the middle of some battle, I asked these people for a lift so that I could reach some quiet place. I have really been unlucky. What are you going to do with me?' Then she feigned some indifference, complaining that she had broken two fingernails. Bellini delle Stelle went back to the room in which Mussolini was held and ordered two partisans to escort Marcello and his family to a hotel. Claretta was locked in a ground-floor room in the town hall. Before they were separated, she managed to give her sister-in-law the last letter Mussolini had written her in Menaggio.[6]

Meanwhile, Lazzaro had been sitting beside Mussolini, drawing up an inventory of the contents of his leather case and of the briefcases of the Fascist ministers that were now stacked on the table. As he started to open Mussolini's case, the Duce touched his arm and said in an undertone: 'Be aware that the documents inside there are secret. I warn you they are of great historical importance.'

Lazzaro hesitated, then opened the case and found inside three or four compartments, and a file in each. One file, marked 'Confidential to Benito Mussolini. Secret', contained documents referring to Trieste, reports on Mellini's talks with Troendle about a Swiss refuge for Fascist families, several newspaper clippings quoting Swiss government statements on this issue and various letters referring to partisan movements in several areas. The second file contained exchanges of correspondence between Hitler and Mussolini, with typed Italian translations of the German letters appended. The third file was a dossier on the Verona trial of Ciano and the other Fascists who had voted against Mussolini. There were many letters written to Mussolini by the condemned men, all bearing the note 'not arrived at destination'. Finally, there was a file referring to the private life of Crown Prince Umberto. At the bottom of the case Lazzaro found 160 gold sovereigns, and he looked questioningly at Mussolini.

'They were for my most trusted friends,' the Duce said. There were also three cheques issued by Italian banks, each for 500,000 lire; one cheque for 50,000 lire, and four for 25,000 lire each. Lazzaro also found a pair of black leather gloves, a handkerchief and a pencil, which he handed over to Mussolini. The money was transferred to a case Casalinuovo had been carrying. Lazzaro offered the Duce a cigarette, which he refused with thanks. But Barracu accepted one.[7]

Suddenly there was a lot of shouting in the square in front of the town hall. A boat came in to the jetty, with three partisans escorting Pavolini and Carradori, still wet from their swim in the lake. The crowd threatened to lynch Pavolini, but he was brought safely into the town hall, wet, bleeding from a wound on his forehead and shivering uncontrollably. Mussolini got up and Pavolini saluted him feebly with a raised forearm. Mussolini nodded to him. The partisans found dry clothes for the two men and they were given cigarettes. As the day wore on, Pavolini asked continually for cigarettes and brandy. He and most of the other prisoners were transferred to the Great Hall on the upper floor of the town hall.

Paolo Porta approached Bellini delle Stelle and tried to ingratiate himself, saying he had 'always esteemed a worthy adversary'. Bellini delle Stelle responded coldly that he could not reciprocate such sentiments, since Porta had tortured and killed partisan prisoners. Porta responded that he had always known during the war where Bellini delle Stelle was hiding and could have killed him if he had wanted. Bellini delle Stelle replied: 'And the thirty or more search operations you carried out? Were they only courtesy visits?'[8]

Lazzaro took the Mussolini and Casalinuovo cases, containing the documents and money, and deposited them that afternoon in a bank at Domaso, a few miles north of Dongo. A statement attesting to the contents was drawn up and signed by six witnesses. With Alois Hoffmann, Lazzaro then went on to Ponte del Passo, at the northern end of the lake and near the entrance to the Valtellina, to take the surrender of the German forces who had escorted Mussolini and now were reported ready to give up. When he arrived, Fallmeyer was reluctant to surrender and Lazzaro threatened to have the guns of nearby Fort Colico fire on the convoy and blow up a bridge ahead of it. The fort was actually still in German hands, and the bridge in fact had not been mined, but Fallmeyer could not have know that. After conferring with his fellow officers, he surrendered. The partisan command agreed the Germans could proceed to Switzerland or wherever they wished after they had given up their remaining weapons.

Driving back to Dongo, Lazzaro encountered a luxurious Fiat by a bridge on the Liro river just outside Domaso. A fat German officer got out and said he and a captain with him had surrendered at Dongo but were now going to Ponte del Passo to recover their baggage from the convoy there. Hoffmann and some partisans accompanied the officers, Captain Ernst Kummel and Second Lieutenant Andreas Hess, to Ponte del Passo. Hoffmann later informed Lazzaro that the Germans, who had been assigned to a naval command at Limbiate near Milan, had handed over to him 33 million lire in notes of 1,000 lire each, and offered to give him 11 million if he would divide the rest between their mistresses, two Italian women they had left behind in Tuscany. On Lazzaro's instructions, Hoffmann temporarily hid the money in his cellar.

During the following night, the Germans still camped at Ponte del Passo burned all the paper money still in their possession, and threw into the Mera river everything that would not burn. The next morning, two fishermen saw gold glittering on the river bed and recovered eighty pounds in weight, most of it gold wedding rings, medals, earrings and other jewellery that ordinary

Italians had given to the state at the time of the Ethiopian war in 1935. The fishermen gave the gold to the partisan command.[9]

The partisan political commissar Francesco Terzi sent a message to Como to report the capture of Mussolini and to ask the local CLN for instructions. At 5.45 p.m. Antonio Scappin of the Finance Guards, who had worked with the partisans, telephoned from Gera Lario to the CLNAI in Milan with the news. At 6 p.m. the Allied Command at Siena, apparently responding to rumours of Mussolini's capture, advised the CLNAI in Milan by radio that it was ready to send a plane to take him if the CLNAI was prepared to hand him over. The surrender agreement that the Badoglio government signed with the Allies in October 1943 stated that Mussolini, his chief Fascist associates and all persons suspected of having committed war crimes 'will forthwith be apprehended and surrendered into the hands of the United Nations. Any instructions given by the United Nations for this purpose will be complied with.' Of course, the CLNAI could legitimately claim that it was not a party to this agreement and therefore not bound by it. The CLNAI had no intention of giving up Mussolini to the Allies, and did not respond to the message from Siena.[10]

The commander of the US First Armored Division arrived in Como that night and at 3.59 p.m. the next day sent a radio message to Allied headquarters: 'The big fish will be handed over to us this afternoon.' At 9.30 p.m. the Allied Command sent a second message to the CLNAI: 'Plane that will come to take Mussolini will land at 6 p.m. tomorrow at Bresso airport Stop Prepare landing signals.'

The CLNAI waited until the following morning, 28 April, to send a reply that was a complete fabrication: 'Sorry not to be able to hand over Mussolini who, tried by a popular tribunal, has been shot in the same place where previously fifteen patriots were shot by Nazis.' This, of course, was a reference to the fifteen people shot in Piazzale Loreto in Milan in the summer of 1944 in reprisal for a partisan truck bombing. The CLNAI message, written hurriedly in pencil and unsigned, was brought to Giuseppe Cirillo, principal radio operator of the CLN, by a messenger. The original copy has never been found. At Siena, the message was received by Antonello Trombadori, a Communist who was then on liaison duty with the Allies. In 1962, General Cadorna told an Italian magazine he had never received orders of any type from the Allies concerning Mussolini, and no Allied authority ever questioned him about what subsequently happened to the Duce. That may have been true, as Cadorna was not directly involved with the CLNAI.[11]

Bellini delle Stelle was concerned that his prisoners might be lynched by local people, or other German forces might arrive to liberate them, before he could get them to a secure location. His fears were well founded; on two successive nights, several other Fascist prisoners were taken from the Dongo jail and shot.

Bellini delle Stelle decided in the late afternoon of 27 April to transfer Mussolini to a secret location. He chose the Finance Guards' barracks in Germasino, a medieval village 3 miles from Dongo and 1,900 feet up in the mountains, about as remote a location as could have been found in that area. At 7 p.m., the partisans were ready to depart with Mussolini and, as there was a spare seat in the car, they decided to take Porta along as well. It was raining heavily and had grown much colder. In the car, Mussolini began to shiver. The rain was coming down so hard that the driver could hardly see the road, which twists and turns up the mountain with beautiful views of the lake when the weather is good.[12]

The prisoners were escorted by Bellini delle Stelle and the partisan Giorgio Buffelli, a Finance Guards sergeant. En route, Bellini delle Stelle reproached Mussolini for allowing his men to torture partisans they had captured. 'No, not this, not this,' Mussolini replied. 'You can't blame me for this. . . . I have never allowed it and I never would have wanted it to happen. And when, unfortunately, I came to know about it, I assure you I also was stunned and saddened.'

Bellini delle Stelle replied: 'If you were truly opposed to these shameful acts, given the post that you occupied, with the power you had, you would certainly have been able to stop them and you should have.'

Striking his knees with his fists for emphasis, Mussolini said: 'With the power that I had! . . . If you knew. . . . So many things should be known. But I repeat to you again, this sad burden of responsibility must not be placed upon me. In time I shall be able to document this in a positive way.'

The barracks in Germasino, now a rather rundown, three-storey apartment building, is at the end of a narrow lane and enjoys a fine view over the valley below and the surrounding mountains. Mussolini was handed over to the Finance Guards and put in a little cell. He was offered dinner and said he would like only cooked vegetables. The Guards mixed some young goat with the vegetables and gave him a slice of cheese and a glass of red wine. Mussolini ate with a hearty appetite. Buffelli, who was left behind to guard him, asked him to testify to his good treatment and he wrote on a sheet of paper, in a nervous hand: 'The 52nd Garibaldi Brigade captured me today Friday 27 April on the piazza of Dongo. The treatment given me during and after the capture has been correct.'[13]

As Bellini delle Stelle was preparing to leave, Mussolini asked him to give his regards to the lady travelling with the Spanish gentleman and tell her not to worry about him. Bellini delle Stelle asked who she was and Mussolini replied evasively, with evident embarrassment, but when the partisan leader pressed him for an answer the Duce whispered in his ear: 'She is Signora Petacci.' The name didn't mean much to Bellini delle Stelle. He promised to pass on the message.[14]

After he had gone, Mussolini had a conversation with Buffelli in which he defended his decision to go to war and denied responsibility for the excesses of the Black Brigades. He talked of his rescue from the Gran Sasso and said afterward, when he told the Führer of his reservations about returning to power, Hitler was furious and said: 'You know that I have lead for my enemies and gas for traitors.' Mussolini added: 'And he intended to gas all Italy.' Buffelli noted that Mussolini was now under arrest for the second time, and the Duce replied: 'Dear boy, dust and altars, altars and dust.' He said he would demonstrate to any tribunal that tried him all he had done in the past eighteen months to save Italy from worse disasters than it had suffered. Buffelli asked where he had intended to go after he left Milan, pointing out that the entire zone was controlled by partisans.

'I knew that very well, and yesterday evening I told the SS commander at Cernobbio about the difficulties of such a trip, but he told me: "I must take you to Germany at all costs, including the cost of my head."' Mussolini said they had intended to stop at Merano, then go up the Stelvio Pass. (This doesn't make sense, since Merano is near the Brenner Pass into Austria and taking the Stelvio, which would have involved some doubling back, would have taken him into Switzerland, where Mussolini did not want to go). Buffelli asked why he had not sought refuge in Switzerland. 'Yesterday they told me I had three hours to accept to enter Switzerland. I refused,' he said. He did not elaborate as to whom he meant by 'they'.[15]

A young partisan guard, Giuseppe Martinoni, said Mussolini sometimes appeared restless that evening, but never frightened or apparently worried by his fate. He told Martinoni and another of the young guards: 'Fine youth, fine youth, yours.' He added: 'Yes, yes, I like young people even if I find myself against them and they are armed.' He asked the two young men about their backgrounds, then took off a gold watch and gave it to them. 'Keep it in memory of me,' he said. He spoke of his visit to the Russian front, and described Stalin as one of the greatest living men. Russia was the real victor in the war, he said, and the British Empire would collapse when it was over. He recognised he had made a mistake in allying Italy with Germany and confessed that from the day he was rescued he was only Hitler's gauleiter for northern Italy. 'I want to speak to the world one last time before dying,' he said. 'I have been betrayed nine times, the tenth by Hitler.' At 11 p.m. he said he was tired and asked to go to bed. He was escorted to a small room with a bed beneath a barred window. Buffelli saw a small black object sticking out of his pocket and thought it was the handle of a pistol. It was a spectacles case.[16]

On his return to Dongo that evening, Bellini delle Stelle went to see Claretta and spent an hour or more with her. He observed her carefully. On her right wrist she wore a gold chain with a little gold padlock and military-style ID disc. On her left wrist, a watch, and on her left hand a wedding ring. She carried a gold face powder compact in her purse. At first, when he delivered Mussolini's message, she denied that she knew him. But when he said Mussolini himself had named her, she admitted her identity and denounced his followers as traitors, interested only in saving 'their miserable lives' while none had thought of saving him. 'All traitors. They have abandoned him in the moment of danger,' she said.

She urged that Mussolini be handed over to the Allies, as he would be safer with them. Bellini delle Stelle said he would do all that he could to make sure that did not happen; only Italians had the right to judge him. When he suggested Mussolini would be put on trial, Claretta said it would be better for him to die immediately. She asked what would happen to her, and he replied he didn't know but suggested she could not escape responsibility as a long-time adviser to Mussolini. Claretta denied ever having involved herself in politics, and broke down in tears when his face showed he did not believe her. Unable to bear her tears, Bellini delle Stelle told her he believed her and she calmed down. Finally, she concluded the partisans intended to shoot Mussolini and she asked him to promise that she could be shot with him. 'Put me with him,' she said. 'I want to die with him. My life would have no meaning after his death. I will die anyway, only less quickly and with greater suffering. This is the only thing I ask of you: to die with him. And you cannot deny that to me.'

Bellini delle Stelle later conferred with Michele Moretti and Luigi Canali, a partisan known as Captain Neri, who agreed they should meet her request. Whether they did so out of kindness or indifference to her fate is not clear.[17]

One young partisan who had gone to Como to report Mussolini's arrest met Virginio Bertinelli, the new prefect. Bertinelli told him to go back to Dongo and tell his commander to hide Mussolini somewhere in the mountains to make sure he was not rescued again. When the partisan returned, he found Bellini delle Stelle had already moved Mussolini to Germasino. Colonel Giovanni Sardagna, the new partisan military commander in Como, also learned of the arrest and contacted General Cadorna's chief of staff in Milan, Colonel Palombo, who promised to call back with orders. At 11.30 p.m. Sardagna received a telegram from Milan: 'Bring Mussolini and the *gerarchi* to Milan as soon as possible.'

Sardagna told Palombo in a later telephone discussion that moving Mussolini would be extremely risky. Palombo suggested that at least Sardagna could find a safe place to hide the Duce for a while. Sardagna had a rich industrialist friend, Remo Cadematori, who owned a large secluded villa with long lake frontage at Blevio, a village 4 miles north-east of Como, and he put in a call to him. He told him he needed to hide someone in the villa and would bring him across by boat from Moltrasio, 4 miles up from Como on the west side of the lake, during the night. If Cadematori was asked who it was, he must say it was a wounded English officer. Cadematori knew instinctively his friend referred to Mussolini. He went outside to wait on the steps of his boathouse with his old gardener for company.[18]

Bellini delle Stelle received a message from the CVL General Command in Milan during the evening, urging him to treat Mussolini with respect and, in case of attempted escape, to let him flee rather than use violence. 'This seemed to us an illogical and excessive order,' he wrote later. 'But it may be that it was dictated by concern to avoid so-called summary justice.' Bellini delle Stelle thought news of Mussolini's whereabouts would leak quickly, and said he had always planned to move him again to another secret location. At 11.30 p.m. he was informed of the plan to take the Duce to the Cadematori villa.

He drove back up the mountain, amid rain and lightning, to collect his prisoner shortly after 1 a.m. He had Mussolini's head bandaged, with only his eyes and mouth showing, to disguise him as a wounded partisan. If they were stopped at roadblocks, they would say they had to get him to a Como hospital urgently. Canali would go ahead in a second car to alert partisan roadblocks, with Michele Moretti and Claretta travelling with him. Claretta would be a Red Cross nurse. Sitting in the back with her would be Giuseppe Frangi ('Lino') and Guglielmo Cantoni ('Sandrino'), both fishermen. In the car with Bellini delle Stelle and Mussolini would be Canali's mistress, Giuseppina Tuissi ('Gianna'), who also would pretend to be a nurse.

Tuissi was a partisan who had only recently been freed after months of Fascist imprisonment and torture. Once she had been stripped almost naked, beaten with a whip and immersed in freezing water. Afterwards she was made to lie naked in the snow, then locked up all night in a wall cupboard with a rat. She was later transferred to Bolzano en route to a German death camp, but a German police captain who knew her took pity on her and freed her on 12 March. She showed Bellini delle Stelle the marks of her beatings and burns on her legs. She also showed him a large revolver and said she would shoot Mussolini if there were anything suspicious along the way. He warned her not to do anything unless he gave the order.[19]

Mussolini came out of the Germasino barracks with a military blanket on his shoulders because it was raining and cold. Buffelli had offered him his German overcoat, but he said: 'No, no. I wouldn't like that German overcoat any more. I've finished now with the Germans. They have betrayed me three times and I don't want their stuff. I prefer something else.'* Buffelli found him

*Mussolini's German overcoat was discovered in a Treasury Ministry storeroom in Rome only in 1999.

a Finance Guard coat, and Mussolini also kept the blanket. The car that carried him down to the lake was met at a bridge on the Albano river by the second car in which Claretta travelled. Despite the terrible weather, everyone got out and the two lovers met, rather formally.

'Good evening, Your Excellency,' Claretta said.

'Good evening, signora,' he replied. There was a pause, then Mussolini said: 'Why have you wanted to follow me?'

'I prefer to. But what has happened?' she asked. 'You are bandaged.'

'Nothing, nothing, it is only a precaution.' With that, everyone got back in the cars and the two lovers set off separately for their rendezvous with death.[20]

Chapter 23

'I'VE COME TO SHOOT THEM'

He would deserve to be killed like a mangy dog.

(Sandro Pertini referring to Mussolini, 27 April 1945)

Benito Mussolini and Claretta Petacci were killed on 28 April. Outside Italy, most historians have generally accepted the 'official' story that responsibility for their deaths lay with a Communist agent named Walter Audisio. Inside the country, it has been a different story; for more than a half century many writers have rejected the identification of Audisio, and the search for a definitive answer as to who killed the couple, and in what circumstances, has remained shrouded in dispute that is compounded by lies and sheer fantasy. Only in 1996 did evidence come to light that some would regard as conclusive, but this has not stilled a controversy that is an Italian equivalent of the American debate over who killed John F. Kennedy and who else, if anyone, was behind the murder. Scores of Italian books have been written on the subject, countless theories put forward, purported 'insider' accounts given, and at least a dozen people named as the killer.

Those who were present at the killings are all dead, and some in their lifetimes contributed to the uncertainty with accounts that differed widely. The evidence supporting some of the competing accounts is either lacking or extremely thin, and some of the scenarios that have been sketched are fairly comic. Many non-Italian historians have viewed the debate largely with indifference because, ultimately, the issue is far less important than the controversy surrounding the death of Kennedy, an assassination that at various times has been attributed to the Soviet Union, Cuba, the Mafia and the Pentagon, among others. The death of Mussolini, by contrast, was an internal affair; beyond doubt, Italian political figures ordered the killing and there is no serious doubt that it was a Communist agent who pulled the trigger. Except as a kind of historical footnote, does it matter much which one? The critical issue thrown up by this debate is really the abysmal standard of accuracy of Italian journalism and historiography, which matches some of the sensationalism that has surrounded the Kennedy debate. It is unfortunate that some writers, rather than admitting that the precise identity of the killer or killers was unknowable at the time they wrote, resorted to constructing scenarios based on questionable speculation, and tried to pass those off as fact. In fact, the killer most probably was Walter Audisio. The account given in this and the following chapter traces the available evidence pointing to this conclusion and, in abbreviated form, relates some of the competing theories that continue to provide an intriguing guessing game for Italians.

The two cars carrying Mussolini and Claretta set off from their rendezvous point outside Dongo at about 2.45 a.m. on 28 April, and headed for Moltrasio. The distance from Dongo to Moltrasio is 31 miles, and occasionally the road winds over hills and around bends. With roadblocks along the way and rain falling, the cars must have proceeded rather slowly even though there was no other traffic in the dead of night. Near Menaggio, a machine-gun burst was fired behind Bellini delle Stelle's car by partisans sheltering on a mountainside. Bellini delle Stelle stopped the car and got out, shouting and waving his arms. The partisans ran down from the mountain and he scolded them, saying this was no way to operate a roadblock. At Cadenabbia both cars were stopped at a roadblock and a partisan, noticing the figure wrapped in bandages, asked: 'Who is that mummy there with you?' A wounded partisan, he was told.

Michele Moretti said later that on the drive down the lake, Claretta insistently questioned him about how people lived in the mountains as partisans, who had helped them and what prize they had been promised for the capture of Mussolini. She also asked what they intended to do with this 'great man' drawn into catastrophe by the Germans. Moretti said he politely but firmly told her what she was saying was not true, because Mussolini after 8 September 1943 could have refused 'to become the servant of Hitler and accomplice of his atrocities'. Claretta also asked Tuissi how she came to be a partisan, and Moretti curtly answered for her: 'From the day you Fascists shot her fiancé.' Claretta fell silent.

When they arrived at Moltrasio, they stopped near the Hotel Imperiale and could see rockets bursting in the sky over Como, 4 miles south, celebrating the arrival of advance elements of the Allied forces. Bellini delle Stelle and Canali got out of their car to survey the situation, and returned fifteen minutes later. There was no boat available to cross the lake. Canali wanted to proceed, arguing that they could drive up into the mountains and go around the centre of Como, but Moretti objected that they might run into Allied troops and be forced to hand over Mussolini. They decided to turn back. Mussolini did not ask why they were going back, and he seemed to Bellini delle Stelle to be calm and resigned. At times he nodded off.[1]

Their destination now was a hiding place suggested by Canali, the farmhouse of a couple named Giacomo and Lia De Maria in the seventeenth-century village of Bonzanigo. The village lies on the side of a mountain overlooking the lake, above the lakeside town of Azzano. The De Marias had often sheltered Canali when he was fighting with the partisans. Azzano is 9 miles north of Moltrasio, and the cars arrived there without incident soon afterwards. Moretti and Tuissi remained with the cars, parked beside the road, but the other occupants proceeded on foot about 250 yards up the mountain along an unpaved mule track. Rain was still falling and Claretta was very tired. Mussolini asked if they could stop for a few minutes so she could rest, and the two of them leaned on a low wall. A full moon appeared dimly through the clouds. When the walk resumed, Claretta, in high heels, kept slipping on the wet stones of the path, so Mussolini and Bellini delle Stelle each took her by an arm to support her. Bellini delle Stelle was suddenly struck by the bizarre image they must have presented: an old man in a coat too long for him, with a blanket over him and his bandaged face appearing white in the moonlight; an elegant lady in high heels; and himself shabby, unshaven and with tousled hair, weapons clanking as he walked. They finally reached the De Maria house at No. 8 Via del Riale near the head of the mule track. It is a substantial, three-storey dwelling, painted white. Today red roses climb up the side of the house, and on a spring day there is the smell of jasmine in the air.[2]

Giacomo De Maria, holding an oil lamp, let them in and they were taken to a spacious kitchen on the second floor, where Lia was lighting a wood fire in a huge fireplace. Mussolini's head was still swathed in bandages, and neither of the De Marias recognised their celebrated visitors. Lia saw in Claretta 'a beautiful young woman, a little tired', and thought 'that older man, rather ugly, was her father'. Mussolini fell down on a bench with Claretta next to him, her arm through his. Canali said: 'They are prisoners. Treat them well. Let them sleep.' The De Marias agreed that the prisoners could sleep in a bedroom normally used by their two sons. Lia offered them something to eat and Giacomo asked: 'What can I get the gentleman?' Mussolini mumbled, shook his head and, not looking up from the fire, said he wanted nothing. Claretta said: 'Coffee for me, please.' Lia told her they only had ersatz coffee, made from roasted barley, and she said that would be fine. While all except Mussolini drank the ersatz coffee, Lia went upstairs to remake the bed with fresh linen after telling her sons, Giovanni and Riccardo, to move to a nearby mountain hut.[3]

When she returned to say the room was ready, Claretta had to coax Mussolini to get up and climb a flight of stone steps to the bedroom. Bellini delle Stelle and Canali departed just after 5 a.m., leaving the two fishermen, Guglielmo Cantoni and Giuseppe Frangi, to guard the prisoners, standing watch outside the bedroom with orders to go inside only if they heard suspect noises. Bellini delle Stelle returned to Dongo while the other three, all Communists, went to Como to report to the Communist Party. Bellini delle Stelle said he had his hands full with various tasks when he returned to Dongo. It seems curious that he did not phone Milan urgently to ask what should now be done with one of the world's principal war criminals, but perhaps his Communist companions had told him they would see to that. He did not seem to have considered the possibility that someone might have recognised his prisoners being taken to the De Maria house and tipped off Fascists, who could come and rescue the Duce. Admittedly, it was a remote possibility but not one that could be entirely overlooked where such an important prisoner was concerned.

The bedroom consigned to Mussolini and Claretta was simply furnished. A large walnut double bed stood against one wall, and beside it was a nightstand with a white enamel bowl and a water jug. The room also contained two little chests of drawers, two chairs with cane seats, a small wardrobe and a small chest. There was a religious print over the bedhead. Mussolini walked towards the window, and although it was twenty feet above the ground, Lia thought he intended to escape. She followed quickly and closed the shutters. Claretta felt the bed and asked for another pillow for Mussolini. She said he liked to sleep with two. Lia noticed that when she gave her another pillow Claretta looked at a darn in the pillowcase and put it on her side of the bed. She put the two pillows for Mussolini on the side near the window. As Mussolini sat down on the bed and started unwinding his bandage, Lia suddenly realised who he was. When Claretta asked if she might wash, Lia gave a start and said: 'We are mountain people. You must excuse us. You will have to go downstairs to wash.'[4]

Lia led Claretta to an outhouse and one of the fishermen looked through a crack in the door while she washed. Later he said she had a good body and nice breasts. He followed her back to the bedroom and said the door would have to be left ajar. Claretta undressed in the dim light and got in bed beside Mussolini. Some reports afterward said that in all the thirteen years they had known each other, this was the first time they spent a night together. That was not true; Claretta's sister Myriam wrote of at least one occasion when they were together overnight. While lightning flashed through the night sky, thunder boomed and the rain continued to fall, they held a whispered conversation of which the guards caught only snatches. They thought they heard the names of Pavolini and Graziani, and believed Mussolini said:

'I'm sure they won't kill me.' Then he said something like: 'Can you forgive me?' but the guards could not hear her response, only a murmur from Mussolini: 'That doesn't matter any more.' Finally the couple stopped talking and the young guards, fearing their prisoners were planning to escape, flung open the door and burst into the room. Claretta pulled the sheet over her face and Mussolini said: 'Go away, boys. Don't do that, don't be naughty.'[5]

Mussolini fell into a deep sleep but Claretta stayed awake for a long time and cried before dropping off. Lia found tear-stained mascara on her pillowcase the next morning. The guards also fell asleep at dawn. Mussolini and Claretta awoke only at 11 a.m. The storm had passed, but a few clouds scudded across the sky and there was snow on the mountains. Lia, who had gone out into her garden, saw Mussolini leaning out of a window looking towards the mountains on the far side of the lake and telling Claretta the names of the peaks. Giacomo went upstairs to ask the prisoners if they would like something to eat, adding that it would have to be simple food. Claretta asked for polenta with milk and the Duce murmured he would have the same.

When they came downstairs, Lia had prepared two portions of polenta with milk and some bread and salami. In the absence of a table, Giacomo brought in a box that was covered with a white tablecloth. Claretta had the polenta while Mussolini preferred the bread and salami, along with a glass of water. Both ate with a hearty appetite, but largely in silence. Mussolini stared at red flowers embroidered on the tablecloth, then asked the guards if it were true the Americans had arrived at Como. They said it was and he nodded, but his face clouded over.

Giacomo later said that on the evening Mussolini and Claretta arrived, a knife went missing from the kitchen. After they had left the next day, he found it in the bedroom. Mussolini was too old to have contemplated attacking his guards with it; had he perhaps thought instead of suicide? Or had Claretta taken the knife without quite knowing what she would do with it?

Mussolini and Claretta returned to the bedroom after their meal and she lay down on the bed, pulled the covers over her and closed her eyes, but apparently did not sleep. Mussolini sat on the edge of the bed with his back to her, looking out of the window at the mountains. 'There will be a day of spring that we will not be around to see,' he said. 'And we will not see either the sun or the trees that bud and we will be underground. Oh, but where? Wherever will we be then?'[6]

* * *

On the previous afternoon, Salvatore Guastoni of the American Office of Strategic Services (OSS) arrived in Como. He had been sent to try to make sure that Mussolini ended in Allied hands and did not fall victim to the Communists. Guastoni held discussions with various Fascist representatives, and afterwards a Fascist group set out to try to reach the Duce's convoy. It was led by Pino Romualdi, the Fascist Party deputy secretary who had just signed the accord handing Como over to the partisans, and it included the Duce's nephew, Vito Mussolini, and Vito's brother-in-law, Vanni Teodorani. Francesco Colombo, the notoriously sadistic leader of the Muti Legion in Milan, also went along.

At Cernobbio, just 3 miles up the lake from Como, partisans would not let the group proceed, and they returned to Como, accompanied by a partisan, to try to resolve the situation. Major Cosimo De Angelis, a member of the CLNAI and the newly appointed military chief of the zone, set out to lead the group on another attempt to reach Mussolini. This time they were accompanied by Navy Captain Giovanni Dessi, who had links with the OSS and the British secret services and was determined to persuade Mussolini to become a prisoner of the Allies. But this time the delegation was stopped at Cadenabbia, halfway up the lake, and was disarmed and arrested. A Carabiniere officer finally persuaded the partisans to allow the delegation to return to Como, with the exception of Colombo, whom the partisans shot a few days later.[7]

That morning, the CLNAI in Milan had discussed what to do with Mussolini if he were captured. Achille Marazza, the Christian Democrat who had participated in the discussions with Mussolini at Cardinal Schuster's residence two days earlier, proposed handing him over to the Allies, but this was rejected. The committee decided to bring the Duce before the partisan tribunal nearest his place of capture, and it was clear most members wanted to see him dead as soon as possible.

Communist Party leader Palmiro Togliatti, then serving as deputy prime minister in the Bonomi government in Rome, later claimed he sent a radio message on the evening of 26 April to Milan to this effect: 'For Mussolini and his direct accomplices, only one thing is needed to decide that they must pay with their lives: the question of their identity. And thus it will happen in Milan, we are sure, if forces extraneous to the will of the nation do not intervene at the last moment.' In other words, keep the Allies out of it. Togliatti said he acted in his capacity as deputy prime minister and secretary general of the Communist Party, thus violating the government commitment to hand Mussolini to the Allies. Bonomi denied this order had the sanction of the government, which was opposed to summary executions but favoured speedy trials by duly constituted judicial organs. Ferruccio Parri, who returned to Italy from Switzerland on 25 April, doubted that Togliatti had ever sent such an order.[8]

Longo said the decision to execute Mussolini came from the General Command 'in application of a decision of the CLNAI'.[9] But later he gave a historian a different version. He said he and Fermo Solari of the Action Party, who was filling in for the absent Ferruccio Parri in the leadership of the Corps of Volunteers for Freedom, made the decision to kill Mussolini. Hardly had the news of the Duce's capture arrived in Milan, he said, than he and Solari looked at each other for a moment, then immediately decided to proceed to the shooting. Longo, who would become leader of the national Communist Party in later years, opened his office door, saw Walter Audisio in the corridor and said to him immediately: 'Go and shoot him.'[10]

In his memoirs, Audisio, a Communist known as Colonel Valerio, gave a somewhat different account. Audisio, who was working out of General Cadorna's office, said partisan military leaders met at 3 p.m. on 27 April in Cadorna's office to discuss Mussolini's fate. This was roughly the time at which Mussolini was captured, and several hours before the capture became known in Milan. Audisio quoted Longo as saying: 'He must be killed immediately, in the worst way, without trial, without theatrics, without historical phrases.' Audisio continued: 'And I added a little as justification: "A long time ago the Italian people pronounced the sentence; it's only a matter of executing it." The other members of the command did not contradict me.'

But Sandro Pertini of the Socialists later confirmed Bellini delle Stelle's statement that the CVL had given unequivocal instructions to the captors of Mussolini to 'transfer him to a secure place, without shooting even in case of attempted escape'. Pertini said he was 'taken aback' on learning that, but Longo told him to keep calm, implying the order would not be obeyed.[11]

Audisio said he received a phone message at 8.30 p.m. on 27 April from Lieutenant Colonel Luigi Villani of the Finance Guards in Como advising him that Mussolini had been taken from Dongo and would be brought to Milan to be jailed. Villani also reported the arrest of Colombo at Cadenabbia. Three hours later, Villani phoned again to say that Mussolini was in the Finance Guards' barracks at Germasino.

Audisio, then aged thirty-six, had been a bookkeeper in Alessandria for the hat-making firm Borsalino and had a long history of opposition to the Mussolini regime. A Communist Party member since 1921, he had been arrested in 1934 and sentenced to five years of internal exile on the island of Ponza near Naples, where Mussolini was held prisoner in 1943. Audisio fought in the Spanish Civil War against Franco, and during the Italian civil war had been commander of the Garibaldi Brigade at Mantua. Along with Luigi Longo and Aldo Lampredi, he was one of three Communist members of the General Command of the CVL. Lampredi, known as Guido, was a high-ranking Communist official, mostly used for diplomatic missions, who had been in exile in France during part of the Mussolini regime.

According to Cadorna, Audisio and Lampredi went to see him and said they had a mandate from the CLNAI to go to Lake Como and execute Mussolini. In his memoirs, Audisio suggested instead that the decision had come from Cadorna and other members of the General Command. The CLNAI, he said, could not have ordered them to do anything because they had no relationship with the CLNAI and because no member of the CLNAI except Longo knew them.

Cadorna's version is that he assumed the order to execute Mussolini came from a small Insurrectional Committee within the CLNAI that was composed of the three leftist parties – the Communists, Socialists and Action Party. He said he had to consider two things: that the CLNAI had always held it would be necessary to execute Fascist leaders after simple recognition, and that the Americans, already in Como, would no doubt have claimed Mussolini 'as war criminal No. 2' (the first being Hitler). Cadorna was unable to contact the CLNAI at such a late hour and said he had to decide what would be in Italy's best interests. An Allied trial of Mussolini, he concluded, would turn into a trial of Italian policy over the last twenty years at a time when it would be extremely difficult to separate the responsibilities of the people from those of their leader.

'Who could presume that, after such discredit, the survival of Mussolini could be useful to the country?' he wrote in his memoirs. 'In no case then would I have voluntarily proceeded to hand over Mussolini to the Allies so he could be judged and executed by foreigners. . . . I acted within the limits of a precise responsibility from which I did not intend nor do I intend to excuse myself.' In short, he endorsed the decision to execute the Duce.

General Emilio Faldella met Cadorna that evening, who told him Mussolini had been captured and the two Communists had gone to bring him to Milan. Faldella phoned the director of the San Vittore jail, asking him to prepare twenty cells for Mussolini and his *gerarchi*. Leo Valiani, the Action Party representative on the CLNAI, came to see Cadorna on the morning of 28 April carrying a CLNAI order to execute Mussolini. Cadorna told him two Communist delegates had come with the same order the previous evening and were already en route to carry it out. Valiani said later that he, Sandro Pertini and the Communists Emilio Sereni and Longo, took the decision during the night of 27–8 April to shoot Mussolini without trial, 'given the urgency of the matter'.[12]

Pertini spoke on Milan Radio on the evening of 27 April and announced: 'The head of this association of delinquents, Mussolini, while yellow with rancour and fear and trying to cross the Swiss frontier, has been arrested. He must be handed over to a tribunal of the people so it can judge him quickly. We want this, even though we think an execution platoon is too much of an honour for this man. He would deserve to be killed like a mangy dog (*cane tignoso*).'[13]

Audisio asked for twelve partisans, armed with hand grenades and machine guns, to accompany him and Lampredi. He specified they should be selected from members of the Oltrepò Pavese Brigade, a Communist unit that had just arrived in Milan, and asked that they be ready to leave at 5 a.m. on 28 April. He also chose a black Fiat 1100 that would be driven by Giuseppe Perotta, a Socialist.

While he was studying maps with an aide to Cadorna, the American OSS agent Captain Emilio Q. Daddario arrived. Like Guastoni, Daddario had been sent by the OSS to try to ensure that Mussolini would be handed over to the Allies. Audisio no doubt told Daddario he was going to bring the Duce back to Milan, because he persuaded him to give him a pass in case he were stopped by Allied troops. Audisio, other than calling himself Colonel Valerio, also carried an ID card in the name of Giovan Battista di Cesare Magnoli. Daddario wrote this note for him in English: 'Milan, April 28th, 1945. Colonel Valerio (otherwise known as Magnoli Giovan Battista di Cesare) is an Italian officer belonging to the General Command of the Volunteers of Liberty. He is sent on a mission by the National Liberation Committee for Northern Italy to Como and its province and must therefore be allowed to circulate freely with his armed escort.' Audisio carried a similar paper in Italian from the CVL General Command.

At 5.30 a.m. Audisio, who already had a pistol with him, took a machine gun from a cupboard in his office and went with Lampredi to a school where the partisans were staying. There they learned to their dismay that the truck that was supposed to have carried the men had broken down. Several partisans were sent out to requisition another truck and came back with a small one belonging to a Milanese electrical firm. Audisio briefed the unit commander, an officer he identified only as Riccardo, on their mission and the three of them set out in their Fiat, followed by the truck carrying the partisans. Other authors have identified Riccardo as Alfredo Mordini, but Lampredi said his name was Riccardo Mordini. On the outskirts of Milan, they ran into heavy rain.

The two vehicles reached the Como prefecture at 8.30 a.m. and Audisio and Lampredi met with twelve members of the local CLNAI, telling them they needed a big covered truck so as not to attract attention and alarm the population. The CLNAI members were suspicious and asked Audisio the nature of his mission. He said it concerned the Fascist *gerarchi* arrested at Dongo. They replied that they had an agreement with the 52nd Garibaldi Brigade to transfer the prisoners to a jail in Como the next day or day after. Audisio informed them he had a precise order to carry out that overrode any local agreement, but they remained firm. He insisted the prisoners must be 'taken to safety in Milan' as quickly as possible. The twelve CLNAI members wanted to be alone to decide, so he and Lampredi went into another room. At 9.45, two of the members came in to have further discussions, while the other ten disappeared. By now angry and impatient, Audisio barked: 'You have just one task: to procure for us a big covered truck.' They promised to search for one and went out.

It was now 10 a.m. and Lampredi suggested phoning Milan. Another hour passed before the call came through. Audisio spoke to Longo, who instructed him to brook no interference and carry out his mission 'with maximum energy and decisiveness'. Longo told Audisio, in regard to Mussolini: 'Either you get rid of him or we will get rid of you.'

Audisio went outside and was chagrined to find that Lampredi and Mordini had left in his car with the driver without saying where they were going. A CLNAI member assured him the truck he wanted would arrive at any moment. Finally, at 11.20, an old truck arrived, a charcoal burner that was belching smoke. Audisio realised it would never complete the journey and demanded another truck. At 11.50, a Red Cross ambulance arrived, the only vehicle the CLNAI could find.

Audisio, shouting, demanded to see the CLNAI president and the military commander of Como. CLNAI secretary Oscar Sforni and the commander, Major Cósimo De Angelis, soon appeared and Audisio ordered them to accompany him and his partisans to Dongo. He requisitioned two cars, and the partisans piled in with him. Sforni and De Angelis went ahead in a military vehicle, but after 100 yards they stopped to talk to a man by the side of the road. De Angelis identified him as a naval officer known to the Information Services, and said he must come along. Audisio said they didn't need his help, and left him behind.[14]

That is Audisio's version. Some Italian historians and Sforni tell it differently: Sforni said the local CLNAI had no confidence in 'the strange envoy' from Milan, and Sforni told Audisio that Mussolini should be put into an ambulance and transported to the San Donnino jail in Como. Audisio, he said, replied in a peremptory tone that within seven minutes he and his men would leave without further delay. 'So I was constrained to go with him,' Sforni said. Historians say Audisio encountered Captain Giovanni Dessi and another agent, 'Carletto', who were at a petrol station and proposing to go in their car to Dongo with him. Gun in hand, he ordered them out of the car. Dessi protested in vain, and Audisio departed.[15]

Just outside Como, Audisio and his men saw a big, yellow covered truck coming towards them and forced it to stop. There were three men in the truck and Audisio ordered them to get out. Behind him in the distance, he could hear applause; the people of Como were welcoming the first Allied troops. Sforni and De Angelis continued toward Dongo and, en route, they were fired upon by partisans thinking they were Fascists. Audisio followed and finally reached Dongo at 2.10 p.m. When Sforni asked him how he intended to deal with the prisoners and the valuables that had been seized, Audisio ordered him and De Angelis arrested. Three partisans, holding machine guns at their backs, escorted them to a cell in the town hall that was still stained with the blood of Pavolini. Shortly afterwards, Marcello Petacci was brought to the same cell.[16]

Bellini delle Stelle was in an office in the town hall when Audisio and his armed men arrived in the piazza. He was informed that the man in charge was asking for the local commander. Not knowing who they might be and fearing they were Fascists, Bellini delle Stelle phoned Lazzaro and asked him to bring some men from Domaso in case there was trouble. He sent word to Audisio that he was waiting in his office. The partisan who delivered the message came back to say that Audisio had flown into a rage and threatened to arrest everyone if his orders were not carried out. He said he was from the General Command in Milan, and demanded that Bellini delle Stelle report to him.

Meanwhile, Lampredi and Mordini arrived in the piazza. Audisio was still angry at Lampredi's unexplained disappearance and the two men had a 'stormy' meeting, according to Lampredi. 'Audisio was beside himself. He attacked me with bitter words without allowing me the possibility of explaining what I had done,' Lampredi said. 'We certainly could not get into a quarrel at that moment and therefore I limited myself to inviting him to calm down and postpone every clarification until we were in Milan.'[17] The reason for Lampredi's disappearance will be explained in the next chapter.

Bellini delle Stelle walked out into the square, arriving in time to hear the last words of the quarrel between Audisio and Lampredi. Audisio said: 'Our personal dispute must not enter into it. . . . I am here to execute my mission and I don't want sticks between the wheels.' The square was deserted except for Audisio and his men, who were in new uniforms and carried sub-machine guns.

Bellini delle Stelle described Audisio as rather tall, dark and going slightly bald. He was energetic and brusque. Audisio identified himself as Colonel Valerio and said he must speak to him in private. Lampredi and Mordini appeared in the corridor as they went to Bellini delle Stelle's office, and Lampredi joined the discussion. Bellini delle Stelle's suspicions about Audisio's true identity were laid to rest when Lampredi confirmed to Canali, who was well acquainted with him, that he and Audisio had been sent by the CVL General Command.

Audisio demanded that Mussolini and his ministers be handed over to him. Bellini delle Stelle said he intended to hand them over to the General

Command. 'There's no question of that. I've come to shoot them,' Audisio replied. Bellini delle Stelle protested that this was not right, but Audisio said: 'It is the sentence of the Liberation Committee and it is an order of the General Command. I am charged with carrying out that order and I intend to do so. You are only a subordinate and I am your superior. You have only the duty of obeying. Let that be very clear.' Years later, Audisio told a court that the decision to shoot the Fascists was 'taken of common accord'. Bellini delle Stelle left the room to confer with Canali and Moretti, who concluded he would have to obey. 'This was the application of the law of an eye for an eye, and that law never seemed to me just or human,' Bellini delle Stelle wrote later. Tuissi, who was also present, objected strongly to handing the prisoners to Audisio, evidently because she mistrusted him and did not believe his statements.

Bellini delle Stelle returned to the room to tell Audisio they would give up their prisoners but would not involve themselves further: 'The rest is up to you.' He gave Audisio a list of the names of his prisoners and, as Audisio read through them, he pencilled a black cross against them in the margin. 'Benito Mussolini . . . death. Clara Petacci . . . death.'

Bellini delle Stelle exclaimed: 'Petacci! But why? You want to shoot a woman? She's not guilty of anything.'

Audisio replied that she was Mussolini's adviser and had inspired his policies for years. 'She's just as responsible as he is.' There was an element of truth in this. As noted in Chapter 5, Claretta had sought to influence Mussolini's appointments, and apparently succeeded in some cases.

Bellini delle Stelle continued to object, but Audisio said angrily: 'I don't condemn her. She has already been condemned. Remember that I execute an order and you must not interfere. I know what I'm doing and I decide what I must do.'[18]

That is Bellini delle Stelle's account and undoubtedly the correct one. Audisio's version is clearly a fabrication. He said he told Bellini delle Stelle that everyone on the list, except the Spanish diplomat and his family, must die, and there were no objections. But then he said they must punish only the most guilty, and again with no objection from Bellini delle Stelle, they compiled a list of seventeen people. Nine of the condemned men were in Dongo, six were in Germasino and Mussolini and Claretta were at Bonzanigo. Audisio claimed they then convoked a war tribunal, with himself as president, and formally condemned these prisoners to death. He named the other members of the tribunal as Lampredi, Bellini delle Stelle, Moretti and Lazzaro. Lazzaro, the only surviving member of that group, insists there was no trial. 'I was convinced Mussolini deserved death,' he said. 'But there should have been a trial according to law. It was very barbarous. I always tried to settle things without violence.'[19]

Bellini delle Stelle suggested he would collect the prisoners held at Germasino, and Canali and Moretti could go for Mussolini and Claretta. They had just agreed on this when a guard brought in Marcello. Audisio asked if he was the Spanish consul and he said he was.

'*Habla usted español?*' asked Audisio, who had learned Spanish when he fought in the civil war.

Marcello hesitated, then said: 'No, but I speak French.'

Audisio said: 'What? A Spanish consul who doesn't speak Spanish?'

Marcello lamely replied: 'Well, what do you expect? I've been living in Italy for twenty years.'

Audisio asked him where he had been born and he said Barcelona, adding that his father still lived there. Audisio asked if he had not spoken to his father in a long time.

'Oh no, about six months ago,' Marcello replied.

'And when you speak to your father, you talk in French?' Audisio asked. (In his version, Audisio said he addressed to Marcello some phrases in Spanish, but he might as well have spoken Ostrogoth, and Marcello remained 'as mute as a fish'.)

Audisio leaped to his feet and, his face turning purple with rage, slapped Marcello hard across the face. 'Hands up, you scoundrel. Get that arm up high or I will shoot you,' he shouted. He aimed his pistol at Marcello, who backed against a wall, terrified, with his hands up. 'I've recognised you, you coward. You're Vittorio Mussolini. . . . Get your hands up high or I will kill you like a dog. You braggart. Against the wall, I said.' Marcello stammered that he was mistaken. Lazzaro was ordered to search him, and took from him a gold cigarette case, gold fountain pen, pencil, handkerchief and box of matches. Audisio instructed Lazzaro to remove Marcello's jacket, then told Marcello to take off his shoes.

'But I am not Vittorio Mussolini, I am Don Juan Muñez,' he protested.

'Silence, imbecile. Silence, or I'll shoot you like a dog.' Audisio pointed the pistol at Marcello's face, and Marcello blanched with terror. Audisio turned to Lazzaro: 'Bill, take this man away and shoot him immediately.' Lazzaro took a gun from his holster and, outside, ordered a group of partisans to take Marcello to an isolated place where he could be shot. People in the square hurled threats and insults at Marcello, and some tried to punch and kick him. 'Look, look how fat he is!' one man cried. 'Your father didn't give you a ration card, you ugly pig.' Someone else shouted: 'Kill that scoundrel!'

Marcello protested that he was not Vittorio, and Lazzaro ordered the crowd back. Marcello was taken to a nearby Capuchin monastery, where he was asked if he wanted a priest and he said that he did. He admitted he was not the Spanish consul or Vittorio, but said he was the head of the Italian

Intelligence Service. The priest arrived and began writing down Marcello's statements in a little notebook. Marcello then admitted his true identity, but this meant nothing to Lazzaro. Marcello said he had always been anti-Fascist and it was thanks to him that the Germans never used secret weapons. He and a man named Grossi had made sensational discoveries that would have changed the course of the war, but they had kept them secret from the Germans. (In the summer of 1942, Mussolini wrote to Hitler saying that an engineer named Grossi had invented a system for transforming methane and another gas into liquid and this discovery would have military applications. Hitler apparently did not reply.)

Lazzaro took Marcello back to the town square, where he found Bellini delle Stelle with the other prisoners he had brought from Germasino. On the trip down the mountain, Bellini delle Stelle observed that the prisoners evidently had no intimation of the fate that awaited them and were almost lighthearted. They commented on the beauty of the lake spread out below them, and Casalinuovo said: 'Who knows why we ended up here? Who suggested to Mussolini to take this road?' Someone else commented that they had advised Mussolini several times against taking that route, but Pavolini even managed to crack a joke that referred to fascism's most famous slogan: 'What do you expect? Mussolini is always right.'

Marcello, seeing the Fascist prisoners when they arrived back in Dongo, told Lazzaro they could identify him, but they denied knowing him. Pale with rage, he insisted they say who he was and finally Barracu admitted he knew him. 'We know him only as Fosco,' he said. Fosco is a first name in Italian but it is also an adjective meaning dark, dismal, or gloomy. Barracu apparently used it in that sense.[20]

Chapter 24

EXECUTION OF IL DUCE: WHODUNNIT?

Aim at my heart.

(Benito Mussolini's last words, addressed to his killer, 28 April 1945)

Audisio's identity was a long-held secret; he was not named as the killer of Mussolini until two years after the event. No doubt the Communist Party, which held the secret, judged it was too risky to name anyone during the immediate aftermath of the war, when revenge killings were taking place all over Italy. The earliest versions of how the killing occurred, which gave only pseudonyms for those involved (Audisio was 'Colonel Valerio'), appeared in the Communist newspaper *L'Unità* over a period of months and years and were bewilderingly contradictory with each new telling. Audisio first spoke publicly about the killing in 1947, and his book on the subject was published only in 1975, two years after he died, compounding the confusion because it was at variance with his own public statements in some respects.

All this suggests that (1) Audisio was a completely hopeless liar, unable even to tell a coherent falsehood; (2) he spread confusion deliberately, for reasons not entirely clear; (3) he was not the lone killer of Mussolini; and (4) he may or may not have been present at the killing, but was chosen by the Communist Party to assume the responsibility. These conjectures spawned a virtual cottage industry output of Italian books about the Mussolini execution, nearly all of them naming someone other than Audisio as the true killer. Italian writers often seemed to operate on the premise that anyone who told as many lies as Audisio had done could not possibly be telling the truth as well.

The starting point for a discussion here of what happened is the one that appeared in Audisio's book. It is a mixture of fact embellished with fantasy, as the evidence uncovered in 1996 makes clear. The elements that seem to belong to the world of fantasy are cited in italics.

While driving up to Bonzanigo, Audisio chose the execution spot, then stopped the car and fired a shot to make sure his gun was working. He continued on foot with his fellow partisans, telling the driver not to move. *As they were walking, he said to Lampredi: 'You know what has occurred to me? I will tell him we have come to free him.' Lampredi replied: 'He isn't an imbecile.'* At the De Maria house, Audisio went up the stairs, which were cut into the rock, and confronted Mussolini and Claretta in the bedroom. Mussolini was standing at the right side of the bed, wearing a uniform and a reddish-brown overcoat. Claretta was dressed but in bed with the covers over her. *Mussolini's lower lip trembled as he looked up and asked: 'What's up?'*

Audisio replied: 'I have come to free you.'

'Truly?'

Audisio replied: 'Hurry, you must hurry, there's no time to be lost.' He asked if Mussolini were armed and the Duce said he was not. Claretta quickly gathered up her personal objects. *As they were going out of the room, Mussolini said: 'I knew they would not abandon me. Bravo. I offer you an empire.'* (Lia De Maria later said that as they were departing she feared the worst and made the sign of the cross.) As they headed back towards the car, with Claretta having difficulty walking in her high-heeled shoes, *Audisio whispered to Mussolini: 'I have also freed your son Vittorio.' Mussolini thanked him and inquired about Paolo Zerbino, his interior minister, and Fernando Mezzasoma, his minister of popular culture. Audisio told him they were being freed also.* Mussolini wore a beret and Audisio told him to take it off. When he did, his identity was obvious, so Audisio told him to put it back on.

Mussolini and Petacci sat on the back seat of the car, and Lampredi sat beside the driver. Moretti stood on the running board opposite Claretta, and Audisio seated himself on the right rear bumper. The car began slowly down the mountain, and Audisio ordered a halt before the gate of the Villa Belmonte, a large house in Giulino di Mezzegra that faces the lake. Giulino di Mezzegra appears on few maps; it is simply a collection of a few houses less than a quarter of a mile up the mountain from the lakeside town of Azzano. Audisio whispered to Mussolini: 'I heard some suspicious noises, I'm going to see.' He got off the car and looked along the road to make sure no one was coming. Lampredi turned to Mussolini and said: 'Your luck has run out.'

Audisio ordered Moretti and the driver to take positions at either end of the road in front of the villa, about 150 to 180 feet from each other. Then he ordered Mussolini out of the car and told him to go along a low wall, which runs in front of the villa, and to stand near the pillar of the gate. 'He walked heavily, dragging his right leg a little. The stitching in one boot was frayed,' Audisio wrote. Claretta got out and quickly moved to Mussolini's side.

Audisio began reading the death sentence: 'By order of the General Command of the Corps of Volunteers of Freedom, I am charged with rendering justice to the Italian people.' He pointed his machine gun at Mussolini, and Claretta threw her arms around the Duce's shoulders. *'Get away from there if you don't also want to die,' Audisio commanded.* She moved back, then drew close to the Duce. Audisio pulled the trigger. Nothing happened; the gun jammed. He tried again after manoeuvring the breech-block, but still the gun didn't fire. Lampredi took out his pistol and tried to fire, but it also jammed. Audisio grabbed his machine gun by the barrel, ready to use it as a club. Then he called in a loud voice to Moretti, who ran up with his machine gun, handed it over and hurried back to his guard post.

'I fired five shots at that trembling body,' Audisio said. 'The war criminal dropped to his knees, leaning against the wall, with his head reclining on his chest. Petacci, beside herself and stunned, moved confusedly. She was hit also and fell to the ground. It was 4.10 p.m.' of 28 April. Benito Mussolini had lived sixty-one years and nine months less one day. His last political incarnation, beginning with his rescue from the Gran Sasso, had lasted 594 days. Audisio identified the gun as a 7.65mm L.MAS, 1938 model-F.20830, and said it had a red ribbon tied to the end of the barrel. Claretta's death, he said, was accidental.

Audisio called to the two fishermen, Cantoni and Frangi, to guard the two bodies and to prevent anyone from passing along the road. Then Audisio, Lampredi and Moretti returned to Dongo to execute the Fascist *gerarchi*. Throughout his account, Audisio described Mussolini as frightened, trembling, stammering with terror, cowardly. This is at variance with other accounts, which suggest he was impassive. But Audisio's version is what might be expected from a Communist determined to portray Mussolini in the worst possible light, and on this point as others it lacks credibility.[1]

Over the next two years *L'Unità* published three versions of the killing, all of them different in several important particulars, and other accounts also differed from Audisio's. The first *L'Unità* article, identifying the killer as Colonel Valerio, appeared on 30 April 1945. It was similar in many respects to the account Audisio gave in his book, but not identical. The article, like the book, quoted the executioner as saying the bedroom in the De Maria house had no window. In fact, it had one. The article said that when Valerio entered the bedroom and ordered Mussolini and Claretta to leave, she began rummaging among the bed covers and he asked her what she was looking for.

'My pants,' she said.

He replied: 'Don't worry about them. Come on, hurry.'

This was not mentioned in subsequent articles or the book. The article quoted Valerio, after describing the death of Mussolini, as saying: 'It was then the turn of Petacci, justice was done.' The second *L'Unità* version later that year also indicated that her killing was deliberate, saying she 'returned to her place' (away from Mussolini) and remained 'petrified' before she was gunned down. The book described her death as accidental, as did the third *L'Unità* version published in 1947. In an interview in 1947 with the journalist Vitantonio Napolitano, Audisio said: 'If she had remained at her place, as I insistently warned her, nothing serious would have happened to her. She turned like someone crazed from one point to another, first right, then alongside, then in front of Mussolini, repeating like an automaton, "Mussolini mustn't die."'[2]

In late 1945, a woman named Francesca De Tomasi, who was secretary to the CVL, a Communist and a friend of Longo's, passed to Ferruccio Lanfranchi, a reporter for the newspaper *Corriere d'Informazione*, a photocopy of a report she said 'Valerio' had dictated to her. She made Lanfranchi swear not to reveal her name and to attribute the report to 'a person who saw it and had then reconstructed it faithfully'. Franco Bandini, who worked with Lanfranchi, said the reporter did not know until a decade later that De Tomasi was Audisio's first cousin (actually, the daughter of his cousin). Although Lanfranchi had serious doubts about the accuracy of the report, that did not stop him from writing eleven articles based on it that appeared in his newspaper in October and November of 1945.

In 1962, De Tomasi said the Valerio report had been dictated to her by Lampredi and Audisio. She said it seemed concocted, and it was her understanding that Lampredi, not Audisio, fired the shots. At the end of the dictation, she said, Lampredi commented to Audisio: 'Then we are in agreement. From this moment you take the part of the hero.' By her account, Lampredi turned to De Tomasi and said: 'This is the version that will have to be handed down to history, always. Is that clear?'[3]

The report, like the book, referred to the 'little' house of De Maria, when no one who has seen it could possibly describe it as such. The report referred to a wooden staircase, and the book accurately said it was carved from stone. The report said 'Valerio' and a second man described only as 'X' left Dongo in a small truck and arrived twenty minutes later in Giulino di Mezzegra. But Audisio's book refers to the Fiat 1100, and the trip from Dongo to Giulino di Mezzegra takes about forty minutes. The report said Valerio, outside the Villa Belmonte, nodded to Mussolini and Claretta to sit on a stone bench while he looked around. There was no stone bench.

In November and December of 1945, *L'Unità* carried twenty-four articles, which it said were based on the report of Colonel Valerio and other documents gathered by the Communist Party. In these articles, Valerio was no longer with 'X' but with 'comrade Guido', who of course was Lampredi. The articles also named the driver of the car – no longer a truck – as Bill (Lazzaro), when in fact Lazzaro had scores of witnesses to say he remained in Dongo. In the car ride to the Villa Belmonte, these articles had Valerio sitting on the bumper of the car, as the book later said; in the preceding *L'Unità* article in April, he was inside the car. These articles said that when Audisio's gun jammed, he called to Bill (not Moretti) to bring him his machine gun; in later accounts, Bill was not mentioned as being present. The articles had Claretta falling 'on the wet grass' when in fact there was no grass near the gate to the villa, only a paved road. This time Valerio fired nine shots, not five. At the time these articles appeared, *Corriere Lombardo* carried a long account signed by Bellini delle Stelle and Lazzaro in which they said Lazzaro was not there.[4]

The Roman newspaper *Il Tempo* published eight articles by the journalist Alberto Rossi between 6 and 16 March 1947, in which Colonel Valerio was identified for the first time as Audisio. Rossi quoted Moretti as saying he fired the fatal shots after Audisio's gun had jammed, then Audisio finished off the two victims with two pistol shots. Several days later, Luigi Longo, speaking at a Communist rally at the Palazzo dello Sport in Milan, denounced what he called unfounded 'rumours' about the identity of Valerio. But a Communist Party statement published on 23 March in *L'Unità* confirmed that Valerio was Audisio, and proposed he be awarded the Gold Medal for military valour. Then, beginning on 25 March, six articles under Audisio's byline appeared in *L'Unità* recounting the killing. He also gave a speech at a Communist rally on 28 March at the Basilica of Maxentius in the Roman Forum in which he declared he had killed Mussolini but gave a confused account, full of contradictions, concerning dates and names. He repeated his claim of responsibility in his interview with the journalist Vitantonio Napolitano on 27 August 1947.[5]

The latest articles and the speech contained more discrepancies. The 'little house' remained a little house. The Villa Belmonte was described as 'plainly deserted', when other reports quoted the partisans as seeing several people seated on the terrace in front of the house and shouting to them, 'Get back, get back!' This time Valerio fired ten shots, not nine or five. Bill was no longer present but was replaced by the unnamed political commissar of the 52nd Garibaldi Brigade (Michele Moretti). These reports also conflicted with earlier *L'Unità* articles on the position of Mussolini's body and the words Audisio pronounced.

Another version was reported in *Tempo* magazine in April 1956 by the journalist John Pasetti. He said he had been approached in Rome in February 1947 by a drunk, the doorkeeper at Communist Party headquarters, who identified Valerio as Audisio. Pasetti asked the Communist Party for an interview with Audisio, which was granted on 3 March 1947. Audisio spoke in French into a tape recorder and ended his account with these words: 'It was I who personally shot Mussolini.' Pasetti, who also worked for Radio Lausanne, took the tape to Switzerland but the government refused to allow it to be broadcast. Just why Pasetti waited nine years to publish his report in *Tempo* was not explained.[6]

Moretti's second account of the killing was published in April 1974 in the magazine *Giorni-Vie Nuove*, and this time he did not claim to be the killer. For the most part, he substantiated Audisio's account. When Claretta tried to protect Mussolini, he said, Audisio shouted: 'Do you want to die too?' When Audisio's gun jammed, Moretti gave his gun to Audisio, who turned and fired a burst. Mussolini and Claretta fell to the ground. Then Audisio asked Moretti for his pistol and fired another shot at Mussolini.[7]

Who was the unnamed driver who took the killers from Dongo to Bonzanigo? The journalist Franco Bandini, in an article published on 4 March 1956 in the weekly magazine *L'Europeo*, said he had discovered the identity of the driver but had promised not to reveal his name. He called him Giovanni, and said he was still working at that time as a driver. Giovanni witnessed the killings from six feet away (not seventy-five to ninety feet as Audisio had suggested). Bandini said the driver was a young man of about twenty-nine who had gone to Dongo out of curiosity on the morning of 28 April in his father's black Fiat 1100 and had been pressed into service by Audisio, Lampredi and Moretti. After he driven them back to Dongo, Bandini said, the driver stayed in bed for three days with a fever of 100 degrees brought on by emotional upset.

In his book, Audisio confirmed that the man was a simple driver and 'we didn't know who he was or from where he came'. He identified him as Giovanbattista Geminazza and said he was born in September 1919. Audisio misspelled the surname; it was Geninazza. Why would Audisio have commandeered Geninazza's car instead of using the one in which he had been driven from Milan? That question has never been answered.[8]

Geninazza later disclosed his real name and gave his account of the killing. He insisted Audisio did not go to the De Maria house to collect Mussolini, but waited near the car in Bonzanigo while Lampredi and Moretti went to the house. (He was the only witness to say that.) As Geninazza sat in the car, he said, he was approached by a woman taking her two dogs for a walk, but he did not want to talk to her. He had been told: 'Be on your guard. You will soon see some people whom you cannot fail to recognise. But forget them immediately. If you don't forget you won't lose just your memory, but your head.'

Soon Moretti and Lampredi returned with Mussolini and Claretta, who was wearing a fur coat and carried a camelhair coat on her right arm. (She had left behind her handbag, which contained a broken mirror, medicines, lipstick and a number of coloured handkerchiefs printed with musical notes and amorous words in French.) As they drove away, Mussolini and Claretta sat close together with their heads almost touching, Mussolini pale and Claretta seemingly calm. When the car stopped, almost in the middle of the narrow road, Audisio opened the door and brusquely ordered: 'Get out!' As they did so, Audisio pushed them against the low wall in front of the villa, levelled his machine gun and 'pronounced a few words very quickly'. The driver said Mussolini remained impassive but Claretta threw her arms around him and began to pull at him frenetically. Audisio shouted: 'Move away from there or I will also kill you!' But she clung to Mussolini, shouting, 'No! No! You mustn't do it. You mustn't!' As Audisio squeezed the trigger and there was a 'click' instead of a gunshot, she rushed at him, grabbed the barrel of the gun in both hands and shouted: 'You cannot kill us like this!' Geninazza saw sweat pouring down Audisio's face as he pulled the trigger a second and third time, then pulled his pistol from his pocket and found that jammed also. After Moretti had given Audisio his machine gun, Mussolini pulled back the lapels of his jacket and said: 'Shoot me in the chest.' Geninazza said: 'His voice was clear; I heard it perfectly. They were his last words.' The first shot killed Claretta and the next hit Mussolini, who stumbled back and slid slowly to the ground with his legs bent under him. He lay on the ground breathing heavily, and Audisio went up to him and shot him again in the chest. Audisio watched him in silence, then turned to Geninazza: 'Look at his expression. Doesn't it suit him?'

Geninazza's account was remarkably detailed, considering that in his interview with Bandini in 1956, he said he did not witness the killings but, out of fear, 'looked the other way'. It also appeared to be wrong on several points, such as Claretta's struggle for the gun, which was mentioned by no other witness.[9]

Cantoni later said that he and Frangi came on foot from Bonzanigo just in time to see Moretti with a machine gun pointed at two bodies already on the ground, and he was convinced that Moretti was the killer. Cantoni gave his statement to Giuseppe Giulini, the Christian Democrat mayor of his hometown of Gera Lario, and Giulini entrusted it to a notary. Later, Cantoni gave contradictory versions of the killing to two writers: first, that Audisio fired a pistol shot that missed before Moretti unleashed the fatal burst of machine-gun fire, then that Audisio only fired his pistol afterwards. But within days of giving his second version, Cantoni issued a denial that was published by *L'Unità* on 25 February 1956. He said he had made the false statement only because he had been promised money for an interview, and admitted he had not been present at the shootings.

This was confirmed by Moretti, who said neither Cantoni nor Frangi was present; they had taken their shoes off when they entered the De Maria house earlier that day, and when Mussolini and Claretta were taken away, their own departure was delayed because they had to put on their shoes. Then, instead of following the road from Bonzanigo down to the Villa Belmonte, they went along the mule track to the lakeside road at Azzano. Moretti said that after the shooting he and the others present scooped up the cartridge cases, then he went down to Azzano and found Cantoni and Frangi. He said he ordered them to go up to the Villa Belmonte and guard the bodies.[10]

Nella Galeffi, a partisan known as Gina, said the word that Moretti killed Mussolini was circulating among partisans from that evening. Another partisan, Ennio Pasquali, said: 'I spoke several times with Michele Moretti in the days after the shooting of Mussolini. He told me not to take seriously what Valerio had said and written, as he had revealed himself to be a demagogue and a man possessed.' He said Moretti told him that after Valerio's gun had jammed, he himself fired, hitting Mussolini first and then Claretta. 'This is the tale Moretti told me several times in the following days. . . . If he officially gave a different version, I believe he did so for party discipline. Besides, this tale was not a personal confidence but was in the public domain among local partisan commanders.'

In the autumn of 1990, Moretti gave an interview to the writer Giorgio Cavalleri in which he started to recount the 'official' version that he handed his gun to Audisio. When Cavalleri challenged this statement, Moretti neither confirmed nor denied that he killed the Duce and Claretta, but Cavalleri said he was convinced Moretti was the gunman. Part of Cavalleri's 'interview' was a word-for-word reproduction of the interview that had appeared sixteen years earlier in *Giorni-Vie Nuove*. Remo Mentasti, a Communist partisan, said Lampredi fired after Audisio's gun had jammed. Mentasti, however, was not present.[11]

The Villa Belmonte, where the killings took place, was occupied by Bernardo Bellini, an engineer, his wife Teresa, Rinaldo and Aminta Oppizzi and the Oppizzis' two little girls, Lelia and Bianca. Teresa was sitting on the terrace, about ten yards from the wall in front of the villa, when the car stopped outside the gate. Her husband and Rinaldo were inside listening to the radio. Lelia was in the garden reading a book, and the Bellini maid Giuseppina Cordazzo was weeding the flower bed behind the gate. Teresa said she saw a heavily built man (Mussolini, in fact) get out of the car wearing what she thought was a black beret, holding the lapels of his coat. He looked 'like a mountaineer holding onto the straps of his rucksack'. Teresa and the others who were outside were ordered to go indoors. She said the partisans heard Claretta whisper to Mussolini: 'Are you happy that I have followed you all the way?' Later, the residents of the villa agreed they had heard ten shots, but the high hedge in front of the villa prevented them from seeing anything.

After the car had left, the maid went out on the pretext of collecting parsley and saw a rigid leg in the mud, covered by a boot with a loose heel. She heard the two fishermen conversing:

'Look, he's still moving.'

'Let it go. It doesn't concern us.'[12]

There is now a plaque at the site of the execution, in black stone with white lettering saying simply: 'Benito Mussolini 28 aprile 1945.' Mussolini sympathisers go there on each anniversary of his death and leave bouquets of flowers tied with ribbons – in the green, white and red colours of the Italian flag – in the hedge rising above the low stone wall. Then they go to a nearby church for a commemorative mass in honour of the Duce. In 2001, Alberto Botta, a businessman who lives not far away and describes himself as a Fascist, and some of his friends erected a plaque at Musso marking the spot where partisans stopped the Mussolini convoy on 27 April 1945. But anti-Fascist Italians smashed the plaque to pieces within days.

In July 1959, Audisio met the journalist Silvio Bertoldi and implied that the truth of what happened had never been told. Bertoldi quoted him as saying: 'If I wished, I would one day make a big journalistic coup, a sensational one. All I would have to do would be to write for a magazine five little chapters as I intend about the history of which I have been the protagonist . . . and I assure you it would reach a circulation . . . a circulation . . . like *Grand Hotel*!' After the war, Audisio was elected twice as a member of the Chamber of Deputies, the lower house of parliament, and twice as a senator. In 1971, he said to a parliamentary group: 'But do you really believe I was the killer?'[13]

What is one to make of the lies and contradictions in Audisio's testimony, his later hints that he in fact did not kill Mussolini and the suggestions that someone else was responsible? Did Audisio offer conflicting accounts in a deliberate attempt to discredit himself, to spread confusion or out of simple carelessness? The last two *L'Unità* reports were prepared in Rome under the eyes of Communist Party officials, and it seems strange that they did not ensure he produced a coherent and believable account. *L'Unità* named him as the killer only as he was preparing to run for parliament, when the publicity clearly would help his campaign.

After the war, the Italian government charged a Milanese military prosecutor, General Leone Zingales, to conduct an inquiry to determine who killed Mussolini. He concluded that Moretti was responsible and tried to have him arrested, but Moretti, facing criminal charges on a related matter, had fled to the Yugoslav republic of Slovenia. The writer Ezio Saini, who conducted a long inquiry into the matter, also concluded Moretti was the killer. On the other hand, some Italian writers have speculated about a host of other people whom they claim did the deed. Among those who have been named are Lampredi, Canali and a former soldier turned partisan named Domenico Tomat. A partisan named Bruno Giovanni Lonati claimed he killed Mussolini with four or five shots and that British Secret Service Captain 'John', working with him shot Claretta. Another claim of British involvement was made by Mussolini biographer Renzo De Felice in 1995. He said a British secret agent of Italian origin – evidently a reference to Max Salvadori – had urged the partisans to kill Mussolini quickly to keep him from revealing that Churchill had carried on a secret correspondence with the Duce during the war. De Felice cited no evidence for this claim, and the suggestion that Churchill corresponded with Mussolini when they were mortal enemies in war is patently ludicrous.

An equally far-fetched account of the killings came from Lorenzo Bianchi, a partisan known as Renzo, in ten articles he wrote for a partisan newspaper beginning on 27 April 1945. He claimed that he and Lazzaro captured Mussolini, and that he finished off Claretta after 'somebody else' had shot her, while Bellini delle Stelle and Audisio killed Mussolini. There is plenty of evidence that Bellini delle Stelle was in Dongo when the killings took place. Several writers also came up with a novel twist in the tale: Mussolini and Claretta were not killed after 4 p.m. but earlier in the day, and a fake second shooting was staged in the late afternoon. This theory was put forward by Bandini, Lazzaro and the former neo-Fascist parliamentarian Giorgio Pisanò, but none of them offered an even barely credible explanation as to why the killer or killers went back and pumped bullets into dead bodies.

Other theories have proliferated over the years: Mussolini and Claretta were shot dead inside the De Maria house, Mussolini naked at the time and dressed afterwards. Communist leader Luigi Longo and the Socialist Sandro Pertini, who later became president of Italy, killed them. As late as 1992 the Communist partisan Pietro Terzi claimed in a magazine article that he was the killer. One author has even suggested that Mussolini committed suicide, and another that both Mussolini and Claretta took cyanide capsules in the De Maria house.[14]

Franco Bandini, who investigated the affair at length, maintained that Audisio, while in Como on the morning of 28 April, did not in fact speak to Longo in Milan at 11 a.m.; Longo had left Milan in the early hours, shortly after Audisio departed, and had decided to become the executioner. Bandini offered no explanation as to why Longo, having sent Audisio to do the job, set out practically on his heels to do it himself. Bandini's unsubstantiated conclusion is that Lampredi, Longo and Mordini, the commander of the Oltrepò partisan unit, and four other men left Como together well before

Audisio departed. He said they went to Dongo to collect Moretti and Canali, and perhaps Tuissi, so these partisans could identify them to the two guards at the De Maria house.

They arrived at the house at around noon. When Mussolini and Claretta were brought into a small square in Bonzanigo, Mordini and Longo opened fire with Czech 9mm machine guns. The bodies were loaded into a car, which was driven into the courtyard of a small house of local Communist sympathisers. Longo returned to Milan. The others went back to Dongo, met Audisio and told him what had happened. To try to hide the participation of such a high-ranking Communist in the killings, Audisio and Moretti went to the De Maria house in the afternoon to stage a mock execution, taking with them one partisan dressed to resemble Mussolini and Tuissi wearing Claretta's coat. These two got out of the car at the Villa Belmonte, while Canali arrived in another car with the dead bodies of the real Mussolini and Claretta. Audisio tried to shoot the bodies but his gun jammed, so Moretti fired two bursts from his machine gun. Bandini said he interviewed Maximilian Mertz, a Swiss who owned a villa at nearby Azzano, who told him he saw men shooting at 'cadavers dead for some time'. He did not explain how Mertz, observing from a considerable distance, could have known they were already dead and for how long. Bandini also quoted two people who said they went to the site the next day and noticed there was very little blood on the ground. He cited several 'witnesses' who merely told him they heard shooting around Giulino di Mezzegra between noon and 1 p.m. on 28 April. None claimed to have seen the shooting of Mussolini and Claretta, but the absence of firsthand witnesses did not deter Bandini from giving a precise, detailed account of how they died. He offered no witnesses who claimed to have seen an execution in the Bonzanigo village square.[15]

Lazzaro, a participant of the events of 28 April who survived until 2006, rejected entirely the idea that Audisio killed Mussolini or was even present at the execution. In 1993, he published a book in which he argued that Valerio was in fact Luigi Longo, and he also claimed there was a double shooting. He said Mordini inadvertently shot Mussolini during a struggle with Claretta, who was trying to wrest away his gun, then Mordini killed Claretta on Longo's orders. The Duce lay wounded on the ground and Moretti finished him off, according to Lazzaro. Furthermore, Lazzaro said the killings took place not after Valerio had reached Dongo at 2.45 p.m. but sometime around 1 p.m. before he came to Dongo. The inadvertent shooting of Mussolini, he said, spoiled Longo's plan to kill the Duce and his minions in Piazzale Loreto in Milan. So, after going to Dongo to arrange the killing of the Fascists being held there, Longo and his companions returned to Giulino di Mezzegra in the late afternoon and staged a fake execution to make it appear as if Mussolini and Claretta had been killed in a deliberate way and not accidentally. One can only ask why; it is an explanation that lacks sense.

Longo and his men then returned to Dongo, executed sixteen Fascists there, went back to Giulino to collect the bodies of Mussolini and Claretta and finally drove to Milan in the evening with a truckload of bodies. This suggestion of Longo bouncing back and forth like a yo-yo – Giulino di Mezzegra to Dongo, Dongo to Giulino, Giulino to Dongo, Dongo to Giulino – seems ludicrous on the face of it. Lazzaro said Lia De Maria confirmed to him in 1981, thirty-six years after the event, that Mussolini and Claretta were taken from her house before 1 p.m. Lazzaro said he recognised that Longo was Valerio when he saw his photograph in May 1945. Oscar Sforni, the Como secretary of the CLNAI who accompanied Valerio to Dongo, agreed with him. But Bellini delle Stelle, after seeing photographs of Audisio, was convinced Audisio was Valerio. It is difficult to understand how this confusion about Colonel Valerio's identity could have arisen; there was little physical similarity between Longo and Audisio.

In his book, Lazzaro said his version of the killing was given to him by someone who was present but insisted on anonymity. Almost six decades later, when all those who had been present were dead, Lazzaro still refused to reveal the name. He said that when he visited the nearly eighty-year-old Lia De Maria in 1981, he showed her photographs of Longo and Audisio and asked which one was Colonel Valerio. After some hesitation and uncertainty, she picked Longo. But that is hardly an identification that would stand up in any court. She had seen Valerio only for a few minutes, and thirty-six years later her memory could not be entirely relied upon. In any case, there is substantial proof that Longo was in Milan on the afternoon of 28 April, not in Dongo or Giulino di Mezzegra. He went to the outskirts of Milan around 2.30 or 3 p.m. that day to meet a partisan division entering the city from the town of Rho, led by a famed partisan named Cino Moscatelli. The division marched into Milan with several Communists, including Longo, leading the way, and a photograph showing him in the march was subsequently published in a book in 1958. The march ended at the Piazza del Duomo in Milan, where Longo and Moscatelli made speeches that were reported in several newspapers the next day.

If any further evidence were needed to establish that Longo was not the killer, there is the fact that General Cadorna saw Audisio and Lampredi leave Milan in the early morning to carry out the killings; that an aide to Cadorna took a phone call from Audisio when he reached the outskirts of Milan in the evening, announcing he had carried out his mission; and that Audisio then drove to the General Command and reported to Cadorna, as Cadorna testified. It is hardly to be believed that a monarchist general and his aide would be party to a Communist conspiracy to protect Longo's identity. Neither Bandini nor Lazzaro offered an explanation as to why Longo was unwilling to be named as the executioner if in fact he was.[16]

Another problem with Lazzaro's version is that Longo, according to Bandini, was in the editorial offices of *L'Unità* in Milan on the evening of 28 April – not travelling back to Milan with the bodies – and wrote a nine-column headline for the newspaper announcing 'Mussolini and His Acolytes Executed in the Name of the People'.[17]

Moretti, Lazzaro and Bellini delle Stelle had a falling out among themselves after the war, and Moretti said Lazzaro's claim that Longo was the killer was 'humbug and stupid'. He also said the theory of the double shooting advanced by Bandini and others was 'absurd and provocatory'. After the war, Lazzaro and Bellini delle Stelle lived for several months in a Como hotel, and Moretti's wife openly accused them of using partisan money to pay for their stay. Moretti once asked Bellini delle Stelle for an account of his spending, and was told there were many things for which Moretti should give an accounting, not vice versa.[18]

To sum up the competing claims of how Mussolini and Claretta died, and who was responsible, it should be noted that witnesses in Dongo agreed that four men set out from Dongo to Bonzanigo that afternoon: the mysterious Colonel Valerio, Lampredi, Moretti and the driver Geninazza. Lampredi always refused to give interviews on the subject, but the other three at one time agreed on the essential facts: the guns of Valerio and Lampredi jammed, and Valerio used Moretti's gun to kill the Duce and his lover. It is true that Moretti offered this version only after claiming he himself was the killer, but his original claim is highly suspect – as a disciplined Communist, it is not likely that he would have disobeyed an order from a superior officer to hand over his weapon nor denied that officer the glory of having carried out a historic act. Nor could he have escaped the wrath of an arrogant, hotheaded man, yet there was no report of Valerio clashing with Moretti at the scene. It should also be noted that Moretti agreed that Valerio was Audisio. Geninazza had no way of knowing who he was. Finally, all three men agreed the killing took place around 4 p.m., not at noon or 1 p.m., and none of the three offered any suggestion of a killing followed by a fake second shooting. The sceptics might contend that Audisio and Moretti were part of a Communist conspiracy to lie about such details, but Geninazza had no such motive.

In 1973 a new, firsthand account of the killings appeared in print for the first time. Over a fourteen-day period, *L'Unità* published five articles giving a detailed account of the events at Dongo and Giulino di Mezzegra. In the last of these articles, Lampredi was quoted for the first time. In all the essential facts, he supported Audisio's account but omitted the apparent fantasies that were cited in italics earlier in this chapter. His comments attracted little attention at the time. No doubt his report seemed to many readers, including historians, as just another of the many conflicting versions of how the Duce and Claretta died.[19]

But in 1996, *L'Unità* returned to the subject with a report that put Lampredi's remarks in a broader and much more significant context. *L'Unità* had made an important discovery as a result of the collapse of the Italian Communist Party in January 1991. After the fall of the Berlin Wall, the party abandoned the last strands of its Marxist ideology and renamed itself the Democratic Party of the Left. The archives of the Communist Party were transferred to the Istituto Gramsci in Rome, and there, amid scores of thousands of documents, reporters for *L'Unità* discovered a report on the killings that had been written in 1972 by Lampredi. It was identical to the report published in 1973, but this new report was published in full along with other material that gave new insights into Lampredi's comments.

'For some time I have thought of making a report to the party on my participation in the shooting of Mussolini and the Fascist *gerarchi*,' he wrote. He said his purpose was to furnish information that would be useful should the party some day want to reconstruct the history of that event, and he said his report would provide a more complete and precise account than that given in the official reports published by *L'Unità* in 1945 and 1947. He said he had hoped to include the reports of comrades whose important roles had always been ignored, but he had not succeeded in obtaining all of them so he had decided to not delay further and to send in the material he had gathered. 'I limit myself to referring to the essential facts and those that interest me the most, overlooking many of those made known by Audisio, even if in regard to those there would be a lot to say,' he went on. 'For another thing, I have forgotten many particulars and I would not be in a position to reconstruct, with true approximation, what I did in the days of the Milan insurrection.' Lampredi sent his report on 22 May 1972 to Armando Cossutta, a member of the Secretariat of the Italian Communist Party.

These circumstances demonstrate why Lampredi's report may be considered trustworthy where others lack credibility. Lampredi did not write for publication; as far as he knew, his report might never see the light of day. But as a dedicated Communist, he wanted his party to be apprised of the facts in case it should one day want to reveal the truth as opposed to the mixture of truth and fantasy that Audisio had presented. Lampredi had no interest in lying to his party's leaders – quite the contrary – and he did not attempt artificially to fill in blanks in his memory that had occurred after a passage of twenty-seven years. Furthermore, he had no reason to credit Audisio with the killings if that was not the case; he and Audisio clearly did not like each other, as his supplementary accounts made clear.

L'Unità, in presenting the Lampredi report, said Longo had decided that Lampredi should accompany Audisio on his mission because he wanted him to oversee the work of a man he considered 'impudent, too inflexible and rash'. Lampredi had the right qualifications for dealing with a hothead. He was a serious and responsible figure in the Communist leadership, more at home in political work than in frontline activism. Jailed by the Fascists when he was young, he later studied in Moscow, then enrolled in the International Brigades during the Spanish Civil War. He became a captain and an instructor in the Spanish republican army, but in 1943 the Communist Party recalled him to Italy and he became one of the political leaders of the partisan movement in the Veneto region. Then Longo made him his principal aide at the General Command of the Corps of Volunteers of Freedom in Milan. People who knew him invariably described him as very reserved and kind. They also used such terms as 'cultivated' and 'honest'. He was forty-six at the time Mussolini and Claretta were killed. Lampredi shared Longo's reservations about Audisio and found it difficult working with him. Nonetheless, his account of the execution of Mussolini and Claretta squares with that of Audisio on the essential point of who fired the fatal shots. But in some respects he also takes issue with him.

Lampredi said he was not present when the decision was made in Milan on 27 April to execute Mussolini and his lover. He returned late that evening to the General Command offices in Palazzo Brera in Milan, and Audisio informed him that he had been entrusted to kill the Duce and Claretta, adding that Longo had decided Lampredi should participate. 'I understood this decision as a party task that was entrusted to me and I conducted myself in that sense,' he wrote. He went on to describe the difficulties he and Audisio encountered in Como with an uncooperative provincial CLN leadership that was intent on seeing Mussolini jailed in Como.

Lampredi thought it was important to get the Communist member of the CLN, Professor Renato Scionti, to break ranks with the other members, so he invited Scionti to accompany him to the Como Communist Federation offices for further discussions while Audisio phoned Longo in Milan. Lampredi gave no explanation as to why he left the Como Prefecture without telling Audisio where he was going and why; perhaps he had had enough of Audisio's arrogant manner at that point and had decided to carry out the mission without him.

At the Federation he found Communist leaders sympathetic to the stand taken by the Como CLN, but he finally convinced them of 'the correctness of the party position'. Two of the local Communists, Giovanni Aglietto and

Mario Ferro, agreed to accompany Lampredi to Dongo to introduce him to Moretti and other Communists and assure them that the Audisio–Lampredi mission had the backing of the party. Having learned that Audisio was no longer at the Como Prefecture, Lampredi travelled to Dongo with Mordini, Aglietto, Ferro and their driver. At Dongo they found Audisio had already arrived, and he and Lampredi then had their 'stormy' confrontation.

In his report, Lampredi ducked the question of whether a popular tribunal had been assembled in Dongo to try Mussolini and condemn him to death, as Audisio claimed and Bellini delle Stelle and Lazzaro insisted did not happen. But Lampredi implied there was no tribunal. 'All that seems to me of little value as it seemed to me then,' he wrote. 'The important thing was to carry out the orders we received and the formalities did not interest me. However, it is a fact that the [52nd Garibaldi] Brigade Command approved the list of *gerarchi* to be executed and contributed to the realisation of this task.' He added that Bellini delle Stelle most certainly was not in agreement on the shooting of the *gerarchi*, and 'tried to complicate things to gain time, hoping for the arrival of the Allies. It is a fact that the execution of Mussolini and Petacci was carried out without his knowledge, since he believed it would happen together with the other *gerarchi* when he had brought them all together in Dongo.' The suggestion that Bellini delle Stelle wanted the Allies to take control of Mussolini ran counter to his own statements that he wanted to avoid such an outcome at any cost.

Lampredi said the atmosphere in Dongo was hostile. The local people and partisans feared a surprise attempt by Fascists to free their captured comrades, and it took the combined efforts of Moretti, Aglietto and Canali to overcome their suspicions. After this problem had been resolved, Lampredi said he, Audisio and Moretti commandeered a car to proceed to the shooting of Mussolini and Claretta. Thus he explicitly denied Audisio's claims that the killing of Claretta was accidental.

Lampredi said he remembered vividly entering the bedroom of the De Maria house and finding Mussolini standing near the door on his right while Claretta lay on the bed. 'I must say that, from that moment, my eyes, all my faculties, were concentrated on Mussolini,' he wrote. 'I remained profoundly struck by the miserable aspect that he presented. Perhaps I was still influenced by the fabled image made of him by Fascist propaganda and I expected to find a vigorous, energetic man. Instead I had before me an old man, white-haired, short, with a dazed air. His forearms were partly raised and with both hands he held a glasses case that I immediately took from him. I don't even know why.'

Lampredi said that with his attention focused on Mussolini he did not follow everything that was happening around him. He did remember the exchange between Claretta and Audisio about her pants, but implied that Audisio had invented the part about telling Mussolini he had come to free him. There was no necessity to calm Mussolini with such remarks, he said, because he could not have been shot on the spot. Nor was the Duce in a position to offer 'an empire' or anything else.

When they drove to the Villa Belmonte, Lampredi said, he approached the car door where Mussolini sat, bent down towards him and remembered saying something to this effect: 'Who would have said that you, who persecuted so many Communists, should have had to settle accounts with them?' (In his account Lampredi used the familiar '*tu*' with Mussolini, evidently as a sign of disrespect.) Mussolini made no reply. Claretta gave Lampredi a long, questioning look 'and she must have found a cold answer in my eyes'.

Mussolini and Claretta were ordered out of the car and made to stand against the low wall of the villa, near the gate, with Claretta on the Duce's right. Lampredi said Audisio did not read the sentence of death he claimed to have pronounced; he may have said a few words, but Lampredi was not sure. He agreed with Audisio's account of how the shooting took place: Audisio's gun jammed, and so did Lampredi's pistol. Then they called to Moretti, who gave his machine gun to Audisio and Audisio proceeded to kill the Duce and Claretta. 'All this happened in a very short time: one or two minutes, during which Mussolini remained immobile and in a stupor, while Petacci shouted that we could not shoot him and moved about near him, as though she wanted to protect him with her person,' Lampredi wrote. 'It was perhaps the behaviour of the woman, so in contrast with his own, that pushed Mussolini at the last moment to give a start, straighten up, and, opening his eyes wide and turning back the lapels of his overcoat, to exclaim: "Aim at my heart." These words seem to me more true than the words mentioned by the driver Geninazza: "Shoot me in the chest."'

Lampredi confirmed Moretti's account that Cantoni and Frangi, the two fishermen who had guarded the prisoners, arrived on foot only after the shooting. It should be noted from Lampredi's account that Mussolini did not act with the combination of cowardice and *naïveté* Audisio ascribed to him.

Lampredi went on to observe that the execution of Claretta had subsequently aroused perplexity and objections even among friends of the Communists, who saw her only as a faithful lover willing to sacrifice her life. He wrote:

> I don't deny there may be this aspect, but I deny she could have been valued objectively in that moment and a different fate assigned to her . . . Petacci was not only a lover but an element closely tied to the Germans

> in whose service she acted in influencing Mussolini. She and her family of voracious profiteers were hated by the people and even by the Fascists. . . . But for me, above all in that moment, there was the painful memory of the atrocities committed by the Nazis and Fascists, of the innumerable innocent victims, of our fallen, of all the suffering borne by the people. All this cried out for justice and punishment. Between me and Audisio there was no discussion concerning Petacci, so normal did it seem to us that she had to follow the fate of Mussolini.

Lampredi's account did not touch on a crucial question that arose some time after the killings about the calibre of bullets used to kill Mussolini and Claretta. This will be discussed in the next chapter. Lampredi closed his report with a postscript: 'I have not spoken with anyone of the final gesture of Mussolini and this is the only writing that refers to it. I will not write nor will I speak even in the future unless the party makes it public. Moretti guaranteed me he will behave in the same way and I believe one can trust him. I don't know what Audisio will do.'

Lampredi attached to his report several revealing documents. In one, he expressed a deep grievance over the fact that the Communist Party had never publicly recognised his role in the events of 28 April. He said Longo and Pietro Secchia, another Communist leader, 'did not know, or knew very little, of what I did at Como' and 'I have always been excluded from everything regarding the events of Dongo'.

'In fact, no director of the party has ever felt the need to ask me what I achieved on that occasion and not even felt the duty, or at least the correctness, to alert me to the publications in *L'Unità* and of what was written about me.' Had they done so, he said, this would have avoided the suspicions that were aroused about his leaving Audisio at the Como Prefecture to go to the Communist Federation, and his superiors might have 'been able to reduce the journalistic hype of the story'. He said he had considerable reservations about Audisio's account of the killings.

Lampredi said he had never been able to explain to himself why the party had obscured his role in the events of that day, but had concluded at one point this was because of Audisio's doubts about him. Some years after 1945, he said, Audisio came to his office and told him that when Lampredi had left him in the lurch at the Como Prefecture he suspected that Lampredi wanted to obstruct his mission or make it fail. 'That Audisio had suspicions about me was clear from the reception I had from him in Dongo,' he said. During the trip from Milan to Como, he said, Audisio had spoken of the enormous importance he attached to his mission because it would put his name into the history books. After Audisio had come to him and expressed suspicions,

Lampredi said it seemed apparent that Audisio believed 'I had tried to take away from him the honour to which he aspired by leaving ahead of him with the same aim in mind'.

Lampredi said he recognised the seriousness of Audisio's allegations and went immediately to Longo to ask if the party knew about Audisio's opinion and had more or less shared it. 'Longo denied that categorically,' he wrote. 'I don't doubt his word, but I don't feel able to rule out the possibility that some other comrade director, who had become aware of it, may not have had some perplexities such as to lead him to the behavior of which I complain.' Lampredi concluded this document in injured tones. He said he regarded his role in the killing of Mussolini and Claretta as a party task, like others he had performed, and did not consider himself 'invested with particular merits and worthy of special recognition. . . . I want to specify I do not have resentments or open problems with the party.' In short, he was aggrieved but had refrained from making his views public.

Another document recounted a meeting he had had with Audisio on 21 February 1972, when Audisio came to his home. Audisio told him that Giovanni Pesce, the famous GAP terrorist during the war, had asked him to write four or five pages on the Dongo mission that Pesce could include in a book he was writing. Pesce told Audisio he planned to make a similar request to Lampredi. Audisio suggested to Lampredi they coordinate their response and thus avoid presenting contradictory accounts, but Lampredi told him he had received no such request from Pesce, and, if he had, he would have turned him down. Audisio then said he also would refuse to write anything for Pesce.

Audisio went on to tell Lampredi he had written a minute account, filling several notebooks, of the Dongo mission and this had never been published. From the conversation, Lampredi gathered that Audisio intended to claim that the shooting of Mussolini and the *gerarchi* was the wish of all members of the General Command and in particular Cadorna, and that Audisio planned to deny a dominant role by the Communist Party in that decision. Lampredi said that this and other details Audisio mentioned were 'contrary to what really happened'.

Audisio also mentioned he had received a generous offer from an American publisher for his memoirs. He suggested they jointly write a book about the Dongo mission, from which they could expect to earn 'some millions' of lire. He said this would be useful to Lampredi, who had a young son to bring up. 'I replied that I had no intention of writing for the public and if I should decide to write something, I would do it as a testimony to be consigned to the party,' Lampredi wrote. He went on to say that Audisio complained of being treated badly by the party and kept away from political activity without explanation.

It is perhaps noteworthy that Lampredi submitted his reports to the Communist Party just three months after this last meeting with Audisio. The supplementary report on that meeting showed clearly that he was perturbed by the prospect of Audisio writing a book that would contain fresh lies about what really happened, and he may have hoped that by alerting the party to Audisio's plans he could be instrumental in thwarting them.

On 21 July 1973, more than a year after Lampredi submitted these documents to the party, and four months after *L'Unità* first published excerpts from his main report, he died unexpectedly while on a trip to Yugoslavia, aged seventy-four. Not surprisingly, publication of the complete documents in *L'Unità* in 1996 failed to convince some writers who had denied that Audisio had carried out the killings. But Giorgio Bocca, a careful and reliable historian and a former partisan, told *L'Unità* that Lampredi's account 'sweeps away all the bad novels constructed over 50 years on the end of the Duce of fascism. . . . There was no possibility that the many ridiculous versions put about in these years were true. . . . The truth is now unmistakably clear.' He did not say so, but one thing that was now unmistakably clear was this: Audisio was as much of a fantasist as the writers who later concocted elaborate accounts of the killings that had no basis in fact. Audisio had the facts, but could not stick to them; he evidently enjoyed embroidering the truth with fanciful and contradictory details, but for the most part these concerned peripheral matters. On the essential fact of who did the shootings, he and Lampredi were in agreement. *L'Unità* reported in 1966 that it had found in the Communist Party archives a document signed by Longo, Ferruccio Parri and others, awarding a gold watch to Audisio in memory of his 'historic mission'.[20]

* * *

Audisio was away from Dongo for about two hours on his trip to and from Bonzanigo. He and Bellini delle Stelle have each supplied accounts of what happened next. Although Audisio clearly lied about some particulars, which will be noted, Lampredi said he had no fundamental quarrel with what had generally been published about the Dongo executions. Audisio returned to the town hall just before 5 p.m. and told Bellini delle Stelle: 'Justice has been done. Mussolini is dead.' Moretti showed Bellini delle Stelle the 7.65 MAS sub-machine gun and said: 'This was the weapon that killed the tyrant.' The gun was war booty, captured from a Fascist militia unit at Gravedona during a partisan attack of 30 March. Audisio told Bellini delle Stelle he now intended to shoot all the *gerarchi* he had previously selected, and proposed that they form a mixed execution squad of men of his escort and partisans of the

52nd Garibaldi Brigade. Bellini delle Stelle refused. 'If you have come to shoot them, you shoot them,' he said.[21]

Audisio went up to a second-floor room to visit the prisoners so that he could ask some questions to establish their identities. Lampredi, in his account, said the prisoners were made to stand on one side of the room, and some Fascists without important posts were told to leave the lineup. Then the prisoners selected for execution were led into the piazza, each accompanied by a partisan with a machinegun pointed at him. Before leaving the room, Mezzasoma asked Lampredi if he could take with him his overcoat that was on a chair. Lampredi told him he would not need it. 'I wonder if he understood what awaited him,' Lampredi wrote. 'I did not go down into the piazza but watched the execution from the balcony of the room that looked out on the lake.'

As Audisio came out of the town hall, he encountered Mayor Rubini, who had come to try to prevent the killings. A local friar, Father Accursio Ferrari, also arrived from his monastery and asked permission to give spiritual consolation to the condemned men.

In his memoirs, Audisio wrote: 'I had no objection but could give him only a few minutes.'

He said the friar replied: 'Three minutes will be enough for me. It is not necessary that they confess one by one.'

Father Accursio's account is very different. He said he told Audisio he needed to go to the hall where the men were held to confer with each one, and Audisio replied: 'No, no, there's not enough time. I can give you only three minutes.' Accursio protested and Audisio cut him off: 'Military requirements do not permit me to do more.'

The friar turned to Rubini: 'Three minutes! I can do nothing except go to the window and send them a blessing from far away.'[22]

Rubini followed the column of condemned men as they were led toward the square, but at the top of the stairs he stopped them and shouted at Audisio: 'You will shoot them in this way, on the main square of the village, in the midst of the crowd, of women and children? I veto that. If you have an order to carry out, go to the cemetery or somewhere around it and better still beyond there, along the deserted bank where there is a landing stage.'

Audisio cut in: 'These are the orders of my superiors.'

Rubini replied: 'The orders of your superiors interest me only to a certain point; I obey rather the orders of my conscience.'

Audisio retorted: 'But perhaps the Germans don't do this sort of thing? The order is to do it in public, this is the order.'

Rubini said: 'But we are Italians. We hate Nazis and Nazi-Fascists precisely because of their barbaric system. I veto it, I forbid it and if my opposition is worth nothing I will clearly separate my responsibility by immediately renouncing the charge conferred upon me. The tribunal of public opinion will judge.'

Walking away, Audisio replied coldly: 'If you are too sensitive, don't come.'

A partisan arrived and whispered to Audisio: 'Colonel, the one with the Spanish documents begs and pleads with us to re-examine his papers. He assures me he does not share the responsibility of the others and insists on being interrogated again.'

Audisio replied: 'Go away, go away. Those papers are not clear. Away, away.' Rubini then informed Audisio he would go home and write out his formal resignation. 'I am a soldier and also a man of the law, not a persecutor,' he said. 'You are losing a wonderful and unique opportunity to begin a new period in the history of the country with systems of civilisation.'[23]

Audisio and Bellini delle Stelle agreed that the fifteen condemned men would be marched out of the town hall in single file, each flanked by one of Bellini delle Stelle's men, to a parapet running along the lakeshore across from the square. Audisio's men would then take charge and carry out the execution. Bellini delle Stelle said he would leave so as not to have to witness the execution, but Audisio flew into a rage: 'You will remain here. You are the local commander and you must be present to testify that the execution has been in order. I therefore order you to attend.'

Bellini delle Stelle replied: 'If it is an order, I will obey you.'

The fifteen prisoners were brought out onto the square and the roll was called. Then the sentence was read out: each man was condemned to be shot in the back. 'About face!' Mordini commanded, and the prisoners turned around. Some of the condemned men raised an arm in the Roman salute, and others shouted, 'Long live Italy!' Father Accursio spoke a few words of comfort and gave a general absolution. Audisio quoted him as delivering these hardly credible remarks: 'In this supreme moment turn your minds to God to ask pardon for the crimes with which you have disgraced yourselves and in the name of God prepare yourselves for death. His mercy is infinite.'[24]

Audisio remembered Marcello, and ordered that he should be shot with the others. Marcello was brought out and the other prisoners began shouting: 'Get away, get away! We don't want him with us. He's a traitor. He mustn't be shot with us!'

Marcello drew back, pale, but Audisio in a great rage shouted: 'Forward! Put him with the others. Finish him off.' Bellini delle Stelle argued that the condemned men should be granted their last wishes, and Audisio ordered that Marcello be led aside.[25]

The Fascist journalist G.G. Pellegrini described the execution:

> The 'colonel' appears at the foot of the square, elegant in his partisan uniform without rank. Face pallid, hard, cold, lips tightly closed. From the line of the *gerarchi*, one, whom I don't know, advances a step to speak to him. It seems he is Captain Calistri [an Air Force officer whom Audisio mistakenly believed was Mussolini's personal pilot; he had joined the Mussolini convoy to get away from Como]. The 'colonel' nods to him to stop, looks at him coldly and immediately proceeds without answering. His entire attitude is complete denial. The *gerarchi* are ordered to move to the back of the railing. Someone throws away the butt of his last cigarette. The one they tell me is Bill reads the names. The 'colonel' has a sheet of paper in hand, but I cannot understand if he reads it. Someone orders attention and about face. The *gerarchi* execute it with the dash of soldiers. The platoon lines up at their shoulders a few metres away. Then, amid the silent dismay of the crowd, a loud shout arises, without echo: 'Long live Italy.'[26]

Francesco Maria Barracu, Mussolini's under-secretary for Cabinet affairs, wore a Gold Medal in his lapel, his decoration for military service. He stepped forward and shouted, showing the medal in his buttonhole: 'I hold the Gold Medal. I have the right to be shot in the chest.'

Bellini delle Stelle tried to persuade Audisio to accede to his request, but Audisio shouted: 'In the back. . . . In the back, like the others. I have had this order and that's how it will be done.' He grabbed Barracu and, with a violent jerk, spun him around.[27]

The execution squad opened fire, and the men crumpled to the ground. Audisio claimed that four of the fifteen members of the squad were Bellini delle Stelle's men, and that Bellini delle Stelle and Lazzaro lied about this, but this appears to be another of his own lies. Mordini commanded the firing squad. There was silence after the shooting, then someone cried: 'Bring out Petacci.' He was carried by two partisans, struggling hard, his face contorted with terror.

'You can't shoot me!' he cried. 'You mustn't. You are committing a huge error. With all that I've done for Italy. You must not.' Suddenly, with a powerful lunge, he broke away from his captors and fled into the crowd, then ran up a narrow street alongside the town hall. A group of ten or twenty men ran after him, and he was captured in front of the Dongo Hotel, 100 yards away. As he continued to struggle and shout incoherently, four men lifted him off his feet, carrying him by each arm and leg to the parapet. Marcello gave one more lunge, shook himself free, ran to the water and, still shouting, threw himself in. He swam away with powerful strokes, but a fusillade of bullets struck him. With his blood staining the water, he sank slowly a few yards from shore. He died three days before his thirty-fifth birthday. For several more minutes, the gunmen went on firing, letting off hundreds of rounds. Some firing came from windows overlooking the scene.

'It is an infernal fire, like that in a war that precedes the assault,' the journalist Pellegrini recalled. 'People shout, terrorised, and flee.' Marcello's elder son Benvenuto, not yet six years old, witnessed his father's death from the window of his hotel room and was so traumatised he later went insane. He spent the rest of his short life in a psychiatric institute, dying in his late twenties.[28]

Rubini was at home, writing his letter of resignation, when he heard the shots. When the shooting stopped, he looked at his watch. It was 5.48 p.m. He went out to hand in his resignation and saw the bodies lying by the parapet, and he remembered Mussolini's last words to him: 'I feel obliged to thank you for the way in which we have been treated.'[29]

Luca Schenini, a Dongo timber merchant, filmed the scene before and during the shooting, but Audisio confiscated the film a few minutes later and it was never returned. Four photographs from the film were published at various times by *L'Unità*, but in none of these can anyone be identified except for the men who were shot. Schenini said the film showed Audisio and the firing squad. This film has never been found. Except for Mordini and Orfeo Landini, the political commissar of the Oltrepò Pavese unit, the names of the firing squad members were never revealed.[30]

Audisio ordered that the bodies of the *gerarchi* be loaded onto the yellow truck he had seized outside Como, and he and his men departed at 6.30 p.m. He had tried to get Bellini delle Stelle to fish Marcello's body from the lake and bury him in a local cemetery, but Bellini delle Stelle made the truck wait until the body was recovered and put with the others. Sand was scattered on the bed of the truck and the bodies were covered with sheets. They drove back to Giulino di Mezzegra, picked up the bodies of Mussolini and Claretta that the two fishermen were still guarding and threw them into the truck on top of the others, then left at 8 p.m. Claretta had with her something that escaped the eyes of the partisans on the truck, a cherished gift from Mussolini. It was a gold pendant with seventeen diamonds that formed the initials of the two lovers, CB. The pendant bore this inscription: 'Clara, I am you, you are me. Ben', and two dates: 24–4–32, 24–4–41. The first was the date of their initial meeting, the second undoubtedly the date on which the pendant was given to Claretta. Morgue attendants in Milan later found it, pinned to her underclothing.[31]

Chapter 25

PIAZZALE LORETO: A SHAMEFUL DENOUEMENT

The insurrection has been dishonoured.

(Sandro Pertini, 29 April 1945)

The sprawling Piazzale Loreto, a mile or so north-east of central Milan, is one of the city's largest squares and certainly among its most hideous. Around the square, which is not square at all but circular like a British circus, is a collection of high-rise modern office and apartment blocks that represent the worst in urban architecture of the postwar period. The piazzale is one of Milan's busiest traffic hubs and is a perpetually noisy place with cars, buses, trucks and motor scooters whizzing around it in an unending stream. In the middle is a patch of green, which no one can reach on foot, covering an underground car park. Off the south-west side, not hugely visible amid such brutalism, is a statue of a St Sebastian-like figure, tied to a tree trunk and pierced with arrows, a monument to the fifteen Italians who were murdered here on 10 August 1944 by Fascist militiamen directed by the SS. It was to Piazzale Loreto, which looked rather different in 1945, that the bodies of Mussolini, Claretta Petacci and the sixteen people slaughtered in Dongo were brought on Sunday morning, 29 April and subjected to an orgy of violence that still shames those who took part.

The yellow truck carrying the bodies left Giulino di Mezzegra for Milan at 8 p.m. on 28 August. Audisio states that he saw an American armoured car ahead just before Menaggio. This makes no sense at all; Menaggio is north of Giulino di Mezzegra, and Audisio would have been travelling south to reach Milan – a typical example of his carelessness with facts. But, as he told it, he stopped his car, got out and told the partisans on the truck: 'Sing, boys, sing partisan songs.' They continued on their way but were stopped at an American roadblock when they entered Menaggio. With a searchlight trained on the car and truck, and the partisans singing, an American soldier said something to Audisio, who did not understand English. He showed the soldier his documents. The soldier looked at them and said: 'Okay, *partisani?*' Audisio replied with one of his few words of English: 'Yes.' The Americans waved them on, not bothering to search the truck. There was another American roadblock at Como, and again the same result. Along the drive from Como to Milan, there were burned-out tanks on the road. The two vehicles reached the outskirts of Milan at 10 p.m. and came upon a roadblock near a Pirelli tyre factory that was manned by partisans affiliated with the Christian Democrats. Audisio stopped to phone the CVL General Command and announce he had carried out his orders. Colonel Pieri, an aide to Cadorna, answered the phone and congratulated him. Audisio asked him for a fresh contingent of partisans, as the men with him had not slept and were tired.[1]

By Audisio's account, he went outside and 'a very strange, nervous captain' grabbed him by the arm and pointed a pistol at him. 'Let's go inside,' the captain shouted. Audisio tried to give an explanation, but the captain refused to listen, disarmed him and put him against a wall with his hands up. When Lampredi and Mordini appeared, the captain put them also against the wall. He ordered the partisans to get down from the truck, two at a time, then went through Audisio's papers and found a list of well-known Fascists that Audisio had brought with him from Milan. The captain began shouting that Audisio and his men were Fascists masquerading as partisans. 'To the wall, hands up. They are Fascists. At the first sign of movement, open fire,' he ordered his men. In his report, Lampredi said: 'The commander of the unit, absolutely beside himself, threatened continually to have us shot if we tried to say a word. The situation had moments such that I truly believed we would not have saved our lives. I thought also that probably we had fallen into the hands of some disguised Fascists.'

He said the Pirelli partisans saved the situation because they understood the need to hear an explanation. Lampredi then told them they should telephone the General Command. As they were telephoning, an officer of higher rank arrived and appeared more reasonable. All this took about three hours. At the end, Audisio refused to accept any apologies but declared the captain, Luigi Vieni, and two of his fellow officers under arrest, disarmed them and made them get on the truck.

The truck proceeded to Piazzale Loreto. Lampredi said the decision to put the bodies there was taken during the return trip, probably at his suggestion. 'What is certain is that when we left Milan, this problem was not raised nor did we think about it,' he said. At 3 a.m., the vehicles finally entered the deserted piazzale and the partisans dumped the bodies in front of a partially constructed Standard Oil petrol station, which no longer exists. Audisio returned to the CVL headquarters an hour later and reported to Cadorna, 'pale and upset', according to the general. Audisio demanded punishment of the partisans who had arrested him. After the war, journalists seeking to determine the identity of 'Colonel Valerio' obtained a list of the people killed at Dongo that Audisio submitted to the CVL. It was signed 'Magnoli', the name he had used on his fake ID card.[2]

From the General Command offices, Lampredi phoned Longo, who was in the former printing plant of *Popolo d'Italia*, where *L'Unità* and other anti-Fascist newspapers were published. Longo asked Lampredi for the names of the Fascists who had been shot, but he listened only briefly because the newspaper was on deadline and he had to hurry to write a report. Longo asked where the bodies had been taken, and when Lampredi told him Piazzale Loreto, Longo expressed disappointment, 'feeling we had profaned the place', according to Lampredi. 'I told him that, according to us,' wrote Lampredi, 'it was an act that rendered justice to all those who had fallen in the liberation struggle and represented a salutary and effective warning.' Lampredi then confirmed that in the early hours of 30 April he and Audisio made a report that was typed 'by the girl of the secretariat who was the daughter of Audisio's cousin'. This was obviously Francesca De Tomasi, the woman who gave a copy of the report to the reporter Ferruccio Lanfranchi and was identified incorrectly by Bandini as Audisio's first cousin.

Some Italians arising that Sunday morning went onto the streets to find news vendors selling copies of *L'Unità* announcing the execution of Mussolini 'and his acolytes'. The article stated: 'Justice has been done. The sinister man of Predappio [Mussolini's birthplace] will no longer pronounce historic phrases and, above all, will not be able to do further evil to the Italian people. The carrion remains of the Duce of evildoers, surrounded by a good number of his acolytes, lie in Piazzale Loreto, exposed to pillory. It is of historical importance that the major war criminals of our country have been given Jacobean-style justice through the unanimous will of our people. This act of popular justice is the inevitable corollary of the national insurrection. It is a severe warning for the present and the future.' Thousands of people would be drawn to Piazzale Loreto that morning by the *L'Unità* report and by an announcement on Radio Free Milan.[3]

At dawn a passer-by took the trouble to arrange the heap of bodies in the square in some sort of order. Mussolini was laid out a little apart from the others with his head and shoulders resting on Claretta's breasts. Two young men arrived and kicked the corpse repeatedly in the jaw. His upper lip was pulled back grotesquely from his teeth so that it appeared he was about to speak. Somebody put a pennant in his hand and squeezed his fingers around it. By 9 a.m. the crowd had grown to a considerable size, and people were shouting and jumping up and down to get a better view. An American who was there described the crowd as 'sinister, depraved, out of control'.

A few were laughing hysterically. One woman produced a revolver and fired five shots into Mussolini's head 'to avenge my five dead sons'. Another woman tore off a strip of his shirt, set fire to it and threw it in his face. Under repeated blows, Mussolini's skull was cracked and one of his eyes fell out of its socket. One woman squatted down, raised her skirt and urinated on his face. Others covered his face in spit. People threw pieces of black bread at the bodies, and one man tried to put a dead mouse in Mussolini's mouth. 'Make a speech now, make a speech,' he chortled. One woman brought a whip to beat Mussolini. The crowd grew and pushed forward, forcing those closest to the bodies to trample on them. Partisans guarding the bodies decided things were getting out of control; they fired in the air, then firemen turned a hose on the crowd. But that had little effect. One large partisan, his bare arms covered with blood, asked the crowd: 'Who is it you want to see?' 'Pavolini,' a man called. Others called out the names of Bombacci, Mussolini, Petacci, and Buffarini-Guidi. (Buffarini was not among the dead.) The partisan lifted each in turn under their armpits, holding them above his head.

'Higher!' people shouted. 'Higher! Higher! We can't see.' A loud voice cried: 'String them up!' Another shouted: 'To the hooks, to the hooks, like pigs.'[4]

The journalist Gaetano Afeltra wrote afterwards: 'It was a very fine day of spring sunshine. The street was full of people who went to see. I was struck by a group of girls on bicycles who pedalled happily in gaudily coloured dresses. . . . From balconies people shouted and cursed. . . . Mussolini was barefoot and in a short-sleeved shirt, Petacci in a gabardine tailleur, without shoes. In that moment they were hanging them by the feet one after the other. . . . I recalled scenes of the guillotine of the French Revolution that I had seen in the cinema, but what I saw now seemed to me worse.'

Another journalist, Indro Montanelli, wrote: 'I had returned the day before from Switzerland and found myself in Piazza San Babila when I was almost knocked over by a swarm of people on bicycles, waving red flags and shouting: "They have taken him! He's in Piazzale Loreto." I followed them on my bicycle and saw a tumultuous crowd that grew dense at a point where flags and banners appeared.' Afterwards, Montanelli left the square with 'a vague sense of shame' and a 'profound hatred' toward those who desecrated the bodies.[5] American correspondents who were present were generally circumspect in their reporting, evidently concluding their readers could not stomach a description of the barbarities they witnessed. Their sanitised dispatches simply obscured an awful truth.

The partisans strung ropes over the girders of the service station, then tied them to the ankles of the cadavers. Mussolini was pulled up first until his head was six feet above the ground. No doubt the partisans acted from instinct rather than historical memory, but in the Middle Ages people had been hung upside down for crimes of infamy. Mussolini's face was splashed with blood and his mouth was open. The crowd cheered wildly. Those in front spat at him and threw rubbish. His underpants showed through the open fly of his military trousers. Claretta was drawn up next, with her skirt falling over her face, revealing that she wore no pants. A partisan chaplain, Don Pollarolo, stood on a box, and amid jeers and shouts tucked her skirt between her legs.[6]

After Claretta's body had been raised, a sudden silence fell over the square. One witness said the air was filled with 'an oppressive quality, an atmosphere of expectancy, as if the whole thing was a dream from which we would awake to find the world unchanged. It was as if we had all in those few seconds shared the realisation that the Duce was really dead at last, that he had been slaughtered without trial and there had been a time when we would have given his dead body, not insults and degradation, but the honours due to a hero and prayers worthy of a saint.'[7]

A man came and poked Claretta's body with a stick, twisting it around the end of the rope. Then four more bodies were raised, amid shouts from the crowd.

American Colonel Charles Poletti, designated as the Allied military governor of Lombardy, arrived in Milan earlier that morning and checked into the Hotel Gallia, having driven through the night with British Colonel Arthur Hancock. Poletti was washing his face when his driver came in and said Mussolini was in Piazzale Loreto. Tired and not thinking clearly, Poletti's first impulse was to believe the Duce was making his last speech. He made his way to the square and en route met armed partisans pushing forward a terrified young girl, evidently a Fascist, with a shaved head. On her head they had painted a red hammer and sickle. In the distance Poletti could hear gunfire. He arrived in the square just as a truck pulled up with another Fascist prisoner, Achille Starace, one of the old, corrupt associates of Mussolini from the earliest days of fascism. Highly unpopular within the party, he served eight years as secretary of the Fascist Party before Mussolini dismissed him in October 1939 and made him chief of staff of the militias. Less than two years later, he fired him from that post. Now in retirement, Starace had gone out jogging that morning, as was his custom, and had been recognised and arrested by partisans. They dragged him into an elementary school for a 'trial' by a revolutionary tribunal of the people and he was quickly condemned to death.

The partisans brought him to Piazzale Loreto in his running gear. An improvised firing squad of three or four men, armed with machine guns, awaited him. Starace was put beneath the hanging bodies and stood at attention, giving the stiff-armed Roman salute to 'my Duce'. He shouted to the firing squad: 'Do it quickly, instead of hitting and insulting a man who is about to be shot.' As Poletti watched, Starace shouted, 'Viva il Duce!' and there was a burst of machine-gun fire. The rope holding Barracu had broken and his body had fallen heavily to the ground. Starace was strung up in his place. Later the rope holding Mussolini was cut and his body fell to the ground, causing brain matter to ooze from his skull and making him almost unrecognisable.[8]

Cardinal Schuster learned what was happening and put in an immediate phone call to Riccardo Lombardi, the new prefect of Milan. Shouting into the phone, he said: 'Either you pull down those cadavers or I will go myself.' Poletti, likewise disgusted and upset, left the square and went to the Prefecture to protest. He later wrote that he had found the scene barbarous and savage, unworthy of a civilised people. He found that most members of the CLNAI shared his indignation, but the Communist Emilio Sereni commented: 'History is made like this. Some must not only die, but die shamefully.' Several years later, Luigi Longo also sought to justify the barbarism of Piazzale Loreto: 'This disturbed many friends of the Committee of Liberation. But I think it was right. Not for sadistic taste. I never went to see them, but it was necessary that people understood that justice had been done. And it was necessary also to cut short other acts of violence and vendettas that would undoubtedly have been unleashed if there had not been the clear sensation that the most important guilty ones had been punished and the chapter was closed.'

Leo Valiani of the Action Party tried to shift the blame for what happened: 'Those in the piazza who insulted the dead were not the partisans moulded in resistance and prepared austerely for years for the insurrection; they were Fascists who until a few weeks earlier had adulated the tyrant.' But the Socialist Sandro Pertini said: 'The insurrection has been dishonoured.' At about 1 p.m. the bodies were taken down, undoubtedly due in part to the protests of Schuster and Poletti, and transferred to the morgue in rough wooden boxes.[9]

Evidently shaken by the protests, the CLNAI decided that afternoon it had better give a semblance of legality to the killings and try to justify the behaviour in Piazzale Loreto. Pertini argued that a statement was necessary to placate the indignation of Allied authorities and said that otherwise the Allies would exploit what happened to Italy's disadvantage. The statement that was issued said the CLNAI had ordered the execution of 'Mussolini and his accomplices' and went on to say: 'Fascism itself is responsible for the explosion of popular hatred that descended on this last occasion to excesses comprehensible only in the climate wanted and created by Mussolini.' But the committee said it would not tolerate further excesses.[10] Achille Marazza, the

Christian Democrat member of the CLNAI, later said the statement had legitimised the executions and therefore the political–juridical question was closed. 'It is not true that this execution was ordered by the CLNAI,' he said. He noted that on 25 April the CLNAI had established the basis for popular tribunals to try Mussolini and other Fascists, and said: 'How could one imagine therefore that three days later the CLNAI issued an order that clearly contradicted that decree?' Ferruccio Parri, who had returned to Italy from Switzerland on April 25, was outraged over the killing of the innocent pilot Pietro Calistri and of Claretta and Marcello Petacci. 'It is terrible and unworthy,' he said. 'It will harm the partisan movement for years to come.' He likened the killing of Claretta to 'an exhibition in a Mexican slaughterhouse'.[11]

Hitler learned of Mussolini's execution from his bunker in Berlin that afternoon, shortly after he had married Eva Braun and a few hours before they committed suicide. Churchill, hosting a dinner at Chequers, rushed in to his guests and announced: 'The bloody beast is dead.' But on 10 May, Churchill was 'profoundly shocked' when he saw a photograph of the scene in Piazzale Loreto. He cabled Alexander: 'The man who murdered Mussolini made a confession, published in the *Daily Express*, gloating over the treacherous and cowardly method of his action. In particular he said he shot Mussolini's mistress. Was she on the list of war criminals? Had he any authority from anybody to shoot this woman? It seems to me the cleansing hand of British military power should make inquiries on these points.' Churchill cited this cable in his war memoirs and added: 'But at least the world was spared an Italian Nuremberg.'[12]

Despite his July 1943 telegram to Roosevelt in which he said he was 'fairly indifferent' as to whether the leading war criminals were shot on the spot or held for trial, Churchill had concluded by November of that year that after a brief kangaroo court at which their identities were verified, they should be 'shot to death . . . without reference to higher authority'. He said in a note to the War Cabinet that he hoped this would avoid the 'tangles of legal procedure' in the cases of some 50 to 100 German, Italian and Japanese leaders. Previously, when the War Cabinet discussed the issue in June 1942, Foreign Secretary Anthony Eden argued: 'The guilt of such individuals is so black that they fall outside and go beyond the scope of any judicial process.' The United States and Soviet Union subsequently rejected quick execution and favoured a full trial of war criminals. Stalin told Churchill when he visited Moscow in October 1944 that executions without trial would leave an impression that 'we were afraid to try them'.

US Treasury Secretary Henry Morgenthau wanted the Axis leaders hunted down and 'put to death by firing squads'. But War Secretary Henry Stimson wrote to Roosevelt condemning this suggestion, saying the American legal tradition would be ill served by lynch law. Churchill raised the subject at the Yalta conference in February 1945 and found Roosevelt and Stalin unwilling to discuss it in detail. The British Foreign Office produced a list of major war criminals in June 1944, including thirty-three Germans and eight Italians, Mussolini and Graziani among them. The Italians later disappeared from the list, as the Allies were then trying to integrate Italy into the democratic community of nations.[13]

* * *

Cadorna, who knew nothing of the scenes at Piazzale Loreto until late in the morning, spent part of that day helping to save Graziani from being lynched. When Graziani left Mussolini at Menaggio on 26 April, he and the generals accompanying him returned to Como. Then, learning that General Wolff was at the Villa Locatelli in Cernobbio, they went there to discuss the fate of the Italian armed forces as the Germans prepared to surrender. Graziani said the Italians expressed their indignation to Wolff over his secret negotiations with the Americans, and the German replied that it had been 'a sad but painful necessity to do it like this'. If he had revealed the negotiations to Mussolini, he said, the essential secrecy would have been blown. Wolff complained that Allied conditions for surrender had recently hardened. Still deceiving himself, he said: 'A month ago we could have obtained much more.'

Graziani gave Wolff the following authorisation, with signed copies in Italian and German: 'With the present proxy I, Marshal of Italy Rodolfo Graziani, in my position as Minister of the Armed Forces, give full powers to General Karl Wolff, supreme head of the SS and of the police and general of the German armed forces in Italy, to conduct on my behalf negotiations with the same conditions as those of the German armed forces in Italy, committing myself for everything that concerns all troops of the Italian army, air force and navy, as well as Fascist militia units.'

Wolff advised Graziani to remain at the SS Command in Cernobbio and await the surrender, as he no longer could reach his headquarters through areas controlled by partisans. Wolff returned to Switzerland early the following morning, en route to the Wehrmacht headquarters in Bolzano via Austria. Graziani phoned Don Bicchierai, Cardinal Schuster's secretary, to inform him he had given Wolff powers to surrender Italian forces. Bicchierai relayed the message to Cadorna.[14]

That afternoon, Graziani heard a loud discussion in Italian in the SS quarters. He found Lieutenant Vittorio Bonetti, an Italian officer who had joined the partisans, having an argument with SS officers. Partisans had taken up positions on hills surrounding the villa, preparing for attack, and

Bonetti had come to the villa with the OSS Captain Daddario to deliver an ultimatum to the Germans to surrender. Eventually the Germans agreed to give up most of their arms and await the arrival of Allied troops to whom they would surrender. They also handed over Graziani to Daddario, and that evening Daddario drove Graziani and the two Italian generals to Milan in a convoy of six cars bearing white flags as well as Italian and Allied flags. As the convoy approached a barracks housing Garibaldi Brigade partisans, it came under machine-gun fire. Three of the cars were put out of action and the other three raked with fire, but no one was injured. Daddario proceeded with the three cars still in working order and later that evening met German officers at the Hotel Regina, where he urged them to surrender. Colonel Rauff postponed giving him a final decision pending the outcome of Wolff's negotiations, and Daddario went on to see Cadorna at around midnight.[15]

The following day, 28 April, Cadorna was preoccupied with German forces still in Milan. Six groups of factories around the city were fortified and occupied by German troops. During the day, Cadorna succeeded in getting other Germans holed up in the aeronautic barracks and in the House of the Student, a building in central Milan, to surrender, even though the German Command had repeatedly ordered its forces not to give in. Cadorna lined up partisan forces in the evening to attack the factories, but this operation was suspended when Colonel Rauff agreed to renewed negotiations.[16]

On 29 April, the partisans had learned that Daddario was holding Graziani and his fellow generals in the Hotel Milan, and Pertini ordered the partisans to 'bring out' Graziani. They surrounded the hotel and were threatening to kill him. Daddario urged Cadorna by telephone to find a more secure place to hide his prisoners. Cadorna went to the hotel and decided to transfer the generals to the San Vittore jail. As they came out of the hotel, Graziani's long Alfa-Romeo, filled with munitions and hand grenades, blew up, and Lieutenant Bonetti was blinded. Cadorna thought the explosion was an accident but Graziani was convinced the weapons had been set off deliberately. Cadorna and the Italian prisoners finally left the hotel, with a hostile crowd lining either side of the street watching and shouting threats. A partisan on a motorcycle ahead of them shouted: 'Here is Graziani, the betrayer of the country.' Finally, Cadorna managed to get him into a cell at San Vittore, and there Graziani signed a document surrendering all Salò troops to General Willis Crittenberger, commander of the US 4th Army Corps. Convinced he would be killed during the night, Graziani asked for a priest. But Colonel John Fisk of Crittenberger's staff took the prisoners away, and Graziani was eventually transferred to a prisoner-of-war camp in Algeria.[17]

After Graziani had been transferred to the San Vittore jail on 29 April, Cadorna and Daddario opened talks with the Germans to try to persuade them to surrender. They met Rauff and General Wening, the commander of the troops, during the afternoon in the Hotel Regina. Daddario told them it was absurd to continue a useless slaughter, and Cadorna warned that he had enough forces on hand to force them to surrender before Allied reinforcements arrived. The Germans said they understood the desperate nature of their situation, but surrender could only be authorised by Wolff and in writing. Finally, Cadorna agreed to suspend attacks if the Germans ordered retreating troops to halt operations while waiting to surrender to the Allies. He was aware that large, well-armed German troop units from Piedmont and elsewhere were headed into Lombardy; he wanted to buy time to allow the Allies to cut off their escape route. He was particularly worried about the situation at Novara, where the Germans had several tanks. Cadorna and Daddario went to the Edison factory, where a direct phone line still functioned, and persuaded a German colonel there to phone Novara and order the local commander to suspend operations.[18]

On 30 April, Cadorna went to the outskirts of Milan to welcome American troops arriving in the city, and asked a group of women he met there if they were happy over the end of the resistance. 'Yes, we are happy, but they killed him too soon,' one woman replied.

'Who?' asked Cadorna.

One woman shouted: 'Mussolini. They should first have carried him around the city so we could cover him with spit.'[19]

The list of Fascists who were arrested on 27 April at Musso and Dongo numbered fifty-one. After the execution of eighteen of them at Giulino di Mezzegra and Dongo the next day, another eight were killed on succeeding nights. The Allies forced the partisans to hand over the other twenty-five by threatening to bomb Dongo. The remaining Fascists were then either freed or charged and sent to internment camps.[20]

* * *

At 7.30 a.m. on 30 April, Professor Caio Mario Cattabeni and two other doctors carried out an autopsy on Mussolini's body at the Institute of Legal Medicine in Milan. Cattabeni then wrote out in longhand a detailed report on his findings. Part of it was written in the margins of a newspaper page, apparently because of a shortage of paper. Cattabeni said the Duce weighed 11 stone 4½ pounds and was approximately 5ft 3in (1.66 metres) tall. But that could not be determined precisely because the skull had been crushed so badly. One version of Cattabeni's report referred to Mussolini having been struck by nine bullets while still alive, another to seven bullets. Death was immediate, caused by four shots near the heart. One bullet pierced the Duce's right forearm, which by Lampredi's account had been raised to pull back his coat. For every entry there was also an exit wound. Cattabeni was silent on the crucial question of the calibre of bullets that hit Mussolini, which is hardly surprising if all the bullets had left his body. In one of his statements, Audisio claimed his last shot at Mussolini was fatal, severing an aorta. But the autopsy report gave no indication that the aorta had been cut.

No autopsy was conducted on Claretta's body, but it was publicly exhumed on 12 April 1947 at the request of her family. *La Notte*, a Milanese newspaper, reported nine years later, on 10–12 May 1956, that two 9mm bullets were found in her body and experts had determined that one was fired from an automatic pistol and the other from a sub-machine gun.

This report provides perhaps the greatest conundrum of all about the death of Mussolini and Claretta. Audisio, Lampredi and Moretti all said they were killed with a 7.65mm weapon. So how does one account for 9mm bullets in Claretta's body? One possible explanation would be that a *coup de grâce* was administered with 9-calibre weapons after they had been shot with the 7.65mm sub-machine gun. But two 9mm bullets from two different weapons in the same body? It seems unlikely, and none of the witnesses mentioned a *coup de grâce* for Claretta; they said she died instantly. Another possible explanation is that the 'experts' who found the bullets in Claretta's body were wrong in identifying them as 9mm, or the newspaper was wrong. Lampredi's 1972 report made no mention of this matter, and it is unlikely the mystery ever will be resolved.

Bandini, the journalist who found the driver Geninazza, quoted him as saying that Audisio collected cartridge cases from the ground after Mussolini and Claretta had been killed, keeping many for himself but giving five to Geninazza as souvenirs. Bandini also found a woman, Clementina Sironi from Monza, who told him she went to the murder site on the morning of 29 April and gathered up a woman's shoe, a handkerchief, two spent bullets and a cartridge case. Bandini said a ballistics examination showed the bullets all came from a 7.65mm weapon and the cartridge case bore the initials SFM (Société Française des Munitions).[21]

After detailing Mussolini's quite extensive wounds, Cattabeni turned to his internal examination. He found only a small scar from Mussolini's ulcer and, despite all the rumours in the past, no evidence that the Duce had ever suffered from syphilis. Colonel James E. Ash, director of the US Army Institute of Pathology, later read Cattabeni's report and said it indicated there was no organic impairment and Mussolini had been 'unusually healthy' for a man of his age. 'It's a rare individual whose body at autopsy doesn't show more impairment,' he said. The only abnormality that showed up, he said, was a small adhesion linking part of the small intestine with the neck of the gall bladder, which could indicate the Duce had a minor gall bladder problem.[22]

Cattabeni was assisted in his examination by Professors Enea Scolar of the University of Catania and Emanuele D'Abundo of the University of Milan. A fourth person who was present took the decision not to have an autopsy on Claretta's body, and he signed simply 'Guido'. This was initially taken to be Professor Piero Bucalossi, a partisan doctor who used that pseudonym. But some Italian authors suggested this Guido was Lampredi, a point Lampredi did not mention in his report. The body of Claretta was buried in a Milanese cemetery under the name Rita Colfosco, and was only consigned to her family eleven years later. In March 1956 the body was reburied in the Roman cemetery of Verano in a pink marble sarcophagus, surmounted by a statue in white marble.[23]

On 4 May 1945, Major Calvin S. Drayer, a psychiatric consultant with the US Fifth Army, wrote to the CLNAI requesting 'as a great favour' that he be allowed to have a small specimen of Mussolini's brain tissue. His letter said the specimen would be sent to Dr Winfred Overholser, director of St Elizabeth's, a psychiatric hospital in Washington, and would be used for scientific purposes only. The specimen was handed over on 29 May. What happened to it after that will be discussed in Chapter 29.[24]

Chapter 26

THE GERMAN SURRENDER

General Schultz . . . asked for immediate authorisation for an armistice. I gave it.

(*Field Marshal Kesselring, 2 May 1945*)

Just over an hour after the bodies of Mussolini, Claretta and the other Fascists had been hauled down and removed from Piazzale Loreto on the afternoon of 29 April, another historic drama was being played out 450 miles south at Caserta, the Allied command headquarters located in a former royal palace north-east of Naples. There, two German officers put their signatures to a document providing for the surrender of all German forces in Italy and in southern Austria. The war was not yet over, but it was about to be, and getting to this point had proved more difficult than anyone had originally imagined, requiring a great deal of determination and courage, and perhaps an element of luck.

The first hurdle was getting Wolff out of Italy, where the route to Bolzano was blocked by partisans, and back into Switzerland so that he could make his way to Bolzano via Austria. Dulles had told Washington that he might be able to induce Wolff to go to Caserta to sign the surrender, but he thought it was probably better to let him go on to Bolzano because it was essential to keep the generals there in line.[1] He cannot have known at the time just how right he was. Wolff returned to Switzerland in the early hours of 27 April and was met at the Chiasso frontier by Gaevernitz, Waibel and Parrilli. Together they went to the Bristol Hotel in Lugano for a last conference. Wolff reaffirmed to Gaevernitz that he would remain true to the commitments he had made. He also said that if Himmler or his emissaries should be present in the Alto Adige when he returned to Bolzano he would have them arrested; the same was true for any soldier or member of the SS who opposed an order to lay down arms. He had instructed Rauff that in an extreme case the Germans in Milan would surrender to the partisans rather than resort to arms. Zimmer and Husmann accompanied Wolff to the Swiss–Austrian frontier that afternoon. Wolff gave

Husmann two letters, one for Husmann himself, the other for Waibel, thanking them for their work in favour of peace. Parrilli remained in Lugano, and said that after all the tension and sleepless nights behind him he suffered a nervous collapse. He later went to a Lucerne clinic to recover, and was found to have dangerously high blood pressure.[2]

Schweinitz and Wenner, the German officers designated to sign the surrender, had been waiting since 23 April at Waibel's house in Lucerne. They were now cleared to go to Caserta. While Wolff was crossing into Austria on 27 April, they took a train to Bern. The next day they were escorted by Gaevernitz to Annecy, in France, where an Allied plane took them to Caserta. Gaevernitz went along as their interpreter. Wally left for Bolzano, escorted over the Swiss–Austrian border by Zimmer. At Feldkirch he was met by an SS car driven by one of Wolff's men, and he changed into an SS uniform. When he reached Bolzano, he was taken to a small room on the third floor of the palace of the duke of Pistoia, where he set up his radio and was in contact with Caserta by noon on 29 April.[3]

During the flight to Caserta, Schweinitz and Wenner wondered aloud if they would be interned if the negotiations broke down. Their plane arrived at 3 p.m. and was met by Lemnitzer and Airey. There were no handshakes. The two Germans were put into one car for the drive to Allied headquarters, while Gaevernitz travelled with the Allied generals. When they arrived at the gate to the Allied encampment, military police told them they were under instructions from General Airey to admit no one. 'I am General Airey,' he said. It took several phone calls to convince the police to let them enter. Schweinitz and Wenner were assigned to a small bungalow, and the first informal talks took place that afternoon over tea. Airey was under the impression that the Germans were prepared to sign an unconditional surrender and would not try to negotiate terms.

The first official meeting took place in the palace at 6 p.m. with other Allied officers present. The Russians had sent two representatives, who were not included at this stage. They were General A.P. Kislenko and a Lieutenant Vraievskiy, who was to act as his interpreter. Kislenko represented the Soviet General Staff and Vraievskiy was a military intelligence officer and Japanese expert. The Reggia, or royal palace, at Caserta was built in the eighteenth century for the Bourbon king of Naples, Charles III, and is the largest palace in Italy with 1,200 rooms – larger than Versailles. Outside, a long series of pools and cascades climbs up to a fountain depicting the goddess Diana and her attendants, and today newly married Italians often go there to be photographed.

Alexander's chief of staff, Lieutenant-General W.D. Morgan, presided at the talks and presented a lengthy document containing the surrender terms. He said there would be a later meeting at 9 p.m. at which the Russians would be present and the Germans could raise questions. Schweinitz and Wenner appeared shocked by the document, which failed to meet Vietinghoff's three requests – to spare the German army from internment, to allow the troops to go home speedily and to permit officers to keep their side arms. At the second meeting, the Germans made a strong plea to allow the German armies to be demobilised on the spot without internment. They also said side arms for officers were necessary to maintain discipline in the uncertain conditions that would prevail at the time of surrender. And they noted that the document made no provision for motor transport; as it would take two or three weeks to carry out the surrender, transport would be necessary to supply the troops with food. Schweinitz made the further point that they could guarantee the surrender of Italian ports but not German naval vessels stationed there, as these were under navy control. The ports at Trieste and Pola, he said, were under the command of General Loehr, the German commander in the Balkans, and Wolff had no authority there.

The Allies agreed to two of the German requests: motor transport would continue to be used, and officers could keep their side arms until the surrender was complete. But they remained firm in opposing the quick demobilisation and return home of the German troops. The Germans were not happy, and Gaevernitz went back to their bungalow with them for a discussion that went on most of the night. Wenner was ready to sign but Schweinitz felt he could not yield on the internment question. Gaevernitz argued that every minute of delay meant more death, destruction and air raids on German cities. Schweinitz weakened, but insisted that Vietinghoff must be informed. At 4 a.m., they completed the draft of a telegram to Vietinghoff, and Gaevernitz drove to Lemnitzer's office, finding the general still at his desk. The telegram was sent to Bern with a request that it be relayed by courier to Bolzano.

Airey, Lemnitzer and Gaevernitz held an informal meeting with the two Germans on Sunday morning. Airey said they could not wait for Vietinghoff's reply and the signing must take place that day. Schweinitz now agreed to sign, and the ceremony was fixed for 2 p.m. The surrender document covered thirty pages, and Gaevernitz inserted the agreed changes by hand. The third official meeting that afternoon took place in the presence of a small group of American and British correspondents who had been flown from Rome and pledged to secrecy until 2 May, when the surrender would take effect. The Germans were shocked by the presence of the reporters. Schweinitz, still unnerved by what he had agreed to do, declared that he was going beyond his powers and assumed Vietinghoff would accept the terms, but Schweinitz could not be entirely responsible. There was a brief stir in the room until Morgan said: 'I accept.' After signing his name, Schweinitz nervously dropped the pen, spilling a few drops of ink. Both Germans signed five copies of the agreement, then Morgan signed. The proceedings ended at 2.17 p.m. The agreement provided that all hostilities would cease at noon on 2 May, and if there were any sabotage or failure to execute orders, the Allies would proceed in conformity with the laws and practices of war.

Lemnitzer had cabled the surrender text to Dulles in Bern that morning and suggested he get a courier to take it to Vietinghoff. Dulles assigned Captain Tracey Barnes of the OSS to drive to Buchs at the Austrian border, find Zimmer and give him the surrender papers. But Barnes and an aide to Waibel, without consulting Dulles, dreamed up another plan: Barnes would fly from Zurich, parachute into Bolzano and make his way on foot to the German High Command. The weather was so bad that day, however, that flying was out of the question. While Barnes waited, Caserta advised it had made contact with Wally in Bolzano and radioed the terms to him.

Gaevernitz and the two Germans flew back to France at 3 p.m. on 29 April and landed at 7.15 p.m. in Annecy. They crossed into Switzerland but missed the last train from Geneva to Bern and were forced to wait until they could contact a local OSS man who provided them with a car. They reached Dulles's house just before midnight, then about an hour later the Germans left for the Austrian frontier, accompanied by Gaevernitz. Just before 7 a.m., Gaevernitz phoned Dulles from Buchs to say the Swiss had sealed the frontier. Dulles contacted the acting Swiss foreign minister, Walter Stucki, at his home and arranged an immediate meeting in his office. Within minutes, Stucki dispatched orders to allow the Germans to cross the frontier. In Austria, they found that Wolff had a car waiting for them. But Wolff sent word that the Austrian gauleiter Franz Hofer was now siding with Kaltenbrunner, and the Gestapo had orders to arrest the two officers when they passed through Innsbruck. Wolff advised them to take a longer southern route to avoid Innsbruck, even though this meant travelling through some places still deep in snow. Meanwhile Höttl, Kaltenbrunner's man in Italy, contacted Dulles that morning (30 April) to say Kaltenbrunner was in Austria and wished to come to the Swiss frontier to discuss peace terms. Dulles ignored this attempt to invalidate Vietinghoff's surrender.[4]

* * *

Wolff reached Bolzano late in the day on 27 April and found himself in a hornet's nest of intrigue and danger that would persist for several days. Much of what happened to him and the other generals attempting to surrender became known to Dulles only after the war. In Germany on 26 April, Dollmann had met Kesselring, who was about to be appointed by Hitler as commander in chief of all forces in southern Germany and Italy, and told him that Vietinghoff wanted his consent to surrender. Kesselring called Vietinghoff and asked him to meet him the next day at a farm outside Innsbruck belonging to Hofer. Ambassador Rahn also was asked to attend. When Vietinghoff arrived, Kesselring told him he was unaware that the overtures to the Americans, which he had previously approved, had already taken the form of negotiations for surrender. He argued that, as officers, they had to obey orders, which forbade surrender unless there were no other way out, and they had to consider the effect on those German forces still fighting north of the Alps. In any case, he could not agree to surrender as long as Hitler was alive. 'The decision met with no opposition,' Kesselring wrote in his memoirs. 'I had the impression that I had stiffened Vietinghoff's back.' Vietinghoff, disheartened, believed he could no longer carry out the surrender. Roettiger was dismayed and had an angry argument with Vietinghoff, accusing him of a lack of personal courage.[5]

Wolff called a meeting of German generals at 2 a.m. on 28 April. Hofer objected to unconditional surrender and demanded that all German forces in his territory be put under his control. Everyone else at the meeting spoke out against his position, and shortly after daybreak Hofer left in a huff. Later that day, Hitler appointed Kesselring commander in the south. On 29 April, Hofer phoned Kesselring to tell him that German officers had gone to Caserta to sign a surrender and to accuse Wolff and Vietinghoff of high treason. When Roettiger learned of this, he had an angry phone conversation with Hofer. Kesselring, presumably unaware the signing was taking place that day, phoned Roettiger and ordered: 'Fight – don't think about negotiating.' The next morning, he removed Vietinghoff and Roettiger and ordered them to report to a secret command post at Blaupunkt in the Dolomites to face a court martial. Wolff was advised that his case had been turned over to Kaltenbrunner for investigation. Vietinghoff obediently left for the Dolomites, but Roettiger remained in Bolzano.[6]

American bombers attacked Bolzano on the night of 29 April, and some bombs fell within fifty yards of Wolff's headquarters. Wally radioed that information the next day, and Dulles cabled Caserta, asking that Bolzano be spared further attacks. But that night the bombers came again. This time the bombs fell wide of the headquarters building.[7]

In Berlin on the afternoon of 30 April, Hitler blew his brains out in his bunker beneath the Reich Chancellery while his bride, Eva Braun, took poison at his side. Thus, within a span of eighteen days, three of the leading personae of the Second World War had died: Roosevelt a stroke victim, Mussolini executed, Hitler a suicide. Within another eighty-seven days a fourth, Churchill, would be thrown out of office by British voters.

Wolff's wife had now arrived in Bolzano, with numerous family members, and according to Colonel Dollmann was making 'demands of every sort'. He said she and Rahn's wife were in dispute over their respective zones of influence.

Schweinitz and Wenner reached Bolzano shortly after midnight on 1 May and showed Wolff and Roettiger the surrender terms they had accepted. The men who had come to replace Vietinghoff and Roettiger, Generals Schultz and Wenzel, told Wolff they could not issue a cease-fire order without Kesselring's approval. With time running out, Wolff and Roettiger became desperate: a group of military police under their orders surrounded the office of Schultz and Wenzel at 7 a.m. on 1 May and told them they were under arrest. Roettiger assumed supreme command of Army Group C and shut down all telephone and teletype communications with Germany. He phoned Generals Traugott Herr and Joachim Lemelsen, commanders of the 10th and 14th armies, but they balked at the arrests and refused to go along with the surrender. At noon, a colonel rushed in to see Wolff and said the deeply compromised Roettiger was considering shooting himself. Wolff talked him out of it and suggested a change of tactics. Schultz and Wenzel were released and Lemelsen and Pohl talked to them, finally persuading them to accept surrender on the condition that Kesselring give his approval. At 6 p.m. Schultz presided at a general conference that was also attended by Herr, Lemelsen and Pohl. Herr and Lemelsen had brought word that only the parachute corps, consisting of 40,000–50,000 men, was still intact and ready to fight. Tempers flared as the talks went on, and none of the generals had had anything to eat or drink since morning. At 8 p.m, Dollmann had an orderly bring in a large dish of slices of cake. After they had eaten, tempers improved.

Schultz again refused to act without Kesselring's approval, but he and Wenzel agreed to try to bring Kesselring around. He and Wolff phoned Kesselring's headquarters but the field marshal was not available and Wolff spoke to his chief of staff, General Westphal, urging the appointment of a new Army Group commander who would be willing to surrender. Westphal said he would speak to Kesselring and get back to them at 10 p.m. He never called back.[8]

At 8.30 p.m., Alexander radioed Wally asking if the Germans intended to carry out the surrender provisions the next day; otherwise he could not order Allied troops to stop fighting. Wolff sent back a message promising a decision within an hour. At about 10.30 p.m., Herr suddenly turned to a staff officer and told him to pass an order to the 10th Army to cease fire at 2 p.m. the next day. Immediately, Wolff, Pohl and Lemelsen issued the same order to forces under their commands. At 11 p.m. German Radio announced the death of Hitler. Just over an hour later, an order arrived from Germany for the arrest of Pohl and one of his staff officers, but it was ignored. Then at 1.15 a.m. came an order from Kesselring for the arrest of Vietinghoff, Roettiger, Schweinitz and several other officers. Wolff, Herr and Lemelsen left the headquarters but found themselves in a group of threatening Nazi officers and had to return later by secret paths. Wolff learned that a Wehrmacht tank unit had been ordered to surround the headquarters. He brought in 350 SS troops armed with machine guns and seven police tanks supplied by Roettiger, and radioed Caserta to request that Allied paratroops be dropped over Bolzano to protect him and his fellow officers. At 2 a.m., Kesselring rang and told Wolff he had learned the surrender order had gone out. In a conversation that went on for two hours, he denounced Wolff, who appealed to him to join the surrender. Wolff pointed out that surrender would free Allied troops to stop the advance of Russian forces into Western Europe, counter Tito's threat to Trieste and put down any Communist uprising in northern Italy. Kesselring, having said five days earlier he would consider surrender when Hitler was dead, promised to call back in a half hour with his decision. It was then 4 a.m. He phoned Schultz at 4.30 with his approval, and withdrew his earlier arrest orders. In his memoirs, Kesselring said: 'My chief of staff reported to me that General Schultz considered any further resistance by his utterly defeated armies useless and asked for immediate authorisation for an armistice. I gave it.'[9]

Wolff radioed Caserta at noon with a message in Kesselring's name, subscribing to surrender but stipulating there should be no public announcement for another forty-eight hours. Caserta advised that the earlier cease-fire orders already had been radioed to the German Tenth and Fourteenth Armies, and there could be no further delay. Kesselring had wanted the extra time to withdraw German troops in Yugoslavia and the Istrian peninsula so that they would not be forced to surrender to the Yugoslavs or Russians. Rahn arrived in Bolzano early that morning and felt it was important that Kesselring reinstate Vietinghoff in command since the surrender had been signed in Vietinghoff's name. Kesselring grudgingly gave in, and Vietinghoff broadcast the news of the surrender to his troops. The 1st and 2nd Parachute Divisions continued fighting for a time, but Vietinghoff renewed his order and they also surrendered. It was just before 5 p.m. Swiss time, 2 May, when Dulles learned that hostilities had ceased. A half million German troops had laid down their arms.[10]

The partisans staged an uprising in the Alto Adige that night, and Bruno De Angelis, their military commander, went to Wolff to demand that he hand over administration of the Alto Adige to the CLNAI. Wolff coldly replied that the surrender agreement did not provide for this, and he would give powers to the German-speaking majority in the province that was in league with

Gauleiter Hofer. De Angelis exploded. He said the fight would continue, Wolff would be responsible and he would be declared a war criminal. Wolff backed down, and Roettiger agreed with De Angelis that control of the Alto Adige would be transferred to him. Wolff signed a paper to this effect without comment, and got Vietinghoff to sign also. De Angelis later became prefect of the province.[11]

One happy result of the surrender was that Wolff had managed to save from destruction, and from Hermann Göring's greed, a considerable number of Italian works of art. Many pieces from the Italian royal house, including busts of the Caesars, the Habsburg emperors and the Savoy kings, as well as King Victor Emmanuel's valuable stamp collection, were stored in sealed cases in the basement of the royal villa at Bolzano. Hofer had also hidden there cases that had been sent to him by Hitler's adjutant Martin Bormann. They contained gold watches with Hitler's signature, which he intended to give to his faithful servants, and gold and silver cigarette cases, as well as pearl necklaces, emeralds from India and diamonds from Brazil.

Hundreds of art works from Florence and other cities were stored in the Alpine valleys just below the Austrian border, near San Leonardo di Pasiria and Campo Tures. So many crates of priceless paintings were taken to Campo Tures from the Uffizi and Pitti Galleries in Florence that they were found piled high in a garage when the Allies and Italian authorities recovered them. Other stolen Italian works were found in a salt mine near Salzburg. Altogether, the Germans looted about 3,600 paintings in Italy and thousands of other art objects. Many were traced and brought back to Italy by the country's famed art detective, Rodolfo Siviero, who had worked with the British and free Italian secret services during the war. Siviero, the '007 of art', died in 1983. In 1996, the Italian government published a list of 1,512 items still missing, some of which may have been destroyed by Allied bombing. One British artillery officer, Anthony Clarke, ordered to bombard San Sepolcro during the war, suddenly remembered that the little town contained 'the most beautiful painting in the world', Piero della Francesca's *Resurrection*, and saved it for posterity.

In his history of the German presence in Italy, Colonel Dollmann gave primary credit for the successful outcome of the surrender negotiations to Parrilli. 'Northern Italy, Senator Ferruccio Parri and with him an infinite number of other people, detained or already sentenced, owe gratitude to Baron Luigi Parrilli,' he wrote. 'I would say that all Western Europe owes gratitude to this able, tireless, fearless Neapolitan.' By helping to hasten the surrender, he said, Parrilli also ensured that the Allies beat the Yugoslav partisans of Tito to Trieste, and thus saved the city from Communist takeover.[12]

The German surrender won widespread acclaim for Dulles, but not all his OSS colleagues were impressed. Captain Max Corvo, who played a key role with the Italian resistance, said Dulles was given exaggerated credit for ending the war, as the disintegration of German resistance meant the war 'had already ended in Italy before the surrender was signed'. This criticism was grossly unfair; the surrender negotiations ensured a more orderly end to the war than otherwise would have been the case, and helped prevent wholesale German destruction of northern Italian infrastructure. But another of Corvo's observations was more to the point. He said an OSS team had been parachuted into Bolzano before Dulles sent Little Wally there, and this team was transmitting appeals from Vietinghoff to General Mark Clark to send emissaries to Bolzano to accept his surrender before Wally began operating. Corvo said officials in Caserta paid little attention to these messages because they were busy with the details of the surrender Dulles had brokered. A few days after the surrender, Dulles showed up unannounced in Milan, and Corvo and a fellow Italo-American, Vincent Scamporino, found him 'insufferable'. Corvo said Dulles's 'autocratic and patronising attitude' caused Scamporino to lose his temper and tell him off in no uncertain terms. Shortly after, Scamporino and Corvo were transferred back to Washington.[13]

* * *

In the week that elapsed between Mussolini's departure from Milan on 25 April and the surrender, partisans staged uprisings all across northern Italy, with Genoa and then Milan the first to fall. One of the bloodiest last-ditch battles was fought in Turin, where workers rose up at dawn on 26 April and met ferocious resistance that was only overcome the next day when the first partisan divisions arrived. There were several hundred deaths in the battle for Turin. Giuseppe Solaro, the Fascist Party leader in Turin and a former cavalry officer noted for his cruelty, was captured and the new regional government sentenced him to be hanged publicly on a site where four partisans had been hanged on 22 July 1944. Terrified, Solaro fell to his knees and said he was an anti-Fascist and a Socialist. The rope that was to hang him was tied to the branch of a plane tree, but the branch broke and he fell to the ground with his hands tied behind his back. There were conflicting versions of what happened next. One was that he was strung up a second time and hanged, the other that his head was smashed in with a club by the father of one of the partisans who had been hanged on the same spot.

After the partisans had won the battle for Turin, the regional government said there were so many dead bodies around that it was forced to throw some in the Po. Solaro's was among them. In Venice, partisans rose up on the night of

26 April, and the CLN took control of the city on 28 April. The German commander was persuaded to withdraw after first threatening to shell the city from the Lido. Partisans in Padua staged an insurrection on 27 April that eventually cost them 400 dead and wounded. Most Fascists surrendered or fled, but the Germans fought back before they eventually abandoned the city.[14]

With victory secured, anti-Fascists began hunting down and killing their enemies across northern Italy. In Milan alone during the first few days after liberation, the Allies reported they found a dozen or more bodies in the streets nightly. Revenge killings were the most numerous in Piedmont. Fascists later claimed the death toll throughout Italy amounted to 300,000, but Giorgio Bocca, one of the historians of the Salò Republic and a partisan fighter, said that was 'an absurd figure'. He estimated the true number was no higher than 18,000. Equally absurd was the estimate of postwar Interior Minister Mario Scelba, who said in 1952 that just 2,344 people were killed in the insurrectionary period. Other authorities have put the figure at 30,000, some as high as 40,000.

Estimates of the number of partisan deaths in the war vary, but not by much. Luigi Longo said 76,500 partisans and 'patriots' died in battle or after capture (some former Italian soldiers who fought with the partisans preferred to be known as patriots). Leo Valiani of the CLNAI gave a figure of 60,000 partisan deaths. Max Salvadori of the British Special Forces said 45,000 to 50,000 were killed in battle or as prisoners, and not fewer than 10,000 civilians were killed for helping the partisans. Of these, up to 9,000 were deported and died in German extermination camps. Another 2,000 Italians were killed fighting with the French resistance, and Salvadori said 90,000 Italian regular soldiers were killed fighting Germans in Italy, the Balkans and the Aegean Islands after the Badoglio government surrendered in 1943. Whatever the correct figure, the partisan losses were extremely high for a force that was relatively modest in size. Longo put partisan strength at 462,000, but most authorities suggested it was never much higher than 200,000. Palmiro Togliatti estimated in November 1944 that partisans numbered 100,000 to 120,000, but there was a surge in membership in the spring of 1945, the closing weeks of the war.[15]

Ferruccio Parri, who had been among the leaders of the CLNAI, gave his critical assessment of the partisan movement in a postwar speech in Rome. 'In the partisan movement there were the good and the bad, the heroes and the looters, the generous and the cruel. There was a people with its virtues and its vices. There were the partisans of the eleventh hour, in general a detestable race. And then the exploiters and profiteers of the partisan movement.'[16]

Field Marshal Alexander said Allied casualties in the Italian campaign totalled 312,000 against German losses of 536,000. General Eisenhower said in his war memoirs that the Italian front absorbed German forces who could have been more usefully employed elsewhere. But Colonel Emilio Canevari, a pro-German Italian Fascist, said the opposite was true: 'The heavy American involvement signified the triumph of Kesselring who . . . without tanks, without planes, without petrol and with transport reduced to vehicles drawn by oxen and horses, knew how to tie down the huge Anglo-American force for twenty months . . .'. The Allies, he said, should have used the forces that fought in Italy in the Balkans instead, and thereby held back Russian expansion in Eastern Europe.[17]

Parri, who had been the Italian representative of an American radio firm in Milan before the war, became Italy's first postwar prime minister. Described by Dollmann as 'a man of limited intelligence', he was unable to cope with the huge array of postwar problems, controlling inflation and the black market, settling regional differences and dealing with a Fascist remnant in government. He lasted only until December, when a new government was formed under the little-known Christian Democrat Alcide De Gasperi, who came to be regarded as one of Italy's outstanding postwar leaders.

The government called a referendum on the monarchy in June 1946, and a month beforehand the unpopular King Victor Emmanuel read the writing on the wall and abdicated, going into exile in Egypt. Umberto II reigned until just 12 June. Italians voted by a nearly 55 per cent majority in favour of a republic, and Umberto left for Portugal on 13 June.[18]

Chapter 27

LAKESIDE MURDERS AND THE DONGO TREASURE

All this will be consigned to the Communist Party because it is the only one that helped us during the entire struggle.

(Giuseppina Tuissi, partisan, speaking of money and jewels seized from Fascists, 28 April 1945)

In the days that followed Mussolini's capture, a vast quantity of Italian and foreign currency, jewellery and other valuable objects that had been seized from him and other Fascists disappeared. In all, this amounted to valuables worth perhaps tens of billions of lire, according to a magistrate who investigated the disappearance. The valuables, which came to be known as the Dongo Treasure, were never found. But all the available evidence pointed to one conclusion: they were, for the most part, stolen by the Italian Communist Party. There were rumours at the time, later confirmed by a Communist official, that the party used this unexpected wealth to buy the building in Via delle Botteghe Oscure in Rome that became its national headquarters. Many Italians still refer to the building as Palazzo Dongo. The disappearance of the valuables was followed by a string of murders, some of which appeared to have been aimed at silencing those who threatened to reveal the thefts. The Como police chief attributed the killings to a secret military unit in the Communist Party. Among those killed were three of the people who had participated in the operation of transferring Mussolini and Claretta Petacci to the De Maria house in the early hours of 28 April: Luigi Canali, Giuseppina Tuissi and Giuseppe Frangi.

As was noted in Chapter 22, on 27 April Urbano Lazzaro confiscated from Mussolini and another Fascist, Vito Casalinuovo, two cases containing documents and money. The Duce's case contained cheques totalling 1,150,000 lire and 160 gold sovereigns. Lazzaro deposited the two cases in a bank at Domaso, a village just north of Dongo. The partisans later discovered that the Germans escorting Mussolini, who surrendered north of Dongo, had thrown into a river three sacks weighing nearly eighty pounds that contained wedding rings, medals, earrings and other jewellery, all donated to the Fascist government by patriotic women at the time of the Ethiopian war in 1935. These sacks were recovered by two fishermen. Two other Germans traveling in an expensive model Fiat also were stopped just outside Domaso and found to be carrying 33 million lire in cash, including 1,020,000 lire that was discovered in a search of their baggage.

Captain Ernst Kummel and Second Lieutenant Andreas Hess consigned this money to Alois Hoffmann, a Swiss citizen living at Domaso, and tried to make a deal with him: if he would give one-third each to their two Italian mistresses they were leaving behind, he could keep the other third for himself. Hoffmann ran to inform Lazzaro, then hid the money in the basement of his villa in Domaso. Lazzaro deposited the funds in the Domaso bank on 28 April.[1]

This was just a part of the valuables that subsequently disappeared. Finance Minister Pellegrini-Giampietro had withdrawn 200 million lire in state funds, and during Mussolini's stop in Como on the night of 25/6 April this money was distributed among various government ministers. Virtually all the Fascists who were in the convoy at Musso on 27 April were travelling with bags and suitcases stuffed with jewels and money as well as clothes with which they hoped to make their escape. Some of their belongings were stolen by local people after their capture, but a great deal ended in the hands of partisans. Interior Minister Paolo Zerbino alone carried 1,170,000 lire, 250,000 Swiss francs (most of which disappeared), 40,000 Spanish pesetas and some gold.

Another significant sum was carried by Rose Marie Mittag, the German wife of Minister of Public Works Ruggero Romano, whom Mittag had left behind at Musso while she went on with the German convoy. She later tried to enter Switzerland, with many of her valuables concealed beneath her dress to make her appear pregnant, but she was turned back and her belongings were seized by a partisan unit. They took from her 1,660,000 lire and a large supply of US dollars, pounds sterling, French and Swiss francs and gold coins, among other things. In 1957, just as a trial concerning the Dongo Treasure was about to begin, Mittag committed suicide by throwing herself from the balcony of her home in Rome. One inventory of valuables taken from government ministers listed 145 pounds of gold, 1,150 gold sterling coins, 147,000 Swiss francs, 160,000 French francs, 10,000 Spanish pesetas and smaller amounts of British, US and Portuguese banknotes. Another report said ministers had 87 million lire in their baggage.[2]

At the Dongo town hall, Lazzaro compiled and signed a five-page typed list of all the objects recovered at Musso and Dongo. After Audisio's departure on the evening of 28 April with the sixteen bodies of those executed at Dongo, Lazzaro saw on a table a rectangular jewel case tied with two ribbons and a metal strongbox for which there was no key. He forced it open and found it contained a large hoard of gold coins, pesetas and Swiss francs, as well as diamonds, jewel-encrusted watches and other valuables. Giuseppina Tuissi, who was with him, counted 76,000 Swiss francs. Lazzaro said she pointed to his inventory and said: 'All this will be consigned to the Communist Party, because it is the only one that helped us during the entire struggle.'[3]

On 2 May, Lazzaro withdrew from the Domaso bank everything he had deposited there, except for 3,020,000 lire that was intended to cover expenses of the 52nd Garibaldi Brigade and local CLNs. The partisans were apparently afraid that the money and other valuables would be stolen or seized by the Allies. They gave this hoard to Don Carlo Gusmaroli, the parish priest of Gera Lario, a village at the northern tip of Lake Como, and he hid it behind the altar of his church. Bellini delle Stelle, Lazzaro and the partisan Antonio Scappin went to see General Cadorna in Milan to inform him of the valuables they had found and to arrange to hand them over. Cadorna agreed to the arrangements.[4] What happened next is outlined by Como Police Chief Davide Grassi in a secret report to postwar Prime Minister Alcide De Gasperi on 16 December, 1945. The report was made public much later.

Grassi said a Como-based employee of the Bank of Italy, accompanied by a police officer, went to Domaso to collect the valuables. 'But with the excuse that it was already evening, the handover was put off until the next morning,' he said. When morning came, the two men were told the valuables had been given to the Communist Michele Moretti (previously named as one of the possible killers of Mussolini) to take to Cadorna's office. Grassi interviewed Moretti's driver, Carlo Maderna, who told him they had driven to Como and stopped the car near a luggage shop owned by Remo Mentasti, a Communist organiser and close friend of Dante Gorreri, the Communist leader in Como. Maderna claimed he was made to go away on a pretext, and when he returned a half hour later the valuables had disappeared. Shortly afterwards, Moretti also disappeared, and he was charged with the theft of state property.[5]

On 7 May, Luigi Canali, a Communist partisan who had been among those escorting Mussolini and Claretta to the De Maria house, disappeared and was never seen again. Grassi said he was killed in Milan 'on the orders of a certain Fabio of the Communist Party' because he had objected to the theft of funds and threatened to reveal what had happened. Canali, who was married, and his lover Tuissi had been arrested in early 1945 by Fascists, but he escaped and later there were rumours that the two of them, under torture, had revealed the names of partisan leaders. They were sentenced to death by the partisans but the sentence was later revoked.

The writer Giorgio Cavalleri said that on 4 May Canali had a furious argument with Gorreri, who had returned from Switzerland six days earlier. Gorreri also had been a Fascist prisoner, and Canali accused him of having revealed names to the Fascists in exchange for a promise to let him flee to Switzerland, then had circulated rumours that Canali was the one who had talked. The partisan Giovanni Tinelli told the newspaper *Il Tempo* on 14 July 1950 that he had witnessed a quarrel in the Como Communist offices in which Gorreri and Moretti had opposed Canali's wish to hand the Dongo Treasure to the state. At a trial in Padua in 1957, Remo Mentasti testified that a Communist gunman, Dionisio Gambaruto, told him on 7 May 1945 that he was awaiting orders of his superiors to shoot Canali. Canali's body was never found, and there were conflicting rumours about what had happened to it: shot at night before car headlights and buried in a cemetery in Milan, thrown into Lake Como, walled up in a building in Milan.[6]

Tuissi vowed to find out who had killed him. A prominent Communist, Pietro Vergani, told her on 9 May that Canali had been executed in the mountains by a partisan unit. 'And if you don't be quiet, I will see that you meet the same end,' he said. But she continued her enquiries, and at the end of May she and Canali's mother Maddalena went to see Ferruccio Lanfranchi, a reporter for *Corriere d'Informazione* in Milan, and Tuissi told him she had a receipt for 280 million lire worth of valuables she had consigned to the Communist Party Federation in Como. She said Canali had opposed the theft of the funds by the party. On 23 June, her twenty-second birthday, she was shot dead near Cernobbio as she was bicycling from Dongo to Como. A young couple hidden by a thicket near the road said later that they heard her shouting and pleading for her life, then heard gunshots and the sound of a motorcycle roaring away. Tuissi's body was thrown in the lake with bullet wounds extending from her abdomen to her throat.[7]

Grassi's report blamed her killing on a partisan called Captain Lince (real name Dino Casinelli) and a man named Maurizio Bernasconi. Lince's band was notorious for having carried out thefts, kidnappings and homicides. Anna Maria Bianchi, a stenographer at the Dongo police headquarters, was a friend of Tuissi's and had spoken to her about the Dongo Treasure. On 5 July, Bianchi's body was recovered from the lake, with two pistol shots to the neck and signs that she had been beaten on her arms and legs. Her father Michele, a Communist, went to the spot where her body was found and threatened to go to the authorities with what he knew. That evening, he was seen being taken away in a small car, and a few days later he was found dead near Cernobbio with two pistol shots to the neck.[8]

Giuseppe Frangi, one of the two sailors who had guarded the prisoners in the De Maria house, was also killed in mysterious circumstances, his body found on 5 May on the bank of the Albano river that empties into Lake Como in the centre of Dongo. Just before the end of the war, four of his comrades had been killed by members of the Black Brigades, and there was one theory that his comrades killed him because they could not tolerate the brutal violence he subsequently used against Fascist prisoners. Another theory was that he was killed by a partisan whom he had accused of giving information to the Fascists.

Grassi's report said there had been 'numerous other homicides or disappearances of people' linked to the disappearance of the Dongo Treasure. 'One can deduce that a very vast and important organisation wants at any cost to maintain the most absolute secrecy around the actual destination of the gold,' he wrote. 'There exists a secret military organisation of the [Communist] party in very close relations with the Russian mission in Milan. They have hidden very many arms, including heavy weapons such as mortars, cannon, machine guns and sub-machine guns.' Grassi said the head of this organisation was Fabio, and Fabio had infiltrated his men into the Como police force – among them a Commander Vinci and Deputy Commander Invernizzi, 'who go at least once a week to the Russian mission'. Grassi said Fabio was Luigi Longo, an identification that would later be disputed.[9]

Grassi's report remained buried for more than a year. The Communists were then serving in De Gasperi's government, and the prime minister may have concluded that keeping his coalition together was of overriding importance. But in 1947, his Christian Democrats and the Communists began feuding, and De Gasperi would expel the Communists from government before the 1948 election. Questions about the Dongo Treasure began to emerge. Longo told *L'Unità* that 'the Dongo Treasure was invented many months after the Liberation'. In early 1947, General Leone Zingales, a military prosecutor entrusted with conducting an inquiry into the events at Dongo, concluded that the missing valuables ended up at the Communist Party in Milan, and the amount stolen exceeded by far the 33 million lire in cash and the gold weighing nearly eighty pounds that had been deposited in Domaso.

He established that these funds arrived at Dongo with the fleeing Fascists and their German escort: 286 million lire from the Bank of Italy in Milan, 310 million from the Bank of Lavoro, 334 million taken at gunpoint by Fascists at the Bank of Novara, 50 million that represented the funds of the Muti Legion, 100 million belonging to the German Navy and more than 50 million belonging to the Luftwaffe. He listed larger sums found in the luggage of the Fascist ministers and estimated the total booty at tens of billions of lire. On 10 February, 1947, Zingales filed charges against Moretti,

Maderna, Mentasti and another partisan named Pietro Terzi, accusing them of the theft of war booty.[10]

Moretti could not be found, but Como Carabinieri arrested Terzi and Mentasti. Maderna, whose nickname was Scassamacchine (car thief), initially escaped, but then went to his mother's home and was arrested there. Terzi testified that in mid-May 1945, he had heard Moretti say he had given all the Dongo Treasure 'to a higher command', which gave him a receipt for it. Terzi also claimed that the Musso partisan leader Davide Barbiere took home some of the money taken from Fascist *gerarchi* and later built a sumptuous villa. Maderna testified that on 2 May 1945, he drove Moretti to Como with 30 million lire wrapped in canvas and a sealed box containing the nearly eighty pounds of gold, and they unloaded it at Mentasti's house. He said Moretti instructed him to say, if he were later arrested, that he had gone to the Como military command to hand over some letters, and when he returned to the car he found the valuables missing.[11]

In an interview published in 1993, Communist Party treasurer Alfredo Bonelli confirmed the Dongo Treasure had been appropriated by the party. Because of the sharp devaluation of the lira after the war, he said, the Communist leadership decided temporarily to invest the money in property in Milan, but later sold it and used the proceeds to build the party headquarters in Rome, to buy a printing plant for *L'Unità* and to acquire a building to host party officials visiting from outside Rome. Remo Mentasti, the Como luggage store owner to whose shop much of the treasure was taken after the war, wrote a memoir in which he said he turned the treasure over to a partisan named Eugenio Tagliabue who came to him with a note from Gorreri. He said he later learned that a sack and strongbox left with him contained the gold objects thrown into the river by the Germans, as well as millions of lire. Some years later he was arrested and accused of appropriating 33 million lire and 77 pounds of gold that were state property. He was imprisoned in Milan for three months, and was then released.[12]

On the evening of 14 March 1947, another killing apparently related to the events at Dongo occurred. Franco De Agazio, editor of the neo-Fascist *Meridiano d'Italia*, was shot dead outside his office. He had been looking into the question of the Dongo Treasure over the previous six months and had been preparing to publish a series of articles about Canali and Tuissi. Urbano Lazzaro, the partisan 'Bill' who captured Mussolini, was convinced, however, that the real target of the killing was himself. He had emerged from the office a half hour earlier than De Agazio, heavily bundled up because of a bad cold, and the killer, he concluded, having failed to recognise him, shot De Agazio by mistake.[13]

Lazzaro said there were two other definite attempts to kill him in September and October 1945, both of which he attributed to Communists. One evening a friend came to visit him at his apartment in Como and, passing through a nearby garden, was approached by two armed men who seized him and took him down to the lake to kill him. But a lamp shone on his friend's face and one of the would-be killers exclaimed: 'But this isn't Bill!' They released their prisoner, who ran to Lazzaro. 'I gave him a cognac, then took a pistol and went outside but I didn't find them,' Lazzaro said. On another occasion, he claimed, he was going to visit a friend and while he waited at the door of his friend's house, a man on a motorbike fired several shots at him. 'I am short, and the bullets went over my head,' he said. Como Prefect Virginio Bertinelli, who later became employment minister in the Italian government, suggested that Lazzaro go to Switzerland for several months at municipal expense and stay at a secret location arranged by Bertinelli. But Lazzaro refused to go into hiding.[14]

As accusations against the Communists surfaced in 1947, Luigi Longo tried to counter them at a rally in Milan. He accused the Fascists of stealing the treasure and said most of it ended in the hands of industrialists who had collaborated with the Salò Republic. He admitted a part of the treasure was 'captured, and therefore saved, by the partisans', and this money served in part to help pay the expenses of various partisan commands and the costs of partisan demobilisation. At the end of March, Pietro Vergani presented himself to magistrates, identifying himself as Fabio and taking responsibility for the disappearance of the treasure. Vergani, former head of the Lombard Communist Party, said he came into possession of valuables seized by partisans and used the money for the expenses of demobilisation. Was Vergani, not Longo, the Fabio named in Grassi's 1945 report? Both Grassi and Bertinelli had identified Longo as Fabio, but his usual *nom de guerre* was Gallo.[15]

General Zingales, the military prosecutor who investigated the disappearance of the Dongo Treasure, came to Rome in March 1947 to deliver a forty-page report on his findings to the Justice Ministry. The morning after his arrival, he was awakened by police, who informed him there had been a theft and fire at the ministry during the night. His report was missing, but he had kept a copy. On 15 March, the ministry's chief of prosecutions, Borsari, announced that Zingales was being replaced because the term of his appointment had expired. Zingales was offered another post but resigned on 18 March, saying: 'The treatment recently accorded me offends my dignity as a magistrate and demolishes the work undertaken by me.'[16]

The Christian Democrats triumphed in the 1948 election, and afterwards the inquiry into the Dongo Treasure and the killings associated with it gained impetus. Dionisio Gambaruto, the Communist gunman, was arrested and accused of murdering Canali. Gambaruto was also widely suspected of having killed De Agazio. Dante Gorreri, the Como Communist leader, was arrested in February 1949 and accused of fraud and homicide for having ordered the execution of Canali, Tuissi and Anna Maria Bianchi. Charges also were pending against Vergani. But in the election of 1954, Gorreri and Vergani were elected as Communist members of parliament and given parliamentary immunity. Both were re-elected in 1958, 1963 and 1968, and a request by magistrates for authorisation to proceed against them afterwards was not acted upon. On 11 April 1952, a Milanese prosecutor absolved Gambaruto of charges of having killed De Agazio.

Magistrates nonetheless opened a trial at Padua on 29 April 1957 concerning the Dongo events. An investigating magistrate had had fifty-one people charged, of whom thirty-four were arrested. Audisio, Gorreri and Vergani were all protected by immunity, and Audisio testified at the trial. But in July it was interrupted when Judge Silvio Andrighetti fell ill. He died on 19 August and there were unsubstantiated rumours that he had committed suicide or had been poisoned. The trial did not proceed, and on 2 June 1959, the government issued a wide-ranging amnesty that covered many of the crimes for which those under arrest had been charged. All crimes in question were covered by a further amnesty on 26 May 1970.[17]

In later years, many of the Communists involved in the events of 1945 said in interviews that they believed Canali and Tuissi had been killed unjustly by fellow Communists. This was officially recognised in May 1991 by the party that succeeded to the Communists, the Democratic Party of the Left, when its Como branch asked that a street, piazza or school in the town be named for Canali and Tuissi, 'victims of a violence that many of the protagonists themselves defined as unjust and illegal'.[18]

So much for the Dongo Treasure and the murders that followed. What about the documents Mussolini was carrying when he was arrested?

Chapter 28

THE MYSTERIOUS CHURCHILL FILE

After the period of struggle and persecutions, these papers absolutely must see the light.

(Benito Mussolini on his personal archive, February 1945)

Just as the money and other valuables that Mussolini and his fellow Fascists carried with them on their flight from Milan largely disappeared, so did some of the Duce's documents. This has given rise to a huge amount of speculation in Italy over the years as to their contents. The most sensational claim, repeated in numerous books and articles, is that Mussolini carried a file of his correspondence with Churchill, some of it conducted secretly when their two nations were at war. Outside Italy, historians without exception have dismissed this speculation and given it scant mention, for good reason: there is a lack of firm evidence to support it, and the idea of Churchill exchanging letters with Mussolini behind the backs of his Allies while Britain and Italy were at war is on the face of it absurd. This has not stopped some Italians from embellishing the tale with wildly improbable details and selling these fantasies to the Italian public. It has all the hallmarks of a historical *giallo*, the Italian term for a crime thriller, but not a very fascinating one because it lacks an essential element of any decent thriller: credibility.

As has been noted previously, Mussolini carried a leather case of documents that was taken from him at Dongo by Urbano Lazzaro on 27 April and deposited in a bank at nearby Domaso the following day. The Duce put other documents into a small truck that left Milan in his convoy on the evening of 25 April but broke down along the way. He was evidently distressed by that loss, but attached greater importance to the documents he carried with him, telling Lazzaro that they were 'of great historical importance'. Lazzaro said the documents were in four files, headed 'Confidential to Benito Mussolini. Secret', 'Umberto di Savoia' (referring to the crown prince), 'Verona trial' and

'Hitler–Mussolini correspondence'. The 'Confidential' file contained assorted newspaper clippings, reports on discussions with the Swiss representative Troendle about a possible Swiss refuge for Fascist families, reports on the situation in Trieste and similar matters.

Travelling aboard the truck that carried documents from Milan were Maria Righini, the personal maid of the Duce; her husband; and a political police officer, Emilio Barsotti. When the truck broke down, they hitched a lift to Como and reported to Mussolini's secretary, Luigi Gatti, who left immediately with three other men to try to recover the documents, which were in a strongbox that was later found to have been forced open and abandoned. Some of the documents were intact but others clearly had been taken from the box. The documents that were found were turned over to the Italian state in 1945 and 1946, and they concerned the Verona trial, government relations with the Vatican, the trial of the men accused of killing the Socialist leader Giacomo Matteotti and the 8 September surrender by the Badoglio government.[1]

As for the documents taken from Mussolini, they were withdrawn from the Domaso bank and hidden in the church at Gera Lario, along with the money and jewels. Lazzaro and Bellini delle Stelle wanted to hand the documents over to members of the CVL in Milan and not solely to General Cadorna. As Bellini delle Stelle explained: 'This is because it worried us to hand to a monarchical general papers that could be exploited in favour of the monarchy.' Most accounts say the documents were handed over on 4 May. Cadorna told a different story. He said two officers of the Finance Guards, Colonel Alfredo Malgeri and an aide named Nanci, came to him on 3 May to say they had taken possession of the documents and wanted them to be given to the government, not to a political party. He said Nanci returned later with Bellini delle Stelle and they renewed the offer of the documents. Cadorna said they were delivered to him on 17 May, and after making a list of the contents he had them all sent on to the Ministry of War in Rome. 'From a summary examination, I did not have the impression there were documents of particular importance,' he wrote. The documents were microfilmed by the British and American governments, and on 2 July 1945, the American military newspaper *Stars and Stripes* reported that the 'voluminous personal correspondence' of Mussolini was being examined at Allied headquarters in Caserta. It said the documents were considered 'of extreme importance', but their publication appeared improbable, at least for the moment.[2]

In April 1950, photocopies of some of these documents were published in *L'Unità*. The originals ended up in the Central Archive of the State in Rome – except for the file on Umberto, which apparently referred to the Prince's private life and allegations of homosexuality. That file was never seen again.[3]

Further information about the Mussolini documents was contained in an anonymous report in the Communist Party archives that only came to light in 1996 when the archives were placed in the Istituto Gramsci in Rome and opened to the public. The report was discovered by reporters for *L'Unità*. It is impossible to verify the statements contained in it without knowing who wrote it. *L'Unità* speculated that it may have been written by an informer of the partisan police or by Michele Moretti, the Communist whose gun was used to kill Mussolini.[4]

The report said Mussolini's leather case and that of Casalinuovo contained 'documents of the utmost national importance'. When Lazzaro deposited the cases in the Domaso bank, it continued, each was wrapped in packing paper and tied with a cord, and the seal of the bank was placed on it. Mussolini's case weighed nearly 12 pounds and Casalinuovo's weighed 10.56 pounds. Also deposited in the bank, according to the report, was an envelope containing the various cheques Mussolini carried, amounting to 1.7 million lire, and an envelope containing his 160 pounds sterling. Each envelope also bore the seal of the bank.

The report said Lazzaro withdrew these documents on 2 May and gave them to Bellini delle Stelle, who in turn gave them to Antonio Scappin, the Finance Guard who had worked with the partisans, and ordered him to hide them in a safe place. Scappin took them on 3 or 4 May to Don Gusmaroli, the parish priest in Gera Lario. Gusmaroli told the author of the report that, around 13 or 14 May, he received a visit from Lazzaro, Bellini delle Stelle and Scappin, who wanted to examine the documents. Gusmaroli brought the packages to his study, where in the presence of the priest the three men cut the cords and broke the seals, then asked Gusmaroli to step outside the room. He said he waited more than half an hour, then was called in and found all the material was now wrapped in just one package, which the three men took away immediately.

The report's author obtained conflicting accounts from Bellini delle Stelle and Lazzaro – the first saying the documents were repackaged in the study and sealed there with the bank's seal, Lazzaro saying the package was taken to a locality he could not remember, and there the documents were repackaged, tied and sealed with the stamp of the bank. 'At this point,' the report noted, 'one has to ask from whom they have had the stamp of the bank and why have they used it when the packages were put together outside the bank.' The report offered no answer to this question, but the author Giorgio Cavalleri, in a book written in 1995, a year before the report surfaced, said Luiselena Rumi, daughter of the Domaso bank director Luigi Rumi, permitted Lazzaro and Bellini delle Stelle to return to the bank to reseal the envelopes they opened. The anonymous report found by *L'Unità* implied that the Rumis had collaborated in a plot to extract from the documents a report by a police officer named Beneduce on an alleged attempt by Crown Prince Umberto to commit 'acts of sexual deviance' with him. The report said Scappin confided to Father Gusmaroli that he had gone to Rome and had spoken directly with Umberto. Later that year, 1945, Luigi Rumi received the title of *cavaliere* (knight) from the royal house. Cavalleri said in his book that Lazzaro was 'of proven monarchical faith', implying that he arranged for the compromising document on Umberto to be given to the crown prince.

The anonymous report said that Bellini delle Stelle instructed Scappin to take the repackaged documents to Milan and hand them over to the General Command of the CVL, but instead, on the advice of Moretti, Scappin gave them to the partisan military command in Como on 16 May. Moretti told a somewhat different story to Cavalleri. He said he and the Finance Guard Giorgio Buffelli, not Scappin, took the documents to Milan on 4 May. Buffelli was about to hand them over to the General Command when Moretti intervened and returned to Como with the documents, handing them to the Communist Party. According to Moretti, that night many of the documents were photocopied. Both reports, of course, were at variance with Cadorna's, which stated that Cadorna received documents on 17 May and forwarded them to the government in Rome, but Cavalleri's book suggested that Cadorna received documents from the truck that broke down, not the documents Mussolini carried. The anonymous report indicated that many of the Mussolini documents were missing when the package arrived in Como. It quoted Lazzaro as saying there had been about 350 documents, but at the Como command, where the documents were photographed by three or four persons working together, there were just twenty-seven letters and documents, covering 72½ pages. Lazzaro had said the Mussolini–Hitler file was voluminous, but in Como it contained only two or three letters.

The partisan Lorenzo Bianchi and a man named Venini from Domaso told the report's author that they saw two other cases of different colours in the Dongo town hall on 28 April. They said these cases contained various documents, including a file on Churchill. Lorenzo Bianchi was the partisan who peddled a palpably false account of the shooting of Mussolini and Claretta to the newspaper *La Voce Partigiana*, so anything he said must be regarded as suspect. The author said he received 'very confidential information' that a Verona lawyer named Segantini, who was staying in Domaso as a displaced person, photographed two important documents, letters or declarations by Churchill to Mussolini in which the British prime minister gave his blessing to the Duce to undertake his war in Ethiopia in 1935 and his intervention in the civil war in Spain in 1936. This report may carry a somewhat greater degree of plausibility than the claims of a

Churchill correspondence with Mussolini during the Second World War. At the time of the events in Ethiopia and Spain, Churchill held no public office, but he was on record as being anxious not to alienate Italy while Mussolini was preparing his attack on Ethiopia. He was also then showing a moderate degree of sympathy with General Franco's uprising in Spain.[5] In his book, Cavalleri identified the Verona lawyer as Luigi Seggatini, not Segantini, and said that Seggatini went to the Domaso bank, where the gold found in the river was displayed on a counter, and filmed it. Cavalleri said a clip from that film was shown on Italian television in 1948. He made no mention of the lawyer having filmed any documents signed by Churchill. It seems extraordinary that a visiting lawyer would have been given access to such documents and allowed to photograph them, even more extraordinary that the bank would have displayed the recovered gold on a counter and allowed it to be filmed. Neither the anonymous report nor Cavalleri gives any explanation for such events.[6]

The report's author accused Bellini delle Stelle, Lazzaro and Scappin of removing documents from the packages that arrived in Como and turning them over to foreign intelligence services, a charge they denied. But the report added that the accusation 'seems to be confirmed by a multitude of witnesses'. It said Colonel Harnold (probably a misspelling), an Allied officer based in Como, gave expensive Swiss watches afterwards to Bellini delle Stelle and Lazzaro. The report went on to say that a group of partisans had drawn up a formal complaint about the theft of documents and the alleged link of Bellini delle Stelle, Lazzaro and Scappin with 'foreign powers', and that this complaint would be forwarded to the prime minister, minister of defence and minister of justice. *L'Unità* said it had been unable to determine whether this complaint was actually sent.[7]

* * *

The claims about a Mussolini–Churchill file apparently originated with an article published in June 1946 by the Roman newspaper *Il Tempo*, which said Churchill had recovered letters he had written to Mussolini. The Geneva weekly *Voix Ouvrière* published substantially the same report on 8 June. It said Churchill recovered and destroyed only the part of his private correspondence with Mussolini relating to the period before the Italian–Ethiopian war of 1935–6.[8] These reports rested on the fact that Churchill, voted out of office in July 1945, came to Lake Como in September for a painting holiday with his daughter Sarah and stayed at the lakeside Villa Apraxin at Moltrasio, put at his disposal by Field Marshal Alexander. During his stay, he painted six large watercolour landscapes and ten smaller pictures, but the mythmakers contend Churchill's real purpose was to recover and burn his incriminating correspondence with Mussolini. The evidence for this is at best circumstantial and at worst ludicrous.

Virginio Bertinelli, the Prefect of Como, said in 1945 that he obtained papers seized from Rachele Mussolini, and that he and Police Chief Davide Grassi decided to hide them rather than let them fall into Allied hands. They hid them inside a gymnastic horse used for exercises in a Como gym, but Bertinelli said a Communist who served as deputy police chief was plied with alcohol and gifts by the Allies on 22 May 1945, and revealed the hiding place. He said Captain Malcolm Smith of the British Field Security Service went to the gym and removed the papers, taking them to the Villa Apraxin where Churchill stayed more than three months later. In a report to Prime Minister Alcide De Gasperi of December 1945, Bertinelli said the papers he saw were from 1934–5. Lazzaro, who initially made no mention of a Churchill file, later said another partisan who examined papers taken from Marcello Petacci found one envelope marked 'Churchill' but did not look inside. Although he cited no evidence, Lazzaro said he believed Mussolini gave one bag of documents to Claretta in Musso before his capture, and asked her to give it to the British ambassador, Sir Clifford Norton, in Switzerland. He said these documents later disappeared. F.W. Deakin, an aide to Churchill who collaborated in the drafting of Churchill's memoirs, said the former prime minister learned of all this only in March 1947 from a story published in the *Daily Herald* in London, and denied immediately having gone to Italy to recover correspondence with Mussolini. Deakin also said there was nothing in the Churchill archives to substantiate such a story.[9]

In his speech of 26 March 1947 in which he boasted of killing Mussolini, Audisio claimed there had been a Churchill file among the Duce's papers. He had never mentioned this before, and even then he did not use the prime minister's name, referring only to 'the man with a cigar in his mouth'. He implied that the file had been taken by the Allies, and he accused Lazzaro of having sold important documents, including letters of Churchill, to a foreign power. There is no evidence that Audisio ever saw any of the Duce's papers.[10]

Without citing a source, Cavalleri contended that on 15 September on the outskirts of Como British secret agents met the Como Communist leader Dante Gorreri, who brought with him a packet of sixty-two letters Churchill had sent to Mussolini before the war. Cavalleri said Gorreri handed over the packet in exchange for 2.5 million lire, which was wrapped in old newspapers. An unnamed former partisan who read the letters, according to Cavalleri, said Churchill had tried to get Italy to join the Allies and had promised Mussolini in exchange all Dalmatia, the Dodecanese Islands, Tunisia and possibly Nice. It goes without saying, of course, that Churchill was in no position to promise foreign territory to Mussolini and would never have contemplated doing so. Cavalleri also claimed that Churchill took tea on 7 September in the Domaso house of Ermanno Gibezzi, who succeeded Rumi as director of the Domaso bank, but Cavalleri did not elaborate on the presumed significance of that gesture.[11]

In 1985, the journalist Flora Antonioni reported in the magazine *L'Europeo* that a government official in Rome had shown her in official files a yellow envelope, bearing three seals, which was marked 'Churchill–Mussolini file'. But she was not allowed to see the contents. Five years later, journalist Ferruccio Lanfranchi claimed that Marcello Petacci had been given a Churchill–Mussolini file and had taken it with him to Switzerland on 18 April 1945, perhaps to contact the British, then returned to Italy on 24 April. But other researchers said Marcello was in Switzerland between 19 and 23 April with his wife and two children, seeking refugee status. When informed that they would be put in an internment camp, he refused the conditions and returned to Italy.[12]

In 1954, the magazine *Oggi* published what it said were photocopies of letters between Churchill and Mussolini during the war. The source was Enrico De Toma, a former lieutenant of Mussolini's Republican National Guard, who claimed Mussolini had given him a case of documents on 22 April 1945, and asked him to take them to Switzerland and turn them over to an Italian Jew living there. If no one claimed the documents after six years, Mussolini supposedly told him, he could reclaim them and use them as he saw fit. In later interviews, De Toma admitted only part of the documents he offered were authentic and said many others had been 'manipulated' to increase the importance of the file. He was arrested, but after having been let out on bail he disappeared. In November 1954, he was photographed at a Paris airport as he boarded a plane for Brazil, and he never returned to Italy. At a trial in 1959, all his documents were declared false and the judge ordered them to be destroyed.

The falsity of the documents was evident from a cursory examination. Some contained grammatical errors that Churchill could not have made. Others were in a clumsy style that could hardly be credited to a man who won the Nobel Prize for literature. Finally, the contents were absurd: Churchill offered to consider Italian claims against France if Italy withdrew from the war. Britain would protect Italian rights in the Mediterranean. Churchill offered Mussolini recognition of the Salò Republic in exchange for the return of his letters. Churchill gave Mussolini assurances about his personal security and expressed 'my personal admiration for you'.[13] Obviously, if Churchill had gone behind the backs of his Allies and his own War Cabinet to make such offers, he would have been at best a fool, at worst a traitor. It is equally obvious that no national leader in his right mind would have written such compromising letters to an enemy who could destroy his career by making them public. Finally, there is the fact that Churchill would not have had to come to Italy to recover the letters, had they existed, but could have had them sent to him in London. Nor does it seem plausible he would have waited more than three months to come for them if they were as compromising as the fantasists insist.

But the absurdities do not stop there. Angelo Tarchi, Mussolini's economy minister, claimed that on the evening of 25 April 1945, Mussolini pulled out and showed him a page from his files marked 'Winston Churchill correspondence' and said this letter – which Tarchi did not read – explained the reason for Italy entering the war in 1940. Mussolini said it was written when 'all seemed lost for England', and Churchill wrote that he approved of Italy's entry into the war because he believed Mussolini would be able to exert a moderating influence on Hitler at the peace table.[14] In short, a treasonous Churchill approved of Italy declaring war on Britain. Other forgeries also have come to light, but they do not merit any detailed attention. This one is cited simply to show the lengths to which fantasists have been prepared to go.

The writer Fabio Andriola is a leading proponent of the theory that there was a Churchill–Mussolini file. He argued in a book published in 1990 that Mussolini's uncertain wanderings around the western side of Lake Como on 26 and 27 April were due to the fact that he intended to hand over his documents to a mysterious Allied agent and waited in vain for him to arrive. Arrigo Petacco, in another book, examined the forgeries of De Toma and concluded that De Toma was 'indubitably a liar'. But Petacco stood logic on its head in discussing the purported letter in which Churchill was supposed to have offered recognition of the Salò Republic in exchange for the return of his letters. 'The absurdity of the text is so clear that, in a certain sense, it argues in favour of its authenticity,' he wrote. 'It is in fact difficult to attribute such evident naïveté to forgers who were very able in other matters.'[15] In fact, they were not 'very able' in other matters, as their amateurish attempts to write English demonstrated.

Even the late Renzo De Felice, Mussolini's principal Italian biographer and a respected scholar, accepted the unsubstantiated claim that Mussolini carried with him a 'careful selection' of his correspondence with Churchill. 'The Churchill "letters"', he said, 'could contain some unpublished surprise. Much more interesting would be to recover certain papers that Mussolini carried that were taken to the Cabinet by an envoy of the CLNAI and then disappeared, perhaps "restored" to the English.'[16]

Finally, it should be mentioned that Mussolini may have sent some secret documents to Switzerland early in 1945. He arranged to have his friend Nino

D'Aroma make three photographic copies of more than 200 documents and said: 'In an opportune time, after the period of struggle and persecutions, these papers absolutely must see the light.' Mussolini later told D'Aroma he had entrusted one set of copies to the Japanese Ambassador Shinrokuro Hidaka, and D'Aroma quoted Hidaka as telling him later: 'I have been in Switzerland and I am happy to tell you, one of his trusted men, that he has been happy with me. Do you understand me?' But after the war, Hidaka denied he had received the file and said he had last visited Switzerland in 1943. 'If I had been in possession of it, I would have handed it to my Foreign Ministry so it could return it to the Italian government,' he told an Italian journalist. The Japanese Embassy said Tokyo ordered anything that could be of use to the victors to be destroyed after Japan's surrender in August 1945.

Mussolini kept a diary, which he mentioned on at least two occasions, but it also disappeared and may have gone to Switzerland. Reuters, the British news agency, reported in late 1945 that the diary was in the possession of someone in Switzerland who intended to sell it for £5,500. The truth of this claim was never verified, and nothing more was heard of the diary. De Felice speculated that Hidaka, tried as a war criminal but absolved, may have made a deal with the Americans to win acquittal in exchange for handing over the diary, which ended 'in some secret archive'.[17] Such speculation is worthless and begs the question why the Americans would suppress for more than a half century a diary that could be of immense benefit to historians.

Dino Campini, the secretary to Education Minister Carlo Alberto Biggini, said Mussolini made three copies of files relating to Italy's relations with Britain and its relations with Germany. He said Mussolini kept one, gave one to Biggini and gave the other to Hidaka. Biggini, he said, confirmed this a few days before he died of cancer in November 1945. Campini said he thought Biggini kept his copy of the documents with him, but learned they were in the Villa Gemma, between Gardone and Maderno on Lake Garda, where Biggini left his wife and son when he had to go into hiding at war's end.

Campini went to the villa and searched, but found the files were not there. Before Biggini died, he said, the former minister confirmed he had left the documents at the villa, and they disappeared in the days following the collapse of the Fascist government.[18] They have never been found.

Chapter 29

THE DEAD SPROUT WINGS

They have stolen Mussolini.

(Headline in Corriere Lombardo, *23 April 1946)*

Even in the grave Benito Mussolini could not rest undisturbed. After the autopsy, he was given a secret burial in field 16, plot 384 of the Musocco Cemetery on the north-eastern outskirts of Milan, with no marker to show where his body rested. But on 22 April 1946, a young Fascist named Domenico Leccisi and two friends who had uncovered the secret stole into the cemetery late at night, and in the early hours of 23 April dug up the body and hauled it away to a hiding place near the Swiss border. Leccisi's means of dramatising his cause may have been eccentric, to say the least, but he was not a madman as some might have thought. He had a precise political aim. In the postwar period, as he later wrote in self-justification, Fascists were being hunted down and killed, placed in internment camps or put before popular tribunals with only a modicum of legality. Many, like himself, were unemployed and struggling to survive. He believed the reconstruction of Italy required a quick end to harsh methods and an integration of Fascists into the new democratic life of the country (an argument that ignored the anti-democratic nature of fascism).

Passing by the Musocco Cemetery, he considered that all the anti-Fascist anger welling up in Italy was focused on one man who lay somewhere in its confines in an unknown grave. 'I began to think that to draw the attention of Italians to the necessity of closing with the past, it was necessary to uncover that sepulchre,' he wrote. 'After a sleepless night of long reflection, I decided to steal the remains of Benito Mussolini.'

The 25-year-old Leccisi, who had a wife and young daughter, hailed from a town near Bari on the southern Adriatic coast. He had migrated to the north and worked in a metallurgical plant at Tremezzo on Lake Como, becoming active in the industrial workers' union of Milan. Believing firmly in the political and social reforms promised by the Salò Republic at its Verona

Congress in 1943, he was determined after the war to carry on the fight for those ideals. He set up the illegal Fascist Democratic Party (the word Fascist in a party name was banned), which initially was a two-man party; his close friend Mauro Rana, aged twenty-six, was the other. He later recruited two or three other friends, and they met in a garret above his apartment in Milan to plot their political campaign.

Always short of money, they did manage to acquire a few pistols and hand grenades, and used those to intimidate workers in private printing plants, forcing them to print an underground tabloid sheet called *Lotta Fascista* (Fascist Struggle), which was written entirely by Leccisi. With these methods, they managed to publish five monthly issues of the paper. On the night of 30 May 1946, they even used their pistols to intimidate workers who operated an electronic news bulletin that flashed high above the Piazza del Duomo in central Milan. They sent out this message: 'The third number of *Lotta Fascista* has come out. Read it. Long live the Duce! Fascism is not dead.'

On 6 April, Leccisi wrote a letter to the Prefect of Milan, the police chief, the newspapers and Cardinal Schuster. He outlined his aims for a pacification programme 'to unite Italians against the common danger of hunger and political devaluation before the world', and threatened violence if his movement was not heeded.

It was common knowledge in Milan that Mussolini had been buried secretly in the Musocco Cemetery. Leccisi, who adopted the underground name of Marco, spent long hours wandering about the cemetery with Rana, who was known as Ferruccio, and Antonio Parozzi, who was known as Rino. Once they had discovered the location of the grave, they planned to seize the building where cemetery workers lived, cut the phone and electricity lines to the cemetery and imprison the custodians while they made off with the body.

They struck up casual conversations with gravediggers, guards and cemetery officials, but had no luck in discovering where Mussolini was buried. Then, on the morning of 20 April 1946, they came upon two young Germans in prisoner-of-war jackets who had been assigned to tend the graves of German officers killed in the Milan insurrection. One of the Germans, who spoke Italian fluently and had worked in the cemetery for six months, proved willing to chat, and Leccisi told him he and his friends, supporters of the Salò Republic, wanted to put a flower on the Duce's grave. He went on talking and the German, smiling, interrupted: 'I know the exact place where the tomb of the Duce lies.' As there were many people about who might overhear their conversation, Leccisi asked him to walk across the field with his hands in his pockets and remove them when he arrived at the grave. The German did so, but he was so far away that Leccisi could not be sure where he had stopped.

To help him out of his difficulty, the German walked across the field again and came back with the number of the grave: 384.

Leccisi had planned to steal Mussolini's body on 28 April, the anniversary of the Duce's death. But on the morning of 22 April, Easter Sunday, he learned that the authorities planned to triple the number of guards on night duty starting at midnight on 24 April. Leccisi decided he and his fellow conspirators had to scrap their original plan and act that night. Luck was on their side. The city police were busy putting down a revolt at San Vittore jail, and Leccisi and his friends would be helped by bright night lighting from a building site next to the cemetery. Ordinarily men would be working at the site during the night, but all work had been suspended for the Easter holidays. Leccisi and his friends spent the rest of 22 April drafting a communiqué and a commentary to appear in *Lotta Fascista*.

They needed a car for their enterprise, but Rana had seen to that, stealing a Lancia Aprilia from a car dealership several months earlier. They had repainted it black and put on false licence plates. Sometime after 11 p.m. they drove to the cemetery, covering the car with a sheet. Then they climbed over the wall and hid among the tombs, waiting for guards with their patrol dogs to make their rounds. Rana had brought a stick fitted with a sharp blade to kill the dogs, while the other two men would overpower the guards and tie them up. Parozzi climbed a cypress tree so that he could jump down on the guards, but an hour passed and no guards appeared.

They decided they needed to move the car closer to the cemetery entrance so they could remove the body. Once they had done that, Parozzi again climbed a cypress tree, but, while they could hear a distant barking of dogs, still no guards came. By 3 a.m. Rana was nervous and wanted to leave before the approaching dawn exposed them to greater risk of capture, but Leccisi persuaded him they had to forget about the guards and act quickly. Rana and Parozzi began to dig in plot 384, using the tools workmen had left nearby and had intended to use to exhume the body of Achille Starace that morning at his family's request. Leccisi kept a lookout. By 4.30 a.m., they were within inches of the wooden casket, and dawn was beginning to break. Leccisi tried with the point of a pickaxe to open the casket, but the wood broke, so he jumped into the grave and pulled it off with his hands. Then he turned on a flashlight. The head of Mussolini was very recognisable. The upper lip was slightly drawn back, giving the Duce a grimace that appeared to Leccisi like a sad smile. He took off his cap out of respect.

Mussolini lay completely naked on a piece of blackened wood, his military trousers placed over the body. There was no time to widen the hole to get the casket out, so they decided to remove only the remains. They managed to get ropes under the chest and legs and drew the body out. Leccisi saw that an opening at the base of the cranium, made to remove the brain, was plugged by plaster or kaolin. He observed numerous gunshot wounds in the chest, pelvis and legs. Mussolini's boots were torn along a seam in the back. Leccisi dropped into the empty grave a copy of the proclamation of the Fascist Democratic Party, accepting responsibility for the theft and explaining the motives. Another copy glued to a piece of cardboard was left at the base of a nearby tree. Leccisi left one of the two boots so that it could be matched later with the other and leave no doubt about the identification of the body. While Rana went to get a sheet from the car, Leccisi and Parozzi washed the body in a cemetery fountain.

By now it was 6 a.m. and the sun was already high. As they struggled to carry the body in the sheet, they saw a wheelbarrow used by gardeners and decided to use it even though it was noisy. In a loud voice, Leccisi said: 'Pardon us, Duce, if we are forced to render funeral honours to you in this way.' He took out a white handkerchief and covered Mussolini's face. They put the body in the car boot and sped toward central Milan. There they went to a doctor, with Rana pretending he had been in a road accident and could not walk properly. The doctor asked no questions, but disinfected their hands and some bruises on Rana's face. When they left the doctor's office, Rana was joined by his wife Silvia and the couple left in the car to take the body to Madesimo, a village in the Valtellina where they had rented a small house. Leccisi and Parozzi went their separate ways on foot.

Several hours later, having made sure he had given the Ranas plenty of time to get away from Milan, Leccisi phoned the newspapers to announce that 'from Musocco the dead have sprouted wings'. *Corriere Lombardo* came out with an extra edition and a headline reading: 'They have stolen Mussolini.'

'We had demonstrated, first of all to ourselves, that the force of the spirit becomes invincible when it reveals itself publicly as a moral conscience,' Leccisi wrote. 'Moved by the memory of the innocent blood of our many murdered comrades, we violated a tomb to reclaim the right to the universal value of respect that is owed to the dead.' The theft of the body, he said, was 'necessary and inescapable because it was imposed by reasons of decorum and national dignity'. In his proclamation, he said Fascists could no longer 'permit the massacres and cannibalistic acts carried out by human scum . . . in offence to a dead man'. He said the body would be handed back to the Italian nation on the day the authorities agreed to permit Mussolini to be buried on the Capitoline Hill 'in that Rome that Mussolini made great'.

The news of the theft flashed around the world, and the Italian press had a field day with feverish speculation. *Corriere d'Informazione* assured its readers the body had been put in a zinc coffin and taken abroad on a British plane. *Milano-Sera* said the body had been cremated.

During the trip to Madesimo, Silvia Rana was overcome by nausea and the couple had to stop so that she could get some fresh air. When they arrived at the house they had rented, they put the body in a chest, which they sealed and left in a corner of the garage where firewood was stored. After piling wood on the chest to hide it, they spent the night in the house, with Silvia sleepless for hours, then beset by nightmares. They returned to Milan on the following day, 24 April.

At 9 a.m. on 29 April, Rana was arrested in Milan's central train station as he prepared to travel to Lodi. A woman who had worked for the former Fascist city government had known of his plans and had tipped off the police, who kept the arrest secret from Silvia and the newspapers. Leccisi, informed by Silvia that her husband had disappeared, packed a bag, destroyed his photos and anything else that could help the police and went to a *pensione* where he checked in using a false identification. Three days later, Rana, acting on police instructions while still under arrest, called him from a public telephone booth and told him he had been arrested (Leccisi did not explain how Rana knew where to find him). Rana said the police had assured him the government was prepared to bury Mussolini in consecrated land and would not press charges if the thieves agreed to return the body. He also said the police had asked for an intermediary to come to them at 4 p.m. the next day, and promised this person would not be arrested.

Leccisi kept the appointment at police headquarters, where two high-ranking officers from Rome awaited him. They assured him they did not know his identity and he could leave the room whenever he wanted. When they outlined their requests, Leccisi said he had not agreed fully with the theft of the body but he would have to consult higher authority. Then he went away. Shortly afterwards, the officers returned to Rome, taking Rana with them.

Leccisi still was not ready to submit to the police conditions. On the day after his meeting with the officers, he went to a monastery called the Angelicum, or Convento dell'Angelo, where he knew two monks, Fathers Enrico Zucca and Alberto Parini, who had helped anti-Fascists during the war, including General Cadorna. He asked if they could hide the body in the monastery, but the monks tried to persuade him to open negotiations with the government to arrive at an honourable conclusion. Leccisi was not to be swayed from his determination to get the body into the monastery.

On 7 May, he went to Madesimo, accompanied by Silvia Rana and Fausto Gasparini, a former officer of the Fascist Republican National Guard. The two men wore Air Force uniforms to help them get through any police roadblocks. Rana had the only key to the Madesimo house, so they had to break a window to get in. They put Mussolini's body in two large rubber sacks, then placed it back in the chest, which they sealed. They returned to Milan with the body, arriving at the monastery at midnight. Father Parini met them at the door and said: 'You cannot demand burial in a church for the body of a man who died, above all else, in mortal sin.' Leccisi and Gasparini muscled their way in with the chest and set it down. Leccisi told Parini that if Mussolini had died without having confessed his sins, it was the fault of his killers. Parini objected: 'Mussolini died with his lover at his side.' Leccisi replied: 'To bury the dead is a human and Christian task which the church cannot refuse.' Parini and Zucca bowed their heads in prayer, then nodded to Leccisi and Gasparini to follow them with the body. They entered the church and, at the fifth chapel on the right, a trapdoor was opened and the body deposited almost beneath the altar.

The referendum that would decide the future of the Italian monarchy was held on 12 June, and afterwards the government decided on an amnesty for political crimes. More than 30,000 Fascists were released from jail or internment camps – an achievement to which Leccisi felt his theft of the body had contributed.

On 22 July, three members of the Fascist Democratic Party including Gasparini went to Como to meet some colleagues, but they fell into a police trap and were arrested. One of them revealed Leccisi's name to the police. On 31 July, as Leccisi was phoning his young daughter from a coffee bar, plainclothes police with guns burst in and arrested him. Meanwhile, the man who had revealed Leccisi's identity also named Parini and Zucca, and the monks were arrested on 10 August. They agreed to talk in return for the promise of a Christian and secret burial for Mussolini. Police recovered the body and took it to the Certosa of Pavia, south of Milan, on 12 August. The two monks were jailed for forty-two days, then released and the charges were dropped. Church authorities transferred them to South America. Leccisi was charged with fourteen crimes, but most of the charges were dropped before he went on trial. He was convicted and served twenty-one months of a six-year term, then was freed under a further amnesty following the 1948 national elections. He was elected to Milan City Council in 1951 on the ticket of the neo-Fascist Italian Social Movement, and two years later was elected to parliament.

After Mussolini's body had been recovered, it was shifted back and forth between the Milan morgue and police headquarters. On 14 August, it was taken to the Institute of Legal Medicine for the second time, primarily for the purpose of securing identification. Government officials in Rome debated what to do next with the body. They eventually decided the burial place should be secret, selected by Cardinal Schuster and known only to eight of the highest-ranking police and government officials. To avoid attracting attention, Milan Police Chief Vincenzo Agnesina had a carpenter prepare a rough wooden crate, bound with metal hoops, saying it was to be used for shipping documents. Agnesina had been in charge of Mussolini's bodyguard on the day in 1943 when the Duce was arrested in Rome, but was conveniently absent at the time. He later told Rachele he 'had to go and get a shave'. She never forgave his betrayal.

Agnesina and a driver left the Milan police headquarters on 25 August with the crate in the back of their car, and were gone for fifty minutes. For the next eleven years, the burial site remained a secret, even from Mussolini's wife and family. It was in fact the Capuchin Monastery of Cerro Maggiore in Milan, as was recorded in the chronicles of the monastery: 'The remains of Benito Mussolini were consigned to us on 25 August 1946. . . . These remains were kept in the interior chapel of our monastery, on the first floor, in a case placed at the side of the small altar, and later in a cupboard intended for sacred vestments, always in the same small chapel.' The move to the cupboard took place in 1950 when exhalations from the wooden case were noticed in the chapel.

In his biography of his brother Arnaldo, published in 1933, Mussolini had written: 'I have only one desire: to be buried alongside my parents in the cemetery of San Cassiano [in Predappio, his birthplace]. I would be really naive if I were to ask to be left in peace after death. Surrounding the tombs of the leaders of those great transformations which are called revolutions, there cannot be peace.' Mussolini's wish for a final resting place in Predappio would be fulfilled, but not for a while yet.[1]

* * *

Rachele, with her children Anna Maria and Romano, was exiled after the war to the island of Ischia, near Naples, and remained there until 1949. Vittorio took refuge in a religious institute, then went to Switzerland and from there to Argentina, where he lived for a number of years and was welcomed by the dictator Juan Perón, an admirer of Mussolini. Vittorio made a number of visits to Italy and returned there permanently in 1968. His marriage then broke up. Romano married Maria Scicolone, a sister of the actress Sophia Loren, but the marriage ended in divorce. Their daughter, Alessandra, now serves in the Italian Parliament. Anna Maria also married, and had two daughters, but died in 1968, just forty years old.[2]

After Rachele's failed attempt to get into Switzerland three days before Mussolini was executed, she said she lost track of time until she heard a voice on the radio on 28 April 1945, proclaiming, 'Justice has been done.' 'I find myself thinking that no ingratitude and no human villainy will be able to reach Benito any longer,' she wrote in her diary. 'He has given everything for Italy – even his life.' Shooting was going on all around the house of the

Blackshirt in which she had taken refuge, and her children were sobbing, but Rachele was so overcome she hardly noticed anything.

At her request, the Blackshirts sent someone to tell the Como CLN where the family was, and shortly afterward three partisans came and began searching the house. One took from her a miniature portrait of her late son, Bruno, telling her: 'This belongs to the people.' She replied: 'Everything belongs to the people because we have always given to the people and my son even gave his life.' A partisan officer made the man give back the miniature and apologise.[3]

Rachele and her children were taken on the afternoon of 29 April to the Como police station, and she was put in a small cell in the women's prison, away from the children. After her arrest, partisans went to the Villa Mantero in Como, where she had previously stayed, and seized a hoard of valuables she had left there, estimated to be worth about 20 million lire. They consisted mostly of official decorations given to Mussolini and included the Collar of the Annunciation, a prized golden decoration that the king awarded to a restricted group of people who were then proclaimed 'cousins' of the monarch; a Persian decoration in gold and diamonds; a pontifical gold medal; a German decoration in gold and diamonds; some Albanian decorations in gold and diamonds; and a long list of similar items, plus gold ingots weighing more than eight pounds. All the decorations were turned over to Como Prefect Virginio Bertinelli, who later restored them to the state.[4]

At the Como jail, none of the women inmates recognised Rachele at first, but then one woman looked at her incredulously and said: 'You here?' Rachele begged her not to reveal her identity and the woman moved away, sobbing quietly. Rachele and the other prisoners could occasionally hear someone in a nearby courtyard pleading for his life, followed by bursts of gunfire, then the rumbling of cart wheels. This was repeated often through the night and women in the cells were distraught. Some of them asked Rachele why she was not crying. 'Haven't you left anyone?' she was asked.

A Carabiniere sergeant came the next day, 30 April, and asked her very courteously to accompany him. She thought her turn had come to be executed, but she was driven in a police car to the American headquarters, set up in a luxurious villa in Como, and an Italian-speaking officer who interrogated her asked at one point: 'How on earth did Mussolini manage to govern these people for twenty years?' He told her not to worry about her children, who would be looked after. Half an hour later, she was called to a room for an emotional reunion with Gina Ruberti, Bruno's widow, and Gina's parents. It was the last time she saw Gina, who drowned in Lake Como after the war. Gina was crossing the lake to attend a wedding reception, along with some British officers, when the boat was hit by a big wave and capsized. She was trapped under the boat and drowned before others could reach her.

Rachele's children were brought to her on 1 May, and the following day the Americans drove mother and children to a building in Milan. On the evening of 3 May, they were put aboard an open truck and taken on an all-night drive to Montecatini in Tuscany, arriving there at 9 a.m. They were lodged in a hotel until the morning of 10 May, when they were handed over to the British and driven to an internment camp located in a synthetic rubber factory in the Umbrian town of Terni. After a few days, Rachele asked the commandant for a job, and went to work in the kitchen. Nearly three months passed before she and the children were transferred to Ischia on 26 July 1945.[5]

It was on Ischia that she learned of the theft of her husband's body in 1946, and its recovery. In her memoirs, she said she was taken to the Institute of Legal Medicine in Milan in 1946 and shown a glass jar shaped like a chalice, containing her husband's brain, which had been labelled with a false name. Professors Caio Mario Cattabeni and Cazzaniga suggested she take away the jar to avoid possible damage by anatomy students, but she declined as she was living on Ischia and could not arrange a proper burial in the family plot in Predappio. She said she could not imagine where she could store the jar in the four-room cottage she shared with her children.

Over the next few years, she pleaded with a succession of Italian prime ministers in the name of compassion and Christian decency for the return and proper entombment of Mussolini's remains. The neo-Fascist Italian Social Movement took up her cause in 1949, but Christian Democrat Prime Minister Mario Scelba replied that the reasons for which the government acted were still valid. 'The rules of civilised life and the eternal precepts of Christianity are not involved in this matter, because there are tens of thousands of relatives who do not know where their dear ones are buried,' he wrote. 'The fault is often that of the infamous policies of fascism . . . its new and old exponents clamour to know where their ex-Duce's tomb is, only so they can create new occasions for political demonstrations.'

But in the summer of 1957, Adone Zoli became prime minister. Not only was he from Romagna, the province in which the Mussolinis had lived; he had employed Rachele's father on his farm and she had been born in a house on his land. For the first time, Rachele found a prime minister prepared to accede to her requests. She had by then been allowed to move back to Predappio. On a stifling day at the end of August, a police officer arrived and told her that Mussolini's body was coming home that day. At noon, a black Packard arrived, disguised with American licence plates (QC 81-12, NY 47). In it were a Father Carlo, a Capuchin monk, and Vincenzo Agnesina, along with Professors Cattabeni and Cazzaniga. Hidden under the back seat was the crate with all that remained of Benito Mussolini. The handle and the metal straps encasing it for the last eleven years had rusted. Those who brought the body had hoped for a quick mass and burial in the family crypt, next to Bruno and Mussolini's parents, Alessandro and Rosa. But Rachele insisted on having the crate opened; she would not accept anyone's word on what was inside, especially the word of the despised Agnesina. 'Is this really the bier they have given you, Benito?' she said when the crate was opened. 'Is everything here? The bones of Mussolini are inside? The government returns you like this after twelve years?'

Cattabeni and Cazzaniga verified to her that the body was that of Mussolini, and after she had satisfied herself on that count she was asked to accept an official statement drawn up by Agnesina and initialled on each page by those present. Rachele objected violently to one phrase: 'The widow Mussolini takes note of all effects of the preceding statement and thanks the Italian Government for the decision adopted.' She was handed the glass chalice containing Mussolini's brain, which had rested all this time in the Institute of Legal Medicine in Milan, and it was placed in the tomb. During the week following the funeral, 8,000 people visited Mussolini's tomb.

On Christmas night 1971, someone placed a bomb at the door of the Mussolini chapel in the cemetery. The bomb caused heavy damage, but the graves were left intact.

Vittorio later claimed that Rachele wrote to US Ambassador James D. Zellerbach to request the return of the brain fragment that had gone to the United States, but there is no record of such a letter or of a reply. She did finally write to Ambassador Frederick Reinhardt on 22 February 1966, 'in the names of my children and my own', to make the request. Dr Overholser of St Elizabeth's Hospital in Washington apparently had found the brain sample insufficient for his purposes. According to an Italian journalist, Overholser, who died in 1964, complained to his wife it was too small, had been crushed and had been mixed with fluid from the ocular bulb. A Washington reporter interviewed Overholser in 1955 and quoted him as saying of the little piece – no bigger than a dice cube – 'There it is: it could have been a discovery, instead it's a failure.'

After Reinhardt passed on Rachele's request to Washington, State Department spokesman Robert McCloskey said there seemed to be no objection to returning the brain fragment, but no one knew where it was. It was located shortly afterward at the Armed Forces Institute of Pathology at Walter Reed Army Medical Center in Bethesda, Maryland, and shipped by diplomatic pouch to the US Embassy in Rome on 21 March 1966. An employee of the American Consulate in Florence took it to Predappio in a yellowish-orange envelope. The envelope was marked: 'Musolinni [*sic*], fragments of brain.' Rachele opened it and saw that it contained pieces of glass used to examine microscopic specimens. The brain cells were presumably on them but they just looked like smears on the glass.

Edda Mussolini Ciano later commented: 'He had an unusual destiny, my father, even in death. His body was shipped like merchandise in a packing crate and his brain in an envelope, like a special delivery letter.' Referring to the misspelling on the envelope, she said ruefully: 'They didn't even respect his name.'[6]

* * *

So Mussolini got his brain back, but what about his reputation? The late Renzo De Felice, who wrote a long, multivolume biography of Mussolini, began a process of trying to partially rehabilitate the Duce and fascism, suggesting that the opprobrium attached to Mussolini in his last years overshadowed his earlier accomplishments. He had modernised the country, defended family values, suppressed the Mafia, made peace with the Roman Catholic Church, and retained much of a liberal bureaucracy. De Felice also pointed to the fact that fascism enjoyed popular support during most of the years Mussolini was in power, and he stressed the differences between Italian fascism and Germany's Nazi creed. Mussolini did not share Hitler's obsession with the Jews, he observed. Other Italian academics have taken up De Felice's theme. Domenico Fisichella, a professor at the University of Rome and a right-wing senator, has commented that fascism adopted a great deal of progressive social and economic legislation that remained valid – and which, he claimed, was taken up in Roosevelt's New Deal. There have been calls in Italy for textbooks on Italian history, which after the war were heavily influenced by Communist academics, to be rewritten 'more objectively'. It remains to be seen whether 'more objectively' in fact means more open to a rehabilitation of fascism.

The Fascist Party was, of course, banned after the war, but its adherents clustered together in the Italian Social Movement, which never attracted more than about 5 per cent of the vote. But a young and able politician, Gianfranco Fini, took over the leadership in the 1990s, changed the party's name to National Alliance and began transforming it into a more respectable right-wing party. In 1994, he created an uproar by calling Mussolini 'the greatest statesman of the twentieth century', but he repudiated that remark in 2002. He has criticised fascism's racial laws and has travelled to Auschwitz and Israel. One of his party members served as a minister in the right-wing government of Prime Minister Silvio Berlusconi, formed in 2000, and Berlusconi himself has said that the good in fascism must be remembered as well as the bad. In 2003, Berlusconi touched off a controversy in Italy when he told a British interviewer: 'Mussolini never killed anyone. Mussolini used to send people on holiday in internal exile.' Such comments could give a younger generation of Italians who have not lived through the Mussolini era and known little of the history of that period a benign view of Il Duce.

The historical revisionism that has been under way in recent years has had that effect to some extent. The legal ban on glorifying fascism is now observed in the breach, with shops selling T-shirts and wine bottles bearing the image of the Duce along with other Mussolini kitsch and news-stands offering a fifteen-video set of Mussolini speeches. His former homes also are being restored and opened to a paying public. The number of visitors to Mussolini's tomb has more than doubled since the early 1990s, with about 70,000 pilgrims descending each year on Predappio, a small town of only 6,000 inhabitants. Since 2000, a group of mostly young neo-Fascists also has mounted a twenty-four-hour guard of honour around Mussolini's tomb. Wearing long black capes and standing rigidly at attention for ten to twelve hours at a stretch, they represent a kind of secular priesthood. On major Mussolini anniversaries marking his birth, rise to power and death, Fascists gather to sing party hymns and give the stiff-armed Roman salute to their fallen hero.[7]

* * *

Those who wish to separate fascism from Nazism are, of course, correct up to a point. For the most part Mussolini exiled his political opponents, even allowing them internal exile on Italian islands rather than killing them, but contrary to Berlusconi's claims, hardly sending them there 'on holiday'. His racial laws were harsh enough in the treatment of Jews, but extremely mild by comparison with those of Hitler, and he never sought to exterminate the Jews. He had territorial ambitions, but not Hitler's megalomania and desire for European domination. His domestic achievements in modernising Italy were real enough. But to attempt to excuse Mussolini on these grounds is nearly akin to suggesting Hitler's construction of the autobahns and his love of flowers and small children demonstrated he was not all bad. The corollary to the revisionist argument, of course, which is never explicitly stated, is that a dose of fascism would still be useful in today's Italy. This is a leap on to dangerous ground.

An essential fact about Mussolini that should never be forgotten – whatever his charisma, his abilities and his achievements – is that he chose to jump into bed with one of the most evil regimes in human history, and was, for a long time, an admirer of Hitler. He never spoke out, even in his private meetings with Hitler, against the barbarities of the concentration camps of which he was fully aware. He applauded Hitler's acts of aggression against neighbouring countries without taking account of the fact that, in a Europe dominated by an all-powerful Germany, Italy could only be reduced to the level of a vassal state. Even in the last twenty months of his life, when he ceased to become a dictator and became simply a front man for a more evil dictatorship, he unpardonably clung to a slim hope of a German victory when it was already clear that this could not possibly be of benefit to the Italian people but would only have the advantage of ensuring the survival of his own regime. Had Germany won the war, Italy would never have regained full independence nor retained all its present territory. Mussolini would have remained a puppet leader in a state garrisoned by German troops, and the northern provinces would have been annexed by the Reich. In the circumstances, no Italian patriot could genuinely have wished after 1943 for a German victory. But Mussolini's professed devotion to the Italian people was always suspect. He did not like Italians as they were, but wanted to transform their character, make them harder, more ruthless. He despised the middle classes, and the man who claimed he returned to office to spare Italy from German destruction was the same man who, in the early stages of the war, exulted in Allied air attacks on Naples because he thought they would toughen the Neapolitan people.

An important fact to remember is the degree to which Mussolini was fanatically determined to subject the Italian people to the anvil of war. Italians were at war longer than any other people, even the Germans, in that violent era. Beginning with the aggression against Ethiopia in 1935, continuing with Italian involvement in the Spanish Civil War, the attack on Albania and going on to the Second World War, Italians in the last decade of his rule shed their blood on widely scattered battlefronts for seven years and eight months. The Mussolini biographer R.J.B. Bosworth calculated that 400,000 Italians died in war, more than half of them in the last phase of the Duce's rule, and fascism may have sent a million or more people to their graves.[8] The blood of all these people is on the hands of Mussolini, who ranks just after Hitler and Stalin in the list of European war criminals of the Second World War. At an early stage he could have chosen, like his fellow Fascist dictator Franco, to remain neutral. But in 1939 he committed Italy to a military alliance with Germany through the Pact of Steel and then the Anti-Comintern Pact, and there was no turning back. He was driven to hitch Italy to the German war machine by a vainglorious lust for territorial expansion; he wanted an empire when the age of imperialism was already passing.

All that was bad enough, but he criminally sent thousands of young Italian men to a needless death because, in straitened economic circumstances, he was unable to provide them with sufficient arms, equipment and winter clothing. Thus he gave the Italian military an enduring reputation for incompetence and cowardice, and made it the butt of cruel jokes that stereotyped it as a kind of cross between the Keystone Kops and comic opera soldiers. In fact, the record shows that when Italian forces were given proper equipment, arms and leadership they fought as bravely as any other troops in the Second World War. Mussolini's actions in the last decade of his rule represented a calendar of crimes against humanity, and against the Italian people in particular, for which he can never be forgiven. Over the centuries, Italy had been ruled by worse men, but never by one who inflicted so much damage.

Mussolini may have done more than any single person to foster the growth of communism in Italy. Many people were attracted to communism as the most effective, if most ruthless, bulwark of opposition to fascism. Thousands of Italian soldiers interned in Germany in the last stages of the war, who were there only because Mussolini had yoked Italy to Germany's destiny, turned to communism for the same reason and came home to instil in their families the same sentiments. The result was that the Italian Communist Party grew to become the largest in the West after the Second World War, and Italian politics was influenced for a half century by the necessity of creating a political system designed to keep the Communists from winning power. The downfall of Mussolini's regime did have two unintended benefits for Italy, however: the eventual repugnance felt by most Italians for fascism ensured a turn to full democracy after the war, and the end of a corrupt and complicit monarchy.

When all this is weighed in the balance, any suggestion that Mussolini's record should be reassessed in light of his domestic achievements appears rather ludicrous, if not obscene. He came to power when Italy was weak and poor. He built it up, then left it virtually in ruins. In the early days of his rule he may have achieved much in a country that has not been notable for outstanding political leaders and which maintains even today a Byzantine political culture, outside the European mainstream, and decidedly corrupt. But only a deeply amoral leader, and perhaps one suffering from a severe personality disorder, could have made such disastrous choices and inflicted so much damage. De Felice argued that Mussolini's return to power in 1943 was motivated purely by a desire to save Italy from Hitler's vengeance, to redeem national honour by remaining loyal to an ally and to overcome Italy's moral inferiority vis-à-vis Germany after the 'betrayal' of 8 September 1943. The last two arguments are entirely spurious. De Felice contended the Salò Republic achieved some of those three objectives, but even he conceded that 'counting the costs and the benefits, the price paid was too high'.[9] The Italian people of Mussolini's time were culpable in their willingness to support his adventures for so long, and the Italian people of today would be guilty of an equal folly in judging him as other than the greatest disaster to befall their country in the twentieth century.

EPILOGUE

Rachele continued to live at Predappio for the remainder of her life, sharing her residence with Vittorio after his return from South America. He looked after a restaurant she owned and tended her land. She died on 30 October 1979, aged eighty-nine. Mussolini's sister Edvige went to Rome after the war. Her son Pino, barely twenty, was killed by partisans at Rovetta in the closing days of the conflict. Edda Mussolini Ciano, who returned to Italy from Switzerland after the war and was briefly exiled to the island of Lipari off the northern coast of Sicily, died on 9 April 1995, aged eighty-five. She never remarried. Vittorio died on 12 June 1997, aged eighty. The last surviving Mussolini child, Romano, died on 3 February 2006, aged seventy-eight.[1] Another significant figure of the Mussolini era – Urbano Lazzaro, the partisan who captured Mussolini – died on 4 January 2006, aged eighty-two.

Graziani and Buffarini were the most prominent survivors of the Fascist ministers who served Mussolini, but Buffarini did not last long. The Finance Guards who captured him handed him over to the Americans in Milan, and during his imprisonment he revealed to OSS Captain Max Corvo the hiding places of files from the Salò Republic's Interior, Foreign Affairs and Armed Forces Ministries. Corvo sent an officer to Lake Garda to recover the documents and complained that James Jesus Angleton, another OSS officer who became a famed chief of counter-espionage for the CIA after the war, claimed credit for this exploit. While undergoing interrogation Buffarini, scheming to the last, implied to Corvo that if he helped him to escape to Switzerland, he would make it worth his while because he had a good deal of money in Swiss banks. Corvo told him the proposal was 'an error in judgement'. Shortly afterwards, the Americans bowed to CLN pressure and handed over Buffarini for trial. A Milanese court convicted him of war crimes on 16 June and fixed the date of his execution for 10 July. Early on the appointed morning, Buffarini swallowed a huge dose of barbiturates in a suicide attempt. Partisan guards revived him, and while he was semi-conscious he was tied to a chair and shot in the back by a firing squad.[2]

Following a number of postponements, a military tribunal tried Graziani in May 1950 and sentenced him to nineteen years in prison, but simultaneously cancelled thirteen of them. As he already had been in detention more than five years, he had only a few more months to serve his sentence, and was released on 29 August.[3] His German counterpart, Field Marshal Kesselring, was tried in Venice in May 1947 on war crimes charges and condemned to death by a British court martial. But Alexander and Churchill intervened to have the sentence commuted to life imprisonment. Kesselring was released on health grounds in October 1952, to the dismay of many Italians, and retired to a villa near Munich. He died in 1960, aged seventy-four.

General Wolff and some of his associates in the surrender negotiations with Dulles were arrested on Sunday, 13 May 1945, Wolff's forty-fifth birthday, as they stood on the lawn of the Royal Palace in Bolzano enjoying a birthday drink. Troops of the 38th Division of the American Fifth Army rolled up in 2½-ton trucks and took away Wolff, Dollmann, Lieutenant Zimmer and others. Wolff, held for four years as a witness and potential defendant in the Nuremberg war crimes trials, sank into depression and paranoia and was for a time confined to a mental hospital. In 1949, testimonials from Dulles and Gaevernitz helped him win acquittal on war crimes charges. A Hamburg court of appeals overturned the acquittal and sentenced him to four years, but he had by then served almost the entire sentence. The West German government tried him again in 1962 when documentary evidence showed he was more knowledgeable about the death camps than he had admitted, and he was sentenced to fifteen years in prison for being 'continuously engaged and deeply entangled in guilt' through his work with Himmler. He was found to have signed a paper in 1942 requesting additional freight wagons for use in Poland, but claimed he did not know they were intended for the transport of Jews to death camps. He was released in the mid-1970s and lived out his retirement in Munich. Ambassador Rahn escaped charges and became an executive of the Coca-Cola Company in Germany.[4]

Parrilli's close friend Lieutenant Zimmer, who helped initiate the surrender negotiations, was cleared of charges and returned to Bavaria, living in poverty until he emigrated to Argentina, where Parrilli helped him get started in business. Parrilli and Gaevernitz also arranged for Zimmer's two children to attend a private school in Switzerland, and paid their fees. General Roettiger, who joined Wolff in the decision to surrender, went to work for the American Army, helping to write the military history of the Second World War. He was chosen as the first inspector general of the new German army that was formed after 1951, and died in the mid-1950s. Schweinitz, the German emissary who went to Caserta to sign the surrender document, joined a German steel company. His boss, General Vietinghoff, died a few years after the war. Major Eugen Wenner, the adjutant to General Wolff, escaped from an Italian prisoner-of-war camp and fled to South America.[5]

Dollmann, the *bon vivant* and artistic-minded SS officer, escaped from a prison camp in Rimini, made his way to Milan and went to Cardinal Schuster to ask for help. Schuster gave him refuge in the Cardinal Ferrari Institute, where Dollmann shared living quarters with recovering narcotics addicts. Parrilli warned him in the summer of 1946 that the Americans were coming for him, so he fled to Rome. Angleton and another OSS officer tracked him down in Rome and asked him to participate in an anti-Russian espionage organisation in Germany. While they awaited his answer, an Italian detective arrested Dollmann in a cinema in Rome on 7 November, 1946, but Angleton and his colleague managed to get him released from Italian custody and transferred to an American military prison in Rome. In the spring of 1947, he was flown to Frankfurt to be imprisoned there, but he escaped, went to Austria and finally made his way back to Italy. Later, he returned to the old family home in Munich to pursue his historic and artistic interests and to use his considerable writing talents to produce two books of highly cynical, sometimes amusing, occasionally untruthful and always colourful memoirs. He also wrote a history of the Nazi presence in Italy that was more straightforward but not lacking in boasts about his achievements. He died in 1985, aged eighty-five.[6]

Colonel Rauff escaped from Italy after the war and settled in South America. Before his transfer to Italy as No. 2 in the SS, he had been accused of being the inventor of gas wagons used to exterminate prisoners on the Eastern front and of killing 96,000 Jews. He was never brought to justice, and died in Santiago, Chile, in May 1984.[7]

While a number of German officers were tried just after the war for atrocities committed in Italy, notably for the Marzabotto and Ardeatine caves massacres, the vast majority of those involved in war crimes escaped punishment. The reason they did so only came to light in 1994 when a cupboard was discovered in the basement of the Military Tribunal offices in Rome, its doors locked and sealed and turned around to face the wall. The 'cupboard of shame', as the Italian press called it, contained 695 files of evidence concerning an estimated 400 cases in which 15,000 Italian civilians were killed by German troops and Italian Fascists during the war. The files were stamped 'temporarily archived'.

A parliamentary commission later concluded that these files had been sealed, and possible prosecutions of the guilty abandoned, because of the exigencies of the Cold War. In 1956, when a number of requests for extradition of former German soldiers were pending, the German government in Bonn was in the process of reconstituting the German armed forces, over the protests of many people in Germany. NATO, faced with the threat of a Soviet invasion of Western Europe, was insistent on the rebirth of the German military, so the Italian government concluded that it would be inopportune to put former German soldiers on trial at such a delicate moment. The discovery of the cupboard led to a huge public outcry in Italy, but it was not until almost ten years later that several cases were reopened against elderly former SS troops living in Germany. But, of course, many potential defendants had died in the intervening years and chances were remote that justice would be done in the majority of the cases that had remained hidden for a half century.

The final word on the Mussolini era may rest with Claretta Petacci. The State Central Archive holds her correspondence with the Duce and her diary, and in 2002 proposed to publish it. But the plan was dropped when Ferdinando Petacci, a surviving nephew who lives in Colorado, threatened to bring suit to protect the privacy of her most intimate thoughts.[8] That safeguard will remain in effect until 2015, when, under Italian law, her right to privacy expires. Whether the publication of her letters and diary will contribute anything to history beyond the romantic banalities of an obsessed young woman is, of course, highly doubtful.

CHRONOLOGY

1943

25 July — Benito Mussolini loses a vote of confidence in the Fascist Grand Council; he is arrested later that day on the order of King Victor Emmanuel III.

8 September — The Italian government announces its acceptance of an armistice with the Allies.

9 September — Just ahead of the German occupation of Rome, the king and Prime Minister Marshal Pietro Badoglio flee for southern Italy. Allied forces invade the Italian mainland, landing at Salerno.

10 September — German troops occupy Rome and begin a roundup of Italian soldiers: 600,000 are shipped to Germany for internment.

12 September — Mussolini is freed from imprisonment on the Gran Sasso mountain in a daring German rescue operation, and is flown to Hitler's headquarters.

18 September — Mussolini addresses the Italian people by radio from Munich, promising to continue the war at Germany's side.

25 September — Mussolini returns to northern Italy to head a puppet government under German tutelage at Gargnano on Lake Garda. The so-called Salò Republic is born.

30 September — Naples is liberated by its own people after a four-day insurrection just before the arrival of Allied troops. It is the first important city under occupation to fall.

16 October — The Germans arrest more than 1,000 Roman Jews and ship them to Auschwitz–Birkenau. Most die in the gas chambers; only fifteen survive the war.

19 October — Mussolini's son-in-law, former Foreign Minister Count Galeazzo Ciano, is brought from Germany and arrested in Verona on treason charges for having voted against the Duce in the Fascist Grand Council meeting three months earlier.

28 October — Mussolini is reunited with his lover Claretta Petacci, who soon takes up residence near him by Lake Garda.

14 November — The reconstituted Fascist Party holds a congress at Verona and adopts an

	eighteen-point political programme for the new government.
18 November	The first of a wave of industrial strikes in northern Italy begins.
30 November	A decree of the Mussolini government orders the arrest of Jews and the confiscation of their property, and provides for the establishment of an Italian concentration camp.

1944

9 January	Edda Ciano flees to Switzerland, a day after her husband, Count Ciano, goes on trial for his life in Verona.
11 January	Ciano is executed at Verona along with four other men who also voted against the Duce.
13 January	A fresh wave of industrial strikes breaks out in northern Italy.
22 January	Allied forces land at Anzio, south of Rome, in a move aimed at speeding up the liberation of the city, but meet stiff German resistance.
12 February	The Fascist Cabinet approves the nationalisation of industry.
20 February	King Victor Emmanuel, under pressure to abdicate, agrees to name his son Prince Umberto as Lieutenant of the Realm on the day the Allies enter Rome.
1 March	Industrial workers in northern Italy stage a general strike, the first and only such to occur in Nazi-occupied Europe.
23 March	Italian partisans, in one of their first big operations, set off a bomb in the Via Rasella in Rome that kills thirty-three German soldiers.
24 March	The Germans execute 335 people in the Ardeatine caves outside Rome in reprisal.
15 April	Partisans in Florence assassinate the philosopher Giovanni Gentile, one of the most prominent Italians associated with fascism.
22 April	Mussolini meets Adolf Hitler at Klessheim Castle in Austria to plead for the return of Italian troops imprisoned in Germany after the armistice, but makes little headway.
4 June	The Germans abandon Rome without a fight and American forces march in: it is the first European capital to be liberated. Badoglio resigns as prime minister and is succeeded by the Socialist Ivanoe Bonomi.
14 June	The United States decides to divert seven divisions from Italy to assist in an invasion of southern France, thus slowing the Allied offensive in Italy.
25 June	General Raffaele Cadorna is appointed as the partisan military commander.
20 July	Mussolini meets Hitler at his headquarters in the East Prussian forest, just hours after the failed attempt on Hitler's life by Claus von

	Stauffenberg. It is the final meeting of the two dictators. Hitler agrees to allow four Italian divisions training in Germany to return to Italy.
25 July	With the war going badly for the Axis, Mussolini permits the formation of a new militia unit, the Black Brigades, to fight the partisans.
10 August	Fifteen Italian prisoners are shot by Fascists in Piazzale Loreto in Milan to avenge a partisan attack on a German truck carrying food.
19 August	Mussolini dismisses the unpopular commander of the Republican National Guard, General Renato Ricci.
1 September	The Allies break through the Gothic Line of German defence in central Italy.
21 September	Milan, Turin and other cities are hit by a fresh wave of strikes.
28–30 September	German forces kill 1,830 people in the Marzabotto area in central Italy, their largest single atrocity of the war in Italy.
24 October	Mussolini's wife, Donna Rachele, has a stormy confrontation with Clara Petacci at Petacci's residence on Lake Garda, but fails to persuade Petacci to abandon the Duce.
13 November	Field Marshal Harold Alexander orders partisan forces to avoid conflict with the Germans and Fascists during the winter months, an order that is ignored.
23 November	Further strikes in northern Italy.
26 November	Bonomi resigns as prime minister, then forms a new government that for the first time includes Communists.
16 December	Mussolini briefly leaves Gargnano to make a major address to the Italian people at the Lyric Theatre in Milan, where he receives an ovation.

1945

21 February	Mussolini dismisses the unpopular Interior Minister Guido Buffarini-Guidi. The Germans retaliate by arresting his secret police chief and former police chief. Earlier in the month, according to his German doctor Mussolini suffers a nervous breakdown.
26 February	Baron Luigi Parrilli, an Italian industrialist, meets an American espionage officer in Switzerland to sound out possibilities of a German surrender in Italy, an initiative that will be crowned with success two months later.
8 March	Parrilli escorts General Karl Wolff, the SS commander in Italy, to Switzerland for a meeting with Allen W. Dulles, head of the US Office of Strategic Services, for the first concrete discussions about a surrender.
9 March	Mussolini sends a priest to Switzerland to present a peace proposal to a Vatican envoy, involving an alliance of Italy, Germany and the

	Allies to defeat Soviet communism. The proposal is not treated seriously.
12 March	Mussolini escapes injury when an Allied fighter plane attacks his convoy of cars near the southern end of Lake Garda.
13 March	Mussolini sends his son Vittorio to Milan to attempt another peace initiative through Cardinal Ildefonso Schuster.
15 March	The Fascist Cabinet considers a plan to retreat to the Valtellina, a valley below the Swiss border, to make a last heroic stand against the Allies.
19 March	General Wolff meets two Allied generals in Switzerland for further surrender talks.
22 March	The Cabinet decides to proceed with further nationalisation of industry.
5 April	The Allies launch their final offensive to drive the Germans from Italy, capturing several towns in central Italy.
12 April	President Franklin D. Roosevelt dies in Warm Springs, Georgia.
18 April	Wolff meets Hitler in Berlin and discloses his negotiations with the Allies. Hitler urges him to get better terms. On the same day, Mussolini goes to Milan to establish his government there, and Claretta follows him.
20 April	Strikes break out in Milan, the prelude to a general partisan insurrection.
22–23 April	Wolff travels to Switzerland, expecting to complete the German surrender, but Dulles is under instructions from Washington not to receive him.
25 April	In a meeting with Cardinal Schuster and partisan political representatives, Mussolini learns that the Germans have been negotiating a surrender behind his back. He leaves for Como that evening with several of his ministers; his departure signifies the collapse of Fascist rule and partisans begin taking over the city.
27 April	Mussolini is captured in the Lake Como town of Dongo, attempting to flee disguised as a German soldier in the back of a German military truck. Other Fascist leaders also are captured, while Claretta Petacci and her brother Marcello are arrested pending an investigation to determine their identities.
28 April	After confessing her identity to a partisan leader, Claretta is taken as a prisoner with Mussolini to a farmhouse in the village of Bonzanigo. Later that day, they are executed by partisans in front of a villa in the nearby hamlet of Giulino di Mezzegra. The partisans then go to Dongo and execute fifteen Fascist leaders as well as Marcello Petacci.
29 April	The bodies are taken to Milan, and those of

	Mussolini, Claretta and several Fascist leaders are strung up by their feet in front of a petrol station in Piazzale Loreto before a large crowd of onlookers, some of whom defile the bodies. On the same day, Rachele Mussolini turns herself in to the partisans and is arrested. She and her two young children are later exiled to the island of Ischia. At Allied headquarters in Caserta, two German officers sign a surrender document.
30 April	Hitler commits suicide in his Berlin bunker along with his bride, Eva Braun.
2 May	The German surrender takes place at noon.

1946

23 April	Three young Fascists dig up Mussolini's body from its secret burial site in a Milanese cemetery and hide it. Authorities later arrest them and recover the body, which is kept in a secret location in Milan for eleven years. In August 1957, the body is returned to Rachele for burial in the family cemetery in Predappio.
12 June	Italians vote to establish a republic, and King Umberto II, after a reign of less than one month (his father abdicated in May), goes into exile in Portugal.

DRAMATIS PERSONAE

AIREY, TERENCE S.: British major-general who helped negotiate the German surrender in Italy
ALEXANDER, HAROLD: British field marshal and commander of Allied forces in Italy
ANFUSO, FILIPPO: Mussolini's last ambassador to Germany
APOLLONIO, EUGENIO: Secret Police chief under Mussolini
AUDISIO, WALTER: Communist member of partisan Corps of Volunteers for Freedom and presumed killer of Benito Mussolini. *Nom de guerre*: Colonel Valerio
BADOGLIO, PIETRO: Marshal of Italy and head of government after Mussolini's overthrow in 1943
BARRACU, FRANCESCO MARIA: minister for Cabinet affairs under Mussolini; executed at Dongo
BASSI, MARIO: Fascist prefect in Milan
BELLINI DELLE STELLE, COUNT PIER LUIGI: head of the partisan brigade in Dongo when Mussolini was captured. *Nom de guerre*: Pedro
BERNARDINI, MONSIGNOR FILIPPO: papal nuncio in Switzerland
BERTINELLI, VIRGINIO: prefect of Como after the collapse of the Fascist government
BICCHIERAI, GIUSEPPE: priest who was also secretary to Cardinal Schuster of Milan and a central figure in the peace negotiations
BIGGINI, CARLO ALBERTO: Mussolini's minister of education
BOMBACCI, NICOLA: former Communist who befriended Mussolini, and was executed at Dongo
BONOMI, IVANOE: Socialist who headed the Italian government in the south after the resignation of Badoglio
BUFFARINI-GUIDI, GUIDO: interior minister under Mussolini; executed after the war
CADORNA, RAFFAELE: military commander of the partisan Corps of Volunteers for Freedom
CALISTRI, PIETRO: Air Force pilot executed at Dongo
CANALI, LUIGI: partisan involved in transporting Mussolini before his execution; later murdered. *Nom de guerre*: Captain Neri
CANTONI, GUGLIELMO: partisan who guarded Mussolini and Claretta Petacci after their capture. *Nom de guerre*: Sandrino
CARITÀ, MARIO: Fascist secret police chief in Florence and notorious torturer
CARUSO, PIETRO: Fascist police chief in Rome, executed after the war
CASALINUOVO, VITO: Mussolini aide and Republican National Guard colonel, executed at Dongo
CIANO, EDDA MUSSOLINI: daughter of Mussolini and wife of Count Ciano
CIANO, COUNT GALEAZZO: Mussolini's foreign minister and son-in-law; executed for treason in January 1944

CLARK, MARK W.: general commanding US Fifth Army in Italy

COLOMBO, FRANCESCO: head of the notorious Fascist Muti Legion in Milan; executed after the war

COPPOLA, GOFFREDO: Mussolini's friend and rector of Bologna University; executed at Dongo

COSTA, VINCENZO: Fascist Party leader in Milan

DAQUANNO, ERNESTO: director of the Stefani news agency, executed at Dongo

DE MARIA, GIACOMO AND LIA: couple in whose farmhouse Mussolini and Claretta Petacci spent their last night

DINALE, OTTAVIO: diarist and long-standing friend of Mussolini's

DOLFIN, GIOVANNI: secretary to Mussolini

DOLLMANN, EUGEN: SS officer in Italy involved in surrender negotiations with the United States

DULLES, ALLEN W.: head of the US Office of Strategic Services in Switzerland (OSS)

FARINACCI, ROBERTO: extreme Fascist leader and critic of Mussolini, executed at the end of the war

FRANGI, GIUSEPPE: partisan who guarded Mussolini and Claretta Petacci after their capture. *Nom de guerre*: Lino

GAEVERNITZ, GERO SCHULZE VON: German-born assistant to Dulles at the OSS

GATTI, LUIGI: last secretary to Mussolini; executed at Dongo

GORRERI, DANTE: Communist Party leader in Como

GRAZIANI, RODOLFO: minister of the armed forces under Mussolini

HARSTER, WILHELM: Gestapo chief in Italy

HÖTTL, WILHELM: SS intelligence chief in southern Europe

HUSMANN, MAX: Swiss citizen involved in negotiations for the German surrender in Italy

KALTENBRUNNER, ERNST: Austrian who headed the Reich High Security Office in Berlin

KAPPLER, HERBERT: Gestapo chief in Rome

KESSELRING, FIELD MARSHAL: Commander of German forces in Italy

KOCH, PIETRO: head of a notorious gang of Fascist assassins and torturers

LAMPREDI ALDO: high-ranking Communist who was in the party that executed Mussolini. *Nom de guerre*: Guido

LAZZARO, URBANO: the partisan who captured Mussolini. *Nom de guerre*: Bill

LEMNITZER, GENERAL LYMAN: American officer who helped negotiate the German surrender in Italy

LIVERANI, AUGUSTO: Mussolini's communications minister; executed at Dongo

LONGO, LUIGI: highest-ranking Communist in northern Italy; one of three leaders of the partisan military organisation, the Corps of Volunteers for Freedom

MARAZZA, ACHILLE: Christian Democrat on the Committee for National Liberation

MAZZOLINI, SERAFINO: under-secretary for foreign affairs under Mussolini

MELLINI PONCE DE LEON, ALBERTO: Italian Foreign Ministry official

MEZZASOMA, FERNANDO: Mussolini's press chief; executed at Dongo

MONTAGNA, RENZO: Mussolini's last police chief

MORETTI, MICHELE: Communist in the party that executed Mussolini. *Nom de guerre*: Pietro

MUSSOLINI, ARNALDO: brother of Benito Mussolini

MUSSOLINI, EDVIGE: sister of Benito Mussolini

MUSSOLINI, RACHELE: wife of Benito Mussolini

MUSSOLINI, VITTORIO, ROMANO AND ANNA MARIA: children of Benito and Rachele Mussolini

NUDI, MARIO: employee of the Fascist Agricultural Federation; executed at Dongo

PARRI, FERRUCCIO: Action Party representative on the Committee for National Liberation and first postwar prime minister of Italy

PARRILLI, BARON LUIGI: Italian businessman who arranged German surrender negotiations with the Americans

PAVOLINI, ALESSANDRO: secretary of the Fascist Party under Mussolini; executed at Dongo

PELLEGRINI-GIAMPIETRO, GAETANO: finance minister under Mussolini

PERTINI, SANDRO: Socialist leader of the partisan Corps of Volunteers for Freedom; later president of Italy

PESCE, GIOVANNI: famed GAP assassin

PETACCI, CLARA: mistress of Benito Mussolini, usually called Claretta

PETACCI, MARCELLO: brother of Clara; executed at Dongo

PETACCI, MYRIAM: sister of Clara

PISENTI, PIERO: justice minister under Mussolini

PIUS XII: the pope whose actions during the Fascist era remain a subject of bitter controversy

PORTA, PAOLO: Fascist leader in Lombardy, executed at Dongo

PREZIOSI, GIOVANNI: defrocked priest who was in charge of the persecution of the Jews under Mussolini

RAHN, RUDOLF VON: German ambassador to the Italian Social Republic

RAUFF, COLONEL WALTER: SS chief for Lombardy, Piedmont and Liguria

RICCI, RENATO: head of Republican National Guard forces under Mussolini

ROETTIGER, GENERAL HANS: chief of staff of the Wehrmacht in Italy

ROMANO, RUGGERO: Mussolini's minister of public works; executed at Dongo

RUBERTI, GINA: Mussolini's daughter-in-law, widow of his son Bruno

RUBINI, GIUSEPPE: mayor of Dongo

SCHUSTER, ILDEFONSO: cardinal archbishop of Milan

SCHWEINITZ, COLONEL VICTOR VON: German who signed the document surrendering German forces in Italy

SILVESTRI, CARLO: journalist and Socialist who befriended Mussolini

TAMBURINI, TULLIO: Italian police chief under Mussolini

TARCHI, ANGELO: economy minister under Mussolini

TOGLIATTI, PALMIRO: leader of the Italian Communist Party

TROENDLE, MAX: Swiss commercial representative in Italy

TUISSI, GIUSEPPINA: partisan who accompanied Mussolini and Claretta Petacci to the De Maria farmhouse; later murdered. *Nom de guerre*: Gianna

UMBERTO: Crown Prince of Italy, reigned as King Umberto II for a month in 1946 before Italy became a republic

UTIMPERGHER, IDRENO: Fascist publicist; executed at Dongo

VALIANI, LEO: Action Party representative on the Committee of National Liberation in northern Italy

VICTOR EMMANUEL III: King of Italy

VIETINGHOFF, GENERAL HEINRICH VON: successor to Field Marshal Kesselring as commander of German forces in Italy

WAIBEL, MAX: Swiss Intelligence major involved in German surrender negotiations

WENING, GENERAL: Wehrmacht commander in Milan

WENNER, MAJOR EUGEN: aide-de-camp to SS General Karl Wolff, joined Schweinitz in signing the German surrender in Italy

WILSON, GENRAL SIR MAITLAND: British commander of Allied forces in the Mediterranean

WOLFF, GENERAL KARL: SS commander in Italy

ZACHARIAE, GEORG: German doctor who treated Mussolini

ZERBINO, PAOLO: last interior minister under Mussolini; executed at Dongo

ZIMMER, GUIDO: SS lieutenant, chief of counter-espionage in Genoa; involved in German surrender negotiations

ZINGALES, GENERAL LEONE: military prosecutor who investigated the killing of Mussolini and the disappearance of his documents and Fascist funds

NOTES

Chapter 1. The Last Spectator

1. Georg Zachariae, *Mussolini si confessa* (Milan: Garzanti, 1948), p. 19.
2. *Ibid.*, p. 28.
3. Benito Mussolini, *Opera Omnia*, vol. 32 (Florence: La Fenice, 1960), pp. 157–61. All subsequent references are to volume 32.
4. Giovanni Dolfin, *Con Mussolini nella tragedia* (Milan: Garzanti, 1949), pp. 27–8.
5. Silvio Bertoldi, *Salò* (Milan: Rizzoli, 1978), pp. 24–5.
6. Ottavio Dinale, *Quarant'anni di colloqui con lui* (Milan: Ciarroca, 1953), p. 244.
7. B. Mussolini, *Opera Omnia*, pp. 168–82.
8. Dinale, *Quaranti'anni di colloqui con lui*, pp. 284, 286, 289.

Chapter 2. After the Fall

1. Ray Moseley, *Mussolini's Shadow* (New Haven, CT: Yale University Press, 1999), pp. 169–75; and R.J.B. Bosworth, *Mussolini* (London: Arnold, 2002), p. 354.
2. Renzo De Felice, *Mussolini l'alleato, II: La guerra civile*, (Turin: Giulio Einaudi, 1997), p. 14 (all subsequent references are to *II: La guerra civile*); and Benito Mussolini, *Storia di un anno* (Milan: Mondadori, 1944), p. 156.
3. De Felice, *Mussolini l'alleato*, pp. 14–43; Giorgio Pini and Duilio Susmel, *Mussolini, l'uomo e l'opera*, vol. 4, (Florence: La Fenice, 1955), pp. 318–20. All subsequent references are to volume 4; Eugen Dollmann, *Roma nazista* (Milan: RCS Libri, 2002), p. 143; Rachele Mussolini, *La mia vita con Benito* (Milan: Mondadori, 1948), p. 209; and Paolo Monelli, *Mussolini piccolo borghese* (Milan: Garzanti, 1950), p. 248.
4. M. de Wyss, *Rome under the Terror* (London: Robert Hale, 1945), p. 98; De Felice, *Mussolini l'alleato*, p. 42; Zachariae, *Mussolini si confessa*, pp. 13–14; and Wilhelm Hoettl, *The Secret Front* (London: Weidenfeld & Nicolson, 1953), p. 230.
5. Zachariae, *Mussolini si confessa*, p. 12.
6. Felice Bellotti, *La repubblica di Mussolini* (Milan: Zagara, 1947), p. 59.
7. Carlo Silvestri, *Mussolini, Graziani e l'antifascismo* (Milan: Longanesi, 1949), pp. 33–4.
8. *Ibid.*, p. 34.
9. Pini and Susmel, *Mussolini, l'uomo e l'opera*, p. 327.

10. Silvestri, *Mussolini*, p. 38; and R. Mussolini, *La mia vita con Benito*, p. 242.
11. Vittorio Mussolini, *Vita con mio padre* (Milan: Mondadori, 1957), pp. 203, 204, 201.
12. *Ibid.*, pp. 199–202.
13. Zachariae, *Mussolini si confessa*, pp. 4, 5.
14. V. Mussolini, *Vita con mio padre*, pp. 192–3.
15. Bruno Spampanato, *L'ultimo Mussolini* (Rome: Rivista Romano, 1964), vol. 2, p. 26.
16. R. Mussolini, *La mia vita con Benito*, p. 220.
17. Moseley, *Mussolini's Shadow*, pp. 182–6.
18. *Ibid.*, pp. 188–9.
19. B. Mussolini, *Opera Omnia* pp. 1–5; and V. Mussolini, *Vita con mio padre*, p. 205.
20. Claretta Petacci, *Il mio diario* (Milan: Garzanti, 1946), p. 180.
21. R. Mussolini, *La mia vita con Benito*, p. 219.
22. Vittorio Mussolini, *The Tragic Women in His Life* (New York: Dial Press, 1973), pp. 3–11.
23. Joseph Goebbels, *The Goebbels Diaries* (London: Hamish Hamilton, 1948), pp. 378–9.
24. *Ibid.*, p. 388.
25. Bellotti, *La repubblica di Mussolini*, p. 65.
26. Silvestri, *Mussolini*, pp. 34–5.
27. Churchill Archives, CHAR 20/116/26—28. These archives are held at Churchill College, Cambridge University.
28. Churchill Archives, CHAR 20/117/10; and William Shirer, *The Rise and Fall of the Third Reich* (New York: Simon & Schuster, 1960), p. 999.
29. Ermanno Amicucci, *I 600 giorni di Mussolini* (Rome: Faro, 1948), pp. 7–12; Max Salvadori, *Breve storia della resistenza italiana* (Florence: Vallecchi, 1974), pp. 61, 71; Luigi Bolla, *Perché a Salò* (Milan: Bompiani, 1982), p. 97; and Richard Lamb, *War in Italy* (London: John Murray, 1993), pp. 14–21.
30. Lamb, *War in Italy*, pp. 129–38.
31. Jane Scrivener, *Inside Rome with the Germans* (New York: Macmillan, 1945), pp. 4–7.
32. Goebbels, *The Goebbels Diaries*, p. 49.
33. Scrivener, *Inside Rome with the Germans*, p. 14.
34. De Wyss, *Rome under the Terror*, pp. 110, 131–2.
35. Scrivener, *Inside Rome with the Germans*, p. 30.
36. Bolla, *Perché a Salò*, pp. 97, 103; and de Wyss, *Rome under the Terror*, p. 11.
37. Giorgio Bocca, *Storia dell'Italia partigiana* (Bari: Laterza, 1966), p. 147.
38. Spampanato, *L'ultimo Mussolini*, vol. 2, p. 36.
39. Bolla, *Perché a Salò*, p. 110.

Chapter 3. Birth of the Salò Republic

1. R. Mussolini, *La mia vita con Benito*, p. 221.
2. Goebbels, *The Goebbels Diaries*, pp. 379, 381, 390.
3. Giorgio Bocca, *La repubblica di Mussolini* (Milan: Mondadori, 1994), p. 34; and Salvadori, *Breve storia della resistenza italiana*, p. 69.
4. Pini and Susmel, *Mussolini, l'uomo e l'opera*, p. 356.
5. Spampanato, *L'ultimo Mussolini*, vol. 2, p. 67.
6. Goebbels, *The Goebbels Diaries*, p. 383.

7. Bocca, *La repubblica di Mussolini*, p. 42.
8. Amicucci, *I 600 giorni di Mussolini*, p. 42.
9. Dollmann, *Roma nazista*, p. 289.
10. Bocca, *La repubblica di Mussolini*, p. 39.
11. Mario Innocenti, *Mussolini a Salò* (Milan: Mursia, 1996), p. 91; Bocca, *La repubblica di Mussolini*, p. 39; Silvestri, *Mussolini, Graziani e l'antifascismo*, p. 35; and Scrivener, *Inside Rome with the Germans*, p. 27.
12. Innocenti, *Mussolini a Salò*, p. 86.
13. Bellotti, *La repubblica di Mussolini*, p. 75; and Bolla, *Perché a Salò*, p. 125.
14. Filippo Anfuso, *Da Palazzo Venezia al Lago di Garda* (Rome: Settimo Sigillo: 1996), p. 405; and Bolla, *Perché a Salò*, p. 125.
15. Goebbels, *The Goebbels Diaries*, p. 387.
16. Dino Campini, *Mussolini e Churchill* (Milan: Italpress, 1950), p. 88; and Elisabetta Cerruti, *Ambassador's Wife* (London: George Allen & Unwin, 1952), p. 228.
17. Bocca, *La repubblica di Mussolini*, p. 79; and Salvadori, *Breve storia della resistenza italiana*, pp. 30, 36.
18. Dollmann, *Roma nazista*, p. 289; and Ernst von Weizsäcker, *The Memoirs of Ernst von Weizsäcker* (London: Victor Gollancz, 1951), p. 291.
19. Bocca, *La repubblica di Mussolini*, p. 41.
20. Dollmann, *Roma nazista*, p. 290.
21. Scrivener, *Inside Rome with the Germans*, pp. 40, 45, 59, 61.
22. De Wyss, *Rome under the Terror*, p. 144.
23. Scrivener, *Inside Rome with the Germans*, p. 63; and de Wyss, *Rome under the Terror*, p. 161.
24. Bocca, *La repubblica di Mussolini*, p. 50; and Bolla, *Perché a Salò*, p. 126.
25. F.W. Deakin, *The Last Days of Mussolini* (London: Penguin, 1962), p. 108; Pini and Susmel, *Mussolini, l'uomo e l'opera*, p. 349; Scrivener, *Inside Rome with the Germans*, p. 29; and Dolfin, *Con Mussolini nella tragedia*, p. 78.
26. Dolfin, *Con Mussolini nella tragedia*, p. 41.
27. *Ibid.*, p. 67.
28. *Ibid.*, pp. 72–4.
29. Bocca, *Storia dell'Italia partigiana*, pp. 161, 163; and de Wyss, *Rome under the Terror*, p. 84.
30. Monelli, *Mussolini piccolo borghese*, p. 319; and Dolfin, *Con Mussolini nella tragedia*, p. 107.
31. Bolla, *Perché a Salò*, pp. 42–3.
32. Pini and Susmel, *Mussolini, l'uomo e l'opera*, p. 371; R. Mussolini, *La mia vita con Benito*, p. 225; and Bolla, *Perché a Salò*, p. 159.
33. Bocca, *La repubblica di Mussolini*, p. 48
34. Maria de Blasio Wilhelm, *The Other Italy* (New York: W.W. Norton, 1988), pp. 35–56; Attilio Tamaro, *Due anni di storia*, vol. 2 (Rome: Tosi, 1948), pp. 76–90; and de Wyss, *Rome under the Terror*, p. 137.
35. Bocca, *La repubblica di Mussolini*, p. 45.
36. Innocenti, *Mussolini a Salò*, p. 123; and Pini and Susmel, *Mussolini, l'uomo e l'opera*, p. 374.
37. Anfuso, *Da Palazzo Venezia al Lago di Garda*, p. 403.

38. Pietro Badoglio, *Italy in the Second World War* (Westport, CT: Greenwood Press, 1976), p. 38; Dolfin, *Con Mussolini nella tragedia*, p. 49; and Dollmann, *Roma nazista*, pp. 243, 247.
39. Dolfin, *Con Mussolini nella tragedia*, p. 50; and Bocca, *La repubblica di Mussolini*, p. 147.
40. Innocenti, *Mussolini a Salò*, p. 46.
41. Anfuso, *Da Palazzo Venezia al Lago di Garda*, p. 406; Eugen Dollmann, *The Interpreter* (London: Hutchinson, 1967), p. 316; and Innocenti, *Mussolini a Salò*, p. 100.
42. Anfuso, *Da Palazzo Venezia al Lago di Garda*, p. 414.
43. Innocenti, *Mussolini a Salò*, p. 48.
44. Bocca, *La repubblica di Mussolini*, p. 145.
45. Anfuso, *Da Palazzo Venezia al Lago di Garda*, p. 420; Dollmann, *Roma nazista*, p. 105; and Giorgio Angelozzi Gariboldi, *Pio XII, Hitler e Mussolini* (Milan: Mursia, 1988), p. 254.
46. Zachariae, *Mussolini si confessa*, pp. 9–19.
47. *Ibid.*, pp. 22, 25.
48. Moseley, *Mussolini's Shadow*, pp. 2, 139; and Zachariae, *Mussolini si confessa*, pp. 79–80.
49. Nino D'Aroma, *Mussolini segreto* (Bologna: Cappelli, 1958), p. 278.
50. Zachariae, *Mussolini si confessa*, pp. 18, 19; and R. Mussolini, *La mia vita con Benito*, p. 228.

Chapter 4. The Fate of the Roman Jews

1. Il ghetto di Roma. www.geocities.com/Paris/Arc/5319/roma-c9i.htm, last accessed 22 February 2003; and John Cornwell, *Hitler's Pope* (London: Viking, 1999), p. 299.
2. Robert Katz, *Black Sabbath* (London: Arthur Barker Ltd., 1969), pp. 19, 20, 25, 27, 33. Katz's book is the definitive work on the Nazi pogrom in Rome.
3. Renzo De Felice, *Storia degli ebrei italiani sotto il fascismo* (Turin: Giulio Einaudi, 1988), p. 466.
4. Katz, *Black Sabbath*, pp. 39–41.
5. Meir Michaelis, *Mussolini and the Jews* (Oxford: Clarendon Press, 1978), pp. 352–3.
6. Katz, *Black Sabbath*, pp. 53–61.
7. Michaelis, *Mussolini and the Jews*, 365; Lamb, *War in Italy*, p. 41; and Katz, *Black Sabbath*, pp. 65–8, 87–93, 97.
8. Katz, *Black Sabbath*, pp. 120–4, 147, 149–50.
9. *Ibid.*, pp. 142–3.
10. *Ibid.*, pp. 157–8, 165–7, 174, 181–2, 184–5.
11. *Ibid.*, pp. 164–5, 175, 186, 190.
12. Silvio Bertoldi, *I tedeschi in Italia* (Milan: Rizzoli, 1994), pp. 136–7.
13. Fulvia Ripa di Meana, *Roma clandestina* (Rome: Polilibraria, 1945), p. 88; and Katz, *Black Sabbath*, pp. 196–7.
14. Scrivener, *Inside Rome with the Germans*, p. 39.
15. Rosetta Loy, *La parola ebreo* (Turin: Einaudi, 1997), pp. 4, 121, 123, 131–2, 138–43, 147.
16. Iris Origo, *War in Val d'Orcia* (London: Jonathan Cape, 1947), p. 109.
17. Katz, *Black Sabbath*, pp. 173, 193, 198, 201–2, 214.
18. Cornwell, *Hitler's Pope*, pp. 304–5.

19. Bertoldi, *I tedeschi in Italia*, p. 137.
20. Katz, *Black Sabbath*, pp. 208–9, 212, 215, 223, 209–10, 220.
21. *Ibid.*, pp. 229, 231–2, 234, 239–40, 242–53, 246, 249–51.
22. *Ibid.*, pp. 255, 267, 269–70, 293.
23. Bertoldi, *I tedeschi in Italia*, pp. 134–6.
24. Katz, *Black Sabbath*, pp. 300–01, 304–06, 310–12; and Angelozzi Gariboldi, *Pio XII, Hitler e Mussolini*, p. 201.
25. Angelozzi Gariboldi, *Pio XII, Hitler e Mussolini*, pp. 148, 214.
26. Robert Katz, *The Battle for Rome* (New York: Simon & Schuster, 2003), pp. 81, 83–4.
27. Cornwell, *Hitler's Pope*, pp. 317–18.

Chapter 5. Mussolini and Claretta

1. Myriam Petacci, *Chi ama è perduto* (Gardolo di Trento: Luigi Reverdito, 1988), pp. 317–18.
2. D'Aroma, *Mussolini segreto*, p. 279.
3. Jasper Ridley, *Mussolini* (New York: Cooper Square Press, 2000), pp. 10, 20–3, 33–4, 52–3, 76–7, 185–6.
4. Asvero Gravelli, *Mussolini aneddotico* (Rome: Latinità, 1976), pp. 277, 278.
5. D'Aroma, *Mussolini segreto*, pp. 422, 427.
6. M. Petacci, *Chi ama è perduto*, pp. 61–4; and Roberto Gervaso, *Claretta* (Bologna: Bompiani, 2002), pp. 20–3.
7. M. Petacci, *Chi ama è perduto*, pp. 68–9.
8. *Ibid.*, 85–89, 92, 94.
9. Gervaso, *Claretta*, p. 31.
10. D'Aroma, *Mussolini segreto*, pp. 431–3, 435; and Bosworth, *Mussolini*, p. 311, quoting Franco Bandini.
11. Cerruti, *Ambassador's Wife*, p. 224.
12. Bosworth, *Mussolini*, pp. 277, 346.
13. Giuseppe Bottai, *Diario 1935–1944*, vol. 2, p. 219.
14. M. Petacci, *Chi ama è perduto*, pp. 152, 180.
15. *Ibid.*, p. 170; Galeazzo Ciano, *Diario*, vol. 2 (Bologna: Cappelli, 1948), p. 188; and De Felice, *Mussolini l'alleato*, p. 1071.
16. De Felice, *Mussolini l'alleato*, p. 1070; and Bottai, *Diario 1935–1944*, vol. 2, p. 337.
17. De Wyss, *Rome under the Terror*, p. 14.
18. De Felice, *Mussolini l'alleato*, pp. 1071–2.
19. Bottai, *Diario 1935–1944*, p. 268.
20. G. Ciano, *Diario*, pp. 86, 143, 149, 167–8.
21. Edda Ciano, *La mia testimonianza* (Milan: Rusconi, 1975), pp. 170–1.
22. G. Ciano, *Diario*, pp. 183, 188.
23. E. Ciano, *La mia testimonianza*, pp. 171–2, 174–6.
24. Bottai, *Diario 1935–1944*, p. 362.
25. G. Ciano, *Diario*, pp. 209, 233.
26. M. Petacci, *Chi ama è perduto*, pp. 182–3.
27. *Ibid.*, p. 269.

28. De Felice, *Mussolini l'alleato*, pp. 1536–40. Carboni's full report is reproduced here as an appendix.
29. M. Petacci, *Chi ama è perduto*, pp. 254–5.
30. D'Aroma, *Mussolini segreto*, p. 431.
31. M. Petacci, *Chi ama è perduto*, p. 283.
32. R. Mussolini, *La mia vita con Benito*, pp. 250–1.
33. M. Petacci, *Chi ama è perduto*, pp. 290, 293, 296.
34. C. Petacci, *Il mio diario*, pp. 1, 11–13, 28, 178–80.
35. M. Petacci, *Chi ama è perduto*, pp. 304–6, 318–21; and Dollmann, *Roma nazista*, p. 294.
36. R. Mussolini, *La mia vita con Benito*, p. 251.

Chapter 6. A Most Unhappy Family

1. Rachele Mussolini, *Benito il mio uomo* (Milan: Rizzoli, 1958), p. 213; and Bolla, *Perché a Salò*, pp. 160–1.
2. Moseley, *Mussolini's Shadow*, pp. 254–5.
3. D'Aroma, *Mussolini segreto*, p. 352.
4. Anfuso, *Da Palazzo Venezia al Lago di Garda*, p. 350.
5. D'Aroma, *Mussolini segreto*, p. 352; and Cerruti, *Ambassador's Wife*, p. 226.
6. Bosworth, *Mussolini*, p. 406; and Zachariae, *Mussolini si confessa*, pp. 26–7.
7. R. Mussolini, *La mia vita con Benito*, p. 228; and D'Aroma, *Mussolini segreto*, p. 372.
8. R. Mussolini, *La mia vita con Benito*, pp. 230–2.
9. Bellotti, *La repubblica di Mussolini*, p. 59; Bolla, *Perché a Salò*, pp. 158, 173–4; and V. Mussolini, *Vita con mio padre*, p. 19.
10. Bolla, *Perché a Salò*, pp. 203–4.
11. Ruggero Zangrandi, *Il lungo viaggio attraverso il fascismo* (Milan: Feltrinelli, 1962), pp. 21–3, 28–32.
12. V. Mussolini, *Vita con mio padre*, pp. 18–19.
13. D'Aroma, *Mussolini segreto*, p. 354; and Moseley, *Mussolini's Shadow*, p. 18.
14. Bosworth, *Mussolini*, p. 311.
15. D'Aroma, *Mussolini segreto*, pp. 311, 349, 353–4.
16. V. Mussolini, *Vita con mio padre*, pp. 72, 79–80, 89, 107, 111, 114–15; and Bosworth, *Mussolini*, pp. 310–11.
17. V. Mussolini, *Vita con mio padre*, pp. 122–4.
18. Benito Mussolini, *Parlo con Bruno* (Milan: Il Popolo d'Italia, 1941), pp. 141, 165–6.
19. De Felice, *Mussolini l'alleato*, p. 41.

Chapter 7. Galeazzo Ciano and Edda

1. Bosworth, *Mussolini*, p. 276.
2. Moseley, *Mussolini's Shadow*, pp. 1, 6–7, 13, 14, 16, 21, 22.
3. *Ibid.*, pp. 57, 60, 255.
4. *Ibid.*, pp. 66, 73, 86, 103, 113.
5. *Ibid.*, pp. 124–5, 132, 165.

6. *Ibid.*, pp. 169, 171, 173, 174, 177, 178, 184, 186–7, 193, 196–7, 199; and D'Aroma, *Mussolini segreto*, p. 283.
7. Moseley, *Mussolini's Shadow*, p. 199.
8. *Ibid.*, pp. 198, 200, 202–03, 206–10; and Bolla, *Perché a Salò*, p. 129.
9. R. Mussolini, *La mia vita con Benito*, p. 234.
10. Moseley, *Mussolini's Shadow*, pp. 211, 213–19; and Bolla, *Perché a Salò*, p. 152.
11. Moseley, *Mussolini's Shadow*, pp. 220–36; and R. Mussolini, *La mia vita con Benito*, p. 229.
12. Moseley, *Mussolini's Shadow*, pp. 236–8; and R. Mussolini, *La mia vita con Benito*, pp. 234, 239.
13. R. Mussolini, *Benito il mio uomo*, pp. 231–2.
14. Moseley, *Mussolini's Shadow*, pp. 244–5, 247–52.
15. *Ibid.*, p. 241.

Chapter 8. Troubles on All Fronts

1. Goebbels, *The Goebbels Diaries*, pp. 411–12.
2. *Ibid.*, pp. 423, 441.
3. Bolla, *Perché a Salò*, pp. 115, 119.
4. Pini and Susmel, *Mussolini, l'uomo e l'opera*, pp. 361–5; and Roberto Battaglia, *Storia della resistenza italiana* (Turin: Giulio Einaudi, 1964), p. 142.
5. Dolfin, *Con Mussolini nella tragedia*, pp. 96–7.
6. Bernard Berenson, *Rumour and Reflection* (London: Constable, 1952), p. 136.
7. Battaglia, *Storia della resistenza italiana*, pp. 146–8; and Luigi Longo, *Un popolo alla macchia* (Milan: Mondadori, 1947), p. 142.
8. Alberto Mellini Ponce de Leon, *Guerra diplomatica a Salò* (Bologna: Cappelli, 1950), p. 194; and Bolla, *Perché a Salò*, p. 124.
9. Dolfin, *Con Mussolini nella tragedia*, p. 116.
10. Bolla, *Perché a Salò*, pp. 122, 126, 139.
11. Battaglia, *Storia della resistenza italiana*, pp. 146–151; Bocca, *La repubblica di Mussolini*, p. 112; and Longo, *Un popolo alla macchia*, pp. 143–5.
12. Bocca, *La repubblica di Mussolini*, pp. 272–6; Mellini, *Guerra diplomatica a Salò*, p. 197; and Dolfin, *Con Mussolini nella tragedia*, p. 137.
13. Bocca, *La repubblica di Mussolini*, pp. 84–5.
14. Battaglia, *Storia della resistenza italiana*, p. 126; Lamb, *War in Italy*, p. 74; Wilhelm, *The Other Italy*, pp. 105–6; Pini and Susmel, *Mussolini, l'uomo e l'opera*, p. 379; and Amicucci, *I 600 giorni di Mussolini*, pp. 62–3.
15. De Felice, *Mussolini l'alleato*, pp. 140–1.
16. Warren F. Kimball, *Churchill and Roosevelt: The Complete Correspondence*, vol. 2 (Princeton, NJ: Princeton University Press, 1984), pp. 503–17, 587, 591, 679.
17. Dolfin, *Con Mussolini nella tragedia*, pp. 184–5.
18. Lamb, *War in Italy*, pp. 56, 94.
19. Harold Alexander, *The Alexander Memoirs* (London: Cassell, 1962), p. 126.
20. *Ibid.*, p. 130.
21. Mark W. Clark, *Calculated Risk* (New York: Harper & Brothers, 1950), pp. 312, 316; and von Weizsäcker, *The Memoirs of Ernst von Weizsäcker*, p. 291.

22. Alexander, *The Alexander Memoirs*, pp. 119–22; Giulio Castelli, *Storia segreta di Roma città aperta* (Rome: Quatrucci, 1959), p. 183; and British Channel 4 television broadcast of 2 April 2003.
23. De Wyss, *Rome under the Terror*, pp. 173, 184; Scrivener, *Inside Rome with the Germans*, pp. 68, 84; report of the International Association of Law and Art; David Roxan and Ken Wanstall, *The Jackdaw of Linz* (London: Cassell, 1964), pp. 111, 157; and Berenson, *Rumour and Reflection*, pp. 226, 242, 299.
24. Pini and Susmel, *Mussolini, l'uomo e l'opera*, p. 394.
25. Dolfin, *Con Mussolini nella tragedia*, pp. 224–5.
26. Bocca, *La repubblica di Mussolini*, pp. 142–4.
27. Dolfin, *Con Mussolini nella tragedia*, p. 145.
28. Bocca, *La repubblica di Mussolini*, pp. 107–8; Tamaro, *Due anni di storia*, p. 196; Innocenti, *Mussolini a Salò*, pp. 76, 79; and Salvadori, *Breve storia della resistenza italiana*, p. 31.
29. Dolfin, *Con Mussolini nella tragedia*, pp. 235–8.
30. Mellini, *Guerra diplomatica a Salò*, p. 197.
31. Bocca, *La repubblica di Mussolini*, 155; and Zachariae, *Mussolini si confessa*, p. 139.
32. Pini and Susmel, *Mussolini, l'uomo e l'opera*, 401; and Deakin, *The Last Days of Mussolini*, p. 166.
33. Dolfin, *Con Mussolini nella tragedia*, pp. 260–1.
34. Bolla, *Perché a Salò*, pp. 150–1, 157.
35. Anita Pensotti, *Rachele* (Bologna: Bompiani, 1983), p. 108; Christopher Hibbert, *Benito Mussolini* (London: The Reprint Society, 1963), pp. 323ff; and R. Mussolini, *La mia vita con Benito*, p. 229.
36. Bocca, *La repubblica di Mussolini*, p. 165; Pini and Susmel, *Mussolini, l'uomo e l'opera*, p. 402; and Longo, *Un popolo alla macchia*, pp. 151–5.
37. Bocca, *La repubblica di Mussolini*, p. 168; and Dolfin, *Con Mussolini nella tragedia*, p. 276.
38. Bocca, *La repubblica di Mussolini*, pp. 171, 188.
39. Kimball, *Churchill and Roosevelt*, vol. 2, pp. 723, 725; *Ibid.*, vol. 3, pp. 28–9, 31, 41, 42; and Wilhelm, *The Other Italy*, p. 204.
40. Pini and Susmel, *Mussolini, l'uomo e l'opera*, p. 401; and Kimball, *Churchill and Roosevelt*, vol. 2, pp. 723, 725, 759–61.
41. Pini and Susmel, *Mussolini, l'uomo e l'opera*, p. 403.
42. *Ibid.*, pp. 406–7.
43. Kenneth Macksey, *The Partisans of Europe in World War II* (London: Hart-Davis, MacGibbon, 1975), p. 164.
44. Churchill Archives, CHAR 9/204 A-C.
45. Pini and Susmel, *Mussolini, l'uomo e l'opera*, p. 406.
46. Dinale, *Quarant'anni di colloqui con lui*, pp. 231–2.
47. Pini and Susmel, *Mussolini, l'uomo e l'opera*, p. 407.
48. *Ibid.*, pp. 408–9; and Bocca, *La repubblica di Mussolini*, p. 215.
49. Pini and Susmel, *Mussolini, l'uomo e l'opera*, p. 404.
50. Bolla, *Perché a Salò*, p. 163.
51. Bocca, *La repubblica di Mussolini*, p. 151; and Dolfin, *Con Mussolini nella tragedia*, pp. 107, 263.

52. Giampaolo Pansa, *L'esercito di Salò* (Rome: Istituto Nazionale per la Storia del Movimento di Liberazione, 1969), pp. 59–60.
53. Bellotti, *La repubblica di Mussolini*, p. 91.
54. Bocca, *La repubblica di Mussolini*, p. 57.
55. Pansa, *L'esercito di Salò*, pp. 24–5; Dollmann, *Roma nazista*, p. 222; and Rodolfo Graziani, *Ho difeso la patria* (Milan: Garzanti, 1948), pp. 436–7, 443.
56. Pansa, *L'esercito di Salò*, pp. 28, 29, 31, 33–4; Graziani, *Ho difeso la patria*, pp. 442–4; Lamb, *War in Italy*, 98; and Amicucci, *I 600 giorni di Mussolini*, pp. 66–7.
57. Pansa, *L'esercito di Salò*, pp. 37–9; and Tamaro, *Due anni di storia*, vol. 3, p.14.
58. Pansa, *L'esercito di Salò*, p. 43; and De Felice, *Mussolini l'alleato*, p. 147.
59. Pansa, *L'escercito di Salò*, pp. 6–7; and Bellotti, *La repubblica di Mussolini*, p. 58.
60. Pansa, *L'escercito di Salò*, p. 9.
61. *Ibid.*, pp. 10, 11, 16–18.
62. *Ibid.*, pp. 20–1; and Amicucci, *I 600 giorni di Mussolini*, pp. 68–9.
63. Deakin, *The Last Days of Mussolini*, p. 191; and Anfuso, *Da Palazzo Venezia al Lago di Garda*, p. 434
64. Graziani, *Ho difeso la patria*, pp. 463–4; Bolla, *Perché a Salò*, pp. 174–5; Pini and Susmel, *Mussolini, l'uomo e l'opera*, p. 411; and Ian Kershaw, *Hitler 1936–1945* (London: Penguin Books, 2000), p. 633.
65. Bolla, *Perché a Salò*, p. 176.
66. Anfuso, *Da Palazzo Venezia al Lago di Garda*, p. 435; Deakin, *The Last Days of Mussolini*, pp. 184–6; Tamaro, *Due anni di storia*, vol. 3, pp. 24, 27; and Bolla, *Perché a Salò*, p. 177.
67. R. Mussolini, *La mia vita con Benito*, p. 238.
68. B. Mussolini, *Opera Omnia*, p. 85.
69. Graziani, *Ho difeso la patria*, pp. 465–6.
70. B. Mussolini, *Opera Omnia*, pp. 39–40.
71. Bocca, *La repubblica di Mussolini*, pp. 237–41.

Chapter 9. The Partisan War Develops

1. Lamb, *War in Italy*, pp. 56–7; and Angelozzi Gariboldi, *Pio XII, Hitler e Mussolini*, p. 230.
2. Katz, *Death in Rome*, pp. 20–2, 37, 70, 71, 74–6.
3. Angelozzi Gariboldi, *Pio XII, Hitler e Mussolini*, p. 231; and Katz, *Death in Rome*, pp. 14–15.
4. Dollman, *Roma nazista*, p. 179; Bertoldi, *I tedeschi in Italia*, pp. 264, 267; Angelozzi Gariboldi, *Pio XII, Hitler e Mussolini*, pp. 229, 232; Katz, *Death in Rome*, p. 83; and Ripa de Meana, *Roma clandestina*, p. 28.
5. Dollmann, *Roma nazista*, p. 183.
6. Lamb, *War in Italy*, p. 58; and Bertoldi, *I tedeschi in Italia*, p. 266.
7. Dollmann, *Roma nazista*, pp. 181–2.
8. Bertoldi, *I tedeschi in Italia*, p. 265.
9. *Ibid.*, pp. 264, 267–8; Lamb, *War in Italy*, p. 59; and Angelozzi Gariboldi, *Pio XII, Hitler e Mussolini*, pp. 242–3.
10. Lamb, *War in Italy*, p. 59; Bertoldi, *I tedeschi in Italia*, p. 266; Angelozzi Gariboldi, *Pio XII, Hitler e Mussolini*, pp. 242, 269; and Katz, *Death in Rome*, p. 168.

11. International Military Tribunal, Trial of the Major War Criminals, vol. 9 (Nuremberg: 1947), pp. 231–2; Lamb, *War in Italy*, p. 60; and Katz, *The Battle for Rome*, pp. 241, 260.
12. Angelozzi Gariboldi, *Pio XII, Hitler e Mussolini*, p. 243; and Dollmann, *Roma nazista*, pp. 85–6, 182, 188.
13. Lamb, *War in Italy*, p. 60.
14. *Ibid.*, p. 61; and R. Mussolini, *La mia vita con Benito*, p. 237.
15. Katz, *Death in Rome*, pp. 285–6; and Bertoldi, *I tedeschi in Italia*, pp. 263–4, 269–70.
16. Katz, *Death in Rome*, pp. 228–9.
17. *Ibid.*, pp. 238–9.
18. Albert Kesselring, *The Memoirs of Field Marshal Kesselring* (London: William Kimber, 1953), pp. 224–5; and Salvadori, *Breve storia della resistenza italiana*, pp. 22, 25–6.
19. Battaglia, *Storia della resistenza italiana*, p. 133; and De Felice, *Mussolini l'alleato*, p. 150.
20. Charles F. Delzell, *Mussolini's Enemies* (Princeton, NJ: Princeton University Press, 1961), pp. 363–70; and Battaglia, *Storia della resistenza italiana*, pp. 117–18.
21. De Felice, *Mussolini l'alleato*, pp. 156–7, 194; Salvadori, *Breve storia della resistenza italiana*, p. 26; Longo, *Un popolo alla macchia*, p. 367; and Wilhelm, *The Other Italy*, p. 119.
22. De Felice, *Mussolini l'alleato*, pp. 158–9.
23. Battaglia, *Storia della resistenza italiana*, pp. 167–8.
24. *Ibid.*, pp. 168, 171; Lamb, *War in Italy*, p. 205; De Felice, *Mussolini l'alleato*, pp. 179, 201; and Salvadori, *Breve storia della resistenza italiana*, p. 171.
25. Battaglia, *Storia della resistenza italiana*, p. 208.
26. *Ibid.*, p. 174.
27. Lamb, *War in Italy*, p. 206.
28. Longo, *Un popolo alla macchia*, p. 179; and Berenson, *Rumour and Reflection*, p. 265.
29. Pini and Susmel, *Mussolini, l'uomo e l'opera*, pp. 409–10; Longo, *Un popolo alla macchia*, p. 195; De Felice, *Mussolini l'alleato*, pp. 184–5; and Tamaro, *Due anni di storia*, vol. 3, p. 9.
30. Bertoldi, *Piazzale Loreto*, pp. 178–82, 186.
31. Origo, *War in Val d'Orcia*, p. 160; De Felice, *Mussolini l'alleato*, p. 319; and International Military Tribunal, *Trials of the Major War Criminals*, p. 223.
32. Battaglia, *Storia della resistenza italiana*, pp. 246–7.
33. *Ibid.*, p. 278; Kesselring, *Memoirs of Field Marshal Kesselring*, pp. 227–8; and De Felice, *Mussolini l'alleato*, p. 194.
34. Battaglia, *Storia della resistenza italiana*, p. 278.
35. Origo, *War in Val d'Orcia*, p. 179.
36. De Felice, *Mussolini l'alleato*, pp. 194, 222–4; and Lamb, *War in Italy*, pp. 207–8.
37. Bocca, *La repubblica di Mussolini*, p. 260.

Chapter 10. Il Duce and the Jews

1. Liliana Picciotto, *Deportazione razziale in Italia*, Union of Italian Jewish Communities, www.ucei.it/giornodellamemoria/storia/shoah/deport, last accessed on 25 February 2003.

2. Bosworth, *Mussolini*, pp. 338, 334.
3. Salvadori, *Breve storia della resistenza italiana*, p. 32.
4. Bosworth, *Mussolini*, p. 335.
5. V. Mussolini, *Vita con mio padre*, pp. 92–3.
6. Cerruti, *Ambassador's Wife*, p. 224.
7. Lamb, *War in Italy*, p. 36.
8. De Felice, *Storia degli ebrei italiani sotto il fascismo*, pp. 441–2, 446; and Michaelis, *Mussolini and the Jews*, pp. 343–4.
9. De Felice, *Storia degli ebrei italiani sotto il fascismo*, p. 464.
10. Michaelis, *Mussolini and the Jews*, p. 398.
11. Bertoldi, *Salò*, pp. 339–41; and Michaelis, *Mussolini and the Jews*, p. 351.
12. Spampanato, *L'ultimo Mussolini*, vol. 2, p. 98.
13. Zachariae, *Mussolini si confessa*, p. 169.
14. Bertoldi, *Salò*, pp. 331–2.
15. *Ibid.*, pp. 332–3, 335–6.
16. Michaelis, *Mussolini and the Jews*, p. 350; and Bocca, *La repubblica di Mussolini*, p. 205.
17. Michaelis, *Mussolini and the Jews*, p. 350; and Bocca, *La repubblica di Mussolini*, pp. 207–8.
18. Lamb, *War in Italy*, pp. 52, 54; and Origo, *War in Val d'Orcia*, p. 112.
19. Michaelis, *Mussolini and the Jews*, p. 386.
20. De Felice, *Storia degli ebrei italiani sotto il fascismo*, p. 461.
21. Michaelis, *Mussolini and the Jews*, p. 389; Lamb, *War in Italy*, p. 54; and Bertoldi, *I tedeschi in Italia*, p. 138.
22. Michaelis, *Mussolini and the Jews*, p. 390.
23. Berenson, *Rumour and Reflection*, p. 138; and Michaelis, *Mussolini and the Jews*, p. 387.
24. De Felice, *Storia degli ebrei italiani sotto il fascismo*, pp. 460–1.
25. Berenson, *Rumour and Reflection*, p. 387; and Michaelis, *Mussolini and the Jews*, p. 389.
26. De Felice, *Storia degli ebrei italiani sotto il fascismo*, p. 451; Michaelis, *Mussolini and the Jews*, p. 386; and Lamb, *War in Italy*, pp. 49–51.
27. De Felice, *Storia degli ebrei italiani sotto il fascismo*, p. 451; and Lamb, *War in Italy*, p. 50.
28. Picciotto, *Deportazione razziale in Italia*, Union of Italian Jewish Communities.
29. De Felice, *Storia degli ebrei italiani sotto il fascismo*, pp. 460, 472; and Michaelis, *Mussolini and the Jews*, p. 392.
30. De Felice, *Storia degli ebrei italiani sotto il fascismo*, pp. 475, 486; and Silvestri, *Mussolini, Graziani e l'antifascismo*, pp. 51–2.
31. Bocca, *La repubblica di Mussolini*, p. 209.
32. Lamb, *War in Italy*, p. 49.
33. D'Aroma, *Mussolini segreto*, p. 290.
34. Bocca, *La repubblica di Mussolini*, p. 209; and De Felice, *Storia degli ebrei italiani sotto il fascismo*, p. 447.
35. De Felice, *Storia degli ebrei italiani sotto il fascismo*, pp. 449, 450; Bocca, *La repubblica di Mussolini*, p. 209; and Origo, *War in Val d'Orcia*, pp. 152–3.
36. Origo, *War in Val d'Orcia*, p. 206; Michaelis, *Mussolini and the Jews*, p. 350; De Felice, *Storia degli ebrei italiani sotto il fascismo*, pp. 456, 457, 459; and Bertoldi, *Salò*, p. 343.

Chapter 11. The Liberation of Rome

1. De Wyss, *Rome under the Terror*, p. 215; Dollmann, *Roma nazista*, p. 201; and von Weizsäcker, *Memoirs of Ernst von Weizsäcker*, p. 292.
2. De Wyss, *Rome under the Terror*, pp. 214–15; Ripa di Meana, *Roma clandestina*, p. 331; and Peter Tompkins, *A Spy in Rome* (London: Weidenfeld & Nicolson, 1962), pp. 338, 334.
3. Scrivener, *Inside Rome with the Germans*, p. 193; and Tompkins, *A Spy in Rome*, p. 337.
4. Ripa di Meana, *Roma clandestina*, pp. 331–2; and Tompkins, *A Spy in Rome*, p. 337.
5. Tompkins, *A Spy in Rome*, pp. 339, 342.
6. Scrivener, *Inside Rome with the Germans*, pp. 199–200.
7. Pini and Susmel, *Mussolini, l'uomo e l'opera*, p. 417; R. Mussolini, *La mia vita con Benito*, p. 241; and Ridley, *Mussolini*, p. 357.
8. Bocca, *La repubblica di Mussolini*, p. 253; Dollmann, *Roma nazista*, pp. 200–1; and Bolla, *Perché a Salò*, p. 195.
9. Roosevelt Archives, FDR Library, Hyde Park, New York.
10. Alexander, *The Alexander Memoirs*, p. 127.
11. De Wyss, *Rome under the Terror*, pp. 190, 208; and Scrivener, *Inside Rome with the Germans*, p. 190.
12. Scrivener, *Inside Rome with the Germans*, pp. 25, 37–8, 72–3, 96–7; and de Wyss, *Rome under the Terror*, p. 190.
13. De Wyss, *Rome under the Terror*, pp. 166–7; Scrivener, *Inside Rome with the Germans*, pp. 103–6; and Michaelis, *Mussolini and the Jews*, p. 390.
14. Scrivener, *Inside Rome with the Germans*, pp. 126, 130, 177, 103, 113, 140, 136; and Bertoldi, *I tedeschi in Italia*, p. 280.
15. Origo, *War in Val d'Orcia*, pp. 153–4; and Bocca, *La repubblica di Mussolini*, p. 265.
16. Scrivener, *Inside Rome with the Germans*, pp. 202–3; and Katz, *Death in Rome*, p. 255.
17. Kimball, *Churchill and Roosevelt*, vol. 3, pp. 176–7, 182, 188–90.

Chapter 12. A Terrible Summer

1. Kesselring, *Memoirs of Field Marshal Kesselring*, p. 225.
2. International Military Tribunal, *Trial of the Major War Criminals*, vol. 9 (Nuremberg: 1947), pp. 220–1.
3. Bocca, *La repubblica di Mussolini*, p. 265.
4. Salvadori, *Breve storia della resistenza italiana*, p. 134; and Lamb, *War in Italy*, pp. 64–5.
5. International Military Tribunal, *Trial of the Major War Criminals*, vol. 9, pp. 222–3.
6. Lamb, *War in Italy*, pp. 65–6.
7. Pini and Susmel, *Mussolini, l'uomo e l'opera*, p. 423.
8. Kesselring, *Memoirs of Field Marshal Kesselring*, pp. 227, 232.
9. Battaglia, *Storia della resistenza italiana*, p. 301.
10. Bocca, *La repubblica di Mussolini*, pp. 254, 266–7.
11. Mellini, *Guerra diplomatica a Salò*, p. 142; and Bolla, *Perché a Salò*, p. 204.
12. Bocca, *La repubblica di Mussolini*, pp. 255–6, 258; Gregory Blaxland, *Alexander's Generals* (London: William Kimber, 1979), p. 148; and David W. Ellwood, *Italy 1943–1945* (Leicester: Leicester University Press, 1985), p. 157.

13. Lamb, *War in Italy*, pp. 206, 210.
14. Bocca, *La repubblica di Mussolini*, p. 272.
15. Battaglia, *Storia della resistenza italiana*, pp. 317–18.
16. *Ibid.*, pp. 329–30.
17. *Ibid.*, pp. 310–11.
18. Raffaele Cadorna, *La riscossa* (Milan: Rizzoli, 1948), pp. 151, 153–4.
19. Pini and Susmel, *Mussolini, l'uomo e l'opera*, pp. 421, 432; and Pansa, *L'esercito di Salò*, pp. 155, 176–7.
20. Denis Mack Smith, *Mussolini* (London: Paladin Grafton, 1983), p. 357; Bocca, *Storia dell'Italia partigiana*, p. 566; Bertoldi, *Salò*, pp. 207–8; Ripa di Meana, *Roma clandestina*, p. 139; and Angelozzi Gariboldi, *Pio XII, Hitler e Mussolini*, p. 247.
21. Bocca, *Storia dell'Italia partigiana*, pp. 558–9; and Bertoldi, *Salò*, pp. 176–7.
22. Bocca, *Storia dell'Italia partigiana*, pp. 559–61; Wilhelm, *The Other Italy*, pp. 99–100; Bertoldi, *Salò*, pp. 214, 220–1; Dollmann, *Roma nazista*, pp. 226–8; and Luciano Garibaldi, *Mussolini e il professore* (Milan: Mursia, 1983), pp. 173, 340.
23. Pini and Susmel, *Mussolini, l'uomo e l'opera*, p. 431.
24. Bocca, *Storia dell'Italia partigiana*, pp. 567–8.
25. Dollmann, *The Interpreter*, pp. 336–8; and *idem*, *Call Me Coward* (London: William Kimber, 1956), pp. 72–3.
26. Dollmann, *Roma nazista*, p. 236.
27. De Felice, *Mussolini l'alleato*, pp. 325, 330, 332, 336.
28. Delzell, *Mussolini's Enemies*, pp. 404, 406; Ellwood, *Italy 1943–1945*, p. 157; and Kimball, *Churchill and Roosevelt*, vol. 3, pp. 225, 227, 299.
29. Cadorna, *La riscossa*, pp. 96, 103–4, 113, 119, 132, 139–41, 150–51, 153–4; and Salvadori, *Breve storia della resistenza italiana*, pp. 121–2.
30. B. Mussolini, *Opera Omnia*, pp. 100, 104.
31. Pansa, *L'esercito di Salò*, pp. 182–3.
32. R. Mussolini, *La mia vita con Benito*, p. 243; V. Mussolini, *Vita con mio padre*, p. 215; Bocca, *La repubblica di Mussolini*, p. 284; Kershaw, *Hitler 1936–1945*, pp. 671–5; Dollmann, *Roma nazista*, p. 315; Pansa, *L'esercito di Salò*, p. 155; and Anfuso, *Da Palazzo Venezia al Lago di Garda*, pp. 450–1, 453.
33. Dollmann, *Call Me Coward*, p. 39; *idem*, *Roma nazista*, p. 316; Kershaw, *Hitler 1936–1945*, p. 684; Paul Schmidt, *Hitler's Interpreter* (London: William Heinemann, 1951), p. 277; and R. Mussolini, *La mia vita con Benito*, p. 244.
34. Deakin, *The Last Days of Mussolini*, p. 216; Bocca, *La repubblica di Mussolini*, pp. 284–5; and Anfuso, *Da Palazzo Venezia al Lago di Garda*, p. 454.
35. Monelli, *Mussolini piccolo borghese*, p. 331.
36. Mellini, *Guerra diplomatica a Salò*, pp. 159–71.
37. Bocca, *La repubblica di Mussolini*, p. 285; and Bolla, *Perché a Salò*, pp. 158–9, 183–5.
38. Bocca, *La repubblica di Mussolini*, 285; and Mellini, *Guerra diplomatica a Salò*, pp. 162–3.
39. Bocca, *Storia dell'Italia partigiana*, pp. 420–2; Pansa, *L'esercito di Salò*, pp. 184–5, 197–8; Amicucci, *I 600 giorni di Mussolini*, p. 76; Anfuso, *Da Palazzo Venezia al Lago di Garda*, p. 460; Deakin, *The Last Days of Mussolini*, p. 246; and Bolla, *Perché a Salò*, p. 199.
40. Delzell, *Mussolini's Enemies*, p. 404; and De Felice, *Mussolini l'alleato*, p. 195.

41. R. Mussolini, *La mia vita con Benito*, pp. 246–7.
42. Battaglia, *Storia della resistenza italiana*, pp. 324–6.
43. *Ibid.*, p. 332; and Berenson, *Rumour and Reflection*, pp. 298–9, 310–11.
44. Battaglia, *Storia della resistenza italiana*, pp. 332–7; Longo, *Un popolo alla macchia*, pp. 262–7; and Berenson, *Rumour and Reflection*, p. 332.
45. Dollmann, *Roma nazista*, pp. 229–30.
46. Wilhelm, *The Other Italy*, pp. 236–7; and Report of the International Association of Law and Art.
47. Bocca, *Storia dell'Italia partigiana*, pp. 432–3.
48. *Ibid.*, pp. 434–9; Lamb, *War in Italy*, p. 68; Battaglia, *Storia della resistenza italiana*, pp. 428–32; and Longo, *Un popolo alla macchia*, pp. 343–4.
49. Bertoldi, *Piazzale Loreto*, pp. 185, 186, 228–30; R. Mussolini, *La mia vita con Benito*, p. 247; and Archives of the Fondazione Fratelli Rosselli.
50. Lamb, *War in Italy*, pp. 66, 72.
51. Pansa, *L'esercito di Salò*, pp. 124–5.
52. Bocca, *La repubblica di Mussolini*, p. 268.
53. *Ibid.*, pp. 264–5; Pini and Susmel, *Mussolini, l'uomo e l'opera*, p. 436; and Lamb, *War in Italy*, pp. 272–3.

Chapter 13. More Atrocities, Greater Despair

1. Battaglia, *Storia della resistenza italiana*, pp. 401–2; Blaxland, *Alexander's Generals*, pp. 28–9; and De Felice, *Mussolini l'alleato*, p. 240.
2. Mellini, *Guerra diplomatica a Salò*, p. 199; and Bocca, *La repubblica di Mussolini*, p. 288.
3. Bocca, *La repubblica di Mussolini*, pp. 288–9; and Mellini, *Guerra diplomatica a Salò*, p. 157.
4. Mellini, *Guerra diplomatica a Salò*, pp. 50–1; and Innocenti, *Mussolini a Salò*, p. 51.
5. Mellini, *Guerra diplomatica a Salò*, p. 200; and Bolla, *Perché a Salò*, p. 227.
6. Bocca, *La repubblica di Mussolini*, pp. 287–8.
7. Lamb, *War in Italy*, pp. 69–70.
8. Wilhelm, *The Other Italy*, pp. 112–16; Bocca, *La repubblica di Mussolini*, p. 289; and Lamb, *War in Italy*, pp. 68, 74–5.
9. Allen W. Dulles, *The Secret Surrender* (London: Weidenfeld & Nicolson, 1967), p. 64; Mellini, *Guerra diplomatica a Salò*, p. 200; and Lamb, *War in Italy*, pp. 74–5, 119–20.
10. Cadorna, *La riscossa*, pp. 154; Battaglia, *Storia della resistenza italiana*, pp. 414, 415, 417; and Lamb, *War in Italy*, pp. 214–26.
11. Mellini, *Guerra diplomatica a Salò*, p. 201.
12. *Ibid.*, p. 44.
13. Longo, *Un popolo alla macchia*, p. 408.
14. R. Mussolini, *Benito il mio uomo*, p. 243.
15. Gervaso, *Claretta*, p. 160.
16. Dolfin, *Con Mussolini nella tragedia*, p. 145.
17. Zachariae, *Mussolini si confessa*, pp. 29–30; Bocca, *La repubblica di Mussolini*, p. 138; and De Felice, *Mussolini l'alleato*, p. 1536.
18. Bocca, *La repubblica di Mussolini*, p. 137; and Gervaso, *Claretta*, pp. 165–6.

19. Gervaso, *Claretta*, pp.167–8; and M. Petacci, *Chi ama è perduto*, pp. 329–32.
20. R. Mussolini, *Benito il mio uomo*, pp. 243–9; and *idem*, *La mia vita con Benito*, p. 253.
21. Gervaso, *Claretta*, p. 173.
22. Dollmann, *Roma nazista*, p. 285.
23. Pensotti, *Rachele*, p. 114; and V. Mussolini, *The Tragic Women in His Life*, pp. 55–7.
24. R. Mussolini, *La mia vita con Benito*, pp. 251–3.
25. *Ibid.*, p. 292; and Pini and Susmel, *Mussolini, l'uomo e l'opera*, p. 442.
26. Bocca, *La repubblica di Mussolini*, pp. 294–5; Amicucci, *I 600 giorni di Mussolini*, p. 207; and Ellwood, *Italy 1943–1945*, p. 157.
27. Bocca, *La repubblica di Mussolini*, pp. 292–3.
28. Battaglia, *Storia della resistenza italiana*, p. 433; Leo Valiani, *Tutte le strade conducono a Roma* (Florence: La Nuova Italia, 1947), p. 305; Ellwood, *Italy 1943–1945*, pp. 163, 171; Longo, *Un popolo alla macchia*, p. 332; and Max Corvo, *The O.S.S. in Italy 1942–45* (New York: Praeger, 1990), p. 211.
29. Battaglia, *Storia della resistenza italiana*, pp. 469–70.
30. *Ibid.*, p. 435; and De Felice, *Mussolini l'alleato*, p. 226.
31. Edgardo Sogno, *Guerra senza bandiera* (Milan: Rizzoli, 1950), pp. 318–23.
32. Longo, *Un popolo alla macchia*, pp. 337–8.
33. Battaglia, *Storia della resistenza italiana*, pp. 441, 471.
34. Mellini, *Guerra diplomatica a Salò*, p. 201.
35. *Ibid.*, pp. 50, 66.
36. Pini and Susmel, *Mussolini, l'uomo e l'opera*, p. 449.
37. R. Mussolini, *La mia vita con Benito*, p. 255; and B. Mussolini, *Opera Omnia*, pp. 128–40.
38. Pini and Susmel, *Mussolini, l'uomo e l'opera*, p. 455.
39. R. Mussolini, *La mia vita con Benito*, p. 255.

Chapter 14. 'I Have Ruined Italy'

1. Edvige Mussolini, *Mio fratello Benito* (Florence: La Fenice, 1957), p. 215.
2. Bocca, *La repubblica di Mussolini*, p. 315; and Richard Collier, *Duce!* (London: Collins, 1971), pp. 305–6.
3. R. Mussolini, *Benito il mio uomo*, p. 256.
4. Roman Dombrowski, *Mussolini: Twilight and Fall* (London: William Heinemann, 1956), p. 149.
5. Pini and Susmel, *Mussolini, l'uomo e l'opera*, pp. 459–60.
6. R. Mussolini, *La mia vita con Benito*, p. 257.
7. Pini and Susmel, *Mussolini, l'uomo e l'opera*, p. 467.
8. *Ibid.*, p. 460.
9. Bocca, *La repubblica di Mussolini*, p. 326; and Longo, *Un popolo alla macchia*, p. 340.
10. Pini and Susmel, *Mussolini, l'uomo e l'opera*, p. 467; Bocca, *La repubblica di Mussolini*, pp. 308–12; and Bertoldi, *Piazzale Loreto*, p. 21.
11. Joseph Goebbels, *The Goebbels Diaries: The Last Days* (London: Secker & Warburg, 1978), p. 10.
12. Bocca, *La repubblica di Mussolini*, pp. 303–4; and Silvestri, *Mussolini, Graziani e l'antifascismo*, p. 61.

13. Bocca, *La repubblica di Mussolini*, p. 304; and R. Mussolini, *La mia vita con Benito*, p. 254.
14. Mellini, *Guerra diplomatica a Salò*, pp. 69–70.
15. Pini and Susmel, *Mussolini, l'uomo e l'opera*, pp. 469–70; and Bocca, *La repubblica di Mussolini*, pp. 304–5.
16. Mellini, *Guerra diplomatica a Salò*, pp. 70–1.
17. *Ibid.*, pp. 69–83.
18. *Ibid.*, pp. 73–5, 84–5; and Bellotti, *La repubblica di Mussolini*, p. 199.
19. D'Aroma, *Mussolini segreto*, pp. 291–3.
20. Pini and Susmel, *Mussolini, l'uomo e l'opera*, pp. 472–3.
21. *Ibid.*, p. 471; Lamb, *War in Italy*, p. 281; and R. Mussolini, *La mia vita con Benito*, p. 256.
22. Zachariae, *Mussolini si confessa*, p. 19; and Tamaro, *Due anni di storia*, vol. 3, p. 508.

Chapter 15. The Secret Negotiations

1. Ferruccio Lanfranchi, *La resa degli 800,000* (Milan: Rizzoli, 1948), pp. 96, 99, 103, 116–26. This book contains a long section written by Baron Luigi Parrilli about his role in the German surrender negotiations. See also Dollmann, *The Interpreter*, p. 342; and *idem*, *Call Me Coward*, p. 82.
2. Lanfranchi, *La resa degli 800,000*, pp. 126–7; and Dulles, *The Secret Surrender*, pp. 67–9.
3. Dulles, *The Secret Surrender*, pp. 70–2; and Lanfranchi, *La resa degli 800,000*, pp. 130–1.
4. Dulles, *The Secret Surrender*, pp. 43–6; Lanfranchi, *La resa degli 800,000*, pp. 44–64; Deakin, *The Last Days of Mussolini*, p. 265; and Dollman, *The Interpreter*, pp. 340–1.
5. Dulles, *The Secret Surrender*, pp. 47–51; and Walter Schellenberg, *The Schellenberg Memoirs* (London: Andre Deutsch, 1956), pp. 370–2.
6. Mellini, *Guerra diplomatica a Salò*, pp. 97–8, 101.
7. Pini and Susmel, *Mussolini, l'uomo e l'opera*, p. 477; and Mellini, *Guerra diplomatica a Salò*, p. 103.
8. Lanfranchi, *La resa degli 800,000*, pp. 133–4; and Dulles, *The Secret Surrender*, pp. 83–6.
9. Dulles, *The Secret Surrender*, pp. 56–7; and Peter Grose, *Gentleman Spy* (London: Andre Deutsch, 1995), p. 231.
10. Lanfranchi, *La resa degli 800,000*, pp. 135–42; and Dulles, *The Secret Surrender*, pp. 73–8.
11. Dollmann, *Roma nazista*, p. 325; and Lanfranchi, *La resa degli 800,000*, pp. 143–53.
12. Mellini, *Guerra diplomatica a Salò* , pp. 106–7.
13. Lanfranchi, *La resa degli 800,000*, pp. 154–60.
14. Dulles, *The Secret Surrender*, pp. 89, 90, 92.
15. Lanfranchi, *La resa degli 800,000*, pp. 167–8; and Hoettl, *The Secret Front*, p. 297.
16. Dulles, *The Secret Surrender*, pp. 91–7.
17. *Ibid.*, pp. 59–60.
18. Lanfranchi, *La resa degli 800,000*, pp. 169–70; and Dollmann, *Roma nazista*, p. 326.
19. Dulles, *The Secret Surrender*, pp. 98–9.
20. Sogno, *Guerra senza bandiera*, pp. 341–3.
21. Grose, *Gentleman Spy*, p. 232.

22. Dollmann, *Roma nazista*, p. 328.
23. Lanfranchi, *La resa degli 800,000*, pp. 171–9; and Dulles, *The Secret Surrender*, pp. 101–5.
24. Dulles, *The Secret Surrender*, pp. 148–50; and Kimball, *Churchill and Roosevelt*, vol. 3, p. 615.
25. Dulles, *The Secret Surrender*, p. 105.
26. Lanfranchi, *La resa degli 800,000*, pp. 180–3; Dulles, *The Secret Surrender*, pp. 106–8; and Pini and Susmel, *Mussolini, l'uomo e l'opera*, p. 479.

Chapter 16. In Search of a Way Out

1. Lamb, *War in Italy*, pp. 296–8.
2. Amicucci, *I 600 giorni di Mussolini*, pp. 246–7; Bocca, *La repubblica di Mussolini*, p. 322; and Pini and Susmel, *Mussolini, l'uomo e l'opera*, pp. 479–80.
3. Bocca, *La repubblica di Mussolini*, p. 322; Pini and Susmel, *Mussolini, l'uomo e l'opera*, p. 478; and Spampanato, *L'ultimo Mussolini*, vol. 2, p. 247.
4. Goebbels, *The Goebbels Diaries: The Last Days*, pp. 78, 134.
5. Mellini, *Guerra diplomatica a Salò*, pp. 111–12.
6. Spampanato, *L'ultimo Mussolini*, vol. 2, pp. 249–50.
7. Cadorna, *La riscossa*, pp. 225–45.
8. Pini and Susmel, *Mussolini, l'uomo e l'opera*, p. 480; and Bocca, *La repubblica di Mussolini*, p. 326.
9. Pini and Susmel, *Mussolini, l'uomo e l'opera*, p. 481.
10. Mellini, *Guerra diplomatica a Salò*, p. 121; and Goebbels, *The Goebbels Diaries: The Last Days*, p. 268.
11. Bocca, *La repubblica di Mussolini*, p. 324; Amicucci, *I 600 giorni di Mussolini*, p. 151; Goebbels, *The Goebbels Diaries: The Last Days*, p. 122; and Mellini, *Guerra diplomatica a Salò*, pp. 128–9.
12. Pini and Susmel, *Mussolini, l'uomo e l'opera*, pp. 486–7.
13. R. Mussolini, *La mia vita con Benito*, p. 259.
14. Pini and Susmel, *Mussolini, l'uomo e l'opera*, p. 487.
15. Anfuso, *Da Palazzo Venezia al Lago di Garda*, pp. 464–6.
16. Goebbels, *The Goebbels Diaries: The Last Days*, p. 260.
17. Pini and Susmel, *Mussolini, l'uomo e l'opera*, p. 488.
18. *Ibid.*, p. 489.

Chapter 17. Peace Hopes in the Balance

1. Lanfranchi, *La resa degli 800,000*, pp. 189–90; and Grose, *Gentleman Spy*, pp. 244–5.
2. Dulles, *The Secret Surrender*, pp. 109–14, 139; and Grose, *Gentleman Spy*, pp. 236–8.
3. Dulles, *The Secret Surrender*, pp. 61, 115–25; and Lanfranchi, *La resa degli 800,000*, pp. 193–8.
4. Lanfranchi, *La resa degli 800,000*, pp. 200–14.
5. Dollmann, *Roma nazista*, p. 329.
6. Dulles, *The Secret Surrender*, pp. 133–5.

7. Hoettl, *The Secret Front*, p. 296.
8. Lanfranchi, *La resa degli 800,000*, pp. 215–21.
9. Kimball, *Churchill and Roosevelt*, vol. 3, pp. 609–15; and Dulles, *The Secret Surrender*, p. 147.
10. Lanfranchi, *La resa degli 800,000*, pp. 222–6.
11. *Ibid.*, pp. 227–8; and Dulles, *The Secret Surrender*, pp. 140–1.
12. Lanfranchi, *La resa degli 800,000*, pp. 231–3; and Dulles, *The Secret Surrender*, p. 156.
13. Lanfranchi, *La resa degli 800,000*, p. 234; and Dollmann, *The Interpreter*, pp. 311–13.
14. Dulles, *The Secret Surrender*, pp. 144, 152–3.
15. Franco Bandini, *Le ultime 95 ore di Mussolini* (Bologna: Sugar, 1959), pp. 31–2; Pini and Susmel, *Mussolini, l'uomo e l'opera*, p. 497; and Anfuso, *Da Palazzo Venezia al Lago di Garda*, pp. 469–70.
16. Dulles, *The Secret Surrender*, pp. 152–4, 157–8, 160–1; and Lanfranchi, *La resa degli 800,000*, p. 243.
17. Dulles, *The Secret Surrender*, pp. 156, 158; and Lanfranchi, *La resa degli 800,000*, pp. 245, 247.
18. Lanfranchi, *La resa degli 800,000*, pp. 248–55; and Dulles, *The Secret Surrender*, pp. 169–80.

Chapter 18. Looming Defeat and Paralysis

1. Pini and Susmel, *Mussolini, l'uomo e l'opera*, p. 492; and Bertoldi, *Piazzale Loreto*, p. 160.
2. Delzell, *Mussolini's Enemies*, pp. 311–12.
3. Bocca, *Storia dell'Italia partigiana*, pp. 570–1.
4. Dinale, *Quarant'anni di colloqui con lui*, pp. 243–51.
5. Graziani, *Ho difeso la patria*, p. 494; and Valiani, *Tutte le strade conducono a Roma*, pp. 326–7.
6. Dollmann, *The Interpreter*, pp. 329–35; *idem*, *Roma nazista*, pp. 303, 330; Spampanato, *L'ultimo Mussolini*, vol. 3, p. 26; Bocca, *Storia dell'Italia partigiana*, pp. 572–3; and Pini and Susmel, *Mussolini, l'uomo e l'opera*, pp. 492–3.
7. Spampanato, *L'ultimo Mussolini*, vol. 2, pp. 334–8.
8. Valiani, *Tutte le strade conducono a Roma*, pp. 328–30.
9. Pini and Susmel, *Mussolini, l'uomo e l'opera*, pp. 493–4.
10. Silvestri, *Mussolini, Graziani e l'antifascismo*, pp. 248–53.
11. B. Mussolini, *Opera Omnia*, p. 460; Anfuso, *Da Palazzo Venezia al Lago di Garda*, pp. 471–7; and Glauco Buffarini-Guidi, *La vera verità* (Milan: Sugar, 1947), p. 195.
12. Pini and Susmel, *Mussolini, l'uomo e l'opera*, p. 496.
13. Mellini, *Guerra diplomatica a Salò*, pp. 136–7; Bocca, *La repubblica di Mussolini*, p. 317; Bertoldi, *Piazzale Loreto*, pp. 152–3; and Collier, *Duce!*, pp. 309–10.
14. Collier, *Duce!*, p. 312.
15. Bertoldi, *Piazzale Loreto*, p. 95; Pini and Susmel, *Mussolini, l'uomo e l'opera*, p. 498; and Bocca, *La repubblica di Mussolini*, p. 327.
16. Campini, *Mussolini e Churchill*, pp. 102–3.
17. R. Mussolini, *La mia vita con Benito*, p. 261.
18. E. Mussolini, *Mio fratello Benito*, pp. 224–7.

19. Silvestri, *Mussolini, Graziani e l'antifascismo*, pp. 273–4.
20. Mellini, *Guerra diplomatica a Salò*, pp. 140–2.
21. B. Mussolini, *Opera Omnia*, pp. 186–90.
22. Collier, *Duce!*, p. 311.
23. R. Mussolini, *Benito il mio uomo*, p. 251, and R. Mussolini, *La mia vita con Benito*, p. 261.
24. Graziani, *Ho difeso la patria*, pp. 498–9.
25. Gervaso, *Claretta*, p. 178.
26. Dulles, *The Secret Surrender*, pp. 158–9.

Chapter 19. A Temporary Loss of Nerve

1. Dulles, *The Secret Surrender*, pp. 162–4.
2. Lanfranchi, *La resa degli 800,000*, pp. 256–7; and Dulles, *The Secret Surrender*, pp. 168, 180–1.
3. Lanfranchi, *La resa degli 800,000*, p. 257; and Dulles, *The Secret Surrender*, p. 165.
4. Lanfranchi, *La resa degli 800,000*, pp. 259–61; and Dulles, *The Secret Surrender*, pp. 165–6.
5. Dulles, *The Secret Surrender*, p. 167; and Lanfranchi, *La resa degli 800,000*, p. 261.
6. Dulles, *The Secret Surrender*, pp. 182–4, 168.
7. Lanfranchi, *La resa degli 800,000*, pp. 261–3.
8. Dulles, *The Secret Surrender*, pp. 185–91; Ildefonso Schuster, *Gli ultimi tempi di un regime* (Milan: La Via, 1946), p. 150; and Cadorna, *La riscossa*, p. 255.
9. Dulles, *The Secret Surrender*, p. 197.

Chapter 20. The Fall of Fascism

1. Corvo, *The O.S.S. in Italy 1942–45*, pp. 248–9; and Collier, *Duce!*, p. 341.
2. Bertoldi, *Piazzale Loreto*, pp. 25, 28, 29.
3. Zachariae, *Mussolini si confessa*, pp. 202–3; and Bertoldi, *Piazzale Loreto*, p. 109.
4. Amicucci, *I 600 giorni di Mussolini*, pp. 250–51; and Spampanato, *L'ultimo Mussolini*, vol. 3, p. 28.
5. Bertoldi, *Piazzale Loreto*, pp. 171–2.
6. Pini and Susmel, *Mussolini, l'uomo e l'opera*, pp. 500–1; Bocca, *La repubblica di Mussolini*, pp. 328–9; and Garibaldi, *Mussolini e il professore*, p. 320.
7. Mellini, *Guerra diplomatica a Salò*, p. 145.
8. Pini and Susmel, *Mussolini, l'uomo e l'opera*, p. 501; and Bertoldi, *Piazzale Loreto*, p. 98.
9. Benito Mussolini, *Testamento politico di Mussolini* (Milan: Tosi, 1948), pp. 25–46.
10. Pini and Susmel, *Mussolini, l'uomo e l'opera*, p. 509.
11. Amicucci, *I 600 giorni di Mussolini*, pp. 251–2.
12. Delzell, *Mussolini's Enemies*, pp. 515–16; Pini and Susmel, *Mussolini, l'uomo e l'opera*, p. 503; Bocca, *La repubblica di Mussolini*, p. 329; Valiani, *Tutte le strade conducono a Roma*, pp. 333–4; Graziani, *Ho difeso la patria*, p. 496; and D'Aroma, *Mussolini segreto*, pp. 320–1.

13. Collier, *Duce!*, pp. 315–16; Amicucci, *I 600 giorni di Mussolini*, p. 252; and Graziani, *Ho difeso la patria*, p. 497.
14. Pini and Susmel, *Mussolini, l'uomo e l'opera*, p. 503; and Amicucci, *I 600 giorni di Mussolini*, p. 232.
15. Amicucci, *I 600 giorni di Mussolini*, p. 253.
16. Pini and Susmel, *Mussolini, l'uomo e l'opera*, pp. 503–4; and Bertoldi, *Piazzale Loreto*, pp. 99–100.
17. Amicucci, *I 600 giorni di Mussolini*, p. 254; and Pini and Susmel, *Mussolini, l'uomo e l'opera*, p. 504.
18. Spampanato, *L'ultimo Mussolini*, vol. 1, pp. 274–5.
19. Garibaldi, *Mussolini e il professore*, p. 321.
20. Pini and Susmel, *Mussolini, l'uomo e l'opera*, pp. 505–6.
21. Schuster, *Gli ultimi tempi di un regime*, p. 135; and Graziani, *Ho difeso la patria*, pp. 495, 500–1.
22. Schuster, *Gli ultimi tempi di un regime*, p. 145.
23. Amicucci, *I 600 giorni di Mussolini*, p. 255; Delzell, *Mussolini's Enemies*, p. 517; Bocca, *La repubblica di Mussolini*, p. 329; Pini and Susmel, *Mussolini, l'uomo e l'opera*, p. 508; and Bandini, *Le ultime 95 ore di Mussolini*, p. 44.
24. B. Mussolini, *Opera Omnia*, p. 202.
25. Graziani, *Ho difeso la patria*, p. 508.
26. Collier, *Duce!*, p. 316; and Bertoldi, *Piazzale Loreto*, p. 155.
27. R. Mussolini, *La mia vita con Benito*, pp. 263–6; and R. Mussolini, Bertoldi, *Benito il mio uomo*, pp. 258.
28. Pini and Susmel, *Mussolini, l'uomo e l'opera*, p. 509.
29. Hoettl, *The Secret Front*, pp. 284–5.
30. Valiani, *Tutte le strade conducono a Roma*, pp. 335–6; and Spampanato, *L'ultimo Mussolini*, vol. 3, pp. 49–50.
31. Mellini, *Guerra diplomatica a Salò*, pp. 148–9.
32. Bocca, *La repubblica di Mussolini*, p. 330.
33. Amicucci, *I 600 giorni di Mussolini*, pp. 255–6; Delzell, *Mussolini's Enemies*, p. 517; Blaxland, *Alexander's Generals*, p. 275; and Battaglia, *Storia della resistenza italiana*, pp. 539, 543; and Valiani, *Tutte le strade conducono a Roma*, p. 337.
34. Bertoldi, *Piazzale Loreto*, p. 101; and Valiani, *Tutte le strade conducono a Roma*, p. 334.
35. Graziani, *Ho difeso la patria*, pp. 518–19.
36. Spampanato, *L'ultimo Mussolini*, vol. 2, p. 279.
37. Collier, *Duce!*, p. 317.
38. Pini and Susmel, *Mussolini, l'uomo e l'opera*, p. 512.
39. Bocca, *La repubblica di Mussolini*, pp. 330–1; and Amicucci, *I 600 giorni di Mussolini*, p. 259.
40. Bertoldi, *Piazzale Loreto*, pp. 91–3.
41. Valiani, *Tutte le strade conducono a Roma*, p. 338; and Mellini, *Guerra diplomatica a Salò*, p. 150.
42. Amicucci, *I 600 giorni di Mussolini*, p. 259; Pini and Susmel, *Mussolini, l'uomo e l'opera*, p. 513; Valiani, *Tutte le strade conducono a Roma*, pp. 338–9; and Blaxland, *Alexander's Generals*, p. 277.

43. Delzell, *Mussolini's Enemies*, pp. 523–4.
44. Pini and Susmel, *Mussolini, l'uomo e l'opera*, pp. 513–14; and Valiani, *Tutte le strade conducono a Roma*, pp. 337–8.
45. V. Mussolini, *Vita con mio padre*, pp. 211–18.
46. Silvestri, *Mussolini, Graziani e l'antifascismo*, pp. 227–8.
47. *Ibid.*, pp. 229–30.
48. Amicucci, *I 600 giorni di Mussolini*, p. 261; and Schuster, *Gli ultimi tempi di un regime*, pp. 162–7.
49. Cadorna, *La riscossa*, p. 250; Bertoldi, *Piazzale Loreto*, pp. 139–40; and Schuster, *Gli ultimi tempi di un regime*, p. 167.
50. Cadorna, *La riscossa*, pp. 250–1; Graziani, *Ho difeso la patria*, p. 513; Schuster, *Gli ultimi tempi di un regime*, p. 168; and Bertoldi, *Piazzale Loreto*, p. 141.
51. Cadorna, *La riscossa*, p. 251; and Schuster, *Gli ultimi tempi di un regime*, p. 169.
52. Bertoldi, *Piazzale Loreto*, p. 142; and Cadorna, *La riscossa*, pp. 251–2.
53. Schuster, *Gli ultimi tempi di un regime*, pp. 169–70; Pini and Susmel, *Mussolini, l'uomo e l'opera*, p. 517; Graziani, *Ho difeso la patria*, p. 515; and Valiani, *Tutte le strade conducono a Roma*, pp. 345–6.
54. Pini and Susmel, *Mussolini, l'uomo e l'opera*, pp. 517–18; Bocca, *La repubblica di Mussolini*, p. 334; Piero Pisenti, *Una repubblica necessaria* (Rome: Giovanni Volpe, 1977), p. 167; and Gravelli, *Mussolini aneddotico*, p. 320.
55. Gravelli, *Mussolini aneddotico*, p. 168; Bocca, *La repubblica di Mussolini*, p. 332; Bertoldi, *Piazzale Loreto*, pp. 93–4; and Graziani, *Ho difeso la patria*, pp. 516–18.
56. V. Mussolini, *Vita con mio padre*, 222–3.
57. Pini and Susmel, *Mussolini, l'uomo e l'opera*, pp. 518–19; Bellotti, *La repubblica di Mussolini*, pp. 221–2; and Gravelli, *Mussolini aneddotico*, p. 319.
58. Amicucci, *I 600 giorni di Mussolini*, pp. 264–5.
59. Bocca, *La repubblica di Mussolini*, p. 334.
60. *Ibid.*, p. 338.
61. Bertoldi, *Piazzale Loreto*, p. 43; and Collier, *Duce!*, p. 320.
62. Cadorna, *La riscossa*, pp. 254–5; and Amicucci, *I 600 giorni di Mussolini*, p. 265.
63. Spampanato, *L'ultimo Mussolini*, vol. 3, p. 64.
64. Collier, *Duce!*, p. 332; and Bertoldi, *Piazzale Loreto*, pp. 53, 55, 58.
65. Cadorna, *La riscossa*, pp. 256, 277.

Chapter 21. Flight and Capture

1. Pini and Susmel, *Mussolini, l'uomo e l'opera*, pp. 519–20; Fabio Andriola, *Appuntamento sul lago* (Milan: Sugar, 1990), p. 60; and Graziani, *Ho difeso la patria*, pp. 521–2.
2. Pini and Susmel, *Mussolini, l'uomo e l'opera*, p. 520; and V. Mussolini, *Vita con mio padre*, p. 224.
3. Urbano Lazzaro, *Dongo: mezzo secolo di menzogne* (Milan: Mondadori, 1993), p. 25; and Cordell Hull, *Memoirs of Cordell Hull*, vol. 2 (London: Hodder & Stoughton, 1948), pp. 1362–3.
4. R. Mussolini, *La mia vita con Benito*, pp. 267–73; and Pensotti, *Rachele*, p. 118.
5. Hibbert, *Benito Mussolini*, pp. 356–7; and Graziani, *Ho difeso la patria*, pp. 523–4.

6. Andriola, *Appuntamento sul lago*, pp. 68–9; Graziani, *Ho difeso la patria*, p. 524; Hibbert, *Benito Mussolini*, pp. 356–7; and Bertoldi, *I tedeschi in Italia*, p. 312.
7. Hibbert, *Benito Mussolini*, p. 357.
8. Pini and Susmel, *Mussolini, l'uomo e l'opera*, p. 523; Gervaso, *Claretta*, pp. 183, 186; and Bertoldi, *Piazzale Loreto*, pp. 110–13, 173.
9. Silvestri, *Mussolini, Graziani e l'antifascismo*, p. 247. The theory that Mussolini awaited Churchill's emissary is a principal theme of Fabio Andriola's 1990 book, *Appuntamento sul lago*.
10. Pini and Susmel, *Mussolini, l'uomo e l'opera*, p. 522; and Andriola, *Appuntamento sul lago*, pp. 70–1.
11. Hibbert, *Benito Mussolini*, pp. 357–9.
12. Andriola, *Appuntamento sul lago*, pp. 76–7; Pini and Susmel, *Mussolini, l'uomo e l'opera*, p. 524; Hibbert, *Benito Mussolini*, p. 359; and Gervaso, *Claretta*, p. 187.
13. Hibbert, *Benito Mussolini*, pp. 359–60; and Andriola, *Appuntamento sul lago*, p. 78.
14. Hibbert, *Benito Mussolini*, p. 360; and Silvestri, *Mussolini, Graziani e l'antifascismo*, p. 247.
15. Pini and Susmel, *Mussolini, l'uomo e l'opera*, pp. 525–6.
16. Pini and Susmel, *Mussolini, l'uomo e l'opera*, pp. 524–5; and Graziani, *Ho difeso la patria*, p.525.
17. Hibbert, *Benito Mussolini*, p. 360; and Andriola, *Appuntamento sul lago*, p. 81.
18. Hibbert, *Benito Mussolini*, p. 361; and Pier Luigi Bellini delle Stelle and Urbano Lazzaro, *Dongo, la fine di Mussolini* (Milan: Mondadori, 1975), p. 96–7. This book was written by Bellini delle Stelle and incorporates passages from an earlier book by Lazzaro. Lazzaro said he knew nothing of the publication of *Dongo, la fine di Mussolini* until it appeared, and it angered him. He disagreed with many of Bellini delle Stelle's statements of fact, interpretations and conclusions. For example, Lazzaro rejected Bellini delle Stelle's account of a conversation with Claretta Petacci, even though he was not present, and in his own book, *Dongo: mezzo secolo di menzogne*, he substituted a seven-page verbatim account that he contends, on no evidence, represented the true conversation.
19. Bellini delle Stelle and Lazzaro, *Dongo, la fine di Mussolini*, pp. 97–8.
20. Marco Luppi, 'Fermarono Mussolini e il parroco raccontò', in *La Provincia Pavese*, 17 December 1995, 21; and Hibbert, *Benito Mussolini*, p. 362.
21. Bellini delle Stelle and Lazzaro, *Dongo, la fine di Mussolini*, pp. 100–1.
22. Hibbert, *Benito Mussolini*, p. 362.
23. Andriola, *Appuntamento sul lago*, p. 92; and Hibbert, *Benito Mussolini*, pp. 362–3.
24. Lazzaro, *Dongo: mezzo secolo di menzogne*, p.33; Bellini delle Stelle and Lazzaro, *Dongo, la fine di Mussolini*, p. 106; and Hibbert, *Benito Mussolini*, p. 363.
25. Lazzaro, *Dongo: mezzo secolo di menzogne*, p. 33; and Hibbert, *Benito Mussolini*, pp. 363–4.
26. Bellini delle Stelle and Lazzaro, *Dongo, la fine di Mussolini*, pp. 105–6, 113; Hibbert, *Benito Mussolini*, pp. 364–5; and Monelli, *Mussolini piccolo borghese*, p. 345.
27. Hibbert, *Benito Mussolini*, p. 365; and Bertoldi, *I tedeschi in Italia*, pp. 307, 309.
28. Luppi, 'Fermarono Mussolini e il parroco raccontò', 21; and Bellini delle Stelle and Lazzaro, *Dongo, la fine di Mussolini*, p. 107.
29. Bellini delle Stelle and Lazzaro, *Dongo, la fine di Mussolini*, pp. 107–13.
30. Hibbert, *Benito Mussolini*, p. 366; Pini and Susmel, *Mussolini, l'uomo e l'opera*, p. 529; and Bellini delle Stelle and Lazzaro, *Dongo, la fine di Mussolini*, p. 160.
31. Bellini delle Stelle and Lazzaro, *Dongo, la fine di Mussolini*, p. 116.

Chapter 22. Mussolini Tamed: The Polite Prisoner

1. Pini and Susmel, *Mussolini, l'uomo e l'opera*, pp. 529–30.
2. Bellini delle Stelle and Lazzaro, *Dongo, la fine di Mussolini*, pp. 117–19.
3. Interview with the author.
4. *Ibid.*, pp. 117–23; and Pini and Susmel, *Mussolini, l'uomo e l'opera*, p. 530.
5. Angelo Colleoni, *La verità sulla fine di Mussolini e della Petacci* (Milan: Lucchi, 1945), pp. 17–19; *Chicago Tribune*, 'Mussolini Shot and Dumped in Public Square', 30 April 1945; and Urbano Lazzaro, *Dongo: mezzo secolo di menzogne*, p. 51.
6. Bellini delle Stelle and Lazzaro, *Dongo, la fine di Mussolini*, pp. 123–29; Anon., 'Sono stato tradito nove volte e la decima da Hitler,' *L'Italia Libera*, 1 May 1945, 1; and Pini and Susmel, *Mussolini, l'uomo e l'opera*, pp. 530.
7. Bellini delle Stelle and Lazzaro, *Dongo, la fine di Mussolini*, pp., 130–31.
8. *Ibid.*, pp., 131–2; and Pini and Susmel, *Mussolini, l'uomo e l'opera*, p. 531.
9. Bellini delle Stelle and Lazzaro, *Dongo, la fine di Mussolini*, pp. 132–7; and Cavalleri, *Ombre sul lago*, p. 28.
10. Hibbert, *Benito Mussolini*, p. 369; Andriola, *Appuntamento sul lago*, p. 92; and Kimball, *Churchill and Roosevelt*, vol. 2, pp. 552–43.
11. Lazzaro, *Dongo: mezzo secolo di menzogne*, pp. 42–3; and Franco Bandini, *Vita e morte segreta di Mussolini* (Milan: Mondadori, 1978), pp. 300–1.
12. Bellini delle Stelle and Lazzaro, *Dongo, la fine di Mussolini*, pp. 138–9; Hibbert, *Benito Mussolini*, p. 369; and Colleoni, *La verità sulla fine di Mussolini e della Petacci*, p. 18.
13. Pini and Susmel, *Mussolini, l'uomo e l'opera*, p. 532; Bellini delle Stelle and Lazzaro, *Dongo, la fine di Mussolini*, pp. 140–3; and Colleoni, *La verità sulla fine di Mussolini e della Petacci*, p. 19.
14. Bellini delle Stelle and Lazzaro, *Dongo, la fine di Mussolini*, pp. 144–5.
15. Andriola, *Appuntamento sul lago*, pp. 114–15; and Anon., 'Sono stato tradito nove volte e la decima da Hitler', p. 1.
16. Pini and Susmel, *Mussolini, l'uomo e l'opera*, p. 532; Hibbert, *Benito Mussolini*, pp. 370–1; Colleoni, *La verità sulla fine di Mussolini e della Petacci*, p. 20; and Anon., 'Sono stato tradito nove volte e la decima da Hitler,' 1.
17. Bellini delle Stelle and Lazzaro, *Dongo, la fine di Mussolini*, pp. 148–58, 161.
18. Hibbert, *Benito Mussolini*, pp. 371–3.
19. Bellini delle Stelle and Lazzaro, *Dongo, la fine di Mussolini*, pp. 163, 165–7, 175–6; Cavalleri, *Ombre sul lago*, pp. 89, 94; and Hibbert, *Benito Mussolini*, pp. 373–4.
20. Pini and Susmel, *Mussolini, l'uomo e l'opera*, p. 534; and Bellini delle Stelle and Lazzaro, *Dongo, la fine di Mussolini*, pp. 173, 175.

Chapter 23. 'I've Come to Shoot Them'

1. Bellini delle Stelle and Lazzaro, *Dongo, la fine di Mussolini*, pp. 176–80; and Giusto Perretta, *La verità* (Como: Actac, 1997), p. 168.
2. Bellini delle Stelle and Lazzaro, *Dongo, la fine di Mussolini*, pp. 180–1.
3. *Ibid.*, p. 181; Hibbert, *Benito Mussolini*, p. 375; Ezio Saini, *La notte di Dongo* (Rome: Corso, 1950), p. 19; and Perretta, *La verita*, xxiii.

4. Bellini delle Stelle and Lazzaro, *Dongo, la fine di Mussolini*, pp. 181–3; Hibbert, *Benito Mussolini*, pp. 375–6; and Andriola, *Appuntamento sul lago*, p. 122.
5. Hibbert, *Benito Mussolini*, pp. 376–7; and Monelli, *Mussolini piccolo borghese*, p. 353.
6. Pini and Susmel, *Mussolini, l'uomo e l'opera*, p. 535; and Hibbert, *Benito Mussolini*, pp. 377–8.
7. V. Mussolini, *Vita con mio padre*, pp. 226–7; and Pini and Susmel, *Mussolini, l'uomo e l'opera*, pp. 533–4.
8. Andriola, *Appuntamento sul lago*, p. 132; Pini and Susmel, *Mussolini, l'uomo e l'opera*, p. 536; and Saini, *La notte di Dongo*, p. 38.
9. Andriola, *Appuntamento sul lago*, pp. 134–5.
10. Wladimiro Settimelli interview with historian Giorgio Bocca, 'Ora il caso è chiuso', *L'Unità*, 24 January 1996, p. 3.
11. Walter Audisio, *In nome del popolo italiano* (Milan: Teti, 1975), pp. 341–2, 348; Cadorna, *La riscossa*, p. 258; and Bandini, *Vita e morte segreta di Mussolini*, pp. 322, 325.
12. Cadorna, *La riscossa*, pp. 258–9; and Andriola, *Appuntamento sul lago*, pp. 145–6.
13. Bandini, *Vita e morte segreta di Mussolini*, p. 323.
14. Audisio, *In nome del popolo italiano*, pp. 346–64.
15. Saini, *La notte di Dongo*, pp. 8–9.
16. *Ibid.*, pp. 9–10; and Audisio, *In nome del popolo italiano*, pp 365–6.
17. Bellini delle Stelle and Lazzaro, *Dongo, la fine di Mussolini*, p. 184; and Aldo Lampredi, 'La fine del Duce', *L'Unità*, 23 January 1996, pp. 2, 3.
18. Bellini delle Stelle and Lazzaro, *Dongo, la fine di Mussolini*, pp. 184, 190–3; and Giacomo Carboni, 'Report of General Giacomo Carboni to the U.S. Office of Strategic Services', archives of the Fondazione Fratelli Rosselli in Italy.
19. Audisio, *In nome del popolo italiano*, pp. 366–71; and Urbano Lazzaro, interview with author.
20. Bellini delle Stelle and Lazzaro, *Dongo, la fine di Mussolini*, pp. 195–206; Luigi Bolla, *Perché a Salò*, p. 193; and Audisio, *In nome del popolo italiano*, p. 371.

Chapter 24. Execution of Il Duce: Whodunnit?

1. Audisio, *In nome del popolo italiano*, pp. 376–83.
2. Bandini, *Vita e morte segreta di Mussolini*, pp. 306–7; and Saini, *La notte di Dongo*, p. 33.
3. Bandini, *Vita e morte segreta di Mussolini*, pp. 308–14; and Andriola, *Appuntamento sul lago*, p. 164.
4. Bandini, *Vita e morte segreta di Mussolini*, pp. 310–11; and Tamaro, *Due anni di storia*, vol. 3, p. 633.
5. Lazzaro, *Dongo: mezzo secolo di menzogne*, pp, 147–8; Saini, *La notte di Dongo*, pp. 158–9; Bertoldi, *Piazzale Loreto*, pp. 236–7; and Tamaro, *Due anni di storia*, vol. 3, p. 636.
6. Saini, *La notte di Dongo*, p. 25; and Bandini, *Vita e morte segreta di Mussolini*, pp. 310, 313–14.
7. Bellini delle Stelle and Lazzaro, *Dongo, la fine di Mussolini*, pp. 210–11.
8. Audisio, *In nome del popolo italiano*, pp. 373–5.

9. Andriola, *Appuntamento sul lago*, pp. 164–5; Hibbert, *Benito Mussolini*, pp. 388; Monelli, *Mussolini piccolo borghese*, p. 356; and Bandini, *Vita e morte segreta di Mussolini*, pp. 433–4.
10. Cavalleri, *Ombre sul lago*, pp. 57f; and Bellini delle Stelle and Lazzaro, *Dongo, la fine di Mussolini*, pp. 209, 211.
11. Andriola, *Appuntamento sul lago*, pp. 166–8; and Cavalleri, *Ombre sul lago*, pp. 70–2.
12. Hibbert, *Benito Mussolini*, p. 387; and Monelli, *Mussolini piccolo borghese*, p. 360.
13. Andriola, *Appuntamento sul lago*, p. 161.
14. Saini, *La notte di Dongo*, pp. 23, 30; Bertoldi, *Piazzale Loreto*, pp. 146–7; Andriola, *Appuntamento sul lago*, pp. 174–6, 181–4; 'Renzo' [Lorenzo Bianchi], *La Voce Partigiana*, 27–28 April 1945; and Cavalleri, *Ombre sul lago*, p. 125.
15. Bandini, *Vita e morte segreta di Mussolini*, pp. 326–32.
16. Lazzaro, *Dongo: mezzo secolo di menzogne*, pp. 111–18, 145–56; Bandini, *Vita e morte segreta di Mussolini*, p. 431; and Cavalleri, *Ombre sul lago*, pp. 179f.
17. Bandini, *Vita e morte segreta di Mussolini*, pp. 430–1.
18. Cavalleri, *Ombre sul lago*, p. 66.
19. Candiano Falaschi, 'Inizia la Grande Inchiesta dell'*Unità*', *L'Unità*, 25 February 1973, p. 3; Candiano Falaschi, 'La cattura di Mussolini', *L'Unità*, 27 February 1973; Candiano Falaschi, 'Missione a Como e Dongo', *L'Unità*, 4 March 1973; Candiano Falaschi, 'La morte del Dittatore', *L'Unità*, 8 March 1973; and Candiano Falaschi, 'I giorni che decisero la fine del fascismo – un taglio netto con il passato', *L'Unità*, 10 March 1973.
20. Unsigned article, 'La vita di Lampredi', *L'Unità*, 23 January 1996, p. 3; Aldo Lampredi, 'La fine del Duce', *L'Unità*, 23 January 1996, pp. 2, 3; Miriam Mafai, 'Un segreto in quei tempi durissimi', *L'Unità*, 24 January 1996, pp. 1, 3; Wladimiro Settimelli, 'Ora il caso è chiuso', *L'Unità*, 24 January 1996, p. 3; Aldo Lampredi, 'Io, partigiano oscurato', *L'Unità*, 25 January 1996, p. 2; and *idem*, 'Quel giorno Walter Audisio venne a casa mia', *L'Unità*, 25 January 1996, p. 2. The Istituto Gramsci records also contain one of the more bizarre forgeries in the former Communist Party archives. A 'proclamation' bearing Mussolini's signature, it is dated 28 April 1945, and states that he has assumed supreme command of Italo-German forces in Italy following the conquest of Berlin and the fall of Hitler and has dissolved the SS. His assumption of command was agreed at his meeting with Hitler on 18 April at Berchtesgaden, according to the document. In fact, Mussolini left Gargnano for Milan on 18 April, and Hitler was then in his Berlin bunker, not Berchtesgaden. And Mussolini was killed on 28 April. Evidently the Communists forged this document well before it became clear that Mussolini would no longer be in power on that date, and their aim was to create a rift between the Duce and the German military leadership in Italy. But they not only failed to anticipate the day of his execution; they were also overly optimistic in assuming Hitler would have fallen by 28 April.
21. Bellini delle Stelle and Lazzaro, *Dongo, la fine di Mussolini*, pp. 206–13; Andriola, *Appuntamento sul lago*, pp. 185–6; and Cavalleri, *Ombre sul lago*, p. 45.
22. Audisio, *In nome del popolo italiano*, p. 384; Saini, *La notte di Dongo*, p. 13; and Aldo Lampredi, 'La fine del Duce', *L'Unità*, 23 January 1996, pp. 2, 3.
23. Andriola, *Appuntamento sul lago*, p. 186; and Saini, *La notte di Dongo*, pp. 13–14.

24. Andriola, *Appuntamento sul lago*, p. 186; Bellini delle Stelle and Lazzaro, *Dongo, la fine di Mussolini*, pp. 213–14; and Audisio, *In nome del popolo italiano*, pp. 384–5.
25. Bellini delle Stelle and Lazzaro, *Dongo, la fine di Mussolini*, p. 214.
26. Saini, *La notte di Dongo*, pp. 14–16.
27. *Ibid.*, p. 16; and Bellini delle Stelle and Lazzaro, *Dongo, la fine di Mussolini*, p. 215.
28. Audisio, *In nome del popolo italiano*, p. 385; Bellini delle Stelle and Lazzaro, *Dongo, la fine di Mussolini*, p. 215; Saini, *La notte di Dongo*, p. 16; and M. Petacci, *Chi ama è perduto*, p. 396. The men shot at Dongo were Alessandro Pavolini, Fascist Party secretary; Francesco Maria Barracu, Paolo Zerbino, Fernando Mezzasoma, Ruggero Romano and Augusto Liverani, all government ministers; Paolo Porta, Fascist inspector for Lombardy; Luigi Gatti, Mussolini's secretary; Goffredo Coppola, rector of Bologna University; Ernesto Daquanno, director of the Stefani news agency; Mario Nudi, employee of the Fascist Agricultural Federation; Vito Casalinuovo, aide to Mussolini; Pietro Calistri, Air Force pilot; Idreno Utimpergher, publicist; Nicola Bombacci, friend of Mussolini's; and Marcello Petacci.
29. Saini, *La notte di Dongo*, p. 14.
30. Bandini, *Vita e morte segreta di Mussolini*, p. 315.
31. Bellini delle Stelle and Lazzaro, *Dongo, la fine di Mussolini*, p. 216; Andriola, *Appuntamento sul lago*, p. 190; Monelli, *Mussolini piccolo borghese*, p. 360; and Paul Ghali, in *Chicago Daily News*, 30 April 1945.

Chapter 25. Piazzale Loreto: A Shameful Denouement

1. Audisio, *In nome del popolo italiano*, pp. 387–8; Paul Ghali, in *Chicago Daily News*, 30 April 1945; and Andriola, *Appuntamento sul lago*, p. 191.
2. Audisio, *In nome del popolo italiano*, pp. 388–9, 391; Lampredi, 'La fine del Duce', pp. 2, 3; Andriola, *Appuntamento sul lago*, pp. 191; Cadorna, *La riscossa*, pp. 260–1; and Saini, *La notte di Dongo*, p. 50.
3. Lampredi, 'La fine del Duce', pp. 2, 3; Andriola, *Appuntamento sul lago*, pp. 197–8; and Bertoldi, *Piazzale Loreto*, p. 243.
4. Hibbert, *Benito Mussolini*, p. 390; Andriola, *Appuntamento sul lago*, p. 198; Tamaro, *Due anni di storia*, vol. 3, p. 641; and Bertoldi, *Piazzale Loreto*, pp. 245–6.
5. Andriola, *Appuntamento sul lago*, pp. 199; and Bertoldi, *Piazzale Loreto*, pp. 249–50.
6. Hibbert, *Benito Mussolini*, p. 391; Andriola, *Appuntamento sul lago*, p. 200; Monelli, *Mussolini piccolo borghese*, p. 362; and Bertoldi, *Piazzale Loreto*, p. 249.
7. Hibbert, *Benito Mussolini*, pp. 391–2.
8. Collier, *Duce!*, pp. 361–3; Andriola, *Appuntamento sul lago*, p. 199; and Bertoldi, *Piazzale Loreto*, pp. 247–9.
9. Andriola, *Appuntamento sul lago*, pp. 196, 199, 201; and Bertoldi, *Piazzale Loreto*, p. 257.
10. Saini, *La notte di Dongo*, pp. 41–2; and Bertoldi, *Piazzale Loreto*, p. 257.
11. Saini, *La notte di Dongo*, pp. 40–1; and Lazzaro, *Dongo: mezzo secolo di menzogne*, p. 46.
12. Collier, *Duce!*, p. 364; Winston S. Churchill, *The Second World War*, vol. 6 (London: Cassell, 1954), p. 461; and *idem*, Churchill Archives, CHAR 20/218/73, 10 May 1945.
13. Richard Overy, *Interrogations* (London: Allen Lane, Penguin Press, 2001), pp. 6–10, 28–9.

14. Graziani, *Ho difeso la patria*, p. 526; and Lanfranchi, *La resa degli 800,000*, p. 263.
15. Cadorna, *La riscossa*, p. 261; Graziani, *Ho difeso la patria*, pp.534, 536; and Corvo, *The O.S.S. in Italy 1942–45*, pp. 251–2.
16. Cadorna, *La riscossa*, p. 262.
17. *Ibid.*, pp. 263–4; Delzell, *Mussolini's Enemies*, p. 536; Graziani, *Ho difeso la patria*, pp. 535, 548; and Corvo, *The O.S.S. in Italy 1942–45*, pp. 253–4.
18. Cadorna, *La riscossa*, p. 264.
19. *Ibid.*, p. 260.
20. Saini, *La notte di Dongo*, p. 212.
21. *Ibid.*, pp. 31–2, 190–1; Lazzaro, *Dongo: mezzo secolo di menzogne*, p.121; and Bandini, *Vita e morte segreta di Mussolini*, pp. 430–1, 435–6.
22. Saini, *La notte di Dongo*, p. 191; Archives of the Fondazione Fratelli Rosselli; Bandini, *Vita e morte segreta di Mussolini*, p. 386; and Associated Press dispatch of 31 January 1946.
23. Bandini, *Vita e morte segreta di Mussolini*, p. 332; and Gervaso, *Claretta*, p. 236.
24. Correspondence in the archives of the Fondazione Fratelli Rosselli.

Chapter 26. The German Surrender

1. Dulles, *The Secret Surrender*, pp. 197–8.
2. Lanfranchi, *La resa degli 800,000*, pp. 262–4.
3. *Ibid.*, p. 264; and Dulles, *The Secret Surrender*, p. 199.
4. Dulles, *The Secret Surrender*, pp. 201–16; and Lanfranchi, *La resa degli 800,000*, pp. 317–19.
5. Dulles, *The Secret Surrender*, pp. 223, 225; Lanfranchi, *La resa degli 800,000*, pp. 321–2; and Kesselring, *Memoirs of Field Marshal Kesselring*, pp. 288–9.
6. Dulles, *The Secret Surrender*, pp. 227–8; and Lanfranchi, *La resa degli 800,000*, p. 337.
7. Dulles, *The Secret Surrender*, pp. 216–17.
8. *Ibid.*, pp. 229–31; Dollmann, *Roma nazista*, pp. 335–6; and Lanfranchi, *La resa degli 800,000*, pp. 338–9.
9. Dulles, *The Secret Surrender*, pp. 219, 233–7; Lanfranchi, *La resa degli 800,000*, p. 339; and Kesselring, *Memoirs of Field Marshal Kesselring*, p. 289.
10. Dulles, *The Secret Surrender*, p. 221; and Lanfranchi, *La resa degli 800,000*, p. 339.
11. Lanfranchi, *La resa degli 800,000*, pp. 349–51.
12. Dollmann, *Roma Nazista*, pp. 340–1, 343, 345, 348; Roxan and Wanstall, *The Jackdaw of Linz*, pp. 109, 111–12; and Mario Bondioli-Osio, report of the Italian Interministerial Commission for Art Works, 15 July 1996.
13. Corvo, *The O.S.S. in Italy 1942–45*, pp. 270–1.
14. Bertoldi, *Piazzale Loreto*, pp. 64–7; Valiani, *Tutte le strade conducono a Roma*, p. 351; Lamb, *War in Italy*, pp. 239–40; and Salvadori, *Breve storia della resistenza italiana*, p. 243.
15. Lamb, *War in Italy*, p. 236; Delzell, *Mussolini's Enemies*, pp. 545–6; Valiani, *Tutte le strade conducono a Roma*, p. 353; Bocca, *La repubblica di Mussolini*, p. 339; Salvadori, *Breve storia della resistenza italiana*, p. 27; Longo, *Un popolo alla macchia*, p. 446; and Giorgio Bocca, *Palmiro Togliatti* (Rome-Bari: Laterza, 1973), pp. 382–3.

16. Delzell, *Mussolini's Enemies*, p. 544.
17. Alexander, *Memoirs of Field Marshal Alexander*, p. 146; and Emilio Canevari, *La guerra italiana*, vol. 2 (Rome: Tosi, 1949), p. 811.
18. Dollmann, *Call Me Coward*, p. 42; and Wilhelm, *The Other Italy*, pp. 258–9.

Chapter 27. Lakeside Murders and the Dongo Treasure

1. Lazzaro, *Dongo: mezzo secolo di menzogne*, pp. 137, 139.
2. *Ibid.*, pp.137, 140–1; Saini, *La notte di Dongo*, p. 204; Andriola, *Appuntamento sul lago*, p. 207; and Cavalleri, *Ombre sul lago*, p. 215.
3. Lazzaro, *Dongo: mezzo secolo di menzogne*, p. 141.
4. *Ibid.*, p. 142.
5. Saini, *La notte di Dongo*,pp. 208–9.
6. Cavalleri, *Ombre sul lago*, pp. 100, 103, 106, 107, 126; Saini, *La notte di Dongo*, pp. 55–7; and Andriola, *Appuntamento sul lago*, pp. 209–10.
7. Andriola, *Appuntamento sul lago*, pp. 212–13; and Cavalleri, *Ombre sul lago*, pp. 104, 111.
8. Andriola, *Appuntamento sul lago*, p. 214; and Cavalleri, *Ombre sul lago*, pp. 110, 111.
9. Saini, *La notte di Dongo*, pp. 209–11; Andriola, *Appuntamento sul lago*, p. 169; and Cavalleri, *Ombre sul lago*, pp. 99f.
10. Andriola, *Appuntamento sul lago*, pp. 215–16; and Saini, *La notte di Dongo*, pp. 144–5, 221.
11. Andriola, *Appuntamento sul lago*, pp. 119–22, 221, 234–5.
12. Cavalleri, *Ombre sul lago*, pp. 211, 223–4.
13. Andriola, *Appuntamento sul lago*, pp. 216–17; Lazzaro, *Dongo: mezzo secolo di menzogne*, p.15; and Cavalleri, *Ombre sul lago*, p. 112.
14. Interview with the author.
15. Andriola, *Appuntamento sul lago*, pp. 217–18; and Saini, *La notte di Dongo*, pp. 158–9.
16. Saini, *La notte di Dongo*, pp. 117, 155–57, 246.
17. Andriola, *Appuntamento sul lago*, pp. 218–19; and Cavalleri, *Ombre sul lago*, pp. 118–19.
18. Cavalleri, *Ombre sul lago*, p. 129.

Chapter 28. The Mysterious Churchill File

1. Cavalleri, *Ombre sul lago*, pp. 158–9; and Andriola, *Appuntamento sul lago*, p. 239.
2. Cadorna, *La riscossa*, p. 270; Andriola, *Appuntamento sul lago*, p. 271; and Arrigo Petacco, *L'archivio segreto di Mussolini* (Milan: Mondadori, 1997), p. 168.
3. Petacco, *L'archivio segreto di Mussolini*, p. 168.
4. The anonymous report, 'Il mistero delle borse', is reproduced in full in *L'Unità*, 25 January 1996, p. 3.
5. Ibid., p. 3; Cavalleri, *Ombre sul lago*, pp. 183, 186–7; and Roy Jenkins, *Churchill* (London: Macmillan, 2001), pp. 464, 482–5, 493.
6. Cavalleri, *Ombre sul lago*, p. 201.
7. Anon., 'Il mistero delle borse', p. 3.

8. Andriola, *Appuntamento sul lago*, p. 259; Arrigo Petacco, *Dear Benito, Caro Winston* (Milan: Mondadori, 1985), p. 58; and Cavalleri, *Ombre sul lago*, p. 193.
9. Andriola, *Appuntamento sul lago*, pp. 228, 230, 259–60, 268–9; Lazzaro, *Dongo: mezzo secolo di menzogne*, pp. 128–30; and Petacco, *Dear Benito, Caro Winston*, p. 46.
10. Andriola, *Appuntamento sul lago*, p. 230; and Petacco, *Dear Benito, Caro Winston*, pp. 61–2.
11. Cavalleri, *Ombre sul lago*, 195, 198–9.
12. *Ibid.*, pp. 145–6, 156.
13. Petacco, *Dear Benito, Caro Winston*, pp. 66–71, 109–17, 123–4.
14. Andriola, *Appuntamento sul lago*, p. 265.
15. Petacco, *Dear Benito, Caro Winston*, p. 112; and Andriola, *Appuntamento sul lago*, p. 250.
16. Renzo De Felice, *Rosso e nero* (Milan: Baldini & Castoldi, 1995), pp. 144–5, 148.
17. Andriola, *Appuntamento sul lago*, pp. 225–8, 249–50; D'Aroma, *Mussolini segreto*, pp. 442, 444–5; and De Felice, *Rosso e nero*, pp. 142–3.
18. Campini, *Mussolini e Churchill*, pp. 134–7, 218, 224, 226.

Chapter 29. The Dead Sprout Wings

1. Domenico Leccisi, *Con Mussolini prima e dopo Piazzale Loreto* (Rome: Settimo Sigillo, 1991), pp. 218–331. This entire account is taken from Leccisi's book, except for a few excerpts from an unpublished American article of 1970 made available to the author.
2. Bosworth, *Mussolini*, pp. 419–20; and V. Mussolini, *The Tragic Women in His Life*, p. 146.
3. R. Mussolini, *La mia vita con Benito*, p. 274.
4. Saini, *La notte di Dongo*, pp. 205, 239–40.
5. R. Mussolini, *La mia vita con Benito*, pp. 275–9; and V. Mussolini, *The Tragic Women in His Life*, p. 131.
6. From the unpublished American article. See also Leccisi, *Con Mussolini prima e dopo Piazzale Loreto*, p. 337; and V. Mussolini, *The Tragic Women in His Life*, p. 147.
7. Richard Boudreaux, 'A New Day for Il Duce', *Los Angeles Times*, 12 May 2002, p. 1; Alexander Stille, 'In Italy, a Kinder, Gentler Fascism', *New York Times*, 29 September 2002, arts section; John Lloyd, 'Marketing Mussolini', *Financial Times*, 4 August 2001, weekend section, p. 1; and Michele Smargiassi, 'Mille mantelli d'orbace per il nuovo culto del duce', *La Repubblica*, 28 October 2002, p. 22.
8. Bosworth, *Mussolini*, pp. 34–5, 409.
9. De Felice, *Rosso e nero*, pp. 114, 115, 120.

Epilogue

1. E. Mussolini, *Mio fratello Benito*, p. 227.
2. Corvo, *The O.S.S. in Italy 1942–45*, pp. 263, 271.
3. Delzell, *Mussolini's Enemies*, pp. 536–7.

4. Grose, *Gentleman Spy*, pp. 244, 253–4; Dollmann, *Roma nazista*, p. 349; Katz, *Death in Rome*, p. 234; and Dulles, *The Secret Surrender*, pp. 252–3.
5. Grose, *Gentleman Spy*, pp. 253–4; Lanfranchi, *La resa degli 800,000*, p. 358; and Dulles, *The Secret Surrender*, p. 252.
6. Dollmann, *Call Me Coward*, pp. 48–64, 83–126; and Grose, *Gentleman Spy*, pp. 253–4.
7. Corvo, *The O.S.S. in Italy 1942–45*, p. 297.
8. Anon., 'Non pubblicate i diari di zia Claretta', *Corriere della Sera*, 7 December 2002.

Bibliography

Archival sources

The Churchill Archives, Churchill College, Cambridge University
CHAR 20/116/26-28 Churchill telegram to President Roosevelt on 26 July 1943; CHAR 20/117/10 Churchill telegram to FDR on 6 August 1943; CHAR 20/218/73 Churchill telegram to Field Marshal Alexander on 10 May 1945; CHAR 9/204 A-C Churchill broadcast of 26 March 1944; and CHAR 9/199 A-D Churchill foreign policy review of 24 May 1944
Fondazione Fratelli Rosselli, Florence
Roosevelt Archives, FDR Library, Hyde Park, New York

Printed sources

Alexander, Harold, *The Alexander Memoirs*, London, Cassell, 1962
Amicucci, Ermanno, *I 600 giorni di Mussolini*, Rome, Faro, 1948
Andriola, Fabio, *Appuntamento sul lago*, Milan, Sugar, 1990
Anfuso, Filippo, *Da Palazzo Venezia al Lago di Garda*, Rome, Settimo Sigillo, 1996
Angelozzi Gariboldi, Giorgio, *Pio XII, Hitler e Mussolini*, Milan, Mursia, 1988
Anon., 'Il mistero delle borse', *L'Unità*, 25 January 1996, 3
——, 'La vita di Lampredi', *L'Unità*, 23 January 1996, 3
——, 'Non pubblicate i diari di zia Claretta', *Corriere della Sera*, 7 December 2002
——, 'Sono stato tradito nove volte e la decima da Hitler', *L'Italia Libera*, 1 May 1945, 1
Audisio, Walter, *In nome del popolo italiano*, Milan, Teti, 1975
Badoglio, Pietro, *Italy in the Second World War*, Westport, CT, Greenwood Press, 1976
Bandini, Franco, *Le ultime 95 ore di Mussolini*, Bologna, Sugar, 1959
——, *Vita e morte segreta di Mussolini*, Milan, Mondadori, 1978
Battaglia, Roberto, *Storia della resistenza italiana*, Turin, Giulio Einaudi, 1964
Bellini delle Stelle, Pier Luigi, and Urbano Lazzaro, *Dongo, la fine di Mussolini*. Milan, Mondadori, 1975
Bellotti, Felice, *La repubblica di Mussolini*, Milan, Zagara, 1947
Berenson, Bernard, *Rumour and Reflection*, London, Constable, 1952
Bertoldi, Silvio, *I tedeschi in Italia*, Milan, Rizzoli, 1994
——, *Piazzale Loreto*, Milan, Rizzoli, 2001

Bertoldi, Silvio, *Salò*, Milan, Rizzoli, 1978

Blaxland, Gregory, *Alexander's Generals*, London, William Kimber, 1979

Bocca, Giorgio, *La repubblica di Mussolini*, Milan, Mondadori, 1994

——, *Palmiro Togliatti*, Rome–Bari, Laterza, 1973

——, *Storia dell'Italia partigiana*, Bari, Laterza, 1966

Bolla, Luigi, *Perché a Salò*, Milan, Bompiani, 1982

Bondioli-Osio, Mario, Report of the Italian Interministerial Commission for Art Works, Rome, 15 July 1996

Bosworth, R.J.B., *Mussolini*, London, Arnold, 2002

Bottai, Giuseppe, *Diario 1935–1944*, vol. 2, Milan, Rizzoli, 1988

Boudreaux, Richard, 'A New Day for Il Duce', *Los Angeles Times*, 12 May 2002, 1

Buffarini-Guidi, Glauco, *La vera verità*, Milan, Sugar, 1947

Cabella, Gian Gaetano, *Testamento politico di Mussolini*, Rome, Tosi, 1948

Cadorna, Raffaele, *La riscossa*, Milan, Rizzoli, 1948

Campini, Dino, *Mussolini e Churchill*, Milan, Italpress, 1950

Canevari, Emilio, *La guerra italiana*, vol. 2, Rome, Tosi, 1949

Castelli, Giulio, *Storia segreta di Roma città aperta*, Rome, Quatrucci, 1959

Cavalleri, Giorgio, *Ombre sul lago*, Casale Monferrato, Piemme, 1995

Cerruti, Elisabetta, *Ambassador's Wife*, London, George Allen & Unwin, 1952

Chicago Tribune, 'Mussolini Shot and Dumped in Public Square', 30 April 1945

Churchill, Winston S., *The Second World War*, vol. 6, London, Cassell, 1954

Ciano, Edda, *La mia testimonianza*, Milan, Rusconi, 1975

Ciano, Galeazzo, *Diario*, vol. 2, Bologna, Cappelli, 1948

Clark, Mark W., *Calculated Risk*, New York, Harper & Brothers, 1950

Colleoni, Angelo, *La verità sulla fine di Mussolini e della Petacci*, Milan, Lucchi, 1945

Collier, Richard, *Duce!*, London, Collins, 1971

Cornwell, John, *Hitler's Pope*, London, Viking, 1999

Corvo, Max, *The O.S.S. in Italy 1942–45*, New York, Praeger, 1990

D'Aroma, Nino, *Mussolini segreto*, Bologna, Cappelli, 1958

Deakin, F.W., *The Last Days of Mussolini*, London, Penguin, 1962

De Felice, Renzo, *Mussolini l'alleato*, vol. II: La guerra civile, Turin, Giulio Einaudi, 1997

——, *Rosso e nero*, Milan, Baldini & Castoldi, 1995

——, *Storia degli ebrei italiani sotto il fascismo*, Turin, Giulio Einaudi, 1988

Delzell, Charles F., *Mussolini's Enemies*, Princeton, NJ, Princeton University Press, 1961

De Wyss, M., *Rome under the Terror*, London, Robert Hale, 1945

Dinale, Ottavio, *Quarant'anni di colloqui con lui*, Milan, Ciarroca, 1953

Dolfin, Giovanni, *Con Mussolini nella tragedia*, Milan, Garzanti, 1949

Dollmann, Eugen, *Call Me Coward*, London, William Kimber, 1956

——, *The Interpreter*, London, Hutchinson, 1967

——, *Roma nazista*, Milan, RCS Libri, 2002

Dombrowski, Roman, *Twilight and Fall*, London, William Heinemann, 1956

Dulles, Allen W., *The Secret Surrender*, London, Weidenfeld & Nicolson, 1967

Ellwood, David W., *Italy 1943–1945*, Leicester, Leicester University Press, 1985

Falaschi, Candiano, 'I giorni che decisero la fine del fascismo – un taglio netto con il passato', *L'Unità*, 10 March 1973

——, 'Inizia la Grande Inchiesta dell'Unità', *L'Unità*, 25 February 1973, 3

Falaschi, Candiano, 'La cattura di Mussolini', *L'Unità*, 27 February 1973
——, 'La morte del Dittatore', *L'Unità*, 8 March 1973
——, 'Missione a Como e Dongo', *L'Unità*, 4 March 1973
Ganapini, Luigi, *La repubblica delle camicie nere*, Milan, Garzanti, 2002
Garibaldi, Luciano, *Mussolini e il professore*, Milan, Mursia, 1983
Gervaso, Roberto, *Claretta*, Bologna, Bompiani, 2002
Ghali, Paul, *Chicago Daily News*, 30 April 1945
Goebbels, Joseph, *The Goebbels Diaries*, London, Hamish Hamilton, 1948
——, *The Goebbels Diaries: The Last Days*, London, Secker & Warburg, 1978
Gravelli, Asvero, *Mussolini aneddotico*, Rome, Latinità, 1976
Graziani, Rodolfo, *Ho difeso la patria*, Milan, Garzanti, 1948
Grose, Peter, *Gentleman Spy*, London, Andre Deutsch, 1995
Hibbert, Christopher, *Benito Mussolini*, London, The Reprint Society, 1963
Hoettl, Wilhelm, *The Secret Front*, London, Weidenfeld & Nicolson, 1953
Hull, Cordell, *The Memoirs of Cordell Hull*, vol. 2, London, Hodder & Stoughton, 1948
Innocenti, Marco, *Mussolini a Salò*, Milan, Mursia, 1996
International Military Tribunal, *Trial of the Major War Criminals*, vol. 9, Nuremberg, 1947
Jenkins, Roy, *Churchill*, London, Macmillan, 2001
Katz, Robert, *The Battle for Rome*, New York, Simon & Schuster, 2003
——, *Black Sabbath*, London, Arthur Barker Ltd, 1969
——, *Death in Rome*, New York, Macmillan, 1967
Kershaw, Ian, *Hitler 1936–1945*, London, Penguin Books, 2000
Kesselring, Albert, *The Memoirs of Field Marshal Kesselring*, London, William Kimber, 1953
Kimball, Warren F., *Forged in War*, London, Harper Collins, 1997
—— (ed.), *Churchill and Roosevelt: the Complete Correspondence*, vols 2 and 3, Princeton, NJ, Princeton University Press, 1984
Lamb, Richard, *War in Italy*, London, John Murray, 1993
Lampredi, Aldo, 'Io, partigiano oscurato', *L'Unità*, 25 January 1996, 2
——, 'La fine del Duce', *L'Unità*, 23 January 1996, 2, 3
——, 'Quel giorno Walter Audisio venne a casa mia', *L'Unità*, 25 January 1996, 2
Lanfranchi, Ferruccio, *La resa degli 800,000*, Milan, Rizzoli, 1948
Lazzaro, Urbano, *Dongo: mezzo secolo di menzogne*, Milan, Mondadori, 1993
Leccisi, Domenico, *Con Mussolini prima e dopo Piazzale Loreto*, Rome, Settimo Sigillo, 1991
Lloyd, John, 'Marketing Mussolini', *Financial Times*, 4 August 2001, weekend section, 1
Longo, Luigi, *Un popolo alla macchia*, Milan, Mondadori, 1947
Loy, Rosetta, *La parola ebreo*, Turin, Einaudi, 1997
Luppi, Marco, 'Fermarono Mussolini e il parroco raccontò', in *La Provincia Pavese*, 17 December 1995, 21
Macksey, Kenneth, *The Partisans of Europe in World War II*, London, Hart-Davis, MacGibbon, 1975
Mack Smith, Denis, *Mussolini*, London, Paladin Grafton, 1983
Mafai, Miriam, 'Un segreto in quei tempi durissimi', *L'Unità*, 24 January 1996, 1, 3
Mellini Ponce de Leon, Alberto, *Guerra diplomatica a Salò*, Bologna, Cappelli, 1950
Michaelis, Meir, *Mussolini and the Jews*, Oxford, Clarendon Press, 1978
Monelli, Paolo, *Mussolini piccolo borghese*, Milan, Garzanti, 1950
Moseley, Ray, *Mussolini's Shadow*, New Haven, CT, Yale University Press, 1999

Mussolini, Benito, *Opera Omnia*, vol. 32, Florence, La Fenice, 1960

——, *Parlo con Bruno*, Milan, Il Popolo d'Italia, 1941

——, *Storia di un anno*, Milan, Mondadori, 1944

——, *Testamento politico di Mussolini*, Milan, Tosi, 1948

Mussolini, Edvige, *Mio fratello Benito*, Florence, La Fenice, 1957

Mussolini, Rachele, *Benito il mio uomo*, Milan, Rizzoli, 1958

——, *La mia vita con Benito*, Milan, Mondadori, 1948

Mussolini, Vittorio, *The Tragic Women in His Life*, New York, Dial Press, 1973

——, *Vita con mio padre*, Milan, Mondadori, 1957

Origo, Iris, *War in Val d'Orcia*, London, Jonathan Cape, 1947

Overy, Richard, *Interrogations*, London, Allen Lane, Penguin Press, 2001

Pansa, Giampaolo, *L'esercito di Salò*, Rome, Istituto Nazionale per la Storia del Movimento di Liberazione, 1969

Pavone, Claudio, *Una guerra civile*, Turin, Bollati Boringhieri, 1991

Pensotti, Anita, *Rachele*, Bologna, Bompiani, 1983

Perretta, Giusto, *La verità*, Como, Actac, 1997

Petacci, Clara, *Il mio diario*, Milan, Garzanti, 1946

Petacci, Myriam, *Chi ama è perduto*, Gardolo di Trento, Luigi Reverdito, 1988

Petacco, Arrigo, *Dear Benito, Caro Winston*, Milan, Mondadori, 1985

——, *L'archivio segreto di Mussolini*, Milan, Mondadori, 1997

Pini, Giorgio, and Duilio Susmel, *Mussolini, l'uomo e l'opera*, vol. 4, Florence, La Fenice, 1955

Pisenti, Piero, *Una repubblica necessaria*, Rome, Giovanni Volpe, 1977

'Renzo' [Lorenzo Bianchi], *La Voce Partigiana*, 27–28 April 1945

Ridley, Jasper, *Mussolini*, New York, Cooper Square Press, 2000

Ripa di Meana, Fulvia, *Roma clandestina*, Rome, Polilibraria, 1945

Roxan, David, and Ken Wanstall, *The Jackdaw of Linz*, London, Cassell, 1964

Saini, Ezio, *La notte di Dongo*, Rome, Corso, 1950

Salvadori, Max, *Breve storia della resistenza italiana*, Florence, Vallecchi, 1974

Schellenberg, Walter, *The Schellenberg Memoirs*, London, Andre Deutsch, 1956

Schmidt, Paul, *Hitler's Interpreter*, London, William Heinemann, 1951

Schuster, Ildefonso, *Gli ultimi tempi di un regime*, Milan, La Via, 1946

Scrivener, Jane, *Inside Rome with the Germans*, New York, Macmillan, 1945

Settimelli, Wladimiro, 'Ora il caso è chiuso', *L'Unità*, 24 January 1996, 3

Shepperd, G.A., *The Italian Campaign 1943–45*, London, Arthur Baker, 1968

Shirer, William, *The Rise and Fall of the Third Reich*, New York, Simon & Schuster, 1960

Silvestri, Carlo, *Mussolini, Graziani e l'antifascismo*, Milan, Longanesi, 1949

Smargiassi, Michele, 'Mille mantelli d'orbace per il nuovo culto del duce', *La Repubblica*, 28 October 2002, 22

Sogno, Edgardo, *Guerra senza bandiera*, Milan, Rizzoli, 1950

Spampanato, Bruno, *L'ultimo Mussolini*, vols 2–3, Rome, Rivista Romano, 1964

Stille, Alexander, 'In Italy, a Kinder, Gentler Fascism', *New York Times*, 29 September 2002, arts section

Tamaro, Attilio, *Due anni di storia*, vols 2–3, Rome, Tosi, 1948

Tompkins, Peter, *A Spy in Rome*, London, Weidenfeld & Nicolson, 1962

Troisio, Armando, *Roma sotto il terrore nazi-fascista*, Rome, Francesco Mondini, 1945

Valiani, Leo, *Tutte le strade conducono a Roma*, Florence, La Nuova Italia, 1947
Venè, Gian Franco, *La condanna di Mussolini*, Milan, Fratelli Fabbri, 1973
Weizsäcker, Ernst von, *Memoirs of Ernst von Weizsäcker*, London, Victor Gollancz, 1951
Wilhelm, Maria de Blasio, *The Other Italy*, New York, W.W. Norton, 1988
Whittle, Peter, *One Afternoon at Mezzegra*, London, W.H. Allen, 1969
Zachariae, Georg, *Mussolini si confessa*, Milan, Garzanti, 1948
Zangrandi, Ruggero, *Il lungo viaggo attraverso il fascismo*, Milan, Feltrinelli, 1962

Websites

www.geocities.com/Paris/Arc/5319/roma-c9i.htm – Il ghetto di Roma; last accessed 22 February 2003
www.ucei.it/giornodellamemoria/storia/shoah/deport – Liliana Picciotto, 'Deportazione razziale in Italia', Union of Italian Jewish Communities; last accessed 25 February 2003

INDEX